1998 NCPEA

TOWARD THE YEAR 2000:
Leadership for Quality Schools

THE SIXTH YEARBOOK OF THE NATIONAL COUNCIL
OF PROFESSORS OF EDUCATIONAL ADMINISTRATION

Edited by

RODNEY MUTH
University of Colorado at Denver

MICHAEL MARTIN
University of Colorado at Denver

With the assistance of
JEAN BONELLI
MARCIA MUTH

TECHNOMIC PUBLISHING CO., INC.
LANCASTER · BASEL

HOW TO ORDER THIS BOOK

BY PHONE: 800-233-9936 or 717-291-5609, 8AM–5PM Eastern Time

BY FAX: 717-295-4538

BY MAIL: Order Department
Technomic Publishing Company, Inc.
851 New Holland Avenue, Box 3535
Lancaster, PA 17604, U.S.A.

BY CREDIT CARD: American Express, VISA, MasterCard

BY WWW SITE: http://www.techpub.com

PERMISSION TO PHOTOCOPY–POLICY STATEMENT

Authorization to photocopy items for internal or personal use, or the internal or personal use of specific clients, is granted by Technomic Publishing Co., Inc. provided that the base fee of US $3.00 per copy, plus US $ .25 per page is paid directly to Copyright Clearance Center, 222 Rosewood Drive, Danvers, MA 01923, USA. For those organizations that have been granted a photocopy license by CCC, a separate system of payment has been arranged. The fee code for users of the Transactional Reporting Service is 1-56676/98 $5.00 + $ .25.

NCPEA OFFICERS FOR 1997

President

Charles M. Achilles, *Eastern Michigan University*

President-Elect

Robert S. Estabrook, *Stephen F. Austin State University*

Past-President

Clarence E. Fitch, *Chicago State University*

Executive Director

Robert H. Beach, *University of Memphis*

Executive Board

Class of 1997
Allen Fisher, *Florida International University*
David Sperry, *University of Utah*

Class of 1998
Thomas C. Valesky, *Florida Gulf Coast University*
Carolyn I. Wanat, *University of Iowa*

Class of 1999
Linda Avila, *Texas A&M University, Corpus Christi*
Cheryl Fisher, *California State University, San Bernardino*
James Smith, *Indiana University, South Bend*

Class of 2000
Leslie Fenwick, *Clark Atlanta University*
Michael Martin, *University of Colorado at Denver*
Louis Wildman, *California State University, Bakersfield*

YEARBOOK COMMITTEE

Charles M. Achilles, *Eastern Michigan University*
Helen Ditzhazy, *Eastern Michigan University*
Michael Martin, *University of Colorado at Denver*
Rodney Muth, *University of Colorado at Denver*
Louis Wildman, *California State University, Bakersfield*

Toward the Year 2000
a**TECHNOMIC** publication

Technomic Publishing Company, Inc.
851 New Holland Avenue, Box 3535
Lancaster, Pennsylvania 17604 U.S.A.

Copyright ©1998 by Technomic Publishing Company, Inc.
All rights reserved

No part of this publication may be reproduced, stored in a
retrieval system, or transmitted, in any form or by any means,
electronic, mechanical, photocopying, recording, or otherwise,
without the prior written permission of the publisher.

Printed in the United States of America
10 9 8 7 6 5 4 3 2 1

Main entry under title:
    Toward the Year 2000: Leadership for Quality Schools—The Sixth Yearbook
        of the National Council of Professors of Educational Administration

A Technomic Publishing Company book
Bibliography: p.
Includes index p. 307

ISBN No. 1-56676-709-1

NCPEA HONOR ROLL OF PRESIDENTS, 1947–1998

1947   Julian E. Butterworth, *Cornell University*
1948   William E. Arnold, *University of Pennsylvania*
1949   Russell T. Gregg, *University of Wisconsin*
1950   Clyde M. Campbell, *Michigan State University*
1951   Dan H. Cooper, *Purdue University*
1952   Walter K. Beggs, *University of Nebraska*
1953   Robert S. Fisk, *University of Buffalo*
1954   Van Miller, *University of Illinois*
1955   Harold E. Moore, *University of Denver*
1956   Walter A. Anderson, *New York University*
1957   A. D. Albright, *University of Kentucky*
1958   Jack Childress, *Northwestern University*
1959   Richard C. Lonsdale, *Syracuse University*
1960   William H. Roe, *Michigan State University*
1961   Howard Eckel, *University of Kentucky*
1962   Daniel E. Griffiths, *New York University*
1963   Kenneth McIntyre, *University of Texas*
1964   Luvern Cunningham, *University of Chicago*
1965   William H. Roe, *Michigan State University*
1966   Willard Lane, *University of Iowa*
1967   Harold Hall, *California State University, Los Angeles*
1968   Kenneth Frasure, *SUNY, Albany*
1969   Samuel Goldman, *Syracuse University*
1970   Malcolm Rogers, *University of Connecticut*
1971   Paul C. Fawley, *University of Utah*
1972   Gale W. Rose, *New York University*
1973   Anthony N. Baratta, *Fordham University*
1974   John T. Greer, *Georgia State University*
1975   C. Cale Hudson, *University of Nebraska*
1976   John R. Hoyle, *Texas A&M University*
1977   J. Donald Herring, *SUNY, Oswego*
1978   Charles Manley, *California State University, Northridge*
1979   Jasper Valenti, *Loyola University of Chicago*
1980   Max E. Evans, *Ohio University*
1981   Lesley H. Browder, Jr., *Hofstra University*
1982   John W. Kohl, *Montana State University*
1983   Bob Thompson, *SUNY, Oswego*
1984   Donald L. Piper, *University of North Dakota*
1985   Robert Stalcup, *Texas A&M University*
1986   Robert O'Reilly, *University of Nebraska, Omaha*
1987   Donald Coleman, *San Diego State University*
1988   Charles E. Kline, *Purdue University*
1989   Larry L. Smiley, *Central Michigan University*
1990   Frank Barham, *University of Virginia*
1991   Paul V. Bredeson, *Pennsylvania State University*
1992   Rosemary Papalewis, *California State University, Fresno*
1993   Don Orlosky, *University of South Florida*
1994   Paula M. Short, *University of Missouri-Columbia*
1995   Maria Shelton, *NOVA Southeastern University*
1996   Clarence E. Fitch, *Chicago State University*
1997   Charles M. Achilles, *Eastern Michigan University*
1998   Robert S. Estabrook, *Stephen F. Austin State University*

NATIONAL COUNCIL OF PROFESSORS OF EDUCATIONAL ADMINISTRATION
51st ANNUAL CONFERENCE
HOSTED BY THE UNIVERSITY OF COLORADO AT DENVER
HELD AT THE VAIL MARRIOTT HOTEL, VAIL, COLORADO, AUGUST 12-16, 1997

Host Institution Staff, University of Colorado at Denver

Ron Emerson, Conference Manager
Sonyae Bolden
Sharon Ford
Holly Nguyen
Melissa McLeod
Felicia Pugh
Dudley Solomon

Hosts

Michael Martin
Rodney Muth

University of Colorado Leadership

David Groth, *Vice-President for Academic Affairs and Research, University of Colorado at Denver*
Georgia Lesh-Laurie, *Chancellor, University of Colorado at Denver*
Michael J. Murphy, *Interim Vice-Chancellor for Academic and Student Affairs, University of Colorado at Denver*
G. Thomas Bellamy, *Dean, School of Education, University of Colorado at Denver*

NCPEA 51st ANNUAL CONFERENCE PROGRAM REVIEWERS:
COLORADO ASSOCIATION OF PROFESSORS OF SCHOOL ADMINISTRATION

Colorado State University

Arnie Danzig
Rich Ginzberg
Chuck Porter
Lonnie Wood

University of Colorado at Colorado Springs

Nadyne Guzmán

University of Colorado at Denver

Sharon Ford
Michael Martin
Michael Murphy

University of Colorado at Denver (*continued*)

Rodney Muth
L. A. Napier
Nancy Sanders

University of Denver

Edwin Steinbrecher

University of Northern Colorado

Bruce Barnett
Gene Hall
Dick King

NCPEA Reporter

Judy Adkison, *University of North Texas*

NCPEA Resource Fair

Carolyn Carr, *University of Texas, Pan American*

Corporate Sponsors

Gracia Alkema, President, Corwin Press
Joe Eckenrode, Technomic Publishing Co., Inc.
Pro-Active Publishing Company

General Session and Preconference Speakers and Presenters

Charles Achilles, *Eastern Michigan University*
Howard Brunner, *Colorado State University*
Gail Carpenter, *Jefferson County School District, Golden, Colorado*
Jill Fellman, *Jefferson County School District, Golden, Colorado*
Mark Gelernter, *University of Colorado at Denver*
Paul Houston, *American Association of School Administrators*
Eugene Howard, *School Climate Associates, Denver, Colorado*
Cherie Lyons, *Jefferson County School District, Golden, Colorado*
Michael Martin, *University of Colorado at Denver*
Martha McCarthy, *Indiana University, Bloomington (Cocking Lecture)*
Joe Murphy, *Vanderbilt University*
Rodney Muth, *University of Colorado at Denver*
Chris Pipho, *Education Commission of the States, Denver, Colorado*
Rod and Beth Pirtle, *Dallas, Texas*
Sharon Rallis, *Harvard University (First Corwin Lecture)*
Louis Rubin, *University of Illinois*
Tom Valesky, *Florida Gulf Coast University*
Eddy Van Meter, *University of Kentucky*

PROPOSAL REVIEWERS, SIXTH ANNUAL YEARBOOK OF THE NATIONAL COUNCIL OF PROFESSORS OF EDUCATIONAL ADMINISTRATION

Charles Achilles, *Eastern Michigan University*
Susan Achilles, *Greenville County Schools, South Carolina*
Raymond Aguilera, *University of Texas at San Antonio*
Linda Avila, *Texas A&M University, College Station*
Bruce Barnett, *University of Northern Colorado*
Cynthia Beekley, *Springfield Schools, Springfield, Ohio*
Jim Beery, *Eastern Michigan University*
Jack Blendinger, *Mississippi State University*
Jean Bonelli, *Boulder Valley School District, Boulder, Colorado*
Fred Bradley, *University of Missouri, St. Louis*
Maynard Bratlein, *Texas A&M University, College Station*
Paul Bredeson, *University of Wisconsin, Madison*
Lesley Browder, *Hofstra University*
John Cochren, *Indiana University/Purdue University, Fort Wayne*
Bryan Cole, *Texas A&M University, College Station*
Don Coleman, *California State University, Fresno*
Douglas Coutts, *Indiana University/Purdue University, Fort Wayne*
Arnie Danzig, *Colorado State University*
John Dayton, *University of Georgia*
Fred Dembowski, *State University of New York, Albany*
Helen Ditzhazy, *Eastern Michigan University*
Harvey Dorrah, Jr., *Central Michigan University*
Linda Farley, *Colorado Children's Museum*
Sharon Ford, *University of Colorado at Denver*
Lenoar Foster, *University of Montana*
Craig Freed, *Northern State University, South Dakota*
Beverley Geltner, *Eastern Michigan University*
Rick Ginzberg, *Colorado State University*
Nadyne Guzmán, *University of Colorado at Colorado Springs*
Catherine Hackney, *Kent State University*
Doug Hemmond, *University of Houston*
Richard Henderson, *University of Arkansas at Little Rock*
John Hoyle, *Texas A&M University, College Station*
Martin Jason, *Roosevelt University*
Bob Johnson, Jr., *University of Utah*
Steve Kaagan, *Michigan State University*
William Keane, *Oakland University*
Dan King, *University of Wyoming*
Richard King, *University of Northern Colorado*
Theodore Kowalski, *Ball State University*
Paul Kussrow, *Florida Atlantic University*
Barbara Martin, *Southwest Missouri State*
Michael Martin, *University of Colorado at Denver*
Kelly McKerow, *Southern Illinois University, Carbondale*
Bob Millward, *Indiana University of Pennsylvania*
Michael Murphy, *University of Colorado at Denver*
Rodney Muth, *University of Colorado at Denver*
L. A. Napier, *University of Colorado at Denver*

Burton Nygren, *North Dakota State University*
Arnold Oates, *Texas A&M University, College Station*
Lucretia Peebles, *Denver University*
Kaye Peery, *University of Nebraska, Lincoln*
George Perrault, *East Carolina University*
Bill Place, *University of Dayton*
Chuck Porter, *Colorado State University*
William K. Poston, *Iowa State University*
P. J. Powers, *University of Wisconsin, Superior*
Al Ramirez, *University of Colorado, Colorado Springs*
Ken Redding, *University of Wisconsin, Superior*
Gwen Schroth, *Texas A&M University, Commerce*
Arthur Shapiro, *University of South Florida*
Mark Shibles, *University of Connecticut*
Eileen Smith-Stevens, *Lehigh University*
Dudley Solomon, *University of Colorado at Denver*
Kathy Sparks, *Clemson University*
Edwin Steinbrecher, *Denver University*
James Strong, *College of William & Mary*
Tom Valesky, *Florida Gulf Coast University*
Eddy Van Meter, *University of Kentucky*
Joyce VanTassel-Baska, *College of William & Mary*
James E. Walter, *University of Missouri, St. Louis*
Scott Wegner, *Southwest Missouri State University*
Kathy Whitaker, *University of Northern Colorado*
Louis Wildman, *California State University at Bakersfield*
Sheri Williams, *Clear Creek School District, Idaho Springs, Colorado*
Elaine Wilmore, *University of Texas at Arlington*
Lonnie Wood, *Colorado State University*

TABLE OF CONTENTS

President's Message — xiii

Contributing Authors — xv

Introduction — xvii

SECTION 1: TOWARD THE YEAR 2000

The "New" Educational Leadership Professor 3
Martha M. McCarthy

Tomorrow's Service Ideal: A Vocational Calling or Token Obligation? 16
Lesley H. Browder, Jr.

Professorial Service: Disseminating Knowledge to Improve Practice 29
C. M. Achilles and Susan H. Achilles

Reconsidering the Role of Research in Educational Administration Doctoral Programs 36
Theodore J. Kowalski and A. William Place

SECTION 2: QUALITY SCHOOLS

Creating Quality Schools: Rethinking the Meaning of and Strategies for Restructuring 49
Bob L. Johnson, Jr.

Reengineering the School for Quality 59
David Weller

Curriculum Alignment: An Approach to Raising Standardized Achievement Scores in High-Risk School Districts 69
Raymond V. Aguilera and Joen M. Hendricks

Performance-Based Rewards as a Model for State School Finance Policy 76
Richard A. King

Should We Have a National Standard of Decency in Our Scholastic Cybernets? 87
Lawrence Lee Oldaker and David Dagley

Free Speech and School Internet Policies: Emerging Law and Its Implications for School Administration 93
John Dayton

The Problematics of Democracy and Schooling 103
James E. Walter

SECTION 3: LEADERSHIP

Special Interest Groups and the Political Nature of Educational Leadership 113
Abe Feuerstein

Leadership for Learning: A Study of the Instructional Leadership Roles of Superintendents in Sweden and Wisconsin 119
Paul V. Bredeson and Olof Johansson

Rethinking School Leadership: Is the Principal Really Needed? 131
Theodore B. Creighton

Staff Development: A Linchpin for Leadership 139
Barbara L. Licklider and Carol Fulton

Principals' Interpersonal Sensitivity Toward Teachers, Central Office Personnel, Parents, Business Leaders, and Community Members 148
John R. Hoyle and Arnold Oates

SECTION 4: PREPARING LEADERS

Imaging Change through the Voices of Teachers and Students: An Ethnographic Approach 157
Frank Pignatelli and Linda Levine

The Portfolio as a Capstone Experience in the Preparation of Educational Leaders 169
Beverley B. Geltner, William J. Price, and Jaclynn C. Tracy

Why Are Cohorts Used or Rejected by Educational Leadership Faculty? 179
Bruce G. Barnett, Margaret R. Basom, Cynthia J. Norris, and Diane M. Yerkes

Emotional Intelligence and Educational Leadership 190
James O. McDowelle and Edwin D. Bell

Can Leadership Be Learned? On Writing and Analyzing the Stories of Educational Leaders 196
Arnold Danzig and Charles Porter

Interactive Television: Reactions of Students and Faculty 208
Earl B. Kaurala

Evolution, Revolution, and Collaboration: Creating New Programs and Paradigms in Doctoral Studies for Educational Leaders 214
Nadyne Guzmán and Rodney Muth

Preparing Future School Leaders to Build School-Home Partnerships through Authentic Learning Experiences 231
Jack Blendinger and Linda T. Jones

Partnerships for Preparing School Leaders: Possibilities and Practicalities 238
W. Michael Martin, Sharon M. Ford, Michael J. Murphy, and Rodney Muth

Integrating Simulations, Extended Internships, and Portfolios in a Principal Preparation Program 247
George Perreault and Lynn Bradshaw

Collaboration Among University Colleagues: A Model for Action Research to Improve Supervision and Teaching 258
Gayle A. Wilkinson and Fred E. Bradley

Why We Need to Strengthen Graduate Training in Educational Administration 268
Gunapala Edirisooriya

A Study of Problem-Based Learning in Teaching Educational Administration Courses 279
Joyce VanTassel-Baska

Toward a Model of Problem-Based Learning for the Preparation of Educational Administrators 289
Robert Rehm and Rodney Muth

Authenticity in Field-Based Preparation Programs for PK–12 School Administrators 299
Mitch Holifield and Gerald Dickinson

Author Index *307*

PRESIDENT'S MESSAGE

Thanks! The 1997 NCPEA meeting at Vail, Colorado, was refreshing, if not breathtaking. After the Herculean task of hosting the NCPEA phalanx, our colleagues at the University of Colorado at Denver took up the challenge of producing the 1998 NCPEA Yearbook which includes selected papers from the 1997 conference. Results of both the "Rocky Mountain High" and the Yearbook reflect the quality that we expected. Thanks to you all.

The 1998 Yearbook's title and contents impel us toward the year 2000 and beyond. This is uplifting. Yet, though it is pressing, the year 2000 still seems too long to wait for the quality schools that America's youngest citizens deserve. Past economic woes were blamed on education, and credit for the roaring economy lately has been claimed by business. Did we ever get a peace benefit to improve schools? Should we expect an economic benefit by the year 2000? Let's pretend. In the meantime, get your own 10 wishes ready. How many of these ideas are lurking in the Yearbook? In the year 2000 . . .

1. Educators will get lots of credit and esteem.
2. Educators will be allowed to do for children what research shows will improve schools and student well-being.
3. We'll find the people who want to be leaders for quality schools.
4. Preparation programs for educational administrators will be able to prepare leaders who will desire and be able to create quality schools.
5. Fewer children will live in poverty and suffer abuse, debilitating problems, and problems that educators are called upon to solve—but can't without lots of help.
6. Children will be allowed to learn for learning and enjoyment, not for economic standards.
7. We'll find the secret to violence-free schools and a less violent society.
8. We'll devote time and resources to solve the "inner-space" problem now that outer-space exploration is becoming routine.
9. We'll divert funds from land mines and weaponry to improving the human condition through education.
10. . . . Wow. Where does it stop?

This list could go on and on. Could this same list have been written five years ago? Ten? More? Things will have to change if the list is to stop growing exponentially, for it's impossible to improve without changing. What will you and I do differently in 2000? Why didn't we do it in 1999? Will the year 2000 be much different from 1999 or 2001 for education and educators? Surely, we hope so. We can help. Let's start. Now.

C. M. ACHILLES
President, NCPEA, 1997

CONTRIBUTING AUTHORS

Charles M. Achilles, *Eastern Michigan University*
Susan H. Achilles, *School District of Greenville County*
Raymond V. Aguilera, *University of Texas, San Antonio*
Bruce G. Barnett, *University of Northern Colorado*
Margaret R. Basom, *University of Wyoming*
Edwin D. Bell, *East Carolina University*
Jack Blendinger, *Mississippi State University*
Fred Bradley, *University of Missouri, St. Louis*
Lynn Bradshaw, *East Carolina University*
Paul V. Bredeson, *University of Wisconsin–Madison*
Lesley H. Browder, Jr., *Hofstra University*
Theodore B. Creighton, *Idaho State University*
David Dagley, *University of Alabama, Birmingham*
Arnold Danzig, *Colorado State University*
John Dayton, *University of Georgia*
Gerald Dickinson, *Arkansas State University*
Gunapala Edirisooriya, *East Tennessee State University*
Abe Feuerstein, *Bucknell University*
Sharon M. Ford, *University of Colorado at Denver*
Carol Fulton, *Iowa State University*
Beverley B. Geltner, *Eastern Michigan University*
Nadyne Guzmán, *University of Colorado, Colorado Springs*
Joen M. Hendricks, *Our Lady of the Lake University*
Mitch Holifield, *Arkansas State University*
John R. Hoyle, *Texas A&M University*
Olof Johansson, *Umea University, Umea, Sweden*
Bob L. Johnson, Jr., *University of Utah*
Linda T. Jones, *Mississippi State University*
Earl B. Kaurala, *Northern Michigan University*
Richard A. King, *University of Northern Colorado*
Theodore J. Kowalski, *Ball State University*
Linda Levine, *Bank Street College of Education*
Barbara L. Licklider, *Iowa State University*
W. Michael Martin, *University of Colorado at Denver*
Martha M. McCarthy, *Indiana University*
James O. McDowelle, *East Carolina University*
Michael J. Murphy, *University of Colorado at Denver*
Rodney Muth, *University of Colorado at Denver*
Cynthia J. Norris, *University of Houston*
Arnold Oates, *Texas A&M University*
Lawrence Lee Oldaker, *University of Alaska Southeast*
George Perreault, *East Carolina University*
Frank Pignatelli, *Bank Street College of Education*
A. William Place, *University of Dayton*
Charles Porter, *Colorado State University*
William J. Price, *Eastern Michigan University*
Robert Rehm, *University of Colorado at Denver*
Jaclynn C. Tracy, *Eastern Michigan University*
Joyce VanTassel-Baska, *College of William & Mary*
James E. Walter, *University of Missouri, St. Louis*
David Weller, *University of Georgia*
Gayle A. Wilkinson, *University of Missouri, St. Louis*
Diane M. Yerkes, *California State University, Fresno*

INTRODUCTION

Toward the Year 2000:
Leadership for Quality Schools

> There is a rumbling in the clouds above us—they are no longer merely on the horizon.
> —H. Beare, 1990

As we draw closer to the beginning of a new century, we are excited and honored to present this sixth annual NCPEA yearbook. Over fifty years have passed since the founding of NCPEA, and during that time the field of educational administration has experienced considerable ferment and turbulence, particularly in the last 15 years. We are fortunate, nevertheless, to be in a dynamic field in which at least 17 domains of knowledge focus our attention on things that matter, ranging from learning theory, leadership, human relations, and systems analysis to school facilities, law, and policy development (Wildman, 1997, p. xi). Policymakers, scholars, practitioners, students, and university leaders have questioned the assumptions of education and educational administration, making innumerable suggestions for change. Much is expected, rightly, both from our field and from the leaders we produce as evidenced by the countless calls for review, reform, restructuring, and renewal of educational institutions. Among these demands for reform are the 1983 *A Nation at Risk: The Imperative for Educational Reform* (National Commission on Excellence in Education) and the 1988 *Leaders for America's Schools: The Report and Papers of the National Commission on Excellence in Educational Administration* (Griffiths, Stout, & Forsyth).

These and other reports have spawned countless reform efforts: school-university partnerships in program design and delivery, field-based problem solving, cooperative learning, cohort training, integrated curricula, standards-based education, distance learning, authentic assessment, and integration of research, teaching, and service (Martin, Ford, Murphy, & Muth, 1996, p. 9). Linking these reforms to more effective schools and to quality learning challenges program developers to overcome past indictments of preparation programs: "follow the leader" internships, fragmented curriculum, overemphasis of theory, uncritical and indefinite use of concepts, professor-centered instruction, irrelevant and unchallenging content, "sit and git" coursework, and incessant swapping of "war stories" by both practitioners and professors.

Rather than dismantle preparation programs as some have suggested, the field continues to demonstrate proactive and energetic responses to these criticisms as evidenced by the chapters in this volume. School leadership must be strengthened at all levels, and this yearbook suggests many ways to overcome the limitations of the past. Current innovations lead the way, including cooperative recruitment and selection of students and collaborative program design, instruction, assessment, and placement of students in such that scholars, practitioners, students, and even private-sector representatives can work together to produce quality leaders (see, for example, Martin, Ford, Murphy, & Muth in this volume). By joining the worlds of the practitioner and the scholar, a "new breed" of educational leader may emerge in the next millennium.

SECTION 1: TOWARD THE YEAR 2000

Martha McCarthy, Indiana University, opens the yearbook by suggesting that the preparation of educational leaders must be transformed if creative, visionary leaders are to bring about fundamental changes in our nation's schools. Her chapter summarizes the results of a comprehensive study of educational leadership faculty members in the United States and Canada. She cites the development of the National Policy Board for Educational Administration, the decade of UCEA conventions, the NCPEA conferences, and the newly created AERA Special Interest Group on Teaching in Educational Administration as signs that reform is receiving increased attention from scholars, practitioners, and policymakers. She cautions, however, that her findings, in combination with data from other studies, suggest that it is still too early to tell the extent to which educational leadership programs will sustain energies for reform.

In the next chapter, Lesley Browder, Jr., Hofstra University, argues that the university must be recast as an institution engaged with the public good if future leaders are to be prepared effectively. He calls for the elevation of teaching and service as part of the reward and recognition structure in universities. Broader definitions of scholarship are essential to achieve this, including the recognition of faculty service as a "vocational calling" rather than merely a set of token obligations to be met.

Charles Achilles, Eastern Michigan University, and Susan Achilles, Greenville County Schools, join Browder in arguing for a broader definition of service. They suggest that knowledge dissemination should be considered an essential dimension of a professor's responsibilities. Achilles and Achilles want professors to apply what research and exemplary practice have shown will improve education, advocating a focus on the implementation of substantive research results and the application of the knowledge base in the field.

In the final chapter in this section, Theodore Kowalski, Ball State University, and William Place, University of Dayton, advocate the reconsideration of doctoral-level research in educational administration. They propose that programs adopt a new research agenda—acknowledging the scholar, practitioner, or practitioner-scholar paradigm and choosing clearly among them. Their preference is for practitioner-scholars who are trained both to know and use the results of research to improve practice.

SECTION 2: QUALITY SCHOOLS

To produce quality schools in the next century, school leaders are charged with challenging the status quo of their public institutions and restructuring and reforming educational programs for the youth of America. Countless authors and reports have suggested the importance of "paradigm shifts" in thinking about teaching, learning, and the governance of public education. Bob Johnson, Jr., University of Utah, maintains that, if we are to create quality schools for the new millennium, we must rethink the meaning of restructuring and the methods of implementing strategies for school improvement. Johnson suggests that careful consideration be given to organizational relationships, motivations for restructuring, and possible barriers to success.

In the next chapter, David Weller of the University of Georgia suggests that educators look to "reengineering," a specific strategy used by the business community to unlock an organizational culture before attempting to introduce a new one. Reengineering requires that school leaders rethink and reassess current educational delivery systems, particularly as they relate to the demands of an ever-increasing global economy and the concomitant yet paradoxical pressures for competition, cooperation, and interdependence. According to Weller, school leaders need to foster proactive behavior and flexible thinking if our educational programs are to improve in quality.

Raymond Aguilera, University of Texas, San Antonio, and Joen M. Hendricks, Our Lady of the Lake University, San Antonio, demonstrate the effectiveness of curriculum alignment as a focused strategy for creating effective learning situations and improving achievement for high-risk students. They outline processes and discuss results of their study of alignment in three school districts.

Another approach for developing quality schools is the use of financial incentives to stimulate improved outcomes for students and school groups. Richard King, University of Northern Colorado, examined the financial reward programs in four states and found that rewards are weaker motivators than the desires to improve and avoid negative consequences. Local and state accountability must be balanced and comparisons made fairly if financial incentives are to be effective. Too narrow a curricular focus or stressful divisiveness may result from overemphasis on state testing, state standards, and curriculum frameworks, thus affecting the ability of the school to offer more comprehensive programs for students.

In two separate chapters, Lawrence Lee Oldaker, University of Alaska Southeast in Juneau, and David Dagley, University of Alabama, Birmingham, as well as John Dayton, University of Georgia, take us into a new and tumultuous arena when they initiate a challenging dialogue on "decency," "free speech," and related legal issues associated with access to the Internet. According to Oldaker and Dagley and to Dayton, recent court decisions have supported First Amendment rights for those using electronic information networks, thus raising issues about what and whose standards should be used to govern educational use of this innovative learning tool.

In the last chapter in this section, James Walter, University of Missouri, St. Louis, raises an important "problematic" associated with democracy in education: whether society wants schooling that promotes democratic cultural values or private values frequently directed toward economic benefit. Walter emphasizes the importance of teachers and administrators in encouraging the moral and intellectual development of students that is necessary for responsible citizenship and ultimately an enlightened democracy.

SECTION 3: LEADERSHIP

Creating quality education in a turbulent environment is a continual challenge to school leaders as we move into the next millennium. The first two chapters in this section examine the role and expectations of educational leaders. Abe Feuerstein, Bucknell University, points to special interest groups and their influence on educational policy making as a new challenge. To encourage such groups to play a constructive role in decision making, he suggests strategies such as coalition building and negotiating as requisite skills for future school leaders. Next, Paul Bredeson, University of Wisconsin, Madison, and Olof Johansson, Umea University, Umea, Sweden, contrast the instructional leadership roles of superintendents in both Wisconsin and Sweden. Despite many cultural differences, they find striking similarities among superintendents in both countries relative to their roles in supporting, delegating, collaborating, and envisioning instructional improvements.

The next three chapters turn to the school-level development of stronger school leaders. Theodore Creighton, Idaho State University, investigates the need for principals as school leadership is reconceptualized and demands for quality increase. He reports on a study of a single elementary (K–8) school which experimented with teams of teachers assuming major administrative responsibilities after eliminating the formal roles of principal and assistant principal.

Transforming staff development for the coming millennium, according to Barbara Licklider and Carol Fulton, Iowa State University, is a major challenge facing school leaders. In their chapter, they recommend more solid underpinnings from the literature on adult learning and staff development. Encouraging more reflective strategies for adult learning, according to the authors, ultimately builds a more effective learning environment for students.

Finally, John Hoyle and Arnold Oates, Texas A&M University, point out the importance of interpersonal sensitivity for school leaders who increasingly deal with stakeholders in stressful, emotional, and conflictual situations. The results of the three studies reported in this chapter challenge school leaders to be more aware of their interactions with teachers, central office, parents, business representatives, and community-agency personnel in an increasingly contentious educational environment.

SECTION 4: PREPARING LEADERS

As a clear indication of the sense of the challenge facing professors of educational administration nationwide, the preponderance of the papers included in this volume focus on preparation issues. The lead chapter in this section, written by Frank Pignatelli and Linda Levine of the Bank Street College of Education, demonstrates the value of using an ethnographic approach for conducting workplace research. This approach can be an effective tool for future leaders, helping them learn how to study the rules, roles, and relationships of embedded cultures. Learning how to apply this spirit of inquiry within a school environment can sharpen an educational leader's moral, political, and pedagogical purpose. The next chapter also examines a particular preparation strategy. Beverley Geltner, William Price, and Jaclynn Tracy, Eastern Michigan University, describe the integration of reflective practice with a summative or capstone portfolio which allows students to direct, document, and evaluate their own learning.

On a larger scale, Bruce Barnett (University of Northern Colorado), Margaret Basom (University of Wyoming), Cynthia Norris (University of Houston), and Diane Yerkes (California State University, Fresno) surveyed educational leadership faculty in America and Canada. Investigating factors and perceptions related to the adoption or nonadoption of cohorts as an innovation, they point out the benefits and deficits reported by both cohort users and nonusers.

The next two chapters examine other ways of understanding leadership and leadership skills. James O. McDowelle and Edwin Bell, East Carolina University, studied the concept of emotional intelligence (in contrast to cognitive intelligence) as an important concept in the tool kit of future school leaders and an essential asset in school leadership. Arnold Danzig and Charles Porter, Colorado State University, introduce a novel idea for preparation programs—writing and analyzing the stories of educational leaders—as a tool for reflection and learning. They contend that leadership can be learned and demonstrate the utility of their reflective and analytical methods through the stories developed by their students from their leadership studies.

Other methods of organizing and delivering preparation programs are discussed in several chapters. Earl Kaurala, Northern Michigan University, introduces us to another view of technology in educational preparation programs—interactive television—and reports on the diverse opinions of students and faculty regarding its use as a learning approach. Nadyne Guzmán, University of Colorado at Colorado Springs, and Rodney Muth, University of Colorado at Denver, describe the strengths and limitations of "evolution, revolution, and collaboration" in designing a new doctoral program in Colorado. They describe the benefits of doctoral-level cohort-based programs (rather than traditional, course-based programs) and of diversity—of faculty, students, and learning experiences—which add considerably to student knowledge and skill development.

Bridges between different educational stakeholders are discussed in the next chapters. Home-school partnerships are the focus of the chapter by Jack Blendinger and Linda Jones, Mississippi State University. They describe learning activities which can foster the knowledge of future school leaders in building this important relationship. With so much emphasis today on building bridges between the university and school districts, Michael Martin, Sharon Ford, Michael Murphy, and Rodney Muth, University of Colorado at Denver, describe issues involved with developing unique partnerships using three distinct models: university-centered, school district-centered, and agency-centered. They outline several components of effective partnerships, illustrating these components with examples from their own practice.

George Perreault and Lynn Bradshaw describe the benefits of extended internships, integrated simulations, and portfolios in their preparation program at East Carolina University as they work to strengthen authentic learning and assessment. An opportunity for collaboration between administrator and teacher preparation programs is identified by Gayle Wilkinson and Fred Bradley, University of Missouri, St. Louis. Based on several years of experience, they outline a model and reflect on its contributions to successful preparation of students in both programs.

Gunapala Edirisooriya, East Tennessee State University, takes on the most recent critics of administrative preparation programs in education and finds their arguments wanting on several counts. Especially in the areas of research methods, data management, and technology, he suggests that preparation programs should be reformed and strengthened, rather than dismantled, to produce the caliber of leaders needed for quality schools in the 21st century.

In the final part of this section on preparing leaders, several chapters explore issues related to problem-based learning. Joyce VanTassel-Baska, College of William & Mary, describes her application of this innovative approach to student learning, providing examples of lessons as well as recommendations for implementation. Robert Rehm and Rodney Muth, University of Colorado at Denver, argue that problem-based learning has some limitations and suggest that "puzzle solving" is a more appropriate metaphor. This new metaphor acknowledges that the problems and issues faced by school leaders require collaboration and action learning instead of simple and immediate solutions to pressing problems of practice. Finally, Mitch Holifield and Gerald Dickinson, Arkansas State University, argue that authentic, field-based learning experiences can overcome the traditional limitations of preparation programs. Surveying exemplary practices of preparation programs, they note a variety of applications of clinical, field-based activities, appropriate for the preparation of leaders for quality schools in the year 2000.

ACKNOWLEDGEMENTS

No volume of this order could be produced without considerable assistance. First, we want to thank our university leadership—David Groth, Georgia Lesh-Laurie, and Michael Murphy—for their encouragement and support of both this volume and the 1997 NCPEA conference which was sponsored by the University of Colorado at Denver and produced most of the papers presented here. We particularly want to express our sincere appreciation to Thomas Bellamy, Dean of the School of Education, for his generous support of the production of this volume. Of course, without the stellar contributions of all of the reviewers, listed elsewhere, we could not have selected easily among the papers originally offered for review—more than 100—or reduced the number to the 31 included here after some very difficult decisions. Finally, we want to thank Joy Chou for all of her work making corrections to successive versions of the manuscripts as they progressed through the editing process, Jean Bonelli for managing the entire review and selection process as well as initial entry of first-round edits, and Marcia Muth for ensuring that this yearbook met high standards of consistency and style.

MICHAEL MARTIN AND RODNEY MUTH
University of Colorado at Denver

REFERENCES

Beare, H. (1990). *Educational administration in the 1990s* (Monograph No. 7). Melbourne, Australia: Australian Council for Educational Administration.

Griffiths, D. E., Stout, R. T., & Forsyth, P. B. (1988). *Leaders for America's schools: The report and papers of the National Commission on Excellence in Educational Administration.* Berkeley, CA: McCutchan.

Martin, W. M., Ford, S., Murphy, M. J., & Muth, R. (1996, October). *The possibilities, potential and practicalities of partnerships in building a learning community in preparing school leaders.* Paper presented to the annual conference of the University Council for Educational Administration, Louisville, KY.

National Commission on Excellence in Education (1983). *A nation at risk: The imperative for educational reform.* Washington, DC: U.S. Department of Education.

Wildman, L. (1997). *Fifth Annual Yearbook of the National Council of Professors of Educational Administration. School administration: The new knowledge base.* Lancaster, PA: Technomic Publishing Co., Inc.

SECTION 1

TOWARD THE YEAR 2000

CHAPTER 1

The "New" Educational Leadership Professor[1]

Martha M. McCarthy

Creative, visionary leaders are needed to bring about fundamental changes in our nation's schools. Because the vast majority of school administrators have advanced degrees in educational leadership, a crucial step in effecting school reform is transforming the preparation of educational leaders. Unfortunately, increasingly strident criticisms have been directed toward the quality of university preparation programs for school leaders and the caliber of faculty staffing these programs (Griffiths, 1988; Heller, Conway, & Jacobson, 1988; Murphy, 1993a). Considerable sentiment suggests that universities have been part of the problem, rather than instigators of reform.

Given that preservice programs leading to certification for school administrators are likely to remain the domain of universities—at least for the foreseeable future—educational leadership faculty will continue to play a key role in determining how future school leaders in our nation are prepared to assume their roles. Developments external to universities, such as the adoption of state and national standards and assessment programs for school administrators (e.g., Council of Chief State School Officers, 1996), certainly have the potential to influence the content and structure of preservice programs, but fundamental transformations are unlikely to take place without substantial commitment from rank-and-file faculty members. To gauge the capacity and readiness of educational leadership faculty members to undertake such a task, we must understand their characteristics, activities, and attitudes.

This chapter summarizes the results of a comprehensive study of educational leadership faculty members in the United States and Canada conducted in 1994 (McCarthy & Kuh, 1997). The study was designed in part to replicate studies conducted in 1972 (Campbell & Newell, 1973) and 1986 (McCarthy, Kuh, Newell, & Iacona, 1988), so that longitudinal comparisons could be made. The 1994 study was sponsored by the National Council of Professors of Educational Administration (NCPEA) and the University Council for Educational Administration (UCEA) with support from the Danforth Foundation, the American Educational Research Association/National Center for Education Statistics/National Science Foundation Grants Program, and Indiana University.

The study entailed two strands, and this chapter focuses primarily on the survey of individual faculty members' characteristics, activities, and attitudes. In this strand, a random sample of 940 faculty members from 371 universities was surveyed, and a 55% response rate was achieved.[2] In the second strand, all 371 educational leadership unit heads were surveyed about the size, structure, and composition of their units, and this survey yielded a response rate of 68%. The first section of this chapter presents a profile of educational leadership faculty members in 1994 and highlights changes in characteristics, activities, and attitudes over time. The second section addresses several trends and their implications for educational leadership units and for the preparation of school administrators in the United States. The concluding section explores the prognosis for reform of educational leadership preparation programs. Throughout, the term "educational leadership" is used to refer to "school administration," "school leadership," or "educational administration" faculty members and units.

Martha M. McCarthy, Indiana University

PROFILE OF EDUCATIONAL LEADERSHIP FACULTY MEMBERS

From the 1970s to the 1990s, the educational leadership professoriate has reflected both stability and change. The typical unit offering graduate degrees in educational leadership in 1994 had 5.6 full-time faculty members, slightly more faculty members than in the mid-1980s ($M = 5.0$, McCarthy et al., 1988) but fewer than in the mid-1970s ($M = 6.5$, Davis, 1978). Although the mean number of faculty members per educational leadership unit has remained fairly constant since 1986, the modal number increased from only two in 1986 to five in 1994. Nonetheless, about two fifths of the educational leadership units in 1994 had fewer than five full-time faculty members, the minimum number considered adequate to staff educational leadership preparation programs (National Commission on Excellence in Educational Administration, 1987; National Policy Board for Educational Administration, 1989).

The faculty increase between the mid-1980s and mid-1990s was primarily a function of an increase in the number of faculty at comprehensive universities[3]; educational leadership units at research institutions continued to decline slightly in faculty size. In 1994, comprehensive universities, which have limited doctoral offerings, housed more than half of all educational leadership units and more than two fifths of all faculty members and students enrolled in graduate degree programs. When units that offer only administrative certification courses are also considered, the proportion of school leaders prepared by comprehensive universities increases substantially (McCarthy, in press).

About 40% of the 1994 educational leadership faculty respondents said that they were hired within the preceding decade, indicating that a substantial influx of new faculty members has occurred. More than one fifth (21%) entered the professoriate within the prior five years, whereas only 14% of the 1986 respondents were new faculty. Given the number of anticipated retirements, continued faculty turnover seems assured into the twenty-first century. New faculty in 1994 were overrepresented at comprehensive universities and programs not affiliated with the University Council for Educational Administration (UCEA), consistent with the finding that non-UCEA programs and those at comprehensive universities have increased in size since the mid-1980s. However, even though UCEA programs and those at research universities have downsized, they still have more faculty members than do other units.

Slightly more than one fourth of the faculty respondents in both 1986 and 1994 were affiliated with units that belonged to UCEA. Fourteen percent of the faculty respondents in 1994 were members of NCPEA, and NCPEA membership was comparable among new and veteran educational leadership faculty members.[4] About one fifth of the NCPEA respondents were employed by units affiliated with UCEA, but only 11% of the respondents from UCEA units were members of NCPEA. Whereas 85% of the UCEA faculty were housed at research institutions, comprehensive universities employed the largest share of NCPEA respondents (44%). The remaining NCPEA respondents were evenly divided between research and doctoral universities.

Personal and Professional Characteristics

Certain characteristics of educational leadership faculty members have changed markedly since the early 1970s. The most significant change pertains to female representation in the professoriate; the percentage of women faculty increased tenfold between 1972 (2%) and 1994 (20%).[5] Almost two fifths of the faculty hired between 1984 and 1994 were women. This dramatic influx of women into the professoriate seems to be slowing, however, as the number of women hired in the five-year period prior to 1994 (39%) was only slightly higher than the number appointed 6 to 10 years earlier (37%).

Among new faculty members in 1994, female representation varied significantly by type of institution and UCEA affiliation. More than half of the new educational leadership faculty members at research institutions (53%) and in UCEA programs (60%) in 1994 were women, whereas women comprised only one fourth of the new faculty at comprehensive institutions and one third of the faculty in non-UCEA programs.

Although not as dramatic as the increase in female faculty members, minority representation increased almost fourfold between 1972 (3%) and 1994 (11%). However, the prospects for race equity do not seem as bright as prospects for gender equity in educational leadership units. It was disappointing that in 1994 minority representation among those hired during the prior five years (10%) was smaller than among faculty hired in the preceding 6 to 10 years (15%). Unlike the findings in 1986, when minority representation was considerably higher among new than among veteran faculty, the intermediate cohort in 1994 (hired between 1984 and 1989) reflected the highest proportion of people of color. This is worrisome because it is difficult to imagine that the educational leadership profession can respond effectively to the changing demographics of American schools and prepare future leaders for those schools without a racially and ethnically diverse professoriate.

As to rank distribution in 1994, the proportions of faculty members at each rank were more similar to those in 1972 than in 1986. The share of faculty at the assistant professor rank declined from 17% in 1972 to 10% in 1986 and then increased to 15% in 1994. Half of the faculty members were professors in 1972 compared to 59% in 1986 and 54% in 1994 at this rank. Educational leadership units continue to be top-heavy with professors compared with other disciplines; across academe at comprehensive, doctoral, and research universities in 1993, 41% of the faculty members had attained the rank of professor (National Survey of Postsecondary Faculty, 1993). Almost three fourths (74%) of the educational leadership faculty members had attained tenure in 1994, with an average of 14 years since tenure was granted.

The educational professoriate was older in 1994 than in the early 1970s; that is, the typical educational leadership faculty member in 1994 (M age = 54) was six years older than his or her counterpart in 1972 (M age = 48). Faculty members hired within the preceding five years in 1994 were on average nine years older when they entered the professorship (M age = 45), compared to faculty with more than 10 years of experience in academe, who on average entered the professorate at age 34.

One third of the total 1994 respondents had served as school administrators before joining the professoriate. New faculty (45%) were far more likely than senior faculty members (28%) to have had administrative experience, which explains in part why new educational leadership faculty members are entering academe at an older age. Faculty who had been school administrators were predominately employed at comprehensive universities. Indeed, of the new faculty *with* administrative experience in 1994, 57% were at comprehensive universities, compared to 24% and 19% at doctoral and research universities, respectively. In contrast, almost one half of the new faculty *without* administrative experience (47%) were employed at research institutions, compared to 22% at doctoral and 31% at comprehensive universities. More than one half of the new faculty in non-UCEA programs, compared to one fourth of the new faculty in UCEA programs, had administrative experience. Recently hired male faculty (54%) also were more likely than their female peers (30%) to have been school administrators.

In terms of compensation, educational leadership faculty members as a group appeared to have lost ground during the past decade, compared with faculty in other disciplines. Campbell and Newell (1973) reported that educational leadership faculty members in 1972 were well paid.

McCarthy et al. (1988) also reported that salaries in educational leadership units compared favorably with those in other areas in 1986. But the 1993 National Survey of Postsecondary Faculty (NSOPF) showed that faculty across disciplines made on average over $7,000 more than educational leadership faculty members in 1993. Of course, within the educational leadership professoriate, significant salary differences occur by type of institution with faculty at research universities on average making $8,000 more than faculty at comprehensive universities ($57,000 compared to $49,000).

An unexpected finding in 1994 was that the gender-based salary differences documented in previous studies of educational leadership faculty members had been eliminated when controlling for rank and length of time in academe. This is particularly surprising, given that faculty salaries across disciplines still reflect a gender discrepancy in compensation (Magner, 1996).

Professional Activities and Preferences

Many responses pertaining to professional activities and preferences remained quite similar across the 1972, 1986, and 1994 cohorts. As in previous studies, the most enjoyable aspect of the professorial role was teaching graduate students, the most preferred periodical was the *Kappan*, and the most important professional organization was the American Educational Research Association (AERA). Another constant between 1986 and 1994 was the least enjoyable professorial activity: faculty governance.

Also similar to prior studies, the largest proportion of faculty members' time in 1994 was devoted to teaching and advising graduate students, with two graduate courses per term the typical teaching load. The difference in average teaching loads of faculty members at comprehensive and research universities was reduced from almost two credit hours per term in 1986 to one credit hour in 1994. Overall, the average amount of time educational leadership faculty devoted to teaching declined between 1986 and 1994, primarily because in 1994 teaching loads for faculty at comprehensive universities were lower and a larger number of faculty did not have teaching assignments due to administrative roles or funded research projects.

Only two of the content areas recommended by the National Policy Board for Educational Administration (NPBEA) for inclusion in leadership preparation programs were among the most frequently reported content specializations of faculty members in 1994: leadership and organizational theory. Leadership was the most frequently mentioned specialization of the 1994 respondents; 16% listed this as their primary focus. The only other topic listed by more than 10% of the 1994 respondents was school law (13%). A small fraction of faculty members specialized in the NPBEA-recommended areas of societal and cultural influences on schooling, teaching and learning processes and school improvement, methodologies of organizational studies and policy analysis, policy studies and politics of education, and the moral and ethical dimensions of schooling. Even though few faculty members listed ethics as their area of primary specialization, the 1994 respondents did strongly support giving greater emphasis to ethics in leadership preparation.

Fewer gender-based differences in content specializations were found in 1994 than in 1986. For example, in 1986 female faculty were far more likely than male faculty to specialize in organizational theory (25% compared to 14%) and far less likely to specialize in economics or finance (1% compared to 8%). By 1994, women were somewhat more likely than men to consider economics or finance their primary specialization (10% compared to 7%) and slightly less likely to specialize in organizational theory (8% compared to 9%). The specializations of women moved more in line with those of men between the two studies.

The content specializations of faculty members in 1994 for the most part mirrored traditional course areas included in leadership preparation programs, which is consistent with findings of prior studies (Norton, 1992; Pohland & Carlson, 1993). In part, this is due to the strong influence that state certification requirements have on the curriculum by requiring course work in traditional areas (e.g., law, finance, organizational theory, supervision) for individuals to be certified as school administrators.

Scholarly productivity of educational leadership faculty members, reflected by the mean numbers of books, monographs, articles, and chapters produced, has increased steadily since 1965 (Campbell & Newell, 1973; Hills, 1965; McCarthy & Kuh, 1997), even though comparisons with faculty across disciplines remain unfavorable (National Survey of Postsecondary Faculty, 1993). The proportion of educational leadership faculty members involved in research increased from 50% in 1965 (Hills, 1965) to 85% in 1994. Faculty members in 1994 on average had written or edited (either alone or with colleagues) 8.6 books or monographs in their careers and had written 12.6 articles or chapters within the preceding five years. NCPEA members had written slightly more articles but had produced slightly fewer books or monographs than had their non-NCPEA peers.

Female faculty members as a group in both 1986 and 1994 exhibited more interest in and devoted more time to research than did their male colleagues. Also, women in 1994 were almost twice as likely as men to designate research as their primary strength (25% compared to 13%). But women on average produced only slightly more articles and chapters than did men in 1994, and men outproduced women in terms of books and monographs, controlling for length of time in academe. People of color were somewhat more likely than Caucasians to list research as their primary strength in 1994, whereas the opposite was true in 1986. The proportion of people of color designating research as their primary strength almost doubled between 1986 and 1994 (from 11% to 19%), and no significant differences in research productivity by race were found in 1994.

Faculty members affiliated with UCEA programs and research universities continued to publish more than their counterparts did. However, the substantial differences by type of institution and UCEA affiliation in amount of time devoted to research and level of commitment to research narrowed considerably between 1986 and 1994, especially among new faculty members. Strong commitment to and a track record in research appeared to be more important in hiring educational leadership faculty members at UCEA programs and research universities in the 1980s than in the 1990s.

Attitudes Toward the Field and Professoriate

Using the early 1970s as a baseline, faculty demographic characteristics have changed more than their job satisfaction and attitudes toward the field and professoriate. In general, faculty members have remained satisfied with their jobs, their students, and their preparation programs. Indeed, faculty members were even more satisfied with various aspects of their work in 1994 than in 1986. More than four fifths of the 1994 respondents were satisfied with their current positions, and most gave high marks to their own preparation program and their students. Also, they identified few topics as rather or very serious problems in their profession.

However, unlike the findings in 1986, at least half of the 1994 faculty cohort felt that the small number of minorities in the profession and the lack of financial support for graduate students were rather or very serious problems. Other concerns that the 1994 respondents voiced pertained primarily to the institutional environment (e.g., lack of university support for their units and for graduate students, insufficient recognition of service activities, politics in academe), external interference in program matters (e.g., increasing state regulation of graduate educational leadership preparation programs), and issues affecting them personally (e.g., heavy teaching, advising, and dissertation loads; low salaries).

A notable development since 1986 has been an increase in the number of faculty interested in strengthening connections with practitioners and emphasizing field-based components in preparation programs. Thus, the NPBEA's (1989) recommendation that relationships with the field should be strengthened apparently is being heeded by educational leadership units. Both program heads and individual faculty members noted that the increase in number and type of connections with the field (e.g., internships, practica, field-based projects) was among the most significant recent developments in their units. Also, the 1994 group ranked "more attention to problems of practice" as the most critical need in the profession, whereas the largest percentage of 1972 respondents ranked "a more extensive knowledge base" first, and the 1986 cohort felt that "curriculum reform" was the most pressing need. Such a shift in preferences among educational leadership faculty members mirrors the efforts in recent years in teacher education programs to tighten the connections between university faculty and schools (Goodlad, 1994; Sizer, 1988).

Another significant finding was that about five sixths of the respondents in 1994 agreed or strongly agreed that ethics should receive more attention in educational leadership preparation programs. In contrast to Farquhar's (1981) findings that little attention was being given to ethical issues in UCEA leadership preparation programs in the late 1970s, by the 1990s most UCEA programs as well as others were addressing the moral and ethical dimensions of leadership in their preparation programs (Beck & Murphy, 1994; Murphy, 1993a).

The attitudes of educational leadership faculty members in 1994 generally did not differ significantly across subgroups (e.g., gender, type of institution, NCPEA membership, race), nor were the differences found in 1986 by gender and UCEA affiliation as pronounced in 1994. Also, the attitudes of newly hired faculty members in 1994 were like those of their experienced colleagues, and many attitudes have remained strikingly similar since the 1970s.

SELECTED TRENDS

Despite calls to alter the dominant paradigm in educational leadership preparation programs (Cambron-McCabe & Foster, 1994), such programs were characterized in the early 1990s as having made only gradual, incremental changes at best (Murphy, 1991; Pohland & Carlson, 1993). Findings from the 1994 study indicate that many features of the professoriate (e.g., faculty attitudes, rank distribution) have endured. At the same time, other results of the 1994 study suggest that the professoriate and university preparation programs may be poised on the brink of a significant transition. Several trends may determine whether a fundamental realignment of educational leadership faculty members and programs will occur: (1) the dramatic increase in the number of female faculty members since 1980, (2) the influx of newly hired faculty members who have served as school administrators, (3) tighter coupling between preparation programs and the field (practitioners and schools), and (4) the escalating homogeneity across units.

The Changing Gender Composition

The impact of the increase in female faculty members on educational leadership preparation programs and knowledge production is difficult to interpret. Although more time must pass to understand the long-range implications of this phenomenon, some things are evident now. Until the mid-1980s, educational leadership units appeared to be inhospitable environments for women. Compared with their male counterparts, for example, female faculty were underpaid and less satisfied with their jobs and their preparation programs (McCarthy et al., 1988). This is no longer the case. Women have become more satisfied, perhaps because they have more female colleagues, and many women have assumed leadership roles in their institutions, putting them in position to influence faculty hires, components of the curriculum, teaching loads, program reform, student recruitment, and so forth. Women also are exerting leadership at the national level. Since the late 1980s, women have been well represented among the leaders of UCEA, NCPEA, Division A of AERA, and specialized organizations that focus on law, finance, and politics of education.

The 1994 data contained some surprises, though. Given the gender-based attitude differences found in 1986, it was expected that the presence of more female faculty members would alter the attitudes and nature of activities that had dominated the educational leadership professoriate (McCarthy et al., 1988). In short, the influx of women was expected to change the professional culture in significant ways. However, this prediction did not materialize. Between 1986 and 1994 the attitudes of women and men toward the field and problems in the profession converged, with women's attitudes becoming more closely aligned with those of men. Thus, instead of women altering the overall culture, it appears that they have adopted the dominant values and beliefs. In addition, gender-based attitude differences were less pronounced among new faculty in 1994 than they were among new faculty in 1986.

According to Shakeshaft (1987), in the mid-1980s female educational leadership faculty members tended to focus more on instructional issues than did male faculty members. But women faculty members were less likely to list teaching as their primary strength in 1994 (60%) than they were in 1986 (71%). They also were far less likely than their male colleagues (73%) in 1994 to view teaching as their primary strength or to have been attracted to academe by an interest in teaching (27% of males; 16% of females). However, women voiced as much interest as men in preparation program development and reform, leaving some ambiguity as to the impact that the shift in gender composition will have on the instructional program.

As noted previously, more than half of the new hires in 1994 at research universities and UCEA programs were women, and female faculty members exhibited a greater affinity for inquiry and devoted more time to research than did their male colleagues. It is possible that female professors at these institutions will become the primary knowledge producers and set the inquiry agenda for the educational leadership profession as males did in earlier decades. However, the lack of significant gender differences in numbers of publications in both 1986 and 1994 is somewhat puzzling. Perhaps, since women as a group have been educational leadership faculty members a far shorter time than have men, females have not yet hit their stride in terms of producing books and monographs and have concentrated instead on refereed articles that receive greater weight in tenure and promotion decisions. The impact of women scholars on the literature in the field warrants study. It would be instructive to examine whether gender differences exist in the research topics addressed, methodologies used, and publication outlets, as has been discovered in other fields (Bean & Kuh, 1988).

Increase in Practice-Oriented Faculty Members

In the mid-1960s, 90% of educational administration faculty members were drawn from the ranks of practitioners; those practice-oriented instructors relied on anecdote and experience in lecturing and conducting class discussions (Hills, 1965). In the next two decades, fewer practitioners and generalists were hired, and more scholars with academic specializations in such areas as law, economics, and political science were appointed. The social sciences were featured in preparation programs throughout the 1970s, and during this time there was a steady increase in the proportion of educational leadership faculty who thought the literature in the field should be more theory based (Campbell & Newell, 1973; Newell & Morgan, 1980). In fact, "theory" was the topic most frequently emphasized in educational administration course work (Nagle & Nagle, 1978).

By the mid-1980s, however, serious concerns were being raised about the relevance of educational leadership preparation to the real world of schools, the dominant role of the social sciences in the curriculum, and the large number of faculty without experience as school administrators (Foster, 1988; Greenfield, 1988). In the 1990s, units have been hiring more individuals with administrative experience, reflecting a change in views about the value of such experience. The appointment of former practitioners has, in turn, contributed to the increased interest within the professoriate in field-based activities and concerns. Also, a substantial proportion of the 1994 respondents indicated that field-based activities warranted greater recognition in university reward systems.

No one argues for a return to the practices of the 1950s when former practitioners delivered most of the educational leadership courses, which lacked firm grounding in theory and research. Yet, this renewed interest in hiring practice-oriented faculty has implications for knowledge production in our field. In 1994, the large group of newly hired faculty members who had served as school administrators was older than the new cohort without such experience and on average had worked about 20 years as precollegiate educators and administrators before joining the professoriate. Also, as a group, newly hired faculty members with administrative experience were less likely to designate research as their primary strength, and they indicated greater interest in problems of practice than did their veteran colleagues or their new peers without such experience. Also, they devoted substantially less time to research than did new faculty members without administrative experience.

Respondents in 1994 were far less likely than their counterparts in the 1970s to think that more of the educational leadership literature should be theory based. Educational leadership faculty members' ambivalence about the merits of theory in guiding practice can be healthy if it represents the realization that theory and research are not the only sources of knowledge and understanding (Murphy, 1992; Sergiovanni, 1991). But this ambivalence will be counterproductive to improving the preparation of educational leaders if it means that inquiry in the field is no longer considered important. The 1994 UCEA cohort (especially new faculty members) was less likely than the 1986 UCEA group to mention "more emphasis on research" and "greater support for research activities" as the most critical needs facing the profession. Indeed, only 2% of *all* new faculty members in 1994 indicated that "more emphasis on research" was the most critical need. Also, the gap doubled from 1986 to 1994 between educational leadership faculty members and those in other disciplines as to the mean amount of their time devoted to research (12% compared to 18% across disciplines in 1986; 14% compared to 26% across disciplines in 1994).

Many of the recently hired faculty members have come to academe from school districts, which have norms and expectations that differ markedly from those of the academy. While program reform and connections with the field are important to the future of the profession, newly hired faculty must be made cognizant of the university's and the profession's expectations for their professorial performance. An appropriate balance needs to be struck within educational leadership programs, one where relevant university resources and inquiry-oriented approaches are used in seeking solutions to problems in the field and in preparing school leaders.

Studies are needed to track the research productivity of practice-oriented faculty and to examine the types of projects being attempted and their influence on preparation programs, leadership practices, and the improvement of learning in our schools. In addition, promotion and tenure patterns of new hires in the educational leadership professoriate should be monitored. How will the new group of faculty with practitioner backgrounds affect the nature and quality of research conducted in the field and the structure and content of preparation programs? Are these faculty members likely to embrace service activities and eschew research? Or will they bring pragmatic inquiry approaches to bear on new and persistent field-based problems?

Strengthening Field Connections

As in other applied areas, connections with the field of professional practice are generally considered to be essential, both for preparing educational leaders and for effective performance of these leaders in the field. Contemporary schools need reflective practitioners who understand and approach complex problems with vision, creativity, and resolve (Mulkeen & Cambron-McCabe, 1994; Schön, 1987). At professional meetings, increasing attention is being given to the moral dimensions of leadership and craft knowledge—the combination of skills, attitudes, and knowledge needed to address current challenges facing schools and educational leaders.

This attention has nurtured efforts to connect schools with preparation program faculty and students, to elevate the status of field service in educational leadership units, and, as discussed above, to underscore the value of preparation program faculty who have practical experience as school leaders.

Some university leaders seem receptive to developing new types of partnerships between the academy and external stakeholders in business, industry, and the local community. And national networks linking schools and colleges of education with public schools are receiving considerable attention (Goodlad, 1994; Sizer, 1988, 1991). In an ideal world, educational leadership units would model how universities can successfully collaborate with these groups and other agencies in mutually beneficial alliances that harness academic resources to improve the quality of life. Equally important, academe would invest in and reward people who are involved in such university-community-school partnerships. But this ideal is far from being achieved.

While much can be applauded about more tightly connecting the professoriate with the field and focusing the preparation program curriculum and faculty research on practical school problems, these shifts can also create tension for some faculty members. Faculty respondents in 1994 pointed to such tensions by indicating that service to school districts and state professional associations is not sufficiently appreciated in university reward systems. Despite efforts to reconceptualize scholarship so that dissemination of innovative instructional approaches and noteworthy observations of practice are also valued in addition to traditional forms of inquiry (Boyer, 1990), little evidence shows that institutions of higher education are embracing an expanded definition of research. University cultures are not fickle; they change slowly, usually reluctantly. Academe has always valued discovery more than application of knowledge. Universities, especially research universities, traditionally have not given high status to applied research and have relegated field-based and other outreach activities to a distant, third tier in the reward system.

It is too soon to know if attempts to change these norms have any chance of succeeding. Such changes are unlikely without additional leverage from outside the field as well as support from national groups, such as the NPBEA and professional associations. Unless institutional norms and policies do change, educational leadership faculty members who are engaged in field-based activities may find themselves disadvantaged in promotion, tenure, and annual reviews compared with their colleagues in other academic areas (Andrews, 1994). Indeed, if faculty *do* focus on activities that run counter to institutional norms, they simply will not survive in academe. If this happens, the pendulum might then swing back, with the emphasis on field connections diminishing and units seeking scholars with strong research records in traditionally valued areas.

Milstein et al. (1993) suggested that perhaps some faculty appointments should be reserved for clinical professors or other non-tenure-track professional staff who would provide leadership for innovative graduate programs and coordinate field activities. This might ameliorate much of the negative tension faculty members experience because of the clash between institutional expectations for research and their involvement with field service and program reform. But it raises other questions about the composition of the educational leadership professoriate and the value of these activities. Should innovation in graduate programs and connections with the field become the responsibility of nontenurable, clinical instructors? And if so, what are the long-term implications for the status of field-based initiatives in academe and the perceived quality of educational leadership programs?

Other issues pertaining to the renewed interest in field connections warrant attention. For example, it is essential to assess whether the nature of current engagement in the field is different from and qualitatively *better* than school linkages in the past. Also, data are needed to ascertain whether field-based preparation programs produce more effective school leaders.

Homogeneity across Programs

A creeping homogeneity seems to be occurring within the educational leadership professoriate. The substantial spread in faculty size among educational leadership units at different types of universities noted in 1986 had been reduced appreciably by 1994. Many other distinctions by type of institution and UCEA affiliation found in 1986 in resources committed to educational leadership programs (e.g., staff support, funds for professional development) had also diminished by 1994. Similarly, the differences noted in 1986 by type of institution, UCEA affiliation, and gender in faculty members' activities and attitudes toward various problems and issues facing the field were not as pronounced in 1994.

Also, differences were not statistically significant by type of institution and UCEA affiliation as to the proportions of faculty members who designated teaching as their primary strength in 1994. Whereas in 1986 the UCEA faculty cohort was far less likely than the non-UCEA group to make this designation, a larger proportion of UCEA faculty members considered teaching their primary strength in 1994. Indeed, UCEA faculty members exhibited a dramatic increase in their interest in and commitment to teaching between 1986 and 1994.

Faculty involvement in research also has become more similar across types of institutions and UCEA affiliation. This can be attributed primarily to faculty members at comprehensive universities and non-UCEA programs increasing their involvement in scholarly activities since 1986. The leveling of scholarly productivity is partly a function of the fact that the majority of educational leadership faculty members are no longer receiving their doctorates from a handful of elite institutions as was true in the 1960s and early 1970s (Campbell & Newell, 1973). No single institution produced even 4% of the faculty members in 1986 or 1994, and the top ten producers combined prepared less than one third of all faculty in both studies.

In 1986, respondents from UCEA programs and research universities were much less likely than peers elsewhere to view their current programs as focusing primarily on the preparation of practitioners, but by 1994 differences were no longer significant in respondents' perceptions of their program orientation by UCEA affiliation and type of institution. More than four fifths of all 1994 respondents indicated that their programs were oriented more toward preparing practitioners than toward preparing researchers and scholars or a balance between the two.

The 1994 respondents listed a much larger number of universities than did the 1986 cohort when asked to rank the five best educational leadership programs nationally (although the top-ranked programs remained quite similar in both studies). Indeed, almost half of all educational leadership units offering degree programs were mentioned at least once across the 1994 respondents' top five choices. Optimistically, this might suggest that more diverse criteria are being applied in judging program quality. Whereas traditionally a unit was judged based on the research publications of its faculty members, perhaps involvement in preparation program initiatives and other activities are now being considered. An alternative explanation, however, is that less distinctiveness exists because of creeping mediocrity across units.

The factors contributing to the increasing homogeneity in faculty activities and beliefs and unit structure and orientation are not known. Possibly faculty whose attitudes and values do not conform to prevailing views are winnowed from candidate pools during the screening process. Or, perhaps they feel unwelcome and undervalued once hired and thus leave academe after a short time. This lack of diversity is troubling if it means that creative thinkers are being excluded from the educational leadership professoriate, as might be suggested by the similarity in attitudes between new and veteran faculty. However, a more positive spin on the movement toward uniformity is that a leveling up has taken place among educational leadership programs: faculty across more units are involved in program reform and knowledge production than was true in the past. Supporting this premise, recent reform initiatives sponsored by the Danforth Foundation have involved faculty from a range of institutions. The roots of the homogeneity probably spring from multiple sources, and whatever the origin, implications of this leveling across units warrants additional attention.

PROGNOSIS FOR EDUCATIONAL LEADERSHIP PROGRAM REFORM

Signals are somewhat mixed regarding whether conditions are favorable for reform in educational leadership units. The slight increase in educational leadership faculty numbers between 1986 and 1994 may facilitate program reform, and a consensus exists among all of the major groups interested in school leadership that preparation program reform is needed. Since 1987, UCEA conventions have focused attention on the improvement of teaching and preparation program reform, and the NPBEA has sponsored workshops and seminars in this regard. Also, program reform has received attention at NCPEA conventions, and an AERA special interest group was established in 1993 to address teaching in educational administration and to provide a forum for faculty members to discuss innovations in preparation programs. In addition, professional publications increasingly have addressed preparation program reform (e.g., Milstein et al., 1993; Mulkeen, Cambron-McCabe, & Anderson, 1994; Murphy, 1993b), so faculty members engaged in such activities have more outlets for manuscripts that address pedagogical and curricular innovations. These activities have given program reform national attention, credibility, and status.

Also, education has become prominent on political agendas (Education Ranks as Major Issue in Elections, 1996), and state legislatures have been increasingly active in the educational policy arena. State mandates focusing on changes in school governance, interagency relationships, student performance standards, school choice, technology, and a host of other topics have affected how and where policy decisions are made, the role of school leaders, and even concepts of what education is and where it takes place. Certain state policies have specifically targeted school administrators and leadership preparation. For example, some states have undertaken extensive assessments of educational leadership programs, resulting in the elimination of some programs. Other states are considering alternatives to traditional certification for school administrators, and a few, such as North Carolina, are making significant fiscal investments in improving the preparation of school leaders (Clark, 1997). Moreover, about half of the states are involved in a consortium to create interstate licensure standards for administrators, which have significant implications for preparation programs (Council of Chief State School Officers, 1996).

The Danforth Foundation has supported two recent initiatives that have encouraged preparation program reform, especially in the participating educational leadership units. One initiative focusing on the improvement of principalship preparation involved 22 universities selected in five cycles from 1987 to 1991. Most of the participating units emphasized clinical experiences and field mentors and collaborated extensively with school districts in offering the principal preparation program. The other project, designed to revitalize educational leadership units, involved 21 institutions from 1987 until 1993. This program created opportunities for faculty members to interact with colleagues from other universities and to engage in comprehensive program development with the assistance of outside consultants. Both of these Danforth initiatives have nurtured a professional culture encouraging "reconstruction rather than simply reshaping existing programs" (Cambron-McCabe, 1993, p. 170).

It is not yet possible, however, to determine how widespread the impact of these initiatives has been and whether leadership preparation has actually improved and become more responsive to the needs of the field as a result of these programs. The effects of recently introduced pedagogical approaches (e.g., use of cohort groups) and curricular innovations (e.g., problem-centered learning) must be rigorously evaluated to determine whether these components of preparation programs are relevant to what school administrators do on the job and if they produce more effective school leaders (Leithwood, Jantzi, Coffin, & Wilson, 1996).

Despite the promising signs mentioned above, some 1994 findings in combination with data from other studies suggest that it is premature to declare that the majority of educational leadership programs are in the midst of something akin to a transformation. For example, most faculty members in 1994 were very satisfied with the quality of their programs and students. One explanation for why faculty are satisfied could be that they have worked hard in the recent past to change their programs and are reveling in their successes. Unfortunately, studies and commentators have not documented such widespread program restructuring (Duke, 1992; Hackman & Price, 1995; Murphy, 1991; Norton, 1992; Pohland & Carlson, 1993). Also, an adequate supply of new faculty members to replenish professorial ranks, much less to assume leadership in program reform, is not assured. Since the 1970s, the number of educational leadership units that place an emphasis on preparing individuals for the professorship has declined steadily. And those individuals who are entering the professoriate are similar to their veteran colleagues in their attitudes and activities.

Cambron-McCabe (1993) observed that the educational leadership professoriate is characterized by a culture of congeniality rather than a culture of collegiality; the latter, she argued, is more conducive to reform efforts. The 1994 results suggest that complacency also is woven into the educational leadership program tapestry. Congeniality and complacency are antithetical to the psychology of successful reform movements. Usually, some combination of external challenges and dissatisfaction with the status quo fosters ferment in the field, resulting in change. Since the majority of faculty do not perceive a need for the radical changes that would bring about a transformation in leadership preparation, it is unclear whether a critical mass of reformers exists to sustain the momentum and energize what appears to be a relatively complacent educational leadership professoriate. Only time will tell if rank-and-file faculty members with the help of professional organizations, such as NCPEA, will rise to the challenge.

ENDNOTES

1 This paper was the basis for the Cocking Lecture at the 1997 National Council of Professors of Education Administration Convention. A revised version of this paper will be published in *Educational Administration: A Decade of Reform*, edited by Joseph Murphy and Patrick Forsyth (in press).
2 See *Continuity and Change* (McCarthy & Kuh, 1997) for a detailed discussion of the procedures and data analysis and for a comprehensive treatment of findings. This paper draws heavily on Chapter 7 of that book.
3 Based on the Carnegie Foundation (1994) classification of institutions of higher education, 27% of the institutions that offer educational leadership graduate degrees are classified as research institutions (awarding 50 or more doctoral degrees each year and receiving annually at least $15.5 million in federal support), 19% are doctoral institutions (awarding at least 10 doctoral degrees in three or more disciplines or 20 doctoral degrees in one or more disciplines), and 55% are comprehensive institutions (awarding at least 20 master's degrees annually in one or more disciplines).
4 Faculty respondents were not analyzed by NCPEA membership in the 1972 and 1986 studies.
5 These data are based on the responses from individual faculty members in 1994. Data provided by 254 educational leadership program heads in 1994 suggested even higher female (29%) and minority (13%) representation than reported by faculty. For a discussion of possible explanations for this discrepancy, see McCarthy and Kuh (1997).

REFERENCES

Andrews, R. (1994). New directions for preparing school leaders. In T. Mulkeen, N. Cambron-McCabe, & B. Anderson (Eds.), *Democratic leadership: The changing context of administrative preparation* (pp. 49–60). Norwood, NJ: Ablex.

Bean, J., & Kuh, G. (1988). The relationship between author gender and the methods and topics used in the study of college students. *Research in Higher Education*, 28, 130–144.

Beck, L., & Murphy, J. (1994). *Ethics in educational leadership programs: An expanding role.* Newbury Park, CA: Corwin.

Boyer, E. L. (1990). *Scholarship reconsidered: Priorities of the professoriate.* Princeton, NJ: Princeton University Press.

Cambron-McCabe, N. (1993). Leadership for democratic authority. In J. Murphy (Ed.), *Preparing tomorrow's school leaders: Alternative designs* (pp. 157–176). University Park, PA: University Council for Educational Administration.

Cambron-McCabe, N., & Foster, W. (1994). A paradigm shift: Implications for the preparation of school leaders. In T. Mulkeen, N. Cambron-McCabe, & B. Anderson (Eds.), *Democratic leadership: The changing context of administrative preparation* (pp. 49–60). Norwood, NJ: Ablex.

Campbell, R. F., & Newell, L. J. (1973). *A study of professors of educational administration.* Columbus, OH: University Council for Educational Administration.

Carnegie Foundation for the Advancement of Teaching. (1994). *A classification of institutions of higher education.* Princeton, NJ: Author.

Clark, D. (1997, March). *The search for authentic educational leadership: In the universities and in the schools.* Paper presented at the annual meeting of the American Educational Research Association, Chicago.

Council of Chief State School Officers. (1996). *Interstate school leaders licensure consortium: Standards for school leaders.* Washington, DC: Author.

Davis, W. J. (1978). Departments of educational administration. In P. Silver & D. Spuck (Eds.), *Preparatory programs for educational administrators in the United States* (pp. 23–51). Columbus, OH: University Council for Educational Administration.

Duke, D. L. (1992). The rhetoric and the reality of reform in educational administration. *Phi Delta Kappan, 73,* 764–770.

Education ranks as major issue in elections. (1996). *College Board News,* 25(1), 2.

Farquhar, R. (1981). Preparing educational administrators for ethical practice. *Alberta Journal of Educational Research, 27,* 192–204.

Foster, W. (1988). Educational administration: A critical appraisal. In D. Griffiths, R. Stout, & P. Forsyth (Eds.), *Leaders for America's schools: The report and the papers of the National Commission on Excellence in Educational Administration* (pp. 68–81). Berkeley, CA: McCutchan.

Goodlad, J. (1994). *Educational renewal: Better teachers, better schools.* San Francisco: Jossey Bass.

Greenfield, T. (1988). The decline and fall of the science in educational administration. In D. Griffiths, R. Stout, & P. Forsyth (Eds.), *Leaders for America's schools: The report and papers of the National Commission on Excellence in Educational Administration* (pp. 131–159). Berkeley, CA: McCutchan.

Griffiths, D. E. (1988). *Educational administration: Reform PDQ or RIP* (UCEA Occasional Paper No. 8312). Tempe, AZ: University Council for Educational Administration.

Hackmann, D., & Price, W. (1995, February). *Preparing school leaders for the 21st century: Results of a national survey of educational leadership doctoral programs.* Paper presented at the meeting of the National Council of Professors of Educational Administration within the annual meeting of the American Association of School Administrators, San Francisco.

Heller, R., Conway, J., & Jacobson, S. (1988). Here's your blunt critique of administrator preparation. *Executive Educator,* 10(9), 18–22.

Hills, J. (1965). Educational administration: A field in transition. *Educational Administration Quarterly, 1,* 58–66.

Leithwood, K., Jantzi, D., Coffin, G., & Wilson, P. (1996). Preparing school leaders: What works? *Journal of School Leadership, 6,* 316–342.

Magner, D. (1996, September 13). The faculty. *Chronicle of Higher Education,* A12-A13.

McCarthy, M. (in press). The evolution of educational leadership preparation programs. In J. Murphy & K. Seashore-Louis (Eds.). *Handbook on research in educational administration.*

McCarthy, M., & Kuh, G. (1997). *Continuity and change: The educational leadership professoriate.* Columbia, MO: University Council for Educational Administration.

McCarthy, M., Kuh, G., Newell, L. J., & Iacona, C. (1988). *Under scrutiny: The educational administration professoriate.* Tempe, AZ: University Council for Educational Administration.

Milstein, M., & Associates (1993). *Changing the way we prepare educational leaders: The Danforth experience.* Newbury Park, CA: Corwin.

Mulkeen, T., & Cambron-McCabe, N. (1994). Educating leaders to invent "tomorrow's" schools. In T. Mulkeen, N. Cambron-McCabe, & B. Anderson (Eds.), *Democratic leadership: The changing context of administrative preparation* (pp. 15–28). Norwood, NJ: Ablex.

Mulkeen, T., Cambron-McCabe, N., & Anderson, B. (Eds.) (1994). *Democratic leadership: The changing context of administrative preparation.* Norwood, NJ: Ablex.

Murphy, J. (1991). The effects of the educational reform movement on departments of educational leadership. *Educational Evaluation and Policy Analysis, 13,* 49–65.

Murphy, J. (1992). *The landscape of leadership preparation: Reframing the education of school administrators.* Newbury Park, CA: Corwin.

Murphy, J. (1993a). Ferment in school administration: Rounds 1–3. In J. Murphy (Ed.), *Preparing tomorrow's school leaders: Alternative designs* (pp. 1–38). University Park, PA: University Council for Educational Administration.

Murphy, J. (Ed.) (1993b). *Preparing tomorrow's school leaders: Alternative designs.* University Park, PA: University Council for Educational Administration.

Murphy, J., & Forsyth, P. (Eds.) (in press). *Educational administration: A decade of reform.* Newbury Park, CA: Corwin Press and University Council for Educational Administration.

Nagle, J., & Nagle, E. (1978). Doctoral programs in educational administration. In P. Silver & D. Spuck (Eds.), *Preparatory programs for educational administrators in the United States* (pp. 114–149). Columbus, OH: University Council for Educational Administration.

National Commission on Excellence in Educational Administration. (1987). *Leaders for America's schools: The report of the National Commission on Excellence in Educational Administration.* Tempe, AZ: University Council for Educational Administration.

National Policy Board for Educational Administration. (1989). *Improving the preparation of school administrators: An agenda for reform.* Charlottesville, VA: Author.

Newell, L. J., & Morgan, D. A. (1980). [Study of professors of higher education and educational administration]. Unpublished raw data.

Norton, M. S. (1992). Doctoral studies of students in educational administration programs in non-member UCEA institutions. *Educational Considerations, 20,* 37–41.

Pohland, P., & Carlson, L. (1993, Fall). Program reform in educational administration. *UCEA Review,* 4–9.

Schön, D. (1987). *Educating the reflective practitioner.* San Francisco: Jossey-Bass.

Sergiovanni, T. (1991). Constructing and changing theories of practice: The key to preparing school administrators. *Urban Review, 23,* 39–49.

Shakeshaft, C. (1987). *Women in educational administration.* Beverly Hills, CA: Sage.

Sizer, T. R. (1988). A visit to an essential school. *School Administrator, 45*(10), 18–19.

Sizer, T. R. (1991). No pain, no gain. *Educational Leadership, 48*(8), 32–34.

U.S. Department of Education. (1993). *National survey of postsecondary faculty* [CD-ROM of restricted data]. Washington, DC: Author.

CHAPTER 2

Tomorrow's Service Ideal: A Vocational Calling or Token Obligation?

Lesley H. Browder, Jr.

The scene is familiar—a group of professors gathered around a conference table. The issues are familiar, too—a deliberation about a colleague's worthiness for tenure or promotion or perhaps the annual discussion of who should receive this year's "meritorious service" award. Sooner or later, however, as part of institutional life, every professor confronts the issue of what *service* means, especially in the context of applying its expectations to oneself and to others, that is, *service* in the sense of doing one's work by fulfilling duties and obligations to others. Depending on the particular case before the professors, it is not uncommon for a deliberating group, in one instance, to consider service as a noble ideal, a "calling," and to weigh it accordingly in their recommendations, while in another case to treat it simply as a matter of token obligations to be met.

The focus here is how we respond to the service portion of our work as professors, generally, and as educational administration professors, particularly. That is, as we approach the third millennium, we need to examine (a) what service means as an ideal—what it is, where it comes from, what it means; (b) how the service ideal has been challenged in today's life; (c) what form of service may lie ahead for tomorrow's professor, generally, and for educational administration professors, particularly; and (d) what service might mean as we move toward the year 2000.

THE SERVICE IDEAL

Nearly thirty years ago, Goode (1969) wrote an oft-quoted essay entitled, "The Theoretical Limits of Professionalization." In it, he claimed that "the two central qualities [of a profession] are (1) a basic body of abstract knowledge, and (2) the ideal of service" (p. 277). Regarding this service ideal, Goode offered four observations:

1. It is the *practitioner* who decides upon the client's needs, and the occupation will be classified as less professional if the client imposes his [sic] own judgment.
2. The profession demands real sacrifice from practitioners as an ideal and, from time to time, in fact (. . . the lawyer defending the unpopular client, the military man sacrificing his life, and so on . . .).
3. The society actually believes that the profession not only accepts these ideals but also follows them to some extent.
4. The professional community sets a system of rewards and punishments such that "virtue pays"; i.e., in general, the practitioner who lives by the service ideal must be more successful than the practitioner who does not. (pp. 278–279)

While Goode does not attempt to be more specific about this service ideal (and what he means by "real sacrifice" where professors are concerned), Hansen (1995) is more obliging. In *The Call to Teach*, Hansen suggests that the service ideal should be epitomized by the term *vocation*, a word originating from the Latin root *vocare*, meaning "to call." Says Hansen, "It denotes a summons or bidding to be of service." He continues, "Many . . .

have felt the kind of magnetic pull toward a life of service exemplified in the idea of vocation" (p. 1). Thus, Hansen's service ideal, as encompassed by the term *vocation*, contains a notion of persons being drawn to what they do, of deriving a sense of meaning and fulfillment from their efforts, and also of contributing something of social (and, for some, of religious) value to society—it "results in service to others and personal satisfaction in the rendering of that service" (p. 3).

In his more formal search for an appropriate definition of *professionalism*, Moore (1970) suggests that professionalism should really be considered as a scale rather than a cluster of attributes, a scale with differing values for each attribute. Among the many attributes of professionalism on Moore's scale are these two: the qualification of a "commitment to a *calling*, that is, the treatment of the occupation and all of its requirements as an enduring set of normative and behavioral expectations" (p. 5) and an expectation that the professional will "exhibit a *service orientation*, to perceive the needs of individual or collective clients that are relevant to his competence and to attend to those needs by competent performance" (p. 5).

Historical Roots of the Service Ideal

Historically, it was Max Weber's classic 1904 work, *The Protestant Ethic and the Spirit of Capitalism*, which brought attention to the linkage of the Reformation's religious sense of a calling to one's work in a manner that permits the existence of a capitalist society. As Weber (1904/1958) wrote, "The only way of living acceptably to God was not to surpass worldly morality in monastic asceticism, but solely through the fulfillment of the obligations imposed upon the individual by his position in the world. That was his calling" (p. 80). Additionally, as David McClelland (1961) points out in *The Achieving Society*, the notion of a calling, as seen through the works of Martin Luther and John Calvin, means continual striving to improve one's self and to achieve. Striving to do one's best religiously may be readily interpreted to mean doing one's best in the post assigned her or him by the Lord, namely one's vocation (as described by Hansen above).

This notion of striving to do one's best in service to the greater glory of God was transplanted to Puritan New England and got woven into the culture of higher education with the founding of Harvard and Yale in the 1600s. As George Mardsden points out in *The Soul of the American University: From Protestant Establishment to Established Nonbelief* (1994), "the primary purpose of Harvard College was the training of clergy" (p. 41). The largely clerical faculty was as equally at ease with the saving of souls as with studying "the natural order" as a revelation of the glories of God in creation. Thus, the service ideal as a calling for professors finds its heavily Protestant religious roots in American higher education from our colonial beginning.

As time has passed from the 1636 founding of Harvard College to the much-expanded version of American higher education today, alterations in the service ideal (as will be more fully explored below) have occurred. For the moment, however, let it be noted that Hansen's (1995) notion of persons being "drawn" to what they do is rarely based today on religious promptings but more on idiosyncratic forms of motivation. So also is deriving a sense of meaning and fulfillment more likely, for many, to find explanation in terms of psychological reasoning rather than in religious apologetics. And finally, the service ideal's sense of contribution is more likely to be perceived today as being more directed at "the common good" as secularly conceived than as reflecting God's glory. In general, today's service ethic has been largely stripped of its religious meaning (DeVitis & Rich, 1996).

Personal Testimony to the Service Ideal

It is rare for educational administration professors to write intimately about their life's work. Campbell's memoir, *The Making of a Professor* (1981), is an exception. In it, he traces his life from start to nearly its finish. This memoir stands as a testimony to Hansen's sense of vocational calling as well as a blending of the secular and religious portions of that calling. Campbell links religious ideals with his service ideals and applies them to the field of educational administration. His memoir is an accounting of his stewardship to the Master, what Campbell did with the God-given talents given him "according to his ability."

But aspects of Campbell's connections also fit the secular world of the professor. The "master" may also represent the employing institution. For example, much latitude is given the servant-professor regarding how the master's resources (wages, opportunities, and so forth) are handled. Academic freedom for the individual professor, for example, normally carries five distinct privileges with it: "classroom autonomy for the teacher, freedom of inquiry for the scholar, extramural freedom for the staff members, tenure protection for the qualified, and academic due process for the accused" (Rich, 1984, p. 57).

At the same time, however, a professor's life has points along the way where he or she will be "called to account" by the institution in one manner or another (tenure and promotion being the most obvious). Like the Master, the university expects to reap results from the professor's service in places where the university may not have "sown" or "planted," beyond its investment of trust that the professor's work will so reward the university.

And the "good" servant-professor shares in the master's happiness—as Goode says, "virtue pays." Persons outside academia, as noted by Anderson (1996, pp. 38–41), may see virtue paying off for the "good professor" in the form of that precious gift, tenure, viewed by the public as a job for life (even if the professor does not teach very well or produces no important writing). Outsiders also see other gifts: a job that is largely self-created in its responsibilities and is usually self-monitored in its activities, a job with generous vacation and free-time flexibility (including sabbatical leaves) as well as a fairly decent insurance package and retirement plan, a job often located in an attractive environment (an environment often sporting swimming pools, tennis courts, faculty parking, and even golf courses for some) with free telephones, computers, fax machines, open library facilities, and sometimes graduate assistants and secretarial help.

Of course, the "unworthy" servant-professor experiences "weeping and gnashing of teeth." If untenured, this experience usually means unemployment for adjunct or junior faculty, many of whom find themselves in Boyer's (1986) new class of "gypsy scholars"—persons who eke out a living by moving from one low-paying, dead-end teaching post to another. If the professor is already tenured, it often means remaining unpromoted in rank and consigned to the darkness of disapproval, most often expressed in the form of being ignored, placed "out of the loop," and, increasingly today, being felt as institutional pressure for the implementation of "posttenure review" systems (Tierney, 1997; Edwards, 1997) to call to account such unfortunate professors.

In *The Call of Service* (1993), Robert Coles attempts to classify various forms of the service ideal, offering a number of possible areas to employ the ideal today—for example, service offered to social and political causes, community service, personal gestures and encounters (going out of one's way), acts of charity, religiously motivated action, government-sanctioned action, service to the country, and mentoring. For Coles, the rewards one receives from performing such acts of service are measured in terms of psychic satisfactions—of doing something and reaching someone, of achieving a moral purpose, of making a personal affirmation, of expressing stoic endurance, or of boosting one's own sense of success.

So, what can be concluded about the service ideal uncritically viewed? Perhaps it is fair to say that, at its best, it is an ideal that includes a zeal for providing service to others which, when rendered, gives the server a personal sense of satisfaction and, rendered over a lifetime, provides a sense of fulfillment. If this represents the ideal, then what is the reality? How is the notion of service realized in practical, less abstract ways in today's academia?

THE SERVICE REALITY

The sociologist Robin Williams (1964) once remarked that the service ideal is usually seen as a sort of secondary ideal of lesser importance to the world at large, and DeVitis and Rich (1996) point out that John Steinbeck expresses Williams's thoughts more plainly in *Cannery Row* (1945):

> "It has always seemed strange to me," said Doc. "The things we admire in men—kindness, and generosity, openness, honesty, understanding, and feeling—are the concomitants of failure in our system. And those traits we detest—sharpness, greed, acquisitiveness, meanness, egotism, and self-interest—are the traits of success. And while men admire the quality of the first, they love the produce of the second."(p. 150)

Views of Faculty Service

Applied to professors, the American Association of University Professor's (AAUP) *Policy Documents and Reports* (1995) offers three views of service for today's professor.

1. *Service as "Enlightened Self-Interest:" An Ideal*: Service represents enlightened self-interest on the part of faculty, for whom work on the curriculum, shared governance, academic freedom, and peer review comprise the scholar's and teacher's contributions to the shaping and building of the institution. In addition, it is through service that the professional disciplines communicate and . . . that the faculties of our colleges and universities offer their professional knowledge, skills, and advice to their communities. (p. 132)
2. *Service as an Equal Part of Faculty Workloads*: Faculty workload combines teaching, scholarship, and service; *this unity of components is meant to represent the seamless garment of academic life, and it defines the typical scholarly performance and career* [emphasis added]. . . . We distort the enterprise of higher education if we attempt to separate these endeavors, or to define them as essentially competitive rather than as complementary. (pp. 129–130)
3. *Service as a Less-Than-Equal Part of Faculty Workload:* . . . *We do not urge that the rewards for service be commensurate with those for dedicated teaching and scholarship* [emphasis added]. On the other hand, we believe that such service is essential to the health of our institutions and can make significant contributions to society. (p. 132)

Limited Rewards for Service

But, while official pronouncements proclaim service to be an ideal (one held as equal to teaching and research . . . well, almost equal to . . . well, at least very important in considering faculty workloads), practice in the trenches offers a different message. While research, teaching, and service are the normal criteria for tenure and promotion, practice indicates that they are not weighted equally. Yes, one is expected to do some service, but few (if any) faculty are denied tenure on the basis of insufficient service (Kasten, 1984). Even outstanding teaching by itself does not guarantee tenure. The decisive factor for tenure and promotion decisions, say many, is published research (Boyer, 1986, 1990; Carnegie Foundation, 1989; Daly, 1994; Daly & Townsend, 1994; Kasten, 1984; Park, 1996). For example, here is a sampling of views held by four experienced educators.

1. Mary Burgan, AAUP General Secretary (1997): "Tenure committees require the measurable; respect, accomplishment, and gratitude of students must be presented in quantitative, preferably comparative, terms to count. *And service doesn't count at all.* [emphasis added]" (1997, p. 5).
2. Craufurd Goodwin, James B. Duke Professor of Economics at Duke University, former Dean of the Graduate School and Vice-Provost for Research, as well as Chair of the University Appointment, Promotion, and Tenure Committee (1995): "You must demonstrate that your career is on a proper upward trajectory and . . . this responsible behavior does not include misusing your scarcest and most precious resource—time, even if for the moment this might seem to answer a pressing need. . . . [One] is likely to encounter gratitude at the moment but a judgment of irresponsibility and unsuitability for a permanent appointment when the tenure decision is at hand" (p. 152).
3. A. Kenneth Pye, former Dean, Duke University Law School, Chancellor of the University, and Samuel Fox Mordecai Professor of Law and former President, Southern Methodist University (1995): "Universities speak of the importance of teaching, research, public service, and service in university affairs, as if all were of equal value. . . . In many institutions, promotion and tenure are conferred only upon those who conduct research and publish work of high quality" (pp. 312–313).
4. Joel Colton, Professor Emeritus of History, Duke University, and former Director for the Humanities, Rockefeller Foundation (1995): "When the times for tenure and promotion and other personnel decisions arrive, attention will be paid, to be sure, to institutional and departmental committee work, but no amount of 'service' . . . is likely to compensate for the absence of publications that signify a continuing commitment to research and scholarship" (p. 323).

So what can be concluded from this sampling? It probably comes as no surprise to professors to learn that, theoretically, service is held in high regard as an ideal, but in practice—in the hard coin of today's academic realm—service does not count at all or counts very little. "Only when a faculty member's research is borderline (adequate, but not outstanding), will her or his teaching or service record become a central focus of the review proceedings" (Park, 1996, p. 48).

And when service is reviewed, what guidelines are usually employed? Park continues:

> Although service, in general, carries little weight in faculty evaluations, certain types of service—such as being an officer or chair of a national professional organization . . . —may be noteworthy. Certainly, such professional service is typically deemed more noteworthy than university service, which, in turn, is deemed more noteworthy than community service. (p. 49)

Thus, in everyday academic life, service usually means solely the meeting of token obligations.

AAUP's General Secretary attempts to explain why service per se draws so little support from professors in today's academic climate:

> These days, many faculty members find themselves enforcing the implementation of standards far more demanding than those under which they themselves passed into tenured ranks. In making cases for hiring when lines are scarce, department faculty are likely to over-promise the administration "a national reputation" with every new hire. And then, in a spirit of "protecting" their younger colleagues from such expectations, they caution them to shield their careers from whatever might look less than perfect in a tenure dossier—the student evaluations from "service" courses or the meager feedback from serving on the faculty senate. (Burgan, 1997, p. 5)

Whether or not Burgan's reasoning suffices as an explanation, it remains clear that for most professors generally, service exists more as an afterthought than as a focused priority. But is this view of service to remain forever fixed? Is it to hold equally for today's professors of educational administration? And if it does hold, should it?

SERVICE, PROFESSORS, AND THE EDUCATIONAL ADMINISTRATION PROFESSOR

Under the leadership of the late Ernest Boyer (1928–1995), the Carnegie Foundation for the Advancement of Teaching released a report, *Scholarship Reconsidered,* in 1990. The goal of this report, said Boyer (1996, p. 130), "was to confront the matter of faculty roles and rewards head on." Pointing out historically that the primary mission of most seventeenth- and eighteenth-century American colleges and universities was a moral and spiritual one, the report contends that this mission shifted with the advent of the land-grant colleges and technical schools toward a more practical and economic focus by the mid-nineteenth century and early twentieth century. In the process of shifting, Boyer (1990) states, "American education, once devoted primarily to the intellectual and moral development of students, *added service as a mission*" [emphasis added] (p. 5).

The Increased Focus on Research

Gradually over the past hundred years, another mission shift occurred, one based on the Germanic PhD model of original research, introducing an imperative for a more theoretical and objective sense of mission in the university's "search of truth." With the advent of World War II and the greatly increased national funding for research, external pressure for research productivity increased and became widely shared among institutions of higher education, not just a limited few. This pressure again shifted mission focus "from the student to the professoriate, from general to specialized education, and from loyalty to the campus [and local community] to loyalty to the profession" (Boyer, 1990, p. 13).

Since this change, research has become the publish-or-perish mantra of higher education, the major yardstick by which faculty are measured. "Even though the diversity of institutions of higher education in the United States is unmatched, the tendency in recent years has been to impose a single model of scholarship on the entire higher education enterprise" (p. 54). This emphasis on professorial research productivity, Cole (1993) suggests, comes from competition among universities "to be 'the best' and to be *perceived* as among the best . . . research excellence . . . legitimates the university's claim to greatness" (p. 24). But must and should this research model of scholarship remain the dominate focus of all American colleges and universities today? And what about tomorrow?

While today the research and publication emphasis among and between academies remains dominant and largely unquestioned (Park, 1996, p. 74), a growing sentiment appears to support unseating the research-and-publication criteria tomorrow—that is, to unseat the research model as the only significant criteria in assessing a professor's work by giving teaching and service greater weight. In part, this sentiment is driven by forces outside the academy. As any regular reader of *The Chronicle of Higher Education* is aware, we live in an age where government funding of research is less certain, where public cries for fiscally leaner and more accountable institutions of higher education are heard more often, where the demographic pool for college-material students is increasingly more competitive, and where public attitudes toward the mission of higher education are often more cynical (Cole, 1993; Miller, 1990; Nichols, 1993; Park, 1996). Within the academy, accreditation-driven pressures continue for increasing faculty diversity and for honoring lofty mission statements in deed as well as word. And finally, educational administration professors face an added pressure—one derived as a residue from the recent educational reform movement's impact on our field of study: how to respond *as professors* to a growing call for "moral leadership" as an imperative in our administrator preparation programs.

Let me now review three trends which tend to add more weight to the service standard in the assessment of a professor's work, generally, and the educational administration professor's work, specifically, as we move toward the year 2000.

The Trend to Enhance Service by Redefining Scholarship

Driven by a sense that priorities in a professor's work are out of balance—that it has become, for example, "far more important for most professors to deliver a paper at the Hyatt in Chicago than to teach undergraduates back home" (Boyer, 1996, p. 131)—the Carnegie Foundation published *Scholarship Reconsidered* (Boyer, 1990). Using the question, "What does it mean to be a scholar?" this study concluded that scholarship was a multifaceted quality containing not one but four "inextricably interlocked" components (p. 16). These redefined components of scholarship include (a) discovery, representing basically our common understanding of "research"; (b) integration, meaning finding a place for new research "discoveries" and integrating them into a larger pattern of knowledge (avoiding the fragmentation and isolation characteristic of overspecialized knowledge); (c) application, meaning how knowledge can be applied usefully and responsibly to consequential problems, thereby avoiding irrelevant scholarship in the social context and requiring the professor to be responsible for both the direction and consequences of her or his research (Boyer, 1996, p. 132); and (d) teaching, representing a transmission of research publication (viewed as a form of teaching through the printed page) into a teaching act richer in scope and dimension than merely the dissemination of knowledge.

Of course, it is this redefined view of service as the scholarship of application that excites attention here. It opens the door for viewing forms of service in a different light in the assessment of faculty work. "Rather than devaluing service as trivial, nonintellectual or even anti-intellectual (because personal commitments compromise objectivity), an institution that acknowledged the scholarship of service would value service as 'serious, demanding work,' which produces as well as applies knowledge" (Park, 1996, p.77).

Braskamp and Ory (1994) parallel this broader definition of service, using the terms *practice* and *professional service* to indicate faculty work aimed at "solving the problems of our society using their expertise, knowledge, and seasoned professional judgment" (p. 43). Their research includes a sampling of recent, more scholarly definitions of service where scholarship is intended to be used, explicitly or implicitly, in solving "societal problems." Accordingly, this view is intended to convey a sense of "the instrumental value of knowledge and the implicit connection between institutions of higher education and society" (p. 44). Here are a few of these broader definitions of service:

1. Professional or Community Service: "The scholarly use of one's academic expertise in areas other than the traditional teaching and research" (Elman & Smock, 1992, p. 11).
2. Scholarship of Practice: "The application of knowledge to the problems of society" (Rice, 1991, p. 125).
3. Public Service: "Public service is a set of activities utilizing faculty expertise to solve societal problems or to help others to do so, intended to benefit the public and contribute to the welfare of society" (Schomberg & Farmer, 1993, p. 17).

4. Public Service: "The practical application of knowledge accumulated at the university through research and other scholarly activities to problems confronting individual citizens, citizen groups, and public and private organizations. It consists of identifying, assessing, managing problems, and developing and transferring useful information to the client or client groups" (McAlister, 1991, pp. 4–5).

In the progression of definitions offered above, a sense is conveyed of the professor being drawn out of his or her cloistered academic environment into the larger world, a world full of problems. Further, an expectation exists that the professor's scholarship can both be actively employed and should matter in dealing with those problems.

The Trend to Enhance Service by Holding Institutions Responsible for Their Mission Statements

With the academically respectable Carnegie Foundation's redefinition of scholarship broadened to include service (under the wing of the "scholarship of application"), it follows naturally to examine how such redefinitions of scholarship fit the academy's mission statements. Both Boyer (1990, 1996) and Metzler (1994), for example, base portions of their arguments for redefining scholarship on the diversity of American institutional missions. They ask: Is it necessary for *all* colleges and universities to ape the faculty assessment criteria of research universities?

Part of the answer lies in our post-World War II history. During times of rapid expansion and growth, academy mission statements tended to serve more as public relations material than as serious guiding documents. With less growth and a greater concomitant need to determine institutional priorities, however, mission statements are receiving closer attention. For example, as institutions discover that they cannot do everything well, they need to determine what they will or will not do at all. At such times, the mission statement gets reappraised.

Often, this reappraisal yields a different view of an institution's mission. Dilts, Haber, and Bialik (1994), for example, argue that publish or perish may be appropriate if publication in leading journals "is all that needs to occur to accomplish the school's mission. If the institution . . . has no goals or mission in teaching or service, or does not expect good citizenship, then publish or perish may serve it well" (p. 42). But this condition seldom fits the case; it is recognized that teaching, service, and good citizenship are required. Dilts et al. reach this conclusion:

> If citizenship, teaching and service are expected, they must be evaluated and weighed in the appropriate personnel decisions. Without such accountability it is unlikely that these objectives will be served. Expressed expectations of citizenship, service or teaching, if left undefined, serve only to mislead, unless research is viewed as predictive of quality in the three other areas. (p. 42)

Lidstone, Hacker and Oien (1996) go further, stating that colleges and universities often have multiple mission statements and a further internal diversity of missions. For example, the typical land-grant institution is likely to have a research-and-outreach mission for its agricultural and biological science units and a teaching-and-service mission for its arts-and-science college. Going further, they point out that various departments within a subunit of the university are likely to have diverse missions: "Within the college of arts and science, chemistry, for example, may have a doctoral degree-granting program with a strong research agenda, whereas the department of health, physical education, and recreation could have a mission oriented toward professional preparation and service to students and the public" (p. 201). It can be argued, they contend, that individual faculty, based on individual forms of knowledge, experience, and expertise, may legitimately serve different aspects of the larger unit's overall mission.

Thus, in a changing academic world moving toward the year 2000, pressure exists to question the dominant research hegemony in assessment of faculty work (one size does not fit all), to broaden the definition of scholarship (service as "the scholarship of application"), and to reexamine the full context of mission statements ("mission is everything" statements). What is the impact of these pressures on the educational administration professor?

The Trend to Enhance Service via the Reform Movement in Educational Administration

While the above trends apply generally to all professors in American colleges and universities, within the field of educational administration exists an additional pressure—the "reform" pressure for moral leadership, a pressure originating from the continuing educational reform waves sparked by the initial 1983 report, *A Nation at Risk: The Imperative for Educational Reform* (National Commission on Excellence in Education). As this first wave of reform swept across American education, it spilled into the field of educational administration also, producing at least two major reports, *Leaders for America's Schools* (National Commission on Excellence in Educational Administration, 1987) and *Improving the Preparation of School Administrators: An Agenda for Reform* (National Policy Board for Educational Administration, 1989).

Although both of these two reports have had their motives and recommendations questioned (Browder, 1988, 1990–1991; Erlandson, 1990; Gibboney, 1987; Hawley, 1990), the reform wave in educational administration has rolled forward with little formal resistance, and the sheer scope of the reform effort makes it revolutionary. As Murphy (1992) reports, nearly all aspects of administrator preparation programs received attention.

Among the "imperatives for reform" of the new National Policy Board for Educational Administration (1989) was a call for the inclusion of the "moral and ethical dimensions of schooling" (p. 19) in administrator preparation programs. For example, " the program must address what is right to do as well as the right way to do it . . . to provide frameworks and tools to assist students in assessing the moral and ethical implications of administrative decisions in schools" (p. 21). However, while educational administration professors are now asked to include moral and ethical material in their courses for preparing school administrators, a large silence is left on the application of these values to the professor's own moral and ethical practices.

Meanwhile, a more fundamental change is afoot in our field with the knowledge base, roles of theorists and practitioners, and accepted practices being questioned (Bosetti, Landry, & Miklos, 1989). In the eyes of many, an enormous shift in thinking has been underway in the field of educational administration (Alexander, 1984; Clark, 1981; English, 1992, 1994; Hodgkinson, 1991; Sergiovanni, 1992; Starratt, 1996). "Earlier frameworks, presuppositions, and bedrock principles have been challenged, modified, discarded, or reworked," writes Starratt (1996), as "scholars assert that the old certainties are clearly inadequate, misguided, inappropriate, or invalid" (p. 39). According to English (1994): *"The old administrative science is dead"* [emphasis added] (p. 231).

But, continues English (1994), "it must not be replaced by a new administrative science, but by a critical reflective approach that is centered in the humanities" (p. 231). While other approaches are available (Downey, 1988; LaRocque, 1989; Nakamura & Smallwood, 1980), critical theory appears to be among our field's preferred responses to the alleged "death" of administrative science. Works like Sergiovanni's *Moral Leadership* (1992) and Starratt's *Transforming Educational Administration: Meaning, Community, and Excellence* (1996) rest heavily on the theoretical underpinnings of the subjectivist work of Greenfield (1975, 1980, 1988) and Hodgkinson (1982, 1991). In such works, the call is for greater risk-taking; school administrators taking activist-reformer roles as contrasted with the more familiar traditional executive leader role often criticized for simply managing the status quo and for playing it safe. As Sergiovanni (1992) suggests, this expanded view of leadership which now includes the moral dimension of leadership "may require us to reinvent the concept of leadership itself" (p. xiii).

During most of this century, our field has attempted to use scientific conceptualizations of business management and social science research upon which to build its leadership theories. Now, however, spurred by efforts of organizations like the Danforth Foundation to help transform society by promoting a vision of school administrators as moral leaders, a series of new leadership metaphors have emerged (Murphy, 1992, pp. 131–135), metaphors heavily laden with terms like "values," "ethics," "purpose-defining," "reflective analysis," "active intervention," and so on. Says English (1994),

> Leadership without morality is little more than bureaucratic technique. Leadership centered in morality is distinctly aware of its own values, and those of the people working in organizations such as schools. Moral leadership is centered on people as centers of action, not merely as recipients of action. Moral leadership re-centers people as agents of change who can shape their environment and the organizations they live and work in to become more fully humane. (p. 231)

And within our field's paradigm shift, it is not unusual to hear professors critical of school administrators. Writing for a group of professors, for example, Berliner (1997) complains about administrators who "take the middle road on all questions, looking for consensus positions" (pp. 14–15). Stating that today's "lack of unified positions on many issues" allows school administrators to "take on the intellectual and moral leadership of a school and community," Berliner urges them "to be leaders in a choir of moral voices raised because our society is in danger" (p. 15). He exhorts school administrators to show moral courage. While the cries do not, so far, include professors of educational administration, nothing prevents educational administration professors from displaying similar moral backbone for the benefit of our students by "speaking out" and serving the same causes as administrators and others engaged in shaping educational policy. The University Council for Educational Administration's "Thousand Voices from the Field" project is an indication that, indeed, some professors are seeking to render such forms of public service (UCEA Goal Activities, 1997).

Thus, because of our field's shift in thinking caused, in part, by the educational reform movement, and because of the greater appreciation of the moral dimension of leadership and the more active consideration of values in decision making, we are under increased pressure to design preparation programs for moral leaders. In turn, in a context of greater moral and ethical sensitivity, pressure exists for professors of educational administration who engage in such programs to confront the following question: Should the educational administration professor be immune from an expectation that he or she should actively participate as a moral leader in educational matters and in the shaping of public policy? Expressed more simply, if you are going to talk the talk, professor, should you not be expected to walk the walk and be actively involved in both public and professional service? If one is to shift from English's "dead administrative science" with its "pretense" of "neutral objectivity and rationality" to a critical reflective approach—one taking moral positions and producing value-laden scholarship—then one is convicted (in this context) as a "false teacher" if one does not live by what he or she teaches. It now becomes both a moral and ethical imperative and, accordingly, a pressure to weigh such service, when rendered, more heavily in the professional and academic assessment of educational administration faculty. The bell of moral leadership tolls for all who would profess it!

In sum, it is contended that at least three trends are currently active in pressing for a more equalized weighting of research, teaching, and service in the assessment of faculty work. Two of these trends—broadening the definition of scholarship and reconsidering the mission statements of academic units to mean what they say—apply to all college and university faculty. The third trend, our field's response to the educational reform movement, is more particular. For professors who now profess moral leadership to their students, it becomes ethically expected to demonstrate some forms of moral leadership in their service—that is, to practice what they preach.

But if so, what are the consequences for educational administration professors embracing moral leadership as a service ideal? What does it mean?

TOWARD THE YEAR 2000: WHAT IT MEANS

And so, as we look toward the new millennium, what might we expect for the service ideal in the assessment of faculty work—a new respect for it as a vocational calling or its mere tolerance as a collection of token obligations to be met? Which seems more likely?

For the present, the dead weight of the current academic tradition is likely to continue—too many faculty have "paid their dues" to the enshrined research model, hold their current positions by virtue of it, and are comfortable with the rewards that flow from this arrangement. What incentive exists for a tenured, full professor to risk changing the rules? Thus, to the basic question, "Will the faculty reward system ever change?" it is easy to anticipate a negative response under current conditions.

But this is the wrong question, suggests Boyer (1996): "The simple truth is that nothing is static, conditions are always changing.... The only two questions that matter are, In which direction is it changing, and how long will it take?" (p. 138). And what does Boyer believe? He claims,

> there is no question that the paradigm of faculty rewards is moving toward greater recognition of teaching.... we have the evidence ... that service is going to reemerge with greater vitality than we have seen in the last 100 years, simply because the university must be engaged if it hopes to survive. The social imperative for service has become so urgent that the university cannot ignore it. I must say that I am worried that *right now the uni-*

versity is viewed as a private benefit, not a public good [emphasis added]. Unless we recast the university as a publicly engaged institution I think our future is at stake. (p. 138)

It is "recasting" the university as a "publicly engaged institution"—one providing a public good—that is likely to raise the service standard for faculty to the level of a vocational calling. Faced with a change-or-perish environment, most institutions can be expected to elect change—change sooner or later, depending on the particular institution. Consider, for example, the impact on public attitudes toward higher education coming from a recent *New York Times* (Better Schools for Teachers, 1997) editorial, declaring that "colleges that train teachers are often no more than diploma mills, offering watered-down courses and marginal preparation for the profession. . . . At some colleges last year, up to 75 percent of prospective teachers failed state certification" (p. A18). In the same *Times* issue is another story about 104 graduating Hostos Community College students who took a required basic English exam which only 13 passed (Arenson, 1997).

Such daily sorts of articles set a tone for change in academia. The increasing appearance of posttenure review committees, peer observation, and similar changes afoot at many universities today already harbinger the feeling of pressure to recaste the faculty-assessment structure. If other pressures appear (e.g., an alteration in the way *U.S. News & World Report* compiles and reports its annual college rankings [Geraghty, 1997]), the recasting pace of change could accelerate.

One might also expect that it will only be a question of time before the AAUP's famous "1940 Statement of Principles on Academic Freedom and Tenure" has its "academic freedom" clause read more closely—particularly the clause declaring professors to be "citizens" (American Association of University Professsors, 1995, p. 4).

This clause is a safeguard and set of rules for faculty if and when they perform citizen-type services as professors in the larger community. It states that they should be free from institutional censorship and discipline, but not from institutional expectation that faculty will perform such services as citizens. Accordingly, one might expect institutional pressures for faculty to perform such roles, say, in responding to the *New York Times* editorial above. At the same time, the quid-pro-quo factor can be expected to increase the weight of rendering such public services in faculty work assessments.

Taken altogether—the broadening of scholarship's definition, the growing recognition that different academic units have different missions and should assess their faculty in accordance with those missions, and the pressures for change coming from both outside and within academia and its different fields of study—what does it mean? To me, it means that one might expect to see an accommodation made in the manner criteria are used in faculty assessment. Such an accommodation would entail official recognition (both in word and deed) of the following: (a) that different institutional and unit missions necessitate different faculty assessment profiles (i.e., an abandonment of the one-size-fits-all criteria); (b) that broader definitions of scholarship require broader acceptance of its demonstration and enlarged standards of evidence; (c) that the increasing needs for institutional and academic subunits to be perceived as "public goods" rather than "private benefits" concomitantly increase need for faculty to be more diligently involved in their (heretofore largely ignored) "citizen" roles, performing services of "good works"; and (d) that faculty service be recognized as a vocational calling rather than merely a set of token obligations to be met.

For today's junior faculty—many coming from what some call "a plantation system" of scarce faculty positions (Leatherman, 1997)—it will come to mean an expectation that the employing academies will increasingly give "three talents" to newly employed faculty: one for research, one for teaching, and one for service. When the academy checks, it will expect to find evidence that each talent has been well maintained and another three talents also produced. While some may now fret that the means of assessing such talents are inadequate, others are more confident (Boyer, 1996; Braskamp & Ory, 1994; Dilts et al., 1994; Lidstone, Hacker, & Oien, 1996; Park, 1996; Seldin, 1984). But the point stands: junior faculty are not likely to hear, "well done, good and faithful servant," from the employing institution unless the new expectations for each of the three areas are well clarified.

And for the educational administration professor identifying with moral leadership, the added expectation is that, in the act of practicing what one professes, one will embrace a vocational calling as a service ideal. If a moral leader is a person concerned with acting responsibly on her or his held ideals and values, a person who is motivated by ethical principles to help others both inside and outside the academy, and a person who seeks to help people by empowering them rather than by controlling them, then a faculty member acting in such a manner will reflect the spirit of moral leadership.

One hopes that at the close of professional careers, ones like Roald Campbell's devoted to fulfilling such standards, it can be said that the service has been faithful. And perhaps, as we move toward the year 2000, that is what the Master intended all along.

REFERENCES

Alexander, E. R. (1984). After rationality what? A review of responses to paradigm breakdown. *American Planning Association Journal, 50*(1), 62–69.

American Association of University Professors. (1995). *Policy documents and reports.* Washington, DC: Author.

Anderson, M. (1996). *Impostors in the temple: A blueprint for improving higher education in America.* Stanford, CA: Hoover Institution Press.

Arenson, K. W. (1997, July 15). A judge tells CUNY to give diplomas to Hostos students. *New York Times,* p. B3.

Berliner, D. C. (1997). Voice training. *UCEA Review, 38*(2), 1, 9, 11, 14–15.

Better schools for teachers. (1997, July 15). *New York Times,* p. A18.

Boyer, E. L. (1986). *College: The undergraduate experience in America.* Princeton, NJ: Carnegie Foundation for the Advancement of Teaching.

Boyer, E. L. (1990). *Scholarship reconsidered: Priorities of the professoriate.* Princeton, NJ: Princeton University Press.

Boyer, E. L. (1996, May). From "scholarship reconsidered" to "scholarship assessed." *Quest, 48*(2), 129–139.

Braskamp, L. A., & Ory, J. C. (1994). *Assessing faculty work: Enhancing individual and institutional performance.* San Francisco: Jossey-Bass.

Browder, L. H. (1988). A commentary on "Leaders for America's Schools." *AASA Professor, 10*(4), 1–4.

Browder, L. H. (1990-1991). Look what they've done to us now! A critical essay on the National Policy Board for Educational Administration's "agenda for reform." *National Forum of Educational Administration and Supervision Journal, 8*(1), 5–40.

Burgan, M. (1997, May/June). Ratcheting up. *Academe, 83*(3), 5.

Campbell, R. F. (1981). *The making of a professor.* Salt Lake, UT: Publishers Press.

Carnegie Foundation for the Advancement of Teaching. (1989). *The condition of the professoriate: Attitudes and trends.* Princeton, NJ: Author.

Clark, D. L. (1981). In consideration of goal-free planning: The failure of traditional planning systems in education. *Educational Administration Quarterly, 17*(3), 42–60.

Cole, J. R. (1993). Balancing acts: Dilemmas of choice facing research universities. *Daedalus, 122,* 1–35.

Coles, R. (1993). *The call of service: A witness to idealism.* Boston: Houghton Mifflin.

Colton, J. (1995). The role of the department in the groves of academe. In A. L. DeNeef & C. D. Goodwin (Eds.), *The academic's handbook* (pp. 315-333). Durham, NC: Duke University Press.

Daly, F., & Townsend, B. K. (1994). The chair's role in tenure acquisition. *Thought and Action, 9,* 125–146.

Daly, W. T. (1994). Teaching and scholarship: Adapting American higher education to hard times. *Journal of Higher Education, 65,* 45–57.

DeNeef, A. L., & Goodwin, C. D. (Eds.). (1995). *The academic's handbook.* Durham, NC: Duke University Press.

DeVitis, J. L., & Rich, J. M. (1996). *The success ethic, education, and the American dream.* Albany: State University of New York Press.

Dilts, D. A., Haber, L. J., & Bialik, D. (1994). *Assessing what professors do: An introduction to academic performance appraisal in higher education.* Westport, CT: Greenwood Press.

Downey, L. W. (1988). *Policy analysis in education.* Calgary, Alberta, Canada: Detselig.

Edwards, R. (1997). Can post-tenure review help us save the tenure system? *Academe, 83*(3), 26–31.

Elman, S. E., & Smock, S. M. (1992). A continuing conversation about professional service. *AAHE Bulletin, 44*(2), 10–13.

English, F. W. (1992). *Educational administration: The human service.* New York: HarperCollins.

English, F. W. (1994). *Theory in educational administration.* New York: HarperCollins.

Erlandson, D. (1990). Agenda for reform: A critical appraisal. *Journal of Educational Policy, 5*(2), 187–191.

Geraghty, M. (1997, July 18). "U.S. News" alters methodology of its controversial college rankings. *Chronicle of Higher Education,* p. A34.

Gibboney, R. A. (1987, April 15). Education of administrators: "An American tragedy." *Education Week,* p. 28.

Goode, W. J. (1969). The theoretical limits of professionalization. In A. Etzioni (Ed.), *The semi-professions and their organization* (pp. 266–313). New York: Free Press.

Goodwin, C. D. (1995). Some tips on getting tenure. In A. L. DeNeef & C. D. Goodwin (Eds.), *The academic's handbook* (pp. 150–157). Durham, NC: Duke University Press.

Greenfield, T. B. (1975). Theory about organization: A new perspective and its implications for schools. In M. G. Hughes (Ed.), *Administering education: International challenge* (pp. 71–99). London: Athlone.

Greenfield, T. B. (1980). The man who comes back through the door in the wall. *Educational Administration Quarterly, 16*(3), 26–59.

Greenfield, T. B. (1988). The decline and fall of science in educational administration. In D. E. Griffiths, R. T. Stout, & P. B. Forsyth (Eds.). *Leaders for America's schools* (pp. 131–159). Berkeley, CA: McCutchan.

Hansen, D. T. (1995). *The call to teach.* New York: Teachers College Press.

Hawley, W. (1990). Policy board proposals ignore real problems. *School Administrator, 46*(10), 8–11, 14–15.

Hodgkinson, C. (1982). *The philosophy of leadership.* Oxford: Blackwell.

Hodgkinson, C. (1991). *Educational leadership.* Albany: State University of New York Press.

Kasten, K. L. (1984). Tenure and merit pay as rewards for research, teaching, and service at a research university. *Journal of Higher Education, 55,* 500–514.

LaRocque, L. (1989). Another perspective on "critical perspectives." *Canadian Administrator, 29*(2), 8–9.

Leatherman, C. (1997, July 18). Should dog walking and house sitting be required for a Ph.D.? *Chronicle of Higher Education,* pp. A10–A11.

Lidstone, J. E., Hacker, P. E., & Oien, F. M. (1996). Where the rubber meets the road: Revising promotion and tenure standards according to Boyer. *Quest, 48,* 200–210.

Lyons, J. D. (1997, March/April). Not so good: The annual report on the economic status of the profession, 1996–97 [Special issue]. *Academe, 83*(2), 12–92.

Marsden, G. M. (1994). *The soul of the American university: From protestant establishment to established non-belief.* New York: Oxford University Press.

McAlister, J. D. (1991). *Report of the committee on the evaluation of faculty effort in extension and service.* Blacksburg: Virginia Polytechnic Institute and State University.

McClelland, D. C. (1961). *The achieving society.* New York: Van Nostrand.

Metzler, M. W. (1994). Scholarship reconsidered for the professoriate of 2010. *Quest, 46,* 440–455.

Miller, L. H. (1990, September/October). Hubris in the academy: Can teaching survive an overweening quest for excellence? *Change,* pp. 9–11, 53.

Moore, W. E. (1970). *The professions: Roles and rules.* New York: Russell Sage Foundation.

Murphy, J. (1992). *The landscape of leadership preparation: Patterns and possibilities.* Beverly Hills, CA: Corwin Press.

Nakamura, R. T., & Smallwood, F. (1980). *The politics of policy implementation.* New York: St. Martin's Press.

National Commission on Excellence in Education. (1983). *A nation at risk: The imperative for educational reform.* Washington, DC: U.S. Government Printing Office.

National Commission on Excellence in Educational Administration. (1987). *Leaders for America's schools.* Tempe, AZ: University Council for Educational Administration.

National Policy Board for Educational Administration. (1989). *Improving the preparation of school administrators: An agenda for reform.* Charlottesville, VA: Author.

Nichols, R. W. (1993). Federal science policy and universities: Consequences of success. *Daedalus, 122,* 197–223.

Park, S. M. (1996). Research, teaching, and service: Why shouldn't women's work count? *Journal of Higher Education, 67*(1), 46–84.

Pye, A. K. (1995). University governance and autonomy: Who decides what in the university. In A. L. DeNeef & C. D. Goodwin (Eds.), *The academic's handbook* (pp. 297–314). Durham, NC: Duke University Press.

Rice, R. E. (1991). Toward a broader conception of scholarship: The American context. In I. T. G. Whitson & R. C. Geiger (Eds.), *Research and higher education: The United Kingdom and the United States.* Bristol, PA: Society for Research into Higher Education and Open University Press.

Rich, J. M. (1984). *Professional ethics in education.* Springfield, IL: Charles C. Thomas.

Schomberg, S., & Farmer, J. A. (1993). The evolving concept of public service and implications for rewarding faculty. Urbana-Champaign: University of Illinois at Urbana-Champaign, Office of Continuing Education.

Seldin, P. (1980). *Successful faculty evaluation programs.* Crugers, NY: Coventry Press.

Seldin, P. (1984). *Changing practices in faculty evaluation.* San Francisco: Jossey-Bass.

Sergiovanni, T. J. (1992). *Moral leadership.* San Francisco: Jossey-Bass.

Starratt, R. J. (1996). *Transforming educational administration: Meaning, community, and excellence.* New York: McGraw-Hill.

Steinbeck, J. (1945). *Cannery row.* New York: Viking Press.

Thom, D. J. (1993). *Educational management and leadership: Word, spirit, and deed for a just society.* Calgary, Alberta, Canada: Detselig.

Tierney, W. G. (1997, May/June). Academic community and post-tenure review. *Academe, 83*(3), 23–25.

UCEA goal activities. (1997, Spring). *UCEA Review, 38*(2), 12.

Weber, M. (1958). *The protestant ethic and the spirit of capitalism* (T. Parsons, Trans.). New York: Charles Scribner's Sons. (Original work published 1904–05)

Williams, R. M., Jr. (1964). Values and beliefs in American society. In M. McGiffert (Ed.), *The character of Americans* (pp. 180–189). Homewood, IL: Dorsey Press.

CHAPTER 3

Professorial Service: Disseminating Knowledge to Improve Practice

C. M. Achilles and Susan H. Achilles

If professors are to be part of improving education in America's schools, they must define service much more broadly, and they must give far greater attention to their service role. In the professorial role's traditional triad of teaching, research, and service, publishing research and teaching get more attention than service. This does seem strange, given professors' self-reported low emphasis on research and on reading of research (e.g., McCarthy & Kuh, 1997; McCarthy, Kuh, Newell, & Iacona, 1988). Although dissemination is a useful part of a professor's role, this publishing is not research. It logically could be service, and this change would add legitimacy to the service role while clarifying the dissemination function of most professional writing. After all, aside from disingenuous puffery, why should publication of nonresearch be considered research? Ideas, advice, thoughts, suggestions all have their value . . . but are these research?

Recall the low estate of education among university colleagues, mere tolerance of educators among politicians and policy people, and near derision from some business folks. Remember the noneducator "Education Summit" of politicos and beneficiaries of corporate welfare? Rather than continue down a path that gets little but scorn, educators should seize the Information and Knowledge Ages (Achilles, 1993) and establish education as a strong and respected social institution. Turn negatives into positives. As an example, educators might show the positive values of the politically conservative rallying cry that "Less is More" by pointing out one educationally sound application: Small classes (Less) offer a plethora of positive student benefits (More). Small classes translate the political slogan "Less is More" into the educationally positive "Small is Better."

When building something substantial or important, people usually start with a solid, firm, strong foundation. A classic example of architects, engineers, and builders not heeding this axiom can be found in the gravity-defying tower of Pisa. Some education critics believe that, if it has not already fallen over, public education is as close or closer to collapse than is the famous leaning tower! The Leaning Tower of Pisa analogy is not farfetched in American education. For one reason or another, educators have not used much of the research available to them to build a solid foundation for educational improvement. This is a complex issue. One concern revolves around the idea of *professional* and its relationship to the idea of *malpractice*. Recall what research has shown about such things as early childhood education, kindergarten, class sizes in K–3, retention in grades, and so forth. Early education in America is not done as well as the research shows that it could be. Kindergarten and even pre-K help pupils prepare for school. Not all states require kindergarten; some have only half-day kindergarten and few kindergarten class sizes are appropriate (1:15 or fewer). The Head Start program is not fully funded. These situations suggest some dire scenarios.

1. Those in charge of education decisions and improvement do not know the substantial research and knowledge base relating to early intervention, early childhood education, and so on.
2. Those in charge of education decisions do know the research and knowledge base, but for various reasons they do not use it.

C. M. Achilles, Eastern Michigan University
Susan H. Achilles, The School District of Greenville County

THE BASIC ARGUMENT

This discussion is rooted in the concept of educator as professional and educational administration as a profession of practice (Achilles, 1994, p. 165). As the standard for *professional*, we mean having such things as (a) a knowledge base that the person applies beneficially to help solve "people" or client problems; (b) a method of inquiry to access, assess, and advance the knowledge base; (c) standards (or licensure) for admission to the profession and requirements for renewal; (d) a specialized language to bring precision to the field; and (e) some regulations or standards and a code of ethics to govern minimal levels of performance in the field. Perhaps the oldest code of ethics for professional conduct is medicine's Oath of Hippocrates (460–375 B.C.). In not using what educators know about education (see Glickman, 1991), do educators follow the Oath of Hypocrites as an ethical guideline? If educators claim that education is a profession of practice (similar to medicine), then they ought to embody at least points (a) to (e) above in a generalized statement about professional ethics and behavior. As one example of inattention to professional stature, why is much of education's rush to "world class" status *not* built on reasonable research results, even as researchers provide new research bases for educational improvements? Is education, as presently practiced, essentially malpractice, and are professors of education largely responsible for this state?

Primum Non Nocere

The foundation of a client-oriented code of ethical behavior is "primum non nocere," which translated liberally is "At the very least, do (the client) no harm." A professional's *base* is, "If you can't help, at least don't cause any harm." Pretty safe, one would suppose. Well, how many educators work in systems where pupils are routinely retained in grade? Glickman's (1991) conundrum, "Pretending not to know what we know" provides a quick starting place to check on "primum non nocere."

Besides Primum Non Nocere?

Other issues impede education's claim to be a profession. A profession has a knowledge base and a method of inquiry to access, assess, and advance the field. A knowledge base? A method of inquiry? *If education had its own knowledge base, why do educators rush to try to make education fit on the Procrustean bed of the knowledge base of other fields?* Many educators advocate "restructuring," but on what research base and with what assurance that this knowledge base produces desired results?

Mitchell and Beach (1993) asked the key question, "If restructuring is the answer, what is the problem?" (p. 266). The lively qualitative and quantitative debate leaves unsettled just what is education's method of inquiry. (Achilles [1994] suggested that it is Q^2 or "Qualiquantitative.") The struggle over standards and licensure evident in the National Council for the Accreditation of Teacher Education's "Curriculum Guidelines for Educational Leadership," the "Interstate School Leaders Licensure Consortium" (ISLLC) of the Council of Chief State School Officers, the American Association of School Administrators' *Professional Standards for the Superintendency* (Hoyle, 1993; AASA Commission on Standards for the Superintendency, 1993) shows that some educator groups are searching for professional status.

WHY SEEK IMPROVEMENT AND HOW? THREE TRIAL SCENARIOS

Real educational improvement will only come when educators use what is known, evaluate it carefully, extend it, and continue a research agenda built upon educational issues. Some "good bets" that are not yet substantiated by research should be advanced as "venture capital" because of their potential to yield positive education results, but the core of educational improvement should be built on positive research results already available that relate to education's technical core. Why isn't this idea well accepted?

Table 1. Presented and Discovered Problem Situations.

---

1. *Presented Problem Situation.* The problem is *given* to the problem solver. It has a known formulation, known method of solution, and known answer. (This situation prevails in schools. Given that the side of a square is four feet, what is the area?) This condition is not really a problem in the sense of professional problem analysis, for essentially it only requires *implementing* someone else's solutions.

2. *Discovered Problem Situation.* A problem exists, and it is formulated by the potential problem solver, not by someone else. It may NOT have a known formulation, known method of solution, or a known solution. It meets the conditions discussed in this chapter in that it is amenable to refinement and offers a problem-finding challenge. Why do children, at about grade 3 or 4, begin to dislike school when almost all children are initially eager to attend school? Does this American phenomenon exist in other cultures?

Note. Table 1 is excerpted from Getzels (1979, 1985). The problem categories show differences in how the problem is formulated (and by whom), in the certainty of the method of solution, and in the complexity of the projected solution.

One way that educators choose to advance education is by considering ideas and innovations that have been developed in other institutions of society, such as business or industry (*Option A*). This is to continue to march to other people's drums and to address what Getzels (1979, 1985) called "the presented problem." (See Table 1.) Some of these ideas are already part of educational literature, as distinct from educational research. Many professors and others peddle "projects" built on this stuff and fluff. ("Have I got a project for you!")

A second way to improve education is to incorporate into its operation those things that research has shown are likely to improve education outcomes (*Option B*). These "things" come from education or related social science fields, such as psychology, and have a substantial research base.

A third option incorporates elements of both options A and B above. In *Option C*, educators might improve education's *structure or infrastructure* by judicious use of borrowed innovations. They might improve education's *technical core* by incorporating research results from education and education-related disciplines. This paper supports Option C, using a balance of externally and internally feasible ideas for education improvement.

THE ROLE OF THE EDUCATIONAL ADMINISTRATION PROFESSOR

If professors teach mainly in Option A, they profess education improvement via things urged on education by noneducators. This is strange, indeed, especially since in this role those outside of education (e.g., business leaders, entrepreneurs) see professors as little more than handmaidens whose function is to advertise and legitimate the work of important people. Listen to Ogawa's (1994) conclusions:

> *Role of academic actors.* We raise a third issue because it hits so close to home. It concerns the role that academic actors played in institutionalizing school-based management. *Academic actors, as reported earlier, were not the chief institutional entrepreneurs* [emphasis added]. . . . As one interview respondent observed, the words of professors carry weight because they are backed by academic credentials.
>
> The relationship of educational scholarship to educational policy and practice has often been a point of concern and not a little contention between academics on the one side, and policymakers and practitioners on the other. Both sides, however, seem to agree that scholarship should have a substantive relationship to policy and practice. In the present instance, scholarship did not drive policy and practice, as some academics believe it should. Nor was it irrelevant, as many policymakers and practitioners believe it to be. *Instead, it served the largely symbolic function of legitimating what institutional entrepreneurs had shaped, which may strike at the legitimacy of educational research* [emphasis added]. (pp. 546–547)

For example, professors may profess things like Total Quality Education (TQE), Site-Based Management (SBM), restructuring generally, ever-increasing expenditures on technology, and so on. These may help the infrastructure of education, but where is substantial evidence that such things have any impact on the technical core of education such as student achievement and development? (See, for example, Smylie, Lazarus, & Brownlee-Conyers [1996, Fall] on the questionable efficacy of SBM to raise student "outcomes" such as test scores.) Education frequently is described in business and factory metaphors (students as workers) and, thus, is "evaluated" by business models like production-function analyses. Let's pursue this a bit.

Both business and education are fields of practice that rely on ideas from disciplines as the bases for their practices. Yet, since the goals of each field differ, why would educators uncritically use procedures developed for business to improve student outcomes? What assures educators that statistical process control would be applied in the same way with the same results in education and in business when the anticipated goals and outcomes of the fields of practice are different? In one case, the outcomes are widgets for profit; in another the outcome is an educated citizenry (Murnane & Levy, 1996).

Consider the "standards" movement. This may be good politics: lots of tough talk and no funds. Educators are the bad guys again, dropouts will increase, and who could be against "higher" standards? Slavin (1996) asked, "Could anyone imagine that tougher high school graduation requirements will motivate third graders to learn more math" (p. 4)? Business deals in dollars. Education deals in sense. The difference yields profits or prophets.

Do educational administration (EDAD) professors teach research results that are of education and influence the technical core of education (Option B)? Unless professors profess Option B things, how will educators know much about them and use them? Consequently, the technical core of education remains stagnant. In Option B, we find things that are specifically of education:

- retention in grade
- class size in early primary grade
- multi-aged classrooms
- corporal punishment
- grouping and tracking
- risks factors

What would happen to educational *outcomes* if professors emphasized Option B with the same interest that they tout Option A ideas? What would happen if EDAD professors encouraged their students to use what research has shown will improve student outcomes? Might Option B provide a substantial education base for "restructuring" since it emphasizes outcomes related to improvements in student learning and development?

If professors do not profess Option B, is it because they believe that this is *not* part of the knowledge base for educators? Is it because they believe that results of educational research are not necessary knowledge for prospective education administrators? Do the professors know this research? Are they happy, as results of Ogawa's (1994) study seem to say, in being mere disseminators who come into the fray late (if at all) and write to legitimate the work of others?

If professors know Option B research, should they take a stand on it? Should they urge educators and others to recognize and use the research, and urge the ethical practice of doing what research shows will work? Is this part of a service role? If EDAD professors equally profess Option B (research about education) *and* Option A (ideas brought to education from the outside), then Option C seems reasonable to improve student outcomes and differentiate between ways to improve the technical core of education and to change the infrastructure and delivery of education.

Without a knowledge base, no profession, no expertise, and nothing much of value can be professed. At issue may be more what is professed than the absence of a knowledge base. If so, then this general topic area seems like a useful place to begin a discussion of educational reforms.

The EDAD knowledge base has been addressed by University Council for Educational Administration personnel who developed seven domains of an EDAD knowledge base:

1. Social and Cultural Influences in Schooling
2. Teaching and Learning Processes

3. Organizational Studies
4. Leadership and Management Process
5. Policy and Political Studies
6. Legal and Ethical Dimensions of Schooling
7. Economic and Financial Dimensions of Schooling

Not everyone in EDAD agrees with these domains. According to Scheurich and Laible (1995), these seven domains contain little of the realities of educational problems, issues, and concerns.

> Nicolaides and Gaynor (1989) confirmed something close to what we have contended are the "central challenges" for schools and, thus, for administrators. They also ratify that the present knowledge base domain structure "is limited to topics and themes shaped by traditional perspectives" and that these perspectives are inconsistent with the nature of our challenges. (p. 318)
>
> In short, the knowledge base project, as presently constituted and structured, moves attention back to the old, inadequate way of doing business and away from the kind of changes and leadership necessary to prepare administrators who are ready and committed to developing—collaboratively with teachers, students and parents—the kinds of schools that are equally successful for all children. (p. 318)
>
> It is not minor change that we need for our purposes; it is not the traditional course structure and focus that we need. It is a major transformation, a major realignment of our entire way of preparing educational administrators. What we need is a knowledge base, a domain structure, a course structure, focused on leadership committed to all children (no exceptions allowed—by race, gender, class, or any other exclusionary category). (p. 319)

Hallinger and Heck's (1996) recent review of the principal's role in school effectiveness suggested that principals do little to improve student outcomes. "It is interesting to note that the findings of these studies reveal either no effects or, at best, weak effects" (p. 20) and "with three exceptions . . . these studies found either relatively weak effects or no effects of principal leadership on school achievement" (pp. 21–22). Hallinger and Heck cited work by Ogawa and Hart showing that the "principal variable accounted for *between 2 and 8 percent of the variance in test scores*" (p. 39, emphasis added). The weak results indicated by Hallinger and Heck, by Smylie, Lazarus, and Brownlee-Conyers (1996), and by other studies offer little solace that educators are using research that makes much difference in schooling outcomes.

THE PROFESSOR'S SERVICE ROLE

If educators expect to improve education, one might expect that they would use what research and practice have shown will improve education. This change to data-driven improvement will not come easily. Professors have a major service role to play in this change, including the difficult task of helping to shape public opinion about education. When research and exemplary practice show clearly, at a point in time, *what* does or does not work, one service role of professors is to help define *how* to do what needs to be done. The "how to" decisions will be political.

EDAD professors need to address the knowledge base of EDAD. The following illuminates the range of the problem. Educators prescribe homework about as regularly as doctors prescribe aspirin, but how many educators know the voluminous research on homework and the correct use of homework? The question of effectively using the range of education's knowledge base will generate considerable healthy debate around such questions as these: How do we know? How certain are we about it? Where might we see the exemplary use of the knowledge base? How, when, and where do we teach this knowledge base?

Table 2 demonstrates one structure for organizing and evaluating education's knowledge base. Using such a structure, groups of educators might work on redefining "the basics" of education's knowledge base to provide direction for the renewed emphasis on service described here. The clarity of the indicators might be rated on a scale of 1 to 5, ranging from very clear to very little empirical evidence.

Table 2. Sample Plan for Organizing the Knowledge Base Elements of Education as a Profession.

I. Assume That Education Is a Profession: What Are Indicators of the Knowledge Base?			II. How Would You Expect to Observe Each Element of the Knowledge Base or Assess It in Practice?
What Is the Knowledge Base?	What Is It Built or Based On?	How Clear Is It?	How Is It Observed in Practice? How Could It Be Assessed?
People learn in different ways	Gradner, Sternberg, Vygotsky, Thorndike	Very clear (1)	Learning centers, learning style (schedule, context, psychosocial settings), use of Multiple Intelligences Theory, multiple assessments
Retention in grade seldom works	Sheperd & Smith; TX Commissioner's Report, Holmes & Matthews (about 400 studies)	Very clear, quite clear (1–2)	"No retention" policies with a range of alternatives: non-grades, extended day, year-around, "hands on," peer or mentor coaching

THE PAST IS PROLOGUE

Educational improvement will happen when educators apply what research and exemplary practice have shown will improve education. Once research has developed a reasonably sound knowledge base for education (determination of what to do), a concerted national leadership needs to advocate that these advances be implemented. Logical service activities for professors are (a) to conduct policy-issue research on options about how to apply what research and best practice have demonstrated should be done to improve education and (b) to help local educators implement these practices. Professorial service-role ideas related to these major activities include the following:

1. Conduct policy-related research to determine how substantive educational research results can be implemented
2. Assist in evaluating local applications of the knowledge base
3. Publish nonresearch as service; articles might be clear, concise, compelling, and cogent dissemination of how to use research-driven education improvement ideas
4. Give equal attention to what does and does not work to help guide practitioners
5. Exert leadership for strong, moral stands to advocate for children

The foregoing serve as a starting point for redefining the service role for professors of EDAD. Attention to strengthening and expanding the service role will provide real content for instruction and will begin to bring a balance to the timely triad of teaching, research, and service. Furthermore, this clarity will add a logical way to separate publishing as research and as service, thus clearing up some of the ubiquitous "research shows" pronouncements presently proffered to fix education.

REFERENCES

Achilles, C. M. (1993). A curmudgeon's view: The onager kicks and rears. (A moonscape?). A synoptic assessment of the intra-palindromadic years (1991–2002) as viewed from 2020. In J. Hoyle & D. Estes (Eds.), *The first yearbook of the National Council of Professors of Educational Administration. NCPEA in a new voice.* (pp. 24–34). Lancaster, PA: Technomic Publishing Co., Inc.

Achilles, C. M. (1994). The knowledge base for education administration is far more than content. In J. Burdin & J. Hoyle (Eds.), *The second yearbook of the National Council of Professors of Educational Administration. Leadership and diversity in education* (pp. 164–173). Lancaster, PA: Technomic Publishing Co., Inc.

Achilles, C. M., Keedy, J. L., & Zaharias, J. B. (1996). *If we're rebuilding education, let's start with a firm foundation.* Paper presented at the annual meeting of the University Council for Educational Administration, Louisville, KY.

Achilles, C. M., & Nye, B. A. (1997). *Reinventing education through school improvement research that has resulted in student gains.* Paper presented at the annual meeting of the Congress for School Effectiveness and Improvement, Memphis, TN.

Getzels, J. W. (1979). Problem finding and research in educational administration. In G. Immegart & W. L. Boyd (Eds.), *Problem-finding in educational administration* (pp. 5–22). Lexington, MA: Lexington Books.

Getzels, J. W. (1985). Problem finding and the enhancement of creativity. *NASSP Bulletin, 69*(482), 55–61.

Glickman, C. (1991, April). Pretending not to know what we know. *Educational Leadership, 48*(8), 4–10.

Hallinger, P., & Heck, R. (1996, February). Reassessing the principal's role: A review of the empirical research. *Educational Administration Quarterly, 32*(1), 5–44.

Hoyle, J., et al. (1993). *Professional standards for the superintendency.* Arlington, VA: American Association of School Administrators.

McCarthy, M., & Kuh, G. (1997). *Continuity and change: The educational leadership professoriate.* Columbia, MO: University Council for Educational Administration.

McCarthy, M., Kuh, G., Newell, L. J., & Iacona, C. (1988). *Under scrutiny: The educational administration professoriate.* Tempe, AZ: University Council for Educational Administration.

Mitchell, D. E., & Beach. S. A. (1993). School restructuring: The superintendent's view. *Educational Administration Quarterly, 29*(2), 249–274.

Murnane, R.J., & Levy, F. (1996). What General Motors can teach U. S. schools about the proper role of markets in educational reform. *Phi Delta Kappan, 78*(3), 109–114.

Ogawa, R. (1994). The institutional sources of educational reform: The case of school-based management. *American Educational Research Journal, 31*(3), 519–548.

Scheurich, J. J., & Laible, J. (1995). The buck stops here—In our preparation programs: Educative leadership for all children. (No exceptions allowed). *Educational Administration Quarterly, 31*(2) 313–322.

Slavin, R. (1996). Reforming state and federal policies to support adoption of proven practices. *Educational Researcher, 25*(9), 4–5.

Smylie, M. A., Lazarus, V., & Brownlee-Conyers, J. (1996). Instructional outcomes of school-based participative decision making. *Educational Evaluation and Policy Analysis, 18*(3), 181–198.

CHAPTER 4

Reconsidering the Role of Research in Educational Administration Doctoral Programs

Theodore J. Kowalski and A. William Place

Many departments of educational leadership currently are considering reshaping professional preparation. The need to do so was identified approximately a decade ago when reports were issued by the National Commission on Excellence in Educational Administration (1987) and the National Policy Board for Educational Administration (1989). These documents suggested weaknesses in traditional preparation programs (shortcomings largely predicated on a perceived disjunction between theory and practice) and presented recommendations for more clinical training and tighter coupling between classroom instruction and the work of principals. More recently, arguments in favor of program reform have been based on the evolving context of practice. The application of decentralization theory, for example, circuitously redefines traditional administrative roles, especially in areas such as leadership, collaboration, and professionalism. Consequently, professors of educational administration are being encouraged to move degree and licensure programs in the direction of instructional and policy leadership (Bjork & Ginsburg, 1995; Clark & Clark, 1996). Experience, however, indicates that programmatic change is an illusive goal. In many instances, well-intentioned reformers have failed because they neither recognized nor understood the intricate mix of political, professional, and academic variables that create organizational realities in departments of educational leadership (Duke, 1992).

This chapter examines issues surrounding the reform of research requirements for doctoral programs. It is based on the assumption that necessary improvements are unlikely unless the process is pursued collaboratively by professors, students, and practitioners who understand the dynamics involved. The first part of the chapter explores current practices and the conditions responsible for them; the second part discusses four recommendations for program improvement.

CURRENT PRACTICES AND UNDERLYING CONDITIONS

The task of improving the research experience for doctoral students is facilitated by basic information about the status quo and an understanding of why things are the way they are. Although there are over 150 doctoral programs in educational administration in the United States, they vary considerably with respect to philosophy, focus, and curriculum.

Current Requirements

Data about specific research course requirements in doctoral programs are quite sparse. A recent request for such data issued to Division A members in the American Educational Research Association produced only limited anecdotal information. Professor M. Scott Norton at Arizona State University, who has done research on doctoral programs, confirmed that data on this subject had not been collected in any systematic manner. The

---

Theodore J. Kowalski, Ball State University
A. William Place, University of Dayton

limited information available strongly suggests that substantial differences exist among universities with some requiring as few as two research courses and others requiring as many as six.

Information also is limited about the extent to which research courses are taught within departments of educational leadership. In their study of faculty specializations, McCarthy and Kuh (1997) found that in both 1986 and 1994, only 5% of educational administration professors identified research as their primary specialization. In 1986, the most commonly cited specialization was organizational theory (16%), and in 1994, it was leadership (16%). Pohland and Carlson (1993) analyzed departmental course listings at 40 University Council for Educational Administration (UCEA) institutions, and they found that 28 of the educational leadership departments (70%) offered one or more courses in research.

Most often, the student population in research classes is heterogeneous. If the courses are taught outside the educational leadership department, students with a wide variety of majors are likely to be enrolled. Even when these courses are taught within educational leadership, enrollees are likely to be in different degree programs (master's versus doctorate) and have a variety of career goals (e.g., public school administrator versus professor). Typically, the student population within educational administration is not sufficiently large to offer specialized sections of these courses. Thus, it is not surprising that a lack of differentiation in research courses for school administrators remains a concern (Pohland & Carlson, 1993).

Quantitative and Qualitative Approaches

Another issue raised by common practice and requirements pertains to quantitative and qualitative courses. In their study of curriculum at UCEA institutions, Pohland and Carlson (1993) looked at balance between the two methodologies. Judging only the courses taught within educational administration departments, they concluded that balance had essentially been achieved; if anything, the current distribution of these courses "may be tipped in favor of qualitative research" (p. 8). This conclusion, however, needs to be considered in light of the fact that they did not examine required research courses taught by faculty in other departments (e.g., statistics classes taught within mathematics or educational psychology). At institutions where doctoral students take these generic research courses, the scale is often tilted toward quantitative courses. Although some view quantitative and qualitative approaches as mutually exclusive choices (Smith, 1983; Smith & Heshusius, 1986), a growing concern within the profession is expressed by many writers who suggest that both methodologies need to be studied (Gage, 1989; Howe, 1988; Howe & Eisenhart, 1990; Place & Reitzug, 1992; Salomon, 1991).

McCarthy and Kuh (1997) found that 68% of educational leadership faculty preferred requirements that placed an equal emphasis on the two approaches. Among the others, 20% preferred a greater emphasis on qualitative approaches, 7% preferred a greater emphasis on quantitative approaches, and 5% preferred that their units (departments or programs) did not emphasize research. Despite the overwhelming preference for balance, only 35% felt their units had achieved an equal emphasis. Among the remaining professors, 29% believed that their units placed more emphasis on quantitative approaches, 17% believed that their units placed more emphasis on qualitative approaches, and 19% believed that their units did not emphasize research.

McCarthy and Kuh (1997) also noted that the results from their most recent survey showed greater faculty involvement in research than was indicated in previous studies. However, "despite the increase in scholarly activity, educational leadership faculty members still devoted less time to research than faculty in other disciplines" (p. 105). Unfortunately, there are no data showing the type of scholarly activity that is taking place. Thus, the precise distribution of qualitative and quantitative studies produced in educational leadership departments is not known. However, both the literature and sentiments of faculty suggest that students must study the two methodologies if they are to understand the breadth of the field.

Although the number of doctoral programs in school administration continues to grow, very few institutions are experimenting with new research requirements. During the 1980s, 17 new EdD programs in school administration were initiated in the United States; virtually all were at regional universities offering their first doctoral program, and most were inclined to adopt traditional degree requirements used by established programs (McLaughlin & Moore, 1990). And despite rhetoric advocating a greater sensitivity to practice-based research, considerable evidence indicates that the incentives for faculty and doctoral students continue to lead them to conform to the traditional arts-and-sciences model.

WHY THINGS ARE THE WAY THEY ARE

Four long-standing issues have influenced attitudes and policies pertaining to educational administration doctoral programs. They include (a) issues surrounding the existence of two doctoral degrees, the EdD and PhD; (b) political and cultural influences within academe; (c) the effects of regulation and competition; and (d) the effects of a professional culture. Every decision about research requirements has probably been influenced by these issues.

Distinctions Between Two Doctoral Degrees

Over time, the EdD became the dominant doctoral degree in school administration; in less than 40 years after it was first granted by Harvard University, the percentage of doctoral graduates in education receiving the PhD dropped to about 20%; in the 1950s, the EdD accounted for approximately two out of every three doctorates awarded in education (Brown, 1990). Traditionally, the EdD has been viewed as a professional degree designed primarily to prepare persons for entering practice in schools or districts (Nelson & Coorough, 1994).

By contrast, the PhD has been viewed as a traditional research degree. In developing programs in educational administration, however, universities did not uniformly adhere to this distinction. Further, since school administration lacks a "national curriculum" for either degree, differences between them have been more imagined than real. For example, a study of UCEA member institutions approximately 10 years ago found that the PhD and EdD were virtually identical pursuits (Norton & Levan, 1987). More recent studies produced the same finding at non-UCEA institutions (Norton, 1992) and for newly developed programs (McLaughlin & Moore, 1990). In the early 1990s, slightly less than half of the universities providing educational doctorates offered both the PhD and EdD; 37% offered only the EdD, and 17% offered only the PhD (Osguthorpe & Wong, 1991).

Since 1960, the PhD has regained its status as the more popular degree in a number of majors within schools of education (e.g., foundations, counseling, and educational psychology); however, the EdD has remained the more prevalent degree in educational administration (Brown, 1990). However, hopes of making the EdD an alternative to the PhD focusing more directly on practice (including alternative research requirements) were often impeded by university governance structures. Graduate deans and faculty councils typically adopted standards predicated on the PhD; institutions starting new EdD programs adopted the same standards, largely because of accreditation agencies and state higher education commissions (McLaughlin & Moore, 1990). This explains why requirements for the EdD have been found to parallel closely those for the PhD.

Debates about the EdD have often centered on the issue of research. Common questions have included: If the degree is aimed at practitioners, should students take fewer or different types of research courses than those taken by PhD students? Should students be required to write dissertations since first professional degrees in medicine and law do not have this requirement? Should research focus primarily on problems of practice rather than theory? While these questions have spawned experimentation at a select number of universities (e.g., completing a doctoral project rather than the traditional dissertation), the prevailing condition remains one in which research requirements for both the EdD and PhD in school administration closely parallel the requirements for all PhD programs.

Institutional Culture

Standards for research also have been discussed in relation to university culture (Calabrese & Bartz, 1991; Erlandson, 1990). Frequently, faculty in education schools, particularly at research institutions, have been placed on the defensive and asked to demonstrate the existence of a distinct body of knowledge and a standard method of inquiry qualifying their specializations as disciplines (Achilles, 1989; Clifford & Guthrie, 1988). In an effort to gain acceptance from the university community, education professors adopted the liberal arts model for research and scholarly publication (Yarger, Mertens, & Howey, 1985).

The importance of campus culture cannot be understated; the closing of schools of education at prestigious private universities such as Chicago and Duke reminds educational administration professors of a widespread expectation that their work comply with established norms. Even schools of education at large state-supported research universities have faced occasional threats (as was the case at the University of Michigan in the mid-1980s). At many institutions, educational administration professors encounter an apparent lose-lose situation. If their research (or that of their doctoral students) does not comply with the liberal arts model, the products may be labeled inferior; if their work complies with these standards, the studies may be criticized as unnecessary and inferior duplications of research already being conducted in other disciplines (e.g., economics, political science, or business administration). Although schools of education are commonly recognized as "professional schools," they rarely are accorded the prestige and independence given more established units in this category (e.g., schools of architecture, law, or medicine). Degree requirements are usually controlled by graduate school councils composed largely of arts-and-sciences professors.

Licensure and Demand for the Degree

Since most doctoral graduates in school administration work in public elementary and secondary education, professional preparation has been influenced considerably by licensure and certification requirements. Clark (1989) observed that, despite many of these requirements being narrow and outdated, curricula in some preparation programs still were based entirely on them. He wrote, "Students routinely complete certification requirements with minimal information about the classroom, the school as an organization, or the social context of schooling" (p. 4). In part, this situation occurs because licensing-related courses already consume a major portion of the minimum credit hours a university requires for a doctoral degree. Similarly, curricula are restricted by competition. Consider three facts in this regard: (a) approximately 500 universities offer graduate courses in school administration; (b) the number of institutions offering the doctorate in educational administration continues to increase; (c) many doctoral students in educational administration seek part-time programs in which they can complete their degrees in as little time as possible. Consequently, decisions about degree requirements, including those in the area of research, are often influenced by pragmatic considerations pertaining to recruiting students.

Professional Culture

Professional cultures also influence academic preparation. As in other professions, educational administration professors expect their doctoral students to enter the community of their discipline. While this rite of passage may be perceived differently across preparation programs, it commonly consists of these actions: (a) sharing a model of knowing that is embedded in research methodology (graduate students are expected to learn this methodology and adopt appropriate language); (b) becoming involved in a research community that extends beyond the student's university to include scholars across the profession who are engaged in research; (c) recognizing scholarly papers and publications as the communicative forums for the community (to publish and be cited is to enter the community's discourse); and (d) initiating graduate students into the research community through the reading and writing they do, through instruction in research courses, and through interaction with peers and professors (Berkenkotter, Huckin, & Ackerman, 1991). These expectations play a foundational role in shaping research requirements. Being in the unique position of primarily preparing practitioners in the context of an arts-and-sciences mentality, educational administration professors frequently hold opposing views on critical issues pertaining to professional preparation. Whereas strong cultures usually unify faculty and students in other professional schools, many schools of education are plagued by weak cultures created by disagreements on fundamental issues such as curriculum, professorial standards, and a commitment to preparing practitioners (Yarger et al., 1985).

The prevalence of part-time study in doctoral programs also is noteworthy. Students who pursue their degrees in this manner simply have less opportunity to collaborate with their professors and peers (Denton, Tsai, & Chevrette, 1987); compared to full-time students, their socialization to scholarly activity is less intense. As a result, their attitudes about the value of research are less likely to change during the graduate school experience. Negative or indifferent dispositions toward the value of research make it more likely that doctoral students will select research topics based on time commitment and cost rather than on relevance to practice or the theoretical knowledge base (Baird, 1992).

A REFORM AGENDA

In discussing the need for reform in school administration, Cuban (1996) wrote that the problem facing those who prepare administrators "is how to help people who want to be effective administrators better understand the dilemma-rich situations in which they work" (p. 15). Since it is most unlikely that the profession will produce and adopt a national curriculum for doctoral study in school administration, this challenge will either be addressed or ignored on a program-to-program basis. Central to Cuban's challenge is the need for problem-based research that will provide useful theory about work in schools and districts. Thus, those seeking to improve the doctoral experience are confronted with questions such as these:

1. Which research standards best serve society and schools?
2. Which research standards best serve the needs of practitioners?
3. Which research standards best serve the profession?
4. Which standards are most apt to guide practitioner-scholars toward using research to solve problems in daily practice?
5. Which standards will be accepted by university cultures?

For purposes of discussion, research-related queries are classified in this chapter as follows: (a) those pertaining to the value of research, (b) those pertaining to methodologies, (c) those pertaining to conceptualizing the researcher's role, and (d) those pertaining to a process for evaluating and changing requirements. Professors seeking to reform their programs are likely to face essential decisions in each category; Table 1 provides a summary of possible negative and positive actions. Collectively, these four categories provide parameters for considering the reform of research requirements.

VALUE OF RESEARCH

Charters (1992) noted that "Nearly 90 percent of the published research in our field, according to several estimates, represents the first and the last studies the authors will ever conduct" (p. 39). If true, these estimates sug-

Table 1. Potential Actions Related to Research Requirements.

Category	Actions Not Recommended	Actions Recommended
Value of Research	Treat research as a rite of passage in graduate study; devalue research; eliminate the dissertation	Connect value to the realities of practice; increase the value of research; encourage practice-based dissertations
Methodology	Emphasize either quantitative or qualitative methods; force students to use the preferred methodology	Emphasize both quantitative and quantitative and methods; encourage studies using mixed methodologies
Orientation	Emphasize theoretical research; practitioner behavior	Emphasize the study of problems environments
Process	Be passive and allow others to set research requirements; be defensive and deny the need for improvement	Treat research as a professional prerogative; engage faculty, students, and practitioners in the process of program reform

gest that either research is not used as a tool for problem solving by practitioners or practitioners do not share their research activities in traditional outlets such as journals. In either instance, the nexus between research and practice appears to be weaker in educational administration than it is in most other professions. This condition has prompted some to suggest that dissertations in school administration programs are unnecessary.

The assumption that research is relatively unimportant to practice in school administration deserves to be challenged, especially given the current trends in school reform. Many who hold this view point to "successful" practitioners who are able to thrive by relying on political skills and common sense. Hence, they conclude that research courses and the dissertation are outdated and impractical rites of passage that should be abandoned. In truth, the current challenges of practice, namely those involving the need to reconstruct the climates and cultures of our schools, indicate that the study of research should be refocused, not abandoned. Decentralization, deregulation, and professionalism require administrators to experiment with new ideas, making knowledge about institutional behavior more essential than ever before. If the disjunction between theory and practice is to be diminished, professors will need to value problem-based research that produces theories that are relevant to the work of principals and superintendents (Hoy, 1996).

The responsibility for valuing research begins with professors. Not only do they exercise considerable control over curriculum, their dispositions and actions are highly symbolic. Why should students believe that research is important to effective practice if they never see professors engaged in the process? Negative perceptions about the importance of school administration research also are fostered by a proclivity to accept almost any suggested topic as relevant and appropriate for dissertations in this major. Rather than focusing on the dilemmas facing principals and superintendents, far too many graduate students are allowed to wander into other disciplines or other specializations in education (e.g., educational psychology).

METHODOLOGIES

For some professors, the debate over quantitative and qualitative methodologies constitutes a "paradigms war" (Gage, 1989); they treat this matter as a win-lose situation. Although qualitative research has gained popularity in education, quantitative approaches continue to be dominant and valued in a number of other disciplines. For example, a recent article in the *Chronicle of Higher Education* discussed how professors with statistical expertise could help political science departments become more scientific (Wilson, 1997). Such value judgments remind professors of educational administration that science is still considered the primary vehicle for theory building. Further, doctoral students in educational administration who aspire to become professors may be placed at a disadvantage if they do not acquire competence in both qualitative and quantitative research.

Arguments in favor of retaining some emphasis on quantitative approaches also can be made with respect to students who intend to become practitioners. Noting that quantitative research courses are of value to all administrators, McNamara and Thompson (1996) suggested that the study of quantitative research "should move (1) closer to administrator preparation programs, (2) away from the traditional conception of statistics as mathematical theory, and (3) closer to the conception of statistics as a process of discovery through data analysis" (p. 381).

During the period from 1950 to 1970, research in educational administration relied almost entirely on quantification, sampling, and survey research. By the 1980s, however, a shift toward qualitative approaches became evident (Owens, 1998). Postmodernists viewed scientific theory as primarily a ruse and an instrument of domination; they commonly disputed basic assumptions of modern social sciences (Hoy, 1996). Rather than sending questionnaires to schools, these researchers actually entered schools to obtain a richer and fuller description of what administrators were experiencing (Owens, 1998). However, qualitative approaches also have been criticized (Fein, 1993; Gambell, 1995). Concerns have included a lack of rigor, inadequate controls, excessive subjectivity, and the influence of political goals (e.g., advancing a personal bias toward a controversial issue). Additionally, properly executed qualitative studies can be extremely expensive and time consuming and thus impractical for many doctoral students.

Given the potential imperfections of both quantitative and qualitative methods, more scholars are advocating the use of mixed methodologies. Some of the most important problems in school administration are situational and practice-related (Hoy, 1996). Consider the issue of organizational culture. To reach the deepest levels of culture, and thus to determine how communication influences behavior in schools, we must rely on multidimensional, multilevel analyses (Kowalski, 1998; Mohan, 1993). Such investigations should explore value orientations and contextual variables, especially with respect to explaining how these variables contribute to differences in school cultures (i.e., differences between strong and weak, positive and negative, and stable and unstable cultures). This form of research requires interpretive paradigms permitting us to observe, measure, and classify organizations (Taylor, 1993). Balance is a conundrum that must be addressed in the context of individual departmental and institutional conditions. At least two issues, however, are universally important. One pertains to questions that practitioners and researchers need to be investigating; the other relates to a sufficient emphasis on research that allows doctoral students to become active in the community of scholars in educational administration.

The selection of appropriate methodologies should be predicated on the types of problems and corresponding research questions that practitioners and researchers need to investigate. Some questions are better answered with a quantitative analysis, some with qualitative approaches, and still others with mixed methodologies. Selecting a methodology on the basis of the problem and research questions assures that "form will follow function." Unfortunately, this often is not the case. What researchers determine to be most important is influenced significantly by their own experiences. For example, they often begin by showing a preference for a methodology (largely because of their training) and then seek a problem to fit their approach.

THE RESEARCHER'S ROLE

School reform activities have heightened an awareness that doctoral programs need to be sensitive to practitioner needs. Orientations toward research in educational administration have generally divided the researcher role into three categories: scientist, practitioner-scientist, and practitioner (Muth, 1989). These orientations provide a framework for reconsidering the role of the educational administration researcher. Table 2 shows role conceptualizations and corresponding purposes and foci based on Muth's orientations and Cuban's (1996) recommendations for improving professional preparation.

To become more sensitive to practitioner needs, doctoral programs need to shift toward practice-based research. For example, Muth (1989) argued that an increased emphasis on the practice of school administration would encourage students to develop research skills in the problems and contexts of real practice. About such a model, he wrote, "It should be inquiry-based and field-based, encouraging strong relationships among research professors and field mentors, universities and schools" (p. 9). Research on practice could focus on areas such as decision making, conflict resolution, or other challenges commonly faced by principals and superintendents. Outcomes would relate to theory, although theory building may not be the primary purpose (Achilles, 1989). Much of this research would demand mixed methodologies as suggested earlier.

Simply focusing on practitioner behavior, however, is insufficient. Behavior needs to be understood in the context of theory and situational variables (i.e., conditions in which practitioners encounter problems and make decisions). Additionally, the political realities of professional preparation—that is, those that were discussed

Table 2. Conceptualizations, Purposes, and Foci for Research in Doctoral Programs.

Conceptualization	Perceived Purposes	Research Activity Foci
Scholar (Scientist)	Building new theory; modifying existing theory	Studying phenomena
Practitioner	Understanding practice	Studying practitioner behavior
Practitioner-Scholar	Improving practice through deeper understandings of dilemma-rich situations	Problems, dilemmas of practice in an institutional context

Table 3. A Framework for Discussing Research in the Context of Program Reform.

Theme	Major Tasks
Context Analysis	• Reviewing the meaning and purpose of doctoral study • Reviewing the traditional role of research in doctoral programs • Defining the institutional culture and its influence on doctoral study • Defining the profession's culture and its influence on doctoral study • Identifying market realities (e.g., supply of students, demand for graduates, competition with other institutions) • Identifying economic and political realities (e.g., accreditation, state approval, funding, alumni expectations) • Identifying program intent (e.g., preparing practitioners, preparing scholars, preparing practitioner-scholars)
Needs Assessment	• Clarifying current practices (e.g., extent and nature of research course work, dissertation) • Assessing and evaluating program outcomes (i.e., What do students learn about research, and to what extent are they able to apply their knowledge?) • Identifying research needs among graduates (i.e., What do graduates identify as their needs? What research skills are associated with effective practice?)
Professional Directions	• Discussing an increased value on research • Discussing an emphasis on mixed methodologies • Discussing an emphasis on practice-based research
Congruence	• Assessing the interface of context, needs, and professional directions • Developing program-specific objectives • Developing recommended reforms

under campus culture—mandate that the quality of research completed in doctoral programs must be acceptable to the academic community on a given campus. Hence, the practitioner-scholar conceptualization constitutes both the most relevant professional choice and the most politically acceptable choice.

PROCESS FOR REFORMING RESEARCH REQUIREMENTS

Professors of educational administration basically have three choices with respect to responding to criticisms about the quality of research they control. They can be passive; they can be defensive; they can collectively engage in reform. The first possible course of action allows others in the university to dictate requirements. Even worse, it may allow faculty in school administration to be perceived as indifferent or incompetent. The second alternative is self-defeating because just defending current practice denies the need for improvement. The third is the only alternative that permits those most directly affected to take charge. It is the only choice permitting professors, students, and practitioners—and not the critics or university administrators—to define what is professionally appropriate.

Reconceptualizing the role of research in educational administration requires those who make change recommendations to understand the conditions that have led to current practices. In this vein, those who are involved benefit as learners. A possible framework for engaging professors, students, and practitioners in the quest to reform research requirements is shown in Table 3.

Context analysis is especially meaningful for understanding the traditions and norms of higher education;

needs assessment encourages candid discussions about professional practice in school administration and the effectiveness of academic preparation; *professional directions* integrates both philosophy and the knowledge base on research into the process; *congruence* encourages a synthesis of context, needs, and professional direction.

Bringing professors, students, and practitioners together to evaluate current programs and to recommend changes is likely to be a conflict-laden process. People will bring different values and beliefs to the process, and the discussions can become contentious. However, tension produced by this collaborative approach can be a catalyst for program improvements. Final decisions about research requirements are more likely to be accepted, both in the university and in the profession, if they are clearly based on defensible criteria associated with improving the practice of school administrators.

CONCLUDING COMMENTS

The current interest in reforming doctoral programs in school administration has resurrected some unsettled issues about the role and importance of research (Achilles, 1994). Yet, the topic of research requirements is almost always avoided when potential curricular changes are considered. A study of doctoral programs in educational administration conducted several years ago, for example, found that only 2 of 126 institutions were planning to revise research requirements (Hackman & Price, 1995). In part, the topic is avoided because professors realize that their philosophies toward research are incongruous; it is also avoided because some faculty elect to maintain passive or defensive postures. Unfortunately, the unwillingness to address research requirements in educational administration has contributed to two negative conditions: the thoughtless emulation of standards and values dominant in the arts-and-sciences model of graduate education and the erosion of standards for studying and conducting research.

This chapter outlines critical issues that provide a basis for redefining an appropriate role for research in doctoral programs in educational administration. Meaningful reform is most likely to be accomplished at institutions where there is a willingness to bring members of the educational administration community together to share a commitment for improving doctoral study.

REFERENCES

Achilles, C. M. (1989, October). *The practice of research on practice.* Paper presented at the annual meeting of the University Council on Educational Administration, Scottsdale, AZ.

Achilles, C. M. (1994). Searching for the golden fleece: The epic struggle continues. *Educational Administration Quarterly, 30*(1), 6–26.

Baird, L. L. (1992, April). *The changing atmosphere for research among graduate students.* Paper presented at the annual meeting of the American Educational Research Association, San Francisco.

Berkenkotter, C., Huckin, T. N., & Ackerman, J. (1991). Social context and socially constructed texts: The initiation of a graduate student into a writing research community. In C. Bazerman & J. Paradis (Eds.), *Textual dynamics of the profession: Historical and contemporary studies of writing in professional communities* (pp. 191–215). Madison: University of Wisconsin Press.

Bjork, L. G., & Ginsberg, R. (1995). Principles of reform and reforming principal training: A theoretical perspective. *Educational Administration Quarterly, 31*(1), 11–37.

Brown, L. D. (1990, April). *A perspective on the Ph.D.-Ed.D. discussion in schools of education.* Paper presented at the annual meeting of the American Educational Research Association, Boston.

Calabrese, R. L., & Bartz, D. E. (1991). Improving educational administration programs. *Journal of School Leadership, 1*(4), 351–362.

Charters, W. W. (1992). *On understanding variables and hypotheses in scientific research.* Eugene: ERIC Clearinghouse on Educational Management, University of Oregon.

Clark, D. C., & Clark, S. N. (1996). Better preparation of educational leaders. *Educational Researcher, 25*(9), 18–20.

Clark, D. L. (1989). Time to say enough! *Newsletter of the National Policy Board for Educational Administration, 1*(1), 1, 4.

Clifford, G. J., & Guthrie, J. W. (1988). *Ed school: A brief for professional education.* Chicago: University of Chicago Press.

Cuban, L. (1996). Reforming the practice of educational administration through managing dilemmas. In S. Jacobson, E. Hickcox, & R. Stevenson (Eds.), *School administration: Persistent dilemmas in preparation and practice* (pp. 3–17). Westport, CT: Praeger.

Denton, J. J., Tsai, C., & Chevrette, P. (1987, February). *Quality of research experience in graduate programs as perceived by faculty, graduates, and current students.* Paper presented at the annual meeting of the Association of Teacher Educators, Houston, TX.

Duke, D. L. (1992). The rhetoric and the reality of reform in educational administration. *Phi Delta Kappan, 73*(10), 764–770.

Erlandson, D. A. (1990). Agenda for reform: A critical appraisal. *Journal of Education Policy, 5*(2), 187–191.

Fein, G. G. (1993). In defense of data adoration and even fetishism. *Early Childhood Research Quarterly, 8*(3), 387–395.

Gage, N. L. (1989). The paradigm wars and their aftermath: A "historical" sketch of research on teaching since 1989. *Educational Researcher, 18*(7), 4–10.

Gambell, T. J. (1995). Ethnography as veneration. *Alberta Journal of Educational Research, 41*(2), 162–174.

Hackman, D. G., & Price, W. J. (1995, February). *Preparing school leaders for the 21st century: Results of a national study of educational leadership doctoral programs.* Paper presented at the conference of the American Association of School Administrators, New Orleans, LA.

Howe, K., (1988). Against the quantitative-qualitative incompatibility thesis or dogmas die hard. *Educational Researcher, 17*(8), 10–18.

Howe, K., & Eisenhart, M. (1988). Standards for qualitative (and quantitative) research: A prolegomenon. *Educational Researcher, 19*(4), 2–8.

Hoy, W. K. (1996). Science and theory in the practice of educational administration: A pragmatic perspective. *Educational Administration Quarterly, 32*(3), 367–378.

Kowalski, T. J. (1998). The role of communication in providing leadership for school restructuring. *Mid-Western Educational Researcher, 11*(1), 32–40.

McCarthy, M. M., & Kuh, G. D. (1997). *Continuity and change: The educational leadership professoriate.* Columbia, MO: University Council for Educational Administration.

McLaughlin, J. M., & Moore, C. E. (1990, October). *The reform movement and Ed.D. expansion.* Paper presented at the meeting of the Midwest Council for Educational Administration, St. Cloud, MN.

McNamara, J. F., & Thompson, D. P. (1996). Teaching statistics in principal preparation programs: Part one. *International Journal of Educational Reform, 5,* 381–389.

Mohan, M. L. (1993). *Organizational communication and cultural vision: Approaches and analysis.* Albany: State University of New York Press.

Muth, R. (1989). Reconceptualizing training for educational administrators and leaders: Focus on inquiry. *Notes on Reform, 2,* 1–20. Charlottesville, VA: National Policy Board for Educational Administration.

National Commission for Excellence in Educational Administration (1987). *Leaders for America's schools.* Tempe, AZ: University Council for Educational Administration.

National Policy Board for Educational Administration (1989). *Improving the preparation of school administrators: The reform agenda.* Charlottesville, VA: Author.

Nelson, J. K., & Coorough, C. (1994). Content analysis of the PhD versus EdD dissertation. *Journal of Experimental Education, 62*(2), 158–168.

Norton, M. S. (1992). Doctoral studies of students in educational administration programs in non-member UCEA institutions. *Educational Considerations, 20,* 37–41.

Norton, M. S., & Levan, F. D. (1987). Doctoral studies of students in educational administration programs in UCEA member institutions. *Educational Considerations, 14*(1), 21–24.

Osguthorpe, R. T., & Wong, M. J. (1991). The Ph.D. versus the Ed.D.: Time for a decision. *Innovative Higher Education, 18*(1), 47–63. (ERIC Document Reproduction Service No. ED 339 685)

Owens, R. C. (1998). *Organizational behavior in education* (6th ed.). Boston: Allyn and Bacon.

Place, A. W., & Reitzug, U. (1992). Educational administration research, practice, and preparation: Lessons from woodworking and American Indian philosophy. *Journal of School Leadership, 2,* 396–409.

Pohland, P. A., & Carlson, L. T. (1993). Program reform in educational administration. *UCEA Review, 34*(3), 4–9.

Salomon, G. (1991). Transcending the qualitative-quantitative debate: The analytic and systemic approaches to educational research. *Educational Researcher, 20*(6), 10–18.

Smith, J. (1983). Quantitative versus qualitative research: An attempt to clarify the issue. *Educational Researcher, 15*(1), 4–12.

Smith, J., & Heshusius, L. (1986). Closing down the conversation: The end of the quantitative-qualitative debate among educational inquirers. *Educational Researcher, 12*(3), 6–13.

Taylor, J. R. (1993). *Rethinking the theory of organizational communication: How to read an organization.* Norwood, NJ: Ablex.

Wilson, R. (1997, September 5). How 4 top graduate students joined the faculty ranks. *Chronicle of Higher Education,* pp. A14–A15.

Yarger, S. J., Mertens, S., & Howey, K. R. (1985). Schools of education and programs for continuing professional development. In C. W. Case & W. A. Matthes (Eds.), *Colleges of education: Perspectives on their future* (pp. 93–113). Berkeley, CA: McCutchan.

… SECTION 2

QUALITY SCHOOLS

CHAPTER 5

Creating Quality Schools: Rethinking the Meaning of and Strategies for Restructuring

Bob L. Johnson, Jr.

Fifteen years have passed since the publication of *A Nation at Risk* (National Commission on Excellence in Education, 1983). Since then, Americans have witnessed an unprecedented effort to reform public education. This reform has found expression in a variety of state, federal, and local initiatives. While the purpose and politics surrounding a number of these initiatives are questionable, most appear to be motivated by the felt need to create and maintain quality schools.

A marked change in the language and logic of reform has occurred in recent years. While the seeds of this change can be traced to the mind-set evoked by the landmark educational report of 1983, calls for a more *systemic* change in schools are of more recent origin (Cuban, 1988; Elmore, 1990; Tye, 1987). Reform advocates argue that it is no longer enough to improve schools as we now know them; the time has come to consider how the very organizations in which teaching and learning are embedded can be *fundamentally restructured*. Such concerns for a more deep-rooted, systemic change continue to define the reform debate and are currently reflected in a number of reform initiatives across the states.

Yet as we move toward the year 2000, the full potential and possibilities of restructuring efforts have not been realized. While isolated efforts to restructure have met with success, many have fallen short of expectations. No doubt, multiple factors contribute to this state of affairs, but one critical factor seems primary: the failure of reform advocates to consider *reflectively* the *meaning* and *nuances* of the restructuring process.

Like similar words associated with reform, restructuring in public education has come to mean everything and nothing. A cursory review of the restructuring literature attests to the ambiguity which surrounds both the concept and its use. One quickly sees that the full significance of the word is overlooked, its richness lost as educators and politicians alike equate any and all change efforts with restructuring. A similar review highlights the scarcity of conceptual work on restructuring. While works on specific restructuring initiatives are prevalent, few focus on the meaning and organizational implications of restructuring efforts (Cuban, 1990, 1988; Elmore, 1990; Fuhrman, 1993; Fullan & Stiegelbauer, 1991; Hallinan, 1995). Moreover, a critical mass of this literature appears to be highly prescriptive in tone.

PURPOSE

In light of this ambiguity and scarcity, the purpose here is to provide educational leaders with a framework for thinking about the restructuring process. Realizing the benefits which accrue to the reflective practitioner who considers multiple frames and models, the rationale for this effort is rooted in the assumption that restructuring initiatives have a higher probability of success if guided by informed models of change.

A specific strategy has been used to pursue this purpose. Using the language and logic of the literature on organizational structure to frame the discussion (Hall, 1991; Mintzberg, 1979; Scott, 1992; Thompson, 1967), careful consideration is given to several dimensions of restructuring: the meaning, motivations, end, focus, scope, and logistics of school restructuring efforts.

Bob L. Johnson, Jr., University of Utah

What Does Restructuring Mean?

A useful point of departure for understanding the restructuring process is with an examination of the meaning of the word. Whether used as a noun or verb, the word picture associated with its Latin root (*structura*) is telling. The referent is that of a building, more specifically a building as defined by the *individual components* used in its construction and by the *relationships* shared between these components.

As a word, *structure* is applied across a variety of contexts. One hears of architectural structure, atomic and molecular structure, geological structure, the structure of a musical composition, social structure, governmental structure, organizational structure, and the structure of science. References are frequently made to the act of structuring. Talk is heard of constructing (i.e., building structures), destructing (i.e., dismantling structures), and restructuring (i.e., rebuilding structures).

Regardless of how *structure* is used, three prominent ideas appear to be associated with its definition. The first is that of *entity*. A structure is an entity defined by its unique composition and arrangement of parts. The second idea is *composition of parts*. A structural entity is composed of individual parts, elements, or constituents which, when arranged together in a specific configuration, give the structure its identity. Although part of the structure, the individual parts, elements, and constituents are not to be confused with the structure itself. A third idea associated with structure is that of *relationship*. It is the nature and combination of the relationships between and among the individual parts of a given entity which define its structure. Given that the degree or extent of alteration may vary, the alteration of these relationships has the potential of changing the very nature of the entity itself. A radical alteration of these relationships often results in a radical alteration of the entity in question.

While an analysis of the etymological origins of *structure* may seem a bit removed from discussions of educational restructuring, the logic and ideas associated with it provide a measure of insight into the dynamics of the restructuring process. This insight is broadened as one considers the definition of structure in the context of organizations and organizational theory.

Mintzberg (1979) has defined organizational structure in terms of the ways in which leaders define and coordinate tasks. Unlike the Latin root, this definition makes no reference to a physical building. However, like the Latin root, Mintzberg's definition implies the existence of individual components and of patterns and relationships among these components. Specifically, structure constitutes the ways that organizational leaders (a) divide or differentiate the work of the organization and (b) coordinate this work once it has been divided. Implied in this definition is the assignment of sets of tasks to individuals, roles, or groups and the relating or coordinating of these tasks toward some larger end.

Scott's (1992) definition is similar: structure consists of the group of features developed in order to distinguish, order, and organize tasks. Scott implies the existence of relationships and commonalities among the individual features of the organization. Unlike Mintzberg, however, he identifies the control of organizational participants as an important function served by organizational structure. In accord with mainstream organizational theory, both definitions clarify the primary components and functions of organizational structure: (a) divide, (b) coordinate, and (c) control the work of individuals and groups within the organization.

A review of the literature on organizational structure suggests that, when seeking to describe how the work is divided, one is speaking of organizational complexity (Hall, 1991; Scott, 1992; Thompson, 1967). This complexity may be characterized in terms of horizontal, vertical (i.e., number of hierarchical levels), and spatial differentiation. When seeking to describe those mechanisms used to coordinate and control the work of individuals and groups, one is speaking of two additional structural components: the distribution of power and the level of standardization or formalization within the organization. The distribution of power within an organization is used to describe the degree to which decision-making power or authority has been centralized, decentralized, or divided within the organization (Hall, 1991; Scott, 1992). Standardization or formalization refers to the extent to which the behavior of organizational participants is governed by written rules and regulations (Hall, 1991; Scott, 1992; Thompson, 1967; Weber, 1947).

While much disagreement exists as to the determinants of organizational structure, a working level of consensus appertains among theorists about the meaning, functions, and components of organizational structure. Consistent with this consensus, to restructure an organization means one or more of the following: (a) to alter the way in which work is divided within the organization, be it in reference to horizontal, vertical, or spatial differentiation; (b) to alter the extent to which the work within the organization is standardized or formalized; or (c) to alter the distribution of decision-making authority within the organization. It is the *purposive alteration* of any or all of these three structural dimensions which provides a conceptual framework for thinking about the meaning of restructuring.

Though variations in school structures exist across the United States, they appear to have an identifiable, generic organizational structure. Visiting elementary schools in Florida and Oregon, one will find a remarkable degree of structural similarity (Bidwell, 1965; Johnson & Licata, 1995; Lortie, 1975; Moore-Johnson, 1990; Willower, 1973). Generally speaking, the work within the school tends to be divided among a variety of roles in rather predictable fashion. This work may be classified in a number of ways. Roles, and the tasks associated with them, may be classified into two larger groups: those performing education-related activities (e.g., teachers, counselors, administrators) versus those performing auxiliary tasks (e.g., custodians, food-service personnel). Those individuals performing education-related activities may be further divided into at least three groups: teachers, administrators, and student-support personnel. For those working at the technical core—namely teachers—the work tends to be divided by subject matter and grade level. A measure of coordination and control of these roles (Gamoran & Dreeben, 1986; Weick, 1976) is achieved through various means: the use of policies, guidelines, and standard operating procedures; resource allocations within and between schools (Barr & Dreeben, 1983); the standardization of the curriculum; and professional socialization (Jackson, 1968; Lortie, 1975; Moore-Johnson, 1990).

Further, this structure consists of a host of other elements, including curricula, students, buildings, classes, equipment, and the relationships among these. Teachers, for example, have instructional authority over students, textbooks tend to be the focal point of curricular activity, instruction is graded, and teachers perform their duties in classrooms isolated from their colleagues. These features, along with many others, come together in complex relationships to define the organizational structure of schools.

To speak, therefore, of the organizational "restructuring" of schools is to speak of (a) adding or removing, in various degrees, individual components which make up the structure of the school (i.e., altering the complexity [vertical, horizontal, spatial] of the school organization), (b) altering the relationships or configurations of these individual components as they relate to each other (i.e., altering the extent of formalization or the distribution of power within the school organization), and (c) potentially altering the structural essence which defines that entity known as the public school (i.e., engaging in deep as opposed to shallow change) (Tye, 1987). Realizing that the degree of intended alteration may vary, these nuances provide a useful frame for thinking about the restructuring process in the schools. This frame is enhanced when other dimensions of the restructuring process are considered.

Why Do Demands for Restructuring Arise?

To understand further the nature of restructuring, consider the motivations behind these efforts. Why restructure? What motivates the demands for educational restructuring? The answers to these questions are found in an examination of the forces operating in and around schools. Organizations such as schools are systems of purposive social interaction (Katz & Kahn, 1978). Although their purposes or goals may be ambiguous or unknown to many organizational participants, the existence of the formal organization presupposes some purpose. This purpose, and the rationality associated with it, are reflected in the organization's structure. While the sophistication of this rationality and the degree to which it is consistent with the purpose of the organization vary across organizations (Meyer & Rowan, 1978), structure may be viewed as the means to achieving desired organizational ends.

To be sure, it is possible for the structure of an organization to be inconsistent with the purpose that has been identified for it. Further, it is possible for organizational participants and environmental actors to disagree over the purpose of a given organization or the means used to pursue this purpose (Pfeffer, 1981). Nonetheless, in the best of all worlds, the individual components and internal forces of the organization are structured to achieve the goals and aims for which the organization was created.

Such a view allows one to speculate on the conditions which make restructuring necessary. It would appear that restructuring in an organization becomes necessary when any one of three conditions is present, either individually or in combination: (a) when disagreements exist about the purpose of an organization, (b) when disagreements exist about the means used to pursue its purpose, or (c) when the purpose of the organization and the means used to pursue this purpose are perceived as incongruent (i.e., a given structure is judged to be ineffective or inappropriate for realizing desired ends). While the presence of one or more of these conditions is *necessary* for restructuring, the presence of one or more of these conditions may not be a *sufficient* cause for the initiation of restructuring efforts. Initiation requires the mobilization of a critical mass of key policymakers and interests.

Two distinguishing features of the school organization—the multiple and diffuse goals defined for it and the ambiguity surrounding the technology of the teaching-learning process (Cohen, March, & Olsen, 1972; Rowan, 1990)—point to the existence of two of the three restructuring conditions noted above. Not only does public education have multiple goals, but disagreements exist about the means (or structure) needed to achieve these goals. Diversity of opinion among practitioners, policymakers, and the public underscore the political nature of debates on the means and ends of education.

Close examination of the internal processes and structure of an organization likewise reveals the existence of influences whose origins lie outside of the organization. Organizations are not only influenced by but dependent on their environments. The environment provides both input and feedback to the organization (Meyer & Rowan, 1978; Scott, 1992, 1995). Schools are particularly vulnerable to their environments. Among other things, the environment of the school organization provides it with financial resources, personnel, ideological support, and legitimacy (Scott, 1995).

In the broadest sense, actors and entities in the environment of the public school play an important role in defining the purpose of the organization and in determining its effectiveness. The survival of the school organization is dependent on the ability of its members to adapt to these environmental influences. Survival of an existing or proposed structural configuration is likewise a function of the adaptability of the structure to environmental demands.

Awareness of the conditions which lead to demands for restructuring and of the relationship shared between an organization and its environment provides the backdrop for understanding current restructuring initiatives. Consider the following example. In light of a perceived decline in economic productivity, it is argued that public education is failing to produce the type of employees needed to meet the demands of the labor market. Concerns about the ability of graduates to engage in reflective thought and master basic technical skills are raised. A subsequent call for the restructuring of public education is issued. Inherent in these concerns is an assumption that the public school, as currently structured, is not achieving the desired end of preparing workers for the workplace. This scenario illustrates how a perceived state of incongruence between the means (organizational structure) and ends (organizational purpose) of public education creates demands for restructuring.

Demands for the restructuring of schools can be motivated by divergent views regarding the ends of education, the means of education, or a perceived incongruence of organizational means (structure) and ends. That such divergent views exist is no surprise. What is forgotten at times is the political means by which a workable level of consensus on purpose and structure is reached in the midst of this diversity.

For the reflective practitioner, conceptualizing the demands for restructuring in this way engenders a proactive stance. Given that the structure of the public school organization has proven remarkably durable (Callahan, 1962; Tyack, 1974), an anticipatory stance of this nature places one in a better position to channel these demands into workable solutions. In light of what we know about the current structure of schools and the teaching-learning process, certain demands for restructuring may have to be rebuffed and the status quo defended. On the other hand, given this same knowledge, other restructuring ideas and strategies may demand serious consideration.

Toward What End Are Restructuring Efforts Aimed?

Values play an indispensable role in defining the end of restructuring efforts. Judgments on the effectiveness or appropriateness of a given structure for achieving desired ends are not only driven by normative conceptions of the purposes of schooling, but also by conceptions of how schools should be structured to achieve these purposes. Such conceptions are expressions of values. While total unanimity on the ends and means of education cannot be assumed, a critical level of consensus is necessary for the identification of desired educational ends and the subsequent creation of a stable and appropriate school structure. The diversity of views on the means and ends of education prohibit the existence of one best method—or, in this case, structure—for schools (Callahan, 1962; Tyack, 1974). The demands and contingencies of a given context provide clues as to an appropriate structure for that setting.

The identification of the goals and purposes of the school organization in a given context and of the appropriate structure for realizing these begins with a fundamental understanding of the current structure of schools and the effects of this structure on organizational behavior. Many restructuring advocates spend inordinate amounts of time rhetorically articulating desired values, ideals, and structural forms, while the specific linkages among these values, their desired forms, and the logistics for achieving these remain cloaked in obscurity. The implications for practice are often equally ambiguous.

A useful way to address this ambiguity is to examine the current structure of the school. To transform an organization from its current state (A) to some desired state (B), some knowledge of the current state of affairs is needed: What is the structure of the current organization? How is this structure similar to the desired structure? How is it different? How do we get from the current state (A) to the desired state (B)?

Logic suggests that successful attempts at restructuring are predicated on a basic understanding of the current structure of schools. This structure, and the world of educational practice, must be examined and understood. What are the individual parts, elements, and components that make up this structural entity known as the school? What is the nature of relationships shared between and among these structural components? How does the current structure differ from the desired structure? What must be done to transform the current structure to the desired structural form? A theory of restructuring builds on such information and should offer a description of restructuring goals and an explanation of how these will be realized.

Restructuring efforts are likewise guided by some theory of pedagogy. The mere existence of restructuring as a reform alternative implies that proponents have an idea of how students learn, how teachers should teach, and the type of organizational structure needed to facilitate both processes. Although the comprehensiveness and full implications of these ideas may indeed be lacking, such ideas define the end of restructuring efforts. Prevailing assumptions on child development, cognition, the psychology of learning, and teaching effectiveness—assumptions inherent in a theory of pedagogy—logically serve as crucial factors in determining the deficiencies of the present structure and the possibilities of the restructured organization.

As an example of how the present structure of schools and prevailing pedagogical theory combine to define and guide restructuring efforts, one need only examine debates about the devolution of decision-making authority in schools (Malen, Ogawa, & Kranz, 1990). The specific structural focus of such restructuring proposals is on the distribution of power within the organization. Cognitive-constructivist models of teaching view the teaching-learning context as a critical factor in determining the most appropriate teaching methods to be used. Given the specific needs of a particular context, the teacher must be given the authority to make decisions about the most appropriate method of instruction. Advocates of this type of restructuring argue that the current structure of schools does not allow teachers this much-needed discretion. Rather, decisions sensitive to teachers and directly affecting classroom activity, they argue, are often made without teacher consent (e.g., allocation of resources, class size, curriculum choices, student assignments, instructional methods and flexibility, ability grouping, and so forth). The frustrations experienced by teachers as a result of exclusion, coupled with the bureaucratic rigidity associated with centralized decision-making structures, threaten the flexibility needed for effective instruction.

Regardless of the desired end of organizational restructuring, the actual end of restructuring efforts would appear to be a function of the perceived incongruities and discrepancies between the consequences of the current school structure and desired consequences. Absent too often from restructuring debates are attempts to build on what we know about the current structure of the schools and to link logically desired educational ends with workable organizational structures.

Conceptualizing the Focus and Scope of Restructuring

Attempts to understand the nature of restructuring must likewise address issues of focus and scope. A reexamination of the definition given to structure will illuminate the significance of both concepts to the restructuring process. As noted earlier, structure may be defined as the unique arrangement of individual components and elements which define the organization as an entity. Key dimensions of this structure, as described in the literature, include complexity, formalization, and the distribution of decision-making authority within the organization. Restructuring occurs when one or more of these dimensions are rearranged, fundamentally altering the relationships between and among organizational components.

Questions about the focus of restructuring center on the identification of those particular organizational parts, elements, or constituents that are the targets of alteration. For example, will the points of leverage targeted by restructuring focus solely on the organization's division of labor, its decision-making structure, its physical layout, or a combination of these? Such questions speak to the focus of restructuring efforts.

Issues about the scope of restructuring center on the extent and breadth of restructuring efforts. To define scope in this manner implies the existence of a restructuring continuum. At one end are restructuring schemes mild in both design and effect; at the other extreme are schemes more radical in nature. Building on the work of Watzlawick, Weakland, and Fisch (1974), Cuban (1988) distinguishes cosmetic and systemic change, first- and second-order change. Hence, restructuring efforts appear to vary in terms of their focus and scope, highlighting some of the difficulties inherent in attempts to conceptualize the restructuring process. The complex, interactive nature of relationships defining the structure of an organization often makes the predictability of restructuring efforts difficult.

A greater understanding of restructuring focus and scope may be gleaned from an examination of the structural complexity found in organized behavior. According to Hall (1991), structural complexity refers to the amount of horizontal, vertical, and spatial differentiation that exists within an organization. Though it would be incorrect to confine definitions of restructuring to this one dimension of organizational structure, it can be argued that many restructuring efforts have as their focus one or more of these aspects of organizational complexity. The complexity that characterizes the present school structure provides a baseline from which to plan and predict both the focus and scope of restructuring efforts. The degree of horizontal differentiation which exists in schools is certainly distinct from that of other organizations (e.g., the U. S. Army, a GM assembly plant, or a shoe repair shop). The division of labor within the school arises from the performance of three basic school functions: managerial, teaching, and support functions. While further differentiation may be made within each of these categories (e.g., teachers are divided by subject and grade, support personnel are divided according to their respective areas of responsibility—cafeteria, maintenance, or classroom aid), the present reward and allocation structure found in schools has as its basis this functional scheme. Rearrangement of this traditional division of labor means focusing on the horizontal dimension of the organization.

Restructuring initiatives which emphasize job-enrichment or job-enlargement opportunities for teachers and other school personnel are indicative of attempts to focus on the horizontal dimension of school structure. Though varying in the extent to which this enlargement or enrichment is achieved and sustained, various career-ladder schemes have been considered and enacted in a number of states. Many questions about the effects of such schemes on the quality of the teaching-learning process remain unanswered.

The vertical dimension of structural complexity refers to the depth or number of hierarchical levels within the organization. Vertical complexity may be viewed as a logical correlate of horizontal complexity: as horizontal complexity increases, vertical complexity typically follows. The logic of this relationship is rather straightforward: the coordination and communication demands created by an organization with an extensive division of labor are greater than the demands of a simpler configuration (Thompson, 1967). The authority patterns, decision-making structure, and degree of centralization peculiar to a given organization are inextricably bound to its vertical depth. An example of a restructuring initiative which has as its focus vertical complexity is the charter-school movement. Concerned with the multi-tiered, bureaucratic governing inertia seen in public education, this movement seeks to reduce or eliminate various layers of governance in an effort to free individual schools from the dysfunctional aspects of this bureaucracy.

The third structural complexity dimension is that of spatial differentiation. Descriptions of spatial differentiation have as their focus the physical location and proximity of central offices, work tools, work activities, and personnel within the organization. The spatial structure of schools is by now well known. Teachers perform the majority of their duties in physically isolated classrooms separated from their colleagues most of the day. Classrooms are located away from the principal's office, sometimes in separate buildings.

Spatial features such as these have implications for the types of relationships which develop between various school personnel. For example, such spatial characteristics affect the nature of supervision exercised by principals and superintendents. Teachers, because of their physical isolation, enjoy less supervision than would otherwise be expected. Likewise, the fact that the school site is physically distanced from the central office prevents tight supervision by the superintendent. Though not deemed successful, attempts in the 1960s to move toward open classrooms (i.e., removing walls which separated smaller clusters of students while making greater use of team teaching) represent restructuring efforts directed at the spatial complexity of schools.

Regardless of focus and scope, the common element in all structural changes would appear to be the restructuring of organizational roles and relationships (Katz & Kahn, 1978). The reconfiguration of structural components has as its consequence the redefinition of organizational roles. This should come as no surprise, particularly when it is realized that organizational structure has consequences for human behavior.

How Is Restructuring Done?

The implementation of a given restructuring plan is guided by several important considerations. The first is that of desired ends. The envisioning of a preferred state of affairs is much like the compass which guides a traveler to a destination. While it may not provide a specific route, it does provide a general direction. Greater specificity is possible as the cause-and-effect linkages associated with a desired structural outcome are considered. While one's experience proves helpful in discerning such linkages, the complex, unpredictable, and interactive nature of these relationships make both the identification and full explanation of these linkages most difficult. As a result, many organizational relationships and much structural variation go unexplained.

In spite of this ambiguity, the rhetoric surrounding calls for restructuring is often loudest from those who assume that these causal links are fully understood and manipulatable. Recent attempts in some districts to move toward a site-based governance model are indicative of this. In its most radical form, site-based management represents a marked departure from current educational-governance forms. In spite of the lack of supporting empirical evidence (Elmore, 1993; Malen, Ogawa, & Kranz, 1990), it is commonly argued that the devolution of decision-making power to individuals at the school site (i.e., teachers, parents, a governing council, and so forth) will not only lead to greater levels of satisfaction among concerned constituents but to higher levels of organizational effectiveness as well. Though research is beginning to emerge that questions these assumptions (Taylor & Bogatch, 1994), a working set of "conventional" assumptions about how site-based management is supposed to work and what effects it will produce are apparent.

In addition to these logistical considerations, it must be remembered that, in spite of the best-laid plans, restructuring does not occur in a vacuum. Discarding the old and implementing the new represent no small tasks. Although not entirely knowable a priori, barriers to restructuring must be anticipated. For example, restructuring may be resisted on ideological grounds. The new set of relationships defined by a given proposal may violate the basic ideological assumptions, traditions, and prevailing cultural norms (Fullan & Stiegelbauer, 1991; Sarason, 1972; Schein, 1985).

Structural constraints inherent in the existing structure of an organization represent yet another source of restructuring barriers. Bureaucratic rigidity and structural inertia constitute formidable obstacles for any type of change. Closely aligned with each of these are various political considerations. Diverse views of the ends and means of education make proposed changes particularly vulnerable to political debate and action (Cohen et al., 1972; Pfeffer, 1981). These should be anticipated with any proposed change.

Regardless of the source of these restructuring barriers, several features of the school organization must be considered when planning for restructuring: the stimulus-overload environment in schools, the teacher-autonomy norm, the pupil-control challenge, and the public-vulnerability issue. Consideration of the possible effects of proposed change on these defining features provides a measure of insight into the success of proposed changed efforts.

Time is a scarce resource, paperwork is abundant, and frustration is often at or near the threshold level. Employees in schools find themselves working in what has been identified as a stimulus-overload, labor-intensive environment (Willower, 1973). When considering a restructuring proposal, the following questions must be asked: Will the proposed change hinder or increase the work level of these individuals? Will it require more time? Unless this work-level issue is addressed, changes that increase the hindrance level of school employees will, in the long-run, meet with resistance.

Rooted in the uncertainty surrounding the teaching-learning process and the subsequent flexibility needed to address the varying needs of individual students, autonomy is a value and norm historically associated with the teaching profession and the public school organization (Jackson, 1968; Lortie, 1975). Teachers tend to guard jealously the boundaries of their classroom from the encroachment of others, be they parents, teaching colleagues, or administrators. Restructuring advocates would do well to consider the potential threats of proposed changes to teacher autonomy. Given the norms of the profession, will the change threaten this autonomy? Will it require teachers to give up critical levels of autonomy?

Closely aligned with notions of teacher autonomy is the theme of pupil control. As has been noted elsewhere, a prominent feature of the school organization is the degree to which it is structured to control the flow and movement of the students (Willower, Eidell, & Hoy, 1967; Willower & Jones, 1967). Given the strength of this norm, the success of a proposed change must be evaluated in terms of how it challenges or threatens the ability of teachers to maintain control. In the context of restructuring efforts, will a proposed change reduce teachers' ability to maintain order in the school and classroom? Will a change enhance or threaten this ability? If successful restructuring is to be achieved, these important questions must be addressed.

A final feature of the school organization which provides further insight into the possible success of proposed reforms is the vulnerability of the public school to its environment. When used to describe education, the adjective public is quite significant. As public institutions supported by tax dollars, schools are accountable to the public and are vulnerable to the demands, supports, and influences of the environment. Not only does the public have a right to raise questions and concerns about schools, the majority of citizens are themselves products of the public school system. The public vulnerability of the school organization creates special problems for educators. School personnel find themselves dealing with a number of functional and dysfunctional environmental influences. Of particular importance are those potentially disruptive influences which threaten the ability of the school to perform successfully the core technology which defines it, namely teaching and learning. Restructuring efforts which increase the public vulnerability of the schools, will—over time, if not initially—encounter resistance from organizational participants.

The need for an awareness of restructuring barriers is underscored by the noted resiliency of the school organization despite structural changes over the years (Callahan, 1962; Fullan & Stiegelbauer,1991). This resiliency stands as testimony to those barriers and unintended consequences which many restructuring advocates and efforts have left unaddressed. As a result, many restructuring initiatives have failed to produce desired ends. If restructuring is to be successful, such barriers must be anticipated and addressed.

CONCLUSION

To speak of the organizational restructuring of schools is to speak of adding or removing, in various degrees, the individual components which define the structure of the school. Restructuring involves altering the relationships or configurations of these individual organizational components as they relate to each other. It becomes necessary when disagreements arise over the ends or means of the organization or when the purposes of the organization and the means used to pursue these purposes are perceived as incongruent. Conceptions of the desired ends of restructuring efforts are rooted in normative ideas about the means and ends of education and assumptions regarding the causal links between the two (i.e., assumptions regarding how the organization is to get from here to there). Questions about the focus of restructuring are concerned with the identification of those organizational components which can become the target of alteration or manipulation. Issues on the scope of restructuring center on the depth and breadth of restructuring efforts.

While many factors are critical to the implementation success of a given restructuring initiative, one in particular is noteworthy: the level of knowledge which exists about internal organizational linkages. That such knowledge is incomplete is well known. The challenges created by this uncertainty represent a major obstacle to most restructuring efforts. Regardless of their nature and source, certain barriers to restructuring can be anticipated. Consideration of the possible effects of proposed change on the defining features of the school organization as it currently exists provides a measure of insight into what some of these barriers might be. Identification of these potential barriers highlights the importance of discussing and planning restructuring in light of what we know about the current structure of schools and of the need to link desired educational ends with workable structures.

The framework for reconsidering restructuring detailed above is a conceptual tool. As such, it can inform current strategies on the meaning, requirements, and demands of restructuring as practitioners seek to create and maintain quality schools. The strength of the framework lies in its attempt to build reflectively on what we know about the change process and schools as organizations.

REFERENCES

Barr, R., & Dreeben, R. (1983). *How schools work.* Chicago: University of Chicago Press.

Bidwell, C. (1965). The school as a formal organization. In J. March (Ed.), *Handbook of organizations* (pp. 972–1022). Skokie, IL: Rand McNally.

Callahan, R. E. (1962). *Education and the cult of efficiency.* Chicago: University of Chicago Press.

Cohen, M. D., March, J. G., & Olsen, J. P. (1972). A garbage can model of organizational choice. *Administrative Science Quarterly, 17,* (1–25).

Cuban, L. (1988). A fundamental puzzle of school reform. *Phi Delta Kappan.*

Cuban, L. (1990). Reforming again, again, and again. *Educational Researcher, 19*(1), 3–13.

Elmore, R. (1990). Reform and the culture of authority in schools. *Educational Administration Quarterly, 23*(4), 60–78.

Elmore, R. (1993). School decentralization: Who gains? Who loses? In J. Hannaway & M. Carnoy (Eds.), *Decentralization and school improvement: Can we fulfill the promise?* (pp. 33–54). San Francisco: Jossey-Bass.

Elmore, R., & Associates. (1990). *Restructuring schools: The next generation of educational reform.* San Francisco: Jossey-Bass.

Fuhrman, S. (1993). *Designing coherent education policy: Improving the system.* San Francisco: Jossey-Bass.

Fullan, M. G., & Stiegelbauer, S. (1991). *The new meaning of educational change.* New York: Teachers College Press.

Gamoran, A., & Dreeben, R. (1986). Coupling and control in educational organizations. *Administrative Science Quarterly, 31*(4), 612–632.

Hall, R. (1991). *Organizations: Structure, process, and outcomes.* Englewood Cliffs, NJ: Prentice-Hall.

Hallinan, M. (1995). *Restructuring schools: Promising practices and policies.* New York: Plenum Press.

Jackson, P. (1968). *Life in classrooms.* New York: Holt, Rinehart, & Winston.

Johnson, B. L, Jr., & Licata, J. W. (1995). School principal succession and teachers on successor effectiveness. *Journal of School Leadership 5,* 394–417.

Katz, D., & Kahn, R. (1978). *The social psychology of organizations.* New York: John Wiley & Sons.

Lortie, D. C. (1975). *Schoolteacher.* Chicago: University of Chicago Press.

Malen, B., Ogawa, R., & Kranz, J. (1990). What do we know about school-based management? A case study of the literature. In W. H. Clune & J. H. Witte (Eds.) *Choice and control in American education: Volume 2. The practice of choice, decentralization, and school restructuring* (pp. 289–342). New York: Falmer Press.

Meyer, J. W., & Rowan, B. (1978). The structure of educational organizations. In M. W. Meyer & Associates (Eds.), *Environments and organizations.* San Francisco: Jossey-Bass.

Mintzberg, H. (1979). *The structure of organizations.* Englewood Cliffs, NJ: Prentice-Hall.

Moore-Johnson, S. (1990). *Teachers at work: Achieving success in our schools.* New York: Basic Books.

National Commission on Excellence in Education. (1983) *A nation at risk: The imperative for educational reform.* Washington, DC: U.S. Department of Education.

Pfeffer, J. (1981). *Power in organizations.* Marshfield, MA: Pitman.

Rowan, B. (1990). Applying conceptions of teaching to organizational reform. In R. F. Elmore & Associates (Eds.), *Restructuring schools: The next generation of educational reform* (pp. 31–58). San Francisco: Jossey-Bass.

Sarason, S. (1972). *The culture of the school and the problem of change* (2nd ed.). Newton, MA: Allyn and Bacon.

Schein, E. H. (1985). *Organizational culture and leadership.* San Francisco: Jossey-Bass.

Scott, W. R. (1992). *Organizations: Rational, natural, and open systems* (3rd ed.). Englewood Cliffs, NJ: Prentice-Hall.

Scott, W. R. (1995). *Institutions and organizations.* Thousand Oaks, CA: Sage.

Taylor, D., & Bogatch, I. (1994). School-level effects of teachers' participation in decision making. *Educational Evaluation and Policy Analysis, 16*(3), 302–319.

Thompson, J. (1967). *Organizations in action.* New York: McGraw-Hill.

Tyack, D. (1974). *The one best system: A history of American urban education.* Cambridge, MA: Harvard University Press.

Tye, B. (1987). The deep structure of schooling. *Phi Delta Kappan, 69*(4), 281–284.

Watzlawick, P., Weakland, J. & Fisch, R. (1974). *Change: Principles of problem formation and problem resolution.* New York: Norton.

Weber, M. (1947). *The theory of social and economic organization.* (A. M. Henderson & T. Parsons, Trans.). New York: Free Press.

Weick, K. (1976). Educational organizations as loosely coupled systems. *Administrative Science Quarterly, 21*(1), 1-19.

Willower, D. J. (1973). Schools, values and educational inquiry. *Educational Administration Quarterly 9,* 1–18.

Willower, D. J., Eidell, T., & Hoy, W. (1967). *The school and pupil control ideology* (Monograph No. 24). University Park: Pennsylvania State University.

Willower, D. J., & Jones, R. (1967). Control in an educational organization. In J. D. Raths, J. R. Pancella, & J. S. Van Ness (Eds.), *Studying teaching.* Englewood Cliffs, NJ: Prentice-Hall.

CHAPTER 6

Reengineering the School for Quality

David Weller

The global marketplace of the 21st century will focus on competition, advanced technology, teamwork, and innovation. Preparing students for this marketplace requires that public schools emphasize critical and high quality thinking skills, the use of and instruction in the latest technology, the use of teams and cooperative learning strategies to solve problems and make decisions, and the ability to adapt and work in fluid, changing environments. Schools, themselves, will have to develop delivery processes which can adjust to the changing demands of the customer as well as future social, economic, and political trends and pressures. New skills and knowledge will have to be delivered by a system whose focus is holistic, not centered on incremental teaching and learning.

LEADERSHIP FOR SCHOOL REENGINEERING

To accomplish these aims, school leaders will have to be creative engineers of the curriculum and instructional delivery process. They will be proactive, use broad-based thinking, and involve the school's constituents in its governance procedures and policy-making efforts. These leaders will reengineer schools for quality outcomes by making decisions from three perspectives: the needs and expectations of a global economy, the design of an organizational structure or process to deliver these requirements, and the individual's role within the context of the organization's delivery system. School leaders will find the conceptual framework for such change and decision making in the business concept of *reengineering*.

Reengineering Defined

Reengineering is a conceptual framework which can help school leaders rethink the context in which they work, how work is done, and how outputs are shaped by inputs. "Reengineering is the fundamental rethinking and radical redesign of business processes to bring about dramatic improvements in performance" (Hammer & Stanton, 1995, p. 3). This definition points to major performance improvements resulting in "dramatic" breakthroughs in achieving predetermined outcomes. The term "radical" calls for the identification and eradication of root problems rather than the indiscriminate attack on symptoms; it means discarding the current way of doing business and inventing a new and better way to produce products and services. "Process" is the result of the reengineering venture, the "redesign" of how work is done, which takes into account the value work has for the employee; the roles and types of employees needed in the new work process; the attitudes, beliefs, and cultural norms needed to support the process; and the kinds of evaluation measures used to assess performance outcomes.

Therefore, reengineering is more than a restructuring of the current structure in an organization; it is more than rearranging hierarchical management and the specialization of employee jobs—it is the way work is per-

---

David Weller, The University of Georgia

formed and the values, attitudes, and set of beliefs that drive the performance of those producing the work (Chaplin, 1996). In essence, the process becomes the catalyst to revolutionize the production of the products and services the organization provides to its customers. As Hammer and Stanton (1995) state, "Reengineering is not about improving what already exists. Rather, it is about throwing it away and starting over; beginning with the proverbial clean slate and reinventing how you do your work. . . . [It] is a process of related tasks that together create value for a customer" (p. 4).

Reengineering versus Restructuring in Schools

Weller and Hartley (1994), Weller (1996a), and English (1994) have noted disillusionment and criticism of school reform models such as site-based management, Total Quality Management (TQM), and the effective schools model. Some school leaders in America, Canada, Great Britain, and Australia have attempted to reform their schools with one or more of these catalysts for change and have failed in their efforts. Yet, the literature is replete with schools and school systems which have adopted these reform models and have enjoyed success (Monk, 1993; Murgatroyd & Morgan, 1993; Schmoker & Wilson, 1993; Short & Greer, 1997; Squires, Huitt, & Segars, 1984; Weller, 1996b; Weller & Hartley, 1994). The success rate far exceeds the failure rate and the positive outcomes of these change models include improved student achievement on standardized achievement tests, increased student self-esteem, and increased teacher morale and self-confidence.

Schools that have successfully adopted the principles of a change model such as Deming's (1986) TQM have undergone more than a paradigm shift: they have transformed the method of schooling (English, 1994). Davies (1994) points out that in TQM schools, teachers' mindsets and their approach to teaching and learning are different. The values and beliefs which influence their thinking and work have undergone a fundamental change. TQM emphasizes teamwork, commitment to the purpose of meeting customer needs and expectations, and internal flexibility and process revision with an emphasis on continuous improvement across organizational boundaries (Weller, 1996a). Bonstingl (1992) notes the importance of the *kaizen*, a systemwide (process) covenant of individuals helping one another pursue excellence on a daily basis. According to Bonstingl, if schools adopted this type of covenants, they would develop new images and new structures with quality products and services specifically addressing student needs and expectations. Bonstingl agrees with Senge (1990) on the importance of a systems approach to school transformation (Senge's fifth discipline) and notes that a holistic process, a new system which is built from the ground up, is essential to meet the challenges and demands of the future. In essence, both Bonstingl and Senge call for *reengineered schools,* schools starting with a clean slate, and TQM provides the essential ingredients necessary for such complete school transformation.

Restructuring, on the other hand, means many things to many people, and "the term is as notable for its ambiguity as for its meaning" (Conley, 1993, p. 7). Usually, Conley adds, restructuring is a rapid adaptation of fragmented programs or practices to maintain or regain competitiveness. Often, what is called restructuring is actually school *renewal* or *reform* with important distinctions between the two: "Renewal focuses on activities that help the organization to do better and/or more efficiently that which it is already doing" (p. 7) while reform "attempts to alter existing procedures, rules, and requirements to allow the organization to adapt the way it functions to new circumstances or requirements" (p. 8). Neither of these processes addresses the fundamental assumptions of schooling, nor do they place emphasis on the primary existence for schools—to promote and demonstrate student learning. Neither process addresses the future; that is, neither is proactive in design. Both are highly reactive to current pressures for change which primarily come from external sources rather than from internal sources of discontent with the status quo.

The basic problems with school restructuring, says Conley, are "the lack of a clear and generally accepted definition of what restructuring really is, the unwillingness or inability to examine the underlying assumptions, values, beliefs, practices, and relationships of quality-producing schools, and the abstract and unclear goals that permeate education" (p. 9). Fullan (1991), also addressing the fundamental problem associated with school restructuring, states that "the incentive system of public schools with its lack of performance scrutiny and a noncompetitive market makes it more profitable politically and bureaucratically to [innovate] without risking the costs of radical change" (p. 28). All of this points to school leaders who fail to embrace radical change, to make drastic shifts in assumptions, beliefs, and practices without significant external pressure to change the nature of schooling. The fear of voluntary, internal change comes from the threats of downsizing, reassignment, and retraining which are implicit in the general concept of fundamental, radical change (Conley, 1993).

The Role of Leadership in the Reengineering Process

"Breakthrough thinking," new, daring, radical thinking, allows for the complete transformation of the organization and is at the heart of the reengineeering process since the act of reengineering negates the incremental changes fostered by incremental thinking and leads to a reshaping of the existing structure. Performance improvement and restructuring do not lend themselves to reengineering since these efforts lack cross-functional, results-oriented processes and possess preexisting hierarchial structures such as departments. Task-oriented thinking must be replaced by thinking which is geared toward final outcomes or goals.

Hammer and Stanton (1995) relate that leaders have the primary responsibility of creating an environment where nontraditional thinking becomes the norm, where brainstorming is a daily activity, and where people feel safe in "dreaming," in thinking the new and expressing nontraditional thoughts. This environment can best be developed by leaders who model this behavior themselves and constantly encourage and take part in "think tank" sessions with and among employees.

Since each organization has its own "underground culture" whose population has progressive and new ideas, environments which encourage and support this kind of thinking allow these ideas to be brought into the open. New and creative ideas are essential since reengineering does not begin with detailed specifications or a predetermined plan for organizational transformation. Reengineering means starting over, beginning with a clean slate. It is about rejecting conventional wisdom and assumptions of the past and searching for new models for organizing work. The new process, in essence, must provide a "best fit" situation for both management and the work force and must be based on the values and beliefs management wants to instill. Reengineering's primary intent is to reorganize the structure and change or modify the culture within the organization. This calls for creative, broad-based thinking on the part of the leader.

Champy (1995) emphasizes the importance of management's role in reshaping the organization's culture. In successful, reengineered organizations, teamwork and employee decision making are highly valued. This is based on the idea that employees will assume ownership of their work and have a vested interest in the organization's success when they share in the problem-solving and decision-making process. The values and beliefs most commonly held in reengineered corporations shift the role of the employee from narrow, task-oriented functions to multidimensional job functions.

Hammer and Champy (1993) and Champy (1995) point out that certain values and beliefs prevail among successfully reengineered corporations. They emphasize that a change in organizational values must exist prior to successful reengineering and that management must discard the traditional role of the authoritarian, the expert in all areas, and become leaders who facilitate the work process and strive to add value to the work of others. They argue that leaders, not managers, know that quality outputs depend more on the employee's attitudes, values, and knowledge and less on policies, procedures, and prescribed ways of performing work. Leaders are those who can influence behavior and reinforce employee values by their own words and deeds.

Values and beliefs central to successful reengineered corporations are as follows:

1. Teams with members who are empowered to solve problems and make decisions and who are free of management's tight, restrictive policies and prescriptive directives
2. Teams that can function across organizational boundaries and be collectively responsible for the quality of products and services provided
3. Rewards based on achievement and not the amount of time spent on narrowly defined tasks; new and increased responsibilities based on ability and overall contributions to the organization
4. Employees and leaders who are customer-centered and work to satisfy the customer since customer satisfaction achieves the goals of the organization
5. Continuous training for employees to keep up with advancements in their job-related knowledge and skill areas (with rewards for individual initiative to improve the quality of work and contribute to the overall efficiency of the organization)

When new values and attitudes compete with existing behaviors, conflict arises both within the organization and individuals themselves. Weller (1996b) explains that, when new ideas or patterns of behavior are required and the old accepted ways of doing things are not fully discarded, traditional practices often win out. Fear of the unknown, threats to individual power and influence, insecurity about learning new skills, and the need to perform tasks differently with different standards threaten comfort zones—the security people derive from work routine. Regardless of the degree of dissatisfaction with their current job or the way the organization functions, change is seen as a threat. Hammer and Stanton (1995) state that "when new process values compete with old process values, the result is [employee] frustration, confusion, cynicism, and cognitive dissonance" (p. 158). Chaplin (1996) notes that, when reengineering fails, it is usually the result of a lack of alignment between the values and beliefs held by management and those of the worker and management's inability to move the work force to accept these new values and attitudes. When reengineering fails, little if any residue of the change process will survive. The values and attitudes of the old process will become even more embedded and future attempts at change more difficult.

What Successful Leaders Need to Do

For leaders to be successful in instilling a new culture, two phenomena associated with change have to be understood. First, every organization consists of employees engaged in multiple interacting linkages which, when taken together, comprise the total work force of the organization. Second, the dynamics of change are basically dichotomous: one force is driving for change while the other force is resisting change (Lewin, 1951).

Lewin's force-field theory holds that prior to change a state of equilibrium exists which balances the driving forces and resisting forces. Change agents, to be successful, must assess the degree of power among these two forces and promote change by increasing the driving forces, reducing the resisting forces, or developing new driving forces, all within the context of the existing multiple interacting linkages. Argyris (1993) maintains that the first step to lasting change is the identification of those "power agents" existing within the informal power-group network among the work force. These informal leaders exert power and influence over their peer groups through competence and knowledge, personality, interpersonal skills, rewards and favors, or cohesion. By working with and through these informal power agents, leaders have a greater probability of achieving their desired outcomes—reducing resistance to change among the work force. Replacing the existing culture is part of reengineering since the new values and expected patterns of behavior will require new organizational structures, policies, and group norms.

Next, to have the work force internalize the new values and attitudes desired by leaders, a program of information giving is necessary. Communicating in clear and concise terms why the old values and behaviors are no longer accepted is essential to convince employees that change is needed. Facts, based on research, become the most powerful persuasive tool, especially when these facts indicate the organization's decline. Communication must be comprehensive and emphasize the positive outcomes of change, the specific reasons for change, and exactly how change will affect and benefit employees.

To reduce change anxiety further, wide participation is needed in planning, designing, and implementing change. During this stage, participants build ownership and commitment by expressing ideas and incorporating them into the change process. Employees will be more tolerant of the new process when they have a vested interest in its success. When a new process is holistically assimilated, the job of the leader becomes easier since the work force helps plan, design, and implement the desired processes, values, and behaviors. Hammer and Stanton (1995) caution against the use of leader coercion in the reengineering process, since this implies threats or reprisals and causes undue frustration, fear, and alienation among the work force. Resistance caused by coercion can result in revenge, poor performance, high turnover rates, and covert activities.

The Role of Leadership in Reengineering Schools

How, then, are schools reengineered into quality-oriented and quality-producing schools? The leader (principal) must first make the decision that the school needs to be transformed through a new set of values and beliefs and a new process to produce quality education. Next, and again central to both reengineering and TQM, is the need for principals to embrace the values and beliefs that they want implemented by modeling these behaviors. Third is the destruction of the school's current culture, the current process for doing things. Reengineering, remarks Champy (1995), necessitates "tearing down" the existing culture, discarding the old process and mindsets, and embracing a new way of thinking, a new way of behaving in the context of work and work outcomes.

The principal will find that dislodging old beliefs and work patterns and infusing new values is not easy. Each organization has its own culture of myths, ceremonies, rituals, and tacit assumptions and beliefs about the purpose and nature of work. Hoy and Miskel (1996) emphasize that organizational values incorporate these cultural components which comprise desirable and acceptable behavior patterns within the organization. In fact, Ouchi (1981) found that the culture of an organization relates directly to its success and that successful organizations share the values of trust, cooperation, teamwork, and egalitarianism. When values are shared, when employees work cooperatively toward the same goals, when employees are customer-oriented and free to innovate, when they have decision-making autonomy, the organization has a process that promotes efficient and effective products. Deal and Kennedy (1984) found similar values and cultural practices in high-achieving schools and specify that values, customs, tacit assumptions, and myths drive the process of schooling. The role of the principal in creating new values and cultural artifacts, Deal and Kennedy maintain, precludes the infusion of the new processes which will be used to transform the outcomes of schooling. Deal and Kennedy also found that successful culture change is a systematic, not a segmented, process. Change must be planned and well organized if it is to be effective in replacing core values in schools.

In changing an organizational culture, the importance of the principal's leadership cannot be overemphasized. Both Hammer and Stanton (1995) and Champy (1995) emphasize leader modeling as the primary, crucial behavior for cultural change. Because transformed organizations depend on new process infusion and new processes depend on employees embracing and practicing new values and beliefs, the modeling of expected behaviors by the leader becomes all important. These writers maintain that employees must be convinced that the new process, and the consequences of this process, are attainable, realistic, and something that they themselves can value and practice.

Schein (1985), who did research on principals and changing a school's culture, found that successful school leaders have a systematic plan for culture change and that their modeling of desired values and behaviors is essential in shaping the culture of the future. Strong principals dedicated to change realize that a school's culture provides the school with its own unique image which conveys to its internal and external publics what the school represents, what its mission is. Conley (1993) adds that the culture of a school determines what and how students learn, how they behave, and what they believe and value. Because teachers deliver the curriculum and, in some schools, develop the curriculum, what the curriculum comprises and how the curriculum is taught directly reflect the beliefs, values, and behaviors of the teaching-learning process.

Schein (1985) refers to the culture of a school as its "hidden curriculum" and suggests that what is learned by and expected of students on a daily basis far more accurately reflects the school's curriculum than any measure assessing instructional content. Conley notes that because culture is such a powerful influence on learning, transformed schools must take care to rid themselves of any vestiges of the old culture so as not to have competing ideas and loyalties over the core values which guide expectations and behaviors.

Gaining Approval of School "Poweragents"

Lunenburg and Ornstein (1996) note the importance of modeling by school leaders to change processes in schools but add that winning the approval and support of informal power agents within the school's culture is equally important to successful change. These informal leaders have peer loyalty, trust, and respect as a result of their knowledge, skills, personalities, and the rewards they can provide. Peers follow these leaders by choice, free of coercion, because they believe that consent will yield personal gain for them within the school.

Many schools have several informal groups which have their own "group leader" and whose influence over their peers is given by group consensus. These group leaders are power agents in schools, and their actions speak for their group membership. They retain power as long as they act in accordance with the norms and values held by their following and can provide personal benefits or rewards to their following. Principals who gain the trust and confidence of these influentials find the path to change easier and more successful since the informal leader's willingness to try new processes or innovative programs will be made known to their followers, thereby reducing the level of cognitive dissonance.

SPECIFIC STEPS FOR LEADERS REENGINEERING SCHOOLS

English (1994) and Davies (1994) emphasize the importance of principals in initiating school change but stress that teacher buy-in is essential for cultural change and true school transformation. Monk (1993), Murgatroyd and Morgan (1993), and Weller and Hartley (1994) document the positive outcomes of TQM as a school transformational process. These include student gains on tests of achievement, improved student self-esteem, and increased teacher morale. These schools have vision, a mission, and empowered teacher teams who participate in school governance. Their constancy of purpose is to improve continuously, and they take pride in their work as they strive to achieve quality performance for themselves and their students.

In this context, the school leader has to think differently about the purpose of schools and the kind of delivery system that will meet the needs and expectations of the core customer. Reengineering in education is about developing a delivery process which is coherent and progressive in scope in order to maximize the learning experiences of students. Since reengineering focuses on coherent processes, not structures, it negates the perpetuation of typical educational structures, such as departments in high schools, and focuses more on sequential, progressive learning through the rearrangement of the curriculum and instruction to address the goals of cohesion and progression. In essence, process follows the strategy for the reengineering of schooling.

Hammer and Champy (1993) indicate that reeingineered businesses plan their process strategy first, teardown their existing organizational structures, and then implement their processes with many processes crossing many organizational boundaries. Boundaries, as opposed to structures, are flexible units that allow for give and take, interdependency, interrelatedness, and integration. In reengineered corporations, the emphasis is on process continuity which is driven by holistic thinking and planning.

How does the school leader move staff members toward such a holistic mental model based on shared and jointly developed vision, mission, and goals? The following steps are suggested.

Information Gathering

Information must be collected which is accurate and based in fact. It is a powerful and persuasive tool to initiate cultural change. Data which are easy to read and understandable (generally free of complicated research designs and statistics) plant seeds of doubt about the existing way of doing things and challenge employees to think beyond the current production processes (Champy, 1995). Literature about successful reengineered schools and their success with TQM sparks interest and triggers questions. Here, the principal becomes a resource person, a supplier of additional information, and a local expert. Pointing to their own modeling behaviors, these principals note that their behaviors coincide with the new process that they want to infuse into their schools. As a result, teachers will begin to question the benefits of the existing culture and to analyze the positive and negative aspects of change.

Not all teachers, however, will question the values, myths, and norms of the school's culture. Some will look at change as a threat to the security of their job functions, their relationships among peers, and their work patterns. Peer leaders who are respected may challenge those who are reluctant to change to look at the data objectively and to replace moral judgments with objective analysis. Some teachers will reject these appeals for open-mindedness and will refuse to be persuaded by the principal, their peers, or the literature, while others will attempt to be intellectually honest. For reluctant teachers, the TQM practice of benchmarking becomes an important part of the cultural change process.

Benchmarking

Benchmarking, the practice of allowing employees to view firsthand exemplary programs and practices, lessens cognitive dissonance and resistance to change by allowing teachers to see the tangible consequences of reengineering. Moreover, in education, nothing has more validity for a teacher than the word of another teacher. Allowing all teachers, both eager and reluctant, to explore the positive and negative effects of TQM as a process for school transformation further reduces resistance to change and answers many practical questions not addressed in the literature. Care should be taken to explore both the process and the results of the process, not just the individual practices themselves. Benchmarking's real value lies in its ability to provide a model to critique, a stimulus for new ideas, not a structure for direct infusion. The primary role of the principal is to select those schools which best exemplify the process design most likely to yield the outcomes targeted for the school.

Focus Groups

Focus groups provide the next step in this systematic change process. Large- and small-group work provide a platform to express discontent and concerns as teachers explore the positive and negative aspects of change. Here, the principal's role becomes one of facilitator who keeps teachers' attention on building a new school yielding quality products and services. Since reengineering is about process design, principals emphasize creative thinking and dreaming and challenge teachers to develop a delivery system that promotes quality teaching and results in quality learning. The principal promotes a "can do" attitude among teachers and serves as a motivator and stimulator to build self-confidence among the staff to undertake cultural change.

In essence, these focus groups go about tearing down the old culture and replacing it with the new values and beliefs that will support and permeate the new process of schooling. This step rests primarily on the following conditions: first, that many of the teachers see a need for change and are willing to explore new and better ways to improve teaching and learning; second, that teachers, for the most part, have the self-confidence and desire to initiate change; and, third, that teachers believe that the new process (TQM) provides viable, realistic, and achievable outcomes.

Brainstorming in Groups

Large-group sessions, well planned with specific topics, greatly facilitate the changing of teachers' perspectives and attitudes. Large-group topics will focus on images of the future, process design, and the TQM philosophy and management principles. In each session, the principal's role in reengineering is that of catalyst and resource person. Images of the future will focus on what teachers believe to be the ideal school, an educational utopia where their dreams can be realized. This session becomes a brainstorming exercise where ideas are generated and free thinking dominates. This stimulates dialogue among teachers and allows for the cross-pollinization of ideas. Some teachers, however, will hold on to some of the existing values, norms, and customs. Old habits, assumptions, and behavior patterns are deeply ingrained and, for some, provide a sense of security in the process of change. Moreover, some aspects of the existing culture may be compatible with the emerging images of the future, and their inclusion will help bridge the gap for those teachers who are most reluctant to change.

Reflection

When brainstorming is completed, small focus groups are formed to allow teachers time to reflect and further explore their feelings and to add to the components of the ideal school. Teachers are free to determine which current practices are compatible with the images of the future and to discuss their merits. For some, small-group interaction is less threatening, and they feel more comfortable in expressing their deepest feelings and opinions. The principal circulates among the small groups, acting as a resource person to provide knowledge and information to address teacher questions and concerns as each group further develops the images of the ideal school and examines the values and norms of the existing culture. The principal must remember that some teachers will want to maintain certain aspects of the current culture and will express strong feelings for their inclusion. When these behaviors and values conflict with future images, the principal's task becomes one of persuader and individual catalyst. The principal addresses each teacher's concerns with fact-based information and, if needed, allows teachers to benchmark additional schools. This process takes time, but it is convincing, and such determined commitment to change is a characteristic of effective leadership.

Vision and Mission Building

Building vision and mission statements and determining the school's core values come next in the transformation process. Vision comes from agreed-upon core values, desired patterns of behavior, and commonly held attitudes and aspirations. Vision is a futuristic statement which clearly projects the organization's direction for at least 30 years (Drucker, 1974). A school's vision embodies beliefs about schooling and its purpose for the future. Mission statements also come from core values and attitudes. A mission statement provides a specific image of the future, is broad in scope, and allows for dreaming but paints a realistic, attainable future. Goals come from the school's core values and state specifically what the school intends to accomplish. Long-range in nature, they are action statements that reflect the vision and mission of the school. Few in number, goals are specific enough to provide the foundation for strategic planning and tangible enough to provide indices to measure the school's progress.

At this critical stage of school transformation, principals must emphasize the importance of consensus in identifying the core values and beliefs that will drive the vision and mission of the school. Moreover, the emphasis on shared ownership must be stressed and permeate the entire process since teachers are now laying the essential foundation upon which the reengineered process will be built. By jointly agreeing upon core values, mission, and vision, teachers and administrators will have a vested interest in making the transformation process a success through a personal commitment to the school's new culture.

Large- and small-group sessions will be used throughout this process to achieve maximum teacher input and promote consensus building. Since core values are the moral and philosophical fabric from which goals are developed, small focus groups follow a large-group session where a list of core values is presented and discussed. Small groups promote close examination of issues and the sharing of intrinsic feelings necessary to open an honest communication among teachers. When these groups have identified their core values, the values are discussed, and consensus is reached in a large-group session. The development of mission and vision statements is conducted in the same format.

TQM as a Transformational Process

The next phase of the transformation is identification of the process that completes the task of reengineering. TQM provides a holistic, empowered, bottom-up approach to transforming schools, and many of the quality management principles are used throughout this reengineering process. Here, principals call on teachers from transformed schools using TQM as their process to help teachers see how the school's goals, mission, and vision can be applied to their professional responsibilities and their classroom instruction. Teachers from TQM schools have the necessary credibility essential for teacher training to be effective. These teachers have gone through a similar process and can answer many of the practical questions teachers may have. They are able to relate personal experiences that add credibility to the effectiveness of TQM as a transformational process. Moreover, teachers realize that, if their peers can adopt TQM as a transformational process and achieve its intended results, they can, too. This results in greater self-confidence and further motivates the staff to embrace the tenets of TQM's management principles.

In reengineering, Champy (1995) maintains that employee satisfaction with the new process precedes quality products and services. Teachers must have ownership in the new process and be satisfied that the goals of schooling are compatible with their own values and attitudes. When teachers' needs are met, they can then concentrate on meeting the needs of their students and on quality outcomes. Because teachers themselves reengineered the delivery system, the issue of accountability is moot. Producing quality products now rests squarely on their shoulders. And because they developed the goals of schooling, they know the evaluation standards and criteria for performance.

In TQM schools, teachers become the decision makers and problem solvers and have the ability, within teams, to cross interdisciplinary boundaries as they work toward implementing the process of schooling—the

TQM principles and management philosophy. When these teams function within and across grade levels or departments, they implement a process that transcends structures and boundaries and makes the curriculum and the instructional delivery system a holistic process devoid of the structural barriers found in traditional schools. Equally important is the ability of these teams to adjust rapidly to the external needs and forces brought to bear on schools. Their empowered base allows for flexibility in the instructional system in order to address the concerns and needs of their primary customer—the student.

CONCLUSION

Senge (1990) believes the problems facing true school transformation lie in the current process of schooling itself and the historical artifacts of the past. Among the most detrimental inhibitors of school transformation are the isolation of teachers in self-contained classrooms, grade levels, or departments; the incremental mental models that dominate our ways of thinking; the targeting for reform and research of symptoms rather than root causes for reform and research; the search for "quick fixes" and the modification of existing programs; and disenchantment with new reform programs which offer panaceas but, like their predecessors, fail to make good on their promises, leaving teachers frustrated and leery of *any* reform movement.

Conley (1993) states that for organizations to survive in the future they will have to be fluid, environmentally responsive bodies which can adapt quickly to changing globalized demands. The only constant is "constant change" with success and survival depending on the organization's response time and ability to adapt successfully to these constant changes. Shifting economic, social, and political trends and their emerging interrelated complexities will be compounded by an increasing dependency on technology and the ability to respond quickly to its rapid innovations. These projected shifts and accelerated changes call for a labor force with new skills and knowledge, a new working environment, and a new way to process products. Incremental thinking with highly departmentalized work structures will be replaced by holistic thinking and cross-sectional configurations which emphasize teamwork and unity of vision, mission, and purpose.

Our schools are no different, and school leaders will have to be flexible enough to respond adequately to these volatile external trends. Establishing proactive patterns of behavior; thinking in broad, contextual frameworks; and preparing the work force for innovations yet to come are the skills that school leaders of the future will have to possess in order to reengineer our schools to meet the demands of the future.

REFERENCES

Argyris, C. (1993). *Knowledge for action: A guide to overcoming barriers to organizational change.* San Francisco: Jossey-Bass.
Bonstingl, J. J. (1992). The quality revolution in education. *Educational Leadership, 50*(3), 4–9.
Champy, J. C. (1995). *Reengineering management: The mandate for new leadership.* New York: HarperCollins.
Chaplin, E. (1996). Reengineering in health-care: The four phase work cycle. *Quality Progress, 29*(10), 105–109.
Conley, D. T. (1993). *Roadmap to restructuring: Policies, practices, and the emerging visions of schooling.* Eugene, OR: ERIC Clearinghouse on Educational Management.
Davies, B. (1994). TQM: A theory whose time has come. *Management in Education 8*(1), 12–13.
Davies, B., & Ellison, L. (1997). *School leadership for the 21st century.* New York: Routledge.
Deal, T. E., & Kennedy, A. A. (1984). *Corporate cultures: The rites and rituals of corporate life.* Reading, MA: Addison-Wesley.
Deming, W. E. (1986). *Out of the crisis.* Boston: Massachusetts Institute of Technology, Center for Advanced Engineering.
Drucker, P. F. (1974). *Management: Tasks, practices, responsibilities.* New York: Harper & Row.

English, F. W. (1994). *Total quality education: Transforming schools into learning places.* Thousand Oaks, CA: Corwin Press.

Fullan, M. G. (1991). *The new meaning of educational change.* New York: Teachers College Press.

Hammer, M., & Champy, J. (1993). *Reengineering the corporation: A manifesto for business revolution.* New York: HarperCollins.

Hammer, M., & Stanton, S. A. (1995). *The reengineering revolution: A handbook.* New York: HarperCollins.

Hoy, W. K., & Miskel, C. G. (1996). *Educational administration: Theory, research, practice* (5th ed.). New York: McGraw-Hill.

Lewin, K. (1951). *Field theory in social sciences.* New York: Harper and Row.

Lunenburg, F. C., & Ornstein, A. C. (1996). *Educational administration: Concepts and practices* (2nd ed.). Belmont, CA: Wadsworth.

Monk, B. J. (1993). *Toward quality in education: The leader's odyssey.* Washington, DC: U.S. Department of Education, Office of Educational Research and Improvement.

Murgatroyd, S., & Morgan, C. (1993). *Total Quality Management and the school.* Bristol, PA: Open University Press.

Ouchi, W. (1981). *Theory z.* Reading, MA: Addison-Wesley.

Schein, E. (1985). *Organizational culture and leadership.* San Francisco: Jossey-Bass.

Schmoker, M. J., & Wilson, R. B. (1993). *Total quality education: Profiles of schools that demonstrate the power of Deming's management principles.* Bloomington, IN: Phi Delta Kappa.

Senge, P. M. (1990). *The fifth discipline: The art and practice of the learning organization.* New York: Doubleday.

Short, P. M., & Greer, J. T. (1997). *Leaders in empowered schools: Themes from innovative efforts.* Columbus, OH: Merrill.

Squires, D. A., Huitt, W. G., & Segars, J. K. (1984). *Effective schools and classrooms: A research-based perspective.* Alexandria, VA: Association for Supervision and Curriculum Development.

Weller, L. D. (1996a). The next generation of school reform. *Quality Progress, 29*(10), 65–70.

Weller, L. D. (1996b). Return on quality: A new factor in assessing quality efforts. *International Journal of Educational Management, 10*(1), 30–40.

Weller, L. D., & Hartley, S. H. (1994). Total quality management and school restructuring: Georgia's approach to educational reform. *Quality Assurance in Education, 2*(2), 18–25.

CHAPTER 7

Curriculum Alignment: An Approach to Raising Standardized Achievement Scores in High-Risk School Districts

Raymond V. Aguilera and Joen M. Hendricks

School districts high in minority populations, high in students qualifying as economically disadvantaged, and traditionally low in achievement scores are being targeted in Texas and the nation as high-risk districts. "Funding the rapidly increasing costs of public elementary and secondary education will be a serious challenge to the people of the nation into the twenty-first century" (Burrup, Brimley, & Garfield, 1996, p. 29), particularly because of the changing demographics in the American educational system. Millions of dollars are being spent annually in hopes of creating districts that are more effective in the delivery of course work. Consequently, districts that can produce positive academic achievement when compared to higher achieving districts and schools will gain appropriate recognition for their efforts to foster quality schools.

Unfortunately, Spring (1994) indicates that the pattern of state involvement in schools shows a continuing search for inexpensive methods of control through increasing requirements and testing but without raising taxes. As the monitoring becomes closer, schools and school districts are targeted for not meeting the standards set.

In attempting to answer the question of how to turn these schools and school districts around, Levine and Havighurst (1984) identified seven characteristics of effective schools in the Connecticut School Effectiveness Project: (a) a safe environment that is conducive to learning, (b) clear school goals, (c) instructional leadership from the principal, (d) a climate of high expectations, (e) a high percentage of time on task, (f) frequent evaluation of student performance, and (g) community support.

More recent studies (Levine & Lezotte, 1995) identify various aspects of school climate and culture. Those cited are "a safe and orderly environment, a shared faculty commitment to improve achievement, orientation focused on identifying and solving problems, high faculty cohesion, collaboration, and collegiality, high faculty input in decision making, and schoolwide emphasis on recognizing positive performance" (p. 525). Teddie, Kirby, and Stringfield (1989) suggest that building principals are the most critical leadership determinant of effective schools. Effective school principals devote considerable time to obtaining additional resources for their schools. Levine and Lezotte (1996) observe that effective principals engaged in "writing grant proposals, soliciting funds or other resources in the community, stretching and bending rules along with skillful politics aimed at acquiring all possible district resources, and in-school fund raising" (p. 525).

Borman and Spring (1984) identified two additional factors critical to effective schools: (a) belief that virtually all students, regardless of their family background, can acquire basic skills and (b) belief that inappropriate school expectations and practices are the major cause of low achievement by low-income and minority students. Others suggest moving away from standardized tests and implementing alternative performance tests and portfolio assessments. Spring (1994), for example, states that "one of the major causes of the unequal distribution of educational opportunities between social classes and racial groups is unequal school expenditures" (p. 90). If schools had more money, many politicians, administrators, and teachers would say, the problems faced by school districts could be solved.

Ferguson (1995) states that district leaders and community people often believe that staffing or organiza-

Raymond V. Aguilera, University of Texas at San Antonio
Joen M. Hendricks, Our Lady of the Lake University

tional changes or the installation of new systems such as computer hardware or software will improve test scores. His research indicates, however, that improvement in test scores are dependent less on these in-school variables than on those related to efforts to sharpen the focus of instruction. Ferguson suggests that well-meaning administrators and staffs spend so much time and money on addressing effective school characteristics that they seldom are able to focus on what he considers the main problem in schools today: the inability of administrators, teachers, students, and parents to focus on curriculum and curriculum issues.

English (1992) defines curriculum as "any document or plan that exists in a school or school system that defines the work of teachers, at least to the extent of identifying the content to be taught children and the methods to be used in the process" (p. 2). Curriculum must be designed by school systems and involves purchasing textbooks and writing curriculum guides. Once designed, English continues, curriculum must be delivered, a process of "implementing, supervising, monitoring, and using feedback to improve the curriculum once it has been created and put it into place in schools" (p. 3). This process leads to the concept of curriculum alignment which is simply "the match or fit between the curriculum (in whatever form it may exist) and the test or tests to be used to assess learners" (p. 18). English calls this "alignment" because it is usually built into the curriculum as it is being developed. "If raising test scores are a concern, tightening the curriculum must be addressed by a school system. This idea refers to actions that bring the written, taught, and tested curricula into alignment or congruence with one another" (p. 19). Tightening the curriculum, then, means that the overlap between the three curricular processes must be increased. The effectiveness of this approach is discussed by Aguilera and Thomson (1992).

STUDY

Three school districts in Southern Texas were identified for this project by central office administrators. The Texas Assessment of Academic Skills (TAAS), a state-mandated examination in all Texas public schools, was used to measure achievement in reading and mathematics. The three districts served low-income communities with large minority populations. The Texas Education Agency placed the participating school districts on an "Accredited Warned" list because of clearly unacceptable performance. Individual schools within these school districts were identified as "Low Performing" by the Texas Education Agency because of the low percentage of students passing the annual TAAS.

With 9,000 students in pre-kindergarten through 12th grade, School District #1 in Texas had an estimated 98% Hispanic population with 40% being migrant students and 78% classified as economically disadvantaged. School District #2 had a pre-kindergarten through twelfth-grade student population of approximately 28,000 students, consisting of 45% Hispanic and 50.2% classified as economically disadvantaged. School District #3 had a pre-kindergarten through twelfth-grade student population of 10,500 students in a low income, high minority district. Ninety-two percent of the population was Hispanic, with 83% classified as economically disadvantaged. The school principals volunteered to participate in a new curriculum alignment program in order to improve low academic achievement test scores.

To address their alignment issues, the three districts participated in a training program and implemented an instructional management program consisting of several steps: curriculum alignment, filling the curriculum gaps, and monitoring student progress. The alignment process, filling in the gaps, and monitoring of student progress using the computerized management system, was the focus of the training.

Step 1: Aligning Curriculum

During the curriculum alignment phase, comparing the curriculum and the TAAS test to be used to assess learners, four criteria were established: (a) the compatibility of conceptual knowledge; (b) the similarity of evaluation, content, and format; (c) the sufficiency of teacher instruction; and (d) the sufficiency of student practice. If a textbook objective and the test met all four criteria, the objective or outcome would be classified at an "Absolute Level." The Absolute Level would be a strong indicator that the materials and approaches at the school were satisfactory for students to perform well on that specific objective. Objectives or outcomes meeting three of the four criteria were classified as "High Partial." Teachers would have to supplement the missing crite-

Table 1. Alignment Results
Reading, 1993 Edition, Grade 8
Correlated to TAAS Reading Instructional Targets.

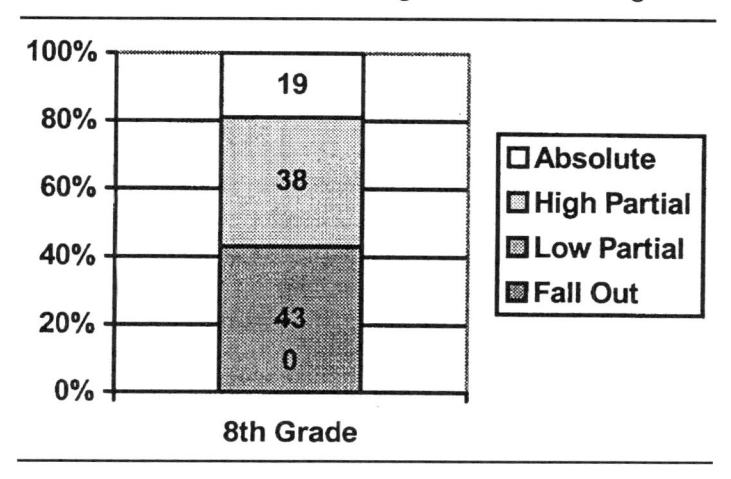

8th Grade:
- Absolute: 19
- High Partial: 38
- Low Partial: 43
- Fall Out: 0

ria with appropriate materials. Objectives that met one or two of the criteria were identified as "Low Partial," again requiring teachers to supplement the missing two or three criteria. If none of the criteria areas were present, objectives were classified as "Fallout." Teachers supplemented all four criterion to ensure students would learn the given objectives. Table 1 displays the criteria levels for the alignment of the TAAS Reading Instructional Targets in grade 8. Similar patterns were found in the 6th- through 8th-grade mathematics alignment.

Table 1 indicates that only 19% of the 8th-grade TAAS instructional targets are absolutely aligned with the reading textbook, and 43% of the targets meet Low Partial criteria. Approximately 81% of the TAAS instructional targets are not covered adequately in this textbook for ensuring student mastery. These results should indicate to school personnel that the lack of curricular alignment within the 81% of instructional targets definitely require more attention if students are to learn more effectively and the tests are to reflect the curriculum.

Table 2 indicates that 14% of the 3rd-grade and 7% of the 4th-grade TAAS instructional targets are not covered by this particular mathematics textbook under the criteria set by this program (Fallout objectives). An addi-

Table 2. Alignment Results
Mathematics, 1991 Edition, Grades 3, 4
TAAS Alignment.

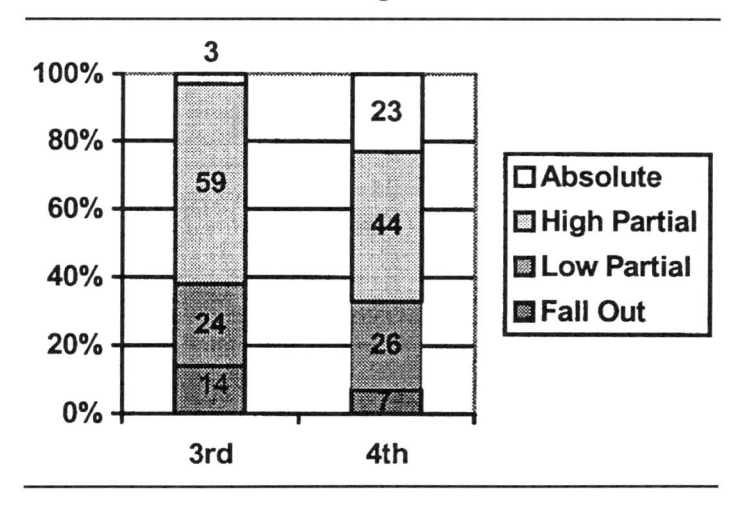

3rd Grade:
- Absolute: 3
- High Partial: 59
- Low Partial: 24
- Fall Out: 14

4th Grade:
- Absolute: 23
- High Partial: 44
- Low Partial: 26
- Fall Out: 7

tional 24% and 26% of the instructional targets respectively only meet the Low Partial criteria. These results indicate that 93% of the 3rd-grade objectives and 77% of the 4th-grade mathematics objectives are not covered adequately by this textbook. Although different textbooks were used in each district, alignment results for each grade level, regardless of textbook used, were similar to the data shown in Tables 1 and 2.

Step 2: Filling the Curriculum Gaps

Having completed the alignment process identified in detailed reports for each instructional objective, the teaching staff begins "filling the gaps" for the missing criterion by purchasing supplementary materials specific to those instructional targets, constructing new materials, developing or purchasing additional testing materials, or increasing instructional time. Once the gaps are filled, teachers can be assured that the instructional materials which they have organized through the alignment process will be sufficient for their students to master the TAAS instructional targets, thus eliminating or reducing the frustration felt by many educators following traditional approaches to raising student achievement.

Step 3: Monitoring Student Progress

Once the curriculum has been aligned and the gaps have been filled, instruction begins with a continuous monitoring of student mastery of those objectives. Students should be monitored regularly by their teacher to ensure that they learn material presented. A computerized management system, allowing teachers to assess students on a formative and summative basis can be used with this program to monitor student progress regularly. If students do not show adequate progress, then teachers must present the material using different approaches, followed again with activities which demonstrate student mastery.

RESULTS

TAAS tests, developed by the Texas Education Agency, were administered the year the alignment process was introduced in each school district, followed approximately 9 to 12 months later by another battery of TAAS tests at the same grade levels. Results for the three participating districts are presented in the following tables.

As Table 3 indicates, the percentage of students passing the TAAS reading examination in District #1 was raised from 25% to 50%. The percentage of students passing the TAAS mathematics exam was raised from 16% to 60%.

Table 3. Texas District #1
Reading, Writing, Mathematics Comparison, Grade 3
Pre-TAAS Testing.

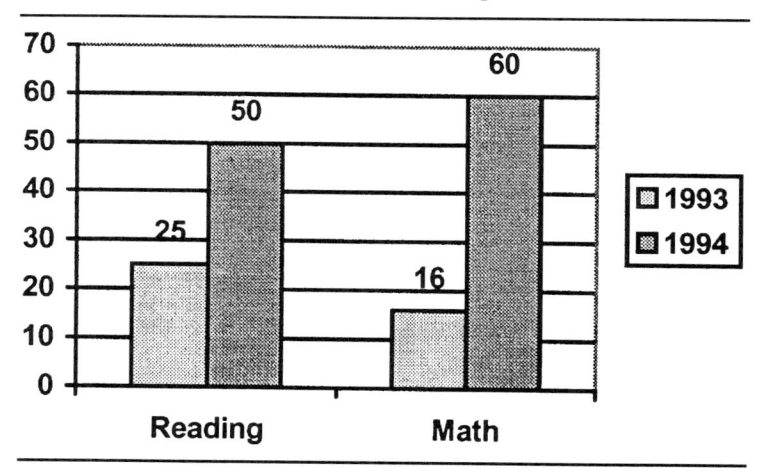

	Reading	Math
1993	25	16
1994	50	60

Table 4. Texas District #2
Grade 4
1993–1994 Reading and Mathematics: School A.

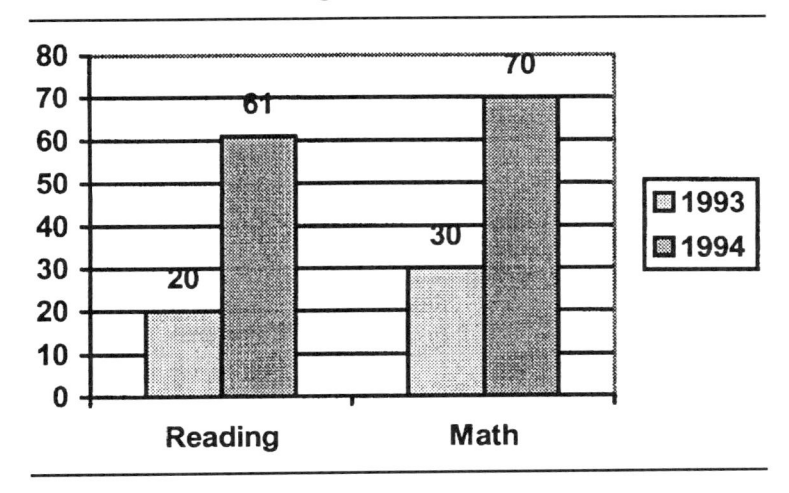

	Reading	Math
1993	20	30
1994	61	70

Table 5. Texas District #2
Grade 4
1993–1994 Reading and Mathematics: School B.

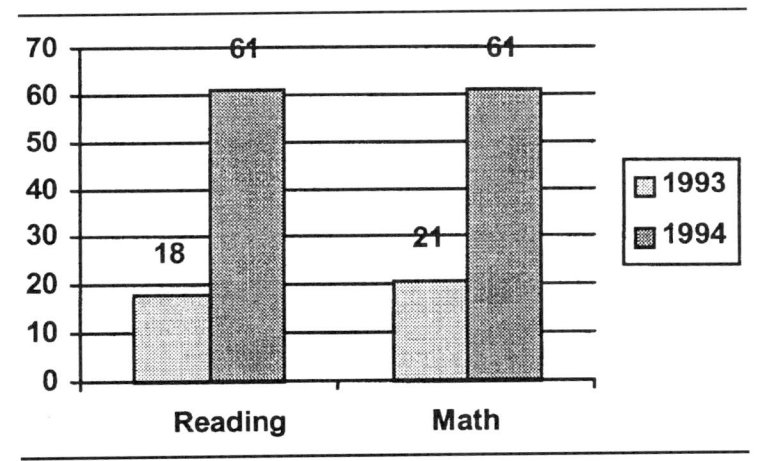

	Reading	Math
1993	18	21
1994	61	61

Table 6. Texas District #3
Grade 4
1993–1994 Reading Results.

[Bar chart showing 1993 and 1994 reading results for schools A, B, C, D:
A: 42 (1993), 62 (1994)
B: 56 (1993), 70 (1994)
C: 22 (1993), 62 (1994)
D: 45 (1993), 78 (1994)]

Participating Schools

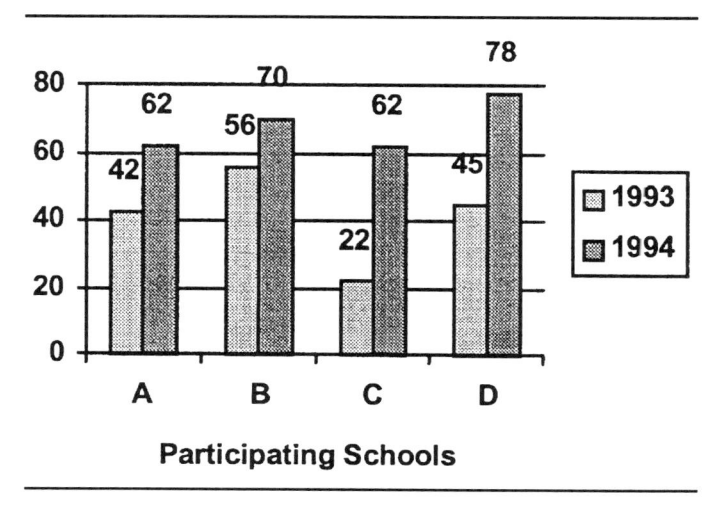

Table 4 demonstrates that the percentage of students passing the TAAS reading and mathematics examination in School A in District #2 increased dramatically from 1993 to 1994. The percentage of students passing the reading examination was raised by approximately 41%. The percentage of students passing the mathematics exam was increased from 30% to 70%.

Table 5 indicates that the percentage of students passing the reading examination in School B in District #2 increased from 18% to over 60% and from 21% to 61% in mathematics.

Achievement scores were raised in the four schools in District #3 at the 4th-grade level, as Table 6 shows. The most dramatic score increase was in School C where the percentage of students passing the reading test was raised from 22% to 62%, a 40% increase in one year. The percentage of students passing the TAAS in all schools was raised above 60%.

Table 7 indicates that in District #3 all four participating schools increased the percentage of students passing

Table 7. Texas District #3
Grade 8
1993–1994 Reading Results.

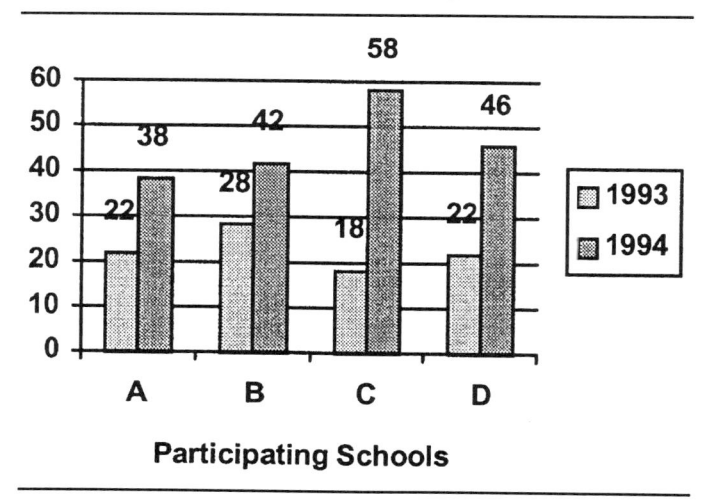

[Bar chart showing 1993 and 1994 reading results for schools A, B, C, D:
A: 22 (1993), 38 (1994)
B: 28 (1993), 42 (1994)
C: 18 (1993), 58 (1994)
D: 22 (1993), 46 (1994)]

Participating Schools

the TAAS reading test. The percentage of 8th-grade students passing the test in School C increased from 18% to 58%, a 40% increase.

DISCUSSION OF THE FINDINGS

An analysis of the sampled textbooks and the TAAS resulted in the identification of objectives or outcomes not covered appropriately by the textbooks. Items classified as fallout, low partial, and high partial then became the targeted instructional objectives for the school year. The objectives or outcomes that were identified as requiring additional materials or supplementary work ranged from a low of 75% to a high of 91%. In short, 75% to 91% of the objectives in the sampled textbooks were inadequately covered, indicating that students were not being taught to pass the TAAS examinations.

After one year of using the curriculum alignment process described here, all participating schools were able to increase their achievement scores substantially.

CONCLUSIONS

Much of the available research would predict that this type of growth is not possible in such school districts until a myriad of parental, societal, and student problems were first addressed and corrected. Then and only then would teachers and administrators stand a chance for making a significant difference in the student achievement scores. The results obtained using the curriculum alignment process described in this project resulted in definite increases in student achievement. If the ultimate goal of our school systems is to address student learning, the results of this study would question the necessity of restructuring the organization of a school district or school, jumping on the proverbial bandwagon of many school movements, or attempting to correct societal problems through our schools. What is needed is a focused curriculum alignment approach, such as the one used in this study, bringing together all the resources a school district has to offer in a more focused manner for our students' ultimate benefit.

REFERENCES

Aguilera, R. V., & Thomson, F. (1992). *Site-based management.* Paper presented at the meeting of the Arizona School Administrators Association Conference, Tempe, AZ.

Borman, K., & Spring, J. (1984). *Schools in central cities.* New York: Longman.

Burrup, P. E., Brimley, V., Jr., & Garfield, R. R. (1996). *Financing education in a climate of change.* Boston: Allyn and Bacon.

English, F. W. (1992). *Deciding what to teach and test: Developing, aligning, and auditing the curriculum.* Newbury Park, CA: Corwin Press.

Ferguson, L. C. (1995). *A strategy to improve student achievement: A detailed step-by step strategy to increase student achievement, particularly in low performing school districts.* Scottsdale, AZ: Evans Newton.

Levine, D. U., & Havighurst, R. J. (1984). *Society and education* (6th ed.). Boston: Allyn and Bacon.

Levine, D. U., & Lezotte, L. W. (1996). Effective schools research. In J. A. Banks & C. A. McBee Banks (Eds.), *Handbook on research on multicultural education* (pp. 525–547). New York: Macmillan.

Ramos, C. (1996, February 2). Group tackles minority TAAS scores. *San Antonio Express News,* pp. D1, D4.

Spring, J. (1994). *American education* (6th ed.). New York: McGraw-Hill.

Teddie, C., Kirby, P. C., & Stringfield, S. (1989). Effective versus ineffective schools: Observable differences in the classroom. *American Journal of Education, 97*(3), 221–236.

CHAPTER 8

Performance-Based Rewards as a Model for State School Finance Policy[1]

Richard A. King

In a performance-based school finance approach, some portion of educational revenue is conditioned on outcome measures to encourage quality schools. The premise is that financial rewards motivate school personnel to adopt effective instructional practices which in turn result in improved student learning. Fourteen states' statutes currently include provisions for team-based rewards for school improvements, and their appropriations are but a small proportion of overall state educational revenue. Nevertheless, an exploration of financial rewards in four states has interesting implications for expanded performance-based accountability systems and school finance policies as inducements for creating quality schools for the future.

PERSPECTIVES UNDERLYING THE MODEL

Performance- or results-based rewards are an important component of "entrepreneurial restructuring" (Boe & Boruch, 1993) and the "new educational accountability" (Elmore, Abelman, & Fuhrman, 1995). Many states have adopted indicators of school success, including student performance on criterion-referenced achievement examinations as well as standards for comparing these performance data by school or district. However, not all accountability systems tie sanctions or other intervention strategies to deficient performance, and even fewer trigger financial rewards for improvements. These emerging models rest on the assumption that externally imposed performance-based rewards and sanctions successfully motivate school improvement.

Many perspectives on human motivation derive from beliefs that people direct behavior toward outcomes that provide pleasure and away from those that produce pain (Atkinson, 1964). For example, Vroom's (1964) expectancy theory suggests that harder work is forthcoming when valued and attainable rewards are anticipated. However, not all research supports such suppositions. Extrinsic factors, including pay, are not necessarily motivators, and competition and fear work against organizational goals (Deming, 1982). More recently, Kohn (1993) observed unintended consequences from individual performance rewards, including undermined relationships among employees and between workers and supervisors, diminished risk taking and work standards, and illegal or unethical behavior as workers identify what is essential to earn rewards.

Intrinsic rewards from work, particularly in schools, are believed to contribute more positively to motivation. Lawler (1994) argued that people work harder because of internal feelings of satisfaction: "For work to be motivating, individuals must feel personally responsible for the outcomes of the work, need to do something that they feel is meaningful, and need to receive feedback about what is accomplished" (p. xix). Although intrinsic rewards may be of greater importance to educators, Hanushek (1991) contended that merit school awards and other extrinsic motivators can successfully motivate school improvement:

> The focus of each of these policies is on providing incentives that would work to improve performance without needing to specify exactly how schools should be run. By providing tangible incentives for improved performance, most decision making could be improved. (p. 450)

Rather than emphasize individual performance pay for teachers, states are turning to team-based rewards.

Richard A. King, University of Northern Colorado

Whereas the competition for individual bonuses often results in divisiveness that undermines collective efforts demanded of work groups (Ballou & Podgursky, 1993; Murnane & Cohen, 1986), team rewards encourage cooperation and foster norms related to good performance. In addition, they can lead to demonstrable gains in organizational performance and worker satisfaction. "Group synergy" and productivity are maximized when tasks are motivationally engaging, when reward systems provide challenging performance objectives and reinforce their achievement, and when interactions promote a shared commitment among members to the team and its work (Galbraith, Lawler, & Associates, 1993; Hackman, 1987; Mohrman, Cohen, & Mohrman, 1995).

Entrepreneurial restructuring within state education policies thus urges rewards that reflect schoolwide performance, and these financial inducements are shared by all personnel or fund schoolwide improvements. Team-based rewards are believed to have incentive effects in advancing educational reforms and enhancing school efficiency (Garris & Cohn, 1996). Further, the avoidance of such undesirable consequences as negative publicity about low performance and formal sanctions that bring uninvited external interventions (Boe & Boruch, 1993) is believed to speed the pace of school improvement.

A STUDY OF PERFORMANCE-BASED REWARDS IN FOUR STATES

Indiana, Kentucky, South Carolina, and Texas are among the fourteen states (Mathers, 1997) that have adopted policies that link financial rewards to school performance measures. These states' accountability systems also call for interventions or sanctions for low-performing schools.

An analysis of performance-based rewards and related interventions (King & Mathers, 1996) included on-site interviews with 82 key influentials in policy development and implementation between February and May of 1996. Selected quotations below refer to individuals and organizations as (a) departments of education, including the chief state school officer or personnel who oversee accountability, rewards, testing, and finance units or both; (b) district offices, including superintendents or their assistants in selected school districts or both; (c) principals at different levels; (d) professional associations, including state associations of school boards or administrators; (e) researchers in universities or independent policy centers; (f) state-level office personnel in various legislative and executive offices (other than departments of education); and (g) teachers association personnel at the state level. It should be noted that views expressed in 1996 may not represent the official positions of organizations then or now.

Tables 1 and 2 present an overview of the financial rewards and performance measures present in the four states.

POSITIVE CONSEQUENCES OF REWARDS AND SANCTIONS

The study methodology permitted only reports of effects since it relied primarily on perceptions of people in positions to influence state policy and local implementation. Despite this limitation, their observations about rewards and sanctions reveal a number of positive consequences:

1. Although performance-based accountability systems are credited with positive improvements, intrinsic aspects of teaching and nonmonetary recognition have greater incentive effects.
2. School-improvement efforts and team building are particularly evident in elementary schools and low-performing schools.
3. Needs of low-performing students receive increased attention when ratings and rewards consider the performance of student groups.
4. The avoidance of negative publicity and sanctions is a powerful motivator.

Do Rewards and Recognition Motivate Improvements?

Just like the literature on extrinsic and intrinsic motivators, views differ on the role of financial rewards. Several reports noted benefits of extrinsic rewards: "We like to say that teachers are not there for the money, but this program brings additional money and recognition, and they are responding" (Kentucky Department of Educa-

Table 1. Overview of Performance-Based Rewards in Four States.

	Indiana	Kentucky	South Carolina	Texas*
Reward program	School Improvement Award Program	Education Reform Act (KERA) Rewards	School Incentive Reward Program (SIRP)	Texas Successful School Awards System (TSSAS)
Date initiated	1987	1990	1984	1984
Appropriations High Low	$10.1 million (1989–90) $3.2 million (1996–97)	$27.2 million (1996–97) $26.0 million (1994–95)	$6.9 million (1985–86) $5.0 million (1996–97)	$20.0 million (1992–93) $5.0 million (1994–95)
Range of rewards	$415–$16,451 per school (1996–97)	$1,155–$2,310 per teacher (1996–97)	$2,500–$63,000 per school (1996–97)	$250–$30,000 per school (1994–95)
Uses	Educational purposes	School improvement or salary bonuses	Instructional improvement	Academic enhancement
Restrictions	No athletics or salary	Teachers decide bonuses	School Improvement Councils advise principal	No salary bonuses

*TSSAS funding was suspended during 1995–96 and 1996–97; the next rewards will be allocated in Fall 1998.

Table 2. Performance Indicators That Determine Rewards.

	Indiana	Kentucky	South Carolina	Texas
Dropout rate		X	X	X
Performance assessments		X		
Retention rate		X		
Student achievement	X	X	X	X
Student attendance	X	X	X	X
Teacher attendance			X	
Transition from high school		X		

Note: Performance measures collected for accountability purposes may add to these determinants of reward recipients.

tion), and "Schools work on the behaviors most related to the reward" (South Carolina Department of Education). In contrast are observations that rewards do not motivate change: "As a result of TSSAS [Texas Successful School Awards System], did the schools engage in systemic change? It is happening, but not because of a reward. It is not even on the teacher's radar screen" (Texas Teachers Association).

Intrinsic aspects of teaching were more evident in discussions: "The real incentive is a desire for students to learn and do the best they can" (Indiana principal), and "The driving force is the desire to do the best job—there is no time to think about rewards and sanctions" (Kentucky principal). In addition, external recognition, including state and local attention to improvement efforts, has at least as large an incentive effect as reward money: "Recognition itself is important enough to induce improvements" (Indiana principal), and "Flags say the school is an incentive-award winner; recognition for a job well done is motivating" (South Carolina state-level office).

What Are the Consequences for School Improvement?

Rewards and sanctions seemed to stimulate improvement efforts in elementary rather than secondary schools. This differentiation was attributed to school cultures or organizational structures: "Elementary and middle school teachers will work hard to implement reforms so they won't look bad—the secondary teachers won't care" (Kentucky researcher), and "The majority of teachers want to be left alone in their classrooms; in the high school they are so department oriented" (South Carolina principal). The misalignment of state examinations with high school students' concerns about college entrance examinations may also be a contributor: "It is difficult to psyche up 11th graders to do well; they do not see the value in the tests after they pass the 10th grade exit exam; they are more concerned with SAT and ACT" (South Carolina principal).

Team-based rewards play a role in improving low performing teachers' skills when teachers assist the poorest teachers: "We have shared responsibility for school improvement and what happens in all classrooms; it has given me the ammunition to say to good faculty, 'Are you going to help this person improve or encourage them to leave?'" (Kentucky principal), and "Individual rewards set up a competitive system; now it is team based and people are concerned about the lowest performing teacher"(South Carolina Department of Education).

Accountability systems are often credited with improved teaching and learning, but specific effects of rewards are elusive. Recent reports of the extensive Kentucky reforms reveal improvements in curriculum and instruction and dramatic changes in formerly low-performing schools. For example, respondents in a survey of Kentucky educators and the general public agreed that "the performance assessments have changed the way teachers are teaching and students are learning" (Kentucky Institute for Education Research, 1995). Another study in four rural districts showed that high-stakes assessments were one of the "major drivers of instructional change" (Appalachian Educational Laboratory, 1996). Interviews in the present study also suggest that accountability consequences affect the classroom: "In the past, not all English teachers in a school were working on writing; having the state expectations and assessments has forced all English teachers to teach writing" (Kentucky Teachers Association).

When the performance of low-socioeconomic-status and minority-group children are considered in accountability systems, their needs are given greater attention: "By emphasizing groups, schools and teachers are encouraged to focus on needs of African American and Hispanic students who often account for the low scores of low-performing schools" (Texas state-level office), and "We're proud that some schools in low SES [socioeconomic status] groups were award winners each year; these lighthouse schools used the money and status to continue to build their strength; the incentive program helped discover this 'nugget' and boost their confidence" (South Carolina Department of Education).

Do Sanctions and Publicity Motivate Improvements?

Reports about technical assistance and sanctions suggest that these strategies more directly encourage school improvements than do financial rewards. For example, Kentucky's "high-stakes" consequences are credited with motivating change: "The sanctions, possibly declaring a school 'in crisis' and dismissing personnel, are more incentive than any other part of KERA [Kentucky Education Reform Act]; teachers see it as a threat to their jobs" (Kentucky state-level office). This report was echoed by teachers in the study of four rural school districts (Appalachian Educational Laboratory, 1996). They "most often told us that *fear of sanctions rather than the promise of rewards motivated the changes.*"

Perhaps an even stronger motivator of change is public awareness of school improvement efforts and related consequences: "No matter the amount of money in the award program, it's the rating, the label, that makes a difference; I want to hold my head up in comparison with other schools" (Texas district office), and "An appropriate sanction is coming before the public; the public does not know what's happening in their schools; public hearings bring public pressure for improvement" (South Carolina Professional Association).

One principal's reflections on rewards, sanctions, and publicity placed students first and money last: "First, we want what's best for kids; second, we do not want to be last; third, no sanctions; and the money comes in a distant fourth" (Kentucky principal).

UNINTENDED CONSEQUENCES OF REWARDS AND SANCTIONS

Assessments of the viability of these models of accountability and school finance must consider unintended, and potentially negative, consequences along with desired benefits. Reports of unintended consequences included the following, although others might argue that they were anticipated and intended outcomes:

1. Curriculum is "narrowed," and instructional practices are altered as school personnel respond to priorities within accountability systems.
2. Purposes of testing are changed as public purposes displace classroom purposes.
3. Unethical or illegal practices become more prevalent as the stakes are raised.
4. High-stakes accountability systems create morale problems and divisions among personnel.

Is Curriculum Narrowed?

When performance is closely monitored, reports of unintended effects on curriculum and instruction arise: "The emphasis on test scores narrowed the curriculum; the teaching strategies directed at these tests are not helping all children learn" (Indiana Teachers Association), and "The state needs to be careful not to give the message that the test is the target and that the state's curriculum frameworks are all that's needed" (Texas principal).

When curriculum is aligned with state standards and criterion-referenced assessments, teachers are teaching to the test, which is not necessarily illegal or unethical: "The intent of the program has been to teach to the test and to rethink curriculum in ways to integrate new assessments into instruction" (Kentucky principal). A similar influence of testing on instructional activities occurs when teachers and students prepare for newly adopted performance assessments: "Portfolios are changing instruction; teachers have stressed language arts and math to the point that they may be neglecting science and social studies" (Kentucky state-level office).

Effects of state assessments are also evident in this principal's concern: "The state does not have a focus on what education must be about; they only emphasize the minimum number of credits and skills tests; there are mixed messages, telling us to broaden the curriculum to meet workplace needs, but assessing and rewarding only the basic core curriculum" (Texas principal).

Do Purposes of Achievement Testing Change?

When stakes are increased, the purposes of testing may change. Norm- and criterion-referenced tests were initially used to assist the diagnosis of student learning needs or to determine school improvement goals to meet state expectations. They have recently become data sources for ranking schools, allocating rewards, or determining job security—and these high-stakes accountability systems shift the way school personnel treat achievement tests: "Because of these public purposes, educators began to teach students how to respond to multiple choice questions, gear the curriculum to the test material, and devote three weeks of instruction to prepare students for testing" (Kentucky Department of Education).

When results are delayed until all accountability measures are available, it becomes apparent that student testing is more for accountability than for classroom purposes: "Test results come back too late to assess student placement for next year; it is OK for curriculum development, but not for student diagnosis" (Texas principal), and "Teachers don't see scores till December; it's too late to understand what changes should be made for this year's students" (South Carolina Professional Association).

Are Illegal or Unethical Behaviors Encouraged?

Some unintended consequences border on illegal behavior, primarily in terms of testing procedures, but very few substantiated incidents exist: "Early on, there was some concern, but not now with greater test security; I don't know of any principals who would tamper with their careers like that" (South Carolina principal). Such unethical or illegal behavior seems to be related more to sanctions than money.

Indiana's performance-based accreditation program creates high stakes for low-performing schools and a code of ethics was developed following several incidents: "A case of blatant cheating was proven by the superintendent and corrections were made; sanctions motivated the principal and staff to falsify data" (Indiana Department of Education). The Kentucky study (Appalachian Educational Laboratory, 1996) disclosed "many allegations" that successful schools cheated, including the retention of a disproportionate number of low-achieving primary students due to fears that they would lower the school's fourth-grade scores. One school was recently cited for "inappropriate test practices"; it was alleged that teachers and the principal typed student portfolios, jeopardizing the elementary school's reward ("Test Violations Uncovered," 1997).

The possibility of rewards or sanctions may influence behavior relative to indicators other than achievement test scores, such as the determination of who is a dropout: "Lots of administrators weed out the poorest students to show gain; it is a great success, and we then create alternative learning centers to warehouse students so they are not classified as dropouts" (Texas Teachers Association), and "When a student desires to drop out, discuss the situation with parents and ask them whether they are home schooling—then the student is not a dropout" (Texas principal).

One report suggests that team-based rewards may discourage such behaviors: "When the reward is shared by the team, it is less likely there will be cheating because collusion among many in the system would be needed to raise scores sufficiently to effect the awards" (South Carolina Professional Association).

Do Personnel Face Unintended Effects?

High-stakes accountability may create unnecessary divisions among school personnel, undermine morale, and inhibit leadership in ways that work against reform goals. Divisions are seen at building and district levels: "It has split the faculty into those who are buying into KERA and are working hard to change versus those who resist change but may be excellent teachers—the division carried into the election of teachers to the school council—now that scores are up, the 'good guys' have won" (Kentucky principal), and "Walking into S—Elementary with nine incentive flags hanging by the entrance is intimidating; this school has one of the lowest per pupil funding levels in the district—but when we celebrated its success at a principals' meeting, there was a real negative strain" (South Carolina district office).

Team-based rewards may create morale problems, perhaps when teachers who do not contribute to school success derive benefits: "Teachers work as individuals, and there are some who could care less about performance in both great and poor schools—team rewards breed resentment among teachers" (South Carolina state-level office), and "Because of conflicts among staff and teachers, rewards are referred to as 'the money from Hell' in some schools" (Kentucky Teachers Association).

Unnecessary stress may affect teachers and principals: "Every two years, the state modifies the system and its indicators—teachers are shooting at a moving target, and it creates tension and stress" (Texas district office). Similarly, as state oversight and public accountability increases, unintended effects may discourage leadership—just the opposite of what is often needed for real school improvement: "We are not rewarding risk taking" (Texas principal).

MAKING PERFORMANCE-BASED SCHOOL FINANCE A VIABLE MODEL

The voices of key informants in Indiana, Kentucky, South Carolina, and Texas suggest ways to strengthen the potential of this model for advancing state educational reforms. Policymakers should address the following in designing performance-based accountability systems and school finance strategies:

1. Finding an appropriate balance of state and local control
2. Identifying indicators tied to school-improvement goals to trigger rewards and sanctions
3. Determining what proportion of revenue should be performance based
4. Encouraging all schools and students to improve performance
5. Targeting funds for capacity building in low-performing schools

Finding an Appropriate Balance of State and Local Control

Performance-based accountability systems and finance policies send clear messages to educators and the public that states are serious about school improvements. However, these strategies may not sufficiently motivate school personnel toward reform goals without local commitments to improvement efforts: "Money won't help if vision and mission are not present; vision must drive practice; learners, both adults and children alike, must be involved in the improvement process; the community as a whole must have a stake in reaching goals" (Indiana Department of Education).

Performance-based accountability systems often appear to local school boards and teachers to be top-down, intrusive, and overly directive. A successful model will find an appropriate balance between state and local control over reform directions as well as between state and local accountability mechanisms. Moreover, meaningful educational improvements will result only when principals and teachers are involved in designing school improvement efforts.

Identifying Indicators to Trigger Rewards and Sanctions

Indicators for performance-based finance models must reflect important school improvement goals, not just those that can be easily measured or have been traditional indicators of school success: "Ask policymakers to broaden the definition of accountability; we swung from exclusively input to exclusively output measures; what of process measures? What goes on within the classroom as a result of testing is critical" (Kentucky Department of Education). Clearly, what is assessed is often addressed within schools and classrooms and too often other important school improvement goals or subject areas may not be emphasized.

Achievement-test results are favored indicators because of their proven validity and reliability and the ease of making comparisons across schools. When instruction is aligned with state standards and curriculum frameworks, the curriculum may be narrowed. Broader indicators of school improvement can assess the quality of curriculum and instructional practices more comprehensively and encourage school personnel to reach other reform goals. However, the lack of valid and reliable measures, the costs of data collection and training raters, controversies between schools and external constituencies (e.g., conservative citizen groups), or the difficulty of determining the contributions of schools to their attainment discourage the adoption of alternative indicators. When Kentucky relied on such performance assessments as portfolios and group problem-solving tasks, school personnel stressed activities to improve students' success. The accountability system was criticized for its reliance on subjective measures of school performance and for emphasizing problem-solving and teamwork goals. A well-conceived performance-based accountability and school finance model must consider desired school improvements and measure them accordingly, rather than reward and sanction school personnel for performance on narrow indicators.

Determining What Proportion of Revenue Should Be Performance Based

A successful model must balance the need for large incentives to stimulate improvements with the potential for large inequities among schools. Keeping in mind the presumption that only valuable and attainable rewards have incentive effects, performance-based funds should represent a substantial proportion of school resources. The four states' appropriations for rewards represent less than one percent of total state and local revenue, and they declined in three of the states over the years. Even though the allocation increased in Kentucky, the amount of money actually earned decreased because more schools met requirements.

It might be argued that a small and declining financial commitment would not result in any changes locally. However, changes occurred, both positive and negative, particularly as sanctions accompanied the rewards. Such unintended consequences as narrowed curriculum, altered purposes of testing, and morale problems resulted. Large proportions of performance-based revenue may bring similar consequences as the stakes are raised.

Large appropriations in a performance-based finance strategy may also pose potential inequities when low-performing schools—which too often are located within low-wealth school districts—are denied needed resources. The equalization of allocations within typical state school finance formulas would divert a relatively larger share of state reward money to deserving poorer districts or schools than currently occurs in "add on" reward structures. Otherwise, conditioning large proportions of state revenue on performance measures outside an equalization formula will raise concerns about perpetuating inequities and ultimately undermine the accountability model's success.

Encouraging All Schools and Students to Improve Performance

Performance-based revenue must be attainable in all schools to stimulate those most in need of reforms toward reform goals. Fairness in a restructured accountability and finance model will result when gains in test scores and other indicators are considered along with or in place of absolute performance standards and when comparisons take into account student socioeconomic status. In addition, procedures that monitor low-performing students' gains, rather than considering only average performance, encourage school personnel to attend to their educational needs.

Accountability systems typically include one of two procedures for determining improvements. Longitudinal gains compare scores of each student from year to year; thus, a fifth grader's performance is compared with her or his performance one year earlier. Even though tracking individual student performance is costly, this approach is preferable because it is more sensitive to the changes made by schools to induce performance gains. A cross-sectional approach compares students' scores at a given grade level with the performance of last year's students at the same grade. This process costs less than tracking individual students, but it is criticized for not providing information on individual student achievement growth: "If you want to reward true learning, you must examine the amount of growth of individual students—longitudinal analysis reveals the schools that are making a difference, whereas cross-sectional comparisons reward high-achieving schools merely for being located in wealthy communities" (South Carolina state-level office). Further, with high student mobility, cross-sectional gains are said to compare apples with oranges.

The relationship between achievement and socioeconomic status of students must also be considered in the design of an effective model. One approach is to construct "comparison bands" of similar schools in terms of community context, but procedures for determining fair comparison groups are complex and controversial. The perceived fairness and ability of the public and educators to understand grouping practices are critical in designing this aspect of accountability systems. For these reasons, states are advised to compare gains made by a school relative to its own prior performance.

Encouraging all students to make performance improvements should be an important goal of a performance-based strategy. If funds rely only on average performance levels or gains, high-achieving students' scores skew the results and create the impression that a school is performing effectively for all students. In contrast, conditioning rewards on the performance of student groups within schools urges school and district personnel to pay attention to the lowest performers. Provisions of the Kentucky and Texas reward programs recognize schools' efforts to raise test results of all student groups: "It has forced districts to spend money in schools most in need; people are paying attention to kids who were previously not served" (Texas Teachers Association).

Targeting Funds for Capacity Building in Low-Performing Schools

The promise of monetary rewards may have little incentive effect on low-performing schools that lack the desire to change. Similarly, when educators have the desire to improve but lack necessary skills and resources, neither rewards nor mandates result in action. Capacity building (O'Day, Goertz, & Floden, 1995; Fuhrman & O'Day, 1996) is a more effective strategy for assisting low-performing schools to make necessary improvements. If this assistance is not effective, then stronger sanctions, including changes in leadership when there is no desire or ability to lead change, are appropriate (Firestone & Corbett, 1988).

Schools that are making satisfactory progress in attaining state and local standards may not need technical assistance or rewards, and public recognition may be a sufficient motivator to maintain performance levels in high-achieving schools. In contrast, deficiencies in far too many schools limit their attainment of performance standards. Schools may have the desire to improve but may lack supplies, textbooks, computers, professional development, and facilities: "Incentives should not be added until there is a basic program everywhere—first fund the basic program adequately" (Texas Teachers Association). Targeting assistance and resources on low-performing schools may be a more effective use of limited state funds than adopting performance-based school finance structures: "The business folks on commissions on improving schools initially want to reward those who are working hard; after they have served for two years and understand the problems of education, they want to help the poor schools" (South Carolina Professional Association).

THE FUTURE OF PERFORMANCE-BASED SCHOOL FINANCE

No doubt the quest for quality schools in the next century will provoke states to align finance structures with indicators of school performance. Many strongly believe that financial rewards are effective incentives for school improvement. The movement will intensify as evidence is gathered that performance-based accountability systems advance the reform agenda and, more importantly, lead to improvements in student learning.

Findings of this study of financial rewards and related sanctions in four states provide such evidence. However, reports also suggest that intrinsic desires to improve teaching and learning, along with the avoidance of negative publicity and sanctions, are stronger motivators of change than promised rewards. Further, potentially harmful consequences may result, particularly when accountability systems rest on limited performance indicators.

Expanded performance-based models for state school finance in the coming century will be received more eagerly at the local level and will result in school improvements if caution is taken in their design. Appropriate balance must exist between state and local control over reform directions, limits on the proportion of state allocations to be performance based, and inclusion of performance rewards within equalization formulas. In addition, provisions to ensure fairness in comparing schools of varying socioeconomic status and to encourage improvements for all students must be included. Policymakers must also realize that a performance-based approach, without targeted capacity building, may do little to advance reforms, create quality education, and foster achievement gains in low-performing schools.

ENDNOTE

1 The research on performance-based rewards was supported by the Spencer Foundation and the University of Northern Colorado's Faculty Research and Publications Board. The author is solely responsible for interpretations of states' policies and observations about performance-based accountability and finance strategies.

REFERENCES

Appalachian Educational Laboratory. (1996). Five years of education reform in rural Kentucky. *Notes from the Field.* Charleston, WV: Author.

Atkinson, J. W. (1964). *An introduction to motivation.* Princeton, NJ: Van Nostrand Reinhold.

Ballou, D., & Podgursky, M. (1993, October). Teachers' attitudes toward merit pay: Examining conventional wisdom. *Industrial and Labor Relations Review, 47,* 50–61.

Boe, E. E. (1992). *Incentive and disincentive phenomena in education: Definitions and illustrations* (Report No. 1992-ER2). Philadelphia: Center for Research and Evaluation in Social Policy.

Boe, E. E., & Boruch, R. (1993). *Performance-based accreditation of public schools.* Philadelphia: Center for Research and Evaluation in Social Policy.

Deming, W. E. (1982). *Quality, productivity, and competitive position.* Cambridge: Massachusetts Institute of Technology, Center for Advanced Engineering Study.

Elmore, R. F., Abelman, C. H., & Fuhrman, S. H. (1995). *The new accountability in state education reform: From process to performance.* Paper presented at the Brookings Institution Conference on Performance-Based Approaches to School Reform, Washington, DC.

Firestone, W. A., & Corbett, H. D. (1988). Planned organizational change. In N. Boyan (Ed.), *Handbook of research on educational administration* (pp. 321–340). White Plains, NY: Longman.

Fuhrman, S. H., & O'Day, J. A. (1996). *Rewards and reform: Creating educational incentives that work.* San Francisco: Jossey-Bass.

Galbraith, J. R., Lawler, E. E., & Associates. (1993). *Organizing for the future: The new logic for managing complex organizations.* San Francisco: Jossey-Bass.

Garris, J. M., & Cohn, E. (1996). Combining efficiency and equity: A new funding approach for public education. *Journal of Education Finance, 22,* 114–134.

Hackman, J. R. (1987). The design of work teams. In J. W. Lorsch (Ed.), *Handbook of organiztion behavior* (pp. 315–342). Englewood Cliffs, NJ: Prentice Hall.

Hanushek, E. A. (1991). When school finance "reform" may not be good policy. *Harvard Journal on Legislation, 28,* 423–456.

Jacobson, S. L. (1988). Merit pay and teaching as a career. In K. Alexander & D. H. Monk (Eds.), *Attracting and compensating America's teachers* (pp. 161–177). Cambridge, MA: Ballinger.

Kentucky Institute for Education Research. (1995). *Results from the 1995 statewide education reform form surveys on issues related to assessment and accountability.* Frankfort: Author.

King, R. A., & Mathers, J. K. (1996). *The promise and reality of rewards for school improvement: Indiana, Kentucky, South Carolina and Texas.* Greeley: University of Northern Colorado.

King, R. A., & Mathers, J. K. (1997). Improving schools through performance-based accountability and financial rewards. *Journal of Education Finance, 23,* 147–176.

Kohn, A. (1993). *Punished by rewards: The trouble with gold stars, incentive plans, A's, praise, and other bribes.* Boston: Houghton Mifflin.

Lawler, E. (1994). From job-based to competency-based organizations. *Journal of Organizational Behavior, 15,* 3.

Lortie, D. C. (1975). *Schoolteacher: A sociological study.* Chicago: University of Chicago Press.

Mathers, J. (1997). *Education accountability systems in 50 states.* Denver, CO: Education Commission of the States.

Mohrman, S. A., Cohen, S. G., & Mohrman, A. M. (1995). *Designing team-based organizations: New forms for knowledge work.* San Francisco: Jossey-Bass.

Murnane, R. J., & Cohen, D. K. (1986). Merit pay and the evaluation problem: Why most merit pay plans fail and a few survive. *Harvard Educational Review, 56,* 1–17.

O'Day, J., Goertz, M. E., & Floden, R. E. (1995). Building capacity for education reform. *CPRE Policy Briefs.* New Brunswick, NJ: Rutgers University, Eagleton Institute of Politics, Consortium for Policy Research in Education.

Test Violations Uncovered. (1997, August 6). *Education Week,* p. 4.

Vroom, V. H. (1964). *Work and motivation.* New York: John Wiley.

CHAPTER 9

Should We Have a National Standard of Decency in Our Scholastic Cybernets?

Lawrence Lee Oldaker and David Dagley

All America and much of the world is flooded by an astonishing array of technological products and services. In America's schools, the walls that once protected our nation's youth are besieged by this tide, and policymakers, administrators, and teachers find themselves challenged to respond appropriately. Classroom teachers are pressed to access technology training effectively and, at the same time, guide student learning activities that have been affected by the tidal waves of information and frank adult experiences that pour through Internet communications. This electronic, globe-spanning vehicle is becoming an all-pervasive phenomena that is capable of conveying instantaneous, expansive, and unrestricted information to libraries, laboratories, and desktops throughout schools in every city and hamlet. No place with electricity and a telephone line is inaccessible.

From this vast change in technology has emerged the troubling question of societal decency, and school systems are not exempt from this question. Also hearing this question, Congress answered by passing the Communications Decency Act of 1996 (CDA) within the statutory provisions of the larger Telecommunications Act of 1996. The CDA was meant to outlaw the electronic transmission of morally objectionable materials to anyone under eighteen years of age, thereby creating a nationwide code of decency for cyberspeech insofar as minors are involved. Judicial reactions were immediate. A large coalition of publishing, business, library, education, and civil-liberty groups, and nonprofit organizations initiated proceedings in two federal district courts that produced injunctions enjoining enforcement of those features of the CDA concerning decency (*ACLU v. Reno,* 1996; *Shea v. Reno,* 1996). The government appealed the pair of legal setbacks to the U.S. Supreme Court. Within one year, a nearly unanimous court added finality to the issue by affirming the unconstitutionality of the CDA (*Reno v. ACLU,* 1997).

Although federal courts over the years have continually protected the welfare of unemancipated youth from behavioral and economic exploitation by adults, the reaffirmation of First Amendment rights in *Reno* placed limits on "overbroad and vague" restrictions on speech that created a chilling effect on the protected speech of adults. But contrary to contemporary critics, the Court did not overturn the will of Congress and did not "legalize obscenity" (Friedman, 1997). Yet, it is within this accusatory atmosphere that an emerging question arises: should the federal government create a youth-focused decency statute for the growing number of Internet users in the nation's public schools, or should the responsibility to govern scholastic technology reside within the authority of local boards of education?

SCHOOLS IN THE "ELECTRONIC COMMUNITY"

The late Canadian scholar, Marshall McLuhan, likened electronic communication discoveries to the importance accorded the invention of movable print at the close of the fifteenth century. The swiftness of modern telecommunications, as McLuhan observed, had indeed transformed the world into a global village (McLuhan, 1964a; McLuhan & Powers, 1989). Our present-day communities, with their public schools, are continuously

---
Lawrence Lee Oldaker, University of Alaska Southeast
David Dagley, University of Alabama at Birmingham

buffeted by cyberage electronic developments. New machines and software impose obsolescence of previously adopted computer and communication programs. As envisioned by McLuhan, each of these new inventions turns its predecessor into an art form to be honored by curators of the past or to be set aside in favor of more recent innovations (McLuhan, 1964b). School policymakers, reflecting the will of citizen-sponsors, are continually challenged to keep pace in the rapidly advancing technoworld of information collection, storage, retrieval, and dissemination. Desktop computers networked to local and distant sites have increased the ability of teachers and students to communicate with respondents far beyond their classroom. What is said and what is observed over these new electronic links raises questions of academic propriety and whether alleged inappropriate expression can be regulated.

This situation confronts the basic tenets of academic freedom, one of the most widely misunderstood concepts in American education. Public school committees and civil courts have been asked to apply a variety of legal standards in settling these disputes. Since the midcentury mark, the U.S. Constitution's First Amendment had been invoked by instructors and students in search of protection from perceived institutional violations of academic freedom. Although the federal courts have demonstrated an occasional willingness to apply the Bill of Rights in reviewing challenged state policies, the jurists tended to refrain from making professional decisions in matters affecting educational governance. Instead, the court often placed the responsibility of operating educational programs within the province of those who are thought best qualified to maintain reasoned institutional needs, the administrators. Recently, federal courts have respected the professional autonomy of school systems by applying judicial abstention, by limiting the scope of constitutionally protected expression, and by strengthening administrative power to control instruction and to set the tenor of preferred behavior in the local school community (*Bethel v. Fraser*, 1986).

But the school community is no longer what it was. Decisions about promoting and preserving propriety in networked computers as they increase in scholarly value must address a corresponding dark side as cybercrimes join the digital rivers and tributaries to and from our schools and classrooms. Once seen as harmless "hacking" into computer networks, prankish actions on the Internet have been the popular subject of recent Hollywood motion pictures such as *War Games*. The more serious computer "pirates" that may inflict felony-level harm, as depicted on film in *The Net*, pose a greater danger to financial and national securities. Although the Electronics Communications Privacy Act of 1994 forbids the unauthorized entry into a closed system and the Constitution guarantees property protection rights, electronic interactive services that support e-mail, bulletin boards, and Internet transmissions have become the most efficient and prevalent forms of communication (Kassel & Kassel, 1995) and a growing venue for fraud.

With the simple click of a mouse or other basic computer skills, almost anyone can obtain information from virtually any worldwide location, and with equally simple keyboard dexterity, almost anyone can access copy-protected intellectual property such as textbooks, novels, and musical works. Any computer operator has the potential of obtaining a free copy of a work protected by law (Clinque, 1995; McCoy & Needham, 1995). The potential to engage in this breach of law confronts school authorities and students on a regular basis. The ease of employing computer-generated materials can save valuable time in investigating a topic, enhancing a lesson plan, or creating a classroom assignment. The mass appearance of these materials confirms their availability and their seductive presence. Here, then, is one aspect of the challenge facing administrators as they seek to exercise the proper and lawful reaction to computer-borne assaults on freedom in academic matters on the one hand and the theft of intellectual property on the other. But an even more challenging matter is that of determining the proper and lawful response in matters generally coming under the name of "public decency" and of maintaining the elusive nature of "community values."

CYBERPERILS AND THE ILLUSION OF COMMUNITY

Tensions related to controversial speech and expression, unresolved at local and state levels, often appear in the federal judiciary for resolution. For several decades, federal district and appellate courts have attempted to create a standard of behavior to judge whether alleged obscene expressions are lawful under First Amendment analysis. The nation's high court ruled, in the landmark 1957 case of *Roth v. United States*, that obscenity was not afforded constitutional protection. From *Roth* to 1973, courts searched in vain for a clear rationale in determining what graphic or verbal speech and expression was permissible. Fifty-five separate opinions evolved from the 31 cases of obscenity that reached the Supreme Court (Huelster, 1995). In *Miller v. California* (1973), the Court crafted a three-pronged test to determine whether materials were obscene based on whether an average person, applying contemporary community standards, would be offended by a work. The *Miller* decision upheld a statewide definition of community, abandoning the lofty and elusive objective of establishing a nationwide standard of expression by stating that "to construct obscenity proceedings around evidence of a national 'community standard' would be an exercise in futility." Further, the Court reasoned

> that there is no provable 'national [obscenity] standard.' ... At all events, this Court has not been able to enunciate one, and it would be unreasonable to expect local courts to divine one. It is neither realistic nor constitutionally sound to read the First Amendment as requiring that the people of Maine or Mississippi accept public depiction of conduct found tolerable in Las Vegas or New York City.

One thoughtful commentator has questioned the efficacy of each local community determining its own obscenity standard (Huelster, 1995). What, after all, constitutes a "local community" within the vaguely defined expanse of the global Internet? New technologies that beam electronic messages between nations—and into our schoolhouse rooms—possess no content restrictions relative to state or local ordinances. To illustrate the complexity that this electronic vehicle carries, a California couple providing on-line pornographic access to adult subscribers was found guilty of violating obscenity standards in Memphis, Tennessee, a metropolitan community nearly half a continent from their West Coast neighbors who did not take exception to such bulletin board services (*United States v. Thomas*, 1994). Should the conviction stand, it would be the first "cybersentence" of a service provider challenged at the site of reception, not at the site of transmission. As this drama and its overarching legal consequences unfold, the nation and the court system may be forced to reevaluate the twenty-five-year-old *Miller* "community standard" concept in light of technological developments and the manner in which they enter public and private computer systems. As observed by Supreme Court Justice O'Connor in *Reno*, such events have caused state and federal legislative bodies to consider enacting bans on behavior that is judged to be unacceptable, especially when minors are or could be involved.

LEGISLATION, COURTS, AND DECENCY

Aside from the urgently needed revisions to a federal communications statute enacted in 1934 (Salomon, Gray, & Kennedy, 1996), Congress and the executive branch—through the controversial CDA provisions—attempted to regulate contemporary Internet transmissions as a means of protecting children from "indecent speech." The statutory measure was designed to restrict "indecent" material from being sent or made available to anyone under 18 years of age. Enraged cyberactivists claimed that the Internet would be transformed into a "Disney cartoon" (Bennahum, 1996). Many also claimed that the proportionality of the ambitious CDA venture offended the free speech clause of the First Amendment because the CDA lacked the narrow tailoring that would reach the specific objective of protecting minors yet not limiting the rights of adults to access and transmit electronic messages. The decency provisions of the enactment are now seen as a politically inept reach to create "adult zones" on the Internet that would make it possible to limit behavior based on age, somewhat akin to physical zones in the "real world" that exclude children from adult-only cinemas and bars serving alcoholic beverages (Lessig, 1996).

Justice O'Connor's concurring and dissenting opinion in *Reno* characterized the adult-zoning concept as a commendable goal embedded among the constitutionally flawed provisions of the statute. Drawing upon the twin characteristics of geography and identity in real-world zoning, she envisioned the fundamentally different electronic world as being malleable enough to construct amenable zoning restrictions through the development of "gateway" technologies that would further isolate patently offensive materials from children. O'Connor opined that such technologies could require Internet users to enter information about themselves before they could participate in certain sectors of cyberspace, somewhat "like a bouncer that checks a person's driver's license before being admitted to a nightclub." This kind of screening, however, is not readily available to Internet users in 1998.

Until these gateway technologies are in place, a workable, proactive step can be taken. Public school policymakers could seek means to create supportable "school zones" in a similar fashion to the "adult zones" sought by CDA proponents. To support this concept, it is plausible that electronic buffers could be erected to shield classroom computers from certain kinds of transmissions. This move would reduce the need to seek legal controls over free expression rights in an Internet system that seems to defy public or private governance. The driving force to approach the objective of creating a "school zone" should be the local boards of education, the rightful educational authority as determined in a 1992 desegregation case. In *Freeman v. Pitts* (1992), the Supreme Court reasoned that the control of the schools by local authorities would bring satisfactory closure to long-ranging conflicts. Concurring Justice Scalia championed the democratic heritage and educational tradition that placed public schooling in the hands of elected authorities acting in concert with parents who wish to place their children in schools nearest their homes. This educational principle of local control strengthens the notion of "community" and the creation of a supervised "school zone" to regulate network activities based on definable local values. Such a move lessens the need to face the improbable task of codifying an acceptable nationwide standard to regulate Internet transmissions.

POLICY DIRECTIONS FOR SCHOOLS

Technology has been a major catalyst for change throughout the centuries. Sensing the need to develop guiding policies to keep the school system apace of the rapidly advancing information age, school boards have the primary role in establishing a comprehensive plan to allocate financial and personnel resources to create sound educational programs that integrate classroom "school zone" activities into the community's "electronic village." A technology planning group, working under the aegis of the school board and the municipal government, could seek to establish long-range goals and immediate objectives to create modern classrooms that are able to exchange voice, video, and print information with computers in facilities throughout the school system, community centers, and individual households. The plan could provide for continuous technology training among the students and community residence. This cooperative training endeavor can strengthen existing technology skills of youths and adults using current telephone systems, facsimile machines, cable television, VCRs, and individual computers (Stokley, 1996). Further, such a plan could be the basis for developing a sense of community by identifying local needs and values.

As an outgrowth of this plan, an Acceptable Use Policy (AUP) could be developed and accepted by all computer users within the system. The AUP could seek to promote and regulate good citizenship in cyberspace. A valuable use policy should cover training and licensing individuals for computer network use, security provisions to protect the integrity of the system, respect for intellectual property, clearly defined expectations of privacy in transmissions, and disciplinary measures that elevate the working concepts of academic freedom and individual responsibility as well as procedural and substantive due process (Oldaker, 1997).

As the fledgling "electronic" school-community develops and Internet transmissions are brought on line, the new telecommunications activities will require close supervision by teachers and parents (Maurer & Davidson, 1998). School authorities may legally control their students' communicative ventures by using commercial computer "blocking" devices, such as "Net Nanny," "Cyber Patrol," "Intergo," "Specs for Kids," "Cybersitter," and other sensorware programs (Venditto, 1996). On-line filtering programs also can prevent students who surf the Internet from visiting known e-mail sites containing obscene text, sound, and graphics (Filters, Ratings Designed to Control Net Surfing, 1996). Some school systems have the capability of monitoring all e-mail site locations, admittedly a labor-intensive task that is necessary until the telecommunications industry can develop futuristic "I-chips" and "C-chips" to govern network *information* and *content* in a manner similar to the CDA-mandated "V-chip" in new television sets. These in-system restrictions could have the effect of creating a safe "school zone" for the scholastic community. This locally responsible action by a school board should become a focal point for local school improvement and thereby remove the external pitfalls of creating an unwieldy "adult zone," tampering with the global Internet, or breaching the constitutionally protected rights to free speech of American adults.

EPILOGUE

As we progress into the information age amid the digital hustle and bustle of electronic traffic, we need to develop school policies that strengthen pronounced educational values by placing greater emphasis on *caring* about each other rather than *judging* each other. Contrary to the praiseworthy but inept creation of the ill-fated Communications Decency Act of 1996, local boards of education are in the best position to define the morally acceptable and educationally effective school programs in their communities. Technology, whether we embrace it or not, is erasing the borders of our world and creating an "electronic village." We can integrate elements of this neocomputer world within existing community and educational values. These lofty objectives on the local level do not depreciate national interests. Although challenges abound in this new age of exploration and discovery, great opportunities also exist to build and strengthen community and to increase the facilitation of learning. Concerted community efforts can provide the practical and acceptable means to reach for prosperity and peace in a new epoch marked by spectacular electronic discoveries.

REFERENCES

ACLU v. Reno, 929 F. Supp. 824 (E.D. Pa. 1996).
Becker, I. (1995, June). Cybercrime: Cops can't keep up with technobandits. *California Lawyer 15,* 47, 91.
Bennahum, D. S. (1966, March 2). The internet's private side. *New York Times,* sec. 1, p. 19.
Bethel v. Fraser, 478 U.S. 675 (1986).
Cavazos, E. A. (1994). *Cyberspace and the Law: Your rights and duties in the on-line world.* Cambridge, MA: MIT Press.
Clinque, R. A. (1995, April). Making cyberspace safe for copyright. *Fordham International Law 14,* 1258–1302.
Cutera, T. A. (1991). The Constitution in cyberspace: The fundamental rights of computer users. *University of Missouri, Kansas City, Law Review 60,* 139–165.
Electronics Communication Privacy Act of 1994.
Fattore, J. (1992). *What Johnny shouldn't read: Textbook censorship in America.* New Haven, CT: Yale University Press.
Filters, ratings designed to control net surfing. (1996, April 5). *School Law News,* 9–11.
Fiss, O. M. (1996). *The irony of free speech.* Cambridge, MA: Harvard University Press.
Freeman v. Pitts, 503 U.S. 467, 112 S.Ct.1430 118 L.Ed. 2d 108 (1992).
Friedman, L. (1997, July 3). High court is flexing too much muscle. *Juneau Empire,* 2.
Harvey, P. (1997, June 28). Paul Harvey news. New York: American Broadcasting Company.
Hentoff, N. (1992). *Free speech for me—and not for thee.* San Francisco: HarperCollins.
Hixon, R. F. (1996). *Pornography and the justices: The Supreme Court and the intractable obscenity problem.* Carbondale: Southern Illinois University Press.
Huelster, P. A. (1995, May). Cybersex and community standards. *Boston Law Review, 75,* 865–888.
Kassel, M. A., & Kassel, J. K. (1995). Don't get caught in the net: An intellectual property practitioner's guide to using the internet. *Journal of Computers and Information Law, 13,* 373–389.

Kuhlmeier v. Hazelwood, 484 U.S. 260 (1988).

Lessig, L. (1996, Summer). Reading the Constitution in cyberspace. *Emory Law Journal, 45,* 869–910.

Masson, D. J. (1996). Fixation on fixation: Why imposing old copyright law on new technology will not work. *Indiana Law Journal, 71,* 1049–1066.

Maurer, M. M., & Davidson, G. S. (1998). *Leadership in instructional technology.* Upper Saddle River, NJ: Prentice-Hall.

McCoy, M. D., & Needham, J. B. (1995, Spring). Cyber-theft: Tyranny on the superhighway. *Wake Forest Law Review, 30,* 169–195.

McLuhan, M. (1964a). *The medium is the message: An inventory of effects.* New York: Bantam Books.

McLuhan, M. (1964b). *Understanding media: The extension of man.* New York: McGraw-Hill.

McLuhan, M., & Powers, B. R. (1989). *The global village.* New York: Oxford Press.

McWilliams, P. (1993). *Ain't nobody's business if you do: The absurdity of consensual crimes in a free society.* New York: Prelude Press.

Miller v. California, 413 U.S. 15 (1973).

Moore, D. W. (1995). *The emperor's virtual clothes: The naked truth about Internet culture.* Chapel Hill, NC: Algonquin Books.

Moykr, J. (1990). *The lever of riches: Technological creativity and economic progress.* New York: Oxford University Press.

Oldaker, L. L. (1997). Supervising school computer networks. In L. Wildman (Ed.), *Fifth Yearbook of the National Council of Professors of Educational Administration. School administration: The new knowledge base* (pp. 262–267). Lancaster: Technomic Publishing Co., Inc.

Perritt, H. H., Jr. (1996). *Law and the information superhighway: Privacy * access * intellectual property * commerce * liability.* New York: John Wiley & Sons.

Reeves, H. S. (1996). Property in cyberspace. *University of Chicago Law Review, 63,* 761–799.

Reno v. ACLU, S. Ct. of U.S., No. 96-511, 1997 WL 348012, U.S. (1997).

Roth v. United States, 354 U.S. 483 (1957).

Salomon, K. D., Gray, T. D., and Kennedy, L. J. (1996, July 25). Implications of the Telecommunications Act of 1996 for schools, colleges, and universities. *Education Law Report, 109,* 1051–1061.

Schools' new challenge: Policing the net. (1996, April 5). *School Law News, 1,* 7–9.

Schools, states struggling to perfect internet policies. (1996, April 5). *School Law News, 1,* 11–12.

Sergent, R. S. (1995). A Fourth Amendment model for computer networks and data privacy. *Virginia Law Review, 81,* 1181–1228.

Shea v. Reno, 930 F. Supp. 916 (S.D.N.Y. 1996).

Shull, M. S. (1996, February). What you should—and shouldn't—say when you send those e-mail messages. *Communications Briefings, 15,* 8a–b.

Stokley, F. J. (1996, April). Creating an electronic village. *The School Administrator, 53,* 36.

Telecommunications Act of 1996, P. L. 104-104, Sec. 502, 110 Stat. 56, 133–35.

United States Constitution, Article I, Clauses 3 (Commerce) and 8 (Copyright and Patent).

United States v. Thomas, No. 94-20019-G (W.D. Tenn.1994).

Venditto, G. (1996). Safe computing: Seven programs that filter Internet access. *Internet World,* 49–58.

Wriston, W. B. (1992). *The twilight of sovereignty: How the information revolution is transforming our world.* New York: Charles Scribner's Son.

Young, J. R. (1996, April 26). "Indecency" on the internet. *The Chronicle of Higher Education,* A21, A23–A25.

CHAPTER 10

Free Speech and School Internet Policies: Emerging Law and Its Implications for School Administration

John Dayton

Internet technology is generating both tremendous opportunities and controversy through the creation of unprecedented communications possibilities. As the U.S. Supreme Court recognized in its recent decision in *Reno v. ACLU* (1997): "The Internet is a unique and wholly new medium of worldwide human communication" (p. 2334). Inevitably, new communications technologies raise new questions concerning freedom of speech. Like the printing press, the Internet has provoked urgent calls for regulation and counter-charges of censorship. School administrators find themselves in the middle of this debate, attempting to protect students from exposure to educationally inappropriate materials while enjoying the rapidly expanding benefits of a free and diverse Internet system. This chapter briefly reviews and discusses the legal history of freedom of speech, the U.S. Supreme Court's recent decision on freedom of speech and the Internet in *Reno v. ACLU*, and the implications of this emerging law for school administration (Dayton, in press).

A BRIEF REVIEW OF THE LEGAL HISTORY OF FREEDOM OF SPEECH

Human desire for freedom of speech is ancient and is a prerequisite to other human liberties (Acton, 1877; Hentoff, 1980). The struggle to secure this essential freedom is a perennial historical theme, and history reflects both successes and failures in obtaining free-speech rights (Fried, 1992, p. 229). Attempts to secure freedom of speech also permeate Anglo-American history. The English Bill of Rights (1689) recognized the importance of freedom of speech to free government by stating that "freedom of speech and debates or proceedings in parliament ought not to be impeached or questioned in any court or place out of parliament" (para. 26). Similarly, the U.S. Articles of Confederation (1778) stated that "Freedom of speech and debate in Congress shall not be impeached or questioned in any court, or place out of Congress" (Art. V, para. 5). The U.S. Constitution (1787) incorporates this principle by declaring that "for any speech or debate in either House [senators and representatives] shall not be questioned in any other place" (Art. I, § 6, para. 1). On citizens' free-speech rights, the U.S. Constitution's (1791) First Amendment states that "Congress shall make no law . . . abridging the freedom of speech, or of the press; or the right of the people peaceably to assemble, and to petition the Government for a redress of grievances."

Although the First Amendment was ratified in 1791, most of the U.S. Supreme Court's decisions on freedom of speech were decided after World War I, with the most significant cases occurring after 1960 (Chamberlin,1992). First Amendment law continues to evolve. Nonetheless, some common themes have emerged, including recognition of the importance of free political speech to the democratic marketplace of ideas, the exposure of truth and falsehood, and the protection of freedom. History demonstrates that, because government officials are not politically neutral, they make very poor judges of what constitutes truth. Instead, as Justice Holmes recognized in his dissenting opinion in *Abrams v. United States* (1919), "the best test of truth is the power of the thought to get itself accepted in the competition of the market" (p. 630). Accordingly, the Court has

John Dayton, The University of Georgia

required great governmental deference to citizens' exercise of freedom of speech, leaving decisions on the merits of ideas to the people instead of allowing government officials to censor the content of speech. Within an evolving hierarchy of protection, the Court generally prohibits content-based censorship, with political speech receiving the greatest protection, commercial speech receiving less rigorous protection, and obscenity falling outside of the scope of constitutional protection (Chamberlin, 1992).

The Court recognizes freedom of speech as a fundamental right under the U.S. Constitution. Government officials may only limit fundamental rights, including constitutionally protected speech, by establishing that limitations are necessary to a compelling interest and narrowly tailored to achieving that interest, a very difficult standard to meet. But the Court has also recognized that government officials may apply reasonable time, place, and manner regulations to speech where these regulations are content-neutral and leave open adequate alternative routes of communication (Downs, 1992b). The Court has recognized the necessity of different standards for different mediums of communication (*FCC v. Pacifica,* 1978, p. 748). For example, the Court has allowed greater restrictions on general broadcast communications than on print media (Chamberlin, 1992, p. 809; *Red Lion v. FCC*, 1969). The Court has also recognized different protections in different contexts, vigorously protecting speech in traditional public forums, such as public streets and parks, and allowing greater restrictions in more limited forums (Downs, 1992a, pp. 692–693).

Disputes over freedom of speech have frequently involved public schools with the Court addressing the proper balance between individuals' free-speech rights and the legitimate needs of the school. In the context of a dispute over the rights of students to express their opposition to government activities in public schools, the Court stated that "it can hardly be argued that either students or teachers shed their constitutional rights to freedom of speech or expression at the schoolhouse gate" (*Tinker v. Des Moines,* 1969, p. 506). The Court in *Tinker v. Des Moines* (1969) recognized that "students in school as well as out of school are 'persons' under our Constitution. They are possessed of fundamental rights which the State must respect, just as they themselves must respect their obligations to the State" (p. 511).

Although recognizing a constitutional right to dissent by students, the Court has also emphasized the importance of teaching children tolerance and civility. The Court stated in *Bethel School District v. Fraser* (1986) that public schools "must inculcate the habits and manners of civility" and that this must "include tolerance of divergent political and religious views, even when the views expressed may be unpopular" (pp. 680–681). In conjunction with rights to freedom of speech, the Court has emphasized the responsibility of teaching civility in communications. The Court noted, "Indeed the 'fundamental values necessary to the maintenance of a democratic political system' disfavor the use of terms of debate highly offensive or highly threatening to others.... The inculcation of these values is truly the 'work of the schools'" (*Bethel v. Fraser,* 1986, p. 683). Courts have recognized that divergent views are tolerated in a democratic society and that civil discourse is the appropriate way to express individual views and opposition to even those views that evoke anger. As Judge Burns stated in *Wilson v. Chancellor* (1976),

> I am firmly convinced that a course designed to teach students that a free and democratic society is superior to those in which freedoms are sharply curtailed will fail entirely if it fails to teach one important lesson: that the power of the state is never so great that it can silence a man or woman simply because there are those who disagree. Perhaps that carries with it a second lesson: that those who enjoy the blessings of a free society must occasionally bear the burden of listening to others with whom they disagree, even to the point of outrage. (p. 1368)

Freedom of speech is protected not only for the benefit of individuals but also to assure the free flow of information that leads to the political, intellectual, and cultural advancement of the community (Chamberlin, 1992, p. 808; Dayton & Glickman, 1994, p. 73). Innovative and productive ideas flourish in a free environment where the only controls these ideas are subjected to are the tests of public debate and the reason of an educated and free people. As Thomas Jefferson stated, "Truth is great and will prevail if left to herself" (Jefferson, 1779/1993b, p. 56). Similarly, ideas that are potentially dangerous to the community are also best refuted in open debate. Open public debate and the reasoning power of an educated and free people are the best protections against threats to democracy. As Thomas Jefferson declared after prevailing in one of the nation's most bitter political battles, "if there be any among us who would wish to dissolve this Union or to change its republican form, let them stand undisturbed as monuments of the safety with which error of opinion may be tolerated where reason is left free to combat it" (Jefferson, 1801/1993a, pp. 62–63). It is against this notable history of freedom of speech that Congress adopted the Communications Decency Act (CDA), prompting a constitutional challenge by the American Civil Liberties Union (ACLU) and other plaintiffs.

THE COMMUNICATIONS DECENCY ACT OF 1996

On February 8, 1996, President Clinton signed into law the Telecommunications Act of 1996. The most controversial part of the Telecommunications Act was the CDA. The CDA provided criminal penalties for certain types of communications and was the subject of intense criticism by civil libertarians and many Internet users. Among the most controversial sections of the CDA were 223(a) and 223(d). According to the trial court in *ACLU v. Reno* (1996), section 223(a) provided in relevant part that

> any person in interstate or foreign communications who, "by means of a telecommunications device," "knowingly . . . makes, creates, or solicits" and "initiates the transmission" of "any comment, request, suggestion, proposal, image or other communication which is obscene or indecent, knowing that the recipient of the communication is under 18 years of age," "shall be criminally fined or imprisoned." (pp. 828–829)

The court noted that section 223(d)

> makes it a crime to use an "interactive computer service" to "send" or "display in a manner available" to a person under age 18, "any comment, request, suggestion, proposal, image, or other communication that, in context, depicts or describes, in terms patently offensive as measured by contemporary community standards, sexual or excretory activities or organs, regardless of whether the user of such service placed the call or initiated the communication." (p. 829)

Shortly after its enactment, the constitutionality of the CDA was challenged by the ACLU in *ACLU v. Reno* (1996) and by an editor of an Internet newspaper in *Shea v. Reno* (1996). Courts in both cases declared the CDA unconstitutional. The CDA provided for a special expedited appeals procedure to the U.S. Supreme Court. The government appealed, and the cases were consolidated in *Reno v. ACLU*. The expedited appeals process resulted in an unusually rapid decision in *Reno v. ACLU*, with the Court issuing an opinion at the end of the 1996–97 term.

RENO v. ACLU

Justice Stevens delivered the opinion of the Court in *Reno v. ACLU* (1997). The Court was unanimous in its judgment that the CDA was an unconstitutional infringement on First Amendment freedom-of-speech rights. The Court held, "Notwithstanding the legitimacy and importance of the congressional goal of protecting children from harmful materials, we agree with the three-judge District Court that the statute abridges 'the freedom of speech' protected by the First Amendment" (p. 2334).

The Status of Internet Speech

An overview of the operation of the Internet is provided in the Court's opinion, with the Court relying on the extensive factual findings of the trial court to explain the complexities of the Internet and its role in contemporary communications (p. 2334, n. 2). The Court noted the extraordinary growth of the Internet and the projection that Internet usage in the U.S. would expand from 40 million users at the time of trial to 200 million by 1999. On the Internet's role as a vehicle for freedom of speech, the Court noted that Internet users have the potential to communicate easily and inexpensively with millions of persons through this unique medium and "any person with a phone line can become a town crier with a voice that resonates farther than it could from any soapbox" (p. 2344). On the scope of issues discussed on the Internet, the Court found that it is "no exaggeration to conclude that the content on the Internet is as diverse as human thought" (p. 2335). Further, the Court stated, "Any person or organization with a computer connected to the Internet can 'publish' information.... No single organization controls any membership in the Web, nor is there any centralized point from which individual Web sites or services can be blocked from the Web," allowing expression of all views without censorship (p. 2335).

But as evidenced by the passage of the CDA, some individuals, organizations, and members of Congress found the vast freedom of the Internet troubling. In *ACLU v. Reno* (1996), the trial court had made this determination:

> True it is that many find some of the speech on the Internet to be offensive, and amid the din of cyberspace many hear discordant voices that they regard as indecent. The absence of government regulation of Internet content has unquestionably produced a kind of chaos, but as one of plaintiffs' experts put it with such resonance at the hearing: "What achieved success was the very chaos that the Internet is. The strength of the Internet is that chaos." Just as the strength of the Internet is chaos, so the strength of our liberty depends upon the chaos and cacophony of the unfettered speech the First Amendment protects. (p. 883)

Although many types of Internet speech may provoke some debate, it is the availability of sexually explicit material on the Internet that has generated the most controversy. The Court in *Reno v. ACLU* (1997) noted that "sexually explicit material on the Internet includes text, pictures, and chat and 'extends from the modestly titillating to the hardest-core' " (p. 2336). However, relying on the factual findings of the trial court, the Court stated the following:

> Though such material is widely available, users seldom encounter such content accidentally. "A document's title or a description of the document will usually appear before the document itself... and in many cases the user will receive detailed information about a site's content before he or she need take the step to access the document. Almost all sexually explicit images are preceded by warnings as to the content." For that reason, the "odds are slim" that a user would enter a sexually explicit site by accident. Unlike communications received by radio or television, "the receipt of information on the Internet requires a series of affirmative steps more deliberate and directed than merely turning a dial. A child requires some sophistication and some ability to read to retrieve material and thereby to use the Internet unattended." (p. 2336)

On technologies designed to restrict access to unwanted sexually explicit materials, the Court made this observation:

> Systems have been developed to help parents control the material that may be available on a home computer with Internet access. A system may either limit a computer's access to an approved list of sources that have been identified as containing no adult material, it may block designated inappropriate sites, or it may attempt to block messages containing identifiable objectionable features. (p. 2336)

Factual findings by the trial court indicated that, through the use of existing commercial services like "Surf-Watch" and "Cyber Patrol," parents could exclude a wide variety of unwanted Internet materials they deemed inappropriate by selecting from categories that included violence or profanity, partial nudity, nudity, sexual acts (graphic or text), gross depictions (graphic or text), racism or ethnic impropriety, satanic or cult, drugs or drug culture, militant or extremist, gambling, questionable or illegal, and alcohol (including beer and wine). Subsequently, their children could not access Internet sites that contained materials falling within the screening parameters of blocking services selected by parents. Although current systems may not eliminate all potentially objectionable materials, the Court concluded that "the evidence indicates that 'a reasonably effective method by which parents can prevent their children from accessing sexually explicit and other material which parents may believe is inappropriate for their children will soon be available' " (p. 2336). After assessing the factual status of Internet speech, the Court turned to an analysis of the constitutionality of the CDA.

The Constitutionality of the CDA

In considering the freedom of speech challenge in *Reno v. ACLU*, the Court's prior cases recognized limited governmental authority in regulating radio and television broadcasting. This authority was premised on legitimate public interests associated with allocating scarce broadcast band resources and the invasive nature of radio and television broadcasts (*Sable Communications v. FCC,* 1989; *Turner Broadcasting v. FCC,* 1994). However, the Court explained that "the Internet can hardly be considered a 'scarce' expressive commodity. It provides relatively unlimited, low-cost capacity for communication of all kinds" (*Reno v. ACLU,* 1997, p. 2344). Further, the Court found that "the Internet is not as 'invasive' as radio or television . . . communications over the Internet do not 'invade' an individual's home or appear on one's computer screen unbidden . . . 'odds are slim' that a user would come across a sexually explicit sight by accident" (p. 2343).

The government's arguments that the CDA merely imposed reasonable time, place, and manner regulations were also rejected by the Court. Although government may impose reasonable time, place, and manner regulations on speech, so long as these regulations are content-neutral and leave open adequate alternative routes of communication, the Court determined that "the CDA is a content-based blanket restriction on speech, and, as such, cannot be 'properly analyzed as a form of time, place, and manner regulation' " (p. 2342). Because the CDA was a content-based restriction on speech, strict scrutiny was appropriate and required "the most stringent review of its provisions" by the Court (p. 2343).

To survive this stringent review, the government had to prove that the CDA's impingement on free-speech rights was necessary to a compelling interest and narrowly tailored to achieving that interest. As the Court noted in *Reno v. ACLU,* "Appellees . . . do not dispute that the Government generally has a compelling interest in protecting minors from 'indecent' and 'patently offensive' speech" (p. 2340, n. 30). In determining whether the CDA was narrowly tailored to achieving that interest, the Court held the following:

> We are persuaded that the CDA lacks the precision that the First Amendment requires when a statute regulates the content of speech. In order to deny minors access to potentially harmful speech, the CDA effectively suppresses a large amount of speech that adults have a constitutional right to receive and to address to one another. That burden on adult speech is unacceptable if less restrictive alternatives would be at least as effective in achieving the legitimate purpose that the statute was enacted to serve. In evaluating the free speech rights of adults, we have made it perfectly clear that "sexual expression which is indecent but not obscene is protected by the First Amendment." . . . "[W]here obscenity is not involved, we have consistently held that the fact that protected speech may be offensive to some does not justify its suppression." . . . "the fact that society may find speech offensive is not a sufficient reason for suppressing it." . . . It is true that we have repeatedly recognized the governmental interest in protecting children from harmful materials. . . . But that interest does not justify an unnecessarily broad suppression of speech addressed to adults. As we have explained, the Government may not "reduc[e] the adult population . . . to . . . only what is fit for children." . . . "[R]egardless of the strength of the government's interest" in protecting children, "[t]he level of discourse reaching a mailbox simply cannot be limited to that which would be suitable for a sandbox." . . . the mere fact that a statutory regulation of speech was enacted for the important purpose of protecting children from exposure to sexually explicit material does not foreclose inquiry into its validity. (p. 2346)

The Court determined that "We agree with the District Court's conclusion that the CDA places an unacceptably heavy burden on protected speech, and that the defenses do not constitute the sort of 'narrow tailoring' that will save an otherwise patently invalid constitutional provision" (p. 2350). The Court noted that in *Sable Communications v. FCC* (1989, p. 127) "we remarked that the speech restriction at issue there amounted to 'burn[ing] the house to roast the pig.' The CDA, casting a far darker shadow over free speech, threatens to torch a large segment of the Internet community" (*Reno v. ACLU,* 1997, p. 2350). The Court concluded, "The interest in encouraging freedom of expression in a democratic society outweighs any theoretical but unproven benefit of censorship" (p. 2351).

DISCUSSION OF THE COURT DECISION

Reno v. ACLU (1997) resulted in a significant victory for advocates of freedom of speech, with a unanimous judgment that the CDA was unconstitutional. The Court held that merely invoking a governmental interest in protecting children from inappropriate materials did not empower Congress to "torch a large segment of the Internet community" (*Reno v. ACLU,* 1997, p. 2350). Congressional passage of the CDA placed "an unacceptably heavy burden on protected speech" (p. 2350). Further, although the CDA restricted free speech, there was substantial evidence that the CDA failed to protect children from pornography on the Internet. As the trial court found in *ACLU v. Reno* (1996),

> [T]he CDA will almost certainly fail to accomplish the Government's interest in shielding children from pornography on the Internet. Nearly half of Internet communications originate outside the United States, and some percentage of that figure represents pornography. Pornography from, say, Amsterdam will be no less appealing to a child on the Internet than pornography from New York City, and residents of Amsterdam have little incentive to comply with the CDA. (pp. 882–883)

The court in *ACLU v. Reno* (1996) also noted that the CDA could cause pornographers to omit warning labels on pornographic materials and relocate or remail materials to evade detection:

> Arguably, a valid CDA would create an incentive for overseas pornographers *not* to label their speech. If we upheld the CDA, foreign pornographers could reap the benefit of unfettered access to American audiences. A valid CDA might also encourage American pornographers to relocate in foreign countries or at least use anonymous remailers from foreign servers. (p. 883, n. 22)

Evidence showed that, in addition to being ineffective, the CDA was superfluous in controlling obscenity. As the Court noted in *Reno v. ACLU* (1997), "Transmitting obscenity and child pornography, whether via the Internet or other means, is already illegal under federal law for both adults and juveniles . . . In fact, when Congress was considering the CDA, the Government expressed its view that the law was unnecessary because existing laws already authorized its ongoing efforts to prosecute obscenity, child pornography, and child solicitation" (p. 2347, n. 44).

In addition to federal laws, states also have laws protecting minors from inappropriate materials. As the trial court found in *ACLU v. Reno* (1996),

> The Government can continue to protect children from pornography on the Internet through vigorous enforcement of existing laws criminalizing obscenity and child pornography. . . . As we learned at the hearing, there is also a compelling need for public education about the benefits and dangers of this new medium, and the Government can fill that role as well. (p. 883)

Given the apparent ineffectiveness of the CDA, its superfluous nature in controlling obscenity, and the likelihood that it was unconstitutional, critics of the CDA may question the wisdom, necessity, and motivations for passage of the CDA. Regarding whether Congress engaged in serious investigations or debates concerning legislation to protect children and promote "decency," U.S. Senator Leahy stated that "The Senate went in willy-nilly, passed legislation, and never once had a hearing, never once had a discussion other than an hour or so on the floor" (*S892: Cyberporn and children*, 1995, pp. 7–8). Available evidence indicated that the CDA was probably both ineffective and unconstitutional, leading some members of Congress to assert that passage of the CDA would "involve the Federal Government spending vast sums of money trying to define elusive terms that are going to lead to a flood of legal challenges while our kids are unprotected" (*Reno v. ACLU*, 1997, p. 2338, n. 24). Despite this evidence and a judicial declaration that the CDA was unconstitutional, politicians continued to make speeches supporting the CDA. Although the CDA's practical and legal problems were evident, arguably, in an election year, some politicians may have been hesitant to vote or speak publicly against any law with the word *decency* in its title. But ultimately, courts reviewing the CDA found that the CDA was ineffective, as well as superfluous, and every court that reviewed the CDA declared it unconstitutional (*ACLU v. Reno*, 1996; *Reno v. ACLU*, 1997; *Shea v. Reno*, 1996).

Responsibility for Protecting Children from Inappropriate Materials

Unquestionably, materials are available on the Internet that are inappropriate for children (Rowe, 1997). One of the central issues underlying the debate over the CDA and the Internet was whether Internet speakers or children's parents should bear the primary responsibility for protecting children from these inappropriate materials. In *Reno v. ACLU* (1997) the Court resolved this question by placing the responsibility on parents: "It is cardinal with us that the custody, care and nurture of the child reside first in the parents" (p. 2341, n. 31). The Court referred to its "consistent recognition of the principle that the parents' claim to authority in their own household to direct the rearing of their children is basic in the structure of our society" (p. 2341). This authority is accompanied by the responsibility of providing parental guidance and proper supervision of the activities of children under their care (*ACLU v. Reno,* 1996, p. 857). The Court also recognized the potential for the CDA to substitute governmental authority for parental guidance, noting that "Under the CDA . . . neither the parents' consent—nor even their participation—in the communication would avoid the application of the statute" (*Reno v. ACLU,* 1997, p. 2341). As the Court recognized,

> Under the CDA, a parent allowing her 17-year-old to use the family computer to obtain information on the Internet that she, in her parental judgement, deems appropriate could face a lengthy prison term . . . Similarly, a parent who sent his 17-year-old college freshman information on birth control via e-mail could be incarcerated even though neither he, his child, nor anyone in their home community, found the material "indecent" or "patently offensive," if the college town's community thought otherwise. (p. 2348)

Schools increasingly are obtaining access to the Internet. When parents place their children in schools, they delegate part of their supervisory responsibilities to educators. Accordingly, educators acquire a duty to supervise the children in their care, including protecting these children from exposure to inappropriate materials on the Internet (McCarthy & Cambron-McCabe, 1992, p. 457). While the Internet offers tremendous educational potential, the presence of pornography and other educationally inappropriate materials on the Internet is an inescapable reality.

Although it is unlikely that children will accidentally be exposed to pornography on the Internet (*ACLU v. Reno,* 1996, pp. 844-845; *Reno v. ACLU,* 1997, p. 2336), inappropriate materials are available for students sophisticated enough to search for them. As the Court noted in *Reno v. ACLU* (1997), sexually explicit materials are available on the Internet including "text, pictures, and chat and 'extends from the modestly titillating to the hardest-core'" (p. 2336). Adequate warnings generally precede these materials. As the Court noted,

> A document's title or a description of the document will usually appear before the document itself . . . and in many cases the user will receive detailed information about a site's content before he or she need take the step to access the document. Almost all sexually explicit images are preceded by warnings as to the content. (p. 2336)

Nonetheless, some of these materials can be accessed without providing any proof of age. But most "hard-core pornography" sites require users to provide an adult access code before access is granted. Further, parents and educators should be aware that, although it is generally unlikely, an imprecise search may retrieve an unwanted sexually explicit site. As the Court noted in *Shea v. Reno* (1996),

> While ordinarily a user must affirmatively seek sexually explicit material to view it, on occasion a search not intended to retrieve sexually explicit material may retrieve a link to a sexually explicit site. For example . . . searches of 'Sleeping Beauty,' 'Babe,' and 'Little Women' produced a handful of links to sexually explicit sites" (p. 931). Nonetheless, these sites generally provide adequate notice that they contain sexually explicit materials before they can be accessed. (p. 931)

Following the Court's decision in *Reno v. ACLU,* the burden is clearly on parents and educators to provide guidance and proper supervision for children in the appropriate use of the Internet. As with all other school activities, educators have a duty to instruct and supervise students properly in their use of the Internet so that they may safely participate and learn. But it should not be forgotten that students capable of understanding and following reasonable school rules also have a duty to obey these rules and can be punished for willful disobedience. As juveniles approach maturity, they must accept increased responsibility for their own actions if they are to become responsible adults. As the Court recognized in *Reno v. ACLU* (1997), "A child requires some sophistication and some ability to read to retrieve material and thereby to use the Internet unattended" (p. 2336). Children sophisticated enough to search for and retrieve indecent Internet materials independently are also likely to be sophisticated enough to understand prohibitions given to them by their parents and teachers and to choose between acceptable and unacceptable conduct. In the absence of this maturity, as the trial court in *ACLU v. Reno*

(1996) found, "parents can supervise their children's use of the Internet or deny their children the opportunity to participate in the medium until they reach an appropriate age" (p. 883).

IMPLICATIONS FOR EDUCATORS

To protect the interests of children, parents, and the school, school administrators should consider whether any Internet screening programs are needed to keep inappropriate materials out of their school. Further, school administrators should also adopt appropriate policies governing the use of their school's Internet resources. Concerning the adoption of appropriate Internet use policies, various professional organizations may offer useful Internet policy suggestions for school administrators. For example, reacting to the Court's recent decision in *Reno v. ACLU*, the American Library Association (1997) released the following statement:

> Like radio, movies and TV before it, the Internet has raised concerns about its possible negative impact on children. To help address these concerns, the American Library Association is launching a new campaign to help parents help their children be "webwise" in connection with the Supreme Court ruling on the constitutionality of the Communications Decency Act.

In addition to other useful information, American Library Association materials provide guidance concerning Internet safety for children and suggested educational Web sites including a list of "50 Great Sites for Kids." These and other similar resources, available on the Internet and through more traditional mediums, may be helpful to school administrators in drafting an Internet policy that is appropriate for their school.

Specific provisions of school Internet policies will vary according to circumstances, including the age and maturity of students, local community standards, and other relevant factors. In some circumstances restrictive Internet policies may be justified, while other situations may require a more permissive policy. Although the U.S. Supreme Court has not definitively ruled on many aspects of students' free-speech rights, the Court's decisions in *Hazelwood v. Kuhlmeier* (1988), *Bethel v. Fraser* (1986), *Board of Education v. Pico* (1982), and *Tinker v. Des Moines* (1969) seem to indicate that while schools enjoy significant discretion in limiting school-sponsored speech based on legitimate pedagogical concerns such as the age and maturity of students and the context of the speech, the school's discretion is not without limitations, and an adequate justification for prohibiting students' individual exercise of freedom of speech is necessary. Nonetheless, schools may generally apply reasonable time, place, and manner restrictions to student speech in schools, including the imposition of reasonable school Internet policies. Students unable or unwilling to comply with reasonable school Internet policies can be denied independent access or all Internet access, and more serious sanctions may be imposed when appropriate. Adequate notice of Internet policies should be provided, and students accused of policy violations should be given appropriate due process (*Goss v. Lopez*, 1975). Taking appropriate precautions and adopting a carefully drafted school Internet policy can help to protect both children and freedom of speech, while maximizing the tremendous educational potential of the Internet.

CONCLUSION

In a unanimous decision in *Reno v. ACLU* (1997), the U.S. Supreme Court declared the CDA unconstitutional. Notwithstanding the governmental interest in protecting children from harmful materials, the CDA with its prohibitions against "indecent" and "patently offensive" communications was not narrowly tailored for achieving that purpose. Instead, the CDA was overbroad and suppressed protected speech, a constitutionally unacceptable result if less restrictive alternatives would be at least as effective in achieving governmental interests. The Court in *Reno v. ACLU* (1997) stated that the government cannot "reduc[e] the adult population [to] only what is fit for children" and "the level of discourse reaching a mailbox simply cannot be limited to that which would be suitable for a sandbox" (p. 2346). Instead, parents and educators must bear the primary responsibility for supervision of children.

Although the Court declared the CDA unconstitutional, children are not left unprotected from pornography. Government can continue to protect children from pornography and obscenity on the Internet and elsewhere by enforcing existing laws. Government can also play a role in educating the public about the potential benefits and dangers of the Internet. But ultimately, it is the duty of parents and educators to provide guidance and proper supervision for children under their care. New technologies can assist parents and educators in blocking unwanted Internet materials. Parents and educators can also instruct children regarding safe and responsible Internet use and enforce appropriate rules for their children. Children capable of conforming to these rules can be held responsible for willful violations. Children incapable of conforming to the rules can be more closely supervised or denied access to the Internet until they can follow appropriate rules for Internet use.

REFERENCES

Abrams v. United States, 250 U.S. 616 (1919).

ACLU v. Reno, 929 F. Supp. 824 (E.D. Pa. 1996).

Acton, J. E. (1993). *The history of freedom* (James C. Holland, Ed.). London: Macmillan. (Original work published 1877)

American Library Association. (1997). The librarian's guide to cyberspace for parents and kids [On-line]. Available: http://www.ala.org/parentspage/greatsites

Bethel v. Fraser, 478 U.S. 675 (1986).

Board of Education v. Pico, 457 U.S. 853 (1982).

Chamberlin, B. F. (1992). Speech and the press. In K. L. Hall (Ed.), *The Oxford companion to the Supreme Court of the United States* (pp. 808–816). Oxford, England: Oxford University Press.

Communications Decency Act, 47 U.S.C. § 223(a)–(h) (1996).

Dayton, J. (in press). Free speech, the Internet, and schools. *West's Education Law Reporter.*

Dayton, J., & Glickman, C. (1994). American constitutional democracy. *Peabody Journal of Education, 69,* 62–80.

Downs, D. A. (1992a). Public forum doctrine. In K. L. Hall (Ed.), *The Oxford companion to the Supreme Court of the United States* (pp. 692–693). Oxford, England: Oxford University Press.

Downs, D. A. (1992b). Time, place, and manner rule. In K. L. Hall (Ed.), *The Oxford companion to the Supreme Court of the United States* (pp. 874–875). Oxford, England: Oxford University Press.

English Bill of Rights. (1689).

FCC v. Pacifica, 438 U.S. 726, 748 (1978).

Fried, C. (1992). The new First Amendment jurisprudence: A threat to liberty. In G. R. Stone et al. (Eds.), *The Bill of Rights in the modern state* (pp. 225–253). Chicago: University of Chicago Press.

Goss v. Lopez, 419 U.S. 565 (1975).

Hazelwood v. Kuhlmeier, 484 U.S. 260 (1988).

Hentoff, N. (1980). *The first freedom.* New York: Delacorte Press.

Jefferson, T. (1993a). Inaugural address. In M. Harrison & S. Gilbert (Eds.), *Thomas Jefferson: In his own words* (pp. 61–66). New York: Barnes & Noble. (Original work published 1801)

Jefferson, T. (1993b). The Virginia statute of religious freedom. In M. Harrison & S. Gilbert (Eds.), *Thomas Jefferson: In his own words* (pp. 53–57). New York: Barnes & Noble. (Original work published 1779)

McCarthy, M. M., & Cambron-McCabe, N. H. (1992). *Public school law.* Boston: Allyn and Bacon.

Red Lion v. FCC, 365 U.S. 367 (1969).

Reno v. ACLU, 117 S. Ct. 2329 (1997).

Rowe, C. (1997, September). Surfing for sex. *Playboy, 44*(9) 82–84.

S892: Cyberporn and children: The scope of the problem, the state of the technology, and the need for congressional action. Hearings before the Senate Committee on the Judiciary, 104th Cong., 1st Sess. (1995) (statement of Senator Leahy).

Sable Communications v. FCC, 492 U.S. 115 (1989).

Shea v. Reno, 930 F. Supp. 916 (S.D.N.Y. 1996).

Telecommunications Act of 1996, Pub. L. No. 104-104, 110 Stat. 56 (1996).

Tinker v. Des Moines Independent School District, 393 U.S. 503 (1969).

Turner Broadcasting v. FCC, 512 U.S. 622 (1994).

United States Articles of Confederation. (1778).

United States Bill of Rights. (1791).

United States Constitution. (1787).

Wilson v. Chancellor, 418 F. Supp. 1358, 1368 (D. Or. 1976).

CHAPTER 11

The Problematics of Democracy and Schooling

James E. Walter

If a nation expects to be ignorant and free, in a state of civilization, it expects what never was and never will be.
—Thomas Jefferson (1816)

As our nation and its educational system approach the year 2000, several groups are engaged in efforts to influence the shaping of a new era, an era that is for many vastly different from that when they were born and in school. Social changes have been described as moving from a modern era to a postmodern world. From regional business and industry to multinational conglomerates, the economy has shifted dramatically. Politically, democracy has protected human and civil rights; these are now debated in economic terms.

In the context of these changes, what is the role of schooling and those who administer in schools? Those who aspire to the principalship or superintendency in our public schools will be addressing different conditions than those which have existed for the past century. This analysis raises questions and describes social, economic, and political tensions which have important implications for the knowledge and skills that school administrators will need in the millennium now upon us.

THE PROBLEMATICS OF DEMOCRACY AND SCHOOLING

Enormous amounts of money expended annually in the United States for schooling testify to its high value in society. But which form of schooling does society want? Various groups desire different things from schooling for their children and for society. Some view public schooling as an instrument to promote private values, often economic. Others argue that schools should instill cultural values (Bennett, 1988, 1992, 1995; Bloom, 1987). Debates about schooling speak to the relationship people believe schooling should have to a democratic society. Issues are resolved for a time, only to be debated again and again.

In the United States, each generation defines what kind of a society it wishes to create and at the same time ensures that the next generation is both capable and free to determine its social policies. The work of democracy and schooling is "always our future challenge and *will never be finished!*" (Glickman, 1995, p. 85). School administrators are increasingly expected to be involved in addressing the *problematics* of schooling (Fenstermacher & Glickman, 1995).

Knowledge and ideas, as expressions of values, are central issues in the problematics of education. The core questions are captured by sociologist and educator Richard Bates (1978) and the philosopher of knowledge Jean-Francois Lyotard (1984): What counts as knowledge? Who determines what counts as knowledge? How is what counts as knowledge organized? How is what counts as knowledge transmitted? How is access to what counts as knowledge determined? What are the intended outcomes? What are the processes of control? What ideological appeal justifies the system?

James E. Walter, University of Missouri, St. Louis

WHICH KNOWLEDGE AND IDEAS ARE NEEDED IN A DEMOCRACY?

At base, what does the role of citizen entail in preserving democratic political structures and the individual rights and freedoms inherent in the American democratic ideal? The founders, informed by Enlightenment ideals, argued that a good citizen engages in lifelong political *praxis* (critical analysis and action) in order to maximize free choice (liberty) for each in the context of the commonweal. Jefferson (1779), in his *Preamble to a Bill for the More General Diffusion of Knowledge*, conceived of a system of public schools to prepare active citizens, arguing that a democracy required educated citizens.

The Impermanence of Knowledge and Ideas

Knowledge and ideas articulated in school curricula and instructional methodology are not fixed. While schools teach the categories of social studies, language arts, science, and so forth, specific content and foci change. So does instructional methodology. No single universal answer addresses what counts as knowledge, how such knowledge is transmitted, or any of the questions posed by Bates and Lyotard. These issues are resolved in the larger political arena and are subject to social, political, and economic changes. If specific content of knowledge and methods have no permanence, what can schools teach in order to ensure the continuance of democracy and the enrichment of personal lives?

Freedom of Thought, Freedom of Speech

Perhaps schools should not engage in an effort to instill in the young a *particular* knowledge. If all citizens think alike, freedom of speech is not operational. Citizen activity and liberty are predicated upon knowledge of multiple perspectives which inform debate and dialogue about social policy. Logically, the idea of educated citizens to preserve justice and equality in a democracy leads to a concern that the state, including schools, not have authority to control a person's thoughts which in turn inform speech. In the words of Justice Jackson in 1943 in *West Virginia State Board of Education vs. Barnette*, "If there is any fixed star in our constitutional constellation, it is that no official, high or petty, can prescribe what shall be orthodox in politics, nationalism, religion, *or other matters of opinion* [emphasis added] . . . ."

Given that it is undesirable in a democracy for schools to promulgate a particular knowledge, is the *function of schooling to ensure freedom of thought and consequently expression (speech) through including multiple perspectives in the curriculum?* Simply put, perhaps schools should not *teach*; instead they should *teach about*.

KNOWLEDGE AND IDEAS TO ACCESS ECONOMIC BENEFITS

Curricular goals are increasingly oriented toward preparing students for the workplace. "Standards" legislation passed in several states is similar to Missouri's legislated Show-Me Standards which are based on workplace demands (Little, 1996). This orientation is not a new phenomenon. After debate at the turn of the century, the Smith-Hughes Act of 1917 located vocational education in the public schools; the 1990 amendments integrated academic and vocational education in the secondary school curriculum (Gough & Smith, 1991). Current reform efforts, reflected in the 1994 federal School-to-Work legislation extends learning workplace skills and attitudes into the elementary school and preschool curriculum.

Higher levels of schooling are expected to result in higher income. Higher earnings contribute to an expanding economy. From one perspective, everyone has benefited materially from such growth; the level of income for the poor among us is substantially higher than for most of the world's population. From another perspective, serious economic disadvantages endure as Jonathan Kozol's *Amazing Grace* (1996), a compelling account of abject poverty and crime in the United States, makes abundantly clear.

Entry into current work and labor structures in our society is closely tied to levels of schooling. In addition, private-sector employers, in an effort to reduce costs and increase profits, expect public schooling (supported in part by their tax dollars) to prepare the next generation of employees in generic workplace skills (e.g., problem solving) and attitudes (e.g., being team players).

Two major factors contribute to the problematics of knowledge and ideas related to accessing the economic benefits of our society. One includes technological increases in productivity and efficiency and changes in management techniques. The other is related to schooling responses to these changes in terms of equity for the benefit of the least advantaged.

Technology for Productivity

Technological developments in the workplace are not new. A craft-oriented, entrepreneurial economy became based on large-scale manufacturing and hired labor. These advances were followed by robotics and software-run numerical control machines. In the search for increased productivity through reduced costs, owners and managers developed new managerial techniques. Taylor's (1911) work signaled the introduction of scientific methods for organizing and controlling labor to extract more from employees. Virtually all management theories today have a similar purpose—to extract more work from employees. The nature and meaning of work changed as ownership of the means of production shifted from individual laborers to corporations.

In the context of knowledge and ideas needed in schools, what should be the content of the curriculum and the related instructional methods? Skills and attitudes appropriate for the workplace change as technology develops, and school curricula usually adapt to reflect such changes. Equally important, though, is for students to be exposed to knowledge about how managers and owners relate to workers. Church (1996, January 15) quotes an expert on the effects of layoffs: ". . . in today's business climate, 'we are all temps' " (p. 45). Employees are resources used as needed and exchanged, sometimes by machines, for increased productivity; in the foreseeable future, this condition is likely to persist.

Equity Issues in Access

Keeping current in terms of employer expectations is, in and of itself, problematic. Differentiating curriculum and instructional methods for presumed differences among students adds another dimension. The way schools deliver knowledge and ideas perpetuates social and economic status differences (Anyon, 1983; Bowles & Gintis, 1976). Schooling does not provide the social mobility often attributed to it. According to some critiques, schools induce in children a willing acceptance of their lot in life. It's just the way things are and, by extension, the way they are supposed to be.

Through testing, differentiation of curriculum and instructional methods, and certain aspects of the hidden curriculum (Giroux & Purpel, 1983), students are denied access to economic levels higher than their parents' and their social class. This condition is especially problematic for children and youth from racial and ethnic groups marginalized in society and for females generally. Tension arises from conflict between the techniques of testing, curricular differentiation, and instructional practices and the ethical and moral requirements of fairness and equity. Which should be privileged over the other? Should the instructional techniques give way to fairness and equity, or vice versa?

CURRENT CONDITIONS IN WHICH SCHOOLS FUNCTION

Current times have been described as "postmodern." Current social, economic, and political conditions are inevitably, as they always have been, expressed in the schools. While the following brief discussion separates social from economic and these from political, the three are dynamically intertwined; the separation serves heuristic purposes only. The implications of such conditions and their interrelationships are subject to disagreement. Thus, school administrators face the daunting task of making sense of such conditions in the context of multiple interpretations and descriptions of causes.

Social Conditions

School administrators will find themselves blindsided unless they "read" the society they serve. Perhaps they can anticipate the consequences of social conditions and prepare appropriate responses. Their responses will be in the context of an increasing distrust of most of the institutions in society, including schools (Hull, 1995). While such distrust stimulates increased personal responsibility, it can also lead to selfishness, "looking out for myself," and little concern for the least advantaged. This distrust fuels a growing number of "gated communities" and the privatization of public services. It appears, Hull notes, that "Americans are preoccupied with trying to *satisfy and protect themselves*" [emphasis added] (p. 60).

This apparent increase in personal responsibility is, ironically, contradicted by reports from medical and social science research that some behaviors are functional disorders rather than a lack of self-discipline (e.g., behaviorally disordered). Disciplinary action is now prohibited, depending upon how the disorder is diagnosed and the treatment prescribed. Has the social meaning of personal responsibility and self-discipline shifted?

Bushweller (1996) reports a major shift in home-school relations, continuing a historical trend of schools progressively taking on more parental functions. Parents' need for happiness and fulfillment have taken precedence over the children's need for safety, security and happiness. Currently 63% of "American adults expect schools to play an equal role with parents in the social and personal development of children" (p. 13) in addition to their academic growth. The nuclear family of a generation ago has given way to single-parent, blended, and two-income families. Economic changes have contributed.

Increasingly, parenting is assumed by social agencies. Schools as caring communities coordinate several social agencies. School districts, now designated P–12, provide prenatal training for parents, latchkey programs, and other forms of assistance in rearing the young. In 1994, public child-care workers were classified as a growing employment category.

Other social conditions could be enumerated. Overall, crime is down, but crime related to youth gangs is rising; the truly poor among us are becoming more so. Such social conditions have several implications for curriculum, discipline, and home-school relations. How can administrators act so that the curriculum does not sort individuals into preordained social slots? Will personal and social growth issues deplete academic learning opportunities? What effect will an apparent shift in personal responsibility have for order and safety in schools? A tendency for parents to seek advantage for their children might disadvantage other children. Do administrators have a responsibility to ensure that the schools serve the common good rather than private interests? What is the common good? How is it defined and by whom?

Economic Conditions

In the span of one generation (1970 to 1995), the earnings of the middle classes have stalled, while the income of the top 5% has increased. In short, "What kind of economy is it in which the numbers of the highest-earning and lowest-earning people are expanding while the middle class is shrinking?" (Church, 1996, p. 38) Despite this, Church notes, materially "Americans are living much better than two decades ago" (p. 38). Can this be maintained for long?

The very meaning of work and labor has changed (Aronowitz & DiFazio, 1994). In their analysis, "work" is no longer a source of personal identity and satisfaction. Quality circles and other forms of team work and problem solving presumably provide identity and meaning, but these could also be other management control devices. Labor, not work, is sold to the highest bidder, if a bidder exists.

In the mid-1980s, workers lost jobs. In the 1990s, management positions are being eliminated by the hundreds of thousands. The advent of computer numerical-control machines (from desktop computers to robots) has made workers redundant as corporations seek to maintain their competitive edge. Aronowitz and DiFazio (1994) argue that "the number of workers—intellectual as well as manual—is reduced by quantum measures in computer mediated labor" (p. 299). They do not "accept the prevailing wisdom that significant levels of investment . . . and consequent economic growth lead to more permanent jobs" (p. 299). Is it possible that the private sector, demanding schooling with specific skills and attitudes, is encouraging the production of a large, skilled labor pool to keep wages and salaries low?

These conditions, and others equally stark, have enormous implications for schooling. Schooling is related to employment, but what if personally, socially, and economically satisfying jobs are not there for the total labor pool? In multiple ways, schooling reinforces the relation of schooling to work, sorting individuals into economic roles. In time, the legitimacy of an institution that implicitly promises that working hard in school will lead to *satisfying* employment is eroded.

What is behind current initiatives for charter schools, vouchers, and other choice plans? Is it parents seeking special advantage to secure admission for their offspring to more prestigious colleges and universities to ensure advantage for employment and careers? Is it possible this phenomenon would have advantages for investors if they had more money (by paying less taxes) to invest? How would the economy change with fewer public programs and more investment in the "productive" private sector?

Political Conditions

In a democracy, an ebb and flow occurs as one set of values ascends and others are subordinated. The process is dialectical and involves capturing and redefining language. The following discussion purposely makes some abstract distinctions in order to frame the tensions.

The polity of the United States can be characterized as revolving around two major views, both interested in ensuring "happiness." In one view, funds are allocated to schools to ensure excellence by investing in human growth for all, especially those who are disadvantaged. Many also advocate a curriculum in which diversity and differences are important themes. A different view holds that a person's worthiness is predicated on the individual's effort and merit. Schools become excellent through structures and processes that encourage competition. Curriculum transmits an objective body of knowledge and cultural truths.

Each view tends to see the other as contributing to undesirable outcomes. One set of critics argues that schools do not need more money, rather individuals need to put forth more effort to learn. Another view argues that schools need more money to provide education so that all can have an equal opportunity to access economic benefits. One side sees the other's policies contributing to social chaos. The opposing side sees the other's policies as exploitive and dominating.

These ideals provide the language by which to capture the imagination of voters in order to ensure the dominance of particular values. Noble-sounding ideals may mask an effort to promote particular private and material interests. In this more skeptical analysis, the question of who benefits becomes salient. As an example, during the Bush administration the Department of Energy's Sandia Laboratories prepared an analysis (Carson, Heulskamp, & Woodall, 1991) contradicting *A Nation at Risk*. An early report draft was scuttled but released (Sandia National Laboratories, 1993) after Bush left office.

In the operational settings of schooling, a pragmatic blurring of these distinctions makes it possible for schools to operate more or less adequately on a day-to-day basis. Schools tend to reflect the pressures of both views. Such pragmatism protects the schools but is also a source of criticisms.

THE "FAILURE" OF SCHOOLING IN AMERICA

In 1983, *A Nation at Risk* (National Commission on Excellence in Education) argued that "Our once unchallenged preeminence ... is being overtaken by competitors throughout the world" (p. 5). It blamed the presumed failure on schooling in inflammatory language: "If an unfriendly foreign power had attempted to impose ... mediocre educational performance ..., we might well have viewed it as an act of war" (p. 5). This assessment created an environment in which schools were also attacked as contributing to dismantling America's culture (Bennett, 1988, 1992, 1995; Bloom, 1987). The report's influence is so pervasive that failure is taken for granted by popular journalists (Church, 1995; Hull, 1995).

Thirteen years later, evidence suggests that the report manufactured a crisis. In 1994, *Time* reported that the nation's economy was rated the most productive in the world (Church, 1993). Again in 1995, a special advertising section in *Time* proclaimed that the U.S was again number one in 1994 (National Association of Manufacturers). Assuming (unrealistically) that reforms were developed and implemented by 1986, the first group of students to have benefited from these would not graduate until 1998. The nation's return to being number one was not a function of school reforms!

Moreover, two recent books (Berliner & Biddle, 1995; Bracey, 1994) have presented data refuting the basic thesis of *A Nation at Risk* and similar reports, mostly referring to each other. A disaggregated analysis of standardized tests used for college entrance (e.g., SAT) and for assessment of school performance (e.g., Iowa Test of Basic Skills [ITBS]) shows a modest gain in scores, not an alarming decline. Scores for whites have been stable with some modest gains; scores for African Americans and Hispanics have risen quite sharply. On international comparisons, Berliner and Biddle (1995) demonstrate that, when opportunity to learn (for example, students who have had algebra) is held constant, American students do as well or better than their foreign counterparts.

Another criticism of contemporary schooling is that students do not seem to have adequate mastery of so-called cultural skills, compared with students of generations past. Bracey (1994) reports a study showing that students of past generations performed no better than students in contemporary times.

The results are even more remarkable when considered in the context of social conditions in America. Income levels are associated more directly with performance on tests than any other single factor. For example, on the SAT, scores fall by 15 points for each drop in $10,000 of family income. In addition, other factors such as number of parents, child abuse, mortality rates, and food-stamp rate are related to the climate in which students learn. Since 1970 the so-called Index of Social Health (Bracey, 1994) has fallen from 70 (on a scale of 0 to 100) to 30 in 1990. In other words, while social health was declining, performance of students on virtually all measures was in fact improving, especially for those traditionally considered to be "disadvantaged." Our nation's schools are doing remarkably well!

THE PRIESTS OF DEMOCRACY

Fenstermacher (1995) and Glickman (1995) suggest that economic interests increasingly dominate the curriculum and instructional methods in schooling. Economic concerns are privileged over knowledge for maintaining democracy. How can principals and other educators engage in praxis (critical analysis and action) which secures liberty for individuals to choose their own ends, maintains democracy, and contributes to economic justice?

Since the 1930s, educators have been indoctrinated not to get involved in politics; they have, in other words, been silenced. Decisions about "what counts as knowledge" for liberty, citizenship, and access to economic benefits are made in a larger political arena. Assuming a willingness to become more involved, activism is justified. In *Board of Education v. Pico* (1982), the Supreme Court held that "the Constitution presupposes the existence of an informed citizenry prepared to participate in governmental affairs . . . It therefore seems entirely appropriate that the state use public schools to . . . Inculcate fundamental values necessary to the maintenance of a democratic system."

In *Wieman v. Updegraff* (1952), the Supreme Court recognized the unique role of educators in preserving a democracy:

> Public opinion is the ultimate reliance of our society only if it be disciplined and responsible. It can be disciplined and responsible only if habits of open-mindedness and *critical inquiry* [emphasis added] are acquired in the formative years of our citizens. The process of education has naturally enough been the basis of hope for the perdurance of our democracy on the part of all our great leaders, from Thomas Jefferson onwards. . . . To regard teachers—in our entire educational system, from the primary grades to the university—as the priests of our democracy is therefore not to indulge in hyperbole. It is the special task of teachers to foster those habits of open-mindedness and critical inquiry which alone make for responsible citizens, who, in turn, make possible an enlightened and effective public opinion. . . .

Because teachers and school administrators are central to any system of schooling, they are strategic in pursuing the American democratic ideal which includes liberty, citizenship, and economic access. Those who occupy school roles are also citizens and can engage in the debates. They are in a strategic position within the broad institution of American public education to buffer effectively attacks on the minds of students by those who seek control of the philosophical character of education policy. This affords them power to influence policy. John Dewey (1935/1987) asked a question still salient as we contemplate schooling in a new millennium:

> Is it the social function of the school to perpetuate existing conditions or to take part in their transformation? One decision will make the administrator a time server. He will make it his business to conform to the pressures exercised by school boards, by politicians allied with taxpayers, and by parents. If he decides for the other alternative, many of his tasks will be harder, but in that way alone can he serve the cause of education. For this cause is one of development, focusing indeed in the growth of students, but to be conceived even in this connection as a part of the larger development of society. . . . He will be on the lookout for ways to give others intellectual and moral responsibilities, not just for ways of setting tasks for them. (p. 347)

REFERENCES

Anyon, J. (1983). Social class and the hidden curriculum of work. In H. Giroux & D. Purpel (Eds.), *The hidden curriculum and moral education: Deception or discovery?* (pp. 143–167). Berkeley, CA: McCutchan.

Aronowitz, S., & DiFazio, W. (1994). *The jobless future: Sci-tech and the dogma of work.* Minneapolis: University of Minnesota Press.

Bates, R. J. (1978). The new sociology of education: Directions for theory and research. *New Zealand Journal of Educational Studies, 13,* 3.

Bennett, W. (1988). *Our children and our country.* New York: Simon and Schuster.

Bennett, W. (1992). *The devaluing of America.* New York: Summit Books.

Bennett, W. (1995). *Moral compass.* New York: Simon and Schuster.

Berliner, D. C., & Biddle, B. J. (1995). *The manufactured crisis: Myths, fraud, and the attack on America's public schools.* Reading, MA: Addison-Wesley.

Board of Education, Island Trees Union Free School District No. 26, v. Pico, 457 U.S. 853, 102 S.Ct. 2799 (1982).

Bloom, A. (1987). *The closing of the American mind.* New York: Simon and Schuster.

Bowles, S., & Gintis, H. (1976). *Schooling in capitalist America: Educational reform and the contradictions of economic life.* New York: Basic Books.

Bracey, G. W. (1994). *Transforming America's schools: An Rx for getting past blame.* Arlington, VA: American Association of School Administrators.

Bushweller, K. (1996, February). Take my kids, pleeze! *American School Board Journal,* 12–16.

Carson, C. C., Huelskamp, R. M., & Woodall, T. D. (1991). *Perspectives on education in America: Annotated briefing—third draft.* Albuquerque, NM: Sandia National Laboratories, Systems Analysis Department.

Church, G. J. (1994, October 24). We're #1 and it hurts: The U.S. outruns the world, but some workers are left behind. *Time,* 50–56.

Church, G. J. (1996, January 15). Disconnected: How AT&T is planning to put 40,000 members of its work force out of service. *Time,* 44–45.

Church, G. J. (1996, January 29). Are we better off? *Time,* 36–40.

Dewey, J. (1935/1987). Towards administrative statesmanship. In J. Boydston (Ed.), *John Dewey: Vol. 11. The later works, 1928–1953* (p. 347). Carbondale: Southern Illinois University Press.

Elkind, D. (1995). School and family in the post-modern world, *Phi Delta Kappan, 1,* 8.

English, F. (1994). *Theory in educational administration.* New York: HarperCollins.

Fenstermacher, G. D. (1995). The absence of democratic and educational ideals from contemporary educational reform initiatives. *Educational Horizons, 2,* 70.

Giroux, H., & Purpel, D. (Eds.). (1983). *The hidden curriculum and moral education: Deception or discovery?* Berkeley, CA: McCutchan.

Glickman, C. D. (1995). Super-vision for democratic education: Returning to our core. *Educational Horizons, 2,* 81.

Gough, P. B., & Smith, B. M. (Eds.). (1991). The rebirth of vocational education. [Special issue]. *Phi Delta Kappan, 72*(6).

Hull, J. D. (1995, January 30). The state of the union [Special report]. *Time,* 53–75.

Interstate School Leaders Licensure Consortium. (1996). *Draft standards for school leaders.* Washington, DC: Council of Chief State School Officers.

Jefferson, T. (1779/1904). Preamble to a bill for the more general diffusion of knowledge (to the Virginia legislature). In P. L. Ford (Ed.), *The works of Thomas Jefferson: Vol. 2* (Federal Edition). New York: G. Putnam's Sons.

Jefferson, T. (1816, January 6 /1892-1899). Letter to Colonel Charles Yancey. In P. L. Ford (Ed.), *The writings of Thomas Jefferson: Vol. 10.* New York: G. Putnam's Sons.

Kozol, J. (1996). *Amazing grace: The lives of children and the conscience of a nation.* New York: Crown Books.

Little, J. (1996, January 19). State adopts school standards: Workplace demands spur reform. *St. Louis Post-Dispatch,* pp. 1, 10.

Lyotard, J. (1984). *The postmodern condition: A report on knowledge.* Minneapolis: University of Minnesota Press.

National Association of Manufacturers. (1995, November 27). Innovation: The key to our past and future success [Special advertising section]. *Time.*

National Association of Secondary School Principals. (1992). *Developing school leaders: A call for collaboration.* Reston, VA: Author.

National Commission on Excellence in Education. (1983). *A nation at risk: The imperatives for educational reform.* Washington, DC: U.S. Department of Education.

Sandia National Laboratories. (1993). Perspectives on education in America: An annotated briefing. *Journal of Educational Research, 86*(5), 259–310.

Taylor, F. W. (1911). *Principles of scientific management.* New York: Harper & Row.

West Virginia State Board of Education v. Barnette, 319 U.S. 624, 63 S.Ct. 1178, 87 L.ED. 1628 (1943).

Wieman v. Updegraff, 344 U.S. 183 at 195-197, 73 S.Ct. 215 at 200-221, 97 L.Ed. 216 at 224 25 (1952).

LEADERSHIP

CHAPTER 12

Special Interest Groups and the Political Nature of Educational Leadership

Abe Feuerstein

As we approach the year 2000, public support for education is anything but solid. Discussions of school choice and vouchers have reached an unprecedented level of legitimacy and threaten the "public" nature of our schools. At the same time, local conflicts over bilingual education, the teaching of values, phonics versus whole language, and bond issues have developed a sharper edge. The situation, however, is not hopeless. Skillful educational leaders, who are able to see the benefits of public debate and its role in consensus building and problem solving, can help their communities avoid the politics of polarization (Duke, 1996). Though battles over the distribution of educational resources are bound to occur, politically astute educational leaders can help focus debate on issues that might truly improve the educational process.

How can educational leaders help their communities focus on important educational issues? Unfortunately, no easy answers are readily available to this question. Political turbulence challenges the authority of school leaders and hinders their ability to implement workable policies. Enduring differences in values, preferences, and beliefs among individuals and groups make a school leader's job difficult if not impossible. Providing leadership under such conditions becomes a process of juggling, bargaining, and negotiating the demands of parents, students, teachers, taxpayers, and minorities. In order to survive, school leaders must learn to forge consensus and compromise in the teeth of endless diversity.

Creating a coherent agenda in a politically turbulent environment is a challenging task for any politician. This task is made more difficult for school leaders than for other politicians because school leaders are expected to be expressly nonpolitical. This expectation, which derives from the special role educators play in imparting moral values to children, makes it difficult for school leaders to take on controversial issues. While other politicians are expected to take sides, educational leaders who do the same are often characterized as self-serving or manipulative. As a result, principals and superintendents must deal with political events, including teacher strikes, student protests, and taxpayer revolts, without appearing overtly political.

Will future educational leaders be prepared for the growing challenge of educational politics? In part, the answer to this question depends on the type of training that these leaders receive. Today, most educational leaders have been trained under a "rationalistic" paradigm, wherein goals precede programs and objectives drive decision making. While this paradigm has served administrators well, times have changed. The decreasing tenure of most superintendents and principals suggests that the rational paradigm may no longer be a sufficient basis for leadership in today's politicized educational environments.

In order to improve this situation, school leadership must be explored from a political perspective. This perspective focuses on differences between group interests and the role of leadership in reconciling those differences. Studies of successful administrators indicate that superintendents and principals will be able to build support for their initiative when they gain the political skills necessary to broker agreements among individuals and groups (Bolman & Deal, 1991). Without these skills, administrators will be unable to develop a following or create lasting change.

What are the political skills that allow some leaders to move their agendas ahead while others fail? Typically,

---

Abe Feuerstein, Bucknell University

these skills relate to the leader's ability to portray politics in a positive light. A positive view of politics increases trust on the part of stakeholders and supports relationship building. In turn, relationship building increases the likelihood that deliberation between or among opposing groups will result in consensus.

In order to illustrate the benefits associated with a positive view of politics, I will outline two perspectives on the participation of educational interest groups in the decision-making process. The first perspective, which I call the adversarial perspective, views educational politics as negative and interest groups as uncompromising organizations responsible for most of the problems with our educational system. In this perspective, groups do not engage in deliberation because they believe that self-interest is the only motivating force behind political action.

The second perspective, which I call deliberative, sees the political process in a more positive light. Actors in this perspective believe that group positions are changeable and attempt to negotiate policy positions. Along with negotiation, group members often attempt to influence and persuade members of other groups to see the merits of their position. In this conception of interest-group activity, self-interest and altruism are considered as political motivations in addition to self-interest alone.

After presenting these perspectives on decision making, I discuss the political nature of educational leadership and provide several suggestions for leaders who must work with a variety of interest groups. These suggestions focus on agenda setting, coalition building, negotiating, and the role of ambiguity in bringing groups with disparate interests together. I conclude the paper by focusing on the moral responsibility of educational leaders in turbulent political settings.

A NEGATIVE VIEW OF INTEREST GROUPS

Interest groups are often depicted as combatants, struggling to define reality in their own terms. Groups vie for influence over the type of knowledge to which students will be exposed in school, raise questions about the equity of educational expenditures and outcomes, and argue about procedural issues such as hiring practices or school board candidate selection (Spring, 1993). According to Wirt and Kirst (1992), the involvement of interest groups in educational governance often creates a complex political environment where schools are driven to serve a variety of different and often conflicting interests.

This adversarial understanding of interest-group activity stems from a conflict-oriented view of democracy. According to Mansbridge (1980), current interpretations of democratic theory assume that differences in individual and group interests are natural and unavoidable. The practice of democracy in such a competitive environment is often reduced to casting and counting votes. Governmental decisions are only able to maintain their legitimacy by giving each individual the right to vote (Mansbridge, 1980).

Though voting is efficient, it does not always serve the best interests of all citizens. In particular, it permits some groups to become permanent minorities unable to influence policy. Disillusionment and distrust of the political system by minority groups and individuals is a predictable outcome of such an arrangement. Another negative outcome associated with voting is the tendency to move quickly from problem definition to problem resolution. Although this may seem to be a positive trait, moving too quickly from debate to resolution does not usually allow enough time for adequate consideration of the issues. According to Mansbridge (1992), the predilection for voting, rather than discussing, is an outgrowth of the assumption that individual and group interests are fixed and unchangeable. After all, why should one bother to debate issues when individuals or group leaders are unwilling to compromise?

Overall, this depiction of interest-group involvement in educational governance is cynical—portraying political decisions as a tug of war where some political groups get more and others get less. As mentioned above, such a view assumes that interest-group positions never overlap and are not open to negotiation. Interpreting interest-group positions in this manner has the effect of reducing debate on the issues. When deadlocks between groups occur, decision making bodies vote rather than "waste time" trying to change people's opinions. As indicated, this reaction may block the expression of important points of view and lead to disillusionment.

A POSITIVE VIEW OF INTEREST GROUPS

While the previous characterization of interest groups as competitors may be accurate in many respects, it is not the only way to view interest-group participation in educational governance. Mansbridge suggests that interest groups often provide decision makers with information that would not be available in their absence. Beyond this function, interest groups also stimulate debate. Debate is important because it is the process by which groups come to recognize their common interests and differences. This recognition can help opposing groups work together to solve shared problems.

When interest groups share information with decision makers and debate issues, they are taking part in a process of defining and acting upon their interests. Deliberative processes of this sort give groups' leaders opportunities to (a) persuade decision makers to their point of view, (b) make public statements concerning their beliefs, and (c) identify interests held in common with other groups. This third point is essential—the recognition of common interests allows groups to build consensus, form alliances, and solve public problems.

Unfortunately, group interests do not always overlap. Sometimes, consensus can only be built through an arduous process of change and development. Discussion and debate can facilitate this process because it helps people to understand issues more clearly and allows them to react to those issues in both rational and emotional ways. Deliberation, therefore, is more than a rational dialogue on the costs and benefits associated with a decision; it is a means of communication that typically involves attempts at persuasion, calls for cooperation, and appeals to loyalty. Recognizing the role that these forces can play in decision making is important because people often make decisions on nonrational grounds (Stone, 1988).

While it is difficult to measure the effects of nonrational forces, a growing consensus in the field of political science and education suggests that rationalistic social models have inherent limits. In education, Sergiovanni (1995) contrasts rational assumptions about organizations as places where, "everyone is motivated by self-interest; everyone is out to maximize their gains and cut their losses," with nonrational assumptions that emphasize the "commitments, obligations, and duties that people feel toward each other" (p. 67). According to Sergiovanni, in nonrational systems felt interdependencies, mutual obligations, and other emotional and normative ties motivate individual and collective decisions. Thus, while self-interest continues to be an important predictor of human behavior, other more emotional motivations, such as a person's sense of duty, are equally important.

Mansbridge (1992) suggests that deliberation can be conceived as a process by which individuals and groups meet, discuss issues, and influence each others' preferences. Face-to-face debate is an important component of this process because it helps to cement relationships among people. Usually, face-to-face debate encourages the participants to find solutions that they all can support (Mansbridge, 1980). Interaction encourages adversaries to think about issues differently. According to Mansbridge (1992),

> Deliberation can involve self-interest and altruism. Altruism in turn derives from both empathy and commitment to principle. The deliberative process is not neutral between self-interest and altruism. The presence of others encourages "we" rather than "I" thinking. (p. 38)

In this fashion, the process of deliberation can encourage a sense of commitment and empathy between and among groups. The danger in face-to-face interaction is the possibility that the consensus expressed will be false. Manbridge (1980, pp. 270–277) suggests that face-to-face interaction can create very different political outcomes than other less personal forms of interaction like voting on a referendum. In particular, she believes that face-to-face interaction can increase concern for the common good by both fostering empathy and increasing fear of conflict. While she admits that face-to-face conversation can suppress conflicts rather than solve them, she believes that face-to-face deliberation should be used when individuals' interest coincide. On the other hand, she supports the use of other techniques when differences are large so that a sense of false unanimity can be avoided.

THE ROLE OF EDUCATIONAL LEADERS IN TURBULENT POLITICAL ENVIRONMENTS

For the process of deliberation to work, group leaders need to recognize the benefits of loosening their preferences and the need to discuss their concerns face to face. They also must be committed to the process of problem solving.

In order to craft workable policy in a turbulent environment, educational leaders must promote a positive view of politics and understand the role of ambiguity in political decision making. Ambiguity allows groups with diverse interests and points of view to come together in productive ways (Stone, 1988). Leaders who are able to use ambiguity effectively are easily recognizable because they are good at agenda setting, coalition building, and negotiating. What is it about ambiguity that helps leaders facilitate good relations among competing groups? According to Stone (1988), ambiguity embodied in common symbols helps transform individual interests and actions into collective results and purposes because the same symbols can mean different things to different groups.

Agenda Setting

Many leadership scholars identify "agenda setting" or "visioning" as the first step in effective political leadership (Bolman & Deal, 1991). In a sense, a vision is the symbolic representation of a complex issue or situation. Leaders develop visions by learning about organizational problems and their causes. Such information is then used to build an "agenda for change" (Kotter as cited in Bolman & Deal, 1991). The symbolic nature of the leader's vision is the source of its power. Leaders are able to aggregate support from different groups for a single policy by carefully choosing meaningful, yet ambiguous symbols. For example, a principal might succeed in bringing together parents who are both for and against the inclusion of handicapped children in regular education classes by creating an understanding of the school as a place which "does its best to help every student achieve her or his potential." While parents may disagree about what constitutes best, both sides are able to support the general goals of the school.

Coalition Building

Another leadership skill useful in turbulent political environments is the ability to build coalitions. According to Kotter, four basic steps are involved in coalition building.

1. Identify the relevant relationships.
2. Assess who might resist cooperation, why, and how strongly.
3. Develop, wherever possible, relationships with those people to facilitate the communication, education, or negotiation process needed to deal with resistance.
4. When step three fails, carefully select and implement more subtle or forceful methods (Kotter, as cited in Bolman and Deal, 1991, p. 210).

An additional step might include the careful selection of symbols around which groups can coalesce. In some cases, symbols allow groups that would benefit from the same policy for different reasons to unite. For example, a group of working mothers may be interested in developing an after-school program so that their schedules and their children's schedules match more closely. At the same time, school reformers may be interested in lengthening the school day for the purpose of increasing instructional time. While the interests of these two groups are different, their goals are similar.

Negotiating

Negotiation skills also are considered to be essential for political leaders. In most situations, some bargaining and negotiating must take place in order to resolve problems. Effective leaders view these negotiations as part of the coalition-building process. Negotiations are particularly useful when two or more groups have both common and conflicting interests. Here, too, ambiguity plays an important role. If potential solutions appear too one-sided, the negotiation process takes on a hard-nosed edge, and participants begin to see the activity as a zero-sum game where one group will win and the others will lose.

On the other hand, if solutions have room for interpretation, groups may see new possibilities that make negotiation mutually beneficial. In this scenario, ambiguity facilitates win-win negotiations because the opponents are able either to craft a more creative solution or because both groups are able to claim victory. For example, a group of parents might be interested in banning a particular book from a school library, while the teachers and the librarian believe the book should stay. A wise political leader might try to create a decision that can satisfy both sides in the argument—perhaps the use of parental permission slips for those interested in having their children use the book. In this situation, the parents' group can claim victory because they gained control over the material that their children could read in school. The teachers and the librarian also can claim victory because they were able to maintain control over the selection and availability of reading materials.

Besides facilitating agenda setting, coalition building, and negotiation, ambiguity also helps leaders build a following. For example, most people do not have coherent and logically consistent belief systems as they relate to education issues and choices. Educational leaders benefit from this lack of clarity because it makes people more amenable to the suggestions that they put forward. In other words, ambiguity allows individuals to support leaders even though discrepancies may exist between the value system espoused by the leader and the internal value system of the follower.

CONCLUSIONS

Based on the previous discussion, it is easy to see that effective educational leaders are essentially effective politicians. However, educational leaders need to be concerned with moral issues as well as the ability to develop support for their agendas. According to Bolman and Deal (1991), "the question is not whether organizations will have politics, but what kind of politics they will have" (p. 223). This sentiment raises several interesting questions. What is a leader's responsibility in maintaining the integrity of the political process? What separates moral leadership from simple manipulation or coercion? Sergiovanni (1995) suggests that leaders are obligated to conduct themselves in a moral fashion because of their responsibility to their followers. He writes,

> Whether intended or not, leadership involves an offer to control. The follower accepts this offer on the assumption that control will not be exploited. In this sense, leadership is not a right but a responsibility. . . . The test of moral leadership under these conditions is whether the competence, well-being, and independence of the follower are enhanced as a result of accepting control and whether the school benefits. (p. 310)

From Sergiovanni's perspective, political activity assumes a positive connotation when leaders maintain their focus on issues that go beyond the narrow confines of self-interest.

On this point, James MacGregor Burns (1978)—the father of modern leadership study—concurs; the relationship between leaders and followers "must be more than merely a personal or self-regarding quest" (p. 448). Instead of seeking individual goals, Burns says leaders and followers become "joint seekers of truth and of mutual actualization" (p. 449).

The bond between leaders and followers is deep and pervasive. Leaders, in a sense, embody the values of followers. In this perception, the use of ambiguity in political relationships is not manipulation but rather part of a reciprocal process of defining goals and aspirations in terms that help leaders and followers achieve those goals together.

Thus, while the practice of educational leadership is inherently political, the recognition that politics can be positive allows new ways to conceive the leadership role. Effective leaders in the political arena will be those that facilitate group interaction, promote deliberation, and help groups understand their interests in rational and emotional ways. Leaders able to open channels of communication and present a vision of the public good that transcends short-term, self-serving agendas may be able to forge a measure of consensus despite what is often characterized as a sea of endless diversity.

REFERENCES

Bolman, L., & Deal, T. (1991). *Reframing organizations: Artistry, choice, and leadership.* San Francisco: Jossey-Bass.

Burns, J. M. (1978). *Leadership.* New York: Harper and Row.

Cibulka, J. (1996). The reform and survival of American public schools: An institutional perspective. In R. Crowson, W. Boyd, & H. Mahwhinney (Eds.), *The politics of education and the new institutionalis* (pp. 7–22). Washington, DC: Falmer Press.

Duke, D. (1996). Seeking a centrist position to counter the politics of polarization. *Phi Delta Kappan, 78*(2), 120–123.

Mansbridge, J. (1980). *Beyond adversary democracy.* New York: Basic Books.

Mansbridge, J. (1992). A deliberative theory of interest representation. In M. Petracca (Ed.), *The politics of interests.* Boulder, CO: Westview Press.

Sarason, S. B. (1994). *Parental involvement and the political principal.* San Francisco: Jossey-Bass.

Sergiovanni, T. J. (1995). *The principalship: A reflective practice perspective* (3rd ed.). Needham Heights, MA: Allyn and Bacon.

Spring, J. (1993). *Conflict of interest: The politics of American education.* New York: Longman.

Stone, D. (1988). *Policy paradox and political reason.* New York: HarperCollins.

Wirt, F., & Kirst, M. (1992). *The politics of education: Schools in conflict.* Berkeley, CA: McCutchan.

CHAPTER 13

Leadership for Learning: A Study of the Instructional Leadership Roles of Superintendents in Sweden and Wisconsin

Paul V. Bredeson and Olof Johansson

Public education in Sweden and the United States has long been viewed as a critical social investment that fires the engines of economic productivity and social progress. As each country deals with the allocation of scarce resources to meet various economic, political, and social demands, educational policymakers at national, state, and local levels are pressed by their constituents to reconcile public expenditures with measurable outcomes. The history, culture, and politics of each country have shaped unique educational institutions. Yet, many similarities exist in the ways in which schools are organized and operated to achieve important social goals: an educated population, the nurturing of democratic values, and contributions to economic progress and individual well-being. The press to improve public education through significant reform initiatives is also something Wisconsin and Sweden have in common.

Within dynamic educational reform environments, the formal and informal roles of educators, including those of superintendents, continue to undergo significant change in Sweden and the United States. For example, the development of national standards and curricula, educational restructuring, the decentralization of authority, the use of standardized assessment practices, and experiments with funding nonpublic schools are among the many reform efforts directed at the improvement of education. These same change efforts reverberate through schools as roles, rules, relationships, and responsibilities continue to be renegotiated and reshaped, including those of the superintendent.

A cross-cultural study of educational reform and the impact of those changes on the work of school superintendents has the potential to offer valuable insights to policymakers and practitioners on both sides of the Atlantic. Specifically, our cross-cultural study examines superintendents' instructional leadership through superintendents' self-descriptions of their administrative work, especially in the areas of curriculum development and instruction. The following questions guided our investigation.

1. How do superintendents in Sweden and Wisconsin describe their primary work as educational leaders?
2. How do superintendents describe their involvement in the areas of curriculum and instruction?
3. Do superintendents' descriptions of their involvement in curriculum development and instruction suggest identifiable role types for superintendents as instructional leaders?
4. In what ways have educational reform initiatives in Sweden and Wisconsin affected superintendents' instructional leadership?

BACKGROUND

Though the cultural and historic roots of the superintendency in Sweden and Wisconsin differ, superintendents have long been major figures in public education in both. Despite the recognized importance of this formal leadership position, scholars describe the superintendency as an underesearched area (Crowson & Glass,

Paul V. Bredeson, University of Wisconsin-Madison
Olof Johansson, Umea University, Umea, Sweden

1991; Glass, 1992). This is not to say research on the superintendency is nonexistent. Recent studies include investigations of leadership skills (Hoyle, English, & Steffy, 1990); the discretionary choices of superintendents (Lidstrom, 1991); gender, politics, and power relationships (Brunner, 1995a, 1995b; Tallerico, Burstyn, & Poole, 1993); demographic profiles, career patterns, preservice preparation and training, and work roles (Carter, Glass, & Hord, 1993; Crowson, 1987; Glass, 1992; Murphy, 1994; Wimpelberg, 1988); and the instructional leadership of superintendents (Bredeson, 1996; Faber, 1994; Floden et al., 1988; Johansson & Kallos, 1994; Johansson & Staberg, 1996; Murphy & Hallinger, 1988).

Superintendents are expected to provide leadership, especially in curriculum and instruction. Cuban (1984) concluded that school improvement could not be achieved without a high level of involvement in curriculum and instruction on the part of superintendents. Peterson and Finn (1985) noted that it was rare to encounter a "high achieving school system with a low performance superintendent" (p. 42) in the area of curriculum and instruction. Other scholars describe the ways in which superintendents are involved in curriculum and instruction, the "technical core" of school (Bjork, 1990; Hord, 1990; Murphy & Hallinger, 1988; Peterson, Murphy, & Hallinger, 1987; Wimpelberg, 1988). As important as the superintendent's engagement in curriculum and instruction is, the workplace realities for most superintendents may be closer to one veteran administrator's characterization: "We're hired for our ideas on curriculum and fired for ones on finance."

Understanding superintendents' perspectives on their work is crucial to understanding the relationships among school reform, leadership, and educational outcomes. Since discrepancies appear between what superintendents say is important and what they actually spend their time doing (Bredeson & Faber, 1994; Cregard, 1996), it is important to examine how superintendents deal with these contradictions. Our examination of the self-reports of superintendents provides a baseline of empirical data on superintendents' descriptions of their involvement in curriculum and instruction in Sweden and Wisconsin.

From these investigations, rich descriptions and better understandings of the work of school superintendents are emerging. However, a paucity of empirical research continues on issues related to superintendents' roles as instructional leaders in their districts. Only limited descriptions of superintendents' beliefs about their work and the ways in which they put those beliefs into practice within highly dynamic and oftentimes highly charged political environments are available. Comparative cross-national studies are even rarer. We believe that the collaborative investigations presented here make an important contribution in these areas.

METHODS

Participants in the two studies included 397 superintendents in Wisconsin and 280 superintendents in Sweden. Superintendents completed a three-page written questionnaire. A total of 326 superintendents, representing 82.1% of the district administrators in Wisconsin, and 207, 74.2% of all superintendents in Sweden, returned questionnaires for analysis. The written survey was developed, piloted, and refined in earlier studies of the superintendency (Bredeson, 1994, 1996). The questionnaire consisted of four types of survey items—demographic information, open-ended queries, Likert-scaled items, and rank-order responses. For use in Sweden, the questionnaire was translated, piloted, and revised for the mailed survey (Johansson & Lundberg, 1995).

Because school governance structures and the work of superintendents in Sweden and Wisconsin share many similar features, we were able to translate all survey items and aggregate the two data sets for meaningful cross-national comparisons. Data analysis was completed in stages. First, we examined each data set separately. After preliminary analyses of each data set, we then made cross-data-set comparisons. Numeric data were analyzed using descriptive statistics. Content analysis and constant-comparative data analysis were used to analyze open-ended responses.

A PROFILE OF SUPERINTENDENTS

The superintendency remains a male-dominated profession both in Sweden (82.0% male) and in Wisconsin (93.5% male) as Table 1 indicates. In Sweden, women superintendents hold 18% of all superintendencies,

Table 1. A Profile of Superintendents in Sweden and Wisconsin.

Characteristic	Sweden	Wisconsin
Gender		
Male	82.0%	93.5%
Female	18.0%	6.5%
Average Number of Years as Superintendent	3.5 years	10.5 years
Average Number of Years in Current District	14.0 years	5.8 years
Former Teachers/ Principals	51.9%	98.0%

nearly triple the percentage of women superintendents in Wisconsin (6.5%) and the United States (6.6%). The range of total years of administrative experience is similar between Swedish superintendents (1 to 30 years) and Wisconsin administrators (1 to 35).

Wisconsin administrators tend to be much more professionally nomadic than their Swedish counterparts. The average number of years Wisconsin superintendents have been in their current school districts is 5.86 years. Swedish superintendents who have moved into their administrative positions from other educational positions tend to remain in the same school district. Swedish superintendents report that they have spent 14 years on average in their current district (municipality).

However, a new career pattern among superintendents is emerging in Sweden. The decentralization of educational authority from the national government to municipalities and various reforms promulgated by the National Agency for Education have resulted in greater mobility of school superintendents among municipalities. Our data indicate that 22% of Swedish superintendents recently made such a move. Similarly, administrator mobility is common in Wisconsin where the average rate of superintendent turnover is between 11% and 13% annually (Kayon, 1993). Novice superintendents generally begin their administrative careers in small, rural school districts. With administrative experience, they then move to larger suburban and urban school districts. Administrators in Wisconsin are encouraged to make such moves because of the increased salaries and enhanced prestige that come with being superintendent of a large, affluent, and often innovative school district.

ADMINISTRATOR CAREER PATHS

Another difference between Swedish superintendents and their counterparts in Wisconsin is their professional career path. For instance, in Sweden only 3.8% of superintendents hold a teacher's license and only 48.1% have been former principals or assistants. It is common for superintendents in Sweden, especially those recently employed as superintendents, to have professional work experience outside of education in such fields as public administration, social services, local municipal government, the military, and business. In Sweden, the number of superintendents who hold a teacher's degree is decreasing. In Wisconsin, with few exceptions, superintendents must have had a minimum of three years of classroom teaching experience to qualify for an administrator's license. Thus, 98% of all superintendents have moved into their positions through teaching and the principalship.

Differences in professional training and career advancement may also help to explain differences in the work relationships among superintendents and teachers and principals. Swedish superintendents describe greater professional distance between themselves and their teachers and principals than do Wisconsin superintendents. In Wisconsin, superintendents' former experiences as teachers and principals, though often many years prior, establish a lasting tie linking superintendents closely to their professional colleagues, teachers and principals.

One reason for the greater distance between superintendents, principals, and teachers in Sweden can be explained in relation to a change in role definition. In recent years, an effective superintendent is seen as one who can successfully deal with decreasing budgets and not with pedagogical innovation, despite its importance in the political rhetoric. This point will be discussed later in the paper under types of superintendent instructional leadership.

SUPERINTENDENTS' WORK: ADMINISTRATIVE TASKS

Respondents were asked to identify the three most important things that they did as superintendents. Their responses yielded 747 (Sweden) and 1,021 (Wisconsin) items describing their work priorities. Our content analysis of each set resulted in 10 and 9 major categories of administrative tasks respectively (see Table 2).

Swedish administrators identified instructional leadership (school development), working with the school board, and budget and finances as their three most important administrative tasks. In Wisconsin, budget and finances, communications and public relations, and personnel administration were the most frequently mentioned tasks.

Next, using a list of administrative tasks previously identified in the literature, we asked superintendents to rank each task by its importance and by the amount of time each required in their daily work (see Tables 3 and 4). Once again, Swedish superintendents ranked school development as their most important administrative responsibility. Planning and goals formulation was ranked as the second most important task and budget and finances as the third. However, when we asked superintendents to estimate the amount of time various administrative tasks required, the order of tasks changed. For Swedish superintendents, school development fell to fourth place, while budget and finances, school board training, and planning and goals formulation ranked first through third. Wisconsin superintendents ranked budget and finances, planning and goals formulation, and communications and public relations as their top three administrative tasks. When asked how they spent their time, budget and finances and public relations were ranked first and third, while personnel administration replaced planning and goals formulation. Instructional leadership, ranked as their fourth most important task fell to seventh in terms of the amount of time superintendents spent in that area.

The responses of superintendents in both countries also suggested that they experienced the stress of role conflicts and work overload. When asked who they would hire if they could hire someone to support their work, su-

Table 2. Superintendents' Most Important Administrative Tasks.

Administrative Task	Rank Order of Importance* Swedish Superintendents	Wisconsin Superintendents
Budget and Finances	3	1
Communications and Public Relations	10	2
Personnel Administration	8	3
Work with School Board	2	4
Leadership, Vision, and Purpose	6	5
Instructional Leadership and Curriculum Development	1	6
General System Administration	5	7
Work with Staff and Others	4	8
Planning	9	9
Evaluation	7	*

*Note. Open-ended responses yielded 10 tasks for Swedish superintendents and 9 tasks for Wisconsin superintendents.

Table 3. Rank Order of Superintendents' Administrative Tasks by Importance.

	Sweden		Wisconsin	
Administrative Task*	Mean Rank	Rank Order	Mean Rank	Rank Order
Budget and School Finance	3.6	3	3.2	1
Planning and Goals Formulation	3.0	2	4.0	2
Community and Public Relations	7.8	7	4.3	3
Curriculum and Instructional Leadership	4.8	5	4.4	4
School Development	3.0	1	—	—
Personnel Administration	8.0	9	4.5	5
Professional Growth and Staff Development	5.0	6	5.8	6
School Board Relations and Training	4.7	4	5.9	7
Legal Issues	9.3	11	6.4	8
Political Issues	8.5	10	*	*
Facilities Management	7.9	8	6.5	9

*Note. Task categories vary slightly.

Table 4. Mean Rank Order of Administrative Tasks by Amount of Time Spent.

	Sweden		Wisconsin	
Tasks*	Mean Rank	Rank Order	Mean Rank	Rank Order
Budget and Finance	2.4	1	2.7	1
Personnel Administration	6.4	7	3.5	2
Community and Public Relations	8.3	10	4.6	3
Facilities Management	6.6	8	5.1	4
Legal Issues	9.1	11	5.4	5
Political Issues	7.9	9	*	*
Planning and Goals Formulation	4.4	3	5.7	6
Curriculum and Instructional Leadership	5.8	5	5.7	7
School Development	4.5	4	*	*
School Board Relations and Training	3.8	2	5.8	8
Professional Growth and Staff Development	6.0	6	6.7	9

*Note. Task categories vary slightly.

Table 5. Assistants Superintendents Would Hire.

Type of Assistant	Number of Times Listed by Respondents Sweden	Number of Times Listed by Respondents Wisconsin	Percent of Total Items Listed Sweden	Percent of Total Items Listed Wisconsin
General Administrative Assistant	135	111	28.1	31.4
Director of Curriculum and Instruction	107	89	22.3	25.1
Business Management (Budget)	92	68	19.2	19.2
Personnel Director	50	24	10.4	6.8
Director for Supervision and Staff Development	43	16	9.0	4.5
Public Relations	21	16	4.4	4.5
Facilities Manager	—	14		4.0
Pupil Services Director	—	9		2.5
Director of Planning	11	4	2.3	1.1
Transportation Coordinator	—	3		<1%
Work with School Board	21	—	4.4	—
Total Times Listed	N = 480	N = 354		

perintendents in both countries simply wanted a general assistant to help share the work (see Table 5). Educational reform mandates, new laws, the proliferation of programs to meet increasingly diverse student needs, and decentralization of authority have added enormous amounts of work, especially paperwork, to comply with state and federal requirements. Swedish superintendents also would hire assistants to help in the area of budget and finances, program evaluation, and personnel administration. In Wisconsin, superintendents would delegate work to assistants in the areas of curriculum and instruction, business management, and personnel administration.

SUPERINTENDENTS' WORK: INSTRUCTIONAL LEADERSHIP

We also wanted to know specifically what superintendents meant when they said that they were involved in curriculum and instruction. We asked them, "Among the various responsibilities of superintendents is instructional leadership. What are the most important things you do as superintendent in the areas of curriculum development and instructional leadership?" Wisconsin superintendents provided a total of 708 responses to this survey question. Using a constant-comparative analysis of these open-ended responses, four major categories, or themes, emerged that captured what superintendents meant when they said that they were involved in curriculum and instructional leadership activities: *instructional vision* ($n = 136$), *instructional collaboration* ($n = 154$), *instructional support* ($n = 265$), and *instructional delegation* ($n = 153$) (Bredeson, 1996). Independent corroboration of these categories was established using an expert outsider, a director of instruction and former superintendent. Using a subset of the 708 open-ended responses, we asked the outside expert to place each response item in one of the four instructional leadership categories. Over 90% agreement was achieved between the initial categorization of items and that of the outside expert. Where any differences occurred, the responses were discussed and then categorized within one of the four categories.

Four Instructional Leader Roles

Next, we used the instructional leadership taxonomy to classify each superintendent by dominant role preference in the area of curriculum and instruction. Based on our analysis of all survey responses, we identified the dominant instructional leadership role reflected in each superintendent's responses across survey items. Table 6 displays the number of superintendents classified by one of four instructional leadership types.

Slightly over 36% of superintendents in Sweden ($n = 103$) and in Wisconsin ($n = 115$) described their primary instructional leadership role as one of support. *Instructional support* to these administrators meant providing financial, personnel, and material resources, logistical and political-system support, psychological support, and emotional encouragement. The second most common instructional role was *instructional delegation*: Sweden ($n = 93$, 33.0%) and Wisconsin ($n = 83$, 26.0%). In this role, superintendents' descriptions suggested that they remained distant from direct personal involvement in curriculum and instructional leadership. One superintendent wrote that, "I hire good people in that area and get the hell out of their way." In both Sweden and Wisconsin, these superintendents viewed themselves primarily as managers of systems whose work, when done effectively, made it possible for teachers, principals, and curriculum directors to carry out their work and be successful instructional leaders. Superintendents' work preferences in the area of instructional delegation centered on monitoring activities, keeping the school board up-to-date on important curriculum issues, employing knowledgeable people in the area of curriculum and instruction, and permitting these educators the autonomy to take the ball and run with it (Johansson & Kallos, 1994).

The superintendent's role, according to most job descriptions for superintendents, is depicted in terms of educational leadership. However, the reality of decreasing budgets for the school sector has forced the superintendent into much more of a role as a managerial leader rather than a leader of pedagogy and educational development. In a 1996 study of principals in Canada and Sweden by Begley and Johansson (1997), the shift from instructional leadership to more traditional managerial leadership tasks was evident for principals as well. The principals in this study were exposed to nine critical situations and asked to describe how they would solve the problem posed. The principals, by a six-to-one ratio, used managerial arguments over educational arguments.

Against this background, it could be argued that for most superintendents organizational stability is more important than organizational development (Johansson & Bredeson, 1997). The difference between the percentages for delegation for superintendents in Sweden and Wisconsin likely reflects two important distinctions. Until 1991 Swedish superintendents were administrators working out of the National Agency for Education. As administrators for the state, they delegated much of the operational duties to others at the municipal level. "In 1991, decisions were made which meant the municipalities became the responsible authority for schools instead of the State. The State's role is now to set the broad goals for education via the School Act and the national curriculum and to follow-up and evaluate the activities in the schools" (Lundberg, 1996). Superintendents in Wisconsin, though ultimately responsible to the state, are employed and evaluated by local school boards. Another important difference is that Swedish superintendents are less likely to have been teachers and principals. Their experiences have been as state education officials or as administrators in fields outside of education.

Table 6. Superintendents Categorized by Instructional Role Type.

Instructional Role Type	Sweden Number	Sweden Percent	Wisconsin Number	Wisconsin Percent
Instructional Visionary	41	14.0%	40	12.5%
Instructional Collaborator	17	17.0%	81	25.4%
Instructional Supporter	103	36.0%	115	36.1%
Instructional Delegator	93	33.0%	83	26.0%

The third type of instructional role for superintendents was *instructional collaboration* (Sweden, $n = 17$, 17.0%; Wisconsin, $n = 81$, 25.4%). In general, instructional collaborators tended to describe themselves as administrators who "rolled up their sleeves" and worked closely with teachers, principals, and others to plan, design, implement, and assess curriculum and instruction in their districts.

Instructional visionary was the fourth type of instructional role. Fourteen percent of Swedish superintendents ($n = 41$) and 12.5% of Wisconsin superintendents ($n = 40$) described how they "painted pictures" and "allowed dreamers' dreams to come true" while they kept the focus and purpose of their work, and the work of others, on student learning and outcomes. These superintendents also described themselves as having a personal interest and stake in teaching and learning.

It is important to point out, however, that the four role types are heuristic categories and that they should not be viewed as "pure administrative types." Overlaps are present in the four instructional leadership roles. The complexities of superintendents' work as well as unique organizational contexts and cultures require that they be versatile administrators who can provide a vision, collaborate and support their professional colleagues, and delegate authority and responsibilities appropriately (Johansson & Bredeson, 1997). Superintendents are not managers deterministically tethered to the characteristics of one instructional role type. Our classifications are meant to be interpretive, not prescriptive of rigid roles.

Reform and Instructional Leadership

Our findings indicate that educational restructuring initiatives have significantly influenced the work of school superintendents. Public pressure through various reform efforts, national and local, has resulted in Swedish superintendents describing school development, planning and goal setting, and budget and finance respectively as their top three leadership tasks. In response to a second query, Swedish superintendents reported that the top three responsibilities for which their governing boards held them accountable were budget and finances ($n = 243$, 34.1%), instructional leadership including school development ($n = 112$, 15.7%), and evaluation of programs ($n = 68$, 9.5%), as Table 7 shows. Superintendents in Wisconsin listed budget and finance, planning and goals, and community or public relations as their top job responsibilities. When Wisconsin superintendents were asked what their boards held them accountable for, analysis of open-ended responses indicated

Table 7. Superintendent Accountability to School Boards: Most Important Responsibilities.

Administrative Responsibility	Number of Times Listed Sweden	Number of Times Listed Wisconsin	Percent of Total Items Listed Sweden	Percent of Total Items Listed Wisconsin
Budget and Finances	243	242	34.1	24.9
Communications and Public Relations	27	175	3.9	18.0
Personnel Administration	49	154	6.9	15.8
General System Administration and Management	52	107	7.3	11.0
Instructional Leadership	112	79	15.7	8.1
Work with School Board and Policy	59	60	8.3	6.2
Climate, Culture and Staff Relations	53	56	7.4	5.6
Leadership, Vision, and Purpose	29	41	4.1	4.2
Accomplishment of District Goals	—	35	—	3.6
Planning	21	23	2.9	2.4
Evaluation	68	—	9.5	—
Total Number of Items	$N = 713$	$N = 972$		

that budget and finances ($n = 242$, 24.9%) was the major response. Communications and public relations ($n = 175$, 18.0%), personnel administration ($n = 154$, 15.8%), and general system administration ($n = 106$, 11.0%) were also listed as major responsibilities.

Instructional leadership and curriculum development were identified as important tasks, ranked 4th and 5th in Wisconsin and Sweden respectively. However, the priority given to budgets and finance represents superintendents' pragmatic understanding that effective leadership requires fiscal and political deftness. The priority also suggests that superintendents' curricular visions may be important, but good fiscal management and efficient use of resources are tasks for which superintendents are held accountable and correspondingly rewarded or sanctioned. In addition, superintendents in both Sweden and Wisconsin have learned through experience that budget and finances are levers of power, both inside and outside their school organizations. With control of these levers, they have greater opportunity to articulate educational priorities and to translate school plans and goals into educational realities. Further, when Swedish superintendents were asked to reflect on beginning their careers again as superintendents and to describe how their education and training could be strengthened, 35.0% indicated that they could use more knowledge about finance and business. In Wisconsin, superintendents wanted more training in finance, politics, and legal issues in education.

SIMILARITIES IN SUPERINTENDENTS' WORK

At the outset of the two surveys of superintendents in Sweden and in Wisconsin, we recognized that they had much in common as educational leaders. However, we were struck by the remarkable similarities, and in some cases nearly identical findings, as we compared Swedish and Wisconsin superintendents. Our classification of superintendents as instructional role types resulted in similar distributions of superintendents as instructional supporters, delegators, collaborators, and visionaries. The structure and mission of public schools in part explain many of the similarities we found. In addition, the nature of administrative work accounts for shared experiences and beliefs about superintendents' primary leadership responsibilities and activities in their districts. These similarities were evident despite very different educational reform agendas, the move to decentralize educational authority in Sweden, and attempts to move toward state standards for curriculum and assessment of student outcomes in Wisconsin.

In contrast, the history of locally governed schools in Wisconsin, and across the United States, has required superintendents to be savvy local politicians who exercise extensive autonomy. The increased politicization of educational issues, magnified public scrutiny of schools and their outcomes, and demand for greater accountability through state-mandated curriculum standards and assessment procedures have all influenced superintendents' professional socialization. Successful leadership of schools, or just survival, requires professional expertise, especially in the areas of local politics and finances.

DIFFERENCES IN SUPERINTENDENTS' WORK

Some important differences were found, however, between superintendents' work in Sweden and Wisconsin. Communications and public relations, legal and political issues, and facilities management were important as well as very time-consuming tasks for Wisconsin superintendents but not for Swedish administrators. The fact that a national curriculum exists, that legal traditions tend toward communal good and rights over individual rights, and that responsibility for facility maintenance is delegated to other school officials accounts for the low priority of any of these task areas for Swedish superintendents.

Superintendents are conflicted by differences, which they freely acknowledge, between what they say about the importance of curriculum and instructional issues in their work and how much time they can actually spend on those tasks. Living with this contradiction is reflected in their responses to our question about hiring an assistant to help relieve role overload. In Sweden and Wisconsin, general administrative assistants and directors of curriculum are the top preferences. This likely reflects superintendents' acknowledgment of their own strengths, based on training and experience, as well as their recognition of the complexities of curricular expertise and leadership in today's school systems.

Perhaps it is unrealistic at the dawn of a new millennium to think of superintendents as "teachers of teachers" or as "the local expert" on education. The professionalization of education through formal training programs in universities and the adoption of state licensure requirements for teachers and administrators have greatly enhanced the levels of professional expertise of all educators. Thus, in Wisconsin a superintendent is no longer "the expert" charged with leading a group of ragtag, semiskilled staff with limited educational training. In Sweden, the importance of school development is recognized as a major leadership responsibility. However, because of the dual political message, newly hired superintendents are employed to be good instructional leaders even though their boards are most interested in cutting budgets and personnel. Thus, though they would like to be instructional leaders, they tend to view their leadership role as supporters, managers, and effective delegators rather than as hands-on instructional leaders. Swedish superintendents, like the majority of their American counterparts, defer to the educational expertise of teachers, directors of curriculum, and principals.

Nonetheless, superintendents remain involved in curriculum and instruction in various ways. Professional and personal interest, the pragmatics of daily work routines, and the politics of educational leadership in their districts have shaped superintendents' interpretations of what it means to be involved in curriculum and instruction. To the 533 superintendents surveyed, curriculum development and instructional leadership meant using their power and expertise to provide instructional support (financial, personnel, material, logistical, and political) and psychological assistance to magnify the efforts of others in their districts working on curriculum and instruction. For nearly a third of Swedish superintendents and over a quarter of those in Wisconsin, instructional delegation was their response to role overload and role conflict. These administrators knew their limitations, remained informed but distant from curriculum and instructional tasks, and delegated to others major responsibilities for curriculum and school development.

Instructional collaboration and instructional vision were also ways in which superintendents described their involvement in curriculum and instruction. Instructional collaboration was more prevalent in Wisconsin than in Sweden, but we believe the explanation for this difference stems from two major differences. First, the principalship in the old centralized Swedish school system was a very important position with considerable formal power. The principal's role in many places is still viewed as it was formerly even though the position today is not supported by law. The idea of a powerful, autonomous principal has been transferred into the newly decentralized school system governed by goals and objectives. This is one likely reason why superintendents tend not to view instructional leadership over principals and teachers as their primary responsibility. Second, even for those superintendents who were trained as educators, the fact that they were formerly state education officials contributed to Swedish superintendents maintaining greater distance from educators and their work than did their counterparts in Wisconsin, nearly all of whom had been teachers and principals.

Superintendents in Sweden and Wisconsin reported similar discrepancies between what they said were their most important responsibilities as educational leaders and what they actually spent their time doing. Superintendents viewed themselves as educational leaders and reported instructional leadership and school development as critically important administrative responsibilities. The decentralization of authority and governance in Sweden has changed the primary responsibility of superintendents, especially in the area of school development. Though the National Agency for Education continues to control the curriculum, the articulation of that curriculum and accountability for it at the municipal level reside with the superintendent and staff while school principals are responsible for the everyday work in schools (Johansson & Lundberg, in press). In Wisconsin, the early history of education defined the role of superintendent as the "teacher of teachers" and "superintendent of instruction."

As formal educational leaders, superintendents always had significant positional power to influence events and direct schools and the people in them. Superintendents also had significant personal power based on their professional expertise in teaching and learning. Teachers, principals, school board members, and local citizens deferred to superintendents' professional educational expertise. Though still important, the primacy of educational expertise has given way to expertise grounded in managerial and political skills. Increased state and federal policy mandates, the unionization of educators, recurring cycles of educational reforms, and the increased politicization of issues surrounding schools require educational leaders who are knowledgeable about budgets and finances, public relations, personnel management, and politics. Wisconsin superintendents reported that they wanted to spend more time on curriculum and instruction but found themselves having to concentrate more and more of their work days on budgets, finances, personnel, and politics than on responsibilities in the areas of curriculum and instruction.

Superintendents in Sweden and Wisconsin have adjusted their work role priorities to meet the demands of state mandates and various educational reform initiatives. To address new social and political realities in local school districts, they recognize the need to make adjustments in their traditional sources of power. Over the past decade in Sweden, superintendents' major sources of power have shifted from influence based nearly exclusively on positional power as national government education officers to sources of power flowing from their emerging local political power. Yukl (1989) reminds us that

> Political action is a pervasive process in organizations that involves efforts by members of an organization to increase their power or to protect existing power sources. Political actions may be carried out by organizational subunits or coalitions as well as by individual managers. Although the ultimate source of political power is usually authority, control over resources, or control over information, political power involves influence processes that transform and magnify the initial basis of power in unique ways. (p. 25)

Swedish superintendents' leadership had traditionally been legitimated through the imprimatur of the state and its authority. With the decentralization of authority to municipalities, superintendents have become much more vulnerable, and accordingly more attuned, to local political pressures. As a result, superintendents need to spend significantly more time legitimating their influence with local constituents and competing with other local officials for scarce resources. The high turnover rate of superintendents in Sweden (every 3.5 years), clearly indicates that the superintendency is a job that requires both administrative and political skills to minimize tensions between the superintendent and the local political board.

As our findings illustrate, superintendents' primary levers of influence in their districts continue to come from formal positional authority, especially the control of resources and information, and from their political power. For superintendents in Sweden and Wisconsin, budget and finances were viewed as their most important administrative task and the responsibility that required the most time. Moreover, control over budget and finance defined what they meant when they said they were involved in curriculum development and instructional leadership.

REFERENCES

Begley, P., & Johansson, O. (1997, March). *Values and school administration: Preferences, ethics, and conflicts.* Paper presented at the annual meeting of the American Educational Research Association, Chicago.

Bjork, L. G. (1990, April). *Effective schools—effective superintendents: The emerging instructional leadership role.* Paper presented at the annual meeting of the American Educational Research Association, Boston.

Bredeson, P. V. (1996). Superintendents' roles in curriculum development and instructional leadership: Instructional visionaries, collaborators, supporters, and delegators. *Journal of School Leadership, 6*(3), 243–264.

Bredeson, P. V., & Faber, R. Z. (1994, April). *What do superintendents mean when they say they are involved in curriculum and instruction?* Paper presented at the annual meeting of the American Educational Research Association, New Orleans, LA.

Brunner, C. (1995a). By power defined: Women in the superintendency. *Educational Considerations, 22*(2), 21–26.

Brunner, C. (1995b, October). *The promising intersection of power and ethics: The superintendency as transformed by Euro-American women.* Paper presented at the annual meeting of the University Council for Educational Administration, Salt Lake City, UT.

Carter, D. S. G., Glass, T. E., & Hord, S. M. (1993). *Selecting, preparing and developing the school district superintendent.* Washington, DC: Falmer Press.

Cregard, A. (1996). *Skolchefers arbete: Om cheksskap styrning inom skolsektorn.* Goteborg, Sweden: Goteborgs Unversitet, CEFOS.

Crowson, R. L. (1987). The local school district superintendency: A puzzling administrative role. *Educational Administration Quarterly, 23*(3), 49–69.

Crowson, R. L., & Glass, T. E. (1991, April). *The changing role of the local school district superintendent in the United States.* Paper presented at the annual meeting of the American Educational Research Association, Chicago.

Cuban, L. (1984). Transforming the frog into a prince: Effective schools research, policy, and practice at the district level. *Harvard Educational Review, 54*(2), 129–151.

Faber, R. Z. (1994). *Superintendents' involvement in curriculum development: Issues of influence in leadership.* Unpublished doctoral dissertation, University of Wisconsin, Madison.

Floden, R. E., Porter, A. C., Alford, L. E., Freeman, D. J., Irwin, S., Schmidt, W. H., & Schwille, J. R. (1988). Instructional leadership at the district level: A closer look at autonomy and control. *Educational Administration Quarterly, 24*(2), 96–124.

Glass, T. E. (1992). *The 1992 study of the American school superintendency.* Arlington, VA: American Association of School Administrators.

Hord, S. M. (1990). *Images of superintendents' leadership for learning.* Austin: Texas Association of School Administrators.

Hoyle, J. R., English, F. W., & Steffy, B. (1990). *Skills for successful school leaders.* Arlington, VA: American Association of School Administrators.

Johansson, O., & Bredeson, P. V. (1997, March). *School reform and administrator work.* Paper presented at the annual meeting of the American Educational Research Association, Chicago.

Johansson, O., & Kallos, D. (1994). Om rektorsrollen vid malstyrning av skolan. In Segerstad (Ed.), *A red skola med styrfart: En antologi om styrning och ledning av skolans verksamhet.* Rektorsutbildningens skriftserie, nr 2 Uppsala.

Johansson, O., & Lundberg, L. (1995). *Skolchefsundersokningen: Questionnaire to Swedish superintendents.* Umea, Sweden: Umea University, Centre for Principal Development.

Johansson, O., & Lundberg, L. (in press). Changing roles for chief education officers and head teachers in Sweden. In C. Hudson & A. Lidstrom (Eds.), *Megatrends and policy vacuums: Local education policies in Sweden and Britain.*

Johansson, O., & Staberg, U. (1996). Kommunal skolutvecklin mojlig via den kommunala skolplanen. In O. Johansson & D. Kallos (Eds.), *Tank utveckling: En antologi om skolans kvalitet och effektivitet: Vad kan ledaren gora?* Rektorsutbildningens skriftserie nr 3, Umea.

Kayon, D. (1993). *Job commitment and turnover of school superintendents.* Unpublished doctoral dissertation, University of Wisconsin, Madison.

Lidstrom, A. (1991). *Discretion: An art of the possible.* Umea, Sweden: University of Umea, Department of Political Science.

Lundberg, L. (1996). *Some notes on principal training in Sweden.* Conversation Session presented at Ft. Lauderdale, FL.

Murphy, J. (1994). *The changing role of the superintendency in restructuring districts in Kentucky.* Paper presented at the annual meeting of the American Educational Research Association, New Orleans, LA.

Murphy, J., & Hallinger, P. (1988). Characteristics of instructionally effective school districts. *Journal of Educational Research, 81*(3), 175–181.

Peterson, K. D., & Finn, C. E. (1988). Principals, superintendents and the administrator's art. In D. Griffiths, R. Stout, & P. Forsyth (Eds.), *Leaders for America's schools* (pp. 88–107). Berkeley, CA: McCutchan.

Wimpelberg, R. K. (1988, May). Instructional leadership and ignorance: Guidelines for the new studies of district administrators. *Education and Urban Society, 20*(3), 302–310.

Yukl, G. A. (1989). *Leadership in organizations.* Englewood Cliffs, NJ: Prentice Hall.

Rethinking School Leadership:
Is the Principal Really Needed?

Theodore B. Creighton

The effective schools research of the 1970s and 1980s indicates that strong administrative leadership is directly related to school improvement efforts and increased student learning (Berman & McLaughlin, 1978; Edmonds, 1979; Fullan, 1982). Though little recent research indicates a direct relationship between principal instructional leadership and student achievement (Hallinger, Blickman, & Davis, in press), the consensus and agreement is that a principal has (at least) an indirect effect on student achievement through actions that shape a school's learning climate (Creighton, 1996). Further, Ogawa and Hart (1995) report that the "principal variable" accounted for 2% to 8% in the variance of student test scores. Though few disagree that principals have an impact on the lives of teachers and students, both the nature and degree of that effort continue to be open to debate (Hallinger & Heck, 1996).

The large number of studies on effective schools of the mid 1960s and early 1970s (Brookover, 1979; Coleman, 1966; Edmonds, 1979) clearly identified strong leadership as a characteristic of good schools. A second wave of effective schools research (Goodlad, 1982; Purkey & Smith, 1983; Steadman, 1987) found the principal's leadership crucial to school effectiveness.

In the 1990s, researchers are describing varied sources of instructional leadership (Austin & Reynolds, 1990; Chubb & Moe, 1990; Levine, 1991; Pajak & Glickman, 1989). In many cases, principals are becoming secondary instructional leaders. Primary instructional leaders vary from system to system but include central office supervisors, assistant principals, department chairs, grade-level leaders, and teams of teachers.

Recently, others have questioned whether a principal is necessary. Fullan (1993) contends that in true learning organizations, the principalship as we know it may disappear. Nias (1992) found in her studies that even the collaborative leader was too strong for the development envisioned in the new work of school leaders and that even the collaborative principal may be too authoritarian for the true learning organization to take shape. Sarason (1997) suggests and supports a proposal to eliminate the principal from the school governance structure.

Though the role of the school principal is being questioned, the research clearly reveals that a characteristic of effective schools is that someone, somewhere, is responsible for and committed to the process, function, and tasks of school leadership (Glickman, 1995).

THE STUDY

This study began with a focus on three elementary schools in Casper, Wyoming, and Boulder, Colorado, which are changing the traditional paradigm of school governance by providing for student learning without the usual principal or vice principal. Visits to the two schools in Colorado revealed a "principal structure," with teacher-leaders or teacher-principals performing the duties of the principal. The leaders taught in the classroom for half a day and performed administrative duties the other half. Only the elementary school in Casper, Wyoming, had a governance structure that truly reflected the absence of a principal. The author selected this school for further study and research.

Theodore B. Creighton, Idaho State University

Two research questions guided the study: (a) are schools without principals maintaining the consistency, control, and effectiveness associated with effective principals? and (b) what are the factors influencing schools to view the principal-less structure as a viable option of school governance?

Methodology: The Empirical Study

Any attempt to relate the character of one school to others should proceed with caution. Likewise, any attempt to suggest one particular model of school governance as having positive or negative implications for other schools must acknowledge its limitations. This study represents a case study of one elementary school and its unique form of school governance.

The elementary school under study includes kindergarten through grade 8 with an approximate enrollment of 200 students. Classes consist of two-grade combinations with two teachers per class. In other words, two teachers share the instruction of combination classes of Grades 1–2, Grades 3–4, Grades 5–6, and Grades 7–8. The student population is predominantly white, medium to high socioeconomic status, with approximately 4% of the students qualifying for free and reduced lunch.

In 1990, a team of teachers presented a proposal for the school's structure to their superintendent and board of trustees. The proposal included a governance structure with no principal or vice principal. Each of the identified responsibilities of a school principal was assigned to an individual and, in some cases, a pair of teachers. For example, two teachers were responsible for personnel issues, two teachers handled school finance, two teachers were in charge of discipline, and so on. Early the next year, the superintendent and board of trustees accepted the proposal and doors opened for students in the fall of 1991.

The present study resulted from research conducted during the 1996–1997 school year and used data gathered through interviews with teachers, administrators, parents, and students. A university teacher education major administered a parent-student survey, and additional phone interviews took place with the former superintendent and board members involved in the original proposal in 1991. Observations conducted at the school site also contributed to the research. The interviews, observations, field notes, and analysis of documents collected in the field form the empirical basis for this study.

Interviews were taped, transcribed, and entered into the Statistical Package for the Social Sciences (SPSS) for analysis. Correlation, multiple correlation, and factor analyses helped to identify significant patterns in the area of school leadership. Leadership constructs identified by the National Association of Elementary School Principals (NAESP) and the 21 knowledge and skill bases established by the National Policy Board for Educational Administration (NPBEA) guided and focused the coding and interpretation of data.

RESULTS AND FINDINGS

Eight major findings emerged from this study. These related to cost savings and student-teacher ratio, managerial duties, leadership, principal as manager, personnel evaluation, communication, district goals and objectives, and standards for effective school leadership.

Finding 1: Cost Savings and Student-Teacher Ratio

Addressing the following question in the study was crucial: What was the rationale for eliminating the role of the principal in the original proposal? In discussion with the school's planning team, the recurring theme for the "principal-less" structure was the desire to use the principal's salary (i.e., $40,000 to $50,000) to accomplish a student-teacher ratio of 18–1. The planning team reasoned that, if the cost of a principal could be saved, the money could be used to reduce the student-teacher ratio in each classroom. Their proposal insisted that the amount saved by the elimination of the principal would remain in the local school's budget and be used to support placement of two teachers in each classroom with 36 students (student-teacher ratio of 18–1).

The former superintendent and two board members concurred that assigning a principal within their district to the proposed school would have been counterproductive to the proposal. They said that they felt a principal might jeopardize teacher-parent responsibility and ownership. The former superintendent stated,

I did not feel that any of our current principals could have stepped in and provided the cooperation and shared decision making which were so important to the proposal. I have come to believe that a principal can be the single greatest roadblock to school improvement.

Finding 2: Managerial Duties

Though the managerial duties of a school principal (e.g., discipline, finance, scheduling, etc.) were equally distributed across the staff, no evidence showed any specialized training or expertise in the areas of assignment. For example, the pair of teachers assigned to finances seemed knowledgeable in math and budgeting but had received no specific training in school finance. The teachers responsible for personnel issues had no background or formal training in crisis management, group dynamics, or the like.

Some parents believed that, when they had a specific concern about an issue, it was difficult to identify the staff in charge of that area (e.g., a problem occurring on the playground or bus). In addition, upon identifying the staff member in charge, it was difficult to talk with that person immediately. The issue often had to wait until lunch time or after school or until it could be placed on an agenda for the weekly staff meeting. A parent shared the following comment:

> I found it difficult to know which staff member to talk with if I had a specific concern. For example, I was recently upset about something happening on the playground and wasn't sure who to talk with about it.

Finding 3: Leadership

Management, the day-to-day operation of the school, seemed to be covered sufficiently by the teacher teams. However, leadership, fostering purpose, passion, and imagination, was absent. Classes met on time, buses arrived and departed on time, and recess and cafeteria duties were carried out as scheduled. Teachers and other staff performed their duties and appropriate instruction occurred in individual classrooms.

Though teachers possessed vision and ideas for the future, a unified common purpose was not evident. Some disagreement existed among staff about future direction and focus. Some felt a need to maintain the status quo from 1991, while others felt an urgency to adjust for the future. Still others felt uncomfortable that they had strayed too far from the school's original proposal.

In addition, considerable managerial responsibilities fell upon teaching personnel, requiring much time away from children and the teaching-learning process. While it can be argued that teachers need more planning and preparation time, using that time for the managerial duties of the principal can undermine instructional time with children.

Finding 4: Principal as Manager

After talking with many teachers, parents, and school board members, an image of a principal emerged as a manager, rather than an educator and instructional leader. The image also emphasized administrative control and authority. The sense was that those interviewed did not view the role of the principal as one focused on teaching and learning. Quite the contrary, indications suggested that some viewed the principal as someone who might actually impede teaching and learning. The former superintendent stated,

> Our concern was that any of our current building principals would actually be counterproductive to the proposal made by the teachers. Each of them would have problems with shared decision making and empowering the teachers and parents.

A former board member echoed this concern:

> We as a board did not view the absence of a principal as an issue. Our concern was that a traditional principal would not have the ability to relinquish individual authority and allow for total shared governance at the school. We believed the existing leadership [principals] in our district would be counterproductive to the proposal.

Finding 5: Personnel Evaluation

The school did not have any consistent or regular system of personnel evaluation and supervision. Since no administrators were in the building to conduct formative and summative evaluation of staff, the district appointed two principals from other schools to conduct teacher evaluations. This system of evaluation created several difficulties: (a) the principals, coming from other buildings, lacked familiarity with the day-to-day instruction in the classroom; (b) the visiting principals were not part of the culture of the building; and (c) evaluation of teacher performance was based on very limited observations.

Finding 6: Communication

Formal channels of communication were absent, especially in regard to organizational goals. Communication is complex and permeates every aspect of school life. The translation of goals into concrete actions and accomplishments depends on regular, ongoing, and successful information exchanges (Hoy & Miskel, 1996). Though the staff communicated through a weekly staff meeting, a lack of daily communication resulted in many issues needing a quick response having to wait. A need existed for someone to serve as an anchor to provide guidance and assistance during times of stress and crisis.

Finding 7: District Goals and Objectives

The connection to district goals and objectives appeared weak and unimportant although school-site goals were fairly obvious and shared by the total staff. Though the school staff had a common direction and focus, the school's relationship to district office appeared unproductive. Little collaboration existed between the local school and the district office. It was not apparent that the local education plan related to the overall vision of the district. In addition, the interviews conducted with other parents, teachers, and administrators in the district revealed an ambivalence toward the school under study. A principal stated,

> I do not believe there is effective leadership at the school. They seem to be doing their own thing and not concerned with the overall mission and goals of the district. Though they have a teacher who attends administrative meetings, how can that person have time to promote the direction of the district and teach also?

Finding 8: Standards for Effective School Leadership

The National Association of Elementary School Principals (NAESP) and the National Policy Board of Educational Administration (NPBEA) have identified several standards for effective school leadership (Creighton, 1996). It makes sense to assume that, if the responsibilities of the principal are distributed to teams of teachers, the identified constructs should still be evident in the school culture. For instance, if school effectiveness is determined by a principal's ability to plan appropriately, this same construct of planning should exist in the operation of a school without a principal.

The identified constructs of effective leadership fall into two categories: (a) management traits and (b) leadership traits. These are listed in Table 1.

Responses from teachers, students, parents, and administrators were analyzed and coded to align with the various constructs of effective leadership. In summarizing the data, a restatement of one of the research questions might be helpful: Are schools without principals maintaining the consistency, control, and effectiveness associated with effective principals?

The significant responses or descriptors (.50 or greater) loaded on five factors. Table 2 identifies the five factors along with the loadings of descriptors when subjected to factor analysis. This procedure identifies the clustering of certain variables with the appropriate factor and assists in the naming or labeling of factors.

Four of the five factors clearly align with management traits (problem solving, organizing, planning, and creativity). However, only one (climate development) falls into the leadership category. The implication is that the elimination of the principal did not greatly affect the management of the school but resulted in many of the

Table 1. Constructs of Effective School Leadership.

Management Traits	Leadership Traits
Planning	Vision
Organizing	Communications
Problem Solving	Instructional Leadership
Creativity	Climate Development
Decisiveness	Team Building
Systems Analysis	Instructional Supervision

Table 2. Clustering of Descriptors on Factors.

Factor 1		Factor 2		Factor 3	
03 Prob. Sol.	.52	04 Organizing	.83	08 Planning	.54
16 Prob. Sol.	.84	17 Organizing	.70	21 Planning	.62
29 Prob. Sol.	.92	30 Organizing	.77	34 Planning	.53
42 Prob. Sol.	.79	43 Organizing	.62	47 Planning	.73
54 Prob. Sol.	.78	56 Organizing	.77	60 Planning	.50
67 Prob. Sol.	.82	68 Organizing	.57	73 Planning	.55
94 Prob. Sol.	.70	81 Organizing	.55	86 Planning	.54

Factor 4		Factor 5	
15 Creativity	.86	41 Climate Dev.	.83
28 Creativity	.70	48 Climate Dev.	.54
40 Creativity	.77	55 Climate Dev.	.65
53 Creativity	.51	61 Climate Dev.	.73
66 Creativity	.50	69 Climate Dev.	.79
93 Creativity	.59		

leadership characteristics and responsibilities being nonexistent. The finding may also imply that management responsibilities lend themselves to teacher teams more than do leadership constructs, which may benefit from a specific person or group responsible for those duties.

DISCUSSION

The most significant and recurring pattern appearing in the data analysis was a common conception of a principal. The teachers, parents, and students interviewed described a principal as a person responsible for discipline, finances, and scheduling. This conception seemed based upon mechanical control and maintenance. Absent was any mention of the principal as an educator, as one who directs teaching and learning. Absent was any mention of the principal as a person who directs efforts to improve student learning and creates a positive school climate.

The important question here is this: Why was this conception of the principal so different from the one we have talked about for two decades? The conception of the principal at the university is much different and focuses on the importance of providing instructional leadership, guiding a district's vision, and working collaboratively with the total staff to promote and sustain increased student performance.

The argument exists that the relationship between university preparation programs and our public schools is generally weak and, in many cases, nonexistent (Murphy, 1992). Though we continually talk about the importance of school-university partnerships, in reality the relationship is more rhetoric than fact.

I realize that sending administrators trained in effective leadership to the public schools often results in the new leader being consumed in an environment focused on management and putting out fires. When the system (or school site) views leadership as managerial, it may be very difficult for a newly trained instructional leader to avoid being "sucked into" the world of management.

Another area of responsibility exists which lies with university teacher preparation programs. Why would an entire staff view the principal's role as consisting of six or eight clearly defined tasks that can be performed by individual staff members? Where in teacher preparation programs do future teachers learn about leadership? Teachers are generally "unsophisticated" in the subject of school governance (Sarason, 1993). Very few teacher preparation programs include training (or dialogue) in the area of school leadership. As a result, teachers are expected to respond to school governance but have had little training in preparation.

Should we teach leadership skills in administrative preparation programs only, or should we also teach leadership skills in our teacher preparation programs? Goodlad (1991) stated that undergraduate and graduate teacher education programs do not regularly include preparation in assuming leadership roles outside the classroom. Lieberman, Saxl, and Mills (1988) reported that teachers need to develop skills in building rapport, dealing with change, and managing the demands of leadership. Other authors (Gehrke, 1991; Goodlad, 1991; Manthei, 1992) have advised that leadership skills would be helpful to classroom teachers.

The suggestion is not to teach leadership skills to teachers for the sole purpose of eliminating the principal. The point is that a dichotomy exists in the conception of a principal's job. Unless we address leadership skills and competencies in our teacher education programs, attempts to improve schools through changes in governance structures may continue to have little effect. Providing leadership training for our future teachers may result in more agreement on the meaning of effective leadership and improvement in relations between teachers and administrators.

Another pattern emerging from the data was the absence of *thinking* about the education of all students in the school. Each teacher had a grasp and understanding of effective education in the individual classroom but was not fully aware of any scope and sequence of all the learning activities occurring in the school. It is this *thinking* about the education of all students that characterizes an effective principal. A question surfaces: Without a principal or administrator, how can this overall *thinking* be promoted and sustained?

Glickman (1995) advances five propositions about teachers' attitudes and awareness that can be promoted via leadership: (a) enhancing teacher beliefs in a cause beyond oneself, (b) promoting teachers' sense of efficacy, (c) making teachers aware of how they complement each other in striving for common goals, (d) stimulating teachers to plan common purposes and actions, and (e) challenging teachers to think abstractly about their work. Clearly, the school studied was not attending to these elements in any coherent way.

CONCLUSION

The research on school-based management and shared decision making reveals disappointing results (Mirel, 1994; Weise, 1995). Many new decision-making structures have led to disaster (Beadie, 1996). One of the most significant studies of decision making in the schools (Weise, Cambone, & Wyeth, 1992) looked at the shared governance structures of 45 schools across the country. The recurring theme across all schools studied was the confusion over who actually had the final word when it came to accepting and implementing a decision. In every case but one, the push toward innovation came from the principal. It was not the inclusion of the teachers in the decision making that precipitated reform, but the commitment of the principals to change the way the school operated (Weise, 1995).

This study revealed a prevalent misconception of the principalship, similar to Senge's (1994) description of the common conception of successful managers in the business world: "being decisive, being in control, knowing what is going on, having answers, and forcefully advocating your views" (p. xvi).

Of particular note is the indication that the teacher teams are handling the management responsibilities rather successfully but are not addressing many of the leadership responsibilities of building principals. This finding does not imply that teachers are incapable of leadership as much as it may indicate that their conception of the principalship is primarily managerial. Little evidence surfaced indicating a view of the principal as one who builds vision, communicates effectively, or provides instructional leadership and instructional supervision.

With current national attention given to schools of choice and charter schools, we will undoubtedly see more and more schools experimenting with alternative governance structures. The role of the principal will continue to be questioned and scrutinized. Those of us who are responsible for the training of educational leaders must continue authentic and ongoing dialogue with public schools and their communities. Unless leadership training and preparation includes genuine communication with teacher education programs and our public schools, confusion and misconceptions about effective leadership and the role of the school principal will continue.

Leadership is not something accomplished as an end in itself but must be viewed as developmental if schools are to become more successful. The new leadership of the 21st century must not only respond to teacher performance but also encourage greater involvement, autonomous thinking, and collective actions by teachers (Glickman, Gordon, & Ross, 1995).

REFERENCES

Austin, G., & Reynolds, D. (1990). Managing for improved school effectiveness: An international survey. *School Organization, 10*(2), 167–178.

Beadie, N. (1996). From teachers as decision makers to teachers as participants in shared decision making: Reframing the purpose of social foundations in teacher education. *Teachers College Record, 98(1)*, 77–103.

Berman, P., & McLaughlin, M. (1978). Implementations of educational innovations. *Educational Forum, 40,* 347–370.

Brookover, W. (1979). *School social systems and student achievement: Schools can make a difference.* New York: Praeger.

Chubb, J., & Moe, T. (1990). *Politics, markets, and America's schools.* Washington, DC: Brookings Institute.

Coleman, J. S. (1966). *Equality of educational opportunity.* Washington, DC: U.S. Government Printing Office.

Creighton, T. (1996). *A construct validation of the Administrative Diagnostic Inventory.* (ERIC Document Reproduction Service No. TM 027 024)

Edmonds, R. (1979). Effective schools for the urban poor. *Educational Leadership, 37,* 15–24.

Fullan, M. (1982). *The meaning of educational change.* New York: Teachers College Press.

Fullan, M. (1993). *Change forces: Probing the depths of educational reforms.* Bristle, PA: Falmer Press.

Gehrke, N. (1991). *Developing teachers' leadership skills.* (ERIC Document Reproduction Service No. ED 330 691)

Glickman, C., Gordon, S., & Ross-Gordon, S. (1995). *Supervision of instruction: A developmental approach.* Needham Heights, MA: Simon & Schuster.

Goodlad, J. (1982, January). *A study of schooling.* Paper presented at the meeting of the Stanford Teacher Education Project, Stanford, CA.

Goodlad, J. (1991). A study of the education of educators: One year later. *Phi Delta Kappan, 73*(4), 311–316.

Hallinger, P., Bickman, L., & Davis K. (in press). School context, principal leadership, and student achievement. *Elementary School Journal.*

Hallinger, P., & Heck, R. (1996). Reassessing the principal's role: A review of the empirical research. *Educational Administration Quarterly, 32*(1), 5–44.

Hoy, W., & Miskel, C. (1996). *Educational administration: Theory, research, and practice.* New York: McGraw-Hill.

Jacobson, S. (1998). Preparing educational leaders: A basis for partnership. In *Transforming schools and schools of education: A new vision for preparing educators* (pp. 71–79). Thousand Oaks, CA: Corwin Press.

Levine, D. (1991). Creating effective schools: Findings and implications from research and practice. *Phi Delta Kappan, 72,* 389–393.

Lieberman, A., Saxl, E., & Mills, M. (1988). Teacher leadership: Ideology and practice. In A. Lieberman (Ed.), *Building a professional culture in schools.* New York: Teachers College Press.

Manthei, J. (1992, April). *The mentor teacher as leader: The motives, characteristics, and needs of seventy-three experienced teachers who seek a new leadership role.* Paper presented at the annual meeting of the American Educational Research Association, San Francisco. (ERIC Document Service No. ED 346 042)

Mirel, T. (1994). School reform unplugged: The Bensinville New American School Project. *American Educational Research Journal, 31,* 481–515.

Murphy, J. (1992). *The landscape of leadership preparation: Reframing the education of school administrators.* Newbury Park, CA: Corwin Press.

Nias, J. (1992). *Whole school curriculum in the primary school.* Bristol, PA: Falmer Press.

Ogawa, R., & Hart, A. (1985). The effect of principals on the instructional performance of schools. *Journal of Educational Administration, 22*(1), 59–72.

Pajak, E., & Glickman, C. (1989). Dimensions of school district improvement. *Educational Leadership, 46*(8), 61–64.

Purkey, S., & Smith, M. (1983). Effective schools: A review. *Elementary School Journal, 83,* 427–452.

Sarason, S. B. (1993). *The case for change: Rethinking the preparation of educators.* San Francisco: Jossey-Bass.

Sarason, S. B. (1997). *How schools might be governed and why?* New York: Teachers College Press.

Senge, P. (1994). *The fifth dimension: The art and practice of the learning organization.* New York: Currency Doubleday.

Steadman, L. (1987). It's time we change the effective schools formula. *Phi Delta Kappan, 69*(3), 215–224.

Thompson, S. E. (Ed.). (1993). *Principals for our changing schools: The knowledge and skillbase.* Fairfax, VA: National Policy Board for Educational Administration.

Weise, C. (1995). The four "I's" of school reform: How interests, ideologies, information, and institution affect teachers and principals. *Harvard Educational Review, 65*(4), 571–592.

Weise, C., Cambone, J., & Wyeth, A. (1992). Trouble in paradise: Teacher conflicts and shared decision making. *Educational Administration Quarterly, 28,* 350–367.

CHAPTER 15

Staff Development: A Linchpin for Leadership[1]

Barbara L. Licklider and Carol Fulton

> As a pivotal institution in the lives of young people, the high school can serve as a linchpin in efforts to improve the American condition, touching the lives of almost every teenager and, consequently, contributing to the betterment of the country.
> —National Association of Secondary School Principals (1996), p. 3

The report, *Breaking Ranks: Changing an American Institution* (National Association of Secondary School Principals, 1996) can be the spark that propels educators to lead one of the most exciting educational eras in American history. The report, by its very title, recognizes that old ways that no longer work must yield to change.

Over the past two decades, a long series of reports issued by various educational organizations and government agencies has called into question the quality and effectiveness of our educational institutions. These reports, all sharply critical of education, agree that institutions are not preparing students to meet the demands of the next century. Such concerns have now reached watershed proportions as the social and economic future of the nation hangs in the balance.

In response, national and state leaders are calling for significant restructuring of education. Few commentators believe that our tradition of "tinkering toward improvement" is likely to lead to desired results. Instead, society's needs require a *fundamental reconceptualization* of the very purposes and practices of education.

The changes for school renewal will happen only through the efforts of the educators practicing within the institution. Regrettably, however, many of those practitioners are not prepared for this mission, making the continuous professional development of our country's educators more critical now than at any time in our history.

Sadly, our traditionally implemented, one-size-fits-all, in-service-based staff development has failed to provide teachers with the skills and knowledges needed to help prepare students for the future (Bennett & Rotheiser-Bennett, 1990; Garmston, 1991; Marczely, 1996; McBride, 1994; Sparks, 1983). Indeed, despite what we now know about learning and the implications for teaching, as well as the vast literature on staff development, little change has occurred during the last century in the way that American teachers teach (Cuban, 1990; Warren, 1985). Fundamental changes in the American high school experience for students have also eluded educators.

Failure to embrace education as a true profession wherein the practitioners have an obligation for their continued, personalized professional growth has contributed to the failure of staff development programs. Marczely (1996) submits that, in the quest "... to provide for the professional development of teachers, we have ignored two of the fundamental traits of a true professional: individuality and self-determination" (p. vii).

Transforming staff development for the year 2000 is a key challenge facing leaders of quality schools. Clearly our casual approach to staff development to date and our failure to heed what we know about how professionals learn and work are intricately linked to the low-quality experience of our students and the lack of educational results as judged by the public. Yet recommended changes (e.g., new curricular frameworks, assess-

---
Barbara L. Licklider and Carol Fulton, Iowa State University

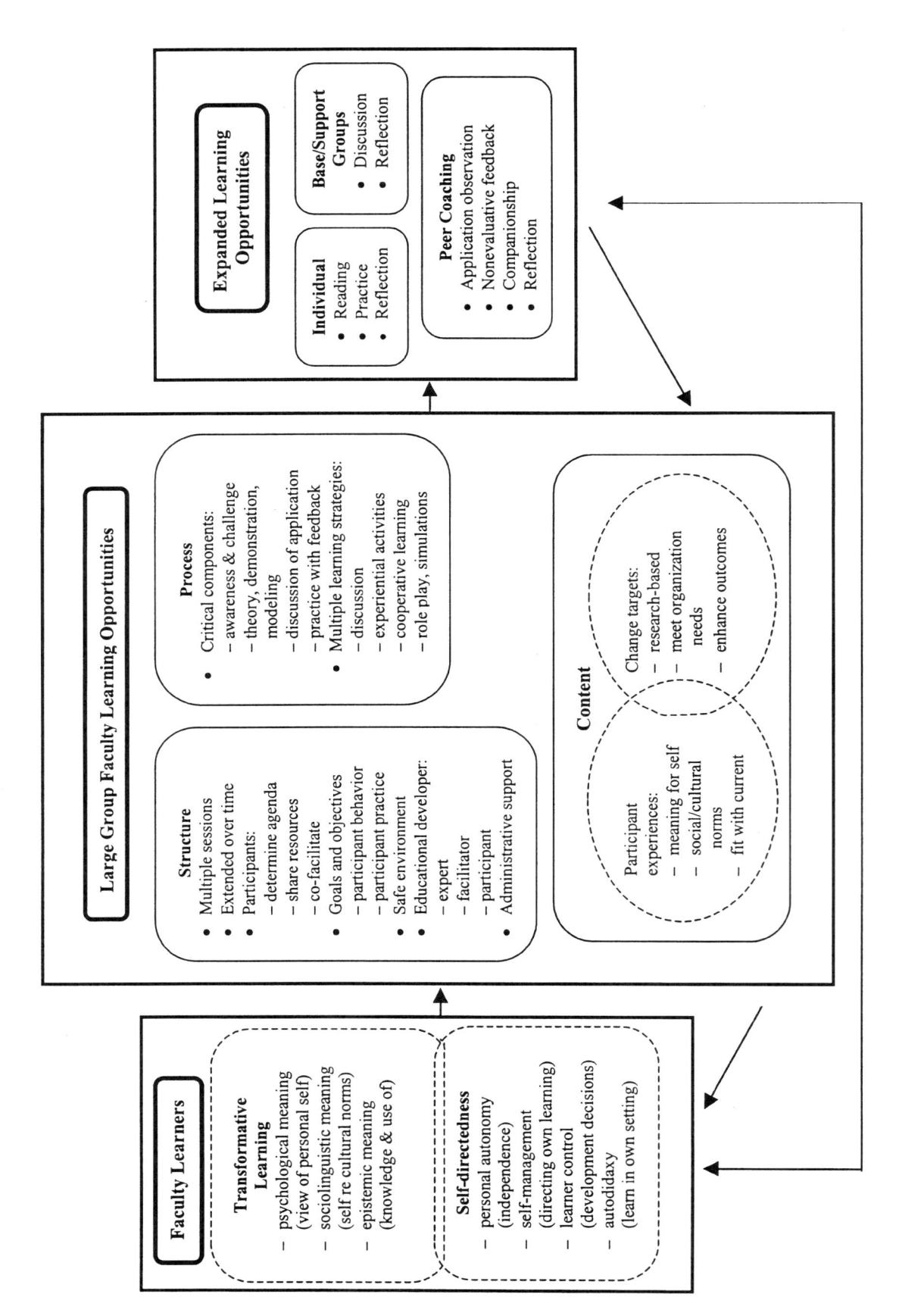

Figure 1. An interactive model of professional development.

ment, and student-centered approaches to learning) alone will not result in gains if faculty do not incorporate them into practice. Seen in this light, staff development is the linchpin to student learning. Improvements in educational outcomes and institutional effectiveness hinge on improvements in the preparation of our staff.

However, such improvements cannot rest entirely on the will of individual teachers. Rather, collective effort and conversation about priorities are needed but are unlikely to happen unless school leaders "expect and invite it into being" (Palmer, 1993, p. 9). Leaders cannot coerce such conversation but they can, in the words of Palmer, "offer people pathways and permissions to do things they want to do but feel unable to do for themselves" (p. 9).

Obviously, a leader's ability to tap the collective wisdom of teachers, create community, and foster dialogue rest on a solid understanding of staff development. Leaders of quality schools need a depth of knowledge in adult education, and staff development research as well as a working model to bring these to life in the schools.

The interactive model of professional development described here (see Figure 1) is buttressed by recent theoretical work in adult education and effective staff development. These two bodies of literature lay the foundation and framework for renewing staff development.

UNDERPINNINGS FROM ADULT EDUCATION

The vast literature on adult education and adult learning is rich in its implications for staff development. This work includes perspectives on self-directed learning (Candy, 1991; Knowles, 1984), transformative learning (Mezirow, 1991), reflective practice (Schön, 1983), and community (Palmer, 1993).

Self-Directed Learning

Theoretical work on self-directed learning highlights the idea that learning occurs all the time. The challenge facing staff developers, then, is to help teachers learn what they want to learn. A self-directed model of professional development would assume that teachers will initiate efforts to improve, make their own decisions about what they want to learn and how learning should occur, and pursue learning apart from sponsored efforts (Cranton, 1994). Further, staff developers in this model cannot do the learning for teachers. Instead, the role of the developer is to provide activities and to offer support, guidance, and expertise as needed.

Reflective Practice

Central to reflective practice is the idea that educators continually examine what they do and the contexts in which they do it. From this perspective, teaching is more than techniques and routine. As teachers pause to reflect critically on their actions and behaviors, they analyze the logic of their thinking, seek to understand what they do and reasons why they do it, and imagine alternative structures and processes. Through such reflective practice, educators improve their teaching and their students' learning.

Transformative Learning

Mezirow's work (1991), like Schön's, highlights the idea that reflection is key to learning. Learners have perspectives that guide how they see and understand the world. Any of these perspectives can be flawed or distorted. It is through the process of critical reflection that learners become aware of flaws, challenge old beliefs, and potentially fashion new understandings.

Building on these ideas, Brookfield (1990, 1995) argues that the key to improving teaching lies in uncovering hidden assumptions. To identify and examine these assumptions, he offers several strategies, including reflection on their autobiographies as teachers and learners, examining teaching practices through the eyes of students, engaging in critical conversations with colleagues and inviting them to watch what we do, and understanding practice in light of theoretical literature.

Community

Current views of staff development emphasize the need for conversation and community. This view is captured by Palmer's appeal for "a good talk about teaching." Such dialogue promotes the sharing of knowledge among educators and fosters the development of a broader identity than that of individual teachers.

UNDERPINNINGS FROM EFFECTIVE STAFF DEVELOPMENT RESEARCH

These insights about adult learners have implications for framing practice. Notions such as reflective practice, community, and transformative and self-directed learning all characterize learning as "over the long haul." Participants in reflective conversation need to spend time evolving ground rules and establishing mutual trust; they need to find ways of talking about their experiences with colleagues; and they need opportunities for demonstration, practice, feedback, and coaching. To accomplish these goals, our tradition of "sit-and-get" inservice must give way to new structures and forms to support adult learners.

These themes long have been echoed in the research on effective staff development (Butler, 1989; Joyce & Showers, 1988; Licklider, 1986; Sparks, 1983). As such, this body of literature provides insights into structuring learning experiences for adult learners and using the structure, content, and process needed to support learning.

Structure

Single-session activities have little effect on educator behavior. Schedules for staff development must include multiple sessions over extended time to provide the opportunity to (a) confront new knowledge and skills in small chunks, (b) try out new learning and adapt it to individual settings, (c) address different concerns of participants that occur at various stages of the change process, and (d) become comfortable trying unfamiliar techniques and talking honestly with each other.

Effective staff development programs have clear, specific goals and objectives. Such goals should be participant driven and connected to teachers' actual work in the classroom. Administrative support is also an important determinant of successful staff development. Where principals support change, participate in learning with teachers, provide incentives for change, reinforce change, and include change in school policies there is far more improvement than where principals are less supportive.

Content

The content of effective staff development efforts is based and paced in accord with participant needs and should engage teachers in the concrete tasks of teaching.

Process

Effective staff development consists of multiple components—diagnosing skills; providing the theory base for new approaches; demonstrating their application, practice, and feedback; and coaching. A variety of instructional strategies may be used, including modeling, videotapes, detailed narrative descriptions, cooperative learning, and experiential activities. Microteaching and role playing are two effective strategies for providing opportunities for practice and feedback.

Base groups or study teams and peer coaching also are effective for expanding learning. Such extended openings provide additional opportunities for dialogue and reflection, promote accountability, and nourish mutual support and companionship to foster a desire for continued development.

AN INTERACTIVE MODEL OF PROFESSIONAL DEVELOPMENT

These lessons from adult education and effective staff development provide the foundation and framework for the interactive model for professional development depicted in Figure 1 (adapted from Licklider, Schnelker, & Fulton, in press). While staff development efforts are typically directed at the improvement of learning and teaching, the model could be applied to any targeted area of school renewal (e.g., curriculum integration, outcome development and assessment, or positive school environment).

Underlying Assumptions about Adult Learners

Transformative learning and self-directedness are assumptions underlying this comprehensive model of faculty development. Mezirow's (1991) discussion of transformative learning applies to teachers just as much as it does to other adult learners. Educators have assumptions about their practice. These assumptions include how they perceive themselves as educators, how they interpret social and cultural roles and expectations, and what epistemic perspectives they hold on "what counts" as effective teaching (Brookfield, 1995; Cranton, 1994). Any of these perspectives may have what Mezirow (1991) calls premise distortions. Changes in practice occur as a result of changed assumptions. Such transformations occur through the process of becoming aware of one's assumptions and examining them through critical self-reflection.

Supporting the preference for self-directedness among adult learners, the model includes provisions to promote and take advantage of participants' predisposition for all aspects of self-directedness: independent thought and action; willingness and capacity to conduct their own education; decision making about goals, strategies, and evaluation of their own development; and pursuit of learning in their own natural settings.

Large-Group Sessions: Structure

Such transformative and self-directed learning is not instantaneous. Integrating new practices can be difficult. Lack of institutional support, student resistance, competing demands for time all play a part in educators' retreating to traditional practices and highlight the need for ongoing support. At the heart of the model is the aim of immersing educators in educational environments to build strong, ongoing support groups to sustain long-lasting change. The following sections describe the framework to support such transformative and self-directed learning.

Schedule

Because adult learners need time to identify, challenge, and modify their beliefs and assumptions as well as their behaviors, a quality staff development model provides for regular sessions over an extended period of time. Such scheduling provides participants ample opportunity to complete the processes of both cognitive and behavior changes.

Participants' Roles

In addition to learning, participants determine the goals and objectives of the program, share resources with each other, and cofacilitate presentation of the program's content.

Goals and Objectives

The most effective development activities are the result of faculty interest in their own professional development and their commitment to shared outcomes. Recall, for example, that programs designed to improve teaching focus on instructional behaviors that affect student performance. Programs designed to examine and change curriculum must target the connections with better preparation of students for productive citizenry in the 21st century. Increasing learner control of goals and objectives enhances the learning environment, and practicing behavior changes gives participants' immediate experiences to discuss and reflect upon, thus intensifying commitment to professional development.

Environment

Changing practice is difficult work. A crucial part of this process is the opportunity for ongoing critical reflection of practice and opportunity for experimentation with new behaviors in a context that is supportive and nonjudgmental (Tiberius & Billson, 1991). Educators need to be comfortable trying unfamiliar techniques, talking honestly with each other about their successes in the classroom as well as their defeats, and openly seeking suggestions. The willingness to be open and genuine can occur only in trusting and collaborative environments.

Educational Developer

In addition to being an "expert" in the target area, the educational developer must help participants become self-directed learners. Recommendations from Cranton (1994) to encourage participant control include (a) withdrawing directiveness gradually over several meetings; (b) asking and expecting faculty to make more and larger decisions over time; (c) using group work and other interactive techniques rather than lecture; (d) encouraging faculty to consult each other and form networks; (e) asking for, using, and relying on faculty members' experiences with teaching; and (f) stating the role of an instructional developer and the expectations of faculty openly and explicitly. Thus, the role of the educational developer moves from expert to facilitator to participant as participants assume greater responsibility for the program.

Principal Support

Modeling risk taking and actively participating in all aspects of the development program are powerful ways for principals to support teachers in their development efforts. Principals must also support participation in development programs by providing opportunities, encouragement, incentives, release time, and financial support. It is also critical that the principal support risk-taking by allowing voluntary participation and keeping participation and performance independent of formal faculty review processes.

Large-Group Sessions: Content

The interactive model is driven by the knowledge of faculty participants, recognizing their prior knowledge and experiences. Beginning where educators are, programs must provide activities that help them fashion deeper understandings. To this end, educators must become learners themselves. Over time, this allows educators to make explicit their beliefs and assumptions. As educators modify their understanding on one topic, questions are raised about other related topics. In this way, participants determine the order in which topics are addressed and the content of the program.

Large-Group Sessions: Process

The process of educator behavior change involves (a) articulating beliefs and assumptions about the targeted area of development, (b) identifying problematic situations, (c) describing behaviors intended to resolve problematic situations, and (d) developing a rationale that links beliefs to new, more effective behaviors (Rando & Menges, 1991). These steps are consistent with the first three phases of effective staff development: (a) diagnosing and building awareness for the need for change, (b) providing the theory and then demonstrating and modeling more effective strategies, and (c) discussing application. The remaining steps (practicing with feedback and coaching) ensure that the modified beliefs and assumptions get translated into actual behavioral change. As coaching usually takes place in the natural setting and not in regular sessions, it is treated in the model as an activity to extend learning rather than as part of a large group session.

Expanded Learning Opportunities

Multiple instructional strategies are used in effective programs. Opportunities for both small- and large-group discussion should be maximized. Between regular, large-group in-service sessions, staff development is facilitated with three types of expanded learning opportunities: individual activities, base groups or study teams, and peer coaching.

Individual activities are included to allow participants the opportunity to pursue their own particular interests as well as promote the goals and objectives of school renewal. Activities might include, but are not limited to, reading assignments, practice in natural settings, and personal reflections about their experiences.

Base groups and study teams provide participants the opportunity to discuss in small groups the content and activities experienced in large-group sessions. Base groups and study teams can also engage in assignments such as additional readings and exercises to increase awareness of more effective skills. Finally, small-group interaction contributes to establishing a nonthreatening environment which promotes growth and development.

Although peer coaching is typically associated with improving teaching and learning, it is included in the model to shape new behaviors targeted in any development program. In general, pairs of participants observe each other, applying new behaviors in the natural setting and providing nonevaluative feedback, companionship and support, and analysis during the application process. For example, partners may observe each others' classrooms to see the application of effective questioning techniques. Pairs may also critique each others' interactions with parents, performance in a faculty meeting, leadership of a committee meeting, or attempts to integrate curriculum.

Evaluation of the Model

The staff development model with its emphasis on instruction, support, and feedback provides a number of sources to study the change process. Reflecting the link between faculty development and student development, this evaluation is twofold: to study the effect of the model on teacher thinking and practice and, subsequently, to determine the impact on students.

For example, group discussion about the content and application of active learning and other effective teaching strategies, five-minute papers about how the program affects views of learning and teaching, and journal entries about strategies and concepts presented in a lesson provide evidence of the impact on teacher thinking and practice as well as insights into the evolution of change. Similarly, a variety of methods can be used to monitor the effect on students (e.g., attitude surveys, achievement tests, and teacher reports on student change). In addition, it would be worthwhile to track student outcomes over time. For example, longer studies of the impact of learner-centered approaches could attempt to address questions such as these: What happens to students who have learner-centered instruction two years in a row? When do attitudes begin to change? Longer studies may shed light on some of the complexities of teaching and learning and provide formative information that can be used to improve the quality of the learning experience for both students and teachers.

STUDENTS AND TEACHERS AT THE CENTER: IMPLICATIONS FOR LEADERSHIP

As we near the turn of the century, American education stands at the crossroads of change, holding onto teacher-directed approaches on the one hand and being pulled toward learner-centered approaches on the other. Our traditional system of education, while still considered by many to be the best in the world, has been found wanting by many others. The host of criticisms and concerns about institutional effectiveness and poor student performance have led to calls for higher standards, curricular changes, and student-centered instructional approaches to improve student outcomes. To many reformers, the success of current restructuring efforts rests squarely on quality staff development (Lieberman, 1995; Darling-Hammond & McLaughlin, 1995).

In recent years, the conviction has been growing that staff development itself must be restructured. No longer can we be content with sit-and-get approaches where educators passively receive knowledge from experts. New conceptions of staff development see educators as learners actively engaged in their own development. Lieberman (1995) points out that much of what we want for our students is the same as what is needed by educators. She writes,

> people learn best through active involvement and through thinking about and becoming articulate about what they have learned. Processes, practices, and policies built on this view of learning are at the heart of a more expanded view of teacher development that encourages teachers to involve themselves as learners—in much the same way as they wish their students would. (p. 592)

School restructuring efforts cannot rest on individual teachers attempting to construct classroom practice in isolation. Teachers need "opportunities to discuss, think about, try out, and hone new practices" (p. 593). To meet these needs, professional development must create new forms of collegiality so that teachers can reflect critically on practice and construct new meanings about content, pedagogy, and learners.

Darling-Hammond and McLaughlin (1995) contend that the

> success of this agenda ultimately turns on teachers' success in accomplishing the serious and difficult tasks of learning the skills and perspectives assumed by new visions of practice and unlearning the practices and beliefs about students and instruction that have dominated their professional lives to date. Yet few occasions and little support for such professional development exist in teachers' environments. (p. 597)

This quote reveals what Palmer (1993) would call the "weak culture of leadership" in education. Educational literature is full of references that document the need for professionals to come together to talk with peers and build on their collective wisdom. Hidden beneath the cloak of "professionalism," however, lies a subtle assumption that the responsibility for these conversations depends entirely on professionals themselves. The pages grow strangely silent on what is needed to bring about these conversations and seldom address the role of leaders in fostering these conversations. This gap reveals what Palmer calls a "silent conspiracy" between educators who "don't want to be led and executives who find it safer to administer than lead" (p. 9).

Palmer (1993), Lieberman (1995), and Darling-Hammond and McLaughlin (1995) all point to the critical role that leaders can (and should) play in current attempts to restructure education. Leaders can invite and expect good conversations about teaching and at the same time create structures that allow professionals to draw on their collective wisdom to enact change.

In the end, the direction that education takes and the success of current reforms depend in good measure on school leaders. Educators' roles and instructional practices are ultimately embedded in organizational arrangements and structures. Leaders with a broad vision of staff development can challenge the status quo that has dominated the lives of educators and subsequently affected the experience of students. Such leaders see staff development not as a frill or luxury that can be dispensed with in times of fiscal stringency but as an imperative for preparing students for citizenship in the 21st century.

ENDNOTE

1 This work is supported by the Center for Teaching Excellence, the College of Education, and the College of Engineering at Iowa State University.

REFERENCES

Brookfield, S. (1990). *The skillful teacher: On technique, trust, and responsiveness in the classroom.* San Francisco: Jossey-Bass.

Brookfield, S. (1995). *Becoming a critically reflective teacher.* San Francisco: Jossey-Bass.

Butler, J. A. (1989). *A review of adult learning theory and staff development research* (ED308334). Washington, DC: Office of Educational Research and Improvement.

Candy, P. (1991). *Self-direction for lifelong learning.* San Francisco: Jossey-Bass.

Cranton, P. (1994). Self-directed and transformative instructional development. *Journal of Higher Education, 65*(6), 726–744.

Cruickshank, D. R. (1987). *Reflective teaching: The preparation of students of teaching.* Reston, VA: Association of Teacher Educators.

Cuban, L. (1990). Reforming again, again, and again. *Educational Researcher, 19*(1), 3–13.

Darling-Hammond, L., & McLaughlin, M. (1995). Policies that support professional development in an era of reform. *Phi Delta Kappan, 76*(8), 597–604.

Gardiner, L. (1994). *Redesigning higher education: Producing dramatic gains in student learning.* Washington, DC: Association for the Studies of Higher Education. (ERIC Higher Education Report, Vol. 23, No. 7)

Garmston, R. J. (1991). Staff development as social architects. *Educational Leadership, 49*(3), 64–65.

Joyce, B. R., Bennett, B., & Rolheiser-Bennett, C. (1990). The self-educating teacher: Empowering teachers through research. In B. Joyce (Ed.), *Changing school culture through staff development: 1990 ASCD yearbook* (pp. 26–40). Alexandria, VA: Association for Supervision and Curriculum Development.

Joyce, B. R., & Showers, B. (1988). *Power in staff development through research on training.* Alexandria, VA: Association for Supervision and Curriculum Development.

Knowles, M. (1984). *Andragogy in action: Applying modern principles of adult learning.* San Francisco: Jossey-Bass.

Licklider, B. L. D. (1986). *Examination of a site-based peer coaching inservice model.* Unpublished doctoral dissertation, Iowa State University, Ames.

Licklider, B. L., Fulton, C., & Schnelker, D. L. (in press). Revisioning faculty development for changing times: The foundation and framework. *Journal of Organization, Staff, and Faculty Development.*

Lieberman, A. (1995). Practices that support teacher development. *Phi Delta Kappan 76*(8), 591–596.

Marczely, B. (1996) *Personalizing professional growth: Staff development that works.* Thousand Oaks, CA: Corwin Press.

McBride, R. E. (1994). Teacher attitudes toward staff development: A symbolic relationship at best. *Journal of Staff Development 15*(2), 37.

Mezirow, J. (1991). *Transformative dimensions of adult learning.* San Francisco: Jossey-Bass.

National Association of Secondary School Principals. (1996). *Breaking ranks: Changing an American institution* (Report of the National Association of Secondary School Principals in Partnership with the Carnegie Foundations for the Advancement of Teaching). Reston, VA: Author.

Palmer, P. (1993). Good talk about good teaching: Improving teaching through conversation and community. *Change, 25*(6), 8–14.

Rando, W. C., & Menges, R. J. (1991). How practice is shaped by personal theories. In R. J. Menges & M. D. Svenicki (Eds.), *College teaching: From theory to practice* (New Directions for Teaching and Learning, No. 45, pp. 7–14). San Francisco: Jossey-Bass.

Ross, D. D. (1989). First steps in developing a reflective approach. *Journal of Teacher Education, 40*(2), 22–30.

Schön, D. A. (1983). *The reflective practitioner: How professionals think in action.* New York: Basic Books.

Sparks, G. M. (1983). Synthesis of research on staff development for effective teaching. *Educational Leadership, 41*(3), 65–72.

Tiberius, R. G., and Billson, J. M. (1991). The social context of teaching and learning. In R. J. Menges & M. D. Svenicki (Eds.), *College teaching: From theory to practice* (New Directions in Teaching and Learning, No. 45, pp. 67–86). San Francisco: Jossey-Bass.

Warren, D. (1985). Learning from experience: History and teacher education. *Educational Researcher, 14*(10), 5–12.

Zeichner, K., & Liston, D. (1987). Teaching student teachers to reflect. *Harvard Educational Review, 57*(1), 23–48.

CHAPTER 16

Principals' Interpersonal Sensitivity Toward Teachers, Central Office Personnel, Parents, Business Leaders, and Community Members

John R. Hoyle and Arnold Oates

As America and its schools move into the next century, leadership for quality schools must improve. The traditional school managers of the past 30 years will not be successful in the years ahead. They must become school leaders who can help shape our schools and communities to become just and moral places. A key attribute that an elementary, middle, or high school principal must have in order to accomplish this is interpersonal sensitivity.

Interpersonal sensitivity, though only one of the 21 performance domains identified by the National Policy Board for Educational Administration, is perhaps the most important. The NPBEA (1993) defines sensitivity as follows: "Perceiving the needs and concerns of others; dealing with others; working with others in emotionally stressful situations or in conflict; managing conflict; obtaining feedback; recognizing multicultural differences; and relating to people of varying backgrounds" (Thompson, 1993, p. 15: 3). Principals may possess skills in the other 20 performance domains but lack the interpersonal sensitivity necessary for working closely with others. This deficit can negatively affect a principal's ability to lead effectively.

Principals who lack interpersonal sensitivity skills often have difficulty seeing themselves as others do. They tend to talk one way but act another. Some believe that they have the sensitivity of Mother Teresa when in reality they treat people in a manner more like that of Attila the Hun. Principals may claim that they value and believe in their staff but turn around and psychologically "drop kick" them to get things done. These principals have learned about the humanizing elements of Theory Y but still apply the dictator tactics of Theory X (Hoyle & Crenshaw, 1996; McGregor, 1960). The results of self-examination measures or ratings of their skills by others may be useful in raising principals' awareness of their interpersonal skill level and foster improvement of these skills.

It is important that principals model sensitivity skills to establish a pattern for others to follow. Unless teachers, staff, and students sense that their principal cares about their needs and their concerns and is making a special effort to involve them in important issues, very little progress will be made toward an empowered, caring community. Thompson (1990), who recognized the importance of interpersonal skills to effective functioning of building principals, wrote that "We know from two national studies of effective principals that they must be competent with people, all kinds of people" (p. 2). However, perhaps the most important relationship is that between the principal and her or his teachers. Barth (1991), the founding director of the Principals' Center at Harvard University, found "no characteristic of a good school more pervasive than a healthy teacher-principal relationship—and no characteristic of a troubled school more common than a troubled, embattled administrator-teacher relationship" (p. 19). Barth suggested that in a given school this relationship has "an extraordinary amplifying effect [and that] it models what all relationships will be" (p. 19). Competent, sensitive principals interact, talk, console, listen, cheer, advise, hug (selectively), cry, and occasionally reprimand as required. These behaviors must be consistent, deeply felt, and honest if principals are to be the kind of leaders needed for schools in the year 2000 and beyond.

Being interpersonally sensitive in school settings is not always easy. Glickman and Pajak (1983) noted that the organizational patterns of the school workplace inhibit interpersonal sensitivity of the entire staff. Factory-

---

John R. Hoyle and Arnold Oates, Texas A&M University

like routines, often the result of policy and administrative directives, frequently regiment the lives of teachers and staff much like those of factory workers. Sensitive principals must strive to change the school environment from routine, noninspiring places of drudgery to joyful centers of learning where teachers and staff are energized by the principal's supportive and caring attitude. And in a time of heightened stress on multiculturalism, gender sensitivity, political correctness, and diversity, all principals need to interact and mix with the entire school community more than ever before (Delpit, 1995). The effectiveness of these interactions will depend to a large degree on the principal's interpersonal sensitivity skills.

Most principals believe that they are sensitive in their daily encounters with teachers, staff, central office personnel, community patrons, and students. However, since interpersonal sensitivity is often in the eye of the beholder, the principal may not be perceived as such by others, thus making the concept difficult to measure in a complex school setting. Bolman and Deal (1993) suggested three steps that principals can take to become more sensitive and to empower others in their school community.

1. Open up communication. (Spend time with people. Listen to them. Attend to their feelings, concerns, and aspirations.)
2. Ask for feedback. (Without feedback, leaders easily become blind to how they're really seen. If the feedback is surprising or negative, listen, acknowledge its importance, and share your own feelings.)
3. Empower everyone. (Increase participation, provide support, share information, and move decision making as far down the organization as possible.) (p. 60)

A SEARCH FOR INTERPERSONAL SENSITIVITY OF PRINCIPALS

A superintendent of a medium-sized South Texas school district consisting of 26 schools conducted a *Gallup Principal Inventory* and discovered gaps in the "Developer" and "Relator" skills of the district's principals. These two skill areas center on facilitating the growth of teachers and collaborative efforts between the principal and the teaching staff. As a result of identifying these two gaps in the skill base of the principals, and in light of other supportive data gathered from central office administrators, board members, and community members, the superintendent engaged the authors to conduct research and staff development in the area of interpersonal sensitivity of principals. The superintendent was interested in helping the principals assess their interpersonal sensitivity toward classroom teachers, central office personnel, parents, business leaders, and community members.

Purpose of the Study

The literature on the principalship is filled with research on leadership style and behavior, instructional leadership, and best practice; however, the research is practically silent on interpersonal sensitivity and how to measure this skill. As stated above, interpersonal sensitivity is in the eye of the beholder, making it a difficult concept to assess objectively. The research reported here was undertaken with these difficult measurement problems in mind. The project had two major purposes: (a) to conduct in-service training for 26 principals and (b) to administer and validate three newly created self-report instruments purported to measure the interpersonal sensitivity of school principals.

Study Participants and Instruments

Data were gathered from 26 principals and their staffs by using three self-report instruments found in *Interpersonal Sensitivity* (Hoyle & Crenshaw, 1996). These instruments are the Staff Sensitivity Scale, Principals' Sensitivity Toward the Central Office Scale, and Parent, Business, and Community Agency Sensitivity Scale. These scales were designed as end-of-chapter skill-building exercises to assist practicing principals in assessing their sensitivity skills and conducting personal research to improve their leadership performance. They were developed from the research literature on interpersonal intelligence and behavior and effective leadership characteristics. After conducting a pilot test of the instruments with graduate students and faculty at Texas A&M University, the developer made alterations to help strengthen the content and construct validity. Written comments about clarity of the items were encouraged and recorded from the participants in the actual study.

The first instrument, a 39-item Staff Sensitivity Scale, was administered to 1,231 teachers in the 26 schools. Of these, 573 (47%) of the Staff Sensitivity Scales were returned and deemed usable for analysis. The second instrument, the Principals' Sensitivity Toward the Central Office Scale, was completed and returned by 18 of the 26 principals. A third measure, the Parent, Business, Community Agency Sensitivity Scale, was completed and returned by 16 of 26 principals. The results from the responses of 573 teachers and 18 principals to these measures provide insights about the strengths and weaknesses in sensitivity skills of the principals.

RESULTS FROM THE STAFF SENSITIVITY SCALE

The authors believe that the data gathered from the Staff Sensitivity Scale are valid since participants were assured that no attempt would be made to identify individual principals by name or school. This assurance was given not only to provide anonymity but also to encourage principals to use the teachers' responses on the 39 items for feedback and self-reflection and to guide them in creating personal professional development plans. If the principals had thought that their interpersonal sensitivity profiles would be shared with colleagues and especially the superintendent, little if any participation by the principals would have occurred.

One major objective of this project was to help principals gain feedback about their interpersonal sensitivity skills, not to conduct precise research which controls as much variation as possible. For this reason and others stated above, no effort was made to disaggregate data from the Staff Sensitivity Scale by individual school or principal. The unit of analysis was, instead, the combined responses of all teachers about 26 of their district's principals. The analysis of the 39 items was conducted using a selective sampling process that included every tenth questionnaire. The object of the sampling was to scan the 573 instruments for trends that could lead to more in-depth item analysis on all 573 instruments.

This sampling of the Staff Sensitivity Scale revealed that, as a whole, the 26 principals exhibit high levels of interpersonal sensitivity. The teachers perceived that their principals listen to them, laugh with them, praise their accomplishments, delegate important tasks to them, are concerned about the teachers' families and, to some extent, their careers, and set high standards for students and teachers. The teachers also perceived that their principals help them improve their performance, give them encouragement, help them deal with parent complaints, accurately evaluate their teaching performance, and provide helpful staff development. Moreover, the teachers believed that their principals are tactful and caring, sensitive to various ethnic, cultural, and gender groups and issues, back them up when needed, communicate clearly, and treat them with respect. In short, these principals make teachers feel important. Teachers also perceived that principals share in their victories and defeats, care for them as unique persons, and inspire them to "be better than they were before." Teachers reported that the principals show their love for all kids, keep their word, maintain confidentiality with teachers, and appear to be servant leaders. They perceived that the buildings are kept clean and safe and that principals acquire needed supplies for each school.

Although no glaring areas of insensitivity appeared in data collected on this Scale, a few areas are worthy of discussion to assist the principals in improving their skills. A complete analysis of the data on two items revealed that 342 of the 573 teachers responded that their principal rarely or never "discusses the teachers' career goals," and 99 said that their principal rarely or never "makes them feel important." Moreover, the sample data on other items showed trends indicating that the principal rarely or never "asks the teachers about their family" and sometimes "doesn't care for all teachers as unique persons" or "give them enough encouragement." To facilitate personal growth, each principal was given a copy of her or his teachers' responses on the 39 items for comparison with the overall aggregate data. Principals were encouraged to use the data in the development of their personal and professional growth plans.

RESULTS FROM THE PRINCIPALS' SENSITIVITY TOWARD CENTRAL OFFICE SCALE

Conflicts often occur between the building principal and personnel in the central office (Hoyle, 1994; Prasch, 1990). Conflict has been heightened in recent years by emphasis on site-based decision making which calls for greater autonomy at the building level (Bailey, 1991). This autonomy can create a barrier between central office administrators, principals, and teachers in the areas of curriculum, budget allocations, staff development, and management. In efforts to serve students more effectively, the sense of "who is in charge" has been moved from solely top-down central office control to include local principals and campus teams. This national effort to share the power at the campus level has produced many success stories about student performance and increased parent and community involvement in the management of schools (Neal, 1991; Patterson, 1993). However, the lines of authority, accountability, and communication can become blurred making conflicts between principals and those they "answer to" almost inevitable.

The Principals' Sensitivity Toward the Central Office Scale was designed to measure some of the conflict indicators so that these can be analyzed and acted on to improve relations between building administrators and central office personnel. The responses of 18 of the 26 principals who completed this measure revealed that in their estimation they exhibit interpersonal sensitivity toward their colleagues in the central office. Almost all of these principals reported that they are sensitive to the restrictions placed on the superintendent by the school board (item 1), and 11 of the 18 reported being sensitive to the feelings of central office staff who think that they are the principals' bosses on all matters affecting the principals' schools (item 2). The data showed, however, that 1 principal is not sensitive to these bosses, and 6 are only "sometimes" sensitive. Sixteen principals are sensitive to collective judgment about which decisions need to be made at the central office and which need to be made at the local school (item 3). Although 15 are sensitive to the feelings of teachers who are told by central office staff to teach certain curriculum (item 4), 1 principal is not so sensitive on the curriculum issue, and 2 principals are "sometimes" sensitive.

Being sensitive to the reasons for screening of teacher applicants first by the central office personnel department was reported by 15 of the respondents, but 3 principals reportedly are not sensitive to these reasons (item 5). Often, site-based teams believe that they should have more control over selecting teachers and administrators since they represent those who will work and socialize with the new staff members. The greatest difficulty being sensitive to central office personnel comes when budgets for site-based programs at a school are cut by the central office staff in favor of another school that makes a stronger case for the funds. Of the 18 principals, 9 reported not being sensitive to such a decision, 5 said they were sensitive, and 2 reported being sensitive "sometimes" (item 6). Most principals are sensitive to the fact that with site-based decision making come greater accountability demands from the central office (item 7). With more autonomy comes greater responsibility to perform. If improvement does not occur over time, the principals must be sensitive to the idea that the central office will eventually intervene and change either the program or the principal (Prasch, 1990).

Responses to item 8 showed almost all of the 16 principals being sensitive to problems they could cause to the central office by leading their school on a tangent that runs counter to district norms and policies. Only 2 principals reported not being sensitive to that concern. In addition, 15 principals said they are sensitive to pressures that parents can place on the superintendent and the board to change a program that a principal's site-based team may have implemented (item 9). Other responses indicated that principals are sensitive to the needs of teachers and school staff and are willing to push central office staff on their behalf (item 10). This act of leadership or defiance is risky for the principal, especially if student performance does not measure up to the standards of the central office. Pushing for faculty concerns while keeping good relations with the central office is a delicate balancing act and must be pursued in the context of good diplomacy and quality performance as a principal and school.

RESULTS FROM THE PARENT, BUSINESS, AND COMMUNITY AGENCY SENSITIVITY SCALE

Research on successful principals emphasizes the critical importance of including parents, businesses, and community agencies in the operation of schools. Principals in this study were asked to rate their sensitivity to issues involving these groups. The results from responses to 11 of the 20 items on the Parent, Business, and Community Agency Sensitivity Scale were not surprising; however, the responses to nine items raised some questions. Most of the 16 principals responding to this questionnaire said that they have an effective parent contact plan (item 1) and a well-designed plan to bring parents into their schools (item 3) and that parents can contact them at any time (item 6). All 16 reported that parents view them as being a partner in helping their child (item 4) and that they listen well to parent concerns (item 8). Two principals, however, reported that they sometimes talk down to low-income parents (item 7). All of these principals believe that the parents trust them with their children (item 9), and most know the important and influential parents (item 10). Most of the principals said they listen well to business leaders about their concerns (item 13), are willing to ask businesses for money and equipment for their students (item 19), and trust other community youth agencies to assist their students (item 16). All of these principals reported working hard to include all races and cultures on advisory groups (item 17). Only one principal does not view herself or himself as a servant leader in the community (item 20). Overall, these principals gave affirmative responses about their close work with parents and community groups and believe that they communicate well and often with these groups.

Despite the responses of principals to items 13 and 19 reported above, the authors of this paper have some reservations about how effectively most of the principals in this study work with the business community. For example, when the principals were asked in item 11 if they had widespread contacts with the business community, 10 (more than half) responded "no"; and only eight reported being on a first-name basis with key community and business leaders (item 14). Seven of these principals have no community advisory group of business people and professionals (item 12), and 10 do not bring in community resource people to tutor and speak to staff and students on a regular basis (item 15). Only 6 of these 16 principals plan regular appearances in business and agency offices (item 18). This low visibility and limited interaction with the business and professional community could inhibit a strong partnership relationship or create barriers when principals seek funding or other forms of support from businesses or agencies.

Research indicates that involving parents and others in schools has a strong, positive impact on student performance in school and attainment of life goals (Henderson & Berla, 1994; Skuza, 1997). These partnerships are viewed by observers of successful schools and effective school leaders as a key to high performance by students and teachers. Although principals who are in tune with their business and agency communities do not always agree with their ideas, they are willing to discuss concerns and explore ways that these valuable resources can be utilized in their schools. Effective principals must be sensitive to the desires of business leaders and others who want workers who can read instructions, write legible letters, show up at the job on time, and work well in teams. The authors hope that feedback to the principals from this study will encourage them to reflect on the need to become more visible and more familiar with business and agency personnel who can provide valuable assistance in improving the quality of school programs.

BENEFITS OF THE STUDY

The results of this study have been beneficial in two primary ways. First, this study provides information that can be used to address a perceived need in the area of interpersonal sensitivity of the 26 principals in a South Texas school district. In response to the superintendent's request for assistance in addressing this need, the authors selected and administered three questionnaires: Staff Sensitivity Scale, Principals' Sensitivity Toward the Central Office Scale, and Parent, Business, and Community Agency Sensitivity Scale.

Although the overall sensitivity of the principals appears to be positive, some areas relating to personal attention given teachers could be improved. For example, when 342 of 572 teachers report that their principal rarely or never discusses career goals with them, considerable room for improvement in the principals' interpersonal sensitivity exists. And when 9 of the 18 principals by self-report are insensitive to central office administrators' decisions to award more money to schools that make a better case for the money, some improvement in sensitivity may be warranted. Finally, when principals report themselves as being sensitive to the needs of parents, business, and community agency groups but are unfamiliar with many of the business and agency personnel and have no planned system to engage community leaders in school programming, a sensitivity gap exists. The authors believe that feedback from this study will be of value to the participating principals and that this project has promoted a closer relationship between the world of theory and the "real world" of the principalship. Perhaps the feedback will help principals become more sensitive to staff needs and will encourage them to become better informed and trained to meet the challenges ahead (Hoyle, 1995).

The second way this study has been helpful is that it provided an opportunity for the first large-scale administration of the three research instruments. Comments and questions from those surveyed indicate that a few of the items created confusion for some respondents. This information will be used in refining the wording or placement of some items on the Scales. Data from this study will also assist in strengthening the validity and reliability of these instruments, a necessary step in determining the potential for more widespread use in future research on the critical area of interpersonal sensitivity.

IMPLICATIONS

Researchers at the Center for Creative Leadership found that insensitivity to others was the "primary reason why successful executives tumble off the track to the executive suite" and that "the ability to understand other people's perspectives" distinguished successful leaders (Kouzes & Posner, 1995, p. 190). Kouzes and Posner concluded that "Managers who . . . are insensitive to others fail, because there's a limit to what they can do by themselves. Those leaders who succeed realize that little can be accomplished if people don't feel strong and capable" (p. 191). Interpersonal sensitivity is an essential skill for effective leadership in schools as much as it is in industry. A sensitive principal encourages staff and students to work toward fulfillment of both personal and campus goals. The principal who is not sensitive will be ineffective and the school will be affected negatively (Barth, 1991).

The first step in development of an appropriate level of sensitivity by any leader is awareness. Most principals, however, do not involve others in a formal evaluation of their leadership performance or skills and may be unaware that they are perceived as insensitive. Assessments by teachers of their principal's sensitivity can increase awareness as can self-assessments related to those with whom the principal interacts (e.g., central office personnel, parents, business leaders, and community members). With the implementation of site-based decision making, principals need to know if they are seen as sensititive to others (both on and off campus) in the areas of shared power, delegation of responsibility, and communication (Wohlstetter, Van Kirk, Robertson, & Mohrman, 1997).

The three assessment instruments used in the study reported in this chapter may be useful in increasing principals' awareness of interpersonal sensitivity. Principals in the study stated that it was often difficult to assess how teachers view them. The Staff Sensitivity Scale in particular provides concrete feedback to the principal in a nonthreatening manner concerning staff and teacher views. This information can be used in setting self-improvement goals. The Parent, Business, and Community Sensitivity Scale assesses how effectively principals relate to the community. Results showed that most of the principals in this study did not have strong working relations with the business community and were not acquainted with many community leaders. Depending on data from this scale, a principal may need to set a goal and develop strategies for improvement of relations with others in the community.

How a principal relates to the superintendent and central office staff can influence the allocation of financial and professional development resources. Principals need to be sensitive to political pressures that the superintendent of schools faces from the school board and state governmental agencies. These pressures preclude superintendents having time to visit school campuses as much today as in the past. Principals often state somewhat critically that they "never see the superintendent anymore." Data from the sensitivity assessment instruments may increase the principal's awareness in this area. The Principals' Sensitivity Toward Central Office Scale assesses the relationship between principal and central office staff and can have implications for improved communications and personal sensitivity.

Knowing her or his level of interpersonal sensitivity as perceived by teachers or staff and from other assessment data provides a principal with information needed to develop a plan for self-improvement. Community relations and interactions, relations with central office staff, and sensitivity toward teachers are critical areas that principals should address in their personal and professional growth plans. Principals who work to improve their level of interpersonal sensitivity improve the organizational culture and climate at the campus level and are more effective in both internal and external relationships.

REFERENCES

Bailey, W. J. (1991). *School-site based management applied.* Lancaster, PA: Technomic Publishing Co., Inc.

Barth, R. S. (1991). *Improving schools from within.* San Francisco: Jossey-Bass.

Bolman, L., & Deal, T. (1993). *The path to school leadership.* Newbury Park, CA: Corwin Press.

Delpit, L. (1995). *Other people's children: Cultural conflict in the classroom.* Newark, NJ: New Press.

Glickman, C., & Pajak, E. (1983). *A cause beyond myself* (Synthesis Policy Paper). Austin, TX: Southwest Development Laboratory.

Henderson, A. T., & Berla, N. (1994). *The family is critical to student achievement.* Columbia, MD: National Committee for Citizens in Education.

Hoyle, J. (1994, January). Can a principal run the show and be a democratic leader? *NASSP Bulletin, 78*(558), 33–40.

Hoyle, J. (1995). *Leadership and futuring: Making visions happen.* Thousand Oaks, CA: Corwin Press.

Hoyle, J., & Crenshaw, H. (1996). *Interpersonal sensitivity.* Larchmont, NY: Eye on Education.

Kouzes, J. M., & Posner, B. Z. (1995). *The leadership challenge.* San Francisco: Jossey-Bass.

McGregor, D. (1960). *The human side of enterprise.* New York: McGraw-Hill.

Neal, R. G. (1991). *School-based management: A detailed guide for successful implementation.* Bloomington, IN: National Educational Service.

Patterson, J. L. (1993). *Leadership for tomorrow's schools.* Alexandria, VA: Association for Supervision and Curriculum Development.

Prasch, J. (1990). *How to organize for school-based management.* Alexandria, VA: Association for Supervision and Curriculum Development.

Skuza, R. (1997). *The impact of an elementary parent center on parent involvement and student classroom performance as perceived by parents and professional staff in Sommerville, Texas.* Unpublished doctoral dissertation, Texas A&M University, College Station.

Thompson, S. (1990). New framework for preparing principals developed by the National Commission for the Principalship. [News release]. Fairfax, VA: National Commission for the Principalship.

Thompson, S. D. (Ed.). (1993). *Principals for our changing schools: The knowledge and skill base.* Fairfax, VA: National Policy Board for Educational Administration.

Wohlstetter, P., Van Kirk, A. N., Robertson, P. J., & Mohrman, S. A. (1997). *Successful school based management.* Alexandria, VA: Association for Supervision and Curriculum Development.

SECTION 4
PREPARING LEADERS

CHAPTER 17

Imagining Change through the Voices of Teachers and Students: An Ethnographic Approach[1]

Frank Pignatelli and Linda Levine

The central premise of this chapter is that guided ethnographic inquiry[2] can provide future school leaders with a significant opportunity for professional growth and enable them to discern ways of making substantive contributions in their workplace. Conducting an ethnographic inquiry project offers practitioners an opportunity to recognize how they might combine their own and others' "funds of knowledge" (Moll & Greenberg, 1989) in efforts to disentangle strands of difficulty and co-construct more promising practices. The authors contend that, despite tensions, technical problems, and time constraints, this mode of inquiry moves future school leaders toward keener awareness of what is problematic and possible in their own and others' school sites. At its best, this mode of inquiry fuels a desire and ability to construct a place for oneself in broader efforts that are and will be needed to advance equity through education. As Schensul and Carroll (1990) note, "Nearly one in three Americans will fall within the Census Bureau's designation of 'minority' by the year 2000. 'By the end of the next century there will be a new majority population in America—a majority of minorities' (United Way of America, 1989, p. 19)" (p. 341).

In preparing future school leaders to value and conduct educational ethnography, we stand with Carr and Kemmis (1986/1993) who argue for

> a form of educational research which is conducted by those involved in education themselves. It takes a view of educational research as critical analysis directed at the *transformation* of educational practices, the educational understandings and educational values of those involved in the process, and the social and institutional structures which provide frameworks for their action. (p. 156)

Our strong emphasis on fostering this mode of inquiry in the preparation of future school leaders reflects the tradition and mission of the graduate school of education where we teach. Bank Street College, in New York City, was founded in 1916 by Lucy Sprague Mitchell, an important progressive voice at a time when progressive education was in its formative stages of development. "Progressivism in education," as historian and educator Vito Perrone reminds us, "was guided historically by a belief that schools needed social power and at their best were rooted in cultural understandings, ethical commitments, and an ongoing struggle for democracy—in other words, large purposes that transcend mere materialism" (Perrone, 1991, p. 9). We agree with his understanding of progressivism's "critical legacy" (Perrone, 1989) and see doing action-oriented ethnographic inquiry (Moll & Diaz, 1987) as an important way to attend to this legacy. As Dewey (1929, as cited in Kincheloe, 1991, p. 16) and Mitchell (Antler, 1987; Mitchell, 1934, 1991) have noted, the role of practitioner as investigator, deliberately cultivating an ethic of personal-professional reflection in action, is an important aspect of the progressive tradition.

ORIENTATION OF THIS STUDY

We encourage research that emerges out of a felt need, a "passionate scholarship . . . grounded upon and moti-

---

Frank Pignatelli and Linda Levine, Bank Street College of Education

vated by our values and solidarities" (Kincheloe, 1991, p. 41). We have found that, in fact, many students are moved to address as well as name occurrences and patterns of inequity through doing ethnographic inquiry in their own professional settings. We are mindful, in our work with future school leaders, that we are endorsing "a new paradigm of social inquiry" (Anderson, Herr, & Nihlen, 1994), one which entails grounded, empirical research conducted by practitioners who seek to improve school practices.

We have learned that a semester-long process of employing ethnographic inquiry methods including participant observation, open-ended interviewing, discourse analysis, and examination of site documents necessarily involves students in an ongoing, reflective process which entails "turning back the lens" (Karp & Kendall, 1982) on their own premises and practices. As Gitlin et al. (1992) put it, "the central aim of Educative Research is to foster voice as a force of protest" (p. 84) and, we would add, an incentive for reconstruction. We recognize, also, that doing effective research of this kind entails the capacity and willingness to draw upon and examine oneself as a person and a developing professional. In this regard, we agree with Kincheloe (1991) that educators "are obligated to become researchers of themselves, revealing the interests implicit in their own teaching" (p. 34). We are concerned also that early optimism about effecting change too often gives way to resignation or hopelessness. How can those of us responsible for preparing these future school leaders help to avert this? In our view, teaching them to conduct educational ethnography provides these students with the opportunity to imagine and actively participate in a process of personal, professional, and institutional change.

We acknowledge the considerable challenge of undertaking ethnographic inquiry. Doing ethnographic research well calls for more than testing one's own assumptions. It means exploring why and how differences come to exist between local claims and practices. It also prompts deeper understanding of how reality can be constructed from different vantage points and perspectives. If undertaken rigorously and authentically, this mode of inquiry teaches the investigator the urgency of remaining open and responsive to unexpected factors which may have significant bearing on problems as well as possibilities for school change. The future school leader as researcher must also become aware of "the fallacy of the ethnographic present" (Heath, 1982). One's specific findings are unlikely to hold for all times and places. The point of the research is not to supply definitive solutions but rather to detect openings as well as impediments to progress and to cultivate an ongoing spirit of inquiry.

For emergent school leaders, learning to track a problematic focus of inquiry in a school context can be a life-redefining experience that holds wider possibilities for the improvement of educational practice. Mindful of the fact that our students are typically novice researchers, we engage and guide them through a systematic study of published educational ethnography, lending support to their use of ethnographic methods in pursuit of their own inquiry topics. Shared exchanges in class and individual conferences about data collection and analysis and action-oriented implications of each study equip students to construct a substantive and coherent ethnographic narrative. By the end of the semester, each student is expected to complete and situate a school-based inquiry project in the light of related research.

DATA COLLECTION AND ANALYSIS

Data sources include field notes from class sessions, notes from open-ended interviews conducted to discuss student work in progress and to mark the formal completion of the research projects, and student research papers. A constant-comparison method of analysis (Glaser & Strauss, 1967) was employed.

Findings

Typically, students in the educational leadership department conduct research in settings where they have worked for several years. Even with mobility, a majority of these students have spent most or all of their careers in the same educational system. The workplace, with its embedded rules, roles, and relationships, has been normalized, its givens uncontested. Yet, leadership that is transformational requires the willingness and ability to interrupt, question, and often dislodge these certainties. The challenge is, as Greene (1988) puts it, "to defamiliarize things, to make them strange" (p. 122) in order "to look at things as if they could be otherwise" (Greene, 1993, p. 14).

This study shows that doing research in a workplace where one has been for a number of years means testing claims put forth by members of one's own school culture in the light of observed practice and questioning what heretofore may have remained unexamined. Further, while the path between inquiry and change is rarely unobstructed, a colleague who steps out of his or her normal role to question claims in the light of practices takes on added risk.

As will be documented below, pursuing meaningful change in one's workplace offers future leaders a chance to affirm, renew, or revisit a commitment to education—to make a difference. As will be seen in "Cristina's" and "Nancy's" stories, bringing to the foreground of one's work silenced or marginalized voices can sharpen an educational leader's moral, political, and pedagogical purpose and provide a clearing for the development of a progressive reform agenda. This is especially important for would-be administrators to remember and carry with them to their future work since so much weight is placed upon the new administrator—indeed, all administrators—to operate in a transactional as opposed to transformational mode. At its best, educational ethnography both draws upon and challenges existing personal and professional understandings and practices. But beyond this, as was the case with "Michael" and "Cristina," it can influence one's workplace culture by surfacing unanticipated problems and yielding new possibilities.

Cristina

Cristina teaches in a school composed exclusively of immigrants from around the world who have been in the United States five years or less. For her, silencing emerged as a critical issue during a discussion with her sex education class about a homosexual teenager dying of AIDS. One student reacted to her suggestion that they invite two homosexuals from a gay rights group to discuss homosexuality by yelling, "They are coming to teach us to be homosexuals." Another student asked the question, "What is a homosexual?" A comment, a question, the general lack of knowledge, and a genuine interest expressed by her students to learn more about a marginalized, stigmatized group prompted her ethnographic study, "What are the attitudes of immigrant students on homosexuality?"

About her topic, she says,

> First of all because I was sincerely interested in discovering and uncovering the attitudes of my students on this extremely controversial topic and because before I had just naturally included the "presentation on homosexuality" in my previous sex education classes without much reflection or thought on what impact this practice was having or not having on my students. [sic] Was it necessary? Was it important? Should I continue with this practice? So the study would help me assess the value of this practice that I had initiated a year ago and now included in my sex education class curriculum."

The issue takes on added significance for Cristina when she decides to interview two gay boys in her school in order to understand better how the culture of her school works to support, accept, or marginalize them as gay people. Giving voice to "the lived experience of gay teenage immigrants," as she puts it, prepares Cristina to follow the effects—sometimes quite subtle, sometimes quite harsh and overt—of power relations in an environment where she has some degree of influence and control. Indeed, this is an environment she shares responsibility for constructing. As the process of doing the research unfolds, the issue of silencing gathers increased urgency and poignancy. She writes compellingly about John, a homosexual student in her school:

> He exuded self-confidence when he spoke, and it was only when speaking of the burden of keeping his homosexuality a secret that he lost his self-assurance and a feeling of sadness and resignation overtook him, but he always seemed to be able to recover himself. I suspected that his ability to recover quickly was a practice he had cultivated over the years.... It was hard to comprehend just how difficult living moment to moment must be for someone who was constantly on guard about protecting who and what he was.

John tells Cristina about a recent episode in class with his sex education teacher.

> John: Mr. Smith said that he'd be talking about homosexuality and all there was to know about it. But as we got to the end of the semester he didn't say anything, he didn't touch the topic. Why didn't he?
> Cristina: Why didn't you remind him?

> John: Because I was afraid he'd know about me or something. I really don't know Mr. Smith very well. I don't know his reaction to homosexuals. I'm careful about some teachers.

And she notes,

> John not only worried about being found out by his peers, but he was also concerned about being found out by his teachers and their reaction to his homosexuality. He also reported that there were seven students in the school that knew and accepted him the way he was. [The school] has 415 students.... John described a Muslim boy being one of the 7 who knew and how he was "shocked" that the Muslim boy had befriended him and not rejected him. However, he made his Muslim friend promise not to tell anyone else, not even his girlfriend.
>
> John [to Cristina]: I told [my Muslim friend] not to tell anyone. I don't want "gay bashings" after school.

What Cristina finds leads her to conclude that inviting homosexuals from a gay advocacy group (which she did do) to her sex education class "is a good first step" but clearly not enough: "there is a need for a more comprehensive approach in which all subject area teachers may participate." The questions she raises confront what she sees as "a conspiracy of silence"—"Why not include gay professionals as speakers in career education classes? Why couldn't biology teachers discuss how human beings are diverse sexual creatures within the context of their discipline? What about the contributions of gay writers as a topic for English classes?"

It is important to note that the school where Cristina teaches, grounded in the principles of progressivism, is widely recognized as a remarkably successful, exemplary school. The school graciously and frequently welcomes visitors who come to study firsthand its achievements in the areas of, for example, interdisciplinary curricula, peer selection and evaluation of teachers, intercultural understanding, and student assessment. The staff of the school is well along in the process of democratic culture building. Still, the urgency Cristina brings to her topic and the sense of possibility and force with which she frames her questions and other comments open spaces for reflection and renewal across the school community. As one student said to another on the final day of the research course, "It sounds like you discovered an area for reform."

Nancy

From the start of the course and throughout the time Nancy conducted her research, she was quite clear that her efforts were intimately tied to her own mixed African American and Native American heritage. Her final research paper begins with a claim: "Afro-Native. This term is the one I have given birth to; it is the term that I have invented to define who I am." Says Nancy, "The research was a personal journey for me.... Afro-Natives are invisible." This sense of invisibility was revealed and reinforced for her in difficulty she encountered gaining access to data from people who, typically, she notes, were reluctant to identify as Afro-Natives or who had convinced themselves such an identity was private—to be shared among family but not publicly. As she put it, "Hearing the data was painful (a word used several times throughout her paper). I'm hearing myself." But this was more than a therapeutic exercise for Nancy. Insisting upon her own cultural hybridity, Nancy found through research a means of resisting and transcending her own marginalization and silence.

Nancy came to her research with "a burning question," as she put it: "How have Afro-Natives managed to teach and learn culture?" In doing the research, she reached out patiently and openly to fellow classmates, other educators, members of her Afro-Native community, and her family trying to understand better their own struggles around this issue, and through them, her own. Leonard was the first person Nancy interviewed. His response to Nancy's question leads to this exchange:

> Leonard: I was born and I had breath. That's about it. I never think about the past. I live in the present and look to the future.
>
> Nancy: [Here I felt I wasn't getting anywhere. I said,] I understand. Sometimes talking about the past can be very painful, and not worth the effort. I've just been wondering how we get to learn about who we are—you know, so we can keep ourselves going.
>
> Leonard: The outside world helps keep you out. They tell you who you are.... There was a time when my people, the Lumbe, were considered the niggers of the Indians.... I don't know why that was ... we never talked about it.... but when I left from down there I wouldn't mention who I was.... I wouldn't say anything.... I

was trying to be somebody else.... But I changed. I accept [who I am] now. I'm not trying to be white anymore. I know I had to suffer.... I've been chaotic in my life.... History is full of lies and deceit. Some of us don't want to face reality. There is a lot of prejudice among Indians; but you've got to get over your hate. I must be mixed with Black. My folks would never say that, but I stopped trying to fight that. I accept that.

Following this and other efforts to gain access in order to find answers to her question, Nancy was plunged into a world of hurt, denial, and prejudice beyond her expectations. Her work, far from disinterested at the outset, took on texture and complexity. She felt anguish and deep regret at what she was finding out. Race, she regretfully learned, could not be disentangled from the issue of culture; indeed, it often occluded or obscured even the discussion of culture. She writes: "The pains of fighting racism and fighting each other has left us very little strength to heal and learn the ways that would sustain us."

To witness and to support the moral purpose, deep commitment, and diligence that Nancy brought to her work was a rare privilege afforded a teacher. But the story does not end here. Near the conclusion of the study, Nancy discusses what for her remains an important consequence of her study of Afro-Natives. She writes: "Being in touch with the individuals from the various organizations mentioned in this study will give me access to issues and developments. I'd like to meet with them on a regular basis, to become active in helping make changes...." Work is needed, she believes, in curriculum writing and more for her to learn about "the customs, sharing the heritage and seeing us becoming a culture known, respected, and allowed to flourish." After the research was completed, Nancy found out, through one of the participants in her study, that an educational resource center for the study of Native Americans funded by the Board of Education was in jeopardy of closing down. She is presently active in seeing that this does not occur.

Michael

Michael teaches in a small, public middle school of choice in a fashionable section of Manhattan. His inquiry centered on understanding what democratic schooling means for the professional staff and assessing how his own school "measured up." As is the case with all of the researchers discussed in this paper, Michael is a member of the school community he intends to analyze and critique. He has no choice but to live his research. And the questions he poses to and for the community are questions he is struggling to answer for himself.

After a lengthy opening quote by Dewey on the meaning of democratic educational administration, he begins his story with an exchange between two colleagues who are also longtime friends:

> Roy: You get yourself involved in situations in which you don't belong and in which you don't have enough information. You didn't hear her [a parent].
>
> Denise: You're right. I didn't hear her. I heard you, and you were being rude. I even asked you, "Are you speaking with a parent?"
>
> Denise [to Michael about the exchange]: That's why I always end up in trouble. I can't keep my mouth shut.

It is clear to Michael that the underlying issue for him and his colleagues is responsibility—when to speak up and why the risk is worth it. While Michael argues later for the inescapability of recognizing the moral dimension of teaching— "[W]e are morally bound to act when we see something inappropriate"—his initial commentary around this exchange is cast in the everyday sensibility and workplace parlance of his school—which he loves dearly. He remarks: "First, there is the issue of comfort. It is uncomfortable confronting a colleague on something that you feel is inappropriate. The question inevitably becomes, 'Why should I put myself in that position?'" What to do, he continues, when the union representative, who is also a colleague, refuses to speak up at a full staff meeting about an issue involving another colleague that has caused much consternation among staff "because she is 'not comfortable doing that.'" Because of its size (240 students) and the fact that half of the staff of a total of 15 have been together since the beginning of the school five years ago, the issue of comfort and the willingness to confront each other on issues about the well-being of the school is a major consideration. While it may be difficult to "disappear" in such an organization, the challenge Michael poses for himself and wishes to examine schoolwide is how deep a commitment can and will he and his colleagues make around building a democratic school. He remains guardedly optimistic as he finds a school "leaning in the direction of democracy." Not surprisingly, governance issues are an important concern for Michael. After its second year of existence, Michael's school applied for status and was accepted as a school-based management (SBM), shared decision-making (SDM) school, a citywide, top-down and bottom-up effort heralded by then Chancellor Fernandez. It would appear that a school such as Michael's would be an ideal location. And the school, according to Michael, did flourish. About the inception of SBM-SDM in his school, he writes the following:

> At that point regular meetings were set up and more input was asked from the staff regarding issues such as philosophy, the curriculum, scheduling. Not only was a philosophy published within the first year of SBM, but a math program which eliminated tracking, focused on enrichment, and offered the ninth grade math curriculum as an after-school program was put into place. Also, through SBM, 'block programming' was brought into the school. Through this scheduling device, eighth-grade English, social studies and art were arranged so that the students in different eighth-grade classes could be easily interchanged allowing for interdisciplinary projects to occur throughout the year.

But around the same time that SBM is building momentum, Michael detects and becomes very concerned about slippage in realizing a democratic school.

> [A]s time went on and the school continued to grow, new teachers entered the school and the communication which had been informal and extensive in the past was now nearly nonexistent among some groups of staff members. The perception of an in-group and an out-group began to appear. Those who perceived themselves as part of the out-group felt that they did not have access to information about the school. As these perceptions began to take hold, positions that had been merely labels—administrator, union representative, SBM chair—began to take on more and more importance and divisions among staff members began to deepen.

Committed to creating a democratic form of school governance among its professional staff, Michael enthusiastically took on the role of chair of SBM meetings last year. Undoubtedly, Michael positioned himself in the middle of a complicated, uncomfortable situation with his colleagues. He takes on an official role, as chair, in the hope of sustaining informal and extensive communication, an aspect of democratic schooling he considers to be essential. He identifies himself with a reform initiative, organizational structure, and vocabulary (SBM) from outside of the local culture of the school. As chair, he becomes aligned with the in-group according to some of his colleagues. He reports one of his colleagues commenting: "[The co-directors] dominate every [SBM] meeting they attend. There is no place for the staff to voice their opinions about the school without them being present. Some people just won't talk when they're around."

Finally, as Michael presently reads the situation, three camps have arisen in his school: one clustering around the union, one clustering around SBM, and one for a status quo. Because of his association with SBM, Michael is drawn into a union discourse of grievances, teacher rights, contractual obligations, and the like and thereby pitted against some of his colleagues as questioning the value and efficacy of the teachers' union and the adversarial role it is often expected to play. Having studied and analyzed carefully the current teachers' contract, he is very clear about the effect it has had upon reform agendas purported to engender democratic schooling as he understands it. "The contract as it stands right now is a minimum-work type contract. It specifies the bare minimum job requirements of a teacher. Unless this is changed, very little is possible as far as reform."

What is remarkable about Michael's research is its dimensionality, its resonance as a record of his felt needs, beliefs, values, and struggles. We recognize what is at stake in desiring change in one's own workplace, how one educator lives change. Michael is "captured" by his situation—fixed (at times, unfairly) within its history, named or silenced through the struggles the school community takes on and the conflict it generates. We understand better through his work how complicity and responsibility haunt one another, how comfortability and appropriateness can mask the uneasiness and messy ethical dilemmas change necessarily entails. Perhaps we understand a little better what it might mean politically and morally to be responsible collectively for nurturing democratic habits in a school. Notwithstanding the inevitable differences of opinion and varied perspectives individuals necessarily bring to a school, committing oneself to democratic schooling in a workplace layered with the scars of past conflicts, past hurts, past indignities is an enormously difficult undertaking, an ongoing challenge. Familiarity among the staff, small size, parental choice, and control over hiring staff—all present in Michael's school—do not, in themselves, guarantee or safeguard that progressive schooling will prevail in the way, for example, that Dewey (1938/1963) means it. Much depends upon the extent to which a school community can agree upon the value of sincere, comprehensible, truthful communication (Burbules, 1993) and create spaces for this to occur.

Drawing upon his own practical knowledge and steeped in a real and less than ideal situation, Michael understands, primarily because he lives it, that "everyone need not be in harmony for a democratic school to move forward." This realization, we believe, did not come cheaply. To speak about and move toward realizing what ought to be in one's own workplace requires both personal and professional risk and principled action. Ethnographic research can serve to clarify what this will require and mean.

SALIENT THEMES IN THE RESPONSES OF FUTURE SCHOOL LEADERS

After presenting an earlier version of this paper, we decided to invite former students to submit a written response to the question: "What has doing ethnographic research meant to you?" The purpose was to discover how the passage of time and subsequent experience affected student-generated connections between doing ethnographic inquiry and effecting change (personal, professional, or institutional).

Fifteen former students in the research course for future school leaders submitted statements. What follows are salient themes from the statements with illustrative excerpts from students' narratives. We then tease out some implications for preparing school leaders from the stories these novice ethnographers have told.

In seeking their perspectives on an earlier learning experience, we were working to extend reciprocal processes of teaching and learning across time. We did so not only to further our present research project but also, as Simon (1992) has urged, in a broader effort to reanimate the past as a way to prompt new possibilities in the present. In his words, a "pedagogy of remembrance" entails a "twofold teaching agenda, helping people develop an understanding of their empirical-ethical present and exploring how this present might inform and be informed by a particular sighting of the past" (p. 151).

1. Conducting Ethnographic Inquiry in One's Own School Setting Presents the Future Leader with a Significant Opportunity to Assume and Manage Risk, an Essential Quality of Leadership

While the research and related class discussions highlighted the risk entailed in doing research in one's own workplace (especially where these educators had spent several years), more than a few responses drew our attention to the depth of risk involved. We believe that the "safety" of time, combined with the chance to reflect upon the experience, surfaced textured, nuanced—indeed, heartfelt—thoughts and emotions about what it meant to recognize the risk involved in doing research effectively and conscientiously.

Consider Paula's comments. A thoughtful, soft-spoken African American woman who teaches in a middle school in Brooklyn, Paula undertook her research in a very familiar school environment, having taught there for several years. Her responses, while not necessarily typical, do point to the kinds of encounters with self, with colleagues, as well with the culture of one's workplace that can emerge for a first-time researcher:

> The school is a setting of immense turmoil and pain for all involved. There is much unrest between the minority population and the teaching staff of the school. The feeling was so strongly disconcerting for me that when it was time for me to share [my inquiry focus with the class near the beginning of the course] I said instead, "I am interested in the effect of music as a nonverbal stimulus for increasing the attention span in adolescents."

Yet, she continues,

> As I began the rationale for the paper, I decided to change this topic and to investigate the topic of school unrest because the school had a near riot situation, and I couldn't help but address it. I decided to take a chance. So I began the process of researching, asking questions, describing what I saw, and all of this was combined with learning about organizational behaviors in my "Foundations of Ed. Administration" class. As I interviewed I dug deeper and deeper into my school culture and gathered data about many unspoken and hidden areas in the day-to-day structure of my school. As I asked questions of the staff about the "event," I was overwhelmed by the impossible dynamics affecting the workplace climate, the history of the school region, and the feelings of

> the school people within the school. The information was explosive. As I got more and more involved, I began to feel fear rear its head again. I switched my topic from looking at "What happens to a school under pressure" to "What happens when African American males teach African American youth." I tried to focus on the study group, but once again the school discord constantly interrupted the process, and once again I was drawn into addressing the issues present in the school culture. I found there was no way I could escape talking about the pain of the students, the teachers and the administration. Most of all, I began to experience my pain. This pain resonated in every fibre of my being. I had to search and *re-search* the question of dominant-minority cultural dynamics. I addressed this issue in the second half of my paper. . . . The search for the truth about what was happening in my school such that students were so angry and violent was one which led me to examine myself and led me to confront the rage within myself about these issues. I had to speak of my feelings in the paper, continue to look, listen, and describe what existed. What a job!!! What a process!!!

Paula's uncertainty about engaging such difficult issues underscores the risk and responsibility taken on by those ready to examine their workplace critically. As instructors, we need to be mindful and sensitive to the context within which this kind of personal research is undertaken. We would be irresponsible ourselves if we did not consider these kinds of engagements as potentially perilous, fearful undertakings. This is not to say we should err on the side of caution. For Paula, it was profoundly important to name her questions and in effect be led by them. We believe she was ready—indeed, needed—to take on the issues she speaks of. Her actual study was an important exercise of moral imagination (Greenfield, 1993), a harbinger of what is at stake for her as an African American woman educator aspiring to a position of educational leadership.

She concludes,

> In looking back on the process now, I've seen the moving forward, the shutting down, the frustrated stumbling through obstacles that continued to confront me. Nevertheless, the question was compelling for me and in reality I could not let it rest. . . . It seems as if this work somehow helped me put on a different pair of glasses. The shift is evident to me in the way I approach my work. It has helped me draw closer to what really matters to me as a professional and has helped me move forward in formulating my vision regarding my role as an educational leader.

How we, as instructors, respond to Paula and others in similar kinds of charged, raw situations and the kinds of supports we can realistically provide become vital, necessary concerns.

Nancy and Serena echo similar kinds of concerns. Nancy writes,

> The research, which I have completed last semester, has brought to life for me a journey towards a deeper sense of self. My topic, which was how people of Afro-Native ancestry teach and learn culture, allowed me to name myself and, in a public way, say who I believe myself to be, and offer a way for others to name themselves. . . . Doing this kind of work for the first time was a bit unsettling, because of the many painful issues that it raised (racism/alienation). But being allowed to do something that helps you believe in who you are and helps you stand up is a great gift.

And Serena, a white woman who teaches in a therapeutic nursery and is preparing to take on larger challenges in her field, writes about the experience of doing research:

> I get excited, I get scared. . . . The two times that I have done lengthy qualitative research I have faced my worst demons and my higher self. My fears haunt me—I can't do this, I'm not smart enough, Who do I think I am? My anger challenges my fears, my inner voice tells me to continue, be disciplined, and trust. I work, I write, it unfolds. I do my research and I search myself. I learn. When I am finished I feel that I have gained a right [sic] of passage, I have passed the test.
>
> Both times I chose material that was important to me. Both times it directly affected my professional work and certainly caused me to be self-reflective. Like meditation, I went to the core—what fuels me. I found what fuels me as a person, fuels me as a professional, there is no boundary.

2. Doing Ethnographic Inquiry Is an Effective Way for Future School Leaders to Commit to Their Own Professional Development as an Ongoing Learning Process

Another theme that emerged from the responses was the generative power of doing research; that doing research of this kind prepares one for further projects of inquiry and opportunities to learn—what Dewey (1938/1963) called collateral learning.

Jen speaks to this point:

> Carrying out the research was a labor... a labor of growth. I became immersed in it, invested in it, driven by it. My colleagues became intrigued with what I was doing, and we entered into long, philosophical discussions about my topic. I began to look at myself, my teaching, and my students with new eyes. I realized that research isn't something "somebody else" does—someone who is "qualified" or has had precise training. It was something I was more than capable of doing.
>
> [Doing and learning about research] gave me a format, an organization, a process by which I could become more reflective. It taught me how to seek out information, to compile it, and to share it with my colleagues. It helped me to collaborate with my colleagues on issues which are important to all educators.

Jen also reports that she received a research grant from her district and plans to continue her research. Wanda, as researcher-practitioner, puts it more succinctly: "There is so much more that the anthropologist in me seeks to discover and the educational practitioner in me wishes to change."

3. Ethnographic Inquiry Can Be a Forceful Prompt for School Transformation

While no clear path exists between inquiry and progressive change, research can make a significant difference if members of a school community took upon themselves and were allowed to formulate what was for them a problematic focus of inquiry. What became more apparent through the analysis of student responses was the vital role research can play in "prompting" change, in providing a "moment of contact" (L. Levine, personal communication, February 1994) for the practitioner as researcher to imagine circumstances differently. Greene (1978), drawing upon the work of Alfred Shutz, addresses the phenomenology of this kind of experience and its place in a larger project of critique and transformation:

> An upsurge of questioning and critique must first occur; I believe this is most likely to occur in response to what Alfred Shutz calls the "experiences of shock," which compel people to break through the limits of one province of meaning and shift "the accent of reality to another one." The point is... that experiences of shock are necessary if the limits or horizons are to be breached. (Greene, p. 101)

Having experienced such shock, the danger, Greene reminds us, is a turn to cynicism or to a thirst for "'positive images' as screen and overlay" (p. 102). The point is to "break with created structures" (p. 103) that disempower, erode creative potential, unfairly limit, or brutally oppress, with the shock serving to spark such a project.

Melissa's response moved us to consider what this moment of shock does and how it can be used to nourish ongoing, worthwhile work. She writes,

> You are present when the question or problem to be researched is created. You are also present when you decide what methods of research you will use, and you are there describing the data as it shows up.... There's a sense of urgency about it. Once you gather the facts you have to respond to them no matter how unpleasant they may be. The facts you gather take a life of their own and demand your attention. They can't be neglected or ignored. One must respond to them.

Melissa (and others) both open up to the shock and are called to respond to what they see or experience. We see here the consequences of being attentive and engrossed in one's work as researcher as part of what Noddings (1993) describes as an ethic of care. Following Noddings, we suggest that this way of caring points to, nourishes, and can serve as a guide to projects of change.

CONCLUSION AND IMPLICATIONS

Continuing to pose problems and challenge assumptions—the heart of ethnographic inquiry and progressivism—is likely to encounter the resistance of those who view reform as prescribed or obvious. Doing ethnography in contexts where service is the preeminent value requires going against the grain, risking old or potential friendships, and testing the limits of collegiality and professional courtesy. This mode of inquiry presents a challenge for future leaders. Most tend to do their research in settings where they have worked for a number of years. With their history and complicity in co-constructing a particular workplace culture, experienced educators can find this enterprise quite stressful, one that calls into question central tenets of their professional identity.

Personal, professional, and institutional transformations do not occur merely because of systematic inquiry. We recognize what Carlson (1992) has termed the "naive optimism of progressive experimentalism" and his claim that progressive-liberal reform efforts in the absence of ideological analysis are unlikely to be sustained and situated within a larger project of democratic schooling. No clear, clean path exists between inquiry and change. Nonetheless, we contend that knowledge generated through inquiry that is site specific, locally informed and oriented, and undertaken by those with a stake in changing what they perceive as oppressive and unfair can be leveraged to prize open unfavorable conditions and can help to frame, guide, and broaden a process and project of institutional change.

These findings suggest that doing ethnographic research serves to intensify the personal and professional investment of future school leaders in struggles in urban education. Gaining the critical distance needed to understand and contextualize urgent issues in fact moves these educators to envision and engage existing practices as though they might be otherwise. Ethnographic inquiry provides the opportunities and the means to understand that seemingly intractable realities are not immutable, that they are and have always been socially negotiated spaces and choices that can be challenged and changed by those with the will and the resources to do so. This becomes an exceedingly powerful stimulus for the "emancipatory project" of educational reform that Giroux (1987) urges educators to undertake.

For future educational leaders who, typically, see themselves as making a long-term commitment to their profession and come to their leadership preparation with a history of involvement in schools, ethnographic inquiry affords opportunities to reflect on "givens" they themselves have helped to create. We argue that the personal and professional exploration this mode of research fosters is singularly well suited for challenging assumptions and opening new options for professional growth.

A factor that deserves special emphasis is the way in which ethnographic research legitimizes the crossing of boundaries that were previously "off limits." Tracking a problematic focus of inquiry means going beyond official claims, seeking out voices of stakeholders who have had little impact on policies, and exploring aspects of a school community that reach beyond one's accustomed terrain. In widening their own understanding of what counts as knowledge—and whose knowledge counts—these educators gain new ideas for collaboration in the service of reforming education. Similarly, scrutinizing familiar documents, aspects of the material culture and social networks that have long been taken for granted can provide fresh insights for dealing with difficult, embedded issues.

What students come to understand by doing ethnographic inquiry is that school culture, like the trajectory of their own lives, is never static. Consequently, new options and roles are always available for themselves and others in its ongoing formation. Conducting inquiry allows them to nurture "ways of exploring possible worlds" and to shape a role for themselves "in constantly making and remaking the culture—an *active* role as participants rather than as performing spectators who play out their canonical roles according to rules when the appropriate cues occur" (Bruner, 1986, p. 123).

ENDNOTES

1 We gratefully acknowledge the efforts and insights of students in the Educational Leadership program at Bank Street College. Our thanks to Nancy Cardwell for her provocative critique and suggestions on an earlier draft of this paper. Responsibility for interpretation of the data rests with the authors.

2 For more information on how to conduct educational ethnography, readers are referred to the following: An-

derson, Herr, and Nihlen (1994), Carr and Kemmis (1986/1993), Merriam (1988), and *Anthropology & Education Quarterly*.

REFERENCES

Anderson, G., Herr, K., & Nihlen, A. (1994). *Studying your own school: An educator's guide to qualitative inquiry.* Thousand Oaks, CA: Corwin Press.

Antler, J. (1987). *Lucy Sprague Mitchell: The making of a modern woman.* New Haven, CT: Yale University Press.

Bruner, J. (1986). *Actual minds, possible world.* Cambridge: Harvard University Press.

Burbules, N. (1993). *Dialogue in teaching: Theory and practice.* New York: Teachers College Press.

Carlson, D. (1992). *Teachers and crisis: Urban school reform and teachers' work culture.* New York: Routledge.

Carr, W., & Kemmis, S. (1993). *Becoming critical: Education, knowledge and action research.* Philadelphia: Falmer Press. (Original work published 1986)

Dewey, J. (1963). *Experience and education.* New York: Macmillan. (Original work published 1938)

Giroux, H. (1987). Schooling and the politics of ethics: Beyond liberal and conservative discourses. *Journal of Education, 169*(2), 9–33.

Gitlin, A., Bringhurst, K., Burns, M., Cooley, V., Meyers, B., Price, K., Russell, R., & Tiess, P. (1992). *Teachers' voices for school change: An introduction to educative research.* New York: Teachers College Press.

Glaser, B. G., & Strauss, A. L. (1967). *The discovery of grounded theory.* Chicago: Aldine.

Greene, M. (1978). *Landscapes of learning.* New York: Teachers College Press.

Greene, M. (1988). *The dialectic of freedom.* New York: Teachers College Press.

Greene, M. (1993). Perspectives and diversity: Toward a common ground. In F. Pignatelli & S. Pflaum (Eds.), *Celebrating diverse voices: Progressive education and equity* (pp. 1–20). Newbury Park, CA: Corwin Press.

Greenfield, W. (1993). Articulating values and ethics in administrator preparation. In C. A. Capper (Ed.), *Educational administration in a pluralistic society.* New York: State University of New York Press.

Heath, S. B. (1982). Ethnography in education: Defining the essentials. In P. Gilmore & A. H. Glatthorn (Eds.), *Children in and out of school: Ethnography and education* (pp. 33–55). Washington, DC: Center for Applied Linguistics.

Karp, I., & Kendall, M. (1982). Reflexivity in fieldwork. In P. Secord (Ed.), *Explaining human behavior: Consciousness, human action and social structure* (pp. 249–273). Beverly Hills, CA: Sage.

Kincheloe, J. (1991). *Teachers as researchers: Qualitative inquiry as a path to empowerment.* London: Falmer Press.

Mitchell, L. S. (1991). *Young geographers.* New York: Bank Street College of Education. (Original work published 1934)

Moll, L. C., & Diaz, S. (1987). Change as the goal of educational research. *Anthropology & Education Quarterly, 18*(4), 300–311.

Moll, L. C., & Greenberg, J. (1990). Creating zones of possibility: Combining social contexts for instruction. In L. C. Moll (Ed.), *Vygotsky and education* (pp. 319–348). Cambridge: Cambridge University Press.

Noddings, N. (1993). Caring: A feminist perspective. In K. A. Strike & P. L. Ternasky (Eds.), *Ethics for professionals in education: Perspectives for preparation and practice* (pp. 43–53). New York: Teachers College Press.

Perrone, V. (1989). Progressive schools: A critical legacy in conservative America. In V. Perrone, *Working papers: Reflections on teachers, schools, and communities* (pp. 86–99). New York: Teachers College Press.

Perrone, V. (1991). Large purposes. In K. Jervis & C. Montag (Eds.), *Progressive education in the 1990s: Transforming practice.* New York: Teachers College Press.

Schensul, J. J., and Carroll, T. G. (1990). Visions of America in the 1990s and beyond: Negotiating cultural diversity and educational change. *Education and Urban Society, 22*(4), 339–345.

Simon, R. (1992). *Teaching against the grain: Texts for a pedagogy of possibility.* New York: Bergin & Garvey.

United Way of America. (1989). *What lies ahead: Countdown to the 21st century.* Alexandria, VA: United Way Strategic Institute.

CHAPTER 18

The Portfolio as a Capstone Experience in the Preparation of Educational Leaders

Beverley B. Geltner, William J. Price, and Jaclynn C. Tracy

New approaches to preparation for professional practice are being developed in many fields—medicine, business, law, and school administration. Barrows' (1984) work with using problem-based learning in the training of physicians informed Bridges and Hallinger (1992) as they modified this approach for use in the preparation of educational administrators. Recent publications by organizations such as the National Policy Board for Educational Administration (1989) and the Danforth Foundation (Milstein, 1993) and by members of the professoriate including Achilles (1994), Bolman and Deal (1994), Murphy (1992), and Schön (1990) have called all aspects of professional leadership preparation into question: program purpose and focus, instructional design and implementation, and teaching methodologies.

What these efforts share is their commitment to develop practitioners who can demonstrate performance excellence and thoughtfulness (not automatic behavior derived from other contexts and simpler times)—practitioners who can master ever larger knowledge bases, confront and analyze complex problems, develop requisite skills to consider alternate solutions, decide and implement their selected choices thoughtfully and effectively, and execute these operations over time in increasingly complex, dynamic environments. To achieve these goals, increasing numbers of professors of educational administration are modifying their programs and infusing their teaching with these new approaches, including problem-based learning, models of case-based instruction, reflective practice, and authentic assessment (Bridges & Hallinger, 1992; Christensen, 1978; Clark, 1986; Dezure, 1993; Hutchings, 1993; Hutchings & Marchese, 1990; Kottkamp & Osterman, 1990, 1991; Langer, 1994; Schön, 1990, 1992; Wiggins, 1993; Wilmore & Erlandson, 1995).

STUDY FOCUS

This chapter describes an innovative approach to the preparation of school administrators developed at Eastern Michigan University (EMU) which integrates two core components of professional preparation: summative portfolio assessment and reflective practice. EMU offers a Master of Arts degree, the Specialists in Arts degree, and the Doctor of Education degree in educational leadership. At the doctoral level, students complete the comprehensive qualifying examination (which is an extensive field-based problem study) and the doctoral dissertation. Both of these experiences provide an intensive capstone to the study of educational leadership and serve as the vehicle by which faculty and the student may assess progress in the mastery of the educational leadership program knowledge base. Similarly, at the educational specialist level, students complete an extensive field-based research study on an educational leadership issue as well as an administrative internship. These capstone experiences also provide opportunity for faculty and student assessment of the student's mastery of the knowledge base. For the master's degree, however, students merely completed the body of course work required by their program of study (12 to 15 courses) and received their degree. Following an internal program review, the faculty realized the need to develop a formal capstone experience which could be utilized at the master's degree level.

Beverley B. Geltner, William J. Price, and Jaclynn C. Tracy, Eastern Michigan University

When considering the various options which could be used as a culminating experience, several of the more traditional approaches were quickly ruled out. A master's thesis, for example, was not considered to be feasible logistically due primarily to the large number of students in the master's program. Faculty were already stretched thin through service on a large number of doctoral dissertation committees and as principal advisors for students' educational specialist research projects. A comprehensive written examination taken upon completion of all master's course work was also eliminated as an option. As other potential options were discussed by department faculty, it soon became clear that a capstone experience was needed that provided an extensive record of the students' progress and growth throughout their entire program of study and that could be of significant value to the students as a major holistic, integrative learning experience. For continuous program review purposes, it was also important that faculty be able to receive constructive feedback and personal reflections from all graduating students as to the overall value of their graduate studies as they completed their degree and left the university. The vehicle that best seemed to fulfill both of these requirements was the professional summative portfolio.

During the 1995–1996 academic year, the entire portfolio process was redesigned as a comprehensive capstone experience for a student's final semester in the program. The redefined purpose of the portfolio was to obtain a comprehensive and holistic assessment of students' learning to confirm that they had mastered and integrated essential program elements. Further, faculty sought to obtain data about students' perceptions of their own growth along with feedback about their perceptions and experience of the program as a whole. The result was a redesigned portfolio assessment model which was aligned directly with official program goals and objectives and which guided students through a process that was initiated at the students' entry, monitored throughout the program, and concluded in the final semester.

The new model was implemented with all graduating students in the master's program the following year. This paper describes the operation and impact of the program as students reframed their perceptions about their own learning and growth, as faculty experienced new opportunities for collaboration and conversation, and as the overall program received rich feedback about design, delivery, and new possibilities.

SOME BACKGROUND ON PORTFOLIO ASSESSMENT

Portfolios as assessment tools have received increasing attention in professional development programs (Paulson & Paulson, 1990; Paulson, Paulson, & Meyer, 1991; Wilmore & Erlandson, 1995). Borrowing from fields with long histories of portfolio assessment—notably in the visual and musical arts and more recently in K–12 education—portfolio assessment is being recognized as a powerful means for students to select and compile multifaceted evidence of performance and growth.

Portfolio Characteristics

Two assumptions underlie the use of the portfolio assessment technique (Nweke, 1991). One is that portfolios complement other assessment methods. This is implied when portfolios are used in conjunction with other methods to document learning. Here, portfolios improve the reliability and validity of evidence. The second assumption is that portfolios yield more relevant and valid data than traditional methods because the evidence is more inclusive and comprehensive.

For Allen (1994), the portfolio represents both an opportunity and a quest for more creative and consequential ways to assess breadth and depth of student learning and thinking. Further, he views the efforts involved in a student's construction of a portfolio as "enabling" work—work that is important in out-of-classroom jobs and careers. According to Allen, the following are conceptual descriptions of enabling work that can occur in the process of portfolio creation:

1. Relevant work, or work perceived by students as being important and worth doing
2. In-context work, or student work perceived as being part of something larger and more important than itself
3. Self-evaluative work, or student work perceived as shaped by students' own scrutinies and criticisms (thus

seeming superior to the more static practice of students routinely submitting work, then waiting for teacher criticisms)
4. Metacognitive work, or student work carefully monitored by themselves and requiring sharp decision-making consequences
5. Engaged work, or student work selected because of a perceived personal dimension or connection
6. Self-directed work, or work guided by self-initiated goals, time allocations, material selections, and completion plans (significantly reducing arbitrary teacher management)
7. Affectively motivated work, or work energized by sustained enthusiasm and positive feelings that the work and its purposes are attractive and self-enhancing

A unique feature of a portfolio when it is used to measure student growth is that it is both a physical and philosophical concept (Valencia et al., 1990). As a physical entity, a portfolio is a container in which the artifacts of student performance can be stored—the examples, documents, and observations that serve as evidence of growth and development. Such artifacts can be infinitely diverse in format and can include anything that documents student learning and applications outside of the classroom—writings, computer programs, audio or video tapes, letters, articles about accomplishments, and reflective statements about personal and professional growth. Modern technology offers the potential to move the portfolio beyond merely documenting a student's written or pictorial work. Thus, a portfolio can be a limitless opportunity for students to display in one collection evidence of what they know, think, and are able to do.

As a concept, a portfolio forces faculty to expand the range of options considered as data to use in evaluating student growth and making instructional decisions. It represents an attitude suggesting that assessment is a dynamic rather than a static process, reflected most accurately in multiple snapshots taken over time. It allows faculty to define achievement in broad, diverse, adaptive, multidimensional terms rather than narrow and restrictive ones. Thus, a portfolio provides a complex and comprehensive view of student performance that encourages faculty to see learning as a complex and multidimensional process. Different from traditional methods of assessment, the portfolio offers the opportunity to observe students in a broader context: taking risks, developing creative solutions, and learning to make judgments about their own performance (Hutchings & Marchese, 1990).

In their work with educational administration interns in Texas, Wilmore and Erlandson (1995) found that the use of portfolio assessment in measuring the professional development of administrative interns gave them a focus for developing the skills most commonly identified as essential to campus-based administrative leadership success. Students reported that having key performance dimensions around which to build their portfolios helped them move from the abstract idea of portfolio assessment to the concrete reality of exactly what to include to make their portfolio evaluation authentic and professionally meaningful.

Portfolio assessment accords with one of the key principles of adult learning—the importance of drawing on students' lived experiences and providing opportunities for independence, self-direction, and personal control of learning (Wilmore & Erlandson, 1995). Through the process of building a portfolio, the student operates as the active agent of the process, not the receiver, as a participant in the process, rather than an object of such a process. Lodging responsibility for the selection and evaluation of worth of such evidence with the student places ownership of the development of professional judgment and expertise with the learner. Through the gathering of ongoing evidence of growth over time based on actual performance, the learner is provided with opportunities to monitor the development of her or his own professional mastery. Further, since portfolio assessment is grounded directly in practice, it is more authentically related to the complexity of schools. By being situated or contextualized in this way, a portfolio more accurately measures leadership behaviors and activities that take place in school settings.

The portfolio process can thus enhance educational leadership development by providing an opportunity for students to document their leadership behaviors over an extended time span in any number of ways: chairing a school improvement committee, conducting a staff development activity, making oral or written presentations, speaking before a board of education or other public body, or designing a new instructional program. Used in this way, the portfolio acquires importance as an instrument of development, of formation over time.

Capstone Portfolios

It is precisely this developmental perspective that enhances the value of the summative portfolio as a capstone professional preparation experience. Unlike a single test score, which represents one piece of information at a particular moment in time, this approach is a continuous, longitudinal, dynamic process, affording students an opportunity to consider what was and to ponder their growth over time. It encourages students to view learning as an incremental process with concrete benchmarks. It recognizes that the learner and the task change with every new situation, that knowledge is cumulative and transferable, and that the basis for future learning comes precisely from growth in understanding, from practice, and from integration of knowledge over time. This approach can have a cumulative, positive effect on student learning and motivation and can serve the psychological needs of adult learners by providing physical evidence of their own growth.

As capstone assessments, portfolios can be final collections of student work, selected and managed by the students for purposes of self-evaluation or self-representation to other evaluators. Such portfolio efforts are *best-work portfolios*. They contain final-draft or product entries meant to portray the best academic, experiential, and preprofessional work which signifies right of graduation, certification, or employment readiness.

In the opinion of Forrest (1990), while the primary "beauty" of the portfolio is its potential to enhance individual student learning, when used as part of the assessment process, portfolios can go beyond evaluation of the student to provide important information for the evaluation of individual courses and an entire program. Thus the addition of just the summative portfolio assessment process alone during the entire course of studies could enhance administrator preparation programs, expanding opportunities to shape desired administrator behaviors and skills, strengthening the collaborative process between student and instructor, and deepening the link between theory and practice. Linked with a second critical dimension of professional preparation—reflective practice—the capstone portfolio assessment process gains even greater significance.

SOME BACKGROUND ON REFLECTIVE PRACTICE

Almost 20 years ago, Argyris and Schön (1974) observed that people's ideas about how things work, their "theories of action," were central to their effectiveness as leaders. To become more effective school reformers, administrators needed to learn not simply new skills, but new "theories of action." In 1983 and 1987, Schön concluded that skilled practitioners were reflective practitioners, using their experience as a basis for assessing and revising existing theories of action to develop more effective action strategies. The concept of reflective practice—the mindful consideration of one's professional actions—has had enormous impact on professional development programs. Beginning with the single premise that ideas shape action, new questions and ideas have unfolded about the nature of professional knowledge and about how professionals learn.

Reflective practice stems from the learning theories of Dewey and Piaget, which hold that learning is dependent upon the integration of experience with reflection and theory with practice. It operates as a dialectic process in which thought is integrally linked with action. When faced with a problem, a discrepancy between the real and the ideal, or between what occurred and what was expected, the reflective practitioner steps back and examines her or his actions and the reasons for these actions.

> Experience provides the basis for learning... An event occurs. The person must make meaning of that event, examine it, appraise it; out of this comes new perspectives, the basis for experimentation. Reflection is the essential part of the process that makes it possible to learn from experience. (Osterman, 1990, p. 137)

Through this dialectic process of moving from theory to practice and back again to theory, the practitioner takes an active role in shaping her or his own professional growth, not merely developing new ideas of theories of action, but eliminating or modifying those old ideas that have been shaping behavior. Thus, by the integration of knowledge and action through thought, reflective practice can alter understanding and behavior and help practitioners improve their practice.

Reflective practice also contains a powerful critical component, moving practitioners to subject their own actions to critical assessment, challenging them to question beliefs and behaviors which preserve an inadequate current system and block reform. Further, reflective practice makes explicit what practitioners often do not talk about. It permits the unconscious thoughts, assumptions, and patterns that guide actions to be raised to a conscious level; it facilitates the articulation of how knowledge, thought, and action are integrated and promotes dialogue among practitioners and the sharing of experiences. In these ways, reflective practice can contribute to professional growth and to the development of a sense of community. Cambron-McCabe (1993) stresses the importance of informing administrative practice by critical reflection—reflection situated in the cultural, political, and moral context of schooling (p. 162). Since schools are sites of cultural conflict, it is imperative for school administrators to understand how in their official roles as leaders they have both the authority and the responsibility to examine the existing structures, practices, and tensions in schools and to work on behalf of the advancement of a just and democratic school environment. Educating for leadership must not lead to mere management but to a thoughtful clarification and consideration of what is in schools—and what ought to be.

Integrating both reflective practice and summative portfolio assessment in an administrator preparation program can further the development of such leaders. Grounding the focus of professional formation in a thoughtful analysis of problems of practice—the real issues and challenges presented in schools—students can develop a deeper understanding of the true responsibilities of their future role in ways not possible with traditional instructional methods.

Thus, such an approach can serve both critical and metacognitive functions, helping students develop their capacity for self-reflection and judgment within a moral context framed by beliefs, purposes, and values.

> Students don't just put material into a portfolio; they reflect upon the material: what they learned, what the material demonstrates, why they are placing it in the portfolio, and how it compares with prior samples. Thus, the portfolio encourages students to develop a set of values, to assess their work according to those values, and to reflect in new ways on their learning and performance. It is these very qualities of reflective practice which distinguish true educational leaders from managers or technicians. (Paulson & Paulson, 1990, p. 11)

Thus, reflective practice linked to portfolio assessment as a capstone experience can serve as a valuable contribution to the development of future school leaders. Theory and practice can be contextualized by reference to actual leadership behaviors in schools, and a critical stance can be exercised in pursuit of educational reform.

THE PORTFOLIO DESIGN

All students pursuing the master's degree in educational leadership at EMU are required to develop a professional portfolio. This portfolio, when completed, represents the formal capstone experience used by the student and educational leadership program faculty to assess the student's overall learning while in the program.

The portfolio is intended to represent an extensive record of the student's progress and growth. It is to be a collection of well-documented papers and other artifacts produced as original work by the student. In addition, the portfolio must contain statements of personal philosophy and goals and other writings indicating deep self-reflection.

The framework for the portfolio is built around seven domains—leadership, research, technology, communication, human relations and cultural diversity, management competency, and professionalism—which collectively represent the educational leadership program's knowledge base and which form the basis of the master's degree program in educational leadership at EMU. Each domain requires a piece of writing or other artifact from the student which clearly demonstrates understandings of and personal reflections on one or more major elements of that domain. Required courses are aligned with each domain, providing students with opportunities to develop competencies in the entire program knowledge base through course work and independent readings and study. Students are also encouraged to include in their portfolios relevant professional staff development activities in which they participated at their work sites and which occurred while enrolled in the master's program.

INTRODUCTION OF THE CAPSTONE PORTFOLIO ASSESSMENT PROCESS

Beginning with the fall 1996 semester, all students entering the master's program in educational leadership at EMU were introduced to the new portfolio assessment process. In preparation for this process, all faculty had collaborated in the development of all portfolio materials and in their own training to serve as advisors for students. Individual portfolio packets were assembled which described the purpose and rationale of the process; the time lines; the introductory, midpoint, and final stages of the process; the specific expectations in terms of artifacts; grading criteria; and the exit interview process with the student's advisor and one additional faculty member.

As the first students were introduced to the process, faculty regularly shared critical aspects of their experiences with colleagues: what happened, how easily understandable were the concepts and steps of the process, how had students responded, what was not yet clear, and what questions or issues had arisen that had not yet been anticipated.

Thus, the very experience of designing and implementing this department-wide assessment process served to reconnect faculty around a core instructional issue—implementation of a significant reform in the evaluation of student progress and program effectiveness. Departmental norms of collaboration, conversation, and creation were enriched as faculty committed themselves to monitoring the process and sharing it with other professional colleagues. A formal process of data gathering was designed in preparation for future scholarly publication and presentation.

RESEARCH DESIGN

This investigation involved a total of 7 professors of educational administration and 32 students who completed a capstone master's portfolio. In each instance, the graduating students prepared two copies of their exit portfolio to be shared with their advisor and one additional faculty member one week in advance of their interview. This provided faculty with sufficient time to review the quality of the portfolio, examine all artifacts (print, audio, or video), identify significant questions or issues to address, and prepare for the personal interview. During the actual interview, students were given approximately 30 minutes to discuss the contents of their portfolio and present their rationale for the selection and inclusion of all items. Faculty then proceeded to question students further on their portfolio, focusing initially on the specific contents and then moving to discussion of larger holistic issues relating to students' perceptions of themselves and of the program. Finally, students discussed the reflective statements which they had written at the end of their program and included in their capstone portfolio for the exit interview.

All participating faculty were interviewed by the authors twice individually and once in a total group. Individual interviews were structured to obtain data about faculty perceptions of the impact of the master's capstone portfolio on (a) students (both affective and cognitive dimensions), (b) self (both affective and cognitive dimensions), (c) the program (both overall and with regard to specific factors), and (d) faculty relationships with their colleagues in the department. Finally, faculty were asked to complete a critical incident report, describing one experience in the capstone portfolio process which they considered of particular significance for them. All data were analyzed according to recognized qualitative research methods (Bogdam & Bilkin, 1982).

ANALYSIS OF THE DATA: STUDENT PERCEPTIONS

Analysis of the perceptions shared by students revealed that the capstone portfolio served as a valuable catalyst for their own reflection. Students consistently reported that the portfolio process served as a vehicle for them to sit down and reflect informally on what they experienced in their program as they were completing their studies. As part of their reflections, students noted the insights that they gained as they attempted to integrate and tie everything together at the end of the program and then render some judgments about it. "I did learn much more than I thought," one student stated. "The capstone portfolio made me look at everything, and I realized just where I was when I began and where I am now. I can hardly believe I'm the same person!"

For another student, the portfolio served a valuable synthesizing function, helping him to organize his learnings and "see the whole and not just the parts." He continued, "It helped me come to closure, even though I know that *I'm* never done and *it's* never done." Another stated, "It permitted me to 'connect the dots' of the curriculum. Now that I'm done, I have a much more complete understanding of what being an administrator entails."

This new awareness—the change in their notion of educational leadership—was frequently reported as students described the impact of their reflection on their personal and professional growth. They began to see leadership not as a single act by an individual but as a collaborative process led by a skilled and thoughtful leader who understands the value of creating an organizational culture that develops and empowers individuals within the organization. As one summarized her thoughts,

> I used to feel, "Just let me at it. I'll turn this place around and really lead this school." Now, I see that while I may want to turn the school around, I will *not* be able to do it all by myself. My job is to motivate others to get on board, to *want* to do it, and to share their best thinking and commitment. I never knew.

A number of students stated that, as a capstone experience, the portfolio caused them to want to put forward their best work. Students no longer saw a term paper as merely satisfying the requirements of an individual class; rather, since they had been prepared in their initial meeting with their advisors for the capstone portfolio requirement at the end of the program, they realized that a paper could also serve as an artifact for possible inclusion in their portfolio. As such, it needed to meet both their standards of excellence and what they assessed was being expected by their instructors. Quite simply, what was needed was their best work—and it was up to them to decide which of their papers or other products best met the desired standards and were representative of their best work in the program. As they came to realize, this was a new experience in setting their own quality standards, moving them to higher levels of self-evaluation as future practicing educational administrators.

Thus, the capstone portfolio review and selection process caused students to reflect on their own cognitive and affective growth. For virtually every student, the new awareness was one of growth—of pride in their own success and accomplishments and in the new knowledge and understanding that they had gained. The process of articulating their final reflective paper in the portfolio served as an opportunity to synthesize their learnings and articulate their new confidence and commitment to serve as educational leaders in whichever arena they might do so. They had formulated a new sense of their leadership potential, and they felt encouraged, empowered, and emboldened. In fact, for several of the students interviewed, the portfolio had already served as the foundation for new professional resumes and interviews as they launched their search for a new career.

> My portfolio was just a blessing! It gave both me and my employer an opportunity to have an important conversation about my educational beliefs and values. They could see that what I believed about leading schools wasn't just something I was saying, but that there was a lot of evidence to show over more than two years of my work.

ANALYSIS OF DATA: FACULTY

One extremely important and somewhat unexpected outcome of the exit portfolio process was the opportunity presented for increased faculty collaboration. During the formal presentation of their portfolios, students met with at least two faculty members and discussed the artifacts that they selected, the reasons for their selection, and their overall experiences in the program. Typically, the presentation became a three-way conversation: the student initiated the presentation, faculty observed and questioned, and an informal dialogue unfolded. Through such conversations, faculty obtained a clearer picture of key aspects of the program: what their colleagues were teaching in their classes, what pedagogical approaches they were using, how students experienced their program, and what connections they made. These exit interviews served as a form of action research in which informants (the students) described their work, their thoughts, and their responses to questions and provided an opportunity for faculty to gain awareness of their program in a breadth and depth that might not otherwise have occurred.

What emerged was an unplanned learning community in which faculty received feedback from students on their instructional efforts and identified what had helped students learn and where omissions or barriers were, giving the opportunity for all parties to explore what changes might enhance teaching and learning. As faculty engaged in conversations with students about their portfolios, it enabled them to see the program through the students' experiences. The portfolio process gave faculty a good picture of strengths and areas where changes might be needed. For example, consistent positive feedback about internships convinced faculty that this was an important program component that was highly valued by students. Students also placed high value on courses that integrated field-based activities within courses and urged continuation of these activities. Thus, a new norm was established in which faculty and students served as partners, engaging in collaborative and open conversation about their shared work, conversing within a common framework and with shared data that could serve as a catalyst for program modification.

The portfolio process allowed faculty to ensure that courses in the master's program reflected the program knowledge base. As faculty collaboratively developed the structure of the portfolio requirements, this process was a way of schematically looking at the relationship between discrete courses and the broad program knowledge base. It was possible for faculty to address the question of "whether or not we are teaching through our courses what it is that we really want students to understand about the nature of school leadership." In other words, it established a kind of curriculum alignment that faculty had felt was missing previously. It also supplied insightful feedback about adjunct professors, about their strengths, needs, and concerns. This feedback provided a source of quality control so that only the finest practitioners were continued as adjunct professors to supplement regular faculty.

Perhaps the greatest contribution of the portfolio process to the structure of the master's program, however, was the development of a culture that structured informal connections between students and faculty and between faculty and faculty throughout the student's entire program. At the front end, when faculty advisors first meet with their advisees, they set in motion the development of a culture that prepares students for their future connection with faculty when they will meet periodically to discuss the student's experiences, growth, and reflection on the entire program experience. This connection creates a community of learners and is a bonding opportunity for students and their professors. At the end, the exit interview serves a ceremonial role—a rite of passage in which students share insights about their personal and professional growth and their future professional goals and aspirations.

This last stage of the interview—discussing a student's future career plans—provides additional opportunity for faculty collaboration. Future possibilities are explored—a new position, further graduate studies, and other educational leadership options. This brings faculty together as they consider whether this is the kind of student who should be mentored and encouraged to pursue advanced studies and whether faculty could and should use their close ties to local school districts to help steer promising candidates toward known job opportunities. Since faculty have just reviewed the student's entire progress, growth, and achievements in the master's program, they are in an excellent position to assess the student's future potential as a school leader. Faculty reported that they would not have had the knowledge of the student's desires had they not engaged in this structured conversation about the student's future career plans.

CONCLUSIONS

While the educational administration faculty at EMU is still gathering data from a new group of program completers, early results continue to indicate that the portfolio process has become an important and viable capstone experience for the master's program in educational leadership. It has become a powerful catalyst for reflection on student growth and understandings, has enhanced faculty collaboration, and has helped improve overall program design and instructional delivery of the master's program. As an alternate assessment technique, the portfolio has created an important opportunity to involve students in directing, documenting, and evaluating their own learning and to engage faculty in meaningful consideration of their programs, their colleagues, and themselves.

REFERENCES

Achilles, C. M. (1994). Searching for the golden fleece: The epic struggle continues. *Educational Administration Quarterly, 30*(1), 6–26.

Allen, R. (1994). *Performance assessment focus.* (Educational Issues Series). Madison: Wisconsin Education Association Council.

Argyris, C., & Schön, D. A. (1974). *Theory in practice: Increasing professional effectiveness.* San Francisco: Jossey-Bass.

Barrows, H. (1984). A specific problem-based, self-directed learning method designed to teach medical problem-solving skills and enhance knowledge retention. In H. Schmidt & M. Volder (Eds.), *Tutorials in problem-based learning* (pp. 16–32). Maastraicht, The Netherlands: Van Gorcum.

Bogdam, R. C., & Bilkin, S. K. (1982). *Qualitative research for education: An introduction to theory and methods.* Boston: Allyn & Bacon.

Bolman, L. G., & Deal, T. E. (1994). Looking for leadership: Another search party's report. *Educational Administration Quarterly, 30*(1), 77–96.

Bridges, E. M., & Hallinger, P. (1992) *Problem-based learning for administrators.* Eugene: ERIC Clearinghouse on Educational Management, University of Oregon.

Cambron-McCabe, N. (1993). Leadership for democratic authority. In J. Murphy (Ed.), *Preparing tomorrow's school leaders: Alternative designs* (pp. 157–176). University Park, PA: University Council for Educational Administration.

Christensen, C. (1987). *Teaching and the case method.* Cambridge, MA: Harvard Business School.

Clark, V. (1986). The effectiveness of case studies in training principals: Using the deliberative orientation. *Peabody Journal of Education, 63,* 187–195.

Dezure, D. (1993). Using cases about teaching in the disciplines. *Change, 25*(6), 40–43.

Erskine, J., Leenders, M., & Mauffette-Leenders, L. (1981). *Teaching with cases.* London, Ontario, Canada: University of Western Ontario, School of Business Administration.

Forrest, A. (1990). *Time will tell: Portfolio-assisted assessment of general education.* Washington, DC: American Association for Higher Education.

Fullan, M. G. (1992). *The new meaning of educational change.* New York: Teachers College Press.

Hutchings, P. (1993). *Using cases to improve college teaching: A guide to more reflective practice.* Washington, DC: American Association for Higher Education.

Hutchings, P., & Marchese, T. (1990). Watching assessment: Questions, stories, prospects. *Change, 23*(5), 12–38.

Kottkamp, R. B. (1990). Means for facilitating reflection. *Education and Urban Society, 22*(2), 182–203.

Langer, G. M., & Colton, A. M. (1994). Reflective decision making: The cornerstone of school reform. *Journal of Staff Development, 15*(1), 2–7.

Milstein, M. M., & Associates. (1993). *Changing the way we prepare educational leaders: The Danforth experience.* Thousand Oaks, CA: Corwin Press.

Nweke, W. C. (1991, November). *What type of evidence is provided through the portfolio assessment method?* Paper presented at the meeting of the Mid-South Educational Research Association Conference, Lexington, KY.

Osterman, K. F. (1990). Reflective practice: A new agenda for education. *Education and Urban Society, 22*(2), 133–152.

Paulson, L. F., & Paulson, P. (1990, August). *How do portfolios measure up? A cognitive model for assessing portfolios.* Paper presented at the annual meeting of the Northwest Evaluation Association. (ERIC Document Reproduction Service No. ED 324 329)

Paulson, L. F., Paulson, P. R., & Meyer, C. A. (1991). What makes a portfolio a portfolio? *Educational Leadership, 48*(5), 60–63.

Schön, D. A. (1983). *The reflective practitioner: How professionals think in action.* New York: Basic Books.

Schön, D. (1990). *Educating the reflective practitioner.* San Francisco: Jossey-Bass.

Slevin, K. (1989). *Portfolio methods of assessment: A sampling of campus practice.* Washington, DC: American Association for Higher Education.

Valencia, S., et al. (1990). *Assessing reading and writing: Building a more complete picture for middle school assessment.* Champaign: University of Illinois at Urbana-Champaign.

Wiggins, G. (1993). Assessment: Authenticity, context, and validity. *Phi Delta Kappan, 75,* 200–208, 210–214.

Wilmore, E. L., & Erlandson, D. A. (1995, January). *Portfolio assessment in the preparation of school administrators.* Paper presented at the annual meeting of the Southwest Educational Research Association, Dallas, TX.

CHAPTER 19

Why Are Cohorts Used or Rejected by Educational Leadership Faculty?

Bruce G. Barnett, Margaret R. Basom, Cynthia J. Norris, and Diane M. Yerkes

Educational leadership programs across the country are undergoing substantial changes in curriculum content, instructional delivery, field placements, and student assessment practices (Milstein & Associates, 1993; Murphy, 1992). One of the more popular innovations is student cohorts, an approach which is becoming more common in master's and doctoral degree programs (Cordiero, Krueger, Parks, Restine, & Wilson, 1992; Norton, 1995). In the typical cohort arrangement, groups of students take all, or a significant portion, of their coursework with an intact group, rather than randomly enrolling in courses at their own pace. In an effort to understand better how cohorts are being conceptualized and used, a variety of studies have emerged, ranging from descriptions of the structural aspects of cohorts (Hackman & Price, 1995; Norton, 1995; Yerkes, Basom, Barnett, & Norris, 1995) to analyses of the effects of cohorts on students and faculty (Burnett, 1989; Herbert & Reynolds, 1992; Hill, 1995; Kasten, 1992; Norton, 1995).

Using student cohorts to prepare educational leaders is not a new program innovation. As early as the 1950s, various educational leadership programs sponsored by foundations and reform initiatives such as the Kellogg Foundation, the Cooperative Program in Educational Administration, and the Leadership in Education in Appalachia Project provided instruction to cohorts of graduate students (Achilles, 1994). These early attempts at using student cohorts, however, tended to wane over time. In many cases, the cohort structure disappeared once the funding from external sources no longer was available, suggesting that this innovation had not become an institutionalized delivery mechanism within the university (Achilles, 1994; Basom, Yerkes, Barnett, & Norris, in press). As we enter a new era of cohort use in higher education, it is essential to understand the factors that affect whether faculty are using or rejecting this delivery structure, especially if this innovation is to become more than a passing fad.

Recent attempts to investigate cohorts in educational leadership preparation programs have been limited by their sampling design. For instance, the populations for these studies tend to be restricted to certain universities (e.g., only programs associated with the Danforth Foundation initiative or members of the University Council for Educational Administration) or specific programs that are using cohorts, thereby ignoring a vast number of universities in which cohorts have been embraced or rejected by the faculty. The study reported here seeks to uncover the perceptions of a wide array of faculty by surveying all educational leadership programs, regardless of whether or not they incorporate cohorts. A study of this magnitude provides a comprehensive examination of cohort usage, rather than the current narrow perspective.

The major purpose of this research study was to examine the perceptions of educational leadership faculty who have made the conscious choice to use or avoid cohorts. This is one of the rare studies to date that examines the perceptions of both cohort users and nonusers. In particular, our research explores the reasons for using cohorts as seen through the eyes of those closest to the innovation—educational leadership faculty using cohorts—as well as the rationale for avoiding this instructional approach by those educational leadership faculty

---

Bruce G. Barnett, University of Northern Colorado
Margaret R. Basom, University of Wyoming
Cynthia J. Norris, University of Houston
Diane M. Yerkes, California State University, Fresno

who refrain from using cohorts. The following research question guided our investigation: *What factors do educational leadership faculty consider when deciding to use or not use cohorts?*

To investigate this question, we begin by briefly reviewing conceptual and empirical literature focusing on the factors influencing the use of innovations in higher education. Next, the data collection and analysis methods are described, followed by a comparison of the reasons faculty provided for embracing or rejecting this instructional approach. Finally, a discussion of these findings is presented, including our major conclusions about cohort use or nonuse as well as suggestions for future research.

INNOVATIONS IN HIGHER EDUCATION

Extant literature on change and innovation delineates the characteristics of innovations as well as the human and structural factors influencing organizational change. For our purposes, an innovation is considered to be a new idea or practice which is accepted by some members of the organization while being rejected by others (Rogers, 1983). An innovation, according to Hall and Hord (1987), can be a product (e.g., a new textbook adoption, a curriculum revision) or a process (e.g., counseling techniques, discipline procedures). The implementation of cohorts, therefore, is a process innovation. In framing our understanding of change and innovation in higher education, we touch briefly on (a) the general factors influencing innovations and (b) the perceptions of nonusers of innovations.

General Factors Affecting Innovations

An emerging literature base deals explicitly with innovations in higher education. Although much of the research in this area is descriptive and speculative rather than empirical, some common factors appear to affect program change and innovation in colleges and universities: conditions within the organization, qualities of the innovation, and conditions outside the organization.

The degree to which new initiatives and improvements become accepted in higher education settings is affected by certain *internal organizational conditions*. Perhaps the most important of these internal conditions is the material, human, and symbolic support allocated to the innovation (Berman & McLaughlin, 1976). Without collegial support for and interest in the innovation, necessary resources will not follow (Fleisher, 1985), and members of the organization will not be as likely to implement the change (Hall, 1976; Hall & Hord, 1987). Further, the experience level of faculty can affect how or if an innovation is used. For example, inexperienced faculty may lack the vision to see the value of a new idea or practice, whereas veteran faculty may need to be much more involved in the decision-making processes surrounding the prospective innovation (Walsh, 1993) if it is to succeed. Finally, organizational structures can enhance or impede the use of an innovation. The incorporation of total quality management in higher-education settings, for instance, has been severely hampered when massive training programs are employed, measurement of performance is overemphasized, and reward structures ignore team performance (Lozier & Teeters, 1993). Likewise, White (1990) found the lack of faculty development programs and large-scale program implementation negatively influences the use of an innovation.

The *qualities of the innovation* itself can affect its implementation. In most cases, the larger the scope and complexity of the innovation, the more difficult it is to implement (Berman & McLaughlin, 1976; Hall, 1976). Rogers' (1983) work on the diffusion of innovations underscores how certain features of innovations influence the rate at which they are adopted. These factors represent the types of questions people in the organization ask as an innovation is being contemplated:

1. Relative advantage: Does the innovation improve what we currently are doing?
2. Compatibility: Does the innovation reflect and honor our values, previous experiences, and needs?
3. Complexity: Can we understand the purpose and use of the innovation?
4. Trialability: Can we use the innovation on a trial basis?
5. Observability: Can we see tangible results of the innovation?

In general, when these questions tend to be answered affirmatively, members of the organization are more likely to experiment with and adopt the innovation.

The qualities of an innovation identified by Rogers (1983) reflect the importance of the organizational context within which the change will occur. Typically, novel practices or ideas which are not adapted to the organizational context can become "watered down," losing their intended impact. For example, the total quality management movement has suffered greatly from this problem, especially when prepackaged, large-scale programs are employed which ignore the unique characteristics of the organization and its members (Lozier & Teeters, 1993). In addition, university writing programs have experienced implementation problems, especially when these programs become a bureaucratic means for monitoring student performance, rather than an innovation aimed at improving students' writing competencies (White, 1990).

Finally, *external organizational factors* can influence how well an innovation is accepted and used although some evidence suggests that these external influences are less problematic than the internal factors mentioned above (Creamer & Creamer, 1986). Federal regulations and policies can enhance or hamper implementation, just as can societal trends (Berman & McLaughlin, 1976). White (1990) provides a striking example of how the country's conservative social, political, and economic policies of the early 1980s severely reduced funding for community psychology programs and evaluation research in colleges and universities.

Nonuser Perceptions of Innovation

Although substantial research has been conducted on how the change process affects those who are using an innovation, some evidence indicates that certain factors affect nonusers' willingness to try a new practice or use a new product. Many of the reservations expressed by nonusers reflect the research on stages of concern summarized in the Concerns Based Adoption Model (CBAM) developed by Hall and Hord (1987). CBAM research indicates that people experience a series of developmental stages—beginning with self-concerns before moving to task and impact concerns—as they consider adopting an innovation. Hall's (1976) early research revealed that nonusers of instructional modules in higher education tended to have lower-level self-concerns, while those faculty using instructional modules expressed higher-level task concerns. This difference indicates that nonusers remained focused on self-concerns since they had no experience with the innovation.

Other research in higher education settings confirms that nonusers' concerns are focused on their personal well-being. For instance, nonusers of instructional television rejected this technological innovation because they were concerned that their teaching role would be diminished and the teaching process would be dehumanized (Koontz, 1989). Similarly, faculty who were not willing to infuse writing into their classroom activities were concerned with the likelihood of an increased personal workload as well as a lack of time and expertise to teach writing (Boice, 1990).

Nonusers also are troubled by other possible consequences of the innovation. Nonusers of instructional television, for instance, believed that the lack of both administrative support and faculty development programs (task concerns) would hamper its use. Further, nonusers also were apt to anticipate problems an innovation might create for students (impact concerns) such as learning would not be improved and students would not be motivated to participate in the new program (Boice, 1990; Koontz, 1989).

These studies of change and innovation in higher education reflect the variety of structural and human factors facilitating or impeding the use of a novel practice or program. With the exception of Hall's (1976) early work on CBAM, few empirical studies have investigated how users and nonusers differ in their reactions to an innovation. This study is intended to shed light on why higher education faculty are motivated to use or reject a particular innovation, student cohorts.

METHODOLOGY

This study is part of a large-scale investigation of educational leadership faculty perceptions of cohorts. Using a survey research design, information was collected using the Cohort Use in Educational Administration/Leadership Programs Questionnaire (see Appendix). One portion of the questionnaire asked respondents to describe various demographic features of the university and the educational leadership preparation program (questions A. 1–5) and focused on factors such as the size of the university and preparation program, the types of programs offered in the department, and the priority placed on teaching, research, and service. In addition, faculty members' perceptions about cohorts, whether they were using this instructional approach or not, were examined using a series of open-ended questions focusing on (a) their definition of a cohort (question B. 1), (b) how cohorts are (or could be) used (question B. 2), (c) the reasons why cohorts are (or are not) being used (question B. 3), (d) the observed (or possible) benefits of and problems with cohorts (question B. 4), (e) the observed (or possible) distinctions between cohort and noncohort students (questions B. 5, 7), and (f) the observed (or possible) differences in how well students are prepared for leadership roles when enrolled in a cohort program (questions B. 6, 8).

Questionnaires were mailed to all educational leadership preparation programs in the United States ($n = 372$) and several Canadian universities ($n = 11$), resulting in a total sample of 383 university programs. Department chairs were asked to complete the questionnaire regardless of whether or not they were using cohorts in their leadership preparation programs. Following the initial distribution to the 383 universities, a follow-up questionnaire was mailed to nonrespondents. These distribution procedures yielded 223 completed and usable questionnaires (58% response rate). Of the final sample of 223 programs, 141 universities (63%) were using cohorts in some or all of the preparation programs and 82 universities (37%) were not using cohorts, revealing cohort use to be quite prevalent. Although this is one of the largest samples of cohort programs ever obtained, over 40% of educational leadership programs are not represented in the study. Therefore, some caution should be exercised regarding the generalizability of the findings to all educational leadership programs.

The following four tables summarize the demographic features of the universities and preparation programs constituting the final sample. Table 1 reveals that cohorts tend to be used more frequently in educational leadership programs housed in larger universities. Similarly, the size of the educational leadership preparation program reflects differences in cohort use (see Table 2).

Smaller programs (i.e., those enrolling up to 100 students) are less likely to use a cohort structure, whereas larger programs (i.e., those enrolling more than 300 students) employ cohorts more frequently. Similar trends in cohort use are reflected in the number of departmental faculty available to teach. Programs employing cohorts tend to have more faculty assigned to their departments than those not using a cohort structure (see Table 3).

Finally, Table 4 indicates cohort programs are more prevalent in universities emphasizing faculty research rather than teaching or service, a finding which probably is related to university size (see Table 1) because larger universities tend to be major research institutions.

As noted above, the questionnaire dealt with a variety of issues about cohorts; however, for this investigation, only the responses to the following question were analyzed and reported: Why have the faculty decided to use or not use cohorts? Data analysis was supported by the QRS NUD-IST qualitative data analysis software package. Separate data files were created for university programs using and not using cohorts. For each file, faculty responses were coded and categories created which reflected the reasons for using or rejecting cohorts. Two members of the research team developed the codes and categories. One member designed the preliminary cod-

Table 1. University Size and Cohort Use.

University Size	Cohorts Used n	Cohorts Used %	Cohorts Not Used n	Cohorts Not Used %	Total n	Total %
Up to 10,000	40	29	42	58	82	39
10,000–19,999	52	38	21	29	73	35
20,000 or more	46	33	10	13	56	27
Totals	138	100	73	100	211	101

Note. Some respondents did not indicate university size. Percentages may total more than 100% due to rounding.

Table 2. Number of Students in Program and Cohort Use.

Number of Students	Cohorts Used n	Cohorts Used %	Cohorts Not Used n	Cohorts Not Used %	Total n	Total %
Up to 100	43	32	34	46	77	37
101–200	45	33	26	35	71	34
201–300	26	19	11	15	37	18
More than 300	22	16	3	4	25	12
Totals	136	100	74	100	210	101

Note. Some respondents did not indicate number of students in the program. Percentages may total more than 100% due to rounding.

Table 3. Faculty FTE and Cohort Use.

Faculty FTE	Cohorts Used n	Cohorts Used %	Cohorts Not Used n	Cohorts Not Used %	Total n	Total %
Less than 4	30	22	37	49	67	32
4–6	53	38	25	33	78	37
7–9	39	28	10	13	49	23
10 or more	16	12	3	4	19	9
Totals	138	100	75	99	213	101

Note. Some respondents did not indicate faculty FTE. Percentages may total more than 100% due to rounding.

Table 4. University Priority on Teaching, Research, and Service Related to Cohort Use.

Priority	Cohorts Used n	Cohorts Used %	Cohorts Not Used n	Cohorts Not Used %	Total n	Total %
Teaching	56	43	43	58	99	51
Research	73	57	30	41	103	49
Service	0	0	1	1	1	1
Total	129	100	74	100	203	101

Note. Some respondents did not indicate priority of teaching, research, and service. Percentages may total more than 100% due to rounding.

ing and categorization scheme for the two data files which were then reviewed by the second researcher. Changes in codes and categories were made following discussions between the two researchers, a process which adheres to the procedures of the constant comparative data analysis method described by Glaser (1965).

FINDINGS

Data analyses revealed similarities and differences between cohort users and nonusers on the rationale for incorporating or rejecting cohorts in their preparation programs. To compare and contrast the reactions of cohort users and nonusers, we first summarize the reasons reported by departments that are incorporating this approach, followed by a similar analysis for departments that have elected not to use cohorts. To highlight chairs' perceptions, major categories capturing their reactions are examined, including the quantity (i.e., relative number of respondents who mentioned a particular reason for using or not using cohorts) and the quality of their responses (i.e., written excerpts from the questionnaire).

Cohort Users

Approximately two thirds of the respondents (141 of the 223 programs or 63%) were currently using cohorts in some or all of their leadership preparation programs. The reasons stated for using cohorts include the following. (Percentages total more than 100% because some respondents reported more than one reason.)

1. Impact on students during their program (66 of 141 programs = 47%)
2. Structural issues associated with cohort programs (66 of 141 programs = 47%)
3. Implications for faculty and programs (18 of 141 programs = 13%)
4. Effect on students after program completion (10 of 141 programs = 7%)

Almost half (47%) of the respondents who were using cohorts mentioned (a) the benefits associated with students' interpersonal relationships and growth (impact on students during their programs) and (b) the ease of scheduling, planning, and delivering the preparation programs (structural issues associated with cohort programs). Users believed that better interpersonal relationships are developed in cohort programs, which subsequently encourage students' growth and development. Their comments repeatedly reinforced the importance of trust, collegiality, networking, student learning, and cooperation. They reported that cohorts provide "a sense of belonging, peer support, learning to work in teams, development of human relationship skills"; "evidence of commitment and collaborative learning among adults"; "enriched student learning experiences"; "supportive networks for students"; and a "community of learners."

Just as important as the growth and development of students was efficient program management. Users left little doubt that their leadership preparation programs were being delivered more efficiently when employing a cohort model. Because many cohort programs tend to schedule courses in a predetermined sequence, users viewed this predictable structure as positively affecting program planning and delivery. The following comments strongly support the managerial benefits of cohorts: "[Cohorts were] encouraged by administration as a means to aid retention toward graduation, recruitment, and planning for a multiple-year schedule"; " economical delivery"; "facilitates our course planning"; "guarantees enrollments for a segment of the overall program"; and "facilitates faculty assignments." Users also saw the cohort as more readily meeting the students' needs, particularly in off-campus programs, as illustrated by these respondents' comments: "[The cohort] assures us that off-campus courses would have adequate enrollment" and "we initiated the cohort group to serve students who found the distance to the university too great."

Finally, a small number of users reported that the cohort model benefits faculty (13%) and provides an avenue for modeling the type of leadership schools of the future will require (7%). Their comments suggested that cohorts will "develop the leadership necessary to restructure schools" and "model site-based decision making [leaders] must use in schools."

Cohort Nonusers

About one third of the respondents (82 of the 223 programs or 37%) indicated they were not using cohorts in any of their leadership preparation programs. Interestingly, respondents who did not use cohorts reported many of the same types of reasons as cohort users, only in different proportions. The reasons and percentages for nonusers are as follows. (Percentages total more than 100% because some respondents reported more than one reason.)

1. Structural issues associated with cohort programs (60 of 82 programs = 73%)
2. Impact on students during their program (26 of 82 programs = 32%)
3. Implications for faculty and programs (20 of 82 programs = 24%)
4. Effect on students after program completion (5 of 82 programs = 6%)

Almost three quarters (73%) of nonusers commented on the difficulties associated with program efficiency, particularly planning, scheduling, and delivering the program. These structural problems were by far the primary reason respondents stated for not using cohorts in their leadership preparation programs. Lack of flexibility and logistical problems were captured in these comments: "scheduling of cohort groups is difficult if not impossible," "insufficient resources," "travel difficulty," "our students can't always attend in lockstep fashion," and "one size does not fit all." Some nonusers hinted, however, that advantages could attend this approach since cohorts could "facilitate scheduling of courses" and "maximize small enrollments."

Nonuser respondents were adamant about the possible detrimental impact on students and faculty (32% and 24% respectively), reinforcing their decision not to use cohorts. Typical comments included: "students do not need to learn at the same rate," "students don't like the restrictive nature of the cohort," and "in real life [cohorts are] not the way administrators work." Nonusers also mentioned that the lack of faculty involvement and commitment influenced their decision to refrain from utilizing cohorts. In many cases, departmental faculty members had either not made a firm decision to use cohorts or the issue of using cohorts had not been raised, as evidenced by comments such as "we are not in the discussion stage of the benefits of going to a cohort," "there has been no decision [about cohorts]," and "[cohorts have] never been discussed as an option." Finally, in terms of meeting students' needs after completing the program, a handful of nonusers (6%) acknowledged that, if students were in cohorts, they could benefit by "learning to work as teams and a community of learners."

DISCUSSION

This investigation of cohorts confirms and expands previous research on change and innovation in higher education in general and cohort use in particular. The following findings are discussed in greater detail: (a) the reasons expressed by nonusers in this study compared with previous literature focusing on faculty who decide not to use innovations and (b) the similarities and differences between users' and nonusers' perceptions of why they chose to incorporate cohorts in their leadership preparation programs.

Concerns of Faculty Not Using an Innovation

Early research on how people react to an innovation indicates that they are more likely to express personal concerns about how the innovation will affect them rather than task or impact concerns (Hall, 1976). More recent research, however, suggests nonusers of an innovation may in fact be concerned about the possible problems of managing the innovation (Koontz, 1989) and the negative impact on students (Boice, 1990; Koontz, 1989). Respondents in this study tended to focus on concerns about program rigidity and organizational problems (task concerns). Almost three fourths of the nonuser respondents expressed serious reservations about scheduling, logistics, and rigidity of program offerings, factors which convinced them to refrain from using cohorts. The influence of cohorts on faculty (self-concerns) and student development (impact concerns) were cited by far fewer nonusers, suggesting that the overriding difficulty of cohorts resides in its perceived rigid program structure.

Being concerned about program management and inflexibility may be a result of the scope and complexity associated with cohorts as an innovation. Some evidence suggests that the more complex the innovation, the more difficult it is to implement (Berman & McLaughlin, 1976). Deciding to move to a cohort model may have ramifications for an entire program, rather than simply affecting a course or an individual faculty member. Because of the magnitude of cohorts as a program innovation, faculty may perceive this structure to be more difficult to implement. The decision to use cohorts is not a trivial matter; reformulating curriculum, altering course sequencing, and revising student assessment affects all, or certainly the majority, of the faculty in an educational leadership department. Furthermore, as Fleisher (1985), Hall (1976), and Hall and Hord (1987) caution, without the investment and support of colleagues and superiors for the innovation, it (i.e., the cohort) may be doomed to failure.

Rogers' (1983) work on the diffusion of innovations also may account for the reluctance of faculty to use cohorts. Given the types of organizational and delivery changes required when moving to a cohort model, nonusers may not view cohorts as having a relative advantage over their current practices. In fact, they may perceive cohorts as quite a disadvantage, especially the restrictions on scheduling courses and meeting individual student's needs. Without being willing to try cohorts, even on a trial basis, nonusers were unable to anticipate or experience the possible tangible benefits for themselves or for students if they chose to implement this innovation.

Comparisons of Cohort Users and Nonusers

This study compares the rationale of both cohort users and nonusers for implementing or rejecting cohorts in their educational leadership programs. Similar reasons for implementing or not implementing cohorts were mentioned by users and nonusers. Both groups made their decisions primarily because of the impact on program delivery and student development. Interestingly, what users see as a viable reason for using a cohort (e.g., program efficiency), nonusers see as a liability. For instance, slightly less than 50% of the users mentioned managerial efficiency as the main reason for deciding to utilize cohorts; however, approximately 75% of nonusers believed the structural and organizational limitations of cohorts do not make them a worthwhile investment.

CONCLUSIONS

Overall, the results of this study suggest several conclusions regarding why faculty choose to use or reject a cohort approach in educational leadership programs:

1. Users believe organizational efficiency and benefits to students' learning and development are prominent reasons for using cohorts.
2. Nonusers' overwhelming concerns about program rigidity and restrictions for students significantly influence their decision not to implement cohorts.
3. Users and nonusers tend not to consider the long-term impact on student development when choosing to use or reject cohorts.

Our findings and conclusions leave us with some curiosity, particularly about what cohort users see as an asset, nonusers see as a liability. A typical comment from a user was: "We decided to use cohorts for scheduling and FTE reasons." Conversely, a nonuser was apt to write: "[We chose not to use cohorts] because of logistical problems in scheduling activities." Besides the possible explanations mentioned earlier, perhaps program size and available faculty resources influence the decision to employ a cohort model. Recall that larger programs tended to use the cohort approach (see Tables 1–3). Because almost two thirds of the respondents are using cohorts, additional research which clarifies this apparent discrepancy might begin to uncover the source of nonusers' discomfort as well as the potential they see in this delivery mechanism. In fact, an analysis of another portion of this data base revealed that some cohort nonusers sensed certain benefits accruing to the program and to students even though they had elected not to employ this delivery mechanism (Barnett, Basom, Yerkes, & Norris, 1997).

Caution should be employed when interpreting these results and conclusions due to the limitations of the research design. On the one hand, over 40% of the educational leadership preparation programs included in the population are missing from the final sample. Generalizing these results to the overall population of preparation programs is somewhat specious. Obtaining a more representative sample of programs would enhance these findings. On the other hand, the study gathered data at one point in time, making it impossible to determine the developmental nature of faculty concerns with cohort use. Even so, the following questions remain unanswered: Do cohort users' concerns change over time? Do cohort users see different benefits or liabilities the longer they use this delivery mechanism? What factors, if any, convince reluctant nonusers to use cohorts? Further, this study examined cohorts only in educational leadership departments, ignoring other university programs which might use a cohort approach. Therefore, future research might investigate the reasons faculty in other disciplines, such as teacher education, business, law, medicine, and physical and social sciences, elect to use or reject this instructional delivery model. Such investigations would broaden our understanding of cohorts, especially how faculty perceive the utility of this approach.

Finally, other aspects of cohorts can be examined in the future. For example, students' perceptions can be explored by determining whether they select leadership preparation programs based on their impressions of cohorts as well as the short- and long-term benefits and challenges they experience in a cohort. In addition, future studies might examine the effects of cohorts on university staffing patterns; faculty workload, compensation, and productivity; and the fiscal efficiency of program delivery. As taxpayers and policymakers continue to call for greater efficiency and increased productivity of university faculty and programs, it will become even more critical for educational leadership faculty to understand and communicate the advantages or threats posed by cohorts to student enrollment, program completion rates, university and program revenues, and faculty workload.

APPENDIX: COHORT USE IN EDUCATIONAL ADMINISTRATION/LEADERSHIP PROGRAMS QUESTIONNAIRE

A. University and Program Information

This section requests information about your university and the educational administration/leadership programs that are offered. Place a check on the appropriate lines in each question.

1. Approximately how many students attend your university?

    Fewer than 5000 _____ 15,000–19,999 _____
    5000–9999 _____   20,000–24,999 _____
    10,000–14,999 _____   25,000 or more _____

2. Rank order the priority your university places on the following in regard to promotion and tenure (with one as highest priority, two as medium, and three as the lowest priority):

    Research _____   Teaching _____   Service _____

3. Check the types of programs offered and whether you use cohorts in these programs:

Program	Offered?	Cohorts Used?	
		Yes	No
Certificate, License, Credential	_____	____	____
Master's Degree	_____	____	____
Educational Specialist Degree	_____	____	____
Doctoral Degree	_____	____	____

4. How many full-time equivalent faculty are assigned to the educational administration/leadership programs reported in Question 3?

   Fewer than 4 _____   4–6 _____   7–9 _____   10 or more _____

5. Estimate how many students are currently enrolled in programs in educational administration/leadership at your university.

   Fewer than 25 _____   151–200 _____
   25–50 _____   201–250 _____
   51–100 _____   251–300 _____
   101–150 _____   More than 300 _____

B. Cohort Information

This section seeks to explore your perceptions of cohorts and how they are used. Please respond as completely as you can, whether or not your educational administration/leadership programs use cohorts.

1. What is your definition of the term "cohort"?
2. How is your educational administration/leadership program using cohorts? If cohorts are not being used, speculate as to how they might be used.
3. Why have the faculty decided to use or not to use cohorts?
4. What do you see as the benefits and difficulties of using cohorts?
   - Benefits
   - Difficulties

If cohorts are used in any of your programs, answer Questions 5 and 6. If cohorts are not being used, answer Questions 7 and 8.

For cohort users:

5. Are there any differences between cohort students and those not in cohorts? If so, please describe those differences.
6. Are students who have been in cohorts better prepared for leadership roles? Why or why not?

For cohort nonusers:

7. What differences might exist between cohort and noncohort students?
8. Would students who have been in cohorts be better prepared for leadership roles? Why or why not?

Please place the survey in the enclosed return envelope. Drop it in the mail. Your time and thoughtful responses are sincerely appreciated.

REFERENCES

Achilles, C. M. (1994). Searching for the golden fleece: The epic struggle continues. *Educational Administration Quarterly, 30*(1), 6–26.

Barnett, B. G., Basom, M. R., Yerkes, D. M., & Norris, C. J. (1997, March). *The benefits and liabilities of cohorts: Perceptions of educational leadership faculty.* Paper presented at the annual meeting of the American Educational Research Association, Chicago.

Basom, M., Yerkes, D., Barnett, B., & Norris, C. (in press). A backward glance: Cohorts in educational leadership programs. *Record in Educational Leadership.*

Berman, P., & McLaughlin, M. W. (1976). Implementation of educational innovations. *Eductional Forum, 40,* 345–370.

Boice, R. (1990). Faculty resistance to writing-intensive courses. *Teaching of Psychology, 17*(1), 13–17.

Burnett, I. E. (1989, August). *Elaboration on working together: A collaborative approach to university/school system principalship career development.* Paper presented at the annual meeting of the National Council of Professors of Educational Administration, Tuscaloosa, AL.

Cordiero, P. A., Krueger, J., Parks, D., Restine, L. N., & Wilson, P. (1992). *Taking stock: A study of the Danforth programs for the preparation of school principals.* St. Louis, MO: Danforth Foundation.

Creamer, D. G., & Creamer, E. G. (1986). Applying a model of planned change to program innovation in student affairs. *Journal of College Student Personnel, 27*(1), 19–26.

Fleisher, M. (1985, March). *Routinization of a community psychology program: Passages and cycles.* Paper presented at the annual meeting of the Eastern Psychological Association, Boston.

Glaser, B. G. (1965). The constant comparative method of qualitative analysis. *Social Problems, 12,* 436–445.

Hackman, D. G., & Price, W. J. (1995). *Results of a national survey of educational leadership doctoral programs.* Unpublished manuscript.

Hall, G. E. (1976). *Longitudinal and cross-sectional studies of the concerns of users of team teaching in the elementary school and instructional modules at the college level.* Austin: University of Texas Research and Development Center for Teacher Education.

Hall, G. E., & Hord, S. M. (1987). *Change in schools: Facilitating the process.* Albany: State University of New York Press.

Herbert, F. T., & Reynolds, K. C. (1992). *Cohort groups and intensive schedules: Does familarity breed learning?* Unpublished manuscript.

Hill, M. S. (1995). Educational leadership cohort models: Changing the talk to change the walk. *Planning and Changing, 26*(3/4), 179–189.

Kasten, K. L. (1992, October). *Students' perceptions of the cohort model of instructional delivery.* Paper presented at the annual convention of the University Council for Educational Administration, Minneapolis, MN.

Koontz, F. R. (1989). Critical barriers to the adoption of instructional television in higher education. *Educational Technology, 29*(4), 45–48.

Lozier, G. G., & Teeters, D. J. (1993). The challenge: Overcoming the pitfalls. *New Directions for Institutional Research, 78,* 127–132.

Milstein, M. M., & Associates. (1993). *Changing the way we prepare educational leaders: The Danforth experience.* Newbury Park, CA: Corwin Press.

Murphy, J. (1992). *The landscape of leadership preparation: Reframing the education of school administrators.* Newbury Park, CA: Corwin Press.

Norton, M. S. (1995, October). *The status of student cohorts in educational administration preparation programs.* Paper presented at the annual convention of the University Council for Educational Administration, Salt Lake City, UT.

Rogers, E. M. (1983). *Diffusion of innovations.* New York: Free Press.

Walsh, S. M. (1993, November). *How to develop a program for writing across the curriculum with an established faculty in a period of retrenchment.* Paper presented at the annual conference of the National Council of Teachers of English, Richmond, VA.

White, E. M. (1990). The damage of innovations set adrift. *American Association for Higher Education Bulletin, 43*(3), 3–5.

Yerkes, D. M., Basom, M., Barnett, B., & Norris, C. (1995). Cohorts today: Considerations of structure, characteristics, and potential effects. *Journal of CAPEA, 7,* 7–19.

CHAPTER 20

Emotional Intelligence and Educational Leadership

James O. McDowelle and Edwin D. Bell

For years, school leaders have attempted to pinpoint that "indefinable something" that separates successful leaders from unsuccessful leaders. Practitioners and university professors agree that success in school leadership is dependent upon more than technical skill and academically defined intelligence (Greenfield, 1980; Griffiths, 1988; Hodgkinson, 1991; Matsumoto & Sanders, 1988; Murphy, 1993; Sergiovanni, 1992). The lack of precise definitions and empirical research to support assertions about these nonobservable variables long has made it difficult to discuss these intangible leadership qualities. As the year 2000 approaches, research associated with the concept of emotional intelligence provides a vocabulary and empirical support for leadership preparation programs in their attempt to pinpoint and develop the intangibles of leadership. The concept of emotional intelligence also may assist public school leaders in their recruitment and assessment of other school administrators.

A VIGNETTE

A real-life incident illustrates the problems caused when a school administrator lacks that "indefinable something." An urban superintendent, plagued by recurring problems in the gifted and talented (G&T) program, promised to get the most capable person available to fill the position. Her search led to a university which featured a state-of-the-art, cutting-edge program in the design and administration of programs for the gifted and talented. A graduate of this program was recruited to come to the urban school system to lead the G&T program. During the selection process, the G&T administrator dazzled the interview committees and the superintendent with his technical mastery, articulate presentation, and high-energy personality. Glowing recommendations accompanied the administrator's exceptional curriculum vitae, and he was hired. Unfortunately, problems emerged as the administrator began to work with the various constituencies involved with the G&T program. Although friendly enough in personal encounters, Mr. G&T appeared dismissive of other viewpoints and preoccupied with his own agenda and task orientation. He saw no reason to enlist the support of others since it was very clear that he possessed more knowledge in this particular area than anyone he encountered. He believed that merely stating the facts that were so obviously clear to him should be enough to convince others to accept his position. Networking with professional colleagues was, therefore, not an option he considered. In addition, he was not empathetic with parents, although in many cases he agreed with their concerns. After meeting with him, they often felt disappointed. Even though he had, in essence, agreed with them. These parents felt that he neither understood nor sympathized with their plight. Eventually, a critical mass of his detractors formed, and the criticisms could no longer be ignored. The administrator was summoned by the superintendent and apprised of the situation. Having worked so hard and been so sure of his direction, he was devastated to learn that his efforts were not appreciated. The devastation was made even greater by the fact that he had no inkling of any problems with his work. Crushed by what he considered to be a very personal rebuke, he reacted in a way that was

---

James O. McDowelle and Edwin D. Bell, East Carolina University

disproportionate to the criticism. He became depressed. His job performance suffered, and he eventually resigned his position.

EMOTIONAL INTELLIGENCE

School leaders frequently have seen variations of this scenario demonstrated in public schools. People with excellent credentials are put in leadership positions and fail because of the absence or presence of certain emotional elements. Until recently, school people have been unable to describe these emotional components with precision or to support their hunches about the effects with empirically verifiable research. Daniel Goleman (1995) provided some insight and direction to help address this dilemma. Goleman described the emotional components that often cause people with high IQs to fail and people with modest IQs to succeed beyond anyone's expectations. His book was on the *New York Times* best-seller list for more than 40 weeks and is now having an impact on business, professional, and educational institutions (Confrey, 1995; Farham, 1996; Gibbs, 1996; Murray, 1996; Nelton, 1996; O'Neal, 1996).

Emotional Intelligence Defined

The concept of emotional intelligence (EQ) was formulated by Salovey and Mayer (1990). They characterized EQ as combining the intrapersonal and interpersonal intelligences described by Gardner (1993). The authors proposed five skill domains that comprise emotional intelligence: (a) being self-aware, knowing yourself and recognizing your feelings; (b) managing emotions, regulating your feelings; (c) motivating yourself, persisting in the face of frustration and difficulties; (d) empathizing, perceiving life as others perceive it; and (e) handling relationships by managing emotions in others. These social skills are used in leadership, teamwork, cooperation, conflict resolution, and negotiation.

The study of the effect of emotions on performance in the workplace, classroom, and personal relationships has been gaining credibility since the mid-1980s (Ashforth & Humphrey, 1995). Prior to the work of Salovey and Mayer (1990), Eysenk, Pearson, Easting and Allsopp (1985) described the emotional development of adults interacting in varied environments. Sternberg (1988) developed the concept of mental self-management and reported research supporting the concept. He described mental self-management as the way in which we order and make sense of events that take place in both our internal and external worlds. Sternberg's mental self-management was a lineal precursor to the concept of EQ.

Emotionality in Organizations

Although his work was not ground breaking, Goleman (1995) popularized the concept of emotional intelligence and raised awareness of the empirical data that have been compiled to support inquiries on the effects of the emotions on intelligence and performance. Much of the fieldwork and research conducted on the importance of the emotions has been related to the study of organizational development and leadership (Ashforth & Humphrey, 1995; House, Woycke, & Fodor, 1988; Howell, 1988; Kahn, 1990; Kelly & Caplan, 1993; Williams & Sternberg, 1988). Ashforth and Humphrey (1995), for example, analyzed the ascendance of the notion of rationality and subsequent displacement of emotionality in organizational development literature. Emotionality either has been neglected or perceived pejoratively. The disregard of emotionality in the literature describing effective organizations may have erroneously circumscribed our perceptions of organizations. If emotions are seen as dysfunctional or as barriers to institutional progress, the study of leadership will be constrained and ultimately stunted.

Ashforth and Humphrey contended that emotionality and rationality are not mutually exclusive concepts and that irrationality is not synonymous with emotionality. The acknowledgment of both elements must occur for an organization to function effectively. For example, the study of motivation within an organization is limited unless human emotion is taken into account. Discussions of motivation must consider the effects of the emotional connection of the person to work (Kahn, 1990). The idea of "flow" (Csikzentmihalyi, 1990), the capacity to become totally engaged in work and to be highly motivated by the work itself, has very little to do with rational incentives but is strongly related to emotional connections to the essence of the work. Emotionality and rationality complement each other in the work world. They can be viewed as inseparable parts of the life of the organization. Rationality and emotionality must both be acknowledged and incorporated into organizational life.

The complementarity of emotionality and rationality in the workplace makes sense because that is the way in which the human brain operates. Proper functioning of the brain is dependent upon the smooth interaction of emotionality and rationality. Goleman (1995) reported that neurological research supports the notion that emotions are indispensable for rational decision making. Rationality is centered in the neocortex region of the brain, and emotional responses are located in the limbic system, specifically the amygdala. Goleman provides an example: a corporate lawyer who suffered damage to the limbic system. Although all his cognitive functions were still intact, he could no longer make even the simplest daily life choices. He could not choose whether to eat french fries or mashed potatoes or whether to wear jeans or a suit. More complex decisions became completely impossible because he had no emotional preference and therefore could not use experience in the decision-making process. The emotional responses that inform and streamline decision making were lost.

EMOTIONAL INTELLIGENCE AND EDUCATIONAL LEADERSHIP

The study of the concept of emotional intelligence is part of a larger movement to expand the belief, knowledge, and skill domains of school leadership (English, 1994; Maxcy, 1991; Rost, 1991; Sergiovanni, 1992). Inquiries into the effect of emotional intelligence on educational leadership will inform discussions about the part that ethics, collaboration, and democratic decision making play in the exercise of school leadership.

The Hegelian dialectic can be used to illustrate how the concept of emotional intelligence is expanding the inquiry about the beliefs, skills, and knowledge necessary for the exercise of school leadership. Hegel posited that knowledge of reality passes through three phases (Taylor, 1975). One's initial conception of reality is the thesis. As one obtains conflicting information about the subject, a second conceptual position, the antithesis, emerges. Eventually, these opposing ideas merge into a final phase or synthesis. Applied to school leadership, this process suggests an initial emphasis on morality and character, placing little value on technical-rational skills, as the thesis. As school leadership evolved as a discipline, English (1994) contends that the antithesis developed, a business ethos focused on technical-rational skills in law, finance, planning, and management. As a consequence, emotions, values, and ethics were not prominent in discussions about school leadership. Now school leadership may be entering an era of synthesis in which both technical-rational skills and character are considered essential.

Applications of EQ to School Leadership

The abilities associated with EQ (Salovey & Mayer, 1990) have clear implications for the exercise of school leadership or any other intense, stressful, activity. Successful school leaders should not be unduly deterred from focusing on their responsibilities by the vicissitudes that are part of the daily events in a school or school district. They should be self-aware and cognizant of the effects that they have on the people that they lead. An effective principal or superintendent must empathize with a variety of stakeholders and constituencies and must work well as a member of a team or as a team leader. An effective leader should be able to transmit the hope that regardless of current problems or issues, things will get better in the future. Recalling the anecdote about Mr. G&T, his inability to empathize with both parents and professional colleagues created the immediate problem. Once the problem surfaced, he was unable to persist in the face of frustration or to keep distress from hindering his ability to confront the situation and learn from his mistakes.

Sarason (1982) described serious problems in the selection and recruitment of future school leaders, making the point that "Choosing a leader is obviously a crucial process and one in which personality and contextual factors fatefully begin to interact..." (p. 47). Other research suggests that standards for admittance in graduate administrative preparation programs are so low and the programs so lax that anyone wishing to become an administrator could receive administrative certification and licensure (Hallinger & Murphy, 1991).

Criticism of selection processes for public school administrators led the National Commission on Excellence in School Administration (1987) to recommend changes in the recruitment practices of universities and school systems. Unfortunately, the commission focused its attention on the performance by future leaders on cognitive tests such as the Graduate Record Examination and the Miller Analogies. Evidence compiled by researchers in areas associated with emotional intelligence suggests that the linkage between cognitive testing and job performance is tenuous. A meta-analysis of cognitive test research conducted by Sternberg, Wagner, Williams, and Horvath (1995) concluded that differences in cognitive test performances accounted for between 4% and 25% of variance in job performance. Therefore, 75% to 96% of the ability to perform a job is related to other variables. Gardner asserts that non-IQ factors play the dominant role in determining an individual's place in society (Goleman, 1995). Among the non-IQ factors cited by Gardner (1993) are interpersonal intelligence, social skills used in interacting with others, and intrapersonal intelligence, self-knowledge, and mental self-management. Intrapersonal intelligence and interpersonal intelligence are closely related to EQ.

Work by Shoda, Mishel, and Peake (1990) offered some direction in devising methods to counter the overreliance on cognitive testing in personnel recruitment and selection. The "marshmallow test" research reported by Shoda et al. described a situation in which a 4-year-old child was given a marshmallow. The child was told that he would be given two marshmallows if he could resist eating the marshmallow while the researcher was out of the room. The ability of the child to delay gratification as measured by the marshmallow test was twice as powerful a predictor of how the child would later perform on the Scholastic Aptitude Test as the child's score on an IQ test. The child's mental self-management and emotional self-control were also greater predictors of success and adjustment to life 12 to 14 years after the test.

Attempts to devise adult versions of the marshmallow test are currently under way (Farham, 1996). Some progress in this vein has been made by Seligman (Gibbs, 1996) who contracted with Metropolitan Life Insurance Company to develop a test that would ascertain the probable chances for future success of newly hired insurance sales representatives. Seligman's test determined levels of optimism or positive attitude in potential employees since insurance salespeople must be able to handle rejection and maintain a stable emotional balance while experiencing setbacks. The ability of the test to predict success based on emotional characteristics appears to be strong. Sales representatives who scored at the superoptimist level outsold the pessimists by 21% the first year and 57% the second year (Gibbs, 1996).

RESEARCH ON EMOTIONAL INTELLIGENCE

Educational leaders should study the research on emotional intelligence and implement practices suggested by empirical data compiled through inquiries about EQ. For example, managers are learning that the necessity for teaming in the modern work world requires greater EQ skills (Nelton, 1996). Williams and Sternberg (1988) found that a lack of EQ skills, or emotional illiteracy, among members of a team created a lack of harmony among the team and lowered what they call "the group IQ." Dysfunctional interaction among the group lessened the group's ability to solve problems and act creatively.

Other research on leadership effectiveness highlights the EQ skills used in networking. Krackhardt and Hanson (1993), for instance, describe how leaders in organizations conducted business through an informal series of networks that operated across both functional and formal boundaries. Conducting this type of networking was premised on EQ skills, and the networks were found to be a much stronger source of organizational communication than those dictated by organizational charts. Kelly and Caplan (1993) studied star performers at Bell Labs and found that the most effective were those who were most adept at networking. They reported that these people were able to rely upon their networks when they encountered difficulties on the job. Conversely, individuals without networks received inadequate assistance when they sought help.

ASSESSING EMOTIONAL INTELLIGENCE

Members of the faculty in the Department of Educational Leadership at East Carolina University (ECU) believe that the empirical data on emotional intelligence offer support for including specific areas of skill development for leaders. At ECU, efforts are underway to include the development of knowledge and skills associated with EQ in the educational leadership curriculum. Some might contend that public school leadership preparation programs already include elements related to EQ. The argument presented here is that the concepts and skills ascribed to emotional intelligence should be systematically and intentionally applied throughout the curriculum for leadership development. The curriculum for school leadership must include attention to both content (the knowledge and theoretical bases of the curriculum) and processes (field experiences, internships, in-class activities, and other clinical activities). Educational leadership preparation programs should plan not only for the development of these capabilities but also for the assessment of EQ skills and knowledge. To this end, the Department of Educational Leadership at ECU is initiating a longitudinal study to measure students' concepts and skills associated with emotional intelligence, ethical analysis, and tolerance of diversity. Pretests and posttests are planned to determine the effect of the curriculum on EQ capabilities. The assessments to be utilized are the EQ Map (Cooper & Sawaf, 1997), the Defining Issues Test (Rest, 1988, 1989, 1995), and the Beliefs about Diversity Scale (Pohan, 1995; Pohan & Aguilar, 1994). Results of this research will be reported as the program progresses.

CONCLUSION

Education is a people business. Exclusion of the emotions, motivations, and drives of the actors engaged in this enterprise is unnecessarily reductive and restrictive. Despite the "pop culture" status of emotional intelligence, it is based upon serious inquiry and research. Practitioners and professors of educational leadership need to recognize the implications of emotional intelligence for preparation and practice implicit in the concept. This will require close scrutiny of the research, fieldwork, and corollary literature linked to emotional intelligence. As a result, internships and clinical experiences which include planned opportunities for teaming, networking, conflict-management and negotiation will be greatly enhanced, and program graduates will not fail, like Mr. G&T, to understand and appreciate others' perspectives in constructive ways.

REFERENCES

Ashforth, B. E., & Humphrey, R. H. (1995). Emotions in the workplace: A reappraisal. *Human Relations, 48*(2), 97–125.

Confrey, J. (1995). A theory of intellectual development. *For the Learning of Mathematics, 15*(2), 36–45.

Csikzentmihalyi, M. (1990). *Flow: The psychology of optimal experience.* New York: Harper & Row.

English, F. W. (1994). *Theory in educational administration.* New York: HarperCollins.

Eysenck, S. B., Pearson, P. R., Easting, G., & Allsopp, J. F. (1985). Age norms for impulsiveness, venturesomeness and empathy in adults. *Personality and Individual Differences, 6*(5), 613–619.

Farham, A. (1996, January 15). Are you smart enough to keep your job? *Fortune, 133,* 34–36, 40, 42, 46, 48.

Gardner, H. (1993). *Multiple intelligences.* New York: Basic Books.

Gibbs, N. (1995, October 2). The EQ factor. *Time, 146,* 60–66, 68.

Goleman, D. (1995). *Emotional intelligence.* New York: Bantam Books.

Greenfield, T. B. (1980). The man who comes back through the door in the wall discovering truth, discovering self, discovering organizations. *Educational Administration Quarterly, 16*(3), 25–59.

Griffiths, D. E. (1988). *Educational administration reform PDQ or RIP* (UCEA Occasional Paper No. 8312). Tempe, AZ: University Council for Educational Administration.

Hallinger, P., & Murphy, J. (1991). Developing leaders for tomorrow's schools. *Phi Delta Kappan, 72*(7), 514–520.

Hodgkinson, C. (1991). *Educational leadership: The moral art.* Albany: State University of New York Press.

House, R. J., Woycke, J., & Fodor, E. M. (1988). Charismatic and non-charismatic leaders: Differences in behavior and effectiveness. In J. A. Conger, R. N. Kanungo, and Associates (Eds.). *Charismatic leadership: The elusive factor in effectiveness* (pp. 98–121). San Francisco: Jossey-Bass.

Howell, J. M. (1988). Two faces of charisma: Socialized and personalized leadership in organizations. In J. A. Conger, R. N. Kanungo, and Associates (Eds.), *Charismatic leadership: The elusive factor in organizational effectiveness* (pp. 213–236). San Francisco: Jossey-Bass.

Kahn, W. A. (1990). Psychological conditions of personal engagement and disengagement at work. *Academy of Management Journal, 33,* 692–724.

Kelly, R., & Caplan, J. (1993). How Bell Lab creates star performers. *Harvard Business Review, 71*(4), 128–139.

Krackhardt, D., & Hanson, D. R. (1993). Informal networks: The company behind the chart. *Harvard Business Review, 71*(4), 104–111.

Matsumoto, D., & Sanders, M. (1988). Emotional experiences during engagement in intrinsically and extrinsically motivated tasks. *Motivation and Emotion, 12,* 353–369.

Maxcy, S. J. (1991). *Educational leadership.* New York: Bergin & Garvey.

Murphy, J. (Ed). (1993). *Preparing tomorrow's school leaders: Alternative designs.* University Park, PA: University Council for Educational Administration.

Murray, W. (1996, April). Are your students emotionally intelligent? *Instructor, 103,* 52–55.

National Commission on Excellence in Educational Administration. (1987). *Leaders for America's schools: The report of the National Commission on Excellence in Educational Administration.* Tempe, AZ: University Council for Educational Administration.

Nelton, S. (1996). Emotions in the workplace. *Nation's Business, 84*(2), 25, 26, 28, 30.

O'Neal, J. (1996). On emotional intelligence: A conversation with Daniel Goleman. *Educational Leadership, 54*(1), 33–39.

Pohan, C. A. (1995, February). *Examining beliefs about diversity: Applications for teacher training.* Paper presented at the annual meeting of the National Association for Multicultural Education, Washington, DC.

Pohan, C. A., & Aguilar, T. E. (1994). The Beliefs About Diversity Scale. Lincoln: University of Nebraska-Lincoln, Center for Curriculum and Instruction.

Rest, J. R. (1988). Why do colleges promote development in moral judgment? *Journal of Moral Education, 17*(3), 183–194.

Rest, J. R. (1989). With the benefit of hindsight. *Journal of Moral Education, 18*(2), 86–96.

Rest, J. R. (1995). Notes for an aspiring researcher in moral development theory and practice. *Moral Education Forum, 20*(4), 11–14.

Rost, J. C. (1991). *Leadership in the twenty-first century.* New York: Praeger.

Salovey, P., & Mayer, J. D. (1990). Emotional intelligence. *Imagination, Cognition, and Personality, 9,* 185–211.

Sarason, S. B. (1982). *The culture of the school and the problem of change* (2nd ed.). Boston: Allyn & Bacon.

Sarason, S. B. (1989). *The creation of settings and the future societies.* San Francisco: Jossey-Bass.

Sergiovanni, T. J. (1992). *Moral leadership: Getting to the heart of school improvement.* New York: Praeger.

Shoda, Y., Mischel, W., & Peake, P. K. (1990). Predicting adolescent cognitive and self regulatory competencies from preschool delay of gratification. *Developmental Psychology, 26*(6), 78–86.

Sternberg, R. (1988). *The triarchic mind: A new theory of human intelligence.* New York: Viking.

Sternberg, R. J., Wagner, R. K., Williams, W. M., & Horvath, J. A. (1995). Testing commonsense. *American Psychologist, 50*(11), 912–927.

Taylor, C. (1975). *Hegel.* London: Cambridge University Press.

Williams, W. M., & Sternberg, R. J. (1988). Group intelligence: Why some groups are better than others. *Intelligence, 12,* 351–377.

CHAPTER 21

Can Leadership Be Learned? On Writing and Analyzing the Stories of Educational Leaders

Arnold Danzig and Charles Porter

It's hard to teach anything that can't be broken down into repeatable and unchanging elements. Driving a car, flying an airplane—you can reduce those things to a series of maneuvers that are always executed in the same way. But with something like leadership, just as with art, you reinvent the wheel every single time you apply the principle.
—Sydney Pollack, Oscar-winning director and producer, when asked if leadership can be taught

The best ways of preparing school leaders continue to be an important debate in the field of educational administration (Hallinger, Leithwood, & Murphy, 1993; Murphy, 1990; Terry, 1993). Articles in three recent issues of *Teaching in Educational Administration* (Cordiero, 1997; English, 1996; Hallinger & Bridges, 1996) raise questions on the relative advantages and limitations of two current approaches: (a) problem-based learning and (b) narrative and biographical approaches to learning. While the two approaches have much in common, they have important differences as well. The problem-based approach adopts a foundationalist epistemology which draws heavily on knowledge domains in educational administration such as those recommended by the National Policy Board in Educational Administration (1989) and represented in the UCEA Primis document base of readings and articles (Hoy, 1994). On the other hand, the narrative approach draws more from cultural and literary analysis and focuses on the historical, biographical, and cultural contexts of leadership. The narrative approach adopts the view from cognitive psychology that story telling and story listening are basic ways that human beings learn (Bruner, 1996).

THE RATIONALE: HOW STORIES HELP PEOPLE LEARN

The assumption of the research reported here is that leadership can be learned. This learning results from life experiences that are brought to the surface and examined for meaning. Stories are one way of subjecting experience to such scrutiny and reflection. Stories connect the explicit, formal, symbolic presentations of knowledge and the practical know-how found in effective actions (Bruner, 1996; Clandinin & Connelly, 1991; Schön, 1991). Stories provide an opportunity for future leaders to examine experiences and practices. The subtleties and nuances of personal relations, organizational culture, values, beliefs, rituals, and myths take on more meaning as they are presented in stories. These underlying concepts are often overlooked or ignored in the rush of daily decision making, and they lose explanatory power if they are presented as abstract principles, divorced from the original situations and contexts in which they occur.

A story allows the careful listener to hear the inner thinking and dialogue of the storyteller. The story is by definition a reconstruction of events which have already occurred. This means a reduction of complexity by the teller. The listener is presented with a vocabulary, values, and constructs which are embedded in the story. Instead of abstract principles, complex life dramas and real people are brought into open discussion. In this way, a story connects theory and practice (Bruner, 1996; Coles, 1989; Schön, 1991).

Arnold Danzig and Charles Porter, Colorado State University

Stories of Education Leaders

A leadership story provides biographical context and details about the personal and practical knowledge of an education leader. While story telling has a long tradition in many fields, the professions have largely remained skeptical, even hostile, to the importance of stories in professional training and development (Bledstein, 1976; Coles, 1989; Lortie, 1975). Traditionally, educational and training programs are built around a knowledge base of theory and consensus around best practices. Leaders' stories and personal experiences are less often a source for the standards of professional practice (Coles, 1989).

The leadership story is a drama that unfolds over time, one in which the leader is the principal character. The leadership story is inevitably a story of identity, one in which leaders are successful in conveying a message to their followers. Gardner (1995) proposes three broad categories of stories: (a) stories about the self, (b) stories about the group, and (c) stories about meaning and values (p. 50). The leader's story is effective in that it is *illuminating*; it makes sense to the audience at a particular moment in time.

Clandinin and Connelly (1991) wrote a story about an urban school principal (Phil) which provides an opportunity to learn about his leadership and administrative decision making. Phil's story is about growing up as an immigrant boy near Toronto. The story explains some of the reasons why Phil values the "school as community." When Phil insists that an end-of-the-year teacher party be part of a larger community celebration, readers are provided a glimpse of what causes him to act this way. Clandinin and Connelly (1991) suggest that more than one explanation exists for events and actions. They ask whether Phil's story is one of a community-spirited principal or one of administrative hegemony, a principal telling his teachers how to celebrate the end of the year. Understanding Phil helps others interpret his actions.

Crafting and Analyzing Leadership Stories

In earlier articles, we have considered the rationale and methods for crafting the stories of experienced school administrators and educational leaders (Danzig, 1997a, 1997b, in press; Danzig & Harris, 1996). We argued that stories allow novices to consider the informal or tacit systems which exist side by side with the manifest systems operating in schools and other organizations. Future leaders have gained from the richer descriptions of the processes by which decision makers classify ambiguous and large amounts of information; they have learned from the descriptions of how leaders view and subsequently act upon problems that contain only partial information and conflicting expectations by parties involved.

The next sections focus more on what is learned in the analysis of stories and on different examples of analysis. Analysis examines the structure of the story. It explores what makes a story believable and possible alternative interpretations. Analysis invites the listener to compare and discriminate among multiple representations of phenomena. Our contention is that analyzing experienced leaders' stories promotes learning by uncovering the underlying theories which inform actions.

Sample

The stories in this research were collected and written by fourteen students in an administrator licensure and PhD program in education at a Carnegie I state university in the western region of the United States. All students were enrolled in a course on leadership development. Students selected a practicing school administrator or leader from their own field of expertise or interest. The storytellers included three school principals, two directors of community agencies, three university administrators (dean, department head, director), one community college vice president, one chief of a campus police unit, one director of a campus ministry, one U.S. Army colonel, and two business entrepreneurs (multimillion dollar businessman and wealthy rancher). Seven of the 14 leaders had been teachers at one time. The administrative experience of the leaders sampled ranged from 3 to more than 10 years, with an average of over 6 years of administrative experience prior to holding their current positions. Eight of the 14 leaders selected were of the same gender as the student doing the interview. All of the mixed gender interviews involved female students interviewing male leaders. Students commented that they used the exercise as an opportunity to spend time with someone whom they admired and as an opportunity to be mentored.

Method

In an initial interview, the leaders were invited to talk about their own personal biographies and entry into their respective fields. In a second interview, they were invited to talk about a *specific* problem or situation in which they had played a leadership role. The problem was to be discrete rather than ongoing and was to involve others inside and outside their organization or institution. The resolution, if any, was also to be discussed. All interviews were audiotaped and transcribed for coding and analysis by the students.

An interview protocol was prepared to provide suggestions on how to begin the interviews, which word-processing system to use, and what the final story should look like. More detailed information about the assignment and interview protocol can be found in Danzig (1997b).

We envisioned a 1,500-to-2,500-word leadership story with an analysis of the central meaning of the story at the end. The goal was for students to write a portrait of *ordinary leaders* in the same way that Gardner (1995) had written stories of *extraordinary leaders* in his book *Leading Minds*. The stories were to include the personal, practical knowledge of the leaders and probe for specifics in their handling of events.

These stories were reviewed by the participating leaders. The goal was to ensure accuracy and to make certain that the storytellers were comfortable with the way that they had been presented in the story. Students were then asked to write their own analysis and reflect on how they might have handled the situation. In the analysis, students were also encouraged to consider the possibility of a counter story, an alternative interpretation of the story, and the limitations of leadership.

FINDINGS

Table 1 presents some of the leadership themes, key values, and examples of practice that were collected. These summaries highlight key concepts found in the leadership stories. The concepts are like qualitative codes and memos; they are derived from the interview data and class discussion of its meaning. Table 1 provides a sense of how leadership is connected to values. Values are in turn related (explicitly and implicitly) to the leaders' actions presented in the examples of practice. These codes/concepts move the reader closer to understanding what leadership means to the storytellers and provide a sense of what is central to the leadership stories.

Commonalities Among the Stories

All of the stories generated student interest. Some of the stories were very dramatic—school fights, vandalism, charges of racism, dealing with sexism, student suicide; others were more mundane—helping a coworker, planning growth of a new program, building a successful business, determining procedures for crowd control at football games. Many of the stories contained dilemmas, where leaders must select from equally unsatisfying options. The rancher in Story L, for example, decided to retire a longtime worker after a stroke, even when he begs for his job. The colonel in Story M refused an out-of-country assignment because of family considerations, to the detriment of his career. These dilemmas provided students an opportunity to probe more deeply into their own value sets, asking what they might have done in similar situations and how they might have acted.

The students were generally approving in their initial stories and descriptions of the leaders and of the leaders' actions. A lack of criticism was not surprising, considering the stories were told from the leaders' perspectives. Also, the assignment to craft a story in the words and from the perspective of the leader decreased the likelihood of a story that was highly critical of the teller. The stories illustrated the connections among biography, personal history, and professional actions.

A Leadership Story: An Example

Excerpts 1 through 6 are part of a larger story taken from Storyteller B (thanks to Mary Ellen Burning for per-

Table 1. Concepts in the Leadership Stories.

Story-Tellers	Leadership Themes Referenced in Story	Key Value(s) Expressed in the Leadership Story	Example of Practice That Is Discussed in Greater Detail
A	Inclusionary leadership; respect in own domain	Discipline and hard work; less comfortable with ambiguity	Vandalism of school bus; dealing with students, parents, and police
B	Leader as resourceful and creative; willing to confront individuals in charge	Unfailing honesty; concern with fairness and the damaging effects of labels on children	Moving the City Council to hire therapeutic recreation specialist for preschool recreation programs
C	Leader as coach, building a team, common goals, common mission, and game plan	Providing every child with an opportunity to be successful	School fight; maintaining credibility with all stakeholders
D	Situational leader with priority on nurturing commitment of others; open relations with others and sharing ideas	Strong family values; allowing everyone the opportunity to realize potential	Serving on administrative bargaining team when faculty formed a union
E	Strong woman leader in predominantly male domain (ministry); leadership is the ability to get people to do things	Quality and integrity in the work one does; facing discrimination in a predominantly male leadership arena	Deciding to suspend long-standing relationship with local community agency for placing volunteers
F	Leaders serve at the pleasure of followers; leadership is being attuned to audience	Concern with moral issues; importance of balance between work and family	Difficulties of personnel evaluation and perceptions of unfairness by faculty
G	Leaders surround themselves with good people; leaders model the characteristics they want to instill in the organization	Need for educators to be empathetic, caring people who love working with children; meeting challenges head on	Student discipline problem results in being charged a racist; using charge as opportunity to address racism in school and community

(continued)

Table 1 (continued). Concepts in the Leadership Stories.

Story-Tellers	Leadership Themes Referenced in Story	Key Value(s) Expressed in the Leadership Story	Example of Practice That Is Discussed in Greater Detail
H	Leaders do not ask others to do what they are not willing to do themselves; no-nonsense approach	Importance of family; encouraging students to express concerns honestly and not cover up situations as a means of learning and personal growth	No specific situation given; general concern with student discipline and new challenges which face youth of the 1990s
I	Leader provides direction and involves staff and colleagues in decision making; keys to leadership are good communication, participation, and information sharing	Importance of balance of personal and professional life; collaboration and partnership part of both	Crowd control at stadium events; developing strategies to involve administrative, student, and community concerns and stakeholders
J	Leaders possess strong self-knowledge, using logical thinking and planning; leader sees herself more as collaborator than commander	Tolerance for diversity and flexibility in conflict situations; balancing goals of organization with individual development	No specific case given; general concerns raised over balancing multiple roles on the job
K	Success in business is the result of *passion* to improve performance; evokes sports metaphor to suggest leadership by example	Passion to win as key	Story of entrepreneur and starting business selling mineral springs water; growth in sales and of company's profitability
L	Leaders must make the difficult decisions	Alienation of man from the land and from his roots	At age 20, deciding to "clean house" and run the family ranch himself
M	Leaders are "reachable"; leaders communicate directly, free from jargon	Openness and honesty; respect for authority	Declining offer to take a new assignment and coping with damage to career
N	Leaders share power with others; leader adopts a teacher role with employees	Importance of relationships; mutual understanding, honesty, trust, caring, and respect prioritized	Developing successful university research center employing 20+ researchers and assistants

mission to use this story). The first and second excerpts give the reader a sense of early family and school experiences. This is followed with excerpts about educational experiences at school and college. The last excerpt looks at a specific leadership situation.

Excerpt One: Growing Up

I was born and raised in rural Illinois in the late 50s, not on a farm, but in a small town of 2,000 people, about 10 miles from the Mississippi River. The agricultural interest was hogs and corn. I lived in town, not in the country. From our town it was 30 miles to a restaurant or a big grocery store. If you wanted to go to the movies, go shopping, things like that, you had to drive 30 to 40 miles. We went to Chicago once in a while, often at Christmas, to see a play or to see the lights. In the summer we'd go to a Cubs game. Chicago was about three-and-a-half hours away.

I had three sisters, and I was the third child. We grew up in an old Victorian brick home that was about 100 years old and walked to school. It was a very kind of storybook childhood. My dad was a businessman, a pharmacist, who had graduated from the University of Iowa. My mom was a registered nurse, who did her nurses training and got her nursing degree at Michael Reese Hospital in Chicago during World War II.

My father was the real authority at home. I just did what he said, and if I didn't, I accepted the consequences. He was real clear about what his expectations were and *if* you didn't meet them, you knew what would happen. So I would make conscious choices about whether I was going to do what he wanted me to do or not. If I didn't I would take my punishment, whatever it might be.

Excerpt Two: Breaking School Rules and Pushing the System

In school, I spent a lot of time in the principal's office or sitting on a little chair outside the principal's office, waiting to see him. We were well acquainted. I didn't see him a lot until I got into 5th, 6th, and 7th grade. I remember that my friends and I would skip school. All the other kids would get their parents to sign an excuse so they could get back into school . . . or they would forge one. I would just go in and say, "I skipped."

The dean would say, "Go see Mr. Pratt" (the principal).

So I'd go see Mr. Pratt, and he'd say, "Where were you yesterday?"

I'd say, "Swimming out at Hall's Pond."

He'd say, "Why did you tell me that? Why didn't you tell me you were sick or tell me your grandma died or something? Now what am I suppose to do with that?"

I'd say, "I don't care. Do whatever you want."

He would usually let me off, but once in a while he would send me to detention—I was Student Council President, so he really had trouble sending me to detention—but a few times he did anyway just to see if it would do any good.

Excerpt Three: College and Early Career Choice

My education, through elementary and high school, happened in the town I grew up in. After that, I went to the University of Illinois in Champaign for 3 years. I transferred to Indiana University for a year and a half and finished up my degree in special education.

I went into special education because one of my early female role models, my aunt, was the director of therapy services for Peoria Association for Retarded Citizens. I would go and live with her for a few weeks each summer. I really idealized her life. She had five kids, worked full-time, and had a great marriage. When I was there, I would volunteer in the classrooms at PARC and those experiences were the reason I went into special education.

Once I had my degree, I taught for 8 years and then I went back and got my master's degree in special education. After another 12 years of teaching, I had my first child. I quit working and started the doctoral program in Special Education Administration. I plowed through coursework up to the dissertation, when I had another child—and that's where I stopped 8 years ago.

Excerpt Four: Early Professional Experiences

I was really frustrated when I was teaching in Indianapolis in a school of 520 kids where every kid had a label of "Trainable Mentally Retarded" or "Severely and Profoundly Handicapped." All these kids were bused to one campus.

One of that district's favorite things to do was to take the worst kids in a black, inner-city school and get them "tested down" to a level so that they could be gotten out of the building. So we had a lot of kids who, were they in school today, would be gang members and that kind of thing. Back then, the idea was to get them out of the building and sent out to our special school in Cold Springs. My lowest point was when I was cornered in a janitor's closet at knife point by one of these incorrectly "labeled" kids who was actually a juvenile delinquent and labeled "TMR." He was very smart, smart enough to figure out how to lure me into a closet and hold me at knife point.

But low points have been balanced out by high points. I can think of times when I've been working with a family who has been beating their head against the wall trying to access something—a service or funding—from the system. I would teach them a trick or show them a strategy or make a phone call that opens the door within the system for them. And then everything falls into place. Events like this are my high points and, gratefully, they happen on a monthly basis.

Excerpt Five: Using Personal Experience to Advocate for Families

I am currently the director of an agency that provides education and support both to families that have a child with a disability and to community professionals who work with those families. This all came about because of Rachel.

Rachel was born—she was very sick when she was born—and she ended up with a "label" of spastic cerebral palsy. As a result of my frustrations, I started working with a group from Denver called the Community Resource Center. I got the idea to start organizing families in the county to reform what was happening at the Community Center Board with their services—their preschool services at the time.

Because of Rachel I started organizing families—to "push" the system. When she started showing significant delays, I had tried to access the system. Here I was, a doctoral student in Special Education Administration, and I couldn't get what I needed for her. That's how crazy the system is and how inaccessible it is. So that said to me, if I can't do it, how would somebody with a degree in advertising or business figure this thing out? So, that's when I decided to use the information I had and the knowledge base I had acquired in graduate school to help families get what they needed for their kids. I wanted to see the system change.

Excerpt Six: Leadership in Practice

I had the opportunity to take a leadership role with the community-based organization that I direct. Two sets of parents came to me a few years ago, and they both had young children with disabilities. They were both physically active families, and they had always thought that when they had kids that they would be involved with their kids in recreation. They were finding out that, because their kids had significant labels, they were denied opportunities to participate in our city's recreation program or that they could participate only if Mom came along.

One of the women's child was two years, and she tried to enroll him in a program at the Lee Martinez Farm. The listed purpose of the program was for kids to learn to separate from Mom in a safe place where they could have fun for an hour. Pretty soon Mom would come back and get them, and so kids were able to learn the early concept that "Mom goes away, but she does come back."

When this mom went to sign her child up and she told them that her child had a disability, they said, "Oh, you'll have to stay here with him." She said, "Wait a minute, I thought the point was to leave him so that he'll learn that I'm coming back." They said, "We can't support (a child like) him."

As a result of this incident, we decided that we needed to do something. Together, we approached the recreation department of the city. They said, "Oh, we would love to do something about that, but we don't have the resources to hire someone to adapt curriculum within our programs or to train volunteers to help do the kinds of things that are needed."

I knew some people from the recreation department from when I used to teach and used to be involved with Special Olympics. The recreation department used to be really active in the Olympics, but they hadn't been in several years and had gotten farther and farther away from programs for kids with disabilities. Because of those contacts within the city government and a conversation with the mayor, I realized that it was possible to present a plan without going in with a hammer. I realized that we would go in with an open hand and work together.

So we formed a coalition and organized a lot of different institutions and organizations— the school district, the community center board, the hospital therapy department, a lot of parents, a lot of concerned citizens within the community—and got them to come together. Our goal was to get the funding resources to support participation in the regular recreation program for kids and people with disabilities. We knew that the recreation department already had a segregated program for adults with disabilities but we didn't want that for our young children. We wanted them to be in the thick of it with everybody else, with their peers.

We worked together to present a thought-out program to the city council with lots of public testimony. As a result, we got them to appropriate funds to hire a therapeutic recreational specialist who has started the kind of program we wanted.

That experience took a lot of leadership. When I realized that people wanted to go in with a hammer and tear things apart and hold up the Americans with Disabilities Act and Section 504 and go the route of filing grievances and complaints, I knew that kind of stuff doesn't usually work. I had to take the reins with this one to turn this action into more of a partnership activity. The only way that it would turn out well was if families could partner with the system to change it.

The excerpts and story from which they are taken portray a woman who sometimes pushes the limits of authority and takes the consequences for her actions. Her story points to a career decision to enter special education and draws on family values, family role models, and gender expectations. Her entry into administration and subsequent actions as director of a community agency are connected to her background, educational and professional experiences, and personal experiences being the parent of a child with a disability.

ANALYZING STORY THEMES

After crafting the story, the goal was for students to analyze significant themes in the story. Students were asked to compare the story that they heard with their own leadership and with how they might have handled events differently. In the analysis of Story B, the student pointed out the storyteller's expertise and commitment.

> She always acts as if her energy and intelligence should be used to help others. Years of graduate education combined with recent years of experience on state-level committees and task forces have created great domain expertise. She knows the laws and the policies that affect early intervention and special education on the local as well as state level. She understands the power structures and the pathways of accountability. Legislator and program administrators know her and her commitment to parents of children with disabilities. Her integrity and her ability to get things worked out has made her a valuable connection on both sides.

The analysis also raised the issue of leadership and empowerment:

> Leadership is empowering other people. In this case, it was empowering the community, the families that were behind the effort—empowering them to do what they needed to do. It was being there with the support and backup that they needed in order to accomplish it. I think the more power you give away, the more you actually have.

The analysis makes explicit the relevance of personal experience—that of having a child with a disability—to the leader's subsequent actions. And the student cites the storyteller's experience:

> I had tried to access the system. Here I was, a doctoral student in Special Education Administration, and I couldn't get what I needed for her. That's how crazy the system is and how inaccessible it is. (Storyteller B)

The quote helps explain the motivation for the storyteller to spend the next two years advocating for enhanced community services for children with disabilities.

Learning from Thematic Analysis

The thematic analysis of a leadership story is an important source of learning for future leaders. The story illustrates how an experienced person thinks about a complex problem. The story presents actions in certain ways that give them meaning. The story requires the student to consider multiple perspectives—a family's need for services versus the limited capacity of city programs to serve disabled children. The leader is also presented in a certain way, one in which her actions are placed in a larger context of personal and institutional concerns.

In the student's analysis, prior personal experiences and professional values are seen as congruent. The student gains understanding of some of the motives of the leader. The student defines the leader's actions in terms of working toward more inclusionary services for children. And the leader is portrayed as someone willing to "challenge city hall" when the situation requires her to do so.

The analyses of the stories raise moral issues to the surface. Students use words such as *tolerance, integrity, honesty, empowering, giving, concerned, fearless, perseverance, genuineness, passion, compassionate,* and *respectful,* to describe the leaders and the leaders' actions in specific situations. These descriptions attribute a moral basis to the leaders' actions that are taken from the stories. Values and how values are enacted in everyday events are common themes raised in all of the stories. An often-repeated narrative was of the altruistic leader who takes the moral high road, with personal and professional risk.

Narrative Analysis and Recognizing Core Leadership Values

Reissman (1993) points out that, "like weight bearing walls, personal narratives depend on certain structures to hold them together" (p. 18). Narrative analysis closely examines what contributes to making something a recognizable story, a story which moves people to action. Narrative analysis focuses on what makes a good story: What gives it power? What makes it believable? What is the core problem? What is the resolution? Narrative analysis explores the inner thinking that is part of the character's decision making and action, leading to a more complete understanding of the structure of the story. Labov (as cited in Reissman, 1993, pp. 18–19) points out that a fully formed narrative includes six common elements: (a) *an abstract* (summary of the substance of the story), (b) *orientation* (time, place, situation, participants), (c) *complicating action* (sequence of events), (d) *evaluation* (significance and meaning of the action, attitude of the narrator), (e) *resolution* (what finally happened), and (f) *coda* (return to the perspective to the present). With these elements, the teller constructs a story, and the significance of events takes on new meaning.

The excerpts presented earlier lead to a thematic analysis of leadership. For example, Excerpt Six: Leadership in Practice illustrated certain leadership themes (e.g., inclusionary leadership, empowerment). The narrative analysis looks for the core values of the story and better addresses the question "What is this a story of?" The narrative analysis displays the data in a different way, to reveal the core values within the story (see Table 2). Analyzing the structure of the story leads to identification of a core value system, working within the system for change. The narrative portrayal of data illustrates the central importance the leader gives to families being a "partner" with the system (as opposed to "going in with a hammer"). This interpretation is consistent with the other excerpts which also illustrate reduced conflict. For example, Excerpt One shows how authority is questioned but within the boundaries of the system. Even though the storyteller breaks the rules, she is not punished severely (if at all), nor does she challenge the basic legitimacy of the rules or of either parental or school authority.

The presentation of data in a narrative form reveals a disposition in which a leader works within the system to make evolutionary change. The point of learning for the student is not the specific steps the leader took to be effective or to reach a desired outcome. Rather, the key point is to illuminate what leaders draw from in choosing one direction or another. The narrative displays the underlying drama and multiple possibilities in the call to action and the leader's responses.

Differences exist between the thematic excerpts and the narrative analysis of the data. The thematic portrayal of the data points to the deliberations that are required to make a program more accessible to all children. The learner defines this as inclusionary leadership, how leaders empower others (here, families and parents). The

Table 2. Narrative Analysis of Excerpt Six: "Partner with the System to Change It."

1. Abstract
   I had the opportunity to take a leadership role with the community-based organization that I direct.

2. Orientation
   Two sets of parents came to me a few years ago, and they both had young children with disabilities. They were both physically active families, and they had always thought that when they had kids that they would be involved with their kids in recreation. They were finding out that, because their kids had significant labels, they were denied opportunities to participate in our city's recreation program or that they could participate only if Mom came along.

3. Complicating action
   When this mom went to sign her child up and she told them that her child had a disability, they said, "Oh, you'll have to stay here with him." She said, "Wait a minute, I thought the point was to leave him so that he'll learn that I'm coming back." They said, "We can't support (a child like) him."
   As a result of this incident, we decided that we needed to do something. Together, we approached the recreation department of the city. They said, "Oh, we would love to do something about that, but we don't have the resources to hire someone to adapt curriculum within our programs or to train volunteers to help do the kinds of things that are needed."

4. Evaluation
   Because of those contacts within the city government and a conversation with the mayor, I realized that it was possible to present a plan without going in with a hammer. I realized that we could go in with an open hand and work together.

5. Resolution
   We worked together to present a thought-out program to the city council with lots of public testimony. As a result, we got them to appropriate funds to hire a therapeutic recreational specialist who has started the kind of program we wanted.

6. Coda
   The only way that it would turn out well was if families could *partner* with the system to change it.

narrative analysis stays closer to the words and story line; it points to how leaders work within the system. For the storyteller, change is the result of "partnering" with the system. Implicit is the view that change is a result of careful planning and orchestration of key players to make things happen.

CONCLUSION

The goal of this paper was to explore whether leadership can be learned. The professional literature points to the need for leadership education and licensure programs to bridge the gap between theory and practice by drawing from communities of practitioners. However, practice does not necessarily mean expert practice, nor does experience guarantee that one has learned from it. Stories allow practice to be more carefully scrutinized.

Multiple outcomes attend collecting, writing, and analyzing leadership stories. One goal was for students to consider and inspect the informal systems which exist side by side with the formal systems operating in schools and other organizations. Issues related to personal relations, values, and beliefs take on more meaning as they are presented in stories of practice. These issues are sometimes overlooked or ignored in the rush of daily experience and in the learning and recitation of abstract principles.

Stories provide an opportunity for active leaders to share their experiences with future leaders. Many people enjoy sharing personal and professional experiences, particularly with someone who is less experienced. Our students report that new relationships and new empathies were formed as a result of the interviewing process.

Many discoveries about biography and leadership also emerged from these stories. Given the opportunity, leaders talked about themselves, their families, their work, and some of the major hurdles that they had faced over a career. Students struggled with capturing the story completely. They expressed concern with maintaining the voice of the storyteller and grappled with how to write a story. Sharing the story with the teller was a more difficult and more authentic assignment than simply writing a paper for a course grade.

How students understood what leaders said and did as they moved from the actual story to an analysis changed. Students began to identify some of the similarities and differences between how they might have constructed the problem and how the storyteller constructed the situation. This led students to consider their own values and make their own choices about what was important in the story versus what was peripheral. Crafting and analyzing the story allowed students to examine their own filters, or biases, in order to get a more complete understanding of what is important to them and how their filters influence their handling of problems or specific situations. And the stories allowed students to probe tacit knowledge related to action, seeking to understand how and why leaders act in certain ways in certain situations. This led to a more general understanding of how leaders define situations as problems, what leaders do in actual situations, and some of the motives behind their actions.

Can leadership be learned? Yes, but first we must recognize that leadership is not understood by breaking it down into abstract component parts. Leadership involves learning to analyze prior experiences in order to understand better how these experiences shape future courses of action; it is learning to reflect on how actions are connected to cultural norms, to initial experiences growing up, to institutional histories, and to professional experiences on the job. Leadership is learning to tell one's story in a way that is understandable to others and learning that other stories are equally powerful determinants of actions.

REFERENCES

Bledstein, B. (1976). *The culture of professionalism.* New York: Norton.

Bruner, J. (1996). *The culture of education.* Cambridge, MA: Harvard University Press.

Clandinin, J., & Connelly, F. M. (1991). Narrative and story in practice and research. In D. Schön (Ed.), *The reflective turn: Case studies in and on educational practice* (pp. 257–282). New York: Teachers College Press.

Coles, R. (1989). *The call of stories.* Boston: Houghton Mifflin.

Cordeiro, P. (1997). For the defense: The case against PBL is unproven. *Teaching in Educational Administration, 4*(2), 6–8.

Danzig, A. (1997a). Building leadership capacity through narrative. *Educational Leadership and Administration, 9,* 49–59.

Danzig, A. (1997b). Leadership stories: What novices learn by crafting the stories of experienced administrators. *Journal of Educational Administration, 35*(2), 122–137.

Danzig, A. (in press). The contribution of stories to leadership development. *International Studies in Educational Administration.*

Danzig, A., & Harris, K. (1996). Building competence by writing and reflecting on stories of practice. *Journal of Educational and Psychological Consultation, 7*(2), 193–204.

English, F. (1995). Toward a reconsideration of biography and other forms of life writing as a focus for teaching educational administration. *Educational Administration Quarterly, 31*(2), 203–223.

English, F. (1996). The problem with PBL (Problem Based Learning). *Teaching in Educational Administration, 4*(1), 1–3.

Gardner, H. (1995). *Leading minds: An anatomy of leadership.* New York: Basic Books.

Hallinger, P., & Bridges, E. (1996). Developing school leaders who are learning through problem-based leadership development. *Teaching in Educational Administration, 3*(2), 1–4.

Hallinger, P., Leithwood, K., & Murphy, J. (1993). *Cognitive perspectives on educational leadership.* New York: Teachers College Press.

Hoy, W. K. (Ed.). (1994). *Educational administration: The UCEA document base.* Hightstown, NJ: McGraw-Hill, Primis.

Leithwood, K., & Steinbach, R. (1993). The relationship between variations in patterns of school leadership and group problem-solving processes. In P. Hallinger, K. Leithwood, & J. Murphy (Eds.), *Cognitive perspectives on educational leadership* (pp. 103–129). New York: Teachers College Press.

Leithwood, K., & Steinbach, R. (1995). *Expert problem solving: Evidence from school and district leaders.* Albany: State University of New York Press.

Lortie, D. (1975). *The schoolteacher: A sociological analysis.* Chicago: University of Chicago Press.

Murphy, J. (1990). Preparing school administrators for the twenty-first century: The reform agenda. In B. Mitchell & L. L. Cunningham (Eds.), *Educational leadership and changing contexts in families, communities, and schools* (pp. 232–251). National Society for the Study of Education Yearbook. Chicago: University of Chicago Press.

National Policy Board for Educational Administration. (1989). *Improving the preparation of school administrators: An agenda for reform.* Charlottesville, VA: Author.

Reissman, C. (1993). *Narrative research.* Thousand Oaks, CA: Sage.

Schön, D. (Ed.). (1991). *The reflective turn: Case studies in and on educational practice.* New York: Teachers College Press.

Terry, R. (1993). *Authentic leadership.* San Francisco: Jossey-Bass.

CHAPTER 22

Interactive Television: Reactions of Students and Faculty

Earl B. Kaurala

Northern Michigan University (NMU) is located in Marquette, a city of 27,000 people situated in Michigan's Upper Peninsula (UP) and on the south shores of Lake Superior. NMU was originally established as a normal school, and of the three universities in the Upper Peninsula, NMU has the most extensive teacher-preparation programs on both the undergraduate and graduate levels. It is the only one of the three to offer a graduate program in educational administration and educational leadership. About 11% (896) of the students are enrolled in graduate programs at the university. Approximately 200 students are in programs leading to degrees in educational administration or educational leadership.

NMU's service area is large. Marquette is somewhat centrally located in the UP, but the distances that students and faculty must travel to take or to teach courses are still extensive. For example, Sault Ste. Marie, one of the sites for extension classes, is 165 miles from campus. Coming to campus for weekend courses from the farthest reaches of the UP is often a trip of two to three hours for many students. Students coming to campus for evening courses from sites closer to Marquette often travel anywhere from 30 to 60 minutes.

During the 1996–1997 academic year, the Department of Education in cooperation with the division of Continuing Education and Sponsored Programs offered five graduate-level courses using interactive television (ITV). The reasons for doing so, of course, are rather obvious when one considers the distances traveled by students and faculty. Then, too, many of the local school districts have been using interactive television instruction for a number of years, so many graduate students had begun to inquire about the possibilities of having courses taught using this technology. Members of the Education Department also wondered about the possibilities that this method would have for lessened travel. (It must be noted, however, that faculty were arguably more hesitant than the students to try the ITV format. During the course of several meetings and conversations, it became apparent that faculty apprehensions were rooted in natural concerns about using a medium so dramatically different and about its impact upon teaching and learning processes.) Recently, an Air Force base located twenty or so miles away from the university closed, causing a drop in total enrollment. Making classes more convenient for students, it was thought, would result in an increase in graduate-school enrollment. Added to this was the fact that the educational administration program had grown, perhaps in response to intensified recruitment efforts. In order to keep these students in the program, courses convenient to them needed to be offered.

Of the five two-way interactive television graduate classes taught during the 1996–1997 year, four were educational administration courses, and one was a seminar for beginning teachers. Two full-time professors and one adjunct professor were the instructors. Two of the courses originated from interactive classrooms on campus, and three originated from classrooms at one of the distance sites.

The study discussed here sought to ascertain perceptions of the students enrolled in the three classes taught by me and to discover the reactions of the three instructors to this method of teaching graduate courses. Four research questions guided this investigation:

1. What are the perceptions of effectiveness by students and faculty?
2. What are advantages perceived by students and faculty?

Earl B. Kaurala, Northern Michigan University

3. What are disadvantages or limitations noted by both groups?
4. What methods of instruction within the ITV format were considered to be effective?

METHOD

The research questions were chosen because of their relevance to questions raised by many of the faculty in the Department of Education and because of my interest in gauging student reactions to this format and in comparing my own reactions to those of the other faculty involved in this project. The questions of effectiveness, of strengths and limitations, and of teaching methods have also been studied by other researchers; consequently, I knew about an established basis against which to compare the findings of this study.

Students were asked to complete surveys during the initial and final class sessions. This paper reports the results from the final class session. We have discovered that graduate students in education department courses are quite vocal about the effectiveness of classes that they have taken and that they have not been reluctant in the past to share their opinions about the advantages and disadvantages of various instructional methods. Nonetheless, I explained to the students that the survey was being conducted for my personal research purposes. Because so many requests for ITV classes had been received, I wanted to allay any fears that negative comments about effectiveness and statements of disadvantages or limitations would result in discontinuance of the instruction via interactive television. I assured them that the university was committed to continuing the format and that their comments would help me to provide the best possible teaching and learning environment for future classes.

The graduate students surveyed consisted of those who were enrolled in the following three courses: ED 544: School Law, ED 533: School and Community Relations, and ED 596: Seminar in Teaching, the First Years. The School Law class originated from the distance learning classroom at Bay de Noc Community College, located in Escanaba. I traveled the 66 miles from campus to this site on Thursday evenings during the fall semester. From Escanaba, the class was sent to an ITV classroom in the Kingsford-Iron Mountain area, 79 miles from campus and about a 45-minute drive from Escanaba. The School & Community Relations course was a Saturday class sent from campus to Hancock, 105 miles from campus. The Seminar in Teaching originated on campus at 3:30 on Monday afternoons and was sent to four distance sites in the Eastern Upper Peninsula; distances from campus to these sites ranged from 100 to over 200 miles.

The two other faculty members were asked to respond in writing to questions about effectiveness, advantages, limitations, and teaching methods. Each of these professors taught one course, both of which originated from distance learning classrooms in Sault Ste. Marie. The classes (School Personnel Administration and Curriculum Development) were sent to St. Ignace. Sault Ste. Marie is a three-hour drive from Marquette as is St. Ignace. St. Ignace is about an hour distant from Sault Ste. Marie. One of the instructors traveled from Marquette, and the other traveled from the Newberry area, approximately an hour distant from the Sault. Both of these professors had previous experience in teaching courses at the graduate level.

I also filled out a questionnaire. In addition, I kept an intermittent journal during the time that I was teaching the courses and a file of any correspondence relating to these classes that I sent to the Education Department head, the director of Continuing Education, and other involved persons.

RESULTS AND DISCUSSION

This section presents the student survey and faculty questionnaire results for each of the research questions, followed by a discussion of those results and a comparison to other research findings.

Effectiveness

The first research question examined the perceived effectiveness of teaching and learning using the ITV format. The student results are presented in Table 1. Only 4 of the 55 total students found ITV to be ineffective.

Table 1. Effectiveness of ITV Format.

	Sending Sites		Receiving Sites		Total of All Sites	
	n	%	*n*	%	*N*	%
Very effective	2	10.52	12	33.33	14	25.45
Effective	10	52.63	15	41.66	25	45.45
No difference	5	26.31	7	19.44	12	21.81
Ineffective	2	10.52	2	5.55	4	7.27
Totals	19		36		55	

Twelve students saw no difference in effectiveness between ITV and the usual method of delivering classes. The other students found this method of instruction to be effective or very effective. A larger percentage of students at the receiving sites felt ITV to be effective or very effective.

One of the faculty stated that the format was "ineffective." The other instructor wrote the following:

> I think that there was some loss of effectiveness because of the fact that the folks at the distance site, in my case St. Ignace, did not have the benefit of participating in groups with the larger number of students in the Soo. I also had the notion that the off-site folks could wool-gather and even do other things while class was going on.

My own perception was that the courses I taught were effective to the degree that essential learning about course content took place. The ITV format and the teaching methods used, however, from my perspective were not conducive to creating "a sense of class." I often had the impression that students at the distance site were watching television rather than participating in a class. After one of the classes, I noted in my journal: "Major concern: How to create a sense of a learning community."

Poole (1996) reported that her examination of teaching effectiveness and student satisfaction revealed that students are generally satisfied with the experience and that they tend to perform as well on examinations as students in more traditional settings. She did find, however, that teachers were less satisfied with the experience than were their students. Although faculty reactions were mixed, teachers with positive reactions still had concerns about classroom interaction and logistics. McCleary and Egan (1989) reported no significant difference in achievement between campus and off-campus students. Bozik (1996) also found a general perception of effectiveness of the teaching strategies used in instruction delivered via an ITV system.

Advantages

The second research question dealt with discovering perceived advantages of the ITV format. The student responses to the open-ended question very naturally fell into two categories: less travel or more convenient and more opportunities. Out of 51 responses, 48 listed travel or convenience and 13 listed more opportunities. Many students expressed their gratitude to the university for making it possible for them to take classes closer to home, saving them travel time and allowing more time for them to spend with their families. Although this category received most of the comments, a number of students also wrote about the increased opportunities afforded by use of this medium. Opportunities listed included greater availability of classes and more opportunity to interact with students from places other than their home communities.

Faculty members listed as advantages less time spent traveling, ability to reach more students, opportunity to learn new technology, no need to prepare special transparencies because of availability of the document camera, easy access to VCR, and the availability of the computer to project information to the students. I had similar responses, although I added that this method also familiarized potential users (classroom teachers and building administrators) with the system. Another advantage from my perspective is that it forced me to look at a variety of teaching methods so that the teaching and learning process could be more effective.

McCleary and Egan (1989) reported apparent student satisfaction with two-way interactive television as measured by student retention through a three-course sequence of classes. Other researchers have recorded student satisfaction to the point of expressing gratitude for the opportunity, indicating that they may not have otherwise been able to take college classes (Poole, 1996).

Disadvantages and Limitations

The third question had to do with disadvantages and limitations felt by the students and instructors. Student responses fell into eight categories in answer to this open-ended question. The results are summarized in Table 2. Four of the responses received the vast majority of comment: (a) problems with sound level and distortion, (b) other technical difficulties (such as loud buzzing noises when a document camera was in use, fuzzy or frozen camera images, inability to see more than one additional site when there were multiple sites, etc.), (c) difficulty of establishing a sense of "connectedness" as a class because of problems interacting through class discussion and just sitting down and chatting with someone, and (d) the absence of the professor which increased some students' sense of isolation and which frustrated others because they could not communicate privately with him.

Disadvantages listed by the faculty responding to the questionnaire noted the difficulty of getting to know students personally at the distance sites, technical difficulties similar to those mentioned by the students, problems with handling cameras and other mechanical aspects when no technician was present, frustration over not being able to use teaching strategies known to be effective, the logistics of preparing and sending handouts and other class materials, and the difficulties that are part of dividing the teacher's attention between two or more sites.

Personally, I found this last disadvantage to be extremely exhausting. I seemed to carry on a constant dialogue in my head referring to the technical aspects as well as to the overall concern about what was going on at the distance site. This became extremely difficult when I had four distance sites, especially knowing that, because of technological limitations, not all sites could see and hear the others. Consequently, I had to become a translator to keep everyone advised of what was happening. The top two limitations for me were (a) the technical problems and (b) the difficulty of creating a sense of a learning community.

Freddolino (1996) discussed the importance of the relationships students have with the instructor and supporting personnel at local sites as well as with the technological aspects and the people involved with the technology. He wrote, "What else do you need in a distance education classroom besides a video monitor to create a quality learning environment? The simple answer to the question is 'Relationships, relationships, relationships'" (p. 206). Bozik (1996) reported that a study of university students involved in ITV courses found that 59% agreed or strongly agreed, 23% were neutral, and 17% disagreed or strongly disagreed with the statement "There is a real advantage to being in the origination site classroom" (p. 100). Poole (1996), reporting the results of her analysis of research findings related to ITV, noted that students reported "turning off the instructor and becoming inattentive" and that students "didn't feel a part of the class interaction with the professor at the remote site" (p. 79).

Table 2. Disadvantages and Limitations of ITV Format.

Response	n	%
Sound or Audio Difficulties	24	22.00
Technical Difficulties	33	30.27
Little Sense of Learning Community	23	21.10
Absence of Professor	21	19.26
Concentration Difficult	2	1.83
Too Much Time Watching Television	3	2.75
Fax Machine in Inconvenient Location or Unavailable	2	1.83
Difficulty of Obtaining Handouts	1	.09
Totals	109	99.14

Other disadvantages or limitations reported in the research literature included (a) difficulties with seeing and hearing and with maintaining attention, (b) less participation in class discussion, (c) fewer questions asked of teachers, (d) difficulty in getting teacher help, (e) disappointment in not being able to establish relationships with the teacher and other students, and (f) problems with delays in receiving materials (Tiene, 1997).

Instructional Methods

The final research question focused on effective methods of ITV instruction. Students indicated their frustration over not being able to engage in the quality of class discussion to which they have become accustomed in more traditional educational settings. They also appeared to value the opportunity to meet in small groups for discussion on site. In general, though, student responses were too inadequate in this area to make any fair assessment of them.

The faculty, however, had no trouble in responding to this area. They found that lecture, limited grouping, student presentations (especially in pairs), and small-group or cooperative-group work were effective. A comment relative to small-group work was that, with larger groups, the instructor can group students differently each time, but that smaller numbers, particularly at some of the distance sites, made this impossible.

In the main, I agreed with the comments of the other faculty. Class discussion was very difficult at times, sometimes because of problems with audio levels but also because many students were reluctant to speak in their "teacher voices" so that they could be picked up by the overhead microphones. I also found that assigning individual mini-investigations, such as locating a bit of information from the School Code for the law class, caused students to share their findings in audible voices. This also generated a good amount of comment, if not discussion, from other students. In fact, after one class I wrote in my journal,

> The second session was much more "classroom like." I believe that was because each student was responsible for sharing a tidbit from the School Code. This led into discussion and comments from students at both sites. They even responded directly to each other rather than through me.

Group work with case studies was another strategy that seemed to work well whether I had all groups working on the same case or assigned different cases to each group. Once again, comments and discussion items were directed to other students or student groups rather than to me as an intermediary.

Bozik (1996) found that students perceived lecture (61%), discussion (91%), demonstration (80%), role playing (76%), and case studies (79%) as being effective or highly effective. Poole (1996) noted that instructors in a study reported by Kendall and Oates indicated that lecture, case studies, and question-answer methods were "more effective in the interactive classroom than in the traditional classroom" (p. 79). Strategies determined by instructors to be not as effective included group discussion, seminar, socratic, and question-answer.

CONCLUSIONS AND SUMMARY

An analysis of the student surveys, responses from the professors involved in teaching the ITV courses, my own reactions, and the findings of other research studies will inform my own practice in future courses taught through the medium of two-way interactive television. Even though students rated ITV as being effective, and even highly effective, despite their having encountered many technical difficulties, I suspect that the convenience factor of not having to travel had much to do with their satisfaction. It remains for the instructor, then, to devise teaching strategies that will contribute to creating a genuine sense of classroom. Once a true community of learners has been established, students will be enabled to reach full satisfaction. Instructors were intensely concerned about effectiveness. Again, developing strategies conducive to establishing a classroom environment making effectiveness possible is crucial for professor satisfaction with the medium.

The importance, then, of developing a relationship with the students at the remote site and of students developing relationships with each other needs to be carefully considered. Familiarizing students with the technology will be a beginning. Using Internet possibilities for e-mail and discussion groups may help in developing a learning community and will certainly facilitate communication.

Technical difficulties became less frequent during the course of teaching three classes. Some difficulties, however, will continue to occur because of the "nature of the beast." Comeaux (1995) found that "Instructors who used a sense of humor in dealing with technical nuances, used a relaxed interpersonal style focusing on the interaction across the sites, and involved students directly in the course content were perceived as more successful on the network" (p. 353). Instructors also need to be well trained in the technology, and readily available technical assistance during class sessions is important as well.

Problem-based learning strategies, small group discussions with consequent sharing of the main points of the discussions with all students, and student presentations and demonstrations are methods that have the potential for providing opportunities for student interaction. These will be the focus of future study as we continue providing instruction through the medium of two-way ITV.

REFERENCES

Bozik, M. (1996). Student perceptions of a two-way interactive video class. *T.H.E. Journal, 24,* 99–100.

Comeaux, P. (1995). The impact of an interactive distance learning network on classroom communication. *Communication Education, 44,* 353–361.

Freddolino, P. P. (1996). The importance of relationships for a quality learning environment in interactive TV classrooms. *Journal of Education for Business, 71,* 205–208.

McCleary, I. D., & Egan, M. W. (1989). Program design and evaluation: Two-way interactive television. *American Journal of Distance Education, 3,* 50–60.

Poole, P. (1996). Teaching via interactive television: An examination of teaching effectiveness and student satisfaction. *Journal of Education for Business, 72,* 78–81.

Tiene, C. D. (1997). Student perspectives on distance learning with interactive television. *TechTrends, 42,* 41–47.

CHAPTER 23

Evolution, Revolution, and Collaboration: Creating New Programs and Paradigms in Doctoral Studies for Educational Leaders[1]

Nadyne Guzmán and Rodney Muth

Two sister institutions, located about 75 miles apart but within the same state system, wished to work collaboratively to bring a field-based, research-based doctoral program for educational leaders to students living in the more southerly regions of the state. Simple as this vision sounds in summary, it raised challenging questions about inter- and intra-institutional cooperation, faculty investment in off-campus programming, on- and off-campus program requirements, and program governance. Despite these challenges, this collaborative effort illustrates how a well-designed program can successfully support the growth of doctoral students as well as encourage faculty and institutions to expand their horizons.

POLITICAL AND STRUCTURAL DILEMMAS

Educational leadership programs in Colorado, as in many states, compete for scarce resources. This competition generally precludes the development of inter-institutional, collaborative programs and has even created barriers to the development of intra-institutional programming within systems. New doctoral programs are limited by governing boards, and some degrees have been terminated or modified to maintain intersystem and intra-institutional missions and status. In addition, state resource allocations have protected the degree "rights" of institutions, although not necessarily the locations of their programs.

These limitations have concentrated doctoral degree-granting capacity in the Denver metropolitan area. All of the doctoral-granting institutions are in the "metropolitan area" (Colorado State University and the University of Northern Colorado are an hour to an hour and one half north of Denver). In addition, the University of Colorado at Denver (UCD) is the sole public institution in the state authorized by the Colorado Commission of Higher Education (CCHE) to grant a PhD in educational leadership in the state. Thus, institutional limitations—and the geographical barriers that they impose—make it difficult, often impossible, for students outside the metropolitan area to obtain degrees unless they are willing to drive great distances, change jobs, or make other significant sacrifices.

In 1994, this history began to change when an alliance was developed between the Schools of Education at UCD and the University of Colorado at Colorado Springs (UCCS). UCD and UCCS sought to respect institutional limitations but respond to the needs of students out of the Denver area. Students in the southern regions of the state and administration program graduates at UCCS wanted access to advanced programming in educational leadership. For too many students, particularly those south of Colorado Springs, the hours—and safety issues—involved in commuting prevented realization of this goal. Thus, it became clear to university faculty and administration at both UCD and UCCS that a collaborative effort was needed.

Inter-Institutional Barriers

Despite this alliance between two state institutions, the barriers to intrasystem cooperation were immense, primarily because the system's bureaucrats could not conveniently pigeonhole the friendly "invasion" of a sis-

---

Nadyne Guzmán, University of Colorado at Colorado Springs
Rodney Muth, University of Colorado at Denver

ter institution's turf. It took six months, for example, to get a memorandum of understanding approved by CCHE, one which simply said that the program is UCD's, that it would be offered in Colorado Springs, and that some of the program credits would go to UCCS. This hold-up meant delays in admitting students, finalizing curriculum, assigning instructors, and finding a workable meeting site. As a result, the UCCS cohort did not first meet until the fall semester of 1995.

While full cooperation within organizations is generally fraught with barriers, collaboration across organizations can include role conflicts, communication gaps, power inequalities, and protection of self-interest (Cooper & Muth, 1994; Muth, 1995). Even assuming a consensus on collaborative goals, further complications can arise from various perspectives on what actually constitutes the "common good" within a given community (Guzmán, 1995). Such was the case throughout the development and implementation of this program.

The issue of program ownership—that is, which institution "owns" the program—surfaced early during "negotiations" with CCHE. This was clearly a deans' issue but one which also troubled CCHE. The UCCS dean, understandably, wanted a strong symbolic and programmatic role so that he could tell his constituents that UCCS was delivering on its promises to facilitate local access to the doctoral degree. CCHE, too, pushed discussions toward building a "cooperative" program which would be governed, according to CCHE policy, by a body spanning both institutions. The UCD dean, also understandably, was not about to give up any authoritative control of the program, particularly since it had just been broadened in its scope from a traditional PhD in educational administration to a schoolwide program with three emphasis areas, all focusing on educational leadership. The struggle for this approval had been protracted and included assurances of nonencroachment to another campus, so the dean was not about to let his faculty's control of the degree be diluted. Off-campus programming also creates additional tuition revenues that come directly to the sponsoring college or school, so sharing a program structure could be costly.

Another issue was one that faces many off-campus programs: travel to a remote site. While UCD faculty were pleased to have a program in Colorado Springs because of the state-supported additional funding for off-campus, "access" programs and the good will it creates, they were reluctant to commit to the weekly drive (about 90 minutes from the Denver campus) required to deliver the program. While several faculty participated in portfolio reviews during the course of the program (one or two trips) and one faculty member gave a guest lecture, only two faculty committed to full-semester participation (12 to 16 trips). This meant that the program's co-directors, one from UCCS and one from UCD, delivered the majority of the academic portion of the program for four of the six semesters.

The low level of faculty participation has important implications for portfolio reviews and dissertation advising. Because the students in Colorado Springs have not met most of the UCD faculty—and the faculty has not met them—it is more difficult for students to make matches with faculty for these essential program requirements. The program's co-directors have worked hard to facilitate such matches by sharing dissertation topic papers with faculty likely to be interested in a student's research interests.

Faculty Concerns

Generally, faculty are concerned about meeting their load requirements. They also want to be recognized for any overload they incur, preferring not to have extra duties simply considered as another contribution to the welfare of the organization. For these reasons, an off-campus program strains faculty good will when it requires travel and consumes far more hours of faculty time for planning and preparation than do convenient, disconnected, on-campus classes.

Load is a significant issue in Colorado since most operating funds are contingent upon enrollments, and if course enrollments are light or classes do not "make," deans get concerned—which concerns faculty. The converse of this, of course, is the willingness of deans to exploit faculty through overloads, either by paying them overload pay (far less than regular pay) or by providing them less costly "perks"—such as part-time graduate assistants or some travel money. The load problem confronted this program because, although UCCS promised to support the program, budget austerity made it very difficult. Often, the UCCS co-director had to contribute time to the program simply to keep a hand in. Some overload support was made available from UCD, however, to make the commitment more palatable, and some credit hours were transferred to UCCS to strengthen programmatic—and fiscal—connections.

NATURE OF THE PROGRAM

The Educational Policy and Administration (EPA) emphasis within UCD's PhD in Educational Leadership and Innovation specifically seeks to prepare highly qualified candidates for senior-level leadership positions in elementary, secondary, and higher education. As part of this preparation, rigorous scholarship is expected for which strong research skills are developed and applied to problems of practice. To this end, EPA focuses on student accomplishments, measured by knowledge and skill outcomes as specified in student portfolios.

The EPA emphasis area requires 70 credit hours, 40 credit hours of course work and 30 credit hours of dissertation research (see Figure 1), beyond the MA. The degree is appropriate for a variety of leadership positions, including state-level administrators, superintendents, district-level administrators, educational leaders in local schools and institutions of higher education, and policy positions in school systems and other educational agencies. Additionally, some PhD students may work toward a Master Certificate through their electives and the preparation of a portfolio that demonstrates expertise beyond the state's professional licensing requirements.

Several aspects of this program's design are unique. First, students meet for extended periods, usually five hours one night per week, to permit more extensive concentration on subject matter and its application to prob-

---

PhD Program Course Work (40 hours minimum)

A. *Schoolwide Core* (9 hours minimum)

  EDUC 7100-3, Leadership and Innovation in Education
  REM 7000-3, Doctoral Seminar in Research Methods
  REM 6100-3, Methods of Qualitative Inquiry, or
  REM 7110-3, Intermediate Statistics

B. *EPA PhD Course Work* (9 hours minimum)

  EDUC 7200-3, Administrative Leadership and Values Appraisal
  EDUC 7210-3, Educational Policy Making for a Democratic Society (required)
  EDUC 7220-3, Leadership, Power, and Authority
  EDUC 7230-3, Organizational Performance in Schools
  EDUC 7250-3, Nature of Work in Schools (required)

C. *EPA Lab Requirements* (9 hours minimum; must be continuously enrolled in 1 or more lab credits through completion of the 40 hours of course work)

  EDUC 7600-1, ST: Laboratory in Educational Leadership and Innovation
  EDUC 7700-1, Doctoral Pro Seminar
  EDUC 8994-1, Doctoral Dissertation, PhD

D. *Doctoral Level Cognate Seminars, Independent Study, and Directed Readings* (3 to 12 hours; tailored to student needs in consultation with an advisor)

E. *School of Education Electives in Master's Level Graduate Course Work* (0 to 9 hours; with approval of a student's program committee)

Dissertation Research (30 hours minimum)
EDUC 8994, Doctoral Dissertation, focuses students on a dissertation research agenda, helping to define and develop a dissertation research problem, a proposal related to the PhD in Educational Leadership and Innovation, EPA emphasis, and the dissertation itself; hours toward the completion of this requirement are included under EPA Lab Requirements; a maximum of 10 hours of 8994 may be taken before admission to candidacy.

Figure 1. EPA emphasis area in Educational Leadership and Innovation PhD program.

lems of practice. Second, "labs"—field-based, action-research activities—are connected to each content area to facilitate successively more sophisticated research opportunities for teams of students to increase their research expertise. Third, from the first semester the students focus on developing dissertation topics, progressively gaining confidence with articulating research problems and methods to study them. Finally, each course and lab activity is designed to help students build portfolio products that demonstrate depth and breadth of knowledge in three topic foci (concentrations), the application of knowledge to problems of practice, and competence with at least two means of conducting research.

The UCD-UCCS program reported here, the third off-campus cohort in educational leadership, has benefited greatly from what has been learned about the timely introduction of doctoral-level research methods, exposure to applied research projects to increase dissertation-related research skills, and development of authentic portfolio products (see Figure 2) that reflect the skills needed by PhD graduates who expect to be leaders in the field.[2]

PhD Committee

When the new, schoolwide PhD program at UCD was approved, a schoolwide faculty committee was developed to govern the program, significantly diminishing the educational leadership faculty's authority and flexibility.[3] While "ownership" issues never overtly surfaced in the school, the UCD co-director's faculty had to devote considerable energy to protecting the integrity of the programming for the Colorado Springs cohort, as that program had been designed and guaranteed before the new schoolwide PhD was entirely in effect. From time to time, members of the committee have needed assurance that the cohort program in Colorado Springs has conformed generally with the overall school program. Assurances have been sufficient, it seems, because the committee has authorized a new cohort for Colorado Springs for Fall 1998.[4] The cohort structure for the Fall 1998 cohort conforms to schoolwide program requirements.

As curricular control now is lodged within the PhD Committee, future cohorts will be approved by that body. The ongoing issues will be the conservative views of many on the PhD committee, which grow out of both their conventional doctoral training experiences and their protectionistic orientation toward the "integrity" and "quality" of their new program as well as some basic philosophical and experiential differences. For example, being traditionally trained, it is difficult for many of the committee to accept recent views on adult learning (Brookfield, 1986; Merriam & Caffarella, 1991), the constructivist paradigm (Brooks & Brooks, 1993; Lambert et al., 1995), or action-oriented research (Schön, 1991; Stringer, 1996).

On a more positive note, the PhD Committee has changed the portfolio process and requirements significantly, and these changes are very beneficial. Because the original requirements were not as well conceptualized as they might have been, the new model should serve the students and faculty better. These changes will be instituted with the Fall 1998 cohort in Colorado Springs as well as the on-campus program for students beginning in Fall 1997.

Emergent Cross-Cultural Challenges

Today's leaders are urged to develop environments in which all participants are continually growing and developing as part of the progression of the organization (Senge, 1990). Beyond that, the expectation that a sense of community should be developed—that vastly different individuals should unite and focus together on the highest good for the organizational mission—has added another dimension to leadership responsibilities. The evolution of the learning community (Sergiovanni, 1990; Guzmán, 1995) is a very real part of today's organizational paradigm and has emerged as an important aspect of the development of this program.

The creation of and agreement upon a common purpose (Guzmán, 1995) is considered to be essential to the cohesion and success of any group. This task becomes especially difficult when the members of the group—such as those in a PhD cohort—are highly competitive, tremendously successful, and intensely focused individuals. The history of these students in educational institutions is based primarily on their ability to compete with others and emerge successfully from that competition. In addition to individual differences, cultures assume many forms (Denison, 1990), and trying to combine several of these simultaneously can lead to some

> ### COLORADO SPRINGS COHORT
>
> The portfolio requirements are intended as vehicles to demonstrate depth and breadth of knowledge in three topic foci as well as the application of knowledge and skills to the improvement of practice. These products also must exhibit knowledge and skill in two research "tools."
>
> **General Criteria:** All documents in the portfolio must (a) be well written and organized; (b) be free of typos, serious grammatical errors, or syntactical problems; (c) use APA style as appropriate; (d) include all appropriate references; (e) be covered by an explanation of the purpose of the product and its relation, if any, to topic focus areas and, where appropriate, the candidate's role in and contribution to the product's development.
>
> **Schoolwide Requirements**
>
> | PRODUCTS | SPECIFICATION | WHERE DEVELOPED |
> |---|---|---|
> | *Goals and Philosophy Statement* | The candidate will prepare a written statement of professional goals and philosophy, giving a rationale for selection of the three content foci in relation to career and academic goals. For EPA students, this includes a statement of personal and professional leadership. | Developed for 1st Annual Review; leadership statement developed throughout (may be combined with reflective essay)

Evaluation Criteria: Clear, well integrated, connects topic foci and portfolio products, reflects growth, and articulates a leadership stance |
> | *Research Review/ Synthesis Paper* | The candidate will prepare a written paper that reviews research in a topic area in a way that adds to the knowledge and application in the field. | Research review for 7220 (Fall 1996) or critical essay/analysis for (Spring 1997)

Evaluation Criteria: An integrated essay that flows from one idea to the next (not a book report) and synthesizes cross-cutting themes into a broader framework; concepts and terms clearly defined |
> | *Research Reviews* | The candidate will review and provide a written critique of at least five articles published or submitted for publication in scholarly journals. | Initially developed in 7100/7240 (Spring 1996) and 7210 (Summer 1996)

Evaluation Criteria: (a) recognizes/identifies strengths/weaknesses of the article, (b) covers major points, (c) summarizes salient points, and (d) flows logically |

Figure 2. Portfolio entries, PhD in Educational Leadership and Innovation, Educational Policy and Administration emphasis area.

	Schoolwide Requirements *(continued)*	
PRODUCTS	SPECIFICATION	WHERE DEVELOPED
Funding Proposal or Application Paper	The candidate will prepare a detailed proposal for application of current knowledge and theory to an applied policy, service or research program, complete with strategies for implementation and management of the program.	Independently developed; alternatives include project proposal and/or management plan Evaluation Criteria: (a) clearly states the problem, (b) clarifies a theoretical framework, (c) outlines a step-by-step research process, and (d) specifies the "value added" to the body of knowledge in the area
Research Proposal	The candidate will design at least one research proposal prior to the dissertation. Each proposal should at least (a) present a rationale for the study, (b) review pertinent research, (c) describe the design and methodology, (d) describe data analysis, and (e) discuss possible outcomes and their significance.	Revision for proposal for 7000/7240 or other research proposal (see Prospectus) Evaluation Criteria: All components are clearly present, sections well connected, thoughts clearly expressed
Research Report	The candidate will plan and conduct at least one research study prior to the dissertation. The study may be done in collaboration with other students or faculty and must be documented in a paper suitable for publication in a professional journal.	Lab reports, AERA papers (must include clarification of role and contribution); 7220 (Fall 1996) study report Evaluation Criteria: The research focus must be clearly stated and the methodology—fully articulated—must match the problem statement with findings clearly derived from data collected, conclusions logically presented as an outcome of the flow from findings, and recommendations flowing from the conclusions

Figure 2 (continued). Portfolio entries, PhD in Educational Leadership and Innovation, Educational Policy and Administration emphasis area.

	Schoolwide Requirements *(continued)*	
PRODUCTS	SPECIFICATION	WHERE DEVELOPED
Inservice/ Consultation/ Teaching	The candidate will plan and conduct at least three different training/consultation events. A planning document must be submitted for each that includes (a) the target audience, (b) the teaching objectives, (c) the materials, (d) the agenda, and (e) plans for evaluation.	Individually developed Evaluation Criteria: All tasks completed and easily understood
Public Information Writing	The candidate will prepare and submit for publication at least three products written for the general public to inform and/or persuade about educational issues (e.g., op. ed. pieces; newsletter articles, news releases about current research).	Developed individually Evaluation Criteria: Understandable by general public; APA not required
Research Management Product	The candidate will develop a method for organizing scholarly information in the topic areas selected that summarizes critical information for useful retrieval.	Developed individually Evaluation Criteria: System used explained clearly and evidence provided as to how information/research can be retrieved quickly and easily
Professional/ Community Participation	The candidate will participate as a member of a public committee, task force, or other group working to improve the quality of educational services and prepare a written, analytic description of the activity. The activity must be outside the candidate's normal job responsibilities.	Developed individually Evaluation Criteria: Provides thorough description of individual role and responsibilities and nature/purpose/impact of group.

Figure 2 (continued). Portfolio entries, PhD in Educational Leadership and Innovation, Educational Policy and Administration emphasis area.

EPA Requirements

PRODUCTS	SPECIFICATION	WHERE DEVELOPED
Background and Briefing Materials	The candidate will prepare three background papers or policy briefings (e.g., speech drafts, talking points, testimony drafts, sound bites, memos that distill critical policy issues).	Individually developed; could be based on critiques, critical essay/analysis, or other research Evaluation Criteria: Clear synopsis, well written, understandable by target audience
Group Project Reports	The candidate will prepare complete versions of all group projects developed during the program, clarifying the candidate's role in and contribution to the project.	Lab, other group reports Evaluation Criteria: Final versions only; strengths/weaknesses of research identified
Reflective Essay	The candidate will prepare an essay that reflectively examines program activities and experiences. This essay should integrate across all formal learning experiences, summarizing what has been learned—and not learned—in the program.	Developed solely for final portfolio review (could be combined with goal/philosophy/leadership statement) Evaluation Criteria: Highlights learning experiences, focusing on important learnings and gaps organized according to individual perspectives and preferences

Figure 2 (continued). Portfolio entries, PhD in Educational Leadership and Innovation, Educational Policy and Administration emphasis area.

	EPA Requirements *(continued)*	
PRODUCTS	SPECIFICATION	WHERE DEVELOPED
Organizational Analysis	The candidate will prepare a written analysis of an organization that demonstrates application of theory to practice and makes specific recommendations for improving organizational performance.	Lab reports; 7220 (Fall 1996) study Evaluation Criteria: Clear identification and connection of problem, theory, methodology, findings, and recommendations for improved organizational practices
Case Study	The candidate will submit a case study of an educational situation that describes the situation in detail, analyzes a key issue within the situation from at least one theoretical perspective, and outlines needed interventions.	Lab reports, 7220 (Fall 1996) study, 7210 (Summer 1996) paper, or AERA paper Evaluation Criteria: Clear identification and connection of problem, theory, methodology, findings, and conclusions
Dissertation Prospectus	The candidate will prepare a prospectus that clearly articulates a dissertation topic, relevant research related to the topic, and one method of conducting research on the topic.	Developed from 7200 (Fall 1995; topic paper) through 7250 (Spring 1997; topic paper); 1st draft in 7230 (Summer 1997) Evaluation Criteria: All components are clearly present; signed by three-member committee

Figure 2 (continued). Portfolio entries, PhD in Educational Leadership and Innovation, Educational Policy and Administration emphasis area.

interesting outcomes. As UCCS and UCD combined to develop and implement the PhD program, they brought together students from multiple K–12 school districts—each with its own cultural perspective—and two institutions of higher education.

Institutional visions—especially within institutions whose mission is primarily educational—have been expanded in recent years to encompass a broader constituency and more inclusive philosophy (Guzmán, 1996). However, individuals may unconsciously adopt and support the cultural assumptions of their own institutions, accepting them as normative influences when they leave their home institutions and enter new environments. It becomes, then, a programmatic imperative to guide students toward the reconciliation of conflicting, culturally based values. Reconciliation becomes one piece of each student's personal process of development, creating a stronger foundation of self-knowledge and, perhaps, a clearer "critical eye" with which to engage in the process of research.

As these values have become clearer within the context of the cohort dialogue and as their dissonance or consonance has emerged, students were invited to examine them individually and collectively in an effort to weave them into the fabric of the cohort experience. Ultimately, this new gestalt has been integrated into the knowledge and skill set of students as they move back into their disparate worlds.

INSTRUCTIONAL AND CURRICULAR ISSUES

Collaborative instruction, team teaching, instructional team building, and integrated programming are difficult to achieve within a single program or school where the ethos continues to support separate courses for separate instructors. Trying to change institutional practices cross-institutionally is even more difficult, as deans—and faculty—tend to like neat structures with few complications.

Problem-Based Learning

Proponents of problem-based learning offer the process as a method for retention and transfer of knowledge in the educational process (Martin, Murphy, & Muth, 1993; Murphy, Martin, Ford, & Muth, 1996; Muth, Murphy, & Martin, 1994). Beginning with problems of practice, this model enables the learner to construct knowledge through reflection on action and reflection in action (Argyris & Schön, 1975; Schön, 1983, 1987).

Problem-based learning in this program concentrates on "*learning that results from designing solutions to significant problems by collaboratively applying relevant knowledge through the use of intellectual tasks* [emphasis in the original]" (Martin, Ford, Murphy, Rehm, & Muth, 1997, p. 389). This means that learning focuses on problems of practice (raised in labs) to which relevant knowledge is applied as the problem becomes "known" and for which approximate solutions might be designed and developed. Such learning engages both students and faculty in collaborative and mutually beneficial learning activities, demonstrated by students in portfolio products. It develops students' analytical and critical thinking skills that lead eventually to self-confidence with research.

Structural Accommodations

Because of classroom shortages on the Colorado Springs campus, a local district with several students in the program offered its professional development center—far more spacious and better equipped than most university facilities—for the cohort sessions held one night per week (and some Saturdays). These five-hour sessions incorporated academic instruction, lab activities, and opportunities for portfolio and dissertation preparation. The credit hours for academic courses varied somewhat from those outlined in Figure 1 because no integrative Pro Seminar was needed to link labs and course work and to provide opportunities to develop portfolios and dissertation topics.

Based on experience with two cohorts in which a seminar on research for doctoral studies came toward the end of the program, the Colorado Springs cohort had a more timely introduction to doctoral-level research methods. Their overview course came in their second semester, following an initial attempt to develop a dissertation topic, and supplied them perspectives on how students might think methodologically about dissertation research. The research projects developed for each semester's lab experience provided exposure to applied research projects and gave students opportunities to build on what they learned. In this way, the program increased their dissertation-related research skills in generally benign circumstances so that students could learn from their mistakes.

These lab activities and their associated content-area projects and products helped students evolve authentic portfolio products that would address the skills and knowledge they needed to complete their portfolio requirements. Each semester contained "building blocks" that successively led to the development of the specific products outlined in Figure 2.

Because of the importance of continuity of instruction in a cohort, classes offered in Colorado Springs have been taught by a team of faculty from both institutions. Students were advised by the program's co-directors, one from each institution, also to ensure continuity. These efforts helped connect classes to one another and to their labs, minimize repetition, and maintain the program's sequential nature.

Integrated Curriculum

This collaborative, UCD-UCCS PhD program was designed to engage students in a series of research-based activities that develop the knowledge and skills necessary to completion of their dissertations. Thus, program structures were developed to ensure that students would be enabled to do so. The program syllabus is outlined in Figure 3 which depicts the integration across "domains" (knowledge "umbrellas" disguised as courses) of labs, the dissertation focus, annual reviews, portfolio products, and reflective-practice journaling.

Collaborative Instruction

Developing the curriculum was a collaborative—often painful—process that involved faculty who developed the initial cohort designs, first with senior executives in the state's largest school district (an effort sponsored by the Danforth Foundation) and then with senior staffers at the Education Commission of the States, as well as other faculty at UCD who joined the process after much of the infrastructure had been developed. The collaboration between UCD and UCCS began after this extensive program-development work. As a result of past experiences, a clear preference on both sides at the faculty level was collaborative, team teaching, not serial instruction.

Often, team teaching is viewed as "You do this week, and I'll do the next week." True team teaching is a collaborative process in which the structures and events for learning are collectively created and implemented. While one faculty member's strengths or preferences may be dominant in one class session (or a related or contiguous set of class sessions) or for a particular activity such as a field project, both are present to work with and off of one another and with students. Their collaboration both enhances the learning process for the students and provides students the opportunity to interact with differing and often divergent perspectives. The interplay of ideas often illustrates clearly that most issues—even orientations—have more than one legitimate perspective and that the challenge is to harness competing perspectives to the task at hand.

Besides these benefits for students, teaming is an excellent way of facilitating faculty growth and development through mutual learning. It provides mentoring opportunities for "junior" faculty and balances instructional abilities and orientations. By ensuring instructional continuity throughout a cohort program, team teaching capitalizes on the serendipity created by synergy and maintains an on-site, knowledgeable presence that assures students that they can get their problems solved locally.

As issues of faculty involvement cited already suggest, team teaching by a limited number of faculty, as at Colorado Springs, can create too much dependence on one instructional team when the program—and students—would profit from more varied instructors and perspectives. Faculty credit is another problem raised by team teaching. Especially in a collaborative arrangement, involved universities may be loathe to give full credit for the extended sessions to each faculty member (although policies on this issue are being developed at UCD).

	Fall 1995	Spring 1996	Summer 1996	Fall 1996	Spring 1997	Summer 1997	Fall 1997
Domains (see syllabi for expectations)	AEDU 7200-4	AREM 7500-3 AREM 7240-1	AEDU 7210-4	AEDU 7220-4	AEDU 7250-3 AEDU 7000-1	AEDU 7230-4	
Lab Activities (research and knowledge applications)	AEDU 7005-1 3 to 4 group projects and reports	LEAD 750-1 3 to 4 group projects and reports	LEAD 750-1 3 to 4 group projects and reports	LEAD 750-1 3 to 4 group projects and reports	LEAD 750-1 3 to 4 group projects and reports	LEAD 750-1 3 to 4 group projects and reports	
Dissertation Focus (emphasizing step-by-step preparation for dissertation proposal)	AEDU 8994-1 topics and groups; topic paper	AEDU 8994-1 groups; methods paper	AEDU 8994-1 groups; revised topic paper	AEDU 8994-1 groups; review of literature	AEDU 8994-1 groups; revised topic paper/review of literature; diss. comm. selection	AEDU 8994-1 groups; preproposal (topic, review, methods)	AEDU 8994-3 groups; prospectus
Annual Reviews (regular quality program reviews)			1st Annual Review: 3 topic foci; *vita*; goals; program plan; GRE scores; course work; portfolio entries; oral			2nd Annual Review: 3 topic foci; *vita*; goals; plan; course work; portfolio entries; oral	Comprehensive Review: paper work; 3 topic foci; *vita*; goals; prospectus; course work; portfolio entries; oral
Portfolio Products (demonstrations of knowledge and skills)	see specifications in *Student Portfolio Entries* and Domain assignments	see specifications in *Student Portfolio Entries* and Domain assignments	see specifications in *Student Portfolio Entries* and Domain assignments	see specifications in *Student Portfolio Entries* and Domain assignments	see specifications in *Student Portfolio Entries* and Domain assignments	see specifications in *Student Portfolio Entries* and Domain assignments	see specifications in *Student Portfolio Entries* and Domain assignments
Reflective Practice Journal (focused deliberation)	personal and ongoing	personal and ongoing	personal and ongoing	personal and ongoing	personal and ongoing	personal and ongoing	personal and ongoing

Figure 3. Program outline for Colorado Springs PhD cohort, 1995–1998. Dissertation studies commence Spring 1998 and for most will end Fall 1998 or Spring 1999.

Rather, each team member is likely to get partial load credit for participating despite generally spending full time preparing, teaching, observing, interacting, and reviewing all student work—thus receiving only half of the credit for the work involved.

Group Lab Projects

One of the main features of the program is the "lab," an opportunity for students to work on research-related projects. The lab asks students to conceptualize research problems, go into the field to collect data, and become familiar with ways of asking questions, developing hypotheses, and analyzing data. Over the course of the Colorado Springs program, the students engaged in at least one group project each semester and three groups remained together for long-term projects that lasted five semesters. These projects resulted in reports on leadership and power in noneducational organizations (an organizational analysis designed to introduce them to literature on organizational behavior and performance outcomes), papers presented at national meetings on policies affecting educational processes in Colorado, and case studies of various schools.

Developmentally, each semester's lab experience was designed both to complement the course work that semester and to assist students in becoming conversant with—and appreciative of—some aspect of research. For example, the leadership and power study gave them the opportunity to learn the complexities of item construction, survey development, and data analysis; the policy studies helped them apply policy analysis models to problems of practice with which they were contending in their work lives.

Structures for Individual Development

Throughout the program, the domains were organized to provide students with access to the foundational knowledge essential for a PhD (see Figure 2). For the cohort, these experiences were arranged over six semesters (see Figure 3) in a rather lockstep fashion because of logistics. Each domain had a connected lab and a dissertation hour to facilitate research activities and growth in the development of dissertation topics. Semester and annual reviews were used to evaluate portfolio products and assess progress toward program completion. Reflective-practice journaling was encouraged both as a means of connecting individuals more explicitly to their learning and as a way for students to keep track of their developing expertise and clarify the linkages between portfolio products and topic foci.

In each semester, activities were developed that both provided practice in skills PhD graduates need and led sequentially to higher-level skills. For example, much of the first semester was spent on "academic" writing, reconnecting active professionals to the writing genres that they would need to master to complete a dissertation. Students worked on problem conceptualization in their lab projects, their initial dissertation topic papers, and book summaries, comparisons, and critiques that prepared them for future literature reviews. Each semester, these building blocks were designed to improve conceptual skills, increase understanding of research issues and processes, develop critical thinking and analysis, and enhance writing abilities.

STUDENT AND PROGRAM EVALUATION

An essential ingredient in any program development process is evaluation (Berk & Rossi, 1990; Brinkerhoff, Brethower, Nowakowski, & Hluchyj, 1983; Cooley & Bickel, 1986). Other than course evaluations, however, many programs do little to assess progress and outcomes. Through outside funding, UCD has been able to evaluate its licensing programs (Martin et al., 1997). Funds and faculty time have not generally been available to evaluate the PhD, although UCD's school of education has an annual program review that develops comparative enrollment and other data. To rectify this deficiency and to learn directly from students about what worked for them and what did not, several strategies were developed, including interviews with students by members of the program's Advisory Board, review of portfolios as assessments of student progress, and a "search process"

(Bunker & Alban, 1997; Rehm, 1997a; Rehm & Cebula, 1997; Weisbord, 1987) designed to develop a contextual approach to program improvement.

Program Evaluation

Although students provide feedback through semester-end faculty course questionnaires (FCQ's) as well as individual and group discussions with instructors, it was determined that additional evaluation data would be beneficial to ongoing program improvement. During the fifth semester of the program, community members from the program's Advisory Board interviewed individual cohort members and the data were compiled by an independent evaluator. Due to scheduling difficulties, two students provided their responses in writing, and three of the seventeen were not interviewed. Students were assured that their identities would remain confidential. Responses were compiled into a summative report.

This evaluation was designed to elicit responses about the following four open-ended issues:

1. Whether or not students believed that the program was helping them meet their individual goals and objectives
2. What recommendations students would make for structural or content changes within the program in order to align it better with individual needs
3. How students perceived and what recommendations they would make about the cohort environment and their relationships with the teaching faculty
4. What suggestions students would make for improving the cohort concept

Strengths of the program were listed as (a) its flexibility to address the needs of a diverse group of students, (b) the breadth of the curriculum, (c) student skill development toward successful completion of the dissertation, (d) field-based research opportunities, (e) location in Colorado Springs, and (f) faculty who demonstrated flexibility and respect for adult learners. Areas suggested for improvement included the following: (a) a broader range of instructional or guest faculty, (b) clearer criteria and more guidance for the portfolios, (c) more structure to class time, (d) timely and consistent discussion of required readings, (e) stronger control by instructors of students who do not honor commitments to small-group projects, and (f) clearer criteria for assignments. Overall, the students indicated a high level of satisfaction with the program and saw it as superior to a traditional program structure.

Student Portfolios as Instruments of Student Evaluation and Program Evaluation

In lieu of a traditional written or oral comprehensive examination, students are required to complete and defend (to a team of program faculty) a portfolio with prescribed products (see Figure 2). Portfolio products are primarily developed as class assignments (e.g., research article critiques, topic papers, etc.) although students are expected to revise them according to faculty feedback before including them in the portfolio. Those products that do not directly relate to the course work (e.g., training/consultation events) are included to allow students to demonstrate skill in professional communication in a setting that differs from their daily work sites.

The utility of the portfolio is that it allows faculty to evaluate student progress in knowledge and skill development and to assess their growing ability to complete the dissertation. Benchmarks include facility in academic writing, development of research foci, skill in critical analysis of research, application of research skills to problems of practice, scholarly depth and breadth, theory development, and integration of the curriculum. This, then, is not only an assessment of individual student success but of instructional and curricular effectiveness as well. Several students found the relative ambiguity of portfolio criteria to be frustrating and asked that the criteria be reviewed and clarified. This created a forum for program improvement, and students provided input into the revision of the portfolio requirements. (See Evaluation Criteria in Figure 2.) While a debate continues as to whether or not portfolio criteria should be defined narrowly, the portfolio requirements have been revised for future cohorts to allow greater student flexibility. Final portfolio reviews are candidacy reviews and include the student's dissertation prospectus, approved by a dissertation committee of three.

Program Development: Global Search Process

As part of the curriculum during the program's last full semester, students studied large-group interventions for creating change for the improvement of systems (Bunker & Alban, 1997; Weisbord, 1987). Students were guided through a global search process (Rehm & Cebula, 1997), based upon a participative design process (Rehm, 1997) that creates a democratic design for a system. One piece of this process involved students in redesigning the cohort experience, and that procedure became, in effect, another evaluation of the program. However, this process was structured and facilitated by a visiting faculty member, permitting greater depth than was achieved by the Advisory Board's external evaluation.

The same strengths and weaknesses of the program were highlighted during this process; however, faculty were included in the dialogue, and the group process revealed ambiguities and disagreements relative to the effectiveness of certain aspects of the curriculum. For instance, some students did not experience difficulty with the portfolio requirements and defended its structure. Another point of disagreement was whether or not faculty should take a stronger hand in controlling cohort processes, particularly work-group problems.

A clear consensus emerged during the search process. According to the participants, the following eight points characterize or should guide future cohort programs.

1. The cohort structure is far superior to traditional course-based programs.
2. The problem-based learning model allows for a natural evolution of learning—even though it is fraught with ambiguities.
3. Diversity of program faculty adds depth and breadth to the program.
4. Assignments, feedback, and additional course work strengthen students' skills in scholarly writing.
5. The K–16 perspective provided by students from elementary and secondary schools and from higher education enriches the experience.
6. Norms should be established early in the program and reclarified periodically.
7. A balance of lecture, dialogue, and small group activities is desirable.
8. Different learning styles and individual expectations create diverse experiences within the cohort.

These and other insights gleaned from all the evaluative data will be used to structure the next cohort. A high probability is that students will be involved in a search process at the beginning and end of the cohort to help design and assess the program.

RECOMMENDATIONS FOR REFORM IN HIGHER EDUCATION

Based on the experiences to date with this third cohort, several lessons emerge. First, in the usual rush to put programs in place to secure enrollments, faculty and administrators often forget that students, particularly successful adults who have active and productive work lives, have much to add to a cohort's collective learning experience. While doctoral work should broaden and deepen student perspectives, the students themselves bring with them extensive experience that should be used as part of the learning process. This is particularly the case for the development of the curriculum structures.

Such students are also very busy and somewhat utilitarian in their perspectives. Thus, greater attention needs to be paid to structure and process and their implications for practical as well as intellectual payoffs—both have import for student retention and success. For example, expecting largely part-time students to act like full-time students and perform the knowledge "integrating functions" that full-time students might be expected to achieve may be unrealistic. Program structures need to facilitate the integration process and the development of the skills needed to complete the doctorate successfully. One reason many students do not complete their programs is that they are not confident researchers. Activities within programs need to lay the foundation for later individual research projects.

On the faculty side, incentives need to be structured which support off-campus programming and encourage faculty to commit to more time-consuming and personally costly instructional activities. Incentives can also drive creative program design and implementation. Finally, all faculty who work with adults need to develop current knowledge and practices that value adult learning theory and its implications for successful adult programming. Like any other students, doctoral students want to be engaged in their learning. For them, however, being respected intellectually, having learning opportunities that are self-managed, seeing practical applications of new knowledge to their everyday world, and learning the skills needed to accomplish important tasks are essential to their effective engagement and program completion.

ENDNOTES

1 An earlier version of this chapter was "virtually published" on the Internet by the *International Journal: Continuous Improvement Monitor*, University of Texas Pan American. It can be found at http://llanes.panam.edu/journal/library/Vol1No2/Guzman.html. Permission to re-publish has been granted by the editor, J. R. Llanes.

2 The on-campus program outlined in Figure 1 is much more highly structured for off-campus cohorts than for on-campus students, primarily because of program logistics. For the Colorado Springs cohort, the program required thirty credit hours, leaving students free to choose ten hours of electives. With the same overall credit requirements, the on-campus program requires only eighteen hours and participation in lab and Pro Seminar, giving students greater flexibility.

3 Inevitably, developing a schoolwide program has led to some structural compromises; none of these, however, has impeded efforts to build a more integrated—and integrating—PhD program for students in policy and administration (see the section on "Integrated Curriculum" below).

4 The demand statewide is so great for access to doctoral programming that current resources are insufficient to the task. Over fifty new inquiries have been received in the Colorado Springs area since the present program began in 1995. Further, program designers are now trying to determine ways to deliver PhD programming to prospective students on the state's Western Slope, geographically separated from the rest of Colorado by the Rocky Mountains. This region has nearly as many potential doctoral students.

REFERENCES

Argyris, C., & Schön, D. A. (1974). *Theory in practice: Increasing professional effectiveness.* San Francisco: Jossey-Bass.

Berk, R. A., & Rossi, P. H. (1990). *Thinking about program evaluation.* Newbury Park, CA: Sage.

Brookfield, S. (1986). *Understanding and facilitating adult learning.* San Francisco, CA: Jossey-Bass.

Brooks, J. G., & Brooks, M. G. (1993). *In search of understanding: The case for constructivist classrooms.* Alexandria, VA: Association for Supervision and Curriculum Development.

Brinkerhoff, R. O., Brethower, D. M., Nowakowski, J. R., & Hluchyj, T. (1983). *Program evaluation: A practitioner's guide for trainers and educators.* Hingham, MA: Kluwer Nijhoff.

Bunker, B. B., & Alban, B. T. (1997). *Large group interventions: Engaging the whole system for rapid change.* San Francisco: Jossey-Bass.

Cooley, W. W., & Bickel, W. E. (1986). *Decision-oriented educational research* (Evaluation in Education and Human Services Series). Hingham, MA: Kluwer-Nijhoff, 1986.

Cooper, B. S., & Muth, R. (1994). Internal and external barriers to change in departments of educational administration. In T. Mulkeen, N. Cambron-McCabe, & B. Anderson (Eds.), *Democratic leadership: The changing context of administrative preparation* (pp. 61–81). Norwood, NJ: Ablex.

Guzmán, N. (1995). The leadership covenant: Essential factors for developing cocreative relationships within a learning community. *Journal of Leadership Studies, 2*(4), 151–160.

Guzmán, N. (1996). Preparing leaders to build a learning community: A reconciliation of conflicting values. In

J. L. Burdin & J. S. Yoon (Eds.), *Fourth Yearbook of the National Council of Professors of Educational Administration. Prioritizing instruction* (pp. 30–35). Lancaster, PA: Technomic Publishing Co., Inc.

Lambert, L., Walker, D., Zimmerman, D. P., Cooper, J. E., Lambert, M. D., Gardner, M. E., & Ford Slack, P. J. (1995). *The constructivist leader.* New York: Teachers College Press.

Martin, W. M., Ford, S., Murphy, M., Rehm, R. G., & Muth, R. (1997). Linking instructional delivery with diverse learning settings. *Journal of School Leadership, 7,* 386–408.

Martin, W. M., Murphy, M. J., & Muth, R. (1993). Problem-based learning: A new approach to preparing school leaders. In J. Hoyle & D. Estes (Eds.), *First Yearbook of the National Council of Professors of Educational Administration. NCPEA: In a new voice* (pp. 141–154). Lancaster, PA: Technomic Publishing Co., Inc.

Merriam, S. B., & Caffarella, R. S. (1991). *Learning in adulthood: A comprehensive guide.* San Francisco, CA: Jossey-Bass.

Murphy, M. J., Martin, W. M., Ford, S., & Muth, R. (1996, October). *Problem-based learning: An idea whose time has come.* Paper presented at the annual meeting of the University Council for Educational Administration, Louisville, KY.

Muth, R. (1995). Craft knowledge and institutional constraints. In R. Donmoyer, J. Scheurich, & M. Imber (Eds.), *The knowledge base in educational administration: Multiple perspectives* (pp. 96–112). Albany: State University of New York Press.

Muth, R., Murphy, M. J., & Martin, W. M. (1994). Problem-based learning at the University of Colorado at Denver. *Journal of School Leadership, 4,* 432–450.

Rehm, R. (1997a, February). *Democratic workplace design.* Unpublished manuscript.

Rehm, R. (1997b, February). *Participative design.* Unpublished manuscript.

Rehm, R., & Cebula, N. (1997, February). *Search conferences.* Unpublished manuscript.

Schön, D. A. (1987). *Educating the reflective practitioner: Toward a new design for teaching and learning in the professions.* San Francisco: Jossey-Bass.

Schön, D. A. (1983). *The reflective practitioner: How professionals think in action.* New York: Basic Books.

Schön, D. A. (Ed.). (1991). *The reflective turn: Case studies in and on educational practice.* New York: Teachers College Press.

Senge, P. A. (1990). *The fifth discipline.* New York: Doubleday.

Sergiovanni, T. J. (1990). *Value-added leadership: How to get extraordinary performance in schools.* San Diego, CA: Harcourt Brace Jovanovich.

Stringer, E. T. (1996). *Action research: A handbook for practitioners.* Thousand Oaks, CA: Sage.

Weisbord, M. R. (1987). *Productive workplaces: Organizing and managing for dignity, meaning, and community.* San Francisco: Jossey-Bass.

CHAPTER 24

Preparing Future School Leaders to Build School-Home Partnerships through Authentic Learning Experiences

Jack Blendinger and Linda T. Jones

The story is told of a first mate who, upon the death of his highly respected captain, inherited command of the ship and the skipper's belongings which included a box that the ship's sailors believed contained the secrets of the captain's success as a leader. Every day before going to the bridge, the captain studied carefully a piece of paper stored in the box. Now the mate had in his possession the secret of the captain's success. Nervously he took the sheet of paper from the box and unfolded it. Written on the paper was the statement, "Port is to the left, starboard is to the right." The moral of the story is it's essential to know the direction you're headed before taking action. Like the captain, future school leaders should acquire the knowledge needed to chart direction and provide guidance in the development of school-home partnerships.

This article shares our experiences in preparing graduate students enrolled in the educational administration program at Mississippi State University to assume a leadership role in planning and implementing effective family involvement programs. Creating quality schools for the approaching millennium requires school leaders who know "best practices" for reaching out to all parents. Investing time and effort on this topic is based on the significant body of research indicating that when parents are involved in children's education, students achieve more and behave better, regardless of socioeconomic status, ethnic-racial background, or the family's educational level (Henderson, 1981; Henderson, 1987; Henderson & Berla, 1994).

The importance of parent involvement is recognized by policymakers, standard setting organizations, and accreditation agencies. The Interstate School Leaders Licensure Consortium of the Council of Chief State School Officers (1996), whose purpose is to develop model standards and assessments for licensing educational leaders, recognized as one of its standards that a school administrator is an educational leader who promotes the success of all students by collaborating with families. The consortium's stand supports one of the eight national education goals:

> Every school will promote partnerships that will increase parental involvement and participation in promoting the social, emotional and academic growth of children.

The National Parent-Teacher Association (PTA) (1997) expanded on the goal by developing standards for parent-family involvement programs that address encouraging school-home communication; promoting and supporting parenting skills; helping parents play an integral role in assisting student learning; volunteering by parents to provide support and assistance at school; involving parents in school decision making and advocacy; and using community resources to strengthen schools, families, and student learning.

The most extensive literature reviews of the connection between parent involvement and children's success in school were completed by Henderson (1981, 1987) and Henderson and Berla (1994). Henderson reviewed 36 studies in 1981 and 49 in 1987 and found overwhelming evidence that parent involvement improves student achievement. In their 1994 report in which 39 new studies were reviewed, Henderson and Berla concluded that the most accurate predictor of a student's achievement in school is the extent to which the student's family creates a home environment encouraging learning, expresses high expectations regarding academic achievement and future career choices, and becomes involved in the child's education. The studies summarized in this report document the following student benefits resulting from schools working with families to support learning: higher grades and test scores, better attendance, more homework completed, fewer placements in special education, more positive attitudes and behavior, and higher graduation rates.

Using both her own research and a review of the literature, Epstein (1992) cites evidence showing family and school partnership practices are more important for children's success than family characteristics such as race, social class, educational level, marital status, income, language fluency, family size, or age of the child. She states, "The more that schools do to involve families, the less these status variables seem to explain parental behavior or children's success" (p. 1147). Epstein reports that, in schools with high parent involvement, teachers have more positive feelings about teaching and their school, parents and principals rate teachers higher in overall teaching ability and interpersonal skills, and school climate is improved.

Epstein (1995, 1996) recently expanded her concept of partnerships to include both the family and the community in helping children succeed in school and in later life. She maintains that such partnerships improve school programs and environments, provide family services and support, increase parents' skills and leadership capabilities, connect families with others, and help teachers with their work. Epstein believes that when parents, teachers, students, and others view one another as partners in education, a caring community forms around students and begins its work.

PARENT/FAMILY INVOLVEMENT CONTINUUM

Preparing future school leaders to reach out to families is seen as a continuum which moves from understanding the importance of taking the initiative in encouraging school staff members to learning specific strategies for putting parent involvement into practice. Modules (self-contained instructional units) designed to develop the necessary knowledge and skills are integral parts of two key courses required for state licensure as an administrator—the principalship and instructional leadership courses. The content of the modules focuses on the research supporting parent involvement and specific activities for communicating with the home, helping parents to assist in their children's learning, encouraging parent participation at school, and planning and implementing parent involvement programs. The term *parents* refers to the child's primary caregivers. Caregivers can be biological parents, adoptive and foster parents, or grandparents and other family members who care for the child. Materials used to teach the modules include books, monographs, and articles (Blendinger & Jones, 1992; Jones, 1991). The modules require students to integrate actual experience at their present schools with a simulated 900 student K–12 school located in a hypothetical Mississippi community reflecting the state's socioeconomic and cultural diversity.

The module in the principalship course emphasizes school-home communication, including parent-teacher conferences, and family participation in school events and activities. This module requires six hours of in-class instruction and an out-of-class assignment requiring approximately nine hours and is initiated with a brief true-or-false quiz. The ten questions on the quiz are designed to activate thinking and discussion:

1. Parent involvement is not identified as a key component for success in effective schools research. (false)
2. Schools that involve parents and those that do not show little difference in student attitudes and achievement. (false)
3. Parent involvement activities should be scheduled only during school hours. (false)
4. Research indicates that teachers' efforts to involve parents in their children's education fall off sharply as children progress through the grades. (true)
5. Teachers who involve parents in their children's learning are rated by the parents as having higher overall teaching ability. (true)
6. Sending home an abundance of written information is the most effective method for building a strong, positive teacher-parent relationship. (false)
7. A businesslike manner will win the respect and support of parents. (false)
8. Parents will not spend time helping their children at home even when given guidance by the teacher about what to do. (false)

9. Home visits are a good way to establish rapport and provide teachers with insights that are not likely to surface in the traditional parent-teacher conference. (true)
10. Meetings involving parents at school are most successful when they involve the whole family and are both social and educational. (true)

Lively interaction among students results from discussing the issues raised in the quiz.

The 900 student K–12 school provides the framework for numerous problem-based case studies. Using the simulated school as the setting, students address questions such as these: How would you describe the problems confronting the principal? What action should be taken to solve them? Students are expected to support their solutions by citing relevant professional literature. An example of one of the problem-oriented case studies follows:

> West Magnolia School enrolls 900 students in grades K–12 and is located in a rural area 15 miles west of a small city. Many of the parents commute 15 to 25 miles to work. The majority of students qualify for free or reduced lunches.
>
> Parents are not involved in their children's education. West Magnolia's teachers think that the lack of parent involvement is typical of low socioeconomic areas. Some teachers do not believe that the parents care about their children's success in school.
>
> Student achievement, as measured by standardized tests, is significantly below the national average, and teachers don't think there is much they can do about it. Teacher job satisfaction is low. As one teacher said, "Both teaching and learning at this school is a lose-lose situation."
>
> When asked, West Magnolia's teachers say they believe that involving parents in their children's education is one of the keys to improving the students' academic performance but they haven't put their beliefs into action. Feedback from parents indicates that they don't understand the school's educational program and don't receive much meaningful information about what is going on at school in general.
>
> There is little communication between teachers and parents. The school does not hold regular parent-teacher conferences, but conferences are held with parents when problems occur. Teachers rarely make telephone calls home or send notes to parents except for disciplinary purposes.
>
> A new principal has recently been hired for the school. How would you describe the problems confronting her or him? What action should he or she take to improve the situation? Be specific.

Students work in teams of four or five to identify the problems inherent in this case study and share their solutions with the class as a whole.

The case study leads to identifying and discussing techniques for communicating with parents. Examples of effective school-home communication strategies include newsletters, good-news calls, success-grams, individual letters and notes, parent-teacher conferences, home visits, and informal methods of communication such as principal-parent coffees. Because parent-teacher conferences offer an excellent means for collaboration through the cooperative development of a plan which the parent and child can carry out at home, methods for holding successful conferences are emphasized. Skills are learned and honed through role-playing so the participants will be able to provide staff development for teachers. Prospective administrators also learn techniques for increasing parent participation in school activities such as back-to-school nights, open houses, book and author events, volunteer and outreach efforts, and after-school programs (Blendinger & Jones, 1992; Jones, 1991).

In addition to activities for improving school-home communication and encouraging parent participation at school, an action-planning process is taught that includes the following:

1. Assessing school-home relationships
2. Forming a planning team
3. Identifying and prioritizing objectives
4. Selecting strategies and activities
5. Monitoring the program and evaluating results

Assessment, the first step of the process, starts with completion of an instrument consisting of questions addressing the quality of school-home relationships. Course participants complete a 30-item instrument to assess school-home relationships using the school where they are presently teaching. The instrument includes questions related to how welcoming the school is, orientation programs for new and transfer students, parent attendance at school functions, support provided to teachers, parent-teacher conferences, outreach programs, methods of communicating with parents, assistance given to parents with home learning activities, work done with volunteers, determinations of parents' needs and interests, health of the parent-teacher organization, and other areas (Blendinger & Jones, 1992). After completing the assessment instrument, students form planning teams of four or five persons and work together using information from the assessment instrument to identify key concerns and needs (e.g., poor parent turnout at back-to-school night) that should be addressed. Each group appoints a facilitator and a recorder. Once the concerns and needs are identified, the groups come together as a whole to develop a composite list.

Next, the planning teams formulate and prioritize goals intended to strengthen the school-home partnership. Each planning team shares its goals with the class as a whole. One student is selected to play the role of principal and take the lead in bringing closure to a small number of schoolwide goals for one school year (e.g., involving more parents in back-to-school night).

After the goals have been identified, each planning team selects activities (e.g., involving the PTA in planning back-to-school night, having children demonstrate what they are learning in their classrooms, and providing child care for preschool-age children) and determines measurement criteria for evaluation purposes (e.g., 90% or more of the parents will attend back-to-school night). Planning teams come together to share their work and create a total school plan containing goals, strategies and activities, and evaluation criteria. Strategies for reaching all parents, including those who are hard to reach, must be part of the plan (Jones, 1991). The final plan is distributed to all members of the class.

Because what parents do to help their children learn is more important to academic success than any other factor, the module supporting children's learning at home, which is taught in the instructional leadership course, includes tips-for-parents brochures, parent-child activity calendars, school-home reading incentive programs, read-aloud activities, homework assignments encouraging parent-child interaction, and workshops for parents. To complete the module, the students are required to implement a month-long project designed to motivate students to read outside of school by choosing a theme that appeals to the level of students they are teaching. The project must include a letter to parents describing the program, a home reading record for parents to sign, a participation certificate, a bulletin board, and books used to encourage reading at home. The assignment is intended to help students realize how important involving parents in their children's reading outside of school is to academic success. At the conclusion of the project, a sample of the materials used and a brief evaluation of how well the project worked are turned in for a grade.

As prospective administrators travel the continuum, they move from building awareness and understanding to participating in authentic parent-involvement learning experiences through field-based research. An example of an action research project carried out by students enrolled in the principalship course during the 1996–1997 school year is presented in the following section.

LEARNING THROUGH ACTION RESEARCH

Action research in this context is defined as structured field-based investigations conducted in school environments that engage teachers preparing to become school administrators in authentic learning experiences. The action research project described was assigned to students enrolled in the principalship course and required them to work in research teams of four or five students. Each team selected an elementary school and obtained permission to investigate the school's parent involvement program. The assignment was structured around five schoolwide activities in which the principal would be expected to play a role: (a) parent-teacher organization, (b) orientation or back-to-school night, (c) parent-teacher conferences, (d) volunteers, and (e) school newsletter.

The research team's first assignment was to determine the principal's opinion about how involved parents were in the school by rating the level of involvement on a nine-point scale with "1" representing very low and

"9" representing very high. After the general rating was given, the principal was asked to explain the reasons for the rating. The team then asked key questions to guide the investigation in each of five activity areas:

1. Parent-Teacher Association or Organization (PTA/PTO): Does the school have a PTA/PTO? Is it healthy and robust? How many parent members does it have? What is the proportion of parent members to potential members? How many teachers or staff members belong? What is the proportion of teachers and staff members to potential members? How many general meetings are held per school year? How many people attend these meetings? What are the organization's major areas of involvement? What activities and events are scheduled? How many people attend these activities and events?
2. Orientation or Back-To-School Night: Does the school hold a back-to-school night? Is it successful? How many parents participate? What is the proportion of actual participants to potential participants?
3. Parent-Teacher Conferences: Does the school hold parent-teacher conferences? How often? What time of day? Are they successful? How does the principal know this? How many parents participate? What is the proportion of actual participants to potential participants? Does the principal provide staff development workshops on the topic of conferencing with parents?
4. Parent Volunteers: Are parents recruited to serve as aides in the school, classrooms, or library? Do parents work on school projects? Does the school have an organized volunteer program? How many parents are involved as volunteers?
5. School Newsletter: Does the school publish a newsletter to keep parents informed? When? How is it sent home? Who prepares it? What content is included? Is it a successful venture? How does the principal know this?

In addition to interviewing the principal and others, the teams collected artifacts (e.g., announcements, reports, memoranda, agendas, minutes, copies of newsletters, membership rosters, and other documents) to support their findings. In the course of investigating these areas, teams often unearth other parent activities unique to a particular school setting, such as schoolwide reading motivation projects, school-home liaison aides, home visits by teachers at the beginning of the school year, workshops for parents, family centers, etc.

After completing field-based investigations, each team wrote a 7- to 10-page research report based on its findings. Collected artifacts were turned in with each paper. Finished reports were evaluated on the quality of content and presentation.

Teams shared their reports in class, discussed knowledge gained from conducting the research, and searched for generalizations derived from considering the five schools. The class then generated ideas for enhancing parent involvement and shared successful ideas. In conjunction with discussing PTA/PTO organizations, involvement of parents in decision making roles on school councils and advisory committees is incorporated through instructor-developed materials (now included in Blendinger and Jones, 1998).

STUDENT FEEDBACK

From 1990 to the present, feedback from the course participants who experienced the parent involvement modules has been overwhelmingly positive. Students enrolled in the principalship and instructional leadership courses were asked to rate their experiences in putting parent involvement to work in terms of authentic learning on a four-point scale ranging from excellent to unsatisfactory; the results are shown in Table 1.

As the data presented in the table and computed chi-square values indicate, students' ratings of their parent involvement experiences were consistently favorable. Representative student comments were as follows:

> Because parents lay the foundation for student attitudes about school, it's crucial that principals become proficient in the area of parent involvement. I now realize how important parent involvement training is for future school administrators.
>
> Parent involvement know-how is a very necessary part of any future principal's preparation program. I sincerely believe that involving parents is one of the keys to helping a school become effective.

Table 1. Student Ratings of Their Parent Involvement Learning Experiences over a Seven-Year Period.

Year	Excellent	Very Good	Satisfactory	Unsatisfactory	χ^2
1996–97	38	9	3	0	72.72
1995–96	39	11	2	0	74.62
1994–95	41	10	2	0	81.72
1993–94	39	8	1	0	84.17
1992–93	42	9	2	0	86.17
1991–92	39	8	1	0	84.17
1990–91	40	10	2	0	79.08

What I have learned about parent involvement will help me to be a better principal.

The hands-on experiences were great. They really helped me to understand the value of parent involvement.

When I become a principal, involving parents in their children's education will be one of my major goals.

Opportunities for working cooperatively with peers by sharing concerns and ideas, interacting with parents in school settings, learning how to develop action plans, and using ready-made materials to implement activities were frequently cited as being helpful.

CONCLUSION

In summary, our experiences for the past seven years in preparing future school leaders to become knowledgeable and proficient in developing skills necessary for putting parent involvement into practice have been very positive. Students become enlightened when engaged in the process of authentic learning through a combination of classroom assignments and field-based projects. When parents, teachers, school staff members, and others view one another as partners in education, a caring community forms and students benefit from the increased support. School-home partnerships should be an integral organizational component of schools to help promote student learning and success. Creating quality schools for the twenty-first century requires preparing school administrators who know "best practices" and can provide leadership for building effective school-home partnerships.

REFERENCES

Blendinger, J. G., & Jones, L. T. (1992). *Putting parent involvement to work.* Dubuque, IA: Kendall/Hunt.

Blendinger, J. G., & Jones, L. T. (1998). *Reaching out to families.* Dubuque, IA: Kendall/Hunt.

Epstein, J. L. (1992). School and family partnerships. In *The encyclopedia of educational research* (Vol. 4, pp. 1139–1151). New York: Macmillan.

Epstein, J. L. (1995). School/family/community partnerships. *Phi Delta Kappan, 76*(9), 701–712.

Epstein, J. L. (1996). Perspectives and previews on research and policy for school, family, and community partnerships. In A. Booth & J. F. Dunn (Eds.), *Family-school links: How do they affect educational outcomes?* (pp. 209–246). Mahaw, NJ: Lawrence Erlbaum Associates.

Henderson, A. T. (Ed.). (1981). *Parent participation—student achievement: The evidence grows.* Columbia, MD: National Committee for Citizens in Education.

Henderson, A. T. (Ed.). (1987). *Parent participation—student achievement: The evidence continues to grow.* Columbia, MD: National Committee for Citizens in Education.

Henderson, A. T., & Berla, N. (Eds.). (1994). *The family is critical to student achievement.* Washington, DC: National Committee for Citizens in Education.

Interstate School Leaders Licensure Consortium. (1996). *Standards for school leaders.* Washington, DC: Council of Chief State School Officers.

Jones, L. T. (1991). *Strategies for involving parents in their children's education* (Fastback 315). Bloomington, IN: Phi Delta Kappa.

National PTA. (1997). *National standards for parent/family involvement programs.* Chicago, IL: Author.

CHAPTER 25

Partnerships for Preparing School Leaders: Possibilities and Practicalities

W. Michael Martin, Sharon M. Ford, Michael J. Murphy, and Rodney Muth

The need for systemic reform in preparation programs for school leaders has been well articulated in the past decade by scholars from a variety of educational sectors (Griffiths, Stout, & Forsyth, 1988; Martin, Murphy, & Muth, 1996; Thompson, 1993). It has long been our contention that contradictions between preparation programs and the practice of educational administration must be resolved to enhance quality, rigor, credibility, and impact. These contradictions culminate in various stereotypical attitudes: professors and university officials often feel that the "ivory tower knows best" and that what preparation programs need is simply a stronger theoretical or research base with which school leaders will be better off. Practitioners, on the other hand, often prefer extensive internships or apprentice-like programs to help them acquire the skills requisite to successful school administration. Achilles (1988), Pitner (1988), and Murphy (1992), however, have much larger concerns about the nature of preparation programs. They indict them for weak knowledge bases, lack of connection to practice, weak clinical experiences, and overemphasis on instructional methods that are disconnected from theories of adult learning.

Our contention is that the creation of significant university-school district partnerships can build a better bridge to excellence in preparing school leaders. Building such partnerships requires a more comprehensive view of change on the part of both the academy and the "real" world of school administration. Achieving this will be difficult for, as Sarason (1990) points out, reform has to be "developmental" and bridge the huge gap between the school and the outside world. By forming meaningful connections between the two sometimes isolated worlds of theory and practice, we have learned that the gulf can be bridged more easily.

POSSIBILITIES OF PARTNERSHIPS

> Partnership is the willingness to give more choice to the people we choose to serve. Not total control, just something more equal . . . As soon as you centralize the point of action at a higher level, you take away real ownership and responsibility from those closest to the work, the touch labor.
>
> Peter Block (1993)

Since 1989, the Administration, Supervision and Curriculum Development (ASCD) Division at the University of Colorado at Denver has networked with local educational agencies to prepare future school leaders cooperatively. Beginning with a joint venture with the Northern Colorado Board of Cooperative Educational Services (BOCES) in Longmont, Colorado, to develop a preparation program for school principals (Welch, Martin, Murphy, Brooks, & Salzman, 1991), we have designed fourteen partnership arrangements at both PhD and MA or licensing levels. Comprehensive networks have been developed to join educational agencies (schools, districts, BOCES, state, and national organizations) with the University of Colorado at Denver. Ward and Pascarelli (1987) argue that bringing together diverse agencies for improvements in education is both "timely and necessary" (p. 193). They state that "collaborative networks are viable and practical vehicles for developing and maintaining the skilled professionals required and for developing improved education programs in a cost-effective manner" (p. 193).

EARLY HISTORY OF UNIVERSITY OF COLORADO PARTNERSHIPS

The educational administration program at the University of Colorado started at Boulder in 1938 and moved to Denver in 1986. When the program was relocated in Denver, it already had a long and valued practice of developing and participating in university-school district partnerships. Through such agencies as the Bureau of Educational Research and Service, the Center for Educational Leadership Services, the North Central Association of Schools and Colleges, and Rockefeller, Danforth, and U.S. Office of Education (USOE) fellowship programs, the university reached out to its clients in Colorado.

Early pioneering efforts to prepare school leaders jointly were begun in the 1970s with pilot programs in locations around Denver, southern Colorado and Pueblo, Cortez, Alamosa, and Durango. These early partnership arrangements were difficult as full-time-equivalency (FTE) instruction was not permitted in off-campus locations by the Colorado Commission of Higher Education (CCHE). These programs had to be offered through the Division of Continuing Education and be self-funded by student tuition. Professors and practitioners who taught in the program were given either overload assignments or a fixed stipend to teach, and their efforts were not counted as part of their regular load within the university. All professors in the educational administration program actively participated in these efforts between 1973 and the late 1980s with none refusing an assignment despite the difficulties created by overload responsibilities in a research-oriented university. Sacrifices made to travel, even during snowstorms, to distant areas by plane, bus, or car were remarkable, given the "out-of-hide" time commitments and low extrinsic rewards within the university for these activities. These arrangements were rarely recognized or valued in merit or other compensation decisions, yet they were continued, being in the best interests of the districts and future leaders being prepared.

Most of these early models were school district-centered partnerships as local districts were constantly searching for outstanding administrator candidates and turned to the University of Colorado as a source of these individuals. In these early efforts, collaboration was mostly in program delivery and the mentorship of administrative candidates in their internships, field-based projects, or individual practicum activities, with the university still controlling the recruitment, selection, program design, curriculum, and assessment of students throughout their program at the university. In the words of Block (1993, pp. 23–32), the "exchange of purpose" was only moderate, practitioners and students had only a low "voice," little "joint accountability" existed, university "patriarchy" was high, and "ownership" of the program by the local or state leaders was minimal.

STRAINS OF INTRA-UNIVERSITY PARTNERSHIPS

The early efforts just described facilitated the development of future university-based partnerships. Intra-university partnerships had early success in the mid-1970s and the early 1980s as the Colorado Springs (UCCS) and Denver (UCD) campuses of the University of Colorado sought and arranged cooperative programs in educational administration with Boulder (UCB). Boulder, however, maintained control of the programs, and this often created turf problems between and among the faculties and administrators at each campus. Faculty teaching loads, advising assignments, library resources, and funding were constant issues between 1973 and 1986 as each campus wanted the visibility and credit hours for its own school of education. The PhD and certification programs were highly prized in educational administration, and despite the early successes of cooperative program delivery and the mutuality of goals for the joint programs, strains were constant. UCB held "all of the cards," having "sole proprietorship" of the program since the late 1930s, and was reluctant to share power, control, or authority with its sister campuses. As Block (1993, p. 23) points out, this is a serious flaw in a partnership. Students and school districts in Denver and Colorado Springs were happy to have classes offered locally while area superintendents vied for stand-alone programs both in Denver and Colorado Springs. The UCCS campus developed its own certification program in the late 1970s, and through the efforts of several aggressive

Denver-area superintendents, all educational administration programs at UCB were moved to UCD by CCHE in 1986.

The ultimate "breakup" of previously successful partnerships was due in part to the lack of concern about the dysfunctional nature of the partnerships as articulated by Block (pp. 23–32): control by one member over another, displacement of purpose, loss of voice, little ownership by sister campuses, excessive "care taking" by UCB, and the vestiges of a "parent-child" relationship between the "flagship" campus and its sister campuses. It was left to the UCD faculty in educational administration in 1989 to design a new "paradigm" for partnerships between the university and its clients. Issues such as "load," FTEs, new models for off-campus credit, changes in reward systems and resources, collaboration, mutuality of goals, systemic change, new models of instructional delivery, and instructional and managerial technology had to be addressed. Curriculum revision and cooperative design were necessary new concepts for partnership to flourish.

REPLACING PATRIARCHY WITH COLLABORATION

> Universities have a mission to create new knowledge. In pursuing this mission in the field of education, universities will benefit from the kind of symbiotic relationship that is possible through a partnership with schools.
> John Goodlad (1985)

Could "patriarchy" be replaced with "partnership" in the newly emerging relationships between UCD and other institutions? Following the admonitions of the scholars who had written extensively about preparation programs over the past few decades, the faculty sought to "dream the best" in concert with practitioners, private sector representatives, and students. Search conferences were held with stakeholder groups (Martin, 1994), advisory committees were formed to conduct cooperative programs, and a waiver was sought from the state to develop an alternative program to prepare future school leaders (Welch et al., 1991).

Block (1993, p. 23) argues that leaders must choose "partnership over patriarchy" in building effective organizations. He states that ineffective organizations overemphasize *control* (which is established when lines of authority are clear, one group makes decisions for another, and people in the middle exist to execute and implement decisions), *consistency* (which is overemphasized when a common or "right" way exists to run an organization and key functions need to be clearly understood by all), and *predictability* (which interferes with organizational effectiveness when overemphasized in terms of measuring specific outcomes, such as students who worry more about grades than learning or teachers who give inflated grades to improve their image). Block points out that when control, consistency, and predictability are imbalanced in leaders, groups, or organizations, then decisions, ownership, satisfaction, and commitment generally remain with the controlling group and are not shared with others who may have a stake in the success of the enterprise.

Based on past experience and Block's and other's admonitions, we have been attempting to build partnerships with schools, districts, BOCES, superintendent groups, and educational agencies where key decisions are made collaboratively and ownership, satisfaction, and commitment are shared by the stakeholder groups. We believe that connecting the university to the field through these partnerships has become indispensable to successful development and implementation of innovative programming at UCD. Whether involving PhD programming for career-oriented executives or standards-based licensing for preservice educators, UCD has collaborated with area superintendents, principals, private-sector representatives, and other administrators to build responsive programs. This "stewardship" (Block) for the preparation of future leaders has resulted in vital and powerful partnerships between the university and its clientele—schools, students, and regional agencies.

Block further identifies four "requirements" that need to be present if partnerships are to achieve their potential. What follows is an integration of Block's requirements with our attempts to implement effective partnerships with our clients.

Exchange of Purpose

The theory, according to Block, is that each party must struggle with defining purpose and then engage in dialogue with others about what is going to be created. It means that all parties in the relationship are responsible for defining the vision and values, with purpose getting defined by the continual dialogue (p. 29). People at each level need to communicate about what they want to create, with each person having to identify the best thinking about the purpose and with all having a voice in discussing what they want the institution to become.

In practice at UCD, we have created partnerships tabula rasa—with only a few "givens"; everything about program design is on the table for dialogue, including purpose, content, delivery, time requirements, instructional teaming, clinical experiences, and balance between theory, research, and practice as well as assignments, activities, and assessment procedures. In this way, power and control issues are minimized, and all stakeholders have an equal voice in the creation of the program. Recently, this collaboration has been expanded to include recruitment, selection, training, and assessment of administrator candidates by all stakeholder groups (Martin, Murphy, & Muth, 1993).

Right to Say No

Block's theory makes a strong case that partners have a "right to say no." This is a fundamental way in which we have reduced our "sovereignty." Block states, "if we cannot say no, then saying yes has no meaning" (p. 30). He claims that partnerships are undermined when people stand up for their ideas and get shot down by a "higher authority." In his view, a partnership does not mean that one partner always get what it wants—it means that "you may lose your argument, but you never lose your voice" (p. 30).

In practice, we have continually sought to make decisions collaboratively with stakeholders and have found little difficulty with this as an operating principle. A set of "ground rules" for stakeholder decision making in our governance or advisory groups has usually been established, with a strong norm emphasizing an equal voice for students, practitioners, and professors. When all members of the partnership can say "no," then all members become more actively engaged in determining purposes, strategies, and activities—often in much more creative ways than in previous designs. This power sharing neither comes easily nor quickly as traditional roles and expectations are hard to break with deference initially given to professors by students and practitioners. If we are to overcome the widespread criticisms of preparation programs, all stakeholders must be encouraged to participate actively in the creation of new program designs. If university personnel continually resist new approaches, then reform will be blocked by the ivory tower, and we will return to "business as usual."

Joint Accountability

The theory, says Block, is that each person is responsible for both the outcomes and the current situation within the partnership with no one else to blame. No one group or individual is responsible for the morale, learning, or career of another—in other words, "bosses resign their caretaking role." The outcomes and quality of cooperation within a group are now "everyone's responsibility" including the maintenance of faith, hope, and spirit. The central point, Block argues, is that, if people want the freedom that partnership offers, then the price is "personal accountability for the success and failure of our unit and community" (p. 30).

In practice, sharing "ownership" and "accountability" with our governance groups and advisory members is not easily achieved, due simply to logistics. Further, the university is viewed as ultimately responsible for a program with professors hired by their university employer and paid to achieve program purposes and outcomes. Since universities have typically been the "gatekeepers" of wisdom and knowledge on the preparation of future leaders, university personnel have to be careful because traditional concerns about turf and territory can easily ruin otherwise superb relationships. Time constraints, more than anything else, interfere with total stakeholder participation. Yet, when purposes, decisions, strategies, and programs are jointly designed and implemented by all stakeholders, accountability is fully shared. Our stakeholder governance groups have (a) testified before the State Board of Education, (b) met with evaluation teams and accrediting agencies, (c) spoken at state and national conferences, and (d) demonstrated ownership and accountability in working directly with our programs. Credit and blame are equally shared when events in each of the programs unfold, and a spirit of mutual inquiry and problem-solving usually prevails.

Absolute Honesty

The theory, according to Block, suggests that one benefit of redistributing power is that people feel less vulnerable and are more open and honest (p. 31). In organizations, patriarchal or parent-child relationships often exist between bosses and subordinates, and the truth often does not get told to avoid a perceived backlash. If a partnership is to be successful, honesty must prevail, and to act otherwise is, according to Block, "betrayal" of the other partners. "Silent watching, folded arms, set jaws," and similar behaviors indicate passive-aggressive behavior which can lead to unhealthy abdication. Block points out that honesty in a partnership arrangement means asking questions, maintaining contact without control, making simple direct statements, and living with not always getting one's way—behaviors that nurture strong and effective partnerships in both professional as well as personal dimensions of life.

In practice, because universities have usually been charged with the responsibility to prepare future leaders, absolute honesty about improving what we do is essential, whether taking the form of suggestions or ideas from new or younger colleagues, a local principal or superintendent, a student, or a private-sector representative. The old cliché, "that's the way we've always done it around here," cannot hold true if partnerships are to be successful. Issues related to professorial turf, experience, and accountability can lead to defensive behaviors by professors and university administrators, particularly when questions are raised by their practitioner or student colleagues. Change in role relationships is difficult, but regular contact and communication have minimized the disruptive behaviors of passive aggression or withdrawal in our partnership relationships. This does not say that professors, practitioners, and students always agree—far from it. Students, like faculty, range from need for structure to tolerance for ambiguity, from the need to emphasize content to the desire to build process skills. Practitioners can lecture students in the same dysfunctional manner as professors, and professors can operate their programs with the same flaws as public school programs. Nobody is perfect, but when "absolute honesty" is a norm, greater receptivity to improvements and new ideas is likely.

Block concludes his ideas about partnerships by stating that seeking clarity of ideas rather than control of the relationship is the appropriate role of leaders, bringing a "value-added" ingredient to a partnership. Block uses the term *stewardship* to signify an essential characteristic of partnerships, the "willingness to hold power, without using reward and punishment and directive authority, to get things done" (p. 32). This applies to the role of professors, practitioners, students, and private-sector representatives in designing a quality preparation program for future school leaders. In accomplishing this end, all stakeholders hold the stewardship for society, schools, and students.

PRACTICALITIES FOR PARTNERSHIPS IN PREPARING SCHOOL LEADERS

> When educational institutions and agencies undertake collaborative efforts in education, an initial tendency is to enter into discussions about how one agency can help the other(s). The predominant notion is that individuals in one setting are more skilled, possess more accurate insights, and are better equipped to bring about a desired improvement than those in the other settings do.... As a result, a work on rather than a work with posture underlies many joint efforts among teachers, schools administrators, university professors and others.
>
> Ward and Pascarelli (1987)

Ward and Pascarelli, drawing upon the research of Sarason, Pascarelli, and Crohn (1985), caution that three crucial factors have inhibited collaborative improvement efforts in the past: (a) promising more than can be delivered, (b) failing to deal effectively with the reality of limited resources, and (c) failing to recognize and initiate opportunities for collaboration and resource sharing. These upsides and downsides to partnerships have caused us to reflect on two dimensions: (a) the types of partnerships created and (b) the lessons learned from their creation.

TYPES OF PARTNERSHIPS FOR PREPARING FUTURE SCHOOL LEADERS

Through our experiences, we have identified three general types of partnerships: (a) university-centered, with two variations (intra-university and inter-university partnerships); (b) school district-centered partnerships with two variations (exclusive partnerships with one district only and inclusive partnerships with multiple districts); and (c) agency-centered partnerships, which have a specific focus and participation by a local, state, or national educational agency. Each has its purposes and its unique characteristics.

University-Centered Partnerships

These appear to be the most fragile partnership arrangements due to the oft-cited turf issues associated with university programs—with student credit hours driving resource allocations, each institution ultimately wants its own program for reasons of prestige, visibility, control, and resources. Efforts must be undertaken constantly to keep the communication open and to share resources to the greatest extent possible. "Parity" is a big issue in developing these models (Ward & Pascarelli, 1987, p. 196): "no agency should work alone to define the ways in which the knowledge and expertise contributed by the participating agencies can be made available to the other members." Achieving parity requires continuous interaction by all parties in the design, planning, and enacting of programs so that the creation is the result of true collaboration rather than one party dominating another. Diverse cultures, expectations, and resource requirements—tuition differentials, courses rather than domains, or lecture vs. group-centered instructional methods—have to be merged if this type of partnership is to be successful.

Intra-University Partnerships

For UCD, intra-university partnerships are those which involve other units within the University of Colorado system. The UCD-UCCS "cooperative" PhD program typifies intra-university partnerships, and professors from both institutions along with practitioners jointly recruit and select students, design the curriculum, and teach and assess students. No one partner is more powerful than another, and "stewardship" of program purposes, goals, objectives, and outcomes is shared by all parties. An advisory board meets regularly to assure program quality, and collaboration has resulted in a highly successful program for doctoral students. Funding for the program comes from the state's "educational access" program in which CCHE authorizes additional resources for programs in locations remote from home campuses. Credit hours, load credits, and similar issues are supported, and all students are on-line through Colorado Education Online, UCD's School of Education's e-mail and conferencing system. Professors are paid mileage for their travel, and support resources come to the School of Education and are shared with ASCD for delivering this off-site program. Most of the flaws in earlier models have been overcome in this new approach, and turf issues have been dormant. Nevertheless, merit and other forms of compensation are still deficient: incentives for developing, implementing, and maintaining this remote program remain small, and faculty at UCCS still have difficulty getting their teaching recognized as part of their regular load.

Inter-University Partnerships

These partnerships exist between one or more higher educational institutions as illustrated by the Denver School Leadership Academy (DSLA) and the Jeffco Leadership Academy (JLA). In this arrangement, the University of Denver and UCD collaborate with the Denver Public Schools (DPS) and the Jefferson County Public Schools (Jeffco) to design and deliver licensing programs for principals in each of the districts. All candidates are collaboratively recruited, selected, trained, and assessed by the three parties in each setting. Potential culture clashes among the three diverse parties—a public university, a private university, and a large urban school system—have largely been avoided by following the ideas of both Block (1993) and Ward and Pascarelli (1987). Purposes are continually clarified through frequent dialogue, and all parties have helped define the vision and values of the programs. All parties have an equal voice in decision making, and no one loses a "voice" in governing the program. "Parent-child" relationships have been avoided through frequent communication and contact among the leaders of each organization, particularly in planning and program assessment—resulting in a high degree of mutual trust over five years with DPS and the last year with Jeffco. Support for students in the DPS program comes from district scholarships, and students receive released time for classes and field activities. Jeffco students get released time for field activities. In the coming year, the two districts, the two largest in Colorado, will join forces to prepare future leaders for their respective districts.

School District-Centered Partnerships

District-centered partnerships are those in which district interests are paramount, and the DSLA and JLA are good examples. At least fourteen partnerships have been formed by UCD since the late 1980s. The premise has been that universities and school districts should join together to prepare future school leaders cooperatively (Martin, Murphy, & Muth, 1993). Initial assumptions that guided the development of these programs were as follows: (a) programs for preparing school leaders could be strengthened if universities (traditional providers) and school districts (employers) collaboratively designed and delivered these programs, cooperatively recruiting, training, and assessing students; (b) programs for the preparation of school leaders could be strengthened if qualified and interested leadership from business contributed to the design and delivery of those programs (such as US West, Storage Technology, IBM, and Hewlett Packard); (c) leadership preparation can be improved through innovative pilot programs that are designed to test new ideas about teaching and learning, curriculum redesign, program delivery, standards-based education, authentic assessment, and so forth; and (d) BOCES and similar school-district partnerships throughout the Denver metropolitan area and the region could design collaborative efforts and replicate them in other sites in the region.

Two types of these school district-centered partnerships exist: *exclusive* and *inclusive*. In the exclusive model, a single district wants its future leaders prepared together in a focused manner. The DSLA is illustrative of this approach. University and district personnel in DPS designed and adapted the program to the Denver setting, and students have worked together as a cohort, receiving district support for some tuition assistance and released time for field activities and some class days.

The advantages of this model include (a) focused time commitments, curricula, and instruction; (b) district sponsorship of future leaders through cooperative recruitment, selection, and training; and (c) more thorough understanding of the school district culture. Disadvantages include (a) too narrow a focus on one school system's "way of doing business" to the exclusion of other perspectives, (b) potential "political" selections or placements of students by district personnel, and (c) "group think" which leads to students emphasizing present practice over other possible approaches to such issues as busing, curriculum design, evaluation of personnel, and so on.

Inclusive partnerships are those relationships in which students are prepared in cohorts from different districts. Examples of this form of partnership are the Denver Area School Superintendents Council (DASSC) program, the Northern Colorado School Leadership Academy, the Western Slope Licensing program in Grand Junction, and the UCD-Jeffco-Danforth PhD program. By selecting students from multiple educational settings, these programs can address some of the limitations of the exclusive model, and cohorts learn alternative approaches to school district practices as they analyze, apply, and integrate their field and classroom experiences.

Agency-Centered Partnerships

UCD has partnered with nondistrict educational agencies such as the Education Commission of the States (ECS) to deliver a "policy" PhD. This emerging model of preparation has initially focused on the improvement of educational policy and practice through collaboration with ECS, the National Conference of State Legislators, and other policy-oriented groups. Cooperative recruitment and selection of high-ability students with policy interests have brought university or college personnel, state department officials, school board leaders, and private-sector consultants into this unique program. This program features many of the innovations identified earlier, with the addition of new approaches such as (a) doctoral "labs" in which students and faculty work together on problems of inquiry and practice, often leading to independent research projects, dissertations, funded research, and publications; (b) pro seminars in which students, faculty, and educational leaders come together to discuss policy and practice issues in education, share topic foci (concentrations) and dissertation topics, and develop lab projects; (c) standards-based expectations with yearly portfolio assessments; (d) dissertation hours taken concurrently with academic work to minimize the "ABDs"; and (e) regular meetings of all doctoral students in the School of Education to focus on common issues. Students are admitted yearly with the expectation that new students will be mentored by more experienced students in areas such as grant writing, project management, research studies, and the like. While the program admits students annually, the pro seminars create vertical cohorts differentiated by their unique research foci and interests. The agency-centered partnership model stemmed from initial development monies from the Danforth Foundation in 1988 and led to the creation of the UCD-Jeffco PhD partnership. Many of the ideas that undergird the ECS-UCD and the UCCS-UCD partnerships owe their intellectual debt to the Danforth-sponsored model which began in 1991 with the first cohort of PhD students.

PARTNERSHIPS—LESSONS BEING LEARNED

Collaborative networks that work on innovative, significant school improvements fail more often than they succeed. ... they require continuous investment of time and energy on the part of each member.... What makes this commitment work is the mutual empowerment, the taking control of problems, and the ability to recognize and use the individual and collective potential of the network for school improvement that sustains such effort.

Ward and Pascarelli (1987)

The work described here must be labeled "under construction," as one of the students in a DASSC cohort put it so aptly. We constantly are working to learn and understand how these partnerships can be refined and improved as new ideas, mistakes, and lessons emerge. We find that some students want more structure in classes and field projects, that many would prefer passively delivered content over the ambiguous world of field projects, that others actively seek the liberation provided by self-directed and problem-based learning activities, that some professors have difficulty with team planning and teaching, and that some practitioners can be more didactic than any professor in delivering content. We plan to continue to meet these and other issues "head-on" and to continue to "walk our talk" about productive partnerships. With some basic issues such as resources, load credit, turf, and others under better control, our time can be spent productively on program refinements and redesign.

Even though we have written extensively about our program experiences here and elsewhere (Martin, Ford, Murphy, Rehm, & Muth, 1997; Martin, Murphy, & Muth, 1993; Muth, Murphy, & Martin, 1994), we still need to be more consistent in documenting what we do, particularly archiving the contributions made to collaborating agencies by our labs and problem-based learning projects and through practica and other field-based learning activities. Further, we need to capture more effectively how our partners benefit from their relations with us. By using the categories outlined here, our continued diligence will ensure continued growth of our partnerships, bringing benefits to all.

REFERENCES

Achilles, C. M. (1988). Unlocking some mysteries of administration and administrator preparation: A reflective prospect. In D. Griffiths, R. Stout, & P. Forsyth (Eds.), *Leaders for America's schools: The report and papers of the National Commission on Excellence in Educational Administration.* San Francisco: McCutchan.

Block, P. (1993). *Stewardship: Choosing service over self-interest.* San Francisco: Berrett-Koehler.

Goodlad, J. I. (1985, September). *Reconstructing schooling and the education of educators.* Paper presented to the National Network of Educational Renewal.

Griffiths, D., Stout, R., & Forsyth, P. (Eds.). (1988). *Leaders for America's schools: The report and papers of the National Commission on Excellence in Educational Administration.* San Francisco: McCutchan.

Martin, W. M. (1994, February). *Discovering common ground: Using futures search conferences to involve students, faculty, administrators and private sector representatives in building a learning community*. Paper presented at the annual Conference-within-a-Conference, American Association of School Administrators, San Francisco.

Martin, W. M., Ford, S., Murphy, M., Rehm, R. G., & Muth, R. (1997). Linking instructional delivery with diverse learning settings. *Journal of School Leadership, 7,* 386–408.

Martin, W. M., Murphy, M. J., & Muth, R. (1994). Problem-based learning at the University of Colorado at Denver. *Journal of School Leadership, 4,* 432–450.

Martin, W. M., Murphy, M. J., & Muth, R. (1993). Problem-based learning: A new approach to preparing school leaders. In J. Hoyle and D. Estes (Eds.). *First annual yearbook of the National Council of Professors of Educational Administration. NCPEA: In a new voice* (pp. 141–154). Lancaster, PA: Technomic Publishing Co., Inc.

Martin, W. M., Murphy, M. J., & Muth, R. (1996). Systemic change as the target of learning in administrator preparation programs: Stirring the comfort zone of participants. In J. Burden (Ed.), *Fourth annual yearbook of the National Council of Professors of Educational Administration. Prioritizing instruction* (pp. 9–17). Lancaster, PA: Technomic Publishing Co., Inc.

Muth, R., Murphy, M. J., & Martin, W. M. (1994, July). Problem-based learning at the University of Colorado at Denver. *Journal of School Leadership, 4,* 432–450.

Thompson, S. (1993). *Principals for our changing schools: Knowledge and skill base.* Fairfax, VA: National Policy Board for Educational Administration.

Pitner, N. (1988). Training of the school administrator: State of the art. In D. Griffiths, R. Stout, & P. Forsyth (Eds.), *Leaders for America's schools: The report and papers of the National Commission on Excellence in Educational Administration.* San Francisco: McCutchan.

Sarason, S., Pascarelli, J. T., & Crohn, L. (1985). *Fulfilling the promise: A fresh look at collaboration and resource sharing.* Portland, OR: Northwest Regional Educational Laboratory.

Sarason, S. (1990). *The predictable failure of educational reform.* San Francisco: Jossey-Bass.

Ward, B. A., & Pascarelli, J. T. (1987). Networking for educational improvement. In J. I. Goodlad (Ed.), *The ecology of school renewal.* Chicago: University of Chicago Press.

Welch, D., Martin, W. M., Murphy, M., Brooks, G., & Salzman, P. (1991). *Final report on the Northern Colorado School Leadership Academy.* Denver: Colorado Department of Education.

CHAPTER 26

Integrating Simulations, Extended Internships, and Portfolios in a Principal Preparation Program

George Perreault and Lynn Bradshaw

Universities, as open systems, are sensitive to wider social pressures, including the widely held perception that we need new ways to prepare school leaders (Clark & Clark, 1996; Lewis, 1997) at the same time as the number of needed new school administrators is rising in our state (North Carolina State Board of Education, 1997) and in others across the nation (Duke, 1992; Jordan, 1994; Southern Association of School, College, and University Staffing, 1996). For these reasons, states, which effectively "own" the licensing procedures within their boundaries, direct universities to reform their programs, and, willingly or not, universities tend to comply. Fortunately, many state mandates are broad enough that universities can respond by developing programs that address skills and knowledge the faculty consider to be especially important; these might include emotional intelligence (Cooper & Sawaf, 1997), collaboration (Wood & Gray, 1991), or sensitivity to diversity (Darling-Hammond, 1995). In addition, program revisions can also focus on new methodologies that promise to be effective, including the use of simulations, extended internships, and student portfolios (Hill & Ragland, 1995; Leithwood, 1995; Thurston, Clift, & Schacht, 1993).

The purpose of this paper is to share the results of three innovative components in one university's preparation program for school administrators: (a) use with student cohorts of the Leadership Early Assessment Program (LEAP) and Springfield simulations of the National Association of Secondary School Principals (NASSP); (b) a full-time, year-long internship during the second year of study; and (c) a required leadership portfolio of evidence demonstrating knowledge, skill, and professional perspectives expected of school leaders. These components were developed in response to a mandate by the North Carolina Legislature for new principal preparation programs in the state which included support for a limited number of "Principal Fellows." Under this provision, a qualified applicant could receive a loan of $40,000 for two years of full-time study, and the loan would be forgiven if the recipient worked as a school administrator in North Carolina for four years. The first cohort of full-time students graduated from the new programs in May 1997.

At the same time, the university has implemented a revised Master's in School Administration (MSA) program for part-time students who are seeking initial administrative licensure. These students complete the same basic course work as do the Principal Fellows, but they do not participate in the simulations, and their internships are more limited in terms of duration and intensity. Except for a four- to six-week full-time experience with a summer school or a year-round program, part-time students typically complete their internships while they are still employed as teachers. In addition to evaluating the use of each component, one of our interests was to assess the relative effectiveness of the two programs.

THE SIMULATIONS

The first cohort of full-time interns participated in NASSP's Springfield development program in January 1997 while they were beginning the second semester of their internships. The Springfield program was chosen

---
George Perreault and Lynn Bradshaw, East Carolina University

as an opportunity for skill development in six areas that were introduced the first day: problem analysis, judgment, organizational ability, decisiveness, leadership, and sensitivity. Participants are given an opportunity to choose two skill areas on which they wish to concentrate and to be observed during the simulation. On the second day, the students chose a role as a principal, assistant principal, or central office supervisor in a seven-hour simulation of the Springfield School District at work. At the conclusion of the simulation, participants have a chance to provide skills-based feedback to others in the simulation. The third day is spent in group feedback sessions with trained mentors and in planning for further professional development.

Most notably, interest in the skill area of sensitivity tended to be higher after the simulation experience. Most students identified sensitivity either as a strength to refine further or as an area for growth in their plans following Springfield. One student identified sensitivity descriptors both as a strength and also as an area for growth, depending on the specific context for the behavior. The student wanted to continue to build her strength in "eliciting perceptions, feelings, and concerns of others," but she saw a need to improve her ability to "express verbal and nonverbal recognition of feelings, needs, and concerns of others."

In her journal, another student described her experience in the area of sensitivity as follows:

> Springfield was an interesting and valuable experience. I was complimented and criticized for sensitivity issues (not on my list of things to work on during the three days). It seems as if everyone got comments about sensitivity. That was certainly the easiest thing to observe. I must work on hiding my facial expressions when I am faced with people who seem momentarily incompetent. I learned in a Myers-Briggs session that, as an ENTJ, I can't tolerate incompetence, and I fear it most in myself. How true that was during Springfield!

Another student noted that "Springfield forced me to be reflective about my affective role as an administrator, to discover my weaknesses in that area, and to take steps to improve."

During the three-day training session and for the rest of the semester, faculty and school district administrators served as mentors for the Principal Fellows. All three groups–faculty, administrators, and students–found that Springfield provided a common language to use to discuss developmental opportunities. One challenge, however, was finding a useful way for tying the Springfield skills together with the course work, the internship experiences, and the knowledge, skills, and professional perspectives of the ten North Carolina standards for school administrators (see Appendix A). Ultimately, it was decided to create a matrix showing the North Carolina Performance Domains down the side and the Springfield skill areas across the top. Using this matrix, students identified areas for focus during the remainder of their internship, merging them wherever practical. One student chose as a goal to "seek input and feedback from staff before making decisions"; another planned "to elicit a firm commitment from others regarding time and work products for increasing classroom performance."

Student reaction to participation in the Springfield simulation was very positive. A few representative comments in response to evaluative questions are shown below.

> Were you able to implement suggestions from your mentors and peers?
>
>> Most definitely. I was told I need to be more sensitive. I have forced myself to think before I act.
>>
>> Yes. Entering into conversations. This is hard for me because I have to learn more about timing. But I did it and was able to contribute more to discussions.
>
> Have you expanded your skills as a result of Springfield?
>
>> Yes! I have developed in the area of problem analysis. I feel as though this is an area which is used every day—and often.
>>
>> Yes—leadership. I helped collaborate to develop the school improvement plan, establish an alternative reading program, and a grant writing committee. I also helped write and do data analysis for a school improvement grant.
>
> What lessons have you learned?
>
>> I have learned that all of the skills and behaviors coupled with the domains play a large part in development as an administrator.
>>
>> That I need to take time and work to involve people meaningfully in decision making.

Other supportive statements on the value of the Springfield experience were contained in the third of our innovative components, the portfolio used for evaluation of the Principal Fellows.

In response to student feedback from the first Springfield experience, the simulation was conducted with the second cohort of Principal Fellows in October 1997. The earlier date was used in order to allow students more time to focus their internship activities on the development of specific skills.

The success with Springfield also prompted the university to begin another effort using NASSP materials and activities, the Leadership Early Assessment Program (LEAP). This decision is in line with the university's commitment to linkages with school districts in our service area, many of which are faced with the need to "grow their own" future leaders. Most districts in our service region, however, have encountered persistent shortages of funding and of qualified internal trainers and have come to rely heavily on the university's MSA and Principal Fellows programs. Since the administrators in these districts are often involved in mentoring activities for our students, both before and during formal university programs, we have initiated a joint project to identify future leaders and to assist in their development.

Twenty LEAP assessors from three pilot districts and the university were trained in February 1997. Mentors for administrators were trained in the spring, and 12 eventually became mentor trainers, establishing internal capacity to expand further. Thirty more assessors, from the pilot districts and other districts, were trained this fall, and two of the pilot districts conducted their own LEAP assessment centers in October 1997. Several participants who were identified "future leaders" are enrolled in the MSA program and can use their district-administered simulation to focus course activities more specifically for individual growth needs.

At the same time, university faculty members have begun the process of assessing the leadership skills of Principal Fellows upon entry to and graduation from the program. The assessment results—the strengths and potential "derailers" for each student—will be used as a basis for individual and program development (see Appendix B). Individual faculty members are incorporating in-basket problems, leaderless group assignments, and other performance-based activities into course instruction. Individual student progress will be monitored through their leadership portfolios and reflective journals. Aggregate data will be used for needs assessment, program development, and program evaluation. For example, a review of the overall results provides the following information about this new cohort of full-time students:

1. Students demonstrated strengths in specific administrative skills, but few students were consistently strong in the broad administrative skill areas.
2. Many students demonstrated strengths in the interpersonal skills area. In the interviews, they tended to describe themselves as being sensitive to the needs and concerns of others. They also demonstrated high levels of motivation. At the same time, certain interpersonal skills were potential derailers in other activities.
3. Although specific communication skills were potential derailers for some students during certain activities, there do not appear to be serious problems with oral or written communication skills.
4. Students have begun to demonstrate some strength in "knowledge of strengths and weaknesses" and in "educational values." These strengths were apparent during the reflective discussion following the in-basket activity and during the interview.

As students have opportunities to practice these skills in course work and field experiences, the expectation is that broad skill areas will emerge as strengths and "potential derailers" will tend to be context specific and relatively minor.

Lessons learned from the pilot effort will be helpful in a broader context if the collaborative efforts are expanded as other districts have requested. A proposal for funding to support additional training of assessors for districts in our service region has been submitted. We see several advantages for the stakeholder groups:

1. Collaborative efforts will increase networking among school district and university personnel and build stronger consensus regarding the skills required for school administrators.
2. Collaborative district leadership development efforts will strengthen the skills of practicing administrators who supervise interns during field experiences.
3. Mixing novices with more experienced administrators in development programs has the potential to broaden the interaction among participants, not only within preparation programs but also throughout their careers as a common language is learned and used.

4. Collaborating groups will share costs of training licenses and coordination. Some costs could be a benefit of membership in existing regional partnerships and could actually be used as a way for strengthening those partnerships.

THE EXTENDED INTERNSHIP

The second new feature of the Principal Fellows program was a year-long administrative internship. The typical schedule for Principal Fellows was to keep Mondays free for campus seminars, but to be committed otherwise to being "on the job" in their school district. Considerable variation existed within the placements that students could arrange. Some were assigned to a single school for the whole academic year, while others spent one semester each at two different instructional levels. Many of the Fellows received supplemental stipends from their districts and clearly were perceived as being part of the administrative team at their sites. Some of them quickly assumed responsibilities in substantive areas (e.g., student discipline and teacher evaluation) while others were assigned "token" responsibilities (such as directing a small project to support school volunteers) and struggled to be viewed as significant contributors to the leadership effort in their schools.

However, in spite of within-group variations, the Principal Fellows as a whole were very satisfied with the experience they gained, and they were clearly better prepared for entry-level administrative positions than their part-time counterparts. For example, full-time interns were much more heavily involved with instructional leadership issues, especially with teacher evaluation. They typically had the opportunity to conduct dozens of classroom observations and numerous conferences with teachers. Some of these were done in conjunction with a principal or assistant principal, but some of the Fellows had responsibility for the complete evaluative process for 12 or 13 or, in one case, for 30 teachers. Since one of the challenges for new school administrators is to overcome the effects of their isolation as classroom teachers, it cannot help but be beneficial to have such experiences as observing "all nontenured certified staff at least once, my cohort of tenured teachers at least thrice, and noncertified staff at least once."

In contrast, part-time interns generally reported few opportunities to be involved in teacher observations. Much of their time was spent doing useful but tangential administrative tasks: developing schedules; chairing the graduation committee; preparing handouts for meetings; completing purchase orders; and serving on regional accreditation committees. In addition, for logistical reasons, part-time students almost invariably take positions within their own districts, and, although they begin to increase their perspective, they do not have the benefit which many Principal Fellows had of "stepping outside the box" and seeing how things are done in different environments.

Not unexpectedly, the Fellows also reported that the internship reinforced concepts that they had acquired during their year of campus work, including the value of teamwork that grew out of cohort experiences. As one put it in a survey, "We all learned, I think, how to accept team members for who they are and, from that point, get work done." They also reported that the sheer "ongoingness" of the internship allowed them to practice listening and other interpersonal skills, afforded opportunities to identify problems and develop plans to solve them, and to become seen as experts in such areas as technology which were stressed in the university program. In reflective comments toward the end of their experience, the Principal Fellows exhibited both a confidence in their emerging skills and an appreciation for the complexity of the systems that they would be entering—a balance which seems appropriate for entry-level leaders and one to which the extended internship may well have contributed.

THE LEADERSHIP PORTFOLIO

The third major innovative component was that each of the Principal Fellows was required to maintain a portfolio of experiences as they related to development of leadership skills. The initial framework for organizing the portfolios was based on the 10 North Carolina leadership domains, but, as the students incorporated their Springfield skills into their internship activities, these also were documented within the portfolios.

Table 1. Example of Student Journal Entry.

Reflections October 17, 1996

The past two weeks have been a great learning experience for me. We have been scheduling preconferences, announced observations, and postconferences for nine ILP [beginning] teachers. It has not been easy.... There were so many other factors that had to be dealt with before trying to get four people (teacher, principal, myself, and mentor) together. I now see the value of what Dr. Glatthorn often discussed in his lectures concerning observations and sound teaching. I find myself looking for three key components: 1. Does the teacher give the students an opportunity to express what they already know prior to the lesson? 2. Does the teacher give the students an opportunity to express what they want to learn during the lesson? 3. Does the teacher give the students an opportunity to discuss what they learned from the lesson?

The past observations were difficult to schedule because of so many conflicts. The next two observations should be a lot easier because they will be unannounced.

Because one of the central functions of the portfolio is documentation of progress toward proficiency in the performance domains, the Principal Fellows kept logs of their activities and provided reflective comments on their efforts. A representative example of these comments is shown in Table 1.

Not unexpectedly, the quality of reflections in student logs varied considerably. Periodic review of the logs by and feedback from university instructors alleviated this to some extent, but some students were rarely as open or as thoughtful in their logs as they were in oral communications, either individually or in seminar situations. On the other hand, a few students seemed to find journaling an activity where they could explore concerns and doubts in a depth not exhibited in public.

Portfolios were also used for students to document their self-assessments and the plans they had for achieving growth. They drew both upon the North Carolina standards and the skills presented during the Springfield simulation. Brief examples of a student assessment and subsequent plans are shown in Tables 2 and 3.

Students were required to provide documentation of actions taken to achieve progress toward proficiency in the several required areas. Conscious effort was made to use their internship placements as clinical sites for skill acquisition; students were encouraged to be open with their district mentors who could then provide immediate feedback on developmental efforts.

To fulfill university requirements, for each item included in the leadership portfolio, a cover sheet was required. Some of the Principal Fellows felt these sheets were redundant, but we found that information was probably the most helpful data collected. Two examples of student cover sheets are included in Tables 4 and 5. This provided a common framework for assessing the impact of various program components and helped the faculty determine progress toward skill mastery. It also greatly facilitated our review of the portfolios which became, in effect, the "text" of the comprehensive examination at the end of the second year. Thus each student's "portfolio defense" was problem based, highly individualized, and truly comprehensive.

THE CHALLENGES AHEAD

The first year of a new program is typically chaotic and exciting as faculty and students struggle to find what works well and what needs more refinement. One of the advantages of this situation is that it models for students the growth process in which we hope they will be engaging during their two years with us. We shared openly with them our use of formative evaluation data to guide program design and, by so doing, invited them to be collaborators with us, a process advocated by Murphy (1993). The challenge for our work with future cohorts is to maintain that spirit of a joint pilgrimage rather than becoming too settled in "doing what we know works."

A related issue is continuing the focus on problem-based learning that was, almost of necessity, a feature of our work with the first cohort. The challenge for us is to remember that we can guide and facilitate students in

Table 2. Example of Student Growth Plan.

Areas of Strength	Areas for Improvement
Vision: • Understands trends, issues, and research in education • Understands the concept of vision	Vision: • Understands community dynamics • Understands group processes
Learning: • Understands curriculum and its alignment with instruction • Knows what instructional resources are available and how to allocate them • Knows how to use assessment to enhance teaching and learning • Knows how different teaching styles impact student learning	Learning: • Knows the formal and informal leaders in the school community who broker the change process • Knows how to organize the school to enhance teaching and learning
Climate: • Understands that learning occurs best when students feel safe • Understands that good morale is essential	Climate: • Understands conflict resolution theory and practice • Understands preventive and responsive strategies for dealing with school problems
Professional Ethics: • Knows the ethical standards of the profession • Knows his/her own convictions and their ethical implications	Professional Ethics: • Understands the complexity of ethical issues in schools • Understands how to analyze situations ethically
Collaboration and Empowerment: • Understands group processes • Knows that stakeholders can contribute • Understands the research on collaboration, empowerment, and school improvement	Collaboration and Empowerment: • Understands the community's political dynamics • Understands the decision-making process
School Operations: • Knows pertinent local, state, and federal laws, policies, and procedures • Understands the budget process	School Operations: • Knows community resources • Knows the school facilities • Knows the school staff

Table 3. Example of Student Action Plan.

Goals for Action Plan/January 1997
<u>Area for Improvement/Goal for Improvement</u>: *Knows the formal and informal leaders in the school community who broker the change process; Understands community dynamics*/After the recent changes in my County Schools that resulted in my move to another school, I feel that I need to learn more about how the community affects and causes changes within the schools. I will talk with school and community members and obtain any available printed information about the influences of community members.
Goals for Action Plan/February 1997 (Springfield Focus Areas)
<u>Area of Strength/Goal for Refinement</u>: *Understands the importance of responding to concerns and doing so in a timely manner*/Communicate all necessary information to the appropriate person(s). I plan to make it a priority to notify others if I cannot meet specific obligations such as meetings, deadlines, etc. I will try very hard to avoid procrastination and idealistic notions so that I am capable of doing everything that I believe needs to be done!! (Sensitivity S5)
<u>Area for Improvement/Goal for Improvement</u>: *Recognizes when a decision is required* / I plan to improve my ability to make needed decisions by anticipating the consequences if a decision is or is not made and asking experienced administrators to give me feedback concerning the quality of my decisions and suggestions for improvement.

Table 4. Example A of Student Portfolio Evidence.

Identification of Item Being Placed in Portfolio:	*Primary Performance Domain:*
Minutes from a meeting of the Student Achievement Committee, a committee which I chair, composed of all the teachers who teach tested subjects.	Vision
	Other Domains (if applicable):
	Collaboration & Empowerment

Description of Problem:
As part of the leadership team I was assigned to chair a committee of teachers. The committee which I was assigned, student achievement, was charged with finding ways to improve student achievement based on EOG scores.

Description of Your Action:
I tried to make sure that my role on the committee was mainly that of a facilitator. I strongly feel that teachers will usually have the best ideas and that it was my job to elicit them. This year the committee analyzed previous-year test scores to look for trends and identify areas that needed improvement. Additionally, the committee also looked into new techniques that would help improve instruction.

What You Demonstrated or Learned:
When I first chaired the committee I came across as too gung ho and too much of a know-it-all. I quickly learned that things went much better when the teachers took control of many of the functions of the committee. I transformed my role to being much more of a supporter and less of a lecturer. The teachers responded well to this change and, after a bumpy start, the committee has run smoothly and implemented a number of new initiatives including setting target scores for the EOG test, looking at center-based instruction, holding a schoolwide science day, and coming up with an after-school detention system.

Link to Primary Performance Domain:
The committee worked well because we were able to develop a vision of student achievement that demanded excellence of both teachers and students.

Link to Other Performance Domains (if applicable):
The vision that was created was due to the amount of time the teachers spent working on things together and collaborating with each other.

Table 5. Example B of Student Portfolio Evidence.

Identification of Item Being Placed in Portfolio: Teacher Observations	*Primary Performance Domain:* Information Management, Evaluation, and Assessment *Other Domains (if applicable):* Development of Self and Others

Description of Problem:
There are two observations presented. One of which is excellent, the other below standard.

Description of Your Action:
After observing teachers, I met with them to discuss my findings. With the below-standard teacher, I had prepared some suggestions and recommendations. She was aware that her lesson was not as good as it could have been. She accepted my recommendations and asked for additional help. I did note some improvement in her performance.

What You Demonstrated or Learned:
When observations are below standard, be prepared with additional resources to help that teacher. Offer suggestions and recommendations for improvement. Allow teacher input into the process. This particular teacher was going through some marital problems, but I could not let this affect my professional judgment about her performance.

Link to Primary Performance Domain:
Works with staff to implement a personnel evaluation process for strengthening classroom performance.
Deals with marginal or incompetent performance effectively.

Link to Other Performance Domains (if applicable):
Mentors the professional growth of others.

---

many ways, but we also have to be respectful of their own search for the specific problems that drive them in their quest to provide leadership in public schools.

We also are conscious of the undesirability of creating a substantively different program for our Principal Fellows and our regularly enrolled MSA students. As the Fellows' experiences with Springfield and LEAP instruct one set of students, pressure will arise to extend these opportunities for all. The simulations are labor-intensive (LEAP, for example, requires one day for the candidates and approximately three days for the assessors), and this continually forces us to reassess our professional commitments.

The issue of continued funding is always an additional concern with programs whose initial efforts are supported by external sources (Fullan & Stiegelbauer, 1991). To some extent, the success of partnership-based efforts using the simulations will be contingent upon the districts moving their contributions into their operational budgets. Unfortunately, in times of fiscal austerity, professional development is an area where budget savings are too often realized.

Another challenge is to continue the conversation we have had as faculty members about what happens in the individual courses we teach, a conversation that conflicts with the prevailing culture of individual autonomy of university faculty. For example, if the students will ultimately be evaluated on the basis of their leadership portfolios, to what extent does that shape the experiences and requirements of preceding courses? If true reflection is a common weakness of our students, how do we as a faculty prepare them to be better at that important task? And as we incorporate problem-based approaches, how do we ensure that our activities support and extend each other's rather than becoming duplicative?

Another challenge is related to the external environment in which we work. North Carolina will be using the examination of the Interstate School Leaders Licensure Consortium to certify entering school administrators. We have a responsibility to prepare students in ways that will facilitate their success on that examination at the same time as we try to take what is best from the state standards and the NASSP simulations that have been so helpful to our students. And then, of course, we have our own concerns with the NCATE process! Relating all of these various standards in a coherent program will require ongoing attention. That said, perhaps we should not worry about our program ever getting too settled and look forward instead to the opportunity of dealing every year with the sort of evolutionary planning we recommend that our students apply in their positions as new leaders in the public schools.

APPENDIX A

North Carolina Standards Board for Public School Administration

Performance Domains for the Principalship

I. VISION: The principal is an educational leader who facilitates the development, implementation, and communication of a shared vision of learning that reflects excellence and equity for all students.

II. LEARNING: The principal is an educational leader who promotes the development of organizational, instructional, and assessment strategies to enhance teaching and learning.

III. CLIMATE: The principal is an educational leader who works with others to ensure a working and learning climate that is safe, secure, and respectful of diversity.

IV. PROFESSIONAL ETHICS: The principal is an educational leader who demonstrates integrity and behaves in an ethical manner.

V. COLLABORATION AND EMPOWERMENT: The principal is an educational leader who facilitates school improvement by engaging the school community's stakeholders in collaboration, team building, problem solving, and shared decision making.

VI. SCHOOL OPERATIONS: The principal is an educational leader who uses excellent management and leadership skills to achieve effective and efficient organizational operations.

VII. HUMAN RELATIONSHIPS: The principal is an educational leader who employs effective interpersonal, communication, and public relations skills.

VIII. DEVELOPMENT OF SELF AND OTHERS: The principal is an educational leader who demonstrates academic success, intellectual ability, and a commitment to life-long learning.

IX. INFORMATION MANAGEMENT, EVALUATION, AND ASSESSMENT: The principal is an educational leader who promotes the appropriate use of reliable information to facilitate progress, evaluate personnel and programs, and make decisions.

X. CONTINUOUS IMPROVEMENT: The principal is an educational leader who fosters a culture of continuous improvement focused upon teaching and learning.

APPENDIX B

National Association of Secondary School Principals

Leadership Early Assessment Program (LEAP): Description of Leadership Skills

Administrative Skills
   Seeking out and interpreting relevant data

Making high quality judgments and decisions based on available information
Planning the use of resources to maximize your work and the work of others

Interpersonal Skills

Facilitating and interacting with a group of individuals to accomplish a task
Ability to perceive the needs, concerns, and feelings of others and to act appropriately
Motivating self and others—creating conditions that focus energy from a group of individuals toward the accomplishment of goals

Communication Skills

Verbal
Written

Knowledge of Self

Knowing areas of strengths and weaknesses
Educational values
Developmental activities

REFERENCES

Clark, D. C., & Clark, S. N. (1996). Better preparation of educational leaders. *Educational Researcher, 25*(9), 18–20.

Cooper, R. K., & Sawaf, A. (1997). *Executive EQ: Emotional intelligence in leadership and organizations.* New York: Grosset/Putnam.

Darling-Hammond, L. (1995). Inequality and access to knowledge. In J. A. Banks & C. A. M. Banks (Eds.), *Handbook of research on multicultural education* (pp. 465–483). New York: MacMillan.

Duke, D. L. (1992, June). The rhetoric and the reality of reform in educational administration. *Phi Delta Kappan, 73*(10), 764–770.

Fullan, M. G., & Stiegelbauer, S. (1991). *The new meaning of educational change.* New York: Teachers College Press.

Hill, M., & Ragland, J. (1995). *Women as educational leaders: Opening windows, pushing ceilings.* Thousand Oaks, CA: Corwin Press.

Jordan, D. W. (1994). *The supply and demand trends of public school principals and administrators in southwestern Louisiana.* (ERIC Document Reproduction Service No. ED 375 525)

Leithwood, K. (1995). Preparing school leaders: What works? *Connections! 3*(3), 1–7.

Lewis, A. C. (1997). Standards for new administrators. *Phi Delta Kappan, 79*(2), 99–100.

Murphy, J. (1993). Alternative designs: New directions. In J. Murphy (Ed.), *Preparing tomorrow's school leaders: Alternative designs* (pp. 225–253). University Park, PA: University Council for Educational Administration.

North Carolina State Board of Education. (1997). Report on the pool of administrative candidates. Raleigh, NC: Department of Public Instruction.

Southern Association of School, College, and University Staffing. (1996). Teacher and administrator supply and demand in the Southeast. Atlanta, GA: Author. (ERIC Document Reproduction Service No. ED 406 336)

Thurston, P., Clift, R., & Schacht, M. (1993). Preparing leaders for change-oriented schools. *Phi Delta Kappan, 75*(3), 259–265.

Wood, D. J., & Gray, B. (1991). Toward a comprehensive theory of collaboration. *Journal of Applied Behavioral Science, 27*(2), 139–162.

CHAPTER 27

Collaboration Among University Colleagues: A Model for Action Research to Improve Supervision and Teaching

Gayle A. Wilkinson and Fred E. Bradley

Critics of administrator preparation programs indicate that new methods of instruction aimed at preparing school leaders must be implemented to assure quality leadership for the year 2000 and beyond. They suggest that preparing leaders for the future must consist not only of providing preservice administrators with a sound knowledge base but also of providing students with opportunities to connect that knowledge to practice (Murphy, 1994). Other critics stress that preservice administrators must learn skills in collaboration if they are to be prepared for the rapid changes that are occurring in the demands on the principalship (National Association of Secondary School Principals, 1992).

We have responded to such critics by demonstrating that linking theory to practice and collaborative skills can be taught in a traditional principal preparation program. The main component in accomplishing this task has been the willingness of the professors to depart from traditional teaching strategies. The professors in our program collaborated to develop opportunities for students to practice the skills and examine the theories traditionally taught. Here, we describe how preservice administrators actually practiced supervision techniques by collaborating with preservice teachers during the regular semester. This process extended over a four-year period, using three levels of collaboration. The three levels were (a) university professors and instructors planning, teaching, organizing, observing, reflecting, and exchanging feedback; (b) preservice administrators observing, planning, reflecting, writing, and discussing with each other in small groups; and (c) graduate and undergraduate students observing, reflecting and providing feedback to each other.

BACKGROUND

As experienced educators but new professors in a traditional school of education, we discussed the effectiveness of our courses in preparing preservice administrators for professional duties in the complex, difficult setting of schools. Most of the students at our midwestern, urban university are described as nontraditional because they commute from a large geographic area and balance university, family, and employment schedules. Considering these constraints, we wondered if our students could help each other transfer the required theory into practice through collaboration. Consequently, we began a four-year journey that has revealed much about the changes in teaching strategies that must occur to achieve quality in preparing school leaders for the future.

Part of this journey was the development of a basis—action research—for changing our practices. Collaborative participation in theoretical, practical, and political discourse is a key feature of educational action research. Action research has two essential aims: to improve and to involve. Action research aspires to improve three areas: (a) practice, (b) understanding of the practice by its practitioners, and (c) the situation in which the practice takes place (Carr & Kemmis, 1986). Odell (1987) describes action research as the process of continually rethinking our understandings, evaluating the questions we are asking, and examining the procedures we use to analyze our students' and our own work. Action research has no tidy beginning or ending: rather it repeats cycles of wondering, exploring, and discovering.

> Clearly, action research engages focusing on the improvement of practitioners' own understanding of their practices by involving practitioners in the systematic development of their own understandings, both in the context of the practices themselves and also in the context of explicitly sharing and examining these understandings through communication between collaborating action researchers. (Carr & Kemmis, 1986, p. 188)

In the past decade, the use of action research as a means for empowering teachers, reforming education, and improving teacher education has increased (Catelli, 1995). Commonly, action research involves collaborations between universities and school districts, agencies, foundations, and individual teachers. Some university faculties have conducted action research to integrate curriculum across disciplines (Gritzer & Salmon, 1992; Lasley & Payne, 1991), improve multicultural education (Noronha, 1992), develop curriculum (Collison, 1993), improve instruction (Schratz, 1993) and coordinate programs with community colleges (Caraway, 1994).

In university-based programs, heavy doses of theoretical course work with few opportunities to learn craft knowledge and do field work often leave new teachers longing for practical skills with which to handle day-to-day management and discipline challenges of the classroom (Dill & Stafford, 1994). Teacher and administrator education programs that mediate theory and practice during an important stage of a practitioner's career should be structured so that the validity of theoretical and practical knowledge is mutually accepted (Cherryholmes, 1988).

Berkey et al. (1990) found that collaboration has become a successful method for transferring theory into practice when teachers are trying to learn complex teaching skills. New teachers can learn to challenge or confirm theories presented to them through collaborative inquiry (Lucas, 1988). Collaboration that assists teachers in learning to teach by promoting reflection on practice must provide these conditions: (a) specific times to participate in the reflective process, (b) a safe environment built on trust and respect, (c) open-ended discussions that allow for individual concerns to surface, and (d) written reports containing specific feedback that can be used for reflection (Berkey et al., 1990).

According to Dornbusch and Scott (1975) feedback must meet three criteria in order to be effective in facilitating teacher growth. First, the observation on which the feedback is based must legitimately represent the teaching that was observed. Second, the comments on the observations must be thoroughly understood by the teacher. Third, the feedback must include concepts that are important to those who were observed. Feedback is most useful in aiding professional development when participants have had time to construct their own answers to the questions that result from their practice before they receive feedback (Kulhavy, 1977). This mindfulness in receiving feedback can assist in changing the professional's practice through stimulating reflection on practice (Dewey, 1933).

THE COLLABORATIVE PROJECT

Four years ago, we designed a collaboration between our students that exchanged written feedback between preservice administrators and preservice teachers. The preservice administrators, experienced teachers who were graduate students, were enrolled in a graduate course on supervision where the primary goal was to prepare them to become proficient in observing and evaluating teachers. The preservice teachers were beginning their study of education and were enrolled in their first course on methods of teaching where microteaching was a major focus. The preservice administrators observed the microteaching videotapes of preservice teachers and wrote concise and specific feedback about the microlessons in formal observation reports. The preservice teachers read these reports and wrote comments to the administrators about the value of this additional feedback in their learning to teach.

In our first cycle of action research, we collected data from the responses by the preservice administrators ($n = 21$) and teachers ($n = 20$) to five open-ended questions about supervising or teaching. From these responses, we composed questionnaires using a Likert-type scale and revised the collaborative project in the second year to focus on a more experimental design by including several sections of the course where the preservice teachers ($n =$

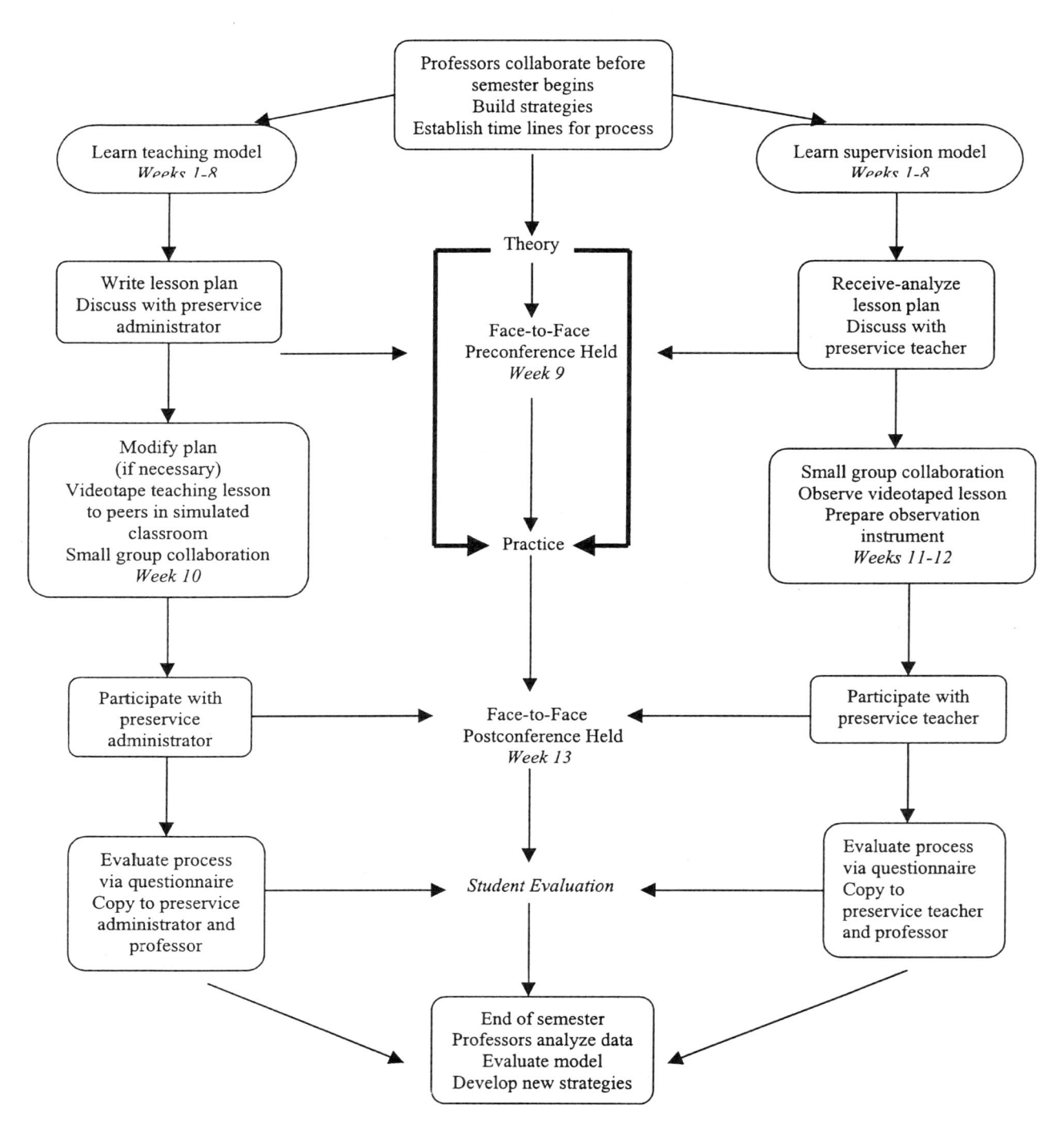

Figure 1. Flow chart for collaborative inquiry process.

99) were assigned to either experimental or control groups. We also designed a similar questionnaire for preservice administrators ($n = 43$). During the third cycle, we composed new open-ended questions for the teachers ($n = 94$), based on the results of the previous year, and added a control group of preservice administrators ($n = 61$). Given our collaboration and the data collected through the various cycles, the materials that the students exchanged and the processes for the collaboration were also modified (Wilkinson, 1996).

Using the results of these previous studies, we hypothesized that collaboration could be more beneficial to both groups of students if they had opportunities for face-to-face conversations rather than only written feedback to each other. Some of our questions included: (a) Will our students be able to benefit from a preconference with a stranger? (b) Will they have enough knowledge about teaching or supervising to benefit from the conversation? (c) Will the supervising preservice administrators be able to use the nondirective approach of clinical supervision rather than the prescriptive approach? (d) How many students would desire to participate in such a conversation? (e) Will these experiences result in better understanding of the theories of supervision and teaching?

We adjusted the project for this cycle to include two face-to-face meetings between the preservice administrators and teachers and increased the number and changed the method of the collaborative discussions among the participating professors. Four types of collaboration occurred in this cycle: (a) university professors and instructors planning, teaching, organizing, observing, reflecting, and exchanging feedback; (b) preservice administrators observing, planning, reflecting, and writing with each other in small groups; (c) preservice teachers observing and reflecting in small groups, and (d) graduate and undergraduate students observing, reflecting, and providing written and verbal feedback to each other.

Originally, we thought that the anonymity of written communication would ensure greater comfort for participants learning new skills. The positive responses from the students made us realize that such safety only inhibited additional, desirable collaboration. It seemed beneficial to the preservice administrators to practice their supervising skills in a preconference with the preservice teachers who could refine the microlesson before it was taught. A postconference would allow the preservice teachers to ask questions about the observation reports. Even though it would make the coordination of the instruction more difficult, it was thought that greater collaboration among the education faculty and students would hold greater potential for preparing novices for the complex processes of schooling.

We shared common goals for our students in transferring theory to practice and sequenced our instruction to provide the needed concepts for our own students and materials for each other's students. The collaboration between our students was sequenced to parallel an actual clinical supervision model (Glickman, 1990). This process included the following steps: (a) preservice teachers wrote lesson plans, (b) preservice teachers met with preservice administrators (preconference), (c) preservice teachers modified their plans (if necessary), (d) preservice teachers were videotaped while teaching a lesson to peers in simulated classrooms, (e) preservice administrators observed the lessons and read the lesson plans, (f) preservice administrators wrote observations in formal reports, and (g) preservice teachers and administrators discussed the observation reports (postconference). The collaboration between the professors, preservice teachers, and the preservice administrators is displayed in Figure 1.

METHODOLOGY

Because we desired to improve our own practice as well as the quality of our students' experiences, we invited a colleague to join the project who was skilled in action research but teaching the introductory methods course for the first time. Throughout the semester, we met eight times to share ideas about teaching and supervision, discuss concerns about the project, solve problems, prepare for the conferences, and discuss observations of our students. We each recorded our reflections, concerns, and questions about the project in a journal after each of the meetings. We also took field notes while observing the conferences between the preservice administrators and teachers.

One week before the preconference, we met to construct the open-ended questions that would provide the evaluation of the preconference by both the preservice teachers and preservice administrators after the preconference. The questions inquired about the benefits of the preconference for learning supervision and teaching and requested suggestions to improve the experience (see Appendix). After discussing the results of the preconference evaluations, we met to design the evaluation of the postconference. We wanted to know which of the activities in the collaborative project were most valued by the students (see Appendix).

Project Data Collection and Analysis

Two sets of data were collected and analyzed. The field notes and reflective journal entries of the professors were collaboratively analyzed to discover the common themes of the discussions about the mechanisms of collaboration within our project. These themes were used to construct a model of collaboration that can be used for other projects: commitment, consistency, coordination, course sequencing, and continued evaluation.

The students were invited to join the action research in order to improve the collaborative project and gave written consent. We assured students that our field notes were evaluative and their responses to questions would be confidential. We collected responses from the students about their collaboration through open-ended questions, rating scales, informal interviews, and reflective journals. The student responses were analyzed for common themes. The rating scales showed the value of the activities for each of the groups.

PROJECT RESULTS

Following the preconference, 23 preservice administrators and 21 preservice teachers returned the completed questionnaires. The preservice administrators reported that the preservice teachers were very responsive in the preconference and actively participated in the conversation. Our observations of the student pairs in preconferences confirmed this. We saw most of them leaning forward, eyes fixed, and intently listening to the other in active, flowing conversation. They exchanged telephone numbers, shook hands, wished each other luck in the upcoming tasks, smiled, and some exchanged business cards. One of the pairs did not converse this actively; the preservice administrator asked the teacher to write comments on the preconference form rather than using it as a note-taking form for a shared conversation. After experiencing the preconference, the preservice administrators felt that they now better understood the process of the preconference and saw the value of discussing the lesson with the new teacher before observing the lesson. A preservice administrator wrote, "If the observer's comments were specific, the preservice teachers should be able to begin to examine their lessons more carefully for the purpose of upgrading their teaching techniques and strategies." They also reported that they could see the theories of supervision being applied in the preconference. One preservice administrator shared, "It allowed me to put the theory of supervision into practice. I internalized concepts more rapidly when I experienced them firsthand." The concern cited most often was the preservice teachers' preoccupation with the "observation form" that would be used and the criteria that the preservice administrator would be using to evaluate the lesson. The preservice administrators thought that this inhibited many conversations about the actual elements of the microlesson. About half of the group had no suggestions for improving the preconference but did make comments such as, "This was a great experience!"

The preservice teachers also reported being more comfortable with the process of supervision. One said, "I feel less threatened by supervision of my teaching. I am more comfortable with the idea of administrative evaluation." They maintained that the conversation with an experienced teacher was very helpful not only in finding flaws in their lesson plans but also in learning specific ways that they could improve their lessons. One preservice teacher wrote, "Laura really opened my eyes about how a lesson plan should work. She gave me a lot of new ideas and approaches to my lesson plan." Most of them described being less nervous about being supervised and found sharing ideas with experienced teachers very beneficial for learning about teaching and preparing lessons. A novice realized, "administrators and teachers are working together to help the students whether this is to improve the teaching or get advice on a problem student."

After the postconference, 19 of the preservice administrators and 21 of the preservice teachers returned their completed questionnaires. The preservice administrators were asked to rate on a Likert-type scale (1 to 5, low to high) the value of the activities included in the project which were (a) preconference, (b) collaboration with peers, (c) viewing the microlesson, (d) writing the observation report, and (e) postconference. The preservice administrators found all activities in the project valuable in their preparation as supervisors (ranged from 4.6 to 4.8 with a mean score of 4.6). Their responses to the open-ended questions on the postconference evaluation form revealed that the two most common benefits were increased confidence in their supervision abilities and using the supervision skills they had learned in their course. One preservice administrator realized, "This was a safe way to practice observing and evaluating. It made me understand the more analytical side to evaluating while at the same time focus in on how to help teachers grow professionally." In response to the question, "Was this project worth the time and effort given by all participants?" all of those participating responded "yes."

The activities for the preservice teachers included (a) writing the lesson, (b) microteaching, (c) peer collaboration, (d) self-evaluation, (e) preconference, (f) postconference, and (g) a written observation report. The preservice teachers found that all of the activities were valuable in preparing them as teachers (ranged from 4.1 to 4.8 with a mean score of 4.4) with the preconference less valuable ($M = 4.1$) and the written observation report from the supervisor ($M = 4.8$) as most valuable. They reported that they did not feel prepared for the preconference and wanted to have more information about the supervision forms and the criteria that the preservice administrators would use when observing their lessons. In response to the open-ended questions, the preservice teachers indicated that the supervision process was more positive than they had expected. One wrote, "It (the postconference) put my mind to ease. I thought it would be a lot worse. More positive feedback was given than I expected." They described greater comfort with being observed by an experienced teacher and saw the benefit of supervision for their professional development. One teacher shared, "Meeting with the administrator allowed us to become acquainted with the process of evaluation and supervision in a nonthreatening way." Another wrote, "The postconference was helpful and gave me a lot of feedback on what could be improved and what was good. The administrator had taken notes very extensively over my lesson and video." All but one preservice teacher found this project to be worth all of the effort that was required by those who participated. He wrote, "Not at all worth it (sorry). The observer (supervisor) needs to be more critical and offer a variety of suggestions." He desired a more direct approach than clinical supervision.

A MODEL FOR COLLABORATIVE ACTION RESEARCH

At the end of the project, we collaboratively analyzed our field notes and journals and found common themes. As we discussed the project details in this cycle and compared them to previous cycles, we discovered that we would be able to guide future collaboration by what we had learned from our own field notes, observations, and reflective journals. This model for collaboration at the university consists of the following elements: commitment, consistency, coordination, course sequencing, and continued evaluation.

Commitment

Professors in the project must be committed enough to the collaboration that they engage in frequent meetings to solve unpredicted problems that occur and to design the strategies necessary for the successful completion of the project. In other semesters, instructors who were not committed to the project failed to prepare materials adequately and follow the time line, reducing the number of opportunities for collaboration between students and professors. One journal entry captured the essence of the foundation for commitment, "I think there are many of us who can work together but think that coordinating our courses is just too difficult when it is really easy. Perhaps this will help some (other professors) begin to think of integrating courses."

Consistency

When participating professors move in and out of the project each semester, the new professors must be informed of all of the project elements so that the students will receive the intended benefits of the collaboration. We found sharing a written description of the process and explaining it often to new participants facilitated the collaboration. One week before the semester one journal included this comment, "We shared ideas that had been successful and solved problems for each other. It seemed to be a very supportive and collegial meeting." When more than one section of the course participates, the curriculum and course requirements, methods of microteaching, student evaluations, and instructor participation should be consistent. To ensure this, the faculty must collaborate and agree on the parameters that affect the project.

Cooperation and Coordination

The processes for the collaboration must be agreed upon early in the project. Any differences among participating faculty must be resolved so that the mechanics of the project assist rather than hinder the collaboration. This requires that participants provide materials on time, coordinate meetings between student groups, identify problems, identify student assignments correctly, and produce all of the necessary materials. We shared equally the responsibilities for identifying student materials, preparing handouts, scheduling meeting rooms, exchanging student telephone numbers, and transferring student files between groups. A journal entry showed this, "Lesson plans and lists from both sections were given to Fred on Wednesday so that he could meet with his class that night to arrange the students into pairs. I did not receive confirmation on the room reservations, so I called to double check."

Course Sequencing

Syllabi must be sequenced to facilitate the collaboration. Compromise usually results in the best plan for all students to benefit from the collaboration. The mechanics of the project will run smoothly if the faculty plan their syllabi together before the semester begins. Estimates must be made about the amount of instructional time needed to move students toward the timeliness of collaboration. In our project, the scheduling of the microteaching and the exchange of the videotapes were critical. We calculated the needs of both student groups and selected dates for the events that would facilitate the collaboration. This meant that each professor had to adjust the sequence of the course enough to meet the time line. It really was not as difficult as it seemed: "We compared the course sequences and discussed the potential for having two conferences between students. We needed to adjust them [the syllabi] a little to accommodate each other."

Continuing Evaluations

We will continue to evaluate the project, looking especially at the changes that were made in response to the research results from this cycle. Our next cycle of action research will investigate the following questions: (a) Does a variety of meeting times for conferences allow more students to participate? (b) Will the preservice teachers benefit more from the preconference because they understand the criteria and forms that will be used by the preservice administrators? (c) Will pairing teachers with administrators who are knowledgeable in their subject areas improve the project for both groups of students? (d) Would establishing pairs earlier in the semester increase student commitment to attend conferences?

REFLECTION ON PROJECT RESULTS

Our students reported enough benefits from the addition of the preconference and postconference that we will continue to improve the process for future students. Even though the students were strangers to each other, they were excited to meet each other and enjoyed the exchange of mutual concerns for learning new skills—one in supervision and the other in teaching. The preservice teachers enthusiastically engaged in conversation about the "real world" of teaching and the preservice administrators eagerly practiced their new supervisory skills. From different sides of experience, both were acutely aware of how much is required to learn to teach. For example, through engaging in conversation about their specific lesson plan in the preconference, the preservice teachers really understood the purposes and functions of lesson plans that had been explained in theory. The preservice administrators learned firsthand the concerns new teachers have about planning lessons and teaching.

We also learned about student concerns that we had not discovered before. The clinical supervision process was easier for the preservice administrators and more difficult for the preservice teachers than we thought. The preservice teachers were preoccupied by "What is the right way?" and "How will I be evaluated?" We needed to explain the observation report and the criteria for the evaluation to the preservice teachers before the preconference so that they could concentrate on the conversation about their lesson plan rather than the forms that would be used. Some suggested that we improve our facilities for videotaping, and others mentioned that we should match preservice teachers to preservice administrators according to subject-area specialties because some felt unprepared to talk about details outside of their area of expertise.

Our evaluations of the project confirmed the students' suggestions. In addition, we realized the need to assess more carefully the level of student commitment to the project. More students were eager to participate than we had expected, but we did not evaluate their level of commitment. Some preservice administrators and teachers who were participating in the project did not meet the other student at the conferences for various reasons. This left one person without a partner to complete the project. Our attempt at pairing unprepared supervisors with teachers did not provide an adequate supervision experience. One such preservice teacher wrote, "I was assigned to an administrator who was unable to attend. As a result, my supervisor had not reviewed my lesson beforehand. The student she had been assigned to was not present either. Although she did not supply any suggestions for my lesson plan, hearing about teaching experiences regarding lesson plans was very interesting."

Perhaps student commitment is really not the reason students did not come to conferences. One student wrote, "Make this preconference at a more accessible time and day. I think it would be more useful to those whose lesson plans need a lot of help." We should try to schedule various times for pairs to meet for conferences and put pairs together who have compatible schedules. Of the 33 preservice administrators, one did not attend either conference and 5 attended only one of the conferences. Of the 35 preservice teachers from two sections of the course, 14 did not attend the preconference and 11 did not attend the postconference. Before the preconference, the preservice teachers who could not attend provided us with telephone numbers. The conferences via telephone did not work as well as we had anticipated, and several of the students did not have any type of conference. A preservice teacher wrote, "We had set up several alternate times to talk again after she reviewed my videotape, but she never got back to me. I did get her observation report and appreciated her written comments." One student reported a successful makeup postconference, "I was scared to meet him, not knowing how the postconference would go. My mom has told me horror stories about her postconferences. Steve was actually nice and helpful by offering me suggestions on the things I said were strong and weak. It was very helpful for me to tell him what I believed first. Overall, the experience was very positive and effective. And I have a contact in his district now."

On both the preconference and postconference evaluation forms, students commented about their increased ability to transfer theory to practice because of their experiences in this project. The preservice administrators learned more about clinical supervision because of their experiences in actually using the skills and theory they had been learning in their course. The preservice teachers understood planning a lesson, reflecting on their own practice, and considering the impact teaching had on students—good or poor. As Goodman (1986) asserts, "the greatest challenge within teacher preparation today is to develop methods courses that are both critical in nature and relevant to students' concerns" (p. 350).

REFLECTIONS ON COLLABORATIVE ACTION RESEARCH

Current literature is blossoming with criticisms of the traditional education methods used by schools of education. This criticism has nearly become an all-out assault, accusing education professors of being disconnected from the changing world, reinforcing archaic educational theories, and insisting that they know how to improve the quality of education in community schools (Clinchy, 1994). In response, traditional schools of education are challenging this image by establishing professional development schools within local school districts and using case studies in the classroom, school-based teacher education models, and clinical cycles to connect theory with real-world practice. The major question facing educators of teachers and administrators is how teacher education programs can bridge the two worlds of theoretical, normatively based canons of practice and inductively derived maxims of reflective practice in the daily action of teaching or administrating (Vare, 1994).

Based on the benefits of this project, we believe that traditional schools of education should realize a concomitant need to continue efforts to identify opportunities for collaboration that assist students to bridge theory and practice in order to increase the students' comfort and establish positive perceptions for those about to begin their first year in a very complex and uncertain profession. Professional preparation programs should consider collaborative projects that are mutually beneficial for students and their instructors. We found that the benefits to our students and to our own professional development more than compensated for the added time that we devoted to this project. Education professors who model action research for their students teach more than the theory of the course: they teach the value of educational research for professional development.

APPENDIX

Preservice Administrators: Preconference Questionnaire

1. How did the preconference with the preservice teacher affect your understanding of supervision?
2. How did the preservice teacher respond to your supervision efforts?
3. What elements of the preconference seemed most helpful to the preservice teacher?
4. How did you benefit from this preconference simulation?
5. What would make this a better experience for future preservice administrators?

Preservice Teachers: Preconference Questionnaire

1. How did the preconference with a preservice administrator help you with your lesson plan?
2. Describe any insights about teaching that you gained through the preconference.
3. How have your perceptions of supervision changed through the experience of the preconference?
4. What were the most beneficial aspects of the preconference?
5. What would you suggest to improve the preconference experience for future preservice teachers?

Preservice Administrators: Postconference Questionnaire

1. Please rate the value of each of the following activities in your preparations for supervising teachers: (a) preconference, (b) collaboration with peers, (c) viewing the microlesson, (d) writing the observation report, and (e) postconference.
2. Describe at least two meaningful interactions or episodes that help us understand your experiences during this supervision project.
3. Describe how participation in this project has affected your level of confidence as a supervisor.
4. Select at least one of the activities listed in question 1, and tell us how we could improve it.
5. Do you think that this project was worth the time and effort given by yourself, the preservice teachers, and the professors?

Preservice Teachers: Postconference Questionnaire

1. Please rate the value of each of the following activities in your preparing for teaching: (a) writing the lesson, (b) microteaching, (c) peer collaboration, (d) self-evaluation, (e) preconference, (f) postconference, and (g) a written observation report.
2. Describe at least two meaningful interactions or episodes that help us understand your experiences during this supervision project.
3. Describe how participation in this project has affected your perceptions of the evaluation and supervision processes.

4. Select at least one of the activities listed in question 1, and tell us how we could improve it.
5. Do you think that this project was worth the time and effort given by yourself, the preservice administrators, and the professors?

REFERENCES

Berkey, R., Campbell, D., Curtis, T., Kirschner, B. W., Minnick, F., & Zietlow, K. (1990). Collaborating for reflective practice: Voices of teachers, administrators, and researchers. *Education and Urban Society, 22*(2), 204–232.

Caraway, G. K. (1994). A community college district/university press co-publishing venture. *Community College Journal of Research and Practice, 18*(5), 465–472.

Carr, W., & Kemmis, S. (1986). *Becoming critical.* London: Falmer Press.

Catelli, L. A. (1995). Action research and collaborative inquiry in a school-university partnership. *Action in Teacher Education, 16*(4), 25–38.

Cherryholmes, C. (1988). *Power & criticism: Poststructural investigations.* New York: Teachers College Press.

Clinchy, E. (1994). Higher education: The albatross of the public schools, *Phi Delta Kappan, 75*(10), 744–751.

Collison, M. N. K. (1993). "Learning communities" for all. *Chronicle of Higher Education, 40*(12), A30.

Dewey, J. (1933). *How we think.* Boston: D.C. Heath.

Dill, V., & Stafford, D. (1994). School-based teacher education, *Phi Delta Kappan, 75*(8), 620–623.

Dornbusch, S. M., & Scott, W. R. (1975). *Evaluation and the exercise of authority.* San Francisco: Jossey-Bass.

Glickman, C. D. (1990). *Supervision of instruction: A developmental approach* (2nd ed.). Boston: Allyn and Bacon.

Goodman, J. (1986). University education courses and the professional preparation of teachers: A descriptive analysis. *Teaching and Teacher Education, 2,* 341–353.

Gritzer, G., & Salmon, M. (1992). Interdisciplinary use of the liberal arts in professional art programs. *Journal of General Education, 41,* 200–216.

Kulhavy, R. W. (1977). Feedback in written instruction. *Review of Educational Research, 47,* 211–232.

Lasley, T. J., & Payne, M. A. (1991). Curriculum models in teacher education: The liberal arts and professional studies. *Teaching and Teacher Education, 7*(2), 211–219.

Lucas, P. (1988). An approach to research based teacher education through collaborative inquiry. *Journal of Education for Teaching, 14*(1), 55–73.

Murphy, J. (1994). A brief prepared by Leon Lynn. *Center on Organization and Restructuring of Schools, University of Wisconsin, 10,* 3–4.

National Association of Secondary School Principals. (1992). *A special report on developing school leaders: A call for collaboration.* Reston, VA: Author.

Odell, L. (1987). Planning classroom research. In D. Goswami & P. Stillman (Eds.), *Reclaiming teacher research as an agency for change* (pp. 128–160). Portsmouth, NH: Heinemann.

Noronha, J. (1992). International and multicultural education: Unrelated adversaries or successful partners? *New Directions for Teaching and Learning, 52,* 53–59.

Schratz, M. (1993). Crossing the disciplinary boundaries: Professional development through action research in higher education. *Higher Education Research and Development, 12*(2), 131–142.

Vare, W. (1994). Partnership contrasts: Microteaching activity as two apprenticeships in thinking. *Journal of Teacher Education, 45*(3), 209–217.

Wilkinson, G. A. (1996). Enhancing microteaching through additional feedback from preservice administrators. *Teaching and Teacher Education, 12*(2), 211–221.

CHAPTER 28

Why We Need to Strengthen Graduate Training in Educational Administration[1]

Gunapala Edirisooriya

Quality schools for the 21st century can be neither created nor sustained without educational leaders of the highest quality. The responsibility of preparing such leaders rests mainly with educational administration preparation programs. The history of these programs shows many phases of evolution and reform efforts (Cooper & Boyd, 1988; Milstein, 1993; Murphy, 1993). In 1988, the National Commission on Excellence in Educational Administration (Griffiths, Stout, & Forsyth, 1988), an offspring of the National Commission on Excellence in Education (1983), prepared an extensive report on how to prepare quality leaders for America's schools. In response, many educational administration preparation programs initiated redesign efforts with foundation support (Murphy, 1993). The Danforth initiative was one such effort (Gresso, 1993; Milstein, 1993). Nevertheless, it is unwise to assume that a large-scale reform movement in educational administration preparation programs commenced (Murphy, 1993) with these efforts.

It would also be a grave mistake to give into the demands of Haller, Brent, and McNamara (1997) who call for dismantling educational administration preparation programs because, they claim, these programs have failed. Such recommendations seem off the mark because educational reform efforts in general, and educational accountability, federal and state policy mandates, and school restructuring with site-based decision making (SBDM) in particular, place a heavy demand on school administrators. Rapid expansion in information and educational technologies impose added requirements (professional knowledge base and technical skills) on future educational administrators. Under these conditions a concerted effort must be made to overhaul rather than dismantle educational administration preparation programs across the country. Such change is necessary in order to prepare a cadre of educational administrators with the necessary professional knowledge base and technical skills to provide the leadership for quality schools for the 21st century. While acknowledging the recommendations of the National Policy Board for Educational Administration (NPBEA) for curriculum guidelines (1996), this paper argues for strengthening research methods, statistics, educational data management, and educational technology as necessary components of educational administration preparation programs to prepare quality leaders for quality schools for the 21st century.

CHALLENGING THE PROGNOSIS OF SOME CRITICS

Ever since the National Commission on Excellence in Education (1983) called for reforms, public education has come under strict scrutiny. Whether *A Nation at Risk* was indeed a "manufactured crisis," as Berliner and Biddle (1996) argue, or not, the onslaught of attack on public education shows no sign of diminishing. No aspect of public education has been able to avoid the microscopic analyses by many groups with differing agendas. Public policy on education (vouchers, charter schools, home schooling, prayer in schools), curriculum (national curricula on history and mathematics, sex education, moral or character education), instruction (conceptual, procedural, hands-on), teacher preparation (Paedia, licensing requirements), and school administration (site-based management, privatization of delivery of services) have all been subjected to their share of scrutiny.

Gunapala Edirisooriya, East Tennessee State University

Graduate programs in educational administration are the latest target of this criticism. For example, Haller et al. (1997) cite five reasons as well as the results of the Schools and Staffing Survey of 1987–88 (SASS87–88) (National Center for Education Statistics, 1991) for their claim that graduate training in education has no positive effect on the performance of school administrators. I see no reason to reexamine their analysis of the decade-old SASS87–88, which collected data on teachers' perception on the effectiveness of their principals. These data do not relate to the present conditions in American public education. In this paper, however, I reexamine their arguments, challenge their prognosis, and substantiate my claim that future educational administrators do need better training, preferably of a different kind.

Argument 1: Quality of Administration in Relation to Formal Training

Haller et al. (1997) argue that our schools are not better administered than those of Germany, Italy, France, Japan, and so on, countries in which little or no formal training in administration is required. In the countries they cite, the opportunities for higher education are much more restrictive than in the U.S. In the U.S., we have an "open-door policy" to provide opportunities for higher education. Clearly, an undergraduate degree in the U.S cannot be considered a clear indicator of proficiency in school administration. Are they also implicitly arguing that access to postsecondary education should be severely restricted in the U.S.?

Argument 2: Graduate Training of Administrators in Private and Public Schools

Haller et al. also maintain that administrators of private schools have significantly less graduate training than do their counterparts in the public sector. Student characteristics, family backgrounds, local communities, policy mandates, school governance, and many other factors differ between the private schools and the public schools. This creates different school environments and different school administrative needs between the two sectors.

Of course, we know that Coleman and Hoffer (1987), Chubb and Moe (1990), and others argue that student outcomes differ between the two sectors with the private sector outperforming the public sector. At the same time, good scholarship dictates that we should not ignore the studies that challenge the findings of Coleman and Hoffer (1987) and Chubb and Moe (1990). Many studies have shown that school resources are positively related to higher student achievement. These studies include Greenwald, Hedges, and Laine (1996); Laine, Greenwald, and Hedges (1995); Hedges, Laine, and Greenwald (1994); Baker (1991); and Spencer and Wiley (1981). What is more surprising than the debate about outcomes is the argument of Haller et al. (1997) about educational training:

> Moreover, the headmasters of *the most prestigious private secondary schools* [emphasis added] in this country are unlikely to have professional training in any aspect of education, much less in educational administration. (p. 223)

Haller et al. compare apples and oranges and conclude that they are different but can be considered equal. Of course, they are different, but I fail to see the point in trying to prove that they are equal. Therefore, no further discussion is necessary on the attempt to compare public schools with the most prestigious private secondary schools in this country.

Argument 3: Anecdotal Report of Professor-Principals Questioning Graduate Training

In arguing that some professors of educational administration who spent their sabbatical years as school principals question the relevance of graduate training for educational administration, Haller et al. refer to two such anecdotal reports. Referring to reflections (which are more than two decades old) of Hills (1975), they state, "Essentially, Hills asked himself if he was using the theories and concepts he taught at the university while he actually served as a principal" (p. 223). Quite to the contrary, Jean Hills, based on his experience as a school principal, argued for revising educational administration programs to produce effective school leaders. In 1975, he was arguing for the need to incorporate in educational administration programs a number of skill areas such as problem-solving skills, analytical skills, situation analysis, and leadership skills. To avoid any misinterpretation, I directly quote Jean Hills (1975):

> Hence, I advocate that a considerable amount of attention be devoted to the development and critical examination of "normative theories" of administration. These need to be firmly grounded in "paradigms" of the human being, human societies, and human organizations, but they must necessarily include value components and less than fully warranted empirical assumptions. Nevertheless, *no administrator should enter practice without a reasonably well-articulated 'theory,' and none should practice who do not update theirs continuously* [emphasis added]. (p. 18)

Haller et al. (1997) interpret reflections of Cross (1983) as follows: "Robert Cross in a career change similar to Hills' [sic], also had doubts about the usefulness of university courses for administrative practice" (p. 223). Quite to the contrary, Cross (1983), based on his experience as an elementary school principal during his sabbatical year, explains the most useful and the least useful aspects of his university's principal preparation program. The areas he found to be most useful were teacher evaluation, teacher selection, budget preparation, student discipline, organization theory, and measurement and evaluation. The areas he found to be least useful were clinical supervision and problem solving through simulated activities. In principal preparation programs, he also suggests covering how to handle children from broken families and providing more information on legal, federal, and state mandates on many aspects of public education. Once again, instead of interpreting, I directly quote Cross's words:

> It is not so much that the program's content in itself is inappropriate. The problem is that we have not sufficiently brought it down to the practical level. We need to summon forth our ingenuity to incorporate more "learning how" into our program, even before the internship phase. The "learning how" must, however, be rooted in a solid base of "learning why." Let me quickly add that I have little sympathy with the disdain for theory and research expressed by some practitioners. *It has always struck me as peculiar that educators would shun intellectuality. The best hope for improving schools is through the artful application of systematized knowledge* [emphasis added]. (p. 22)

No further explanation is required on the findings and the recommendations of Hills (1975) and Cross (1983). Briefly, a careful review of the reflections of Hills and Cross clearly shows that they earnestly spoke of strengths and weaknesses of educational administration programs, arguing for strengthening them, not for abolishing them.

Argument 4: Administrator Perceptions of the Usefulness of Training

Haller et al. (1997) also maintain that educational administrators do not perceive graduate training in educational administration as useful in their daily activities. They use the findings of survey research studies in a number of doctoral dissertations and Educational Resources Information Center (ERIC) documents in support of their argument. In these studies, researchers have surveyed educational administrators on their perception of the usefulness of graduate training in their job performance. Of these, Haller et al. claim that the studies conducted in 1987, 1988, and 1989 support their position, while the other study conducted in 1991 (Wildman, 1991) had concluded that graduate training in educational administration was considered valuable by the respondents in that study.

My reading of Goldman and Kempner (1988) gave me the impression that Oregon educational administrators were not complaining so much about *course content* but about the packaging of instructional delivery. To quote Goldman and Kempner (1988),

> We see in many responses a pronounced preference for short, intense, practical workshops rather than the traditional course work that dominates certification programs.... In the view of these administrators, the packaging and delivery of certification and professional development programs suffers from market mismatches. Certification courses attuned to the academic calendar (semester or quarters) and those offered on college campuses are less attractive than weekend or summer courses and those brought to communities or districts. (p. 9)

Argument 5: Impact of Training on Administrative Performance

Finally, Haller et al. (1997) argue that studies show that graduate training had no positive impact on school administrators' performance. They cite a number of studies in support of this argument. Again, two of the studies were conducted in the 1960s, and the other two studies were based on data collected in the 1980s. What is especially puzzling is their use of SASS87–88 data collected during the 1987–88 school year to question whether graduate training in educational administration has improved American schools. They conclude, "Together with the results of earlier studies, this research casts further doubt on the presumption that graduate training for school administrators has improved U.S. schools" (p. 227). What is important is how they use this conclusion. Their recommendation, which deserves to be challenged, is the following:

> We suggest that the current interest in substantially changing graduate training in educational administration is well founded. Unfortunately, the nature of the changes needed is far from clear and seems likely to remain so. It is not evident that we require more training or even different training. *Perhaps, we should require less. Or none at all* [emphasis added]. (p. 227)

Even if we accept the reported results of some of the studies with decades-old data, I fail to see the logic of the argument that future educational administrators need no training beyond the baccalaureate degree. On the contrary, I argue that future educational administrators need better training, preferably of a different kind. American schools have changed significantly during the last decade, and all the indications point to the need for continuous adaptation to the changing political, economic, social, cultural, and technological conditions in the 21st century. Therefore, future educational administrators need more professional, technological, and administrative knowledge and skills to face the forthcoming challenges in the 21st century.

A WAVE OF CHANGE

In education, rhetoric and reality scarcely converge. Despite the overwhelming "cries" for upgrading the electronic-technological infrastructure in education, Cochrane's (1995) assertion seems to hold true: "Imagine a school with children who can read and write, but with teachers who cannot. You have a metaphor of the information age in which we live" (p. 25). This description can very well be applied to every layer of organization in American public education. For example, in 1994, after implementing an extensive information automation system, a superintendent of an urban school system on the East coast lamented, "I have a big computer on my desk, and I don't know what to do with it; besides, I have no time to learn how to use it. So, I asked them to remove it." It is rather disheartening to hear a statement like this from a superintendent of a school system. Current research findings (Cochrane, 1994; Mehlinger, 1996; Morton, 1996; Peha, 1996; U.S. Congress Office of Technology Assessment, 1995) on the use of technology in education validate such anecdotal records.

Of course, Haller et al. (1997) can use this superintendent as a fine example for their point of view—the failure of graduate preparation in educational administration. I totally agree with this point, but not with their recommendation that educational administrators need no graduate training. My argument is that this superintendent is a typical educational administrator who was trained, as Jean Hills (1975) phrased it, in normative theories of administration. No doubt, educational administrators trained in this way as well as future educational administrators need more training in an array of skills and professional knowledge, especially in educational technology. Therefore, it is not for debate that the educational administrators for the 21st century have to be competent in a repertoire of rapidly expanding knowledge-base and professional skills, encompassing statistics, research methods, data management, and educational technology, if they are to function effectively. Two issues arise here: one is the retraining of educational administrators and the other is the restructuring of educational administration preparation programs, which is the remaining focus of this paper. One major barrier to revamping educational administration preparation programs is the pervasiveness of the traditional thinking among the scholars and the practitioners in this field.

Policy Issues and Traditional Practices

Historically, first order universities conducted educational research. On the basis of such research, policymakers at the high echelon of the educational ladder set educational policies. To implement such policies, second order universities trained educational administrators. Consequently, traditional educational leadership preparation programs concentrated on leadership skills, especially geared toward administrative and supervision skills. This practice perpetuated the infamous perception that educational administrators are not researchers but are consumers of research. Therefore, traditionally, educational administrators were "not supposed to know too much" about statistics and research methods. Because they were not supposed to engage in research in school systems, the designers of educational administration programs saw no reason to provide rigorous training in statistics and research methods for prospective school administrators (Cooper & Boyd 1988; Murphy, 1993). Consequently, research and evaluation activities in school systems were contracted out to universities or other organizations.

This arrangement worked well when federal, state, and local funds were flowing smoothly to school systems. The current emphasis on a balanced budget at every layer of government calls for fiscal responsibility and restraints on resource allocation. Across the country, no school system has been able to escape the impact of this drive, which is commonly called educational accountability. The demand for educational accountability is quite appealing in an era in which the distrust of big government is rampant. The drive for educational accountability calls for school systems to account for their educational dollars spent. This inevitably requires a monitoring and evaluation system in every sphere of activities in a school system. Cross (1983) eloquently highlighted the need for training in these areas for school administrators. Further, as Cross pointed out, the functions and responsibilities of local school systems are changing rapidly as a result of the need to respond to changing social, political, and economic factors locally and nationally.

Legal and policy mandates at the national and the state levels (for example, compliance on inclusion and nondiscriminatory practices) have created additional responsibilities for school administrators (Underwood, 1997; U.S. Department of Education, 1995). Underwood (1997), in her overview of the major changes for school districts in the Individuals with Disabilities Education Act Amendments of 1997, states that "school districts already should be addressing the law's changes, especially those that impact student discipline, funding of services at private schools and individual education plan meetings" (p. 4). These responsibilities create additional demand for data collection and analysis. Further, the decision-making process at the building site has become more complex than ever. The demand for SBDM, an offspring of the current educational reform efforts, comes from educational practitioners who insist on local control of their educational enterprise and from parents who advocate more involvement in their children's education (Cohen, 1995).

While educational reform proposals call for downsizing educational enterprises, legal and policy mandates enforce more responsibilities on school administrators. Furthermore, the SBDM approach demands information at the building site. The cumulative impact of these factors calls for a new cadre of educational administrators. Nevertheless, policymakers at the state and local levels seemed not to have grasped the full implications of this confluence. Similarly, a great majority of our educational leadership preparation programs have yet to recognize and respond to this need—preparing a cadre of educational administrators with the required professional and technical skills to meet the challenges faced by school systems.

Integrating Services for the Future

Educational administrators for the 21st century must be able to wear many different hats. They have to perform, either individually or collectively, an array of activities: conflict resolution, problem solving, maximization of resource use, application of technology, data collection, data management, computer programming, data analysis, program evaluation, project administration, report preparation, dissemination of research findings, and policy formulation. In the traditional, centralized system of school administration, many of these activities were exclusively carried out by the central-office professionals. Again, this practice evolved from the long-established belief that analytical and policy decision-making functions were the exclusive prerogatives of the central-office personnel, and the school principals were the leaders entrusted with supervising the employees and providing instructional leadership at their building sites. Only the extent of these activities varied across school systems. In a typical medium or large school system, many of the analytical functions were structured in separate departments, divisions, or units. School systems perceived data management and data analysis as two different functions and organized them as two different entities. The data management function was housed at data centers, while educational accountability functions were organized as separate departments or units. The latter units were organized under research, evaluation, student testing, assessment, or any combination of them. This way of organizing related functions continues to create inefficiencies.

Generally, data centers are managed by personnel with backgrounds in computer programming, and often they are less familiar with research, evaluation, or student assessment activities. Similarly, the professionals in the latter units rarely possess a knowledge base in data management. Lack of communication and understanding between data management personnel and data analysts about their respective functions creates problems in service delivery. For effective management, school system leaders must therefore have a basic knowledge of the interrelationship between these functions. Traditional educational administration preparation programs were not designed to equip prospective educational administrators with a sufficient knowledge base, either in the area of data analysis or in data management.

It is time to change this thinking. One reason is that we live in an information age. Whether we like it or not, the information superhighway is being laid all around us. Not much choice is left for educators at every level expect to learn to navigate and join the information superhighway. E-mail communication is becoming an integral part of routine communication procedures within and between organizational units. User-friendly text-and-data-transfer protocols, among different computer platforms, are going to boost data and text exchange and will be a tremendous incentive for research and information exchange. Multimedia capabilities offer rich potentials for effective instructional delivery. The World Wide Web offers an array of opportunities for enhancing instructional effectiveness. In the near future, it does not matter whether data collection is carried out in a centrally administered school system or in a SBDM system because of the possibilities for data transfer across locations and systems.

The information superhighway brings current research findings and discussions to any office, and school administrators must possess the necessary background to understand and participate in the discussions and forums about current research and ideas. These technological developments will open many doors for students, classroom teachers, and educational administrators at every level. Educational administrators should have the knowledge base to use these potentials. Every school system has to allocate sufficient resources to afford these technological transformations, and every preparation program has to be restructured to incorporate training in the required technical skills. No other choice is left, except to the concept of translate the 21st-century classroom into reality. This is a real dilemma every school system has to confront at a time of drastic cutbacks in funding allocations, which, in turn, is another outcome of current educational reform efforts.

Furthermore, in a SBDM system, many of the educational accountability activities will have to take place at the building site. If the professional cadre in educational accountability in a centralized school administration is not sufficiently trained, then the question of whether or not educational administrators at the building site can handle the activities related to educational accountability in a SBDM system becomes redundant. Decision makers should know the existing abilities of an organizational unit to make sound decisions. Setting standards and policies and preparing strategies to implement them demand a clear understanding of the organizational structure of the site. These tasks can be accomplished only through accurate data collection, analyses, and interpretations. If these activities are to be carried out at the building site, this creates an added responsibility for the site-based management team because it is hard to find a cadre of professionals with the required training and skills necessary to perform such activities. Therefore, the demand for educational accountability and SBDM is unattainable unless the conditions conducive for fulfilling such obligations are met, especially the professional manpower required for conducting technical and professional functions. Policymakers must realize the need for such manpower at every building site, and the educational leadership preparation programs must come to grip with the changing repertoire of required skills of school administrators.

PREPARATION NEEDED FOR EDUCATIONAL ACCOUNTABILITY

My experience tells me that neither first order universities nor second order universities adequately prepare skilled personnel to perform the activities and functions related to educational accountability. Even in a centralized school system, the task of acquiring the necessary professional skills at the workplace as part of on-the-job training is too much to be desired. Under a SBDM system, how can we expect the building-site administrators to acquire such an array of professional skills as a part of on-the-job training, when none is available? Ironically, this is one of the major bottlenecks the current school restructuring efforts have faced. In an evaluation of a school restructuring pilot project, Edirisooriya (1992) found that the most needed training, as indicated by the school restructuring committee members, was in the following areas: identifying data requirements, understanding the interpretation and implications of data, doing financial planning and budget forecasting, and planning and monitoring implementation. Wohlstetter (1995), in her study of 44 SBDM schools, identified six strategies for success. Two of these strategies are (a) creating a well-developed system for sharing school-related information with a broad range of constituents and (b) focusing on continuous improvement with schoolwide training in functional and process skills and in areas related to curriculum and instruction. Further evidence can be found in Tye (1992). Therefore, I strongly argue that, if we are to prepare educational accountability personnel with the required professional skills, especially in an SBDM system, then it is imperative to place more emphasis on research methods, statistics, educational technology, and educational data management as a core area of studies for future educational administrators.

A Personal Testimony

To put this in a more practical context, I will explain my personal experience with educational accountability as related to this issue. After graduating from a research university, I joined an administrative staff of a newly created educational accountability division in a large urban school system on the East coast. Soon, I realized that I was totally unprepared for that job. I was not convinced that my new colleagues were prepared for those responsibilities either. Nevertheless, I wasted no time in acquiring the necessary professional skills through self-study and trekking on unknown trails on a trial-and-error basis. The perseverance paid off, and I acquired the necessary professional skills and developed many useful techniques and procedures to carry out numerous educational accountability functions. This process was not easy, and I hardly think that it was the best way to go about it. I conducted many activities: data collection, data management, computer programming, data analysis, program evaluation, project administration, report preparation, dissemination of research findings, and policy formulation. These activities comprise a major function for every educational system, especially large school systems. The confluence of SBDM, policy mandates, and educational accountability will multiply the need for professionals with an array of educational accountability skills. Leaving the task of acquiring the required technical and professional skills at the workplace as part of on-the-job training for educational leaders is not a desirable option. Therefore, I continue to urge (Edirisooriya, 1996) more emphasis on research methods, statistics, educational technology, and educational data management as a necessary area of studies for future educational administrators. To this end, we need to change commonly held perceptions and to restructure educational administration preparation programs with enhanced resources.

Attitudinal Changes Needed

Students in master's programs in education are generally required to take a course in research methods, but rarely in statistics. Doctoral programs in educational administration often require students to take a statistics course in addition to a course in research methods. A research methods course is designed to provide the necessary background knowledge in research procedures; a course in statistics covers basic descriptive and inferential statistics. A commonly held attitude toward statistics and research methods among graduate students and some faculty in education administration can be summed up by the following statement, which I used to hear frequently, "You may want to get that course (or those courses) out of the way." Graduate students in educational administration often consider the courses in statistics and research methods as "pain-in-the-neck" courses that are irrelevant for their studies or some unnecessary requirement that interferes with their essential or more interesting studies. Why are these courses considered difficult or irrelevant for the advancement of professional careers of educational administrators? Once again, the reason for the pervasiveness of this perception is the influence of traditional thinking about educational administration preparation programs. When faculty members consider statistics and research methods as irrelevant, students consider them a blessing. A common excuse used by many students is, "I cannot do math; therefore, I hate statistics." So, the fear of numbers is reinforced by the perception of the irrelevance of numbers to their professional careers. Therefore, the bulk of the burden of changing this perception rests with the educational administration faculty. Not only curriculum reforms, but also reforms in instructional methods in statistics, research methods, and related areas must take place. The latter issue is beyond the scope of this paper. In brief, educational administration preparation programs have to reevaluate their teaching methods in statistics, research methods, and other related areas.

NPBEA Guidelines

The call for curriculum reforms in educational administration programs is not an idiosyncratic viewpoint. In fact, the NPBEA (1996) for the Educational Leadership Constituent Council has fully recognized the need for restructuring the educational leadership preparation programs, and due emphasis is given in its Proposed National Council for the Accreditation of Teacher Education (NCATE) Curriculum Guidelines. In NPBEA's proposed guidelines, one of the two Strategic Leadership Area components is Information Management and Evaluation. Professional skills identified in this category include the following:

1. Conduct needs assessments by collecting information on the students, staff, and school environment; family and community values, expectations, and priorities; and national and global conditions affecting schools
2. Use qualitative and quantitative data to inform decisions; plan and assess school programs; design accountability systems; plan for school improvement; and develop and conduct research
3. Engage staff in an ongoing study of current best practices, relevant research, and demographic data; and analyze their implications for school improvement
4. Analyze and interpret educational data, issues, and trends for boards, committees, and other groups, outlining possible actions and their implications (NPBEA, 1996, p. 18)

One of the four areas of Organizational Leadership is Technology and Information Systems. Professional skills identified in this category include the following:

1. Use technology, telecommunications, and information systems to enrich curriculum and instruction (e.g., CAI systems, CD ROM retrieval systems, online networks, distance learning, interactive video, etc.)
2. Apply and assess current technologies for school management and business procedures
3. Develop and monitor long range plans for school and district technology and information systems, making informed decisions about computer hardware and software, and about staff development, keeping in mind the impact of technologies on student outcomes and school operations (NPBEA, 1996, p. 27)

Commenting on these new standards, Lewis (1997) approvingly remarks, "So, how could administrators themselves stay outside the standards movement for so long?" (p. 109). With no further elaboration, the gamut of professional skills deemed required of prospective educational administrators by NPBEA speaks well in favor of the argument for restructuring educational administration programs. This is questioned by Haller et al. (1997) in their examination of decades-old data of teachers' perception of principals' effectiveness and by interpreting the findings of some decades-old research on this issue.

Many universities have taken initiatives, individually and collectively, to redesign their educational administration preparation programs. The Danforth Foundation, for example, has helped a consortium of universities in their restructuring efforts (Gresso, 1993; Leithwood, 1995; Milstein, 1993). Many other colleges across the country have taken steps to revise their educational administration preparation programs (Murphy, 1993) as a result of national calls for change. A concerted effort still has to be made to convince other colleges and universities of the need to redesign their programs to prepare the type of educational leaders we need for the 21st century. As Murphy (1993) points out in his synthesis of a number of alternative designs of educational administration preparation programs,

At one level, a book about alternative designs for preparation programs may encourage readers to conclude that a large scale reform movement has commenced, with these programs representing its vanguard. However, a thoughtful review of the history of innovation in school administration preparation programs would lead one to be careful about making this deduction. (pp. 225–226)

It is important, therefore, to review McCarthy's (1988) call for proactive measures to redesign the educational administration preparation programs, "Never have academe in general and educational administration programs in particular been more in need of creative leadership. No longer can we afford simply to react to changing social conditions that affect our field—*action is needed*" (p. 330).

CONCLUSION

A gamut of professional, technological, and leadership skills is required to be an effective educational leader of a quality school. Educational administration programs in America have to come to grips with reality and recognize this need. Without wasting time on unwise solutions such as "dismantle these programs" (Haller et al., 1997), we must search for meaningful solutions. Instead of dismantling, a more rational and farsighted approach is to reform and strengthen programs to produce the caliber of educational leaders needed for quality schools in the 21st century.

ENDNOTE

1 I greatly appreciate Donn Gresso's efforts in convincing me of the need for preparing this paper and thank him for his assistance. Any errors are my sole responsibility.

REFERENCES

Baker, K. (1991). Yes, throw money at schools. *Phi Delta Kappan, 72*(8), 628–631.

Berliner, D. C., & Biddle, B. J. (1996). Molehills out of molehills: Reply to Lawrence Stedman's review of *The manufactured crisis. Educational Policy Analysis Archives, 4*(3), 1996.

Chubb, J. E., & Moe, T. M. (1990). *Politics, markets, and America's schools.* Washington, DC: Brookings Institution.

Cochrane, P. (1994). Education, technology, and change: A personal view. *IEE Computing and Engineering Journal, 5*(2), 52–54.

Cochrane, P. (1995, June 23). A guide at the side or a sage on the stage: Desperate race to keep up with children. *Times Educational Supplement,* p. S25.

Cohen, D. K. (1995). What is the system in systemic reform? *Educational Researcher, 24*(9), 11–17.

Coleman, J. S., & Hoffer, T. (1987). *Public and private high schools: The impact of communities.* New York: Basic Books.

Cooper, B. S., & Boyd, W. L. (1988). The evolution of training for school administrators. In D. E. Griffiths, R. T. Stout, & P. B. Forsyth (Eds.), *Leaders for America's schools: The report and papers of the National Commission on Excellence in Educational Administration* (pp. 251–272). Berkeley, CA: McCutchan.

Cross, R. (1983). Down from the ivory tower. *Principal, 62*(4), 18–22.

Edirisooriya, G. (1992, April). *Lessons from a first year evaluation of a school restructuring pilot project.* Paper presented at the annual meeting of the American Educational Research Association, Atlanta, GA.

Edirisooriya, G. (1996). Preparing educational administrators for the 21st century. *AASA Professor, 19*(2), 4–5.

Goldman, P., & Kempner, K. (1988, October). *The administrator's view of administrative training.* Paper presented at the annual meeting of the University Council for Educational Administration, Cincinnati, OH. (ERIC Document Reproduction Service No. ED 325 979)

Greenwald, R., Hedges, L. V., & Laine, R. D. (1996). The effects of school resources on student achievement. *Review of Educational Research, 66*(3), 323–340.

Gresso, D. W. (1993). Genesis of the Danforth Preparation Program for School Principals. In M. M. Milstein & Associates (Ed.), *Changing the way we prepare educational leaders: The Danforth experience* (pp. 1–16). Newbury Park, CA: Corwin Press.

Gresso, D. W., Burkett, C. W., & Smith, P. L. (1993). Time is not of the essence when planning for a quality education program: East Tennessee State University. In J. Murphy (Ed.), *Preparing tomorrow's school leaders: Alternative designs* (pp. 109–128). University Park, PA: University Council for Educational Administration.

Griffiths, D. E., Stout, R. T., & Forsyth, P. B. (1988). The preparation of educational administrators. In D. E. Griffiths, R. T. Stout, & P. B. Forsyth (Eds.), *Leaders for America's schools: The report and papers of the National Commission on Excellence in Educational Administration* (pp. 284–304). Berkeley, CA: McCutchan.

Haller, E. J., Brent, B. O., & McNamara, J. H. (1997). Does graduate training in educational administration improve America's schools? *Phi Delta Kappan, 79*(3), 222–227.

Hedges, L. V., Laine, R. D., & Greenwald, R. (1994). Does money matter? A meta-analysis of studies of the effects of differential school inputs on student outcomes. *Educational Researcher, 23*(3),14.

Hill, M., Gresso, D., & Hill, F. (1994). The Tazewell experience: Applying The Alliance in the real world. *NASSP Bulletin, 78*(559), 10–13.

Hills, J. (1975). The preparation of administrators: Some observations from the firing line. *Educational Administration Quarterly, 11*(3), 1–20.

Individuals with Disabilities Education Act, Amendments of 1997 (1997). 105th Congress. (P. L. 105-17).

Laine, R. D., Greenwald, R., & Hedges, L. V. (1995). Money does matter: A research synthesis of a new universe of educational production function studies. In L. O. Picus (Ed.), *Where does the money go? Resource allocation in elementary and secondary schools* (pp. 44–70). Newbury Park, CA: Corwin Press.

Leithwood, K., Jantzi, D., & Coffin, G. (1995). *Preparing school leaders: What works?* (Preliminary report of a study examining the relationship between aspects of school leadership and characteristics of formal preparation programs prepared for the Danforth Foundation.) Ontario, Canada: Ontario Institute for Studies in Education.

Lewis, A. C. (1997). Standards for new administrators. *Phi Delta Kappan, 79*(2), 109–110.

McCarthy, M. M. (1988). The professoriate in educational administration: A status report. In D. E. Griffiths, R. T. Stout, & P. B. Forsyth (Eds.), *Leaders for America's schools: The report and papers of the National Commission on Excellence in Educational Administration* (pp. 317–331). Berkeley, CA: McCutchan.

Mehlinger, H. D. (1996). School reform in the information age. *Phi Delta Kappan, 77*(6), 400–407.

Milstein, M. M., & Associates. (1993). *Changing the way we prepare educational leaders: The Danforth experience.* Newbury Park, CA: Corwin Press.

Morton, C. (1996). The modern land of Laputa: Where computers are used in education. *Phi Delta Kappan, 77*(6), 416–419.

Murphy, J. (Ed.). (1993). *Preparing tomorrow's school leaders: Alternative designs.* University Park, PA: University Council for Educational Administration.

National Center for Education Statistics. (1991). *1987–88 schools and staffing survey: Data file users manual.* Washington, DC: Author.

National Commission on Excellence in Education. (1983). *A nation at risk: The imperative for educational reform.* Washington, DC: U.S. Department of Education.

National Policy Board for Educational Administration. (1996). *NCATE guidelines: Curriculum guidelines for advanced programs in educational leadership for principals, superintendents, curriculum directors, and supervisors.* Alexandria, VA: Author.

Peha, J. M. (1996). How K–12 teachers are using computer networks. *Educational Leadership, 53*(2), 18–25.

Spencer, B. D., & Wiley, D. E. (1981). The sense and nonsense of school effectiveness. *Journal of Policy Analysis and Management, 1*(1), 43–52.

Tye, K. A. (1992). Restructuring our schools: Beyond the rhetoric. *Phi Delta Kappan, 74*(1), 9–14.

Underwood, J. K. (1997). Four implications of IDEA's reauthorization: An overview of the major changes for school districts in the revamped federal law governing special education. [On-line]. *School Administrator, 54*(10). Available: http://www.aasa.org/SchoolAdmin/ nov9701.htm

U.S. Congress, Office of Technology Assessment. (1995). *Teachers and technology: Making the connection.* Washington, DC: Author.

U.S. Department of Education. (1995). *Individuals with Disabilities Education Act Amendments of 1995* (Report No. 1995 399-370/40166). Washington, DC: Author.

Wildman, L. (1991, August). *Does the doctorate make a difference?* Paper presented at the annual meeting of the National Council of Professors of Educational Administration, Fargo, ND. (ERIC Document Reproduction Service No. ED 336 827)

Wohlstetter, P. (1995). Getting school-based management right. *Phi Delta Kappan, 77*(1), 22–26.

CHAPTER 29

A Study of Problem-Based Learning in Teaching Educational Administration Courses

Joyce VanTassel-Baska

Active learning is one of the clarion calls that heralds school reform from preschool through graduate school. The impetus for active learning emerges from a constructivist orientation which holds that meaning and knowledge are constructed by the individual. According to Bruning, Schraw, and Ronning (1995), the goal of teaching, from a constructivist perspective, is "not so much to transmit information, but rather to encourage knowledge formation and development of the metacognitive processes for judging, organizing, and acquiring new information" (p. 216). Encompassing far more than active learning, constructivism transforms the entire instructional system by changing the role of the teacher, by focusing on the need for active participation by the learner, and by placing a renewed emphasis on the context of the instruction (Margetson, 1994; Phillips, 1995). This paper explores the concept of problem-based learning as a manifestation of constructivist theory in teaching educational administration courses.

Problem-based learning (PBL) has been widely used in medical schools (Barrows, 1985), in elementary and secondary science classrooms (Boyce, VanTassel-Baska, Burruss, Sher, & Johnson, 1997), and to some extent in educational administration programs (Bridges, 1992; Chickering & Gamon, 1991). The model, therefore, has already demonstrated its utility in a variety of contexts and for different purposes, populations, and age groups. As an approach to enhancing leadership skills in school administrators, it appears to be particularly promising.

The definition of PBL varies depending on the educational context and profession employing it. In this study, PBL refers to a student-centered learning approach in which students are expected to assume responsibility for their own learning as they develop skills in higher-order thinking and self-directed learning under the guidance of a teacher in the role of facilitative tutor or coach. Learning centers around ill-structured problems that are found in the real world and that stimulate students to learn in domains relevant to the curriculum. It shares many characteristics with other inquiry-based models of teaching (Joyce & Weil, 1996) but is also distinctive in its overall structure and approach.

IMPLEMENTATION OF THE PROCESS OF PBL

For purposes of this study, which employed the strategy of PBL as an embedded technique in a course on administration and policy in gifted education, certain key features were central to its implementation. One central feature was the use of an ill-structured, real-world problem rather than one with a neat, ready-made solution waiting to be discovered. Students dealt with limited data and made decisions about how to gain more. Students needed to understand what the problem actually was and determine how to deal with it. Moreover, they had to recognize that each problem can be approached and dealt with in multiple ways, that each problem has unique and constantly shifting components, and that each problem solver is unique as well. A final aspect about ill-structured problems is their inherent ambiguity because of incomplete information, conflicting data, and the need to make decisions anyway. Carter (1988) has articulated a direct contrast between ill-structured and well-structured problems, noting the activation of intrinsic motivation of the learner as a central response to ill-structured problems.

A second key feature of the problem-based approach used in this study was the explicit use of the concept of stakeholder. Because educational administrators deal with multiple audiences and constituency groups on a daily basis, it was essential that students understand the concept of stakeholder groups in order to function effectively in their roles. Understanding of these roles was also important in understanding the nature of real-world problems, which are fundamentally social constructions that demand different perspectives in order to understand them (Phillips, 1995). Through such a focus, students also learned the effect of bias, that real-world problem solvers are not objective or all-seeing. In the PBL process, they gained ownership of the problem and experienced the real nature of being an educational administrator.

A third key feature of the PBL approach was the role of the teacher. She had to assume a role of tutor, not just to individual students but to the problem itself. Even though the problem was ill-structured, it required the teacher to plan carefully the various possible directions students might take it, to be ready to provide new branches to heighten complexity, and to be a pathfinder for resources to be consulted. The teacher also needed to be effective in conducting discussions that guided the development of the problem at various stages. She had to keep the discussion focused on the problem, provide wait time for student responses, and model the inquiry pro-

Table 1. Problem Statement and Movement of Problem.

Week 1	Problem and Follow-Up Log
	Problem Statement: You are a new gifted program coordinator in a medium-sized school district. On Friday afternoon, your supervisor asks you to investigate and resolve a situation in the school district involving an influential parent whose child has not been identified for the gifted program. It is common knowledge that several parents have direct questions about their children not being identified. The gifted program also is currently being reviewed by the state, and you cannot locate records of student treatment or of student progress. The program has been in operation with students meeting with selected teachers for 2 hours a week for 8 years. The teachers are very popular with students, faculty, and administration. You personally know a student in your neighborhood who attends local university classes for the gifted but does not participate in the school program. There is a superintendent's meeting scheduled 2 weeks from today at which time you must present new directions for the gifted program since the district is uncertain of its current value.
	Problem Log: 1. What do you perceive the problem to be at this time? Describe it fully. 2. What strategies will prove most useful in addressing this problem? Order them according to importance. 3. What data sources will you tap in order to address the problem?
Week 2	New Data and Questions
	New Data: On Monday morning you discover that the influential parent is an attorney who is a senior partner in the first minority-run law firm in the area.
	Questions: 1. How does the new information impact your understanding of the problem? 2. How will you process the new information into your work on the problem? 3. What implications does the new data have for your movement on the problem? (i.e., Need-to-Know board)

Table 1 (continued). Problem Statement and Movement of Problem.

Week 3	New Data and Questions
	New Data: On Tuesday morning you find out that the state team monitoring the gifted program wants to interview you tomorrow.
	Questions: 1. How does the new information impact your understanding of the problem? 2. How will you process the new information into your work on the problem? 3. What implications does the new data have on your movement on the problem? (i.e., Need-to-Know board)
Week 4	New Data and Questions
	New Data: On the Monday of the meeting with the superintendent, you find out that your supervisor has resigned.
	Questions: 1. How does the new information impact your understanding of the problem? 2. How will you process the new information into your work on the problem? 3. What implications does the new data have on your movement on the problem? (i.e., Need-to-Know board)
Week 5	Resolution Session: Mock Cabinet Meeting

cess to be employed by the small groups in proceeding to problem resolution. Using open-ended questions also was important, allowing for student trial and error in the thinking-it-through process (Gallagher, 1997; Gallagher, Sher, Stepien, & Workman, 1995).

Another key feature of PBL relevant to this study was the sequence of behaviors that students need to undertake in the real world when confronted with problems, situations, or tasks in their careers (Barrows, 1994). These steps typically would include the following behaviors:

1. Generation of multiple hypotheses about causes, solutions, or both
2. Reasoning through the problem, using deductive inquiry, synthesis, and analysis, identifying inadequate knowledge and skills
3. Use of external information sources and collaboration with other students
4. Application of new information back to the problem to achieve deeper understanding for movement to resolution
5. Articulation and elaboration of what has been learned verbally and in writing, relating new understandings to past knowledge
6. Self-evaluation and peer evaluation

Inherent in all of these steps was higher-order thinking, characterized as nonalgorithmic, complex, and uncertain (Resnick, 1987). These sequential behaviors then were monitored by the instructor during a PBL episode.

The role of metacognition in PBL was also central to its successful implementation. Because of the ambiguity and complexity of real-world problems, considerable reflection on the problem was required at all stages of the process (Margetson, 1994; Perkins, Simmons, & Tishman, 1990). This reflective stance of the learner was reinforced by the constant shift in the problem and the uncomfortable sense that no right answer existed to which the learner could turn. Moreover, self-assessment and peer assessment were core processes employed by the learner in each behavioral mode. (See Table 1 for problem statement and weekly new data.)

PURPOSES

The purposes of the use of PBL in educational courses are manifold, but in the class described in this study the following student outcomes related directly to the use of PBL:

1. To enhance independent learning so that each student is responsible for "real" learning
2. To enhance information search strategies (i.e., how will I find out what I need to know?)
3. To assess real problems found in the professional practice of gifted-education administration
4. To abstract and generalize from the specific problem to larger issues in the practice of educational administration

Sample

The study sample was comprised of 26 graduate students taking a doctoral-level semester course in educational administration and policy in gifted education during 3 consecutive years from 1995 to 1997. The course was taught to 8 to 10 students each of the 3 years. Student demographics were somewhat diverse in respect to gender and ethnicity: 25% of the students were male, 75% were female, and 12% were minority. The greatest diversity among the students was in respect to prior administrative experience. Only 23% had held administrative posts prior to taking the class. Most students were employed as classroom teachers, special resource teachers, or full-time graduate students not employed in schools.

Methodology

Student portfolios and questionnaires were used to assess the effectiveness of the PBL module over the 3-year period. Student products included four types: (a) individual student logs that reflected on the problem and new data provided over the 5 weeks that the PBL episode was used, (b) student-team resolution papers that served as a handout for the final presentation to the superintendent's cabinet, (c) student-team presentations that simulated the PBL scenario, and (d) an individual student reflection paper that considered individual learning benefits of using PBL as an instructional approach.

Each cohort group of students over the 3 years submitted copies of all the above products required in the course. These products were content analyzed, based on the stated purposes for using PBL and other emerging themes. Presentations were videotaped and content analyzed for overall efficacy, using a 1 to 5 Likert-type scale for assessment. Log notes were also kept by the instructor and analyzed for central themes. Student assessment data on the approach of PBL were also analyzed for common issues and themes.

Movement of the Problem: Procedures

Administration at all levels in schools must work on complex problems that are critical to future career success. By focusing on such problems through 5 to 6 weeks of a course in educational administration, students in small study groups can engage in productive problem-finding and problem-solving strategies. The role of the instructor during this period is to structure the problem, provide ongoing information relevant to it, and assist in considering relevant information resources to tackle. The project culminates with class presentations on proposed ways of dealing with the problem, using the rest of the class as participants in a special cabinet meeting at which the problem is discussed.

The overall effectiveness of PBL episodes rests largely with the planning and skill of the teacher in moving students through the various phases of the problem. In Week 1, students must encounter the problem for the first time and become individually aware of group and individual responsibility to take charge of it. As a group, the class completes the "need-to-know" board and discusses it. For homework, a first problem log is completed. In Week 2, students begin to investigate the problem in earnest. They receive "data files" on the program under study and are encouraged to use the data to help define the problem further and search for solutions. The search continues for data beyond the files provided. In Week 3, students engage further in building toward resolution.

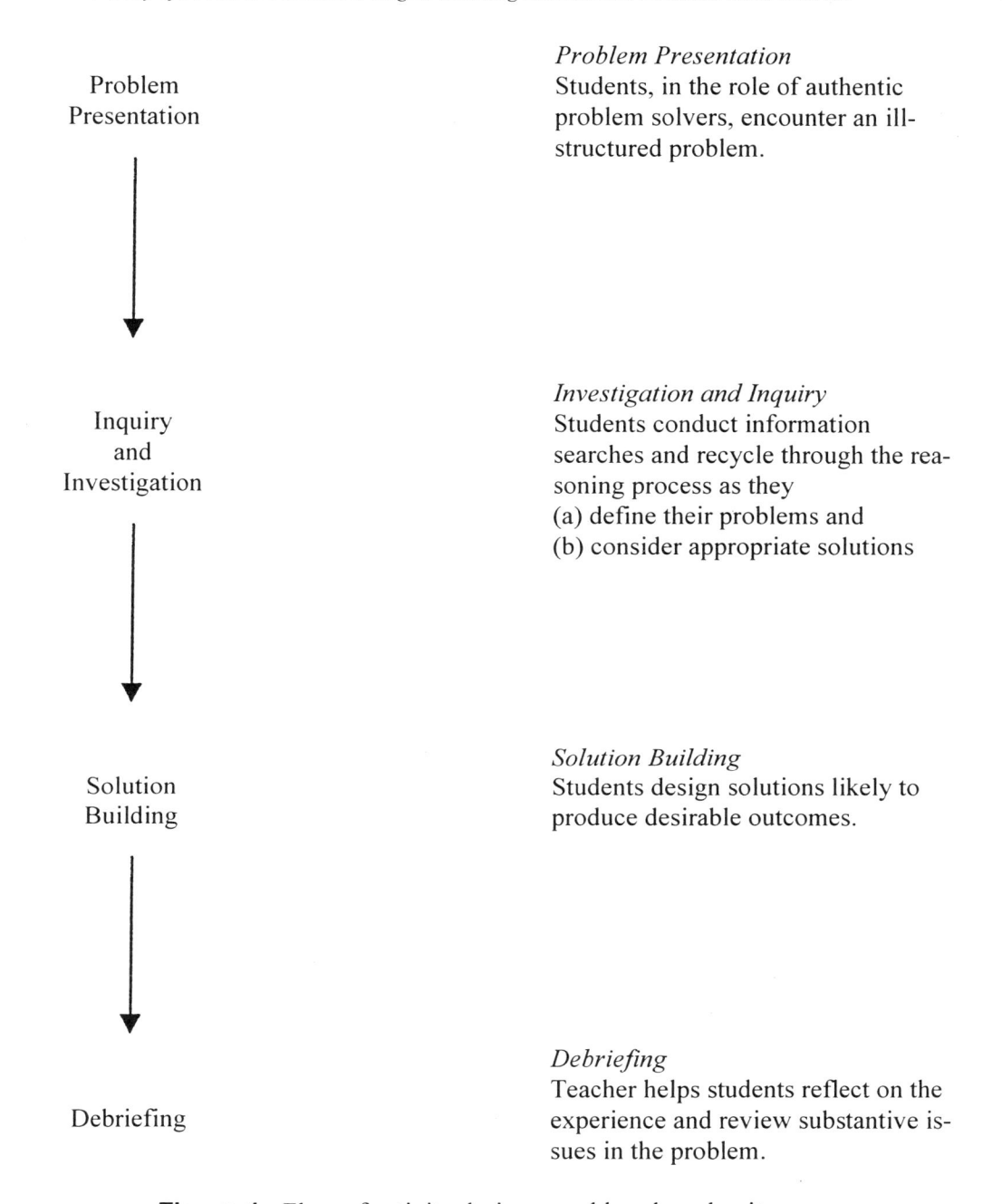

Problem Presentation	*Problem Presentation* Students, in the role of authentic problem solvers, encounter an ill-structured problem.
↓	
Inquiry and Investigation	*Investigation and Inquiry* Students conduct information searches and recycle through the reasoning process as they (a) define their problems and (b) consider appropriate solutions
↓	
Solution Building	*Solution Building* Students design solutions likely to produce desirable outcomes.
↓	
Debriefing	*Debriefing* Teacher helps students reflect on the experience and review substantive issues in the problem.

Figure 1. Flow of activity during a problem-based unit.

They take stock of their role, the role of other stakeholders in the problem, and the demands of the context, and they prepare a handout to accompany an oral presentation of 30-minute duration. During Weeks 2 and 3, new data are received, and problem logs continue to be completed individually.

In Week 4, students present their resolutions as the rest of the class assumes specific roles in a mock superintendent's cabinet meeting. Students query each other about the proposed solution, keeping in character with the role assigned.

In Week 5, students and teacher debrief the PBL episode in respect to the issues it has raised about their being administrators, about programmatic concerns, about the frustrations with the process, and about the nature of the learning that has occurred through the experience. (See Figure 1 showing the flow of activity during the units.)

RESULTS

Results of the 3-year study yielded comparable positive findings across the various data sources. In respect to student-log data, student-reflection papers, and student assessment, results were clustered into three categories for ease of reporting. These categories were group strategies employed, learnings about administration, and benefits of using the strategy of PBL. The results of the content analysis may be found in Table 2.

All students indicated that they would use PBL themselves as teachers and that they would like more opportunities to learn using PBL. Key learnings about group process and principles of administration were also strongly in evidence.

In respect to the prepared paper and presentation, instructor assessment across the 3 years averaged 4.6 on a 5-point scale for all students, indicating a high degree of quality in the student work resulting from the use of PBL. Student papers went well beyond expectations, and presentations were carefully crafted, based on the predetermined nature of the audience.

In respect to congruence with the stated purposes for using PBL, Table 3 reflects the mean student ratings over 3 years, also using a Likert-type scale of 1 to 5, with 5 being the highest rating. On average over 3 years, ratings above 4.0 were obtained for three of the four goal areas.

In respect to instructor perceptions, central themes were identified and may be seen in Table 4. These instructor reflections mirror both the student perceptual data obtained and the objective assessment of student performance.

Table 2. Consensus of Student Responses to PBL over 3 Years and 3 Cohort Groups.

Major Group Strategies Employed
- Problem definition
- Organization of the problem
- Alternative solutions
- Delegation of responsibilities
- Time management and setting priorities
- Exploration of long-term versus short-term solutions
- Collaboration

Key Learnings About Being an Administrator
- The fluidity, complexity, and integrative quality of the role
- Consideration of stakeholders, their roles, and anticipated reactions to problem resolution
- Lack of total knowledge for decision making
- Need to be able to work under unanticipated changes and pressure
- The difficulty of "doing things right"
- The political overtones of all decision making
- Being well prepared, optimistic, yet expecting challenges to one's position
- The need to understand multiple perspectives and work with them to form a higher synthesis
- The insufficiency of good reasoning and data alone to impact decision makers

Benefits of PBL as a Teaching Strategy (endorsed by 100% of each year's cohort)
- Engaged learners actively in global program planning
- Encouraged risk-taking
- Engaged learners in complex real-world problems that required sophisticated approaches to solution
- Encouraged an awareness of dealing with unanticipated change
- Encouraged self-assessment of administrative skills and understanding of schools

Table 3. Mean Student Ratings.

	Year 1	Year 2	Year 3
Independent learning	4.0	4.2	4.6
Information search	3.1	3.3	3.4
Real problem assessment	4.4	4.4	4.7
Transfer to other ed. admin. class work (i.e., policy papers)	4.0	3.8	4.5

Table 4. Instructor Perspectives on PBL.

- Enhanced group process skills, especially in problem solving and collaboration
- Heightened student appreciation for the concept of "audience," in both oral and written contexts
- Forced students to see gifted education as an embedded issue
- Helped students understand firsthand the tension between academic and real-world decision making, between theory and practice
- Enhanced metacognitive reflection at all stages of student work through use of problem logs
- Heightened awareness of school districts as complex organizations nested in states and local communities
- Highlighted student strengths and weaknesses in both content and process dimensions

DISCUSSION

Based on the study results, it appears that one of the most potent uses of the PBL strategy is to expose students with no background in educational administration to its realities, thus providing a well-structured apprenticeship learning experience for the novice. Implications for experienced administrators may be more subtle, yet appear to center on enhanced motivation to solve complex problems and to recognize the importance and need of others in the process, not only to determine multiple perspectives but also to assist in problem solution. Schools could only benefit from administrators well socialized to these understandings. Moreover, the finding that students benefit from being exposed to the complexity of administrative problems and decision making is a useful insight even for the experienced administrator who may feel something is "wrong with her or him" in a given context because particular problems do not go away.

PBL also appears to create a climate of high motivation and persistent reflection, both favorable conditions for learning and for problem solving. These conditions appear to affect the synergy of the group work undertaken as well as the self-assessment of individual students in the process. The use of problem logs was clearly an important tool to assist this process but so too was the use of "debriefing" at key stages of the process and at the conclusion of the episode.

Perhaps the most interesting finding was how effective the PBL process was at helping students understand "real" political issues and the way politics work differently at state and local levels. Through the PBL episode, students gained a deep appreciation of the need to respond to problems at both a political and substantive level, using political knowledge and skills as the lead for positive change. This insight for novice administrators in particular was invaluable and is difficult to convey under traditional teaching-learning paradigms.

CONCLUSIONS

Based on the approaches employed to assess the effectiveness of problem-based learning in a selected educational administration class, results appear to be uniformly favorable. Students self-reported substantial learning in the areas of group process, administration principles, and key benefits of the strategy. Objective assessment of student products revealed consistently high quality across 3 years. Instructor holistic assessment of student outcomes also yielded strong congruence between desired student behaviors and observed behaviors. Finally, instructor reflections on the teaching and learning process of PBL also yielded positive results.

Implications

The use of PBL provides an important framework for integrating classroom and work experiences for would-be school administrators. Implications for use of the strategy include the following recommendations for use in educational administration programs.

1. Curriculum Based on "Realistic" Problems

Because the problem is "real" and localized, students can relate to the problem at a practical level. They can use a rich variety of school-based resources to address the problem. They can visit school sites and talk to the people who would actually be involved in coordinating a response to the type of problem posed.

2. Use of Resources

Graduate students need to demonstrate facility in the use of real-world resources in order to do a successful thesis or dissertation. Through the PBL episode, they consult local resources, journals, experts locally and across the country via the Internet, and other relevant databases. Such multiple resources enrich the creation of students' solutions for the problem.

3. The Teacher Variable

The degree to which problem-based learning can be employed successfully as a tool is related to the readiness of faculty to engage in it, readiness related to educational background, attitude, energy, enthusiasm, and perceived support in their own context for implementation.

4. Transfer Effect

Because problem-based learning promotes so well the motivational aspects of learning, it appears to be an excellent enhancer of learning transfer. Evidence on this point, however, is still limited in educational administration settings (Bridges, 1992).

Use of problem-based learning in educational administration courses should be employed to some degree if the course has similar purposes to those noted in this study. Yet many questions remain to be examined, and implications for further study are manifest. One of them is the extent to which students learned more using PBL than they would have learned under more traditional instruction. Thus, a study directly comparing the results of different methodologies would be helpful. Moreover, it would be interesting to study the impact of PBL beyond the confines of one semester to ascertain if transfer effects are discernible.

REFERENCES

Barrows, H. (1994, June). *Presentation on problem-based learning.* Paper presented at the meeting of the Sixth International Conference on Thinking, Boston.

Barrows, H. S. (1985). *How to design a problem-based curriculum for the preclinical years.* New York: Springer.

Boyce, L. N., VanTassel-Baska, J., Burruss, J., Sher, B. T., & Johnson, D. T. (1997). A problem-based curriculum: Parallel learning opportunities for students and teachers. *Journal for the Education of the Gifted, 20,* 363–379.

Bridges, E. M. (1992). *Problem-based learning for administrators.* Eugene, OR: ERIC Clearinghouse on Educational Management, University of Oregon. (ERIC Document Reproduction Service No. ED 347 617)

Bruning, R. H., Schraw, G. J., & Ronning, R. R. (1995). *Cognitive psychology and instruction* (2nd ed.). Englewood Cliffs, NJ: Prentice Hall.

Carter, M. (1988). Problem solving reconsidered: A pluralistic theory of problems. *College English, 50*(5), 551–565.

Chickering, A. W., & Gamson, Z. F. (Eds.) (1991). *Applying the seven principles for good practice in undergraduate education* (New Directions for Teaching and Learning: No. 46). San Francisco: Jossey-Bass.

Gallagher, S. (1997, March). *Problem-based learning: Preparing for the 21st century.* Paper presented at the meeting of the South Carolina Consortium on the Gifted and Talented, Columbia, SC.

Gallagher, S. A., Sher, B. T., Stepien, W. J., & Workman, D. (1995). Implementing problem-based learning in science classrooms. *School Science and Mathematics, 95,* 136–145.

Joyce, B., & Weil, M. (1996). *Models of teaching* (5th ed.). Boston: Allyn & Bacon.

Margetson, D. (1994). Current educational reform and the significance of problem-based learning. *Studies in Higher Education, 19,* 5–19.

Perkins, D. N., Simmons, R., & Tishman, S. (1990). Teaching cognitive and metacognitive strategies. *Journal of Structural Learning, 10,* 285–303.

Phillips, D. C. (1995). The good, the bad, and the ugly: The many faces of constructivism. *Educational Researcher, 24*(7), 5–12.

Resnick, L. (1987). *Education and learning to think.* Washington, DC: National Academy Press.

Treffinger, D. J., Isaksen, S. G., & Dorval, K. B. (1994). Creative problem-solving: An overview. In M. A. Runco (Ed.), *Problem finding, problem solving, and creativity* (pp. 223–236). Norwood, NJ: Ablex.

CHAPTER 30

Toward a Model of Problem-Based Learning for the Preparation of Educational Administrators

Robert Rehm and Rodney Muth

A principal of a large metropolitan high school recently told us a familiar, but disturbing, story. She came home from a long day at work in which she had solved one problem after another—disciplining students for fighting, meeting unhappy parents, putting out one fire after another. She was bewildered, perplexed, confused, and baffled by the complexity of the situations she faced that day. And on top of these daily crises, she is expected to transform the prevailing paradigm in the school to some new state in which teachers are empowered, decisions are shared, stakeholders are involved, and students experience continuous, lifelong learning. She throws up her hands. "It's a puzzlement!" she says. She can only admit to her loved ones that she is at wit's end about what to do next. And nothing in her formal education had prepared her for anything like this.

THE GENESIS OF PROBLEM-BASED LEARNING

The development of problem-based learning (PBL) is well documented (Barrows, 1994; Bridges, 1992; Duffy & Cunningham, 1996; Martin, Murphy, & Muth, 1993; Savery & Duffy, 1995). Constructed as an alternative to conventional teaching methods in American medical schools (Barrows, 1994; Nova, 1988), PBL was designed to prepare medical students for the real world of doctoring by reversing the usual passive-learning approach (Hannum & Briggs, 1982), providing opportunities to learn in authentic situations (Duffy & Cunningham, 1996; Grabinger, Dunlap, & Duffield, 1997). Traditionally, medical students spent their first years listening to time-honored lectures and burying their noses in books on biology and anatomy. PBL inverted this paradigm by placing students in small tutorial groups in which they work on real-life "problems of practice" and with real, live patients—right away. With the assistance of teaching doctors, the student groups investigate and diagnose a patient's problem and project a course of treatment. Through PBL processes, students worked collaboratively, often with other agencies (Barrow, 1994), learned "hands on" the skills of diagnosis and treatment, and learned medical theory and practice through inquiry linked to real problems of medical practice. The results were dramatic—doctors prepared for handling real-life medical problems tended to be better diagnosticians (Harfmann, 1990; Kaufman et al., 1989; Schmidt, Norman, & Boshuizen, 1990) than traditionally prepared students and perform just as well on medical exams (Kaufman et al., 1989).

Leaders in the field of educational administration, inspired by innovations in medical schools, have applied PBL principles in university programs for the preparation of school administrators (Bridges, 1992; Martin, Murphy, & Muth, 1993). Although significant variety exists in the adaptation of PBL from the medical-school approach, some patterns have emerged. Generally, in educational administration settings, a problem is defined by the instructor and presented to students, Getzels' (1979) "presented" problem. The problem is a discrete situation that has been identified as linked to important knowledge or administrative skill needed by anyone seeking to become a school administrator. Problems usually come to students well formed and defined. Or at least they can be presented easily as a "problem statement."

Robert Rehm and Rodney Muth, University of Colorado at Denver

Such problems might include dealing with a budget issue, increasing student attendance, restructuring a curriculum, or responding to community complaints. Students are formed into small working groups and given instructions on how to work together, such as determining who is responsible for various group tasks. The instructor takes on a facilitative role, perhaps providing background readings and research. Students are given time to work out the problem and make a presentation. They are then evaluated through a combination of peer and instructor processes. In addition to simulations confined to classrooms, problem-based field activities often involve students with real-world problems in schools.

THE PROBLEM WITH "PROBLEMS"

Problems are situations that need to be solved, and they often need to be solved quickly with the "right" answer. School administrators spend much of their day fire fighting, addressing one crisis after another. Problem-based learning helps them learn how to put out the fires. This kind of routine problem solving is genuinely important for school administrators to master (Leithwood & Steinbach, 1995). To prepare aspirants for administrative positions, realistic cases are presented to them to solve: handle a grievance, discipline a student, manage a difficult parent situation, or deal with community concerns. Prospective administrators learn to solve these problems by breaking the problem down, applying some standard problem-solving steps, and submitting an answer on how to fix the problem.

As Barrett (1995) points out, such processes often are mechanistic, focusing on what is "wrong" (a deficiency orientation), seeking to fix whatever it is that is broken. He also suggests that this approach is inherently conservative and limiting, validates the status quo, leads to coping behavior, and seeks "feasible" solutions. Accordingly, a problem-focused methodology tends to be fragmented, rather than holistic, and can inhibit collaboration.

Both in established practice and in preparation, such *problem fixing* generally focuses attention on control processes and outcomes. Medicine, law, and business, for example, approach problem fixing in fairly mechanical, linear ways, breaking complex problems into their constituent parts (e.g., circulation systems, due process, or markets) and analyzing the parts somewhat discretely (Barrett, 1995). Variables are identified that, when isolated and manipulated, often lead to intended outcomes. In application, this tends to be a fairly "transactional" process (Burns, 1978).

In each case, the focus is "getting it right": isolating the condition to cure the abnormality and return the body to a healthy state, marshalling evidence and law to convince a jury of the validity of one side's arguments and win a decision, or examining trends and predicting market outcomes. Although no one "right way" exists in any of these fields and no consensus exists universally on "how to do it," the dominating paradigm is one oriented generally toward finding a right way to do whatever it is. In education, though, competing perspectives, values, solutions, ideologies, and so on often make it hard to "get it right" because no agreement exists about what is "right." Further, it often is challenging just to label a problem (reading? perception? motivation? attention?), let alone isolate it from the multitude of other factors (social class? parental support? community values? resource adequacy?) operating in a school or district that may be producing or affecting the conditions noted.

We think, however, that a whole other side to school administration is overlooked when the focus is on distinct problems. In today's school environment, we ask administrators not only to solve difficult problems of practice, but we also ask them—not too gently—to transform schools to meet future and unknown societal demands (Quantz, Cambron-McCabe, & Dantley, 1991). Increasingly, school administrators are expected to be change agents (Leithwood, Begley, & Cousins, 1992) who know how to involve people in paradigm shifting (Kuhn, 1962). Problem-based learning, in its present form, may not give aspiring administrators the hands-on skills required for *system change* or *transformative leadership*. Problem-based learning also tends not to be oriented to solutions that evolve from the collaboration of those for whom the problems have day-to-day meaning.

Administrators have always dealt with difficult problems of practice. What is different now is the *turbulence* in the social environment (Emery, 1977) in which schools exist. This environment requires a different form of organizational leadership, developed through preparation programs that examine alternative learning models.

The PBL model, although very constructive, needs to be "stretched" to address the complexity of educational problems, the nature of the systems of education and those in which education is embedded, and the improbability of achieving lasting solutions. For administrators in today's schools, the solution process generally is more important than the actual or long-term solution itself, as no permanent solutions are possible in evolving systems, systems open to external influences from their environment.

WHAT DO TODAY'S SCHOOL ADMINISTRATORS NEED TO BE ABLE TO DO?

Today's educational leaders need conceptual and practical skills for navigating the complex (Achilles, Reynolds, & Achilles, 1997), turbulent environment (Emery, 1977) in which education now exists. Educational administrators are expected to be visionary leaders who know how to work collaboratively with the school system and an increasingly diverse community. Expectations are higher than ever. For example, the licensing standards for administrators and principals (Principal and Administrator Professional Standards Board, 1994a, 1994b) that became effective in 1994 in Colorado are based in national efforts to clarify expectations for administrator preparation (Griffiths, Stout, & Forsyth, 1988). Among these standards are the following requirements for school leaders:

1. Model and set high standards for student performance
2. Build a school that promotes belief that children can learn and succeed
3. Make sure that stakeholders are involved in decision making
4. Lead teams committed to student learning
5. Empower others (teachers, parents, students, community) to be leaders themselves
6. Engage school communities in envisioning new possibilities
7. Demonstrate high moral development, maturity, and continuous self-learning
8. Promote ethics, the ideals of a democratic society, and contributions to a culturally diverse society
9. Understand multicultural dynamics and the implications of ethnic, religious, cultural, socioeconomic, physical, and intellectual diversity
10. Provide emotionally and physically safe educational environments

These "transformative" skills and abilities require leaders who can build vision, work cooperatively with all stakeholders, and focus the school community on a preferred future of performance. School transformers are system shapers (Oshry, 1992), and they need to understand that their schools as systems exist in turbulent environments and that their role is to transform these systems to even higher levels of performance. Times of constant change require new sets of skills. In preturbulent times, school administrators could concentrate on day-to-day management issues. Issues were generally few and often predictable—and generally resolvable in known and accepted frameworks. Today's school administrators, however, need to be transformers of culture, change agents for new paradigms, and leaders of intensely complex domains with diverse, often conflicting, interests among stakeholders.

THE CHANGE AGENT VERSUS THE EXPERT PROBLEM SOLVER

In the process of transferring PBL from medical to administrative education, some weaknesses in the doctor-patient analogy have become clear. First, schools and their personnel are not patients; "schools" are not as tractable, the problems are more complex and interrelated, schools cannot be separated from their environments, and school leaders simply do not have the store of knowledge that most doctors command. Second, because of their knowledge, doctors as expert problem solvers diagnose problems, breaking them into solvable chunks, and then prescribe treatments—but for a *mostly passive patient*, which schools are not. Trained to be optimizers, doctors often think that they know the problem and simply have to search through existing knowledge in order to arrive at a solution (Weisbord, 1987, p. 184).

Expert problem solving is based primarily on rational, analytical reasoning (Leithwood, Begley, & Cousins, 1992; Leithwood & Steinbach, 1995). Experts are trained to see two dimensions: the probable efficiency of different paths and the relative value of outcomes (Emery, 1977). In contrast, change agents are people who move in and around a system *trying to change the whole toward some purpose* (Bushe, 1990). The key point is that change agents have a sense of a higher vision and purpose for themselves and the system that they lead, and they rivet their attention on involving people throughout the system in aligning themselves around a common, shared vision for the future. *The change agent* (transformative leader) *sees the system as a complex puzzle to solve, and the school leader as change agent engages the school and community* (all the puzzle pieces) *in a process of co-creating the most desirable school.*

While expert problem solvers are concerned with finding the right paths to solve the problem at hand, change agents realize that many ways lead to a goal—and all possibilities are open to consideration. What is fundamentally important is the intrinsic and shared value of any course of action to those who choose to take it, and it is crucial that the "choosers" are intimately involved in the choice. Because values are involved, it is never easy to identify and agree upon the ideals that change is supposed to serve and the kinds of paths most in line with the articulated ideals. Thus, participation in the choice of paths will reflect intrinsic values to those traversing them.

Where the expert problem solver uses analysis and research to understand and solve a problem, the change agent knows that sharing and agreeing on human ideals and values produce a future worth living and working in. The change agent develops a collaborative relationship with the system. It can be seen as a consultant-client relationship, but it is a collaborative working relationship, not an expert-consulting model. The consultant-client relationship is one in which both work collaboratively to diagnose the problem and agree on a course of action. The relationship between them is the key to change.

For these reasons, the medical model for PBL needs to be adjusted in the context of educational leadership. In the medical environment, problems are broken down, analyzed, and treatments prescribed. The medical practitioner interacts transactionally with the "problem." In education, leaders need to be transformers and change agents as well as transactors. This transformational focus requires a more expansive, systemic view of problems, a view that is more contextual, focused on the future and on possibilities. Adapting PBL to the preparation of educational leaders means stretching the model.

THE PUZZLE METAPHOR FOR PROBLEM SOLVING

In a turbulent, uncertain environment (Emery, 1977), educators face *puzzles*, not problems. A problem focus by its very nature is reductionist and oriented to emphasizing deficiencies (Barrett, 1995). Reframing problems into puzzles offers the opportunity to see problems as pieces of an overall whole within a larger context. If you ever have opened a box containing a complex jigsaw puzzle and dumped the pieces on the table, then you know what a mess you have to work with. We suggest that the jigsaw puzzle is a good metaphor describing what school administrators face every day when they enter a school. What they face is less a series of separate problems that can be disaggregated into smaller parts and more a puzzle needing to be pieced together to form a whole. And the whole, in the case of school, is the picture of the *preferred future of the school.* Some call it vision, and it is essential to successful leadership in schools (Leithwood & Steinbach, 1995).

Using a problem-centered approach, you pick up a piece and start analyzing it, but not in the context of the other pieces. When one piece is "fixed," you go on to another, and then to another. In contrast, a puzzle approach means connecting the first piece with other pieces until a picture starts to take shape. This involves ecological learning (Emery, 1993) in that you look at the bits, trying them this way and that, until a pattern emerges.

> In problem solving it is typical to have the insightful "Eureka" experience when a solution suddenly becomes apparent, and after that it is just a matter of work to put the pieces together. In a puzzle one does not get this. The relation between the pieces is very much a matter of local determination. One can determine what is required for the piece to fit but, until that piece is found one has very little idea of what is going to be required of

the piece after that. Previous experience or training cannot enrich the repertoire of solutions; at best they may help a person "learn how to learn." This is very different from the usual expert approach in which the expert problem solver has a kit full of expert solutions for the problem at hand. (Emery, 1977, p. 125)

As Emery (p. 126) notes from the *Oxford English Dictionary*, a problem is a "thing thrown or put forward. In physics or math: a question or inquiry which starting from some given conditions investigates some fact, result or law." Chess problems, for example, are similarly defined as deriving from a given arrangement of pieces and set of rules.

In contrast, a puzzle is a state of mind, a case of Getzels's (1979) "discovered" or, more likely, "created" problem in which the *questions asked* about it are critical (Getzels, 1985). It is from this state of being puzzled or bewildered, confused, or perplexed about how to act or decide that a person or group can achieve a result that seems impossible to obtain. As a verb, puzzle means "to search in a bewildered or perplexed way; to fumble, grope for something; to *puzzle* out: to make out by the exercise of ingenuity and patience" (Emery, 1977, p. 126). As a noun, *puzzle* describes the object itself (a jigsaw puzzle, for example) as well as the state one is in when perplexed or challenged by a "mystery."

Too often, educators assume that we need more and more information when all the knowledge available cannot help a puzzle solver arrange a puzzle. What actually is needed is knowledge of human values and ideals (Lasswell, 1971). Because puzzles emerge in unpredictable ways, they require ingenuity and creativity to solve them. Thus, puzzles profit from collaboration (Emery & Emery, 1997) since multiple perspectives generally improve decisions (Collins & Guetzkow, 1964). (Recall how much faster, how much more fun, and how much better your puzzle constructing activities have been when a friend or loved one helped you!)

OPEN SYSTEMS AND TURBULENT ENVIRONMENTS

In the early 1960s, Emery and Trist (1973) first observed that the texture of our global environment was changing. They called the emerging environment "turbulent." *Turbulent* refers to the way the current social environment is producing change by its own dynamism and consequently creating uncertainty for any system within it. Changes in the worldwide social environment are happening at such a pace, according to Emery and Trist, that life is becoming more uncertain and unpredictable. "Today's global environment is turbulent, changing faster than our institutions" (F. E. Emery, personal communication, 1993). In this environment, rules of problem solving and planning centered on cause and effect are no longer useful.

Emery and Trist (1973) predicted that, unless we get a grip on our turbulent environment, dire consequences will result. They predicted that the most pervasive change would be a movement to more and more dissociation in society. People would become increasingly segmented and alienated, not experiencing one another as important to their future.

Educators find themselves struggling in this turbulent environment. All around the school, changes are happening at a breakneck pace and include rapidly changing technology, increasing movement toward a global economy, intensifying environmental problems, increasing diversity of cultures and demands, progressive empowerment in the workplace, increasing gaps between rich and poor, and an expanding breakdown of the traditional family. In the immediate social environment of any school in the U.S., we find increasing juvenile crime, families under stress, community resources stretched to the limit, heightened expectations for schools to deal with broad social goals beyond educating children, and on and on.

The open systems approach (Emery, 1969) suggests that any system should have an open relationship with its social environment if it is to be adaptive. The relationship between any system and its environment is co-implicative: the system and environment affect one another. In open-system terms, any event is the result of a system and environment interaction. Systems both get feedback from their environment that facilitates adjustments to the environment as well as act on their environment. In the educational context, a school as a system needs to develop an adaptive relationship with its external environment. That does not necessarily mean responding faster to keep pace with the turbulence. It does mean planning and problem solving—puzzle solving—to reduce the uncertainty and turbulence of the school's environment.

A PUZZLE-SOLVING APPROACH

Puzzle solving (Emery, 1982) in turbulent environments requires analyses built on clarity of ideals and values. For this reason, puzzle solving has several elements. It is contextual, collaborative, appreciative, transformative, and reality based.

Contextual

Puzzle solving is contextual in the sense that any system is a whole moving through time and space (Lasswell, 1971; Pepper, 1942). The only constant in the world view of contextualism is change. Like the complex jigsaw puzzle, every school is a whole system that must constantly recreate itself. No puzzle piece, or problem, exists in a vacuum. To survive and flourish, systems cannot exist in stasis. To be successful, a system must look forward with its collectively created vision (Leithwood & Steinbach, 1995) to realize future preferred states (Lasswell, 1971) that only will change as the environment changes.

Collaborative

Puzzle solving is collaborative because it takes people with knowledge of all the pieces to solve the puzzle. The school leader of today and tomorrow cannot be an expert in every aspect of the puzzle. Instead, as a "constructivist" (Lambert et al., 1995) the school leader must know how to bring people together, both inside and outside the school, to collaborate towards shared solutions within a shared vision (Leithwood & Steinbach, 1995). We use collaboration here in the sense of bringing people with diverse perspectives together and expecting creative solutions to emerge.

Appreciative

Puzzle solving is appreciative (Barrett, 1995; Weisbord, 1992). Machines break down; they naturally depreciate. Many problem-solving methods are based on this kind of machine metaphor; they are depreciative. Human beings, on the other hand, can appreciate. Since schools are human systems, composed of human beings, they can appreciate as well. But in order for any system such as a school to appreciate, it needs processes that are focused on what is possible and desirable, not on what is broken. We know from research that problem solving is by its very nature depressing (Weisbord, 1987); the depreciating process of breaking problems down like deconstructing a machine and applying analytical steps robs the human spirit. Appreciative approaches, on the other hand, are energizing, often resulting in deep commitment to making creative solutions happen. Appreciative puzzle solving involves the generation of ideals and values to guide change. It is a process in which envisioning a desirable future, as opposed to correcting a mistake, is the reference point.

Transformative

A puzzle-solving approach has the potential of transforming a problem. Transforming is about reframing, challenging and changing assumptions, or applying double-loop learning (Argyris, 1976), turning the problem from a symptom in need of a cure to a vision to enact. The transformative perspective enables people to change the culture of the school in profound ways.

Reality-Based

Puzzle solving, as we describe it, deals with real problems. The typical problem-solving approach in many administrator preparation programs can be done at a distance. Problem solvers can pretend that they are dealing with an objective problem—knowing that they are not part of it. The puzzle solver, conversely, gets intimately involved in the puzzle-solving process. While the problem solver fixes the problem, the puzzle solver joins the system, working with its members to clarify and develop preferable futures. The corollary of puzzle solving is consequential change.

TOWARD A TYPOLOGY

Even though PBL is a superior alternative to traditional instructional approaches (Bridges, 1992; Martin, Murphy, & Muth, 1993), educators need to broaden PBL because of its narrow focus, its sometimes perceived pathological orientation, and its "fix-it" perspective. Our thinking about PBL has evolved to the point where we now view PBL as a subset of puzzle solving. While events clearly present themselves which require a problem-solving approach, the view here is that problem solving's—and PBL's—short-term orientation leads a system to become locked into short-range thinking. A puzzle-solving approach, on the other hand, is holistic, long-range, and oriented to system change. And, if school administrators are to be the transformers as many expect, then they must be prepared to take the broader, transformative orientation inherent in the puzzle-solving metaphor.

Two other perspectives on PBL that have emerged recently are practice-based learning (Barrows, 1994) and project-based learning (Glover, 1993). Pointing as well to the need to be contextual, according to Barrows (1994) practice-based learning emerged as a concept because

> the term "problem" is somewhat narrow in its implications for learning. The term "problem" also wrongly suggests that it is the problems of individual patients that are used. They are not the only problems physicians must face in their work, as they must understand and work with the health problems of the community and groups of people as well. (p. 3)

According to a brochure from the Autodesk Foundation, sponsor of project-based learning activities in schools in northern California as well as an annual conference, project-based learning is all of the following:

> A strategy that recognizes that significant learning utilizes students' inherent drive to learn, capability to do important work, and need to be taken seriously. Engaging learning experiences that involve students in complex real-world projects through which they develop and apply skills and knowledge. Learning that requires students to draw from many disciplines in order to solve problems that don't have predetermined results. Experiences through which students learn to manage and allocate resources such as time and materials.

Thus, puzzle solving can incorporate problem-, project-, and practice-based learning as strategies for effecting improvements in educational systems. Each has a role, and each its necessary orientation. It is the encompassing nature, contextuality, and system orientation of the puzzle-solving metaphor that makes it more appealing than other alternatives.

ACTION LEARNING FOR PUZZLE SOLVING

An additional enabling feature for puzzle solving is action learning (Morley, 1989). Action learning is an open-systems tool for helping any system become adaptive in a turbulent, uncertain environment. The focus of action learning is on "creating domain settings for collaborative learning as a basis for initiating strategies for change" (p. 182). The substance of this definition can be found in the words *domain, collaborative learning,* and *change*.

In action learning, the context for learning is the system within its broader social environment. Applying action learning to school leadership means producing learning opportunities that focus on the school within the educational domain. Action learning is collaborative because it builds working relationships between students (administrators in preparation) who act as change-agent consultants to clients from the system. Students and clients join together to learn about the system and to change it towards some agreed-upon higher purpose and vision. Action learning is about change because the result is a system that is adaptive in its environment.

Action learning is based in action research (Argyris, Putnam, & Smith, 1987; Trist, 1981). But it is quite different from traditional notions of action research in which experts formally gather and analyze data through questionnaires, surveys, and other research methods. In this model, the consultant (researcher) acts as an expert in identifying, analyzing, and diagnosing problems. The result of a typical action-research project is a set of recommendations formulated by the consultant to solve the identified problem. In our experience, these recommendations normally sit on shelves gathering dust because the results are the work of the consultants. They are neither developed nor owned by the system.

In contrast, action learning means bringing together people to discover and co-create their future. Both the researcher and the "researched" mutually establish a relationship through their common concern. A collaborative relationship develops, one that is not distant, neutral, or objective. The relationship is collaborative, mutually respectful, and trusting. The specialized knowledge and experience of the researcher, and the local and tacit knowledge of the researched, combine in a process of joint learning, co-discovery, and co-creation. Like other puzzle-solving activities, the action-learning process can engage all of the relevant participants in a social relationship around a common focus.

POSTSCRIPT

This is an initial attempt to conceptualize a broader based, more effective, contextual, and client- and system-oriented approach to the preparation of school administrators than currently exists. Puzzle solving was chosen as the metaphor to illustrate the part-and-whole (Lasswell, 1971), back-and-forth nature of problem solving in the real world and to make clear the importance of the "client" in any approach to improving practice in schools. Based both on our research and experience, puzzle solving, coupled with action learning, may be key to transforming education and the preparation of school administrators. The next step for us is to develop a nonprescriptive model, advancing the concepts outlined here, that is suggestive of practical and effective ways to prepare future school leaders as collaborative, client-centered change agents.

REFERENCES

Achilles, C. M., Reynolds, J. S., & Achilles, S. H. (1997). *Problem analysis: Responding to school complexity.* Larchmont, NY: Eye on Education.

Argyris, C. (1976). Single-loop and double-loop models in research on decision-making. *Administrative Science Quarterly, 21*(3), 363–375.

Argyris, C., Putnam, R., & Smith, D. M. (1987). *Action science: Concepts, methods, and skills for research and intervention.* San Francisco: Jossey-Bass.

Barrett, F. J. (1995). Creating appreciative learning cultures. *Organizational Dynamics, 24*(2), 36–49.

Barrows, H. S. (1994). *Practice-based learning: Problem-based learning applied to medical education.* Springfield: Southern Illinois University School of Medicine.

Bridges, E. M., with Hallinger, P. (1992). *Problem based learning for administrators.* Eugene: ERIC Clearinghouse on Educational Management, University of Oregon.

Brooks, J. G., & Brooks, M. G. (1993). *In search of understanding: The case for constructivist classrooms.* Alexandria, VA: Association for Supervision and Curriculum Development.

Burns, J. M. (1978). *Leadership.* New York: Harper Colophon.

Bushe, G. (1990). Predicting OD consulting competence from the MBTI and Stage of Ego Development. *Journal of Applied Behavioral Science, 26*(3), 338–350.

Checkland, P. (1981). *Systems thinking, systems practice.* Chichester, England: John Wiley.

Collins, B., & Guetzkow, H. (1964). *A social psychology of group processes for decision making.* New York: John Wiley.

Duffy, T. M., & Cunningham, D. J. (1996). Constructivism: Implications for the design and delivery of instruction. In D. H. Jonassen (Ed.), *Handbook of research for educational communications and technology* (pp. 170–198). New York: Macmillan.

Emery, F. E. (Ed.) (1969). *Systems thinking.* Harmondsworth, England: Penguin.

Emery, F. E. (1977). *Futures we are in.* Leiden: Martinus Nijhoff Social Sciences Division.

Emery, F. (1993). Educational paradigms: An epistemological revolution. In M. Emery (Ed.), *Participative design for participative democracy.* Canberra: Australian National University, Centre for Continuing Education.

Emery, F., & Emery, M. (1997). *Toward a logic of hypotheses: Everyone does research.* Cook, Australia.

Emery, F. E., & Trist, E. L. (1973). *Toward a social ecology.* New York: Plenum.

Emery, M. (1982). *Searching: For new directions, in new ways, for new times.* Canberra: Australian National University, Centre for Continuing Education.

Getzels, J. W. (1979). Problem-finding and research in educational administration. In G. L. Immegart & W. L. Boyd (Eds.), *Problem-finding in educational administration* (pp. 5-22). Lexington, MA: D. C. Heath.

Getzels, J. W. (1985, September). Problem finding and the enhancement of creativity. *NASSP Bulletin,* pp. 55–61.

Glover, T. (1993). *The teaching of educational psychology through project-based learning.* Paper presented at the meeting of the Midwest Association of Teachers of Educational Psychology, Anderson, IN.

Grabinger, S., Dunlap, J. C., & Duffield, J. A. (1997). Rich environments for active learning in action: Problem-based learning. *Alt-J, 5*(2), 5–17.

Griffiths, D. E., Stout, R. T., and Forsyth, P. B. (1988). *Leaders for America's schools: The report and papers of the National Commission on Excellence in Educational Administration.* Berkeley, CA: McCutchan.

Hannum, W., & Briggs, L. (1982). How does instructional system design differ from traditional instruction? *Educational Technology, 22*(1), 9–14.

Harfmann, B. (1990). Medical education in the 90's: The alternative curriculum program at Rush Medical College. *The Magazine.* Chicago: Rush-Presbyterian-St. Luke's Medical College.

Kaufman, A., Menin, S., Waterman, R., Duban, S., Hansbarger, C., Silverblatt, H., Obenshain, S. S., Kantrowitz, M., Becker, T., Samet, J., & Wiese, W. (1989). The New Mexico experiment: Educational innovation and institutional change. *Academic Medicine, 64*(6), 285–294.

Kuhn, T. (1962). *The structure of scientific revolutions.* Chicago: University of Chicago Press.

Lambert, L., Walker, D., Zimmerman, D. P., Cooper, J. E., Lambert, M. D., Gardner, M. E., & Ford Slack, P. J. (1995). *The constructivist leader.* New York: Teachers College Press.

Lasswell, H. D. (1971). *A pre-view of policy sciences.* New York: American Elsevier.

Leithwood, K., Begley, P. T., & Cousins, J. B. (1992). *Developing expert leadership for future schools.* Washington, DC: Falmer Press.

Leithwood, K., & Steinbach, R. (1995). *Expert problem solving: Evidence from school and district leaders.* Albany: State University of New York Press.

Martin, W. M., Murphy, M. J., & Muth, R. (1993). Problem-based learning: A new approach to preparing school leaders. In J. Hoyle & D. Estes (Eds.), *First yearbook of the National Council of Professors of Educational Administration. NCPEA: In a new voice* (pp. 141–154). Lancaster, PA: Technomic Publishing Co., Inc.

Morley, D. (1989). Frameworks for organizational change: Towards action learning in global environments. In S. Wright & D. Morley (Eds.), *Learning works: Searching for organizational futures* (pp. 163–190). Toronto, Canada: York University, Faculty of Environmental Studies, ABL Group.

Nova. (1988). *Can we make a better doctor?* [video]. Boston: WGBH. Oshry B. (1992). *Space work.* Boston: Power & Systems Training.

Pepper, S. (1942). *World hypotheses.* Berkeley: University of California Press.

Principal and Administrator Professional Standards Board. (1994a, May). *Standards for school administrators in Colorado.* Denver: Colorado State Board of Education.

Principal and Administrator Professional Standards Board. (1994b, May). *Standards for school principals in Colorado.* Denver: Colorado State Board of Education.

Quantz, R. A., Cambron-McCabe, N., & Dantley, M. (1991). Preparing school administrators for democratic authority: A critical approach to graduate education. *Urban Review, 23*(1), 3–19.

Savery, J. R., & Duffy, T. M. (1995). Problem based learning: An instructional model and its constructivist framework. In B. G. Wilson (Ed.), *Constructivist learning environments: Case studies in instructional design* (pp. 135-148). Englewood Cliffs, NJ: Educational Technology.

Schmidt, H. G., Norman, G. R., & Boshuizen, H. P. A. (1990). A cognitive perspective on medical expertise: Theory and implications. *Academic Medicine, 65*(10), 611–621.

Thompson, S. D. (Ed.) (1993). *Principals for our changing schools: The knowledge and skill base.* Fairfax, VA: National Policy Board for Educational Administration.

Trist, E. (1981, June). *The evolution of socio-technical systems: A conceptual framework and an action research program* (Occasional Paper No. 2). Ontario, Canada: Ontario Quality of Working Life Centre.

Weisbord, M. R. (1987). *Productive workplaces: Organizing and managing for dignity, meaning, and community.* San Francisco: Jossey-Bass.

Weisbord, M. R. (1992). *Discovering common ground.* San Francisco: Berrett-Koehler.

CHAPTER 31

Authenticity in Field-Based Preparation Programs for PK–12 School Administrators

Mitch Holifield and Gerald Dickinson

This review addresses one essential question about preparation programs for school administrators: What are the defining characteristics of authentic, field-based learning experiences in exemplary administrator preparation programs?

Focusing on this question is particularly relevant due to severe criticism leveled against university-based preparation programs for school administrators. In their call for authenticity, Holifield, Cline, and Holman (1995) address some criticisms relevant to the lack of authenticity in preparation programs.

1. Disjunction: The common complaint of practitioners and the consistent observation of critics are that the knowledge and skills required on the job are not taught in administrator preparation programs (Peper, 1988). Both the knowledge base and dissertation research are experienced as academic abstractions (Muth, 1989). Substance is lacking on at least four counts: field-related experiences dealing with current problems, lack of attention to skills, weak clinical programs, and disregard of issues of diversity in school and community.

2. Instruction: Courses are designed and taught by professors working in isolation. The lecture discussion format continues to dominate, emphasizing written communication while ignoring reality-based learning experiences. As a consequence, students are disengaged from content and process as opportunities are not available for students to personalize their learning experiences (Mulkeen & Tetenbaum, 1990).

3. Performance and Assessment: Conventional paper-pencil examinations serve as summative oriented, student-progress monitoring devices that seldom evaluate substantive learning experiences. Since instruction is aimed at knowledge acquisition rather than skills or skill applications, assessment is knowledge-oriented rather than performance-driven and is professor controlled rather than interactive or collaborative. Not only are student performance standards lacking or unrelated to the work of the profession (Peterson & Finn, 1985), bargains and compromises with students in exchange for enrollments militate against standards (Mann, 1975).

CRITERIA FOR AUTHENTIC TASKS

These criticisms call for the inclusion of authentic tasks and assessment in administrator preparation programs. But what are the criteria for authenticity for field-based learning experiences? In part, the answer is found in Bridges and Hallinger's (1995) principles of problem-based learning, Wiggins's (1993) factors for authentic testing, Barnett's (1991) core learning experiences, and Smith's (1993) Authentic Teaching, Learning, and Assessment Model. Each lends insight to criteria for developing tasks congruent to reality:

1. Addressing essential, intriguing, field-based problems or questions requiring attention and work over a sustained time period (Bridges & Hallinger, 1995; Smith, 1993; Wiggins, 1993)

2. Employing cooperation and teamwork to incorporate various viewpoints in the investigation of the problem or question (Barnett, 1991; Bridges & Hallinger, 1995; Smith, 1993)

Mitch Holifield and Gerald Dickinson, Arkansas State University

3. Including clinicians in interdisciplinary teaching approaches (Bridges & Hallinger, 1995)
4. Understanding people and environments by centering "on how demography, cultural diversity, politics, governance, law, and finance influence policies and operations and the ways in which educators can impact these external environments" (Barnett, 1991)
5. Producing a quality product or performance (Wiggins, 1993) including, in addition to analysis and reflection, implementation of a plan that addresses the actual proposed problem (Bridges & Hallinger, 1995)
6. Incorporating assessors-assessees interaction to justify actions and to receive diagnostic feedback (Bridges & Hallinger, 1995; Wiggins, 1993)
7. Using self-analysis of beliefs and values about leadership, organizational governance, and curriculum (Barnett, 1991; Smith, 1993) in field experiences as well as in course work so that students confront their own personal values and beliefs through vehicles for reflection such as journals, logs, reflective seminars, or portfolios
8. Holding students accountable for guiding and directing their own learning (Bridges & Hallinger, 1995)

FIELD-BASED LEARNING EXPERIENCES

Adherence to these criteria would seemingly help provide authenticity to any learning experience, particularly the internship. However, the purpose of this review is not to ascertain the extent to which preparation programs utilize these criteria. We only offer these criteria, followed next by descriptions of programs utilizing internships and unique university-school collaboration methods to afford field-based learning activities (see Table 1).

Internships

The means for employing field-based learning experiences most often mentioned in the literature is the internship, often fashioned after characteristics suggested by the Danforth Foundation for principalship preparation programs (Ubben, 1991):

1. Joint university-district selection of interns
2. Cohort experiences for interns
3. Mentors acting as site supervisors for interns
4. Collaborative planning by faculty and practitioners
5. Full-time internship of at least 720 hours
6. Internship to be completed in part outside educational institutions

In addition to the characteristics for the internship provided by the Danforth Foundation, the National Policy Board for Educational Administration suggests content for principal preparation programs applicable in an internship experience. With support from the Danforth Foundation, the Geraldine Rockefeller Dodge Foundation, the Lilly Endowment, and the major professional organizations representing professors of educational administration and the various levels of school administration, the Policy Board has published *Principals for Our Changing Schools* (Thompson, 1993). This resource describes key knowledge and skills in 21 domains appropriate to the principalship.

Exemplary Uses of the Internship

Contributors to *Preparing Tomorrow's School Leaders: Alternate Designs* (Murphy, 1993) describe various universities' versions of internship and practicum applications to enhance authenticity in their leadership preparation programs. In addition to this source, phone interviews were conducted in spring 1997 with knowledgeable representatives from each university preparation program noted.

Table 1. Comparison of Internship Aspects of Selected Preparation Programs.

Institution	Internship Terms	Sites	Stipends	Internship Content	Assessment	On-Campus Debriefing Reflections
University of New Mexico	2 semesters	home school; miscellaneous social agencies	university stipend	school-based problems	portfolio & formal paper	none
Stanford University	1 academic year	home school	none	school-based problems	portfolio, final report, & site-mentor evaluation	none
East Tennessee State University	90 days	schools at miscellaneous sites	none	school-based problems	handbook requirements	none
University of Central Florida	two 12-day summer terms	outside home school & miscellaneous agencies	none	action plan regarding Florida certification	portfolio self-assessment	weekly
University of Connecticut	90 days	outside home school/miscellaneous agencies	none	school-based problems	portfolios & journals	monthly
University of Washington	700 hours	home school & two other schools	none	pre-determined administration duties	portfolios, mentor evaluation, & evaluation over instructional modules	weekly
Brigham Young University	1200 hours	multiple school levels	none	six pre-determined areas	portfolios & journals	weekly
Indiana University	15 weeks	home school	none	pre-determined administration duties	developed education platform/school improvement plan	none

University of New Mexico

A participant in this administrator preparation program engages in a year-long (two-semester) internship. Candidates forgo a portion of their annual salaries at the school districts where employed but receive monthly fellowship stipends through the university. The internship is dedicated to the candidate identifying a school-based problem, devising solutions jointly with staff, providing leadership in addressing the problem, and evaluating the outcomes. A site supervisor, after receiving mentorship training, serves as the intern's mentor throughout this process. The student must submit a paper describing the problem and the process for addressing it (Milstein & Krueger, 1993). In a phone interview, Dr. Breta Bolta stated that students also may arrange internships with social agencies and that assessment also includes student portfolios.

Stanford University

Students engage in a practicum and an internship. The practicum, which is 40% of the preparation program's curriculum, consists of a series of projects. Each project focuses on a problem likely to confront principals: for example, selecting a new teacher, mainstreaming a special-needs child, or creating a school-improvement plan.

The one-year internship requires that a professor and a building principal supervise the intern. The student must devise a portfolio about these experiences. The portfolio might contain a description of the student's projects, documents (such as reports, newsletters, and brochures) prepared by the student, reflective notes or logs, and a final report prepared with the site supervisor (Bridges, 1993).

In an interview, Dr. Edwin Bridges indicated that interns view videotapes which portray situations and subsequently engage the intern in a decision-making process. University staff analyze the intern's responses and provide feedback. The intern also critiques the responses and discusses the results with the site mentor. Assessment of the intern includes a written evaluation by the site-level administrator and feedback on the structured video simulations completed by the intern during the year.

East Tennessee State University

The internship lasts a minimum of one semester; the 90 days required may be divided among various schools with different grade levels and a company or public agency with a CEO or administrator (Gresso, Burkett, & Smith, 1993). In a phone interview, Dr. Don Gresso said that students work closely with university professors who have responsibility for their supervision and with mentors in participating site schools. Each intern and mentor is given a handbook in which expectations and criteria for success are addressed.

The content of the internship is problem based, and university faculty attempt to connect classroom theory with reality. Course work is enhanced by the student completion of six modules which include actual day-to-day field experiences addressing predetermined competencies and domains. Assessments include evaluation by the faculty advisor of the intern's records and the examination of the student's activities to ensure that they meet specified criteria.

University of Central Florida

Students as a cohort undertake two internships in the summer at schools other than their home schools. During the 12-day period in each summer session, students serve at two sites with different grade levels, including one site at least 20% different in student demographics from those found at the intern's home school. The intern, faculty supervisor, and field mentor develop intern action plans that address Florida certification skills and competencies. Interns compile portfolios of the internship experience and discuss field experiences when the cohort convenes in "get-togethers" prior to scheduled classes or in sessions at the program coordinator's home on Saturday mornings or evenings (Millstein, 1993).

In a follow-up conversation, Dr. David Hernandez noted that students may arrange internship outside the educational setting in personnel management for defense industries, police departments, or mental health agencies, for instance. Assessment of the intern is conducted by the faculty supervisor who makes four visits to the host site and by the intern performing a self-assessment.

University of Connecticut

Internships span at least 90 days at a site other than the student's home school, 30 days during the academic year and 60 days during two summers. In monthly reflective seminars, mentors and interns analyze and discuss events in the schools related to their internship activities. Interns keep logs, journals, and portfolios "to provide a holistic perspective of the exercise" (Milstein, 1993). Dr. Paula Cadero stated in an interview that students participate in problem-based internship activities in site schools, private agencies, regional service centers, or any community agency whose needs may be met by the intern.

University of Washington

Interns, rather than shadowing and observing, develop a plan establishing the internship's purpose, activities, and evaluation. This plan requires the intern to assume responsibility for predetermined administrative duties. Three experiences, of which two must be outside the student's home district, are expected. The internship lasts a minimum of half a year or 700 hours to be completed during the school year with facilitation from a principal functioning as a site mentor and from a university faculty supervisor (Milstein, 1993).

In an interview, Dr. Ken Sirotnik indicated that, rather than traditional three-hour-credit course work, the program uses instructional modules or academic sessions that require interaction with various topical areas and academic units. Each Thursday from noon to 7:00 p.m., students engage in reflection on the internship and work with the academic units. Assessments include a combination of portfolios, mentor evaluations, and evaluations over the various instructional modules.

Brigham Young University

The Leader Preparation Program at Brigham Young University strives to provide a variety of experiences to prospective administrators. A major goal is to achieve a greater integration of theory and more meaningful practice than had previously occurred (Muse & Randall, 1994). In a phone interview, Dr. Ivan Muse stated that fifteen individuals are selected each year for participation. They must be released from their positions in their schools and complete 1200 hours of internship. The participants work one year as a full-time intern, during which time they serve on the elementary, middle, and secondary levels. University faculty serve as advisors and school principals serve as mentors. Mentors selected for the program receive in-service training. Students create portfolios that focus on leadership competencies established by the National Association of Secondary School Principals. In addition, interns keep journals of interactions with others. Following each entry, students indicate what qualities or traits they had to exhibit to work successfully through that situation. These entries are later discussed with university supervisors who offer suggestions for improvement as needed.

Indiana University

Students at Indiana University participate in an internship program for a period of fifteen weeks during which time they work in their own schools. During that period, university faculty members serve as supervisors for the internship and on-site school principals serve as mentors. During their participation in the program, interns take responsibility for conducting a number of tasks such as planning staff development, handling discipline, observing and evaluating teachers, developing budgets and grants, and scheduling classes.

Throughout the year, course work is integrated with the intern's field-based experiences. Activities include readings from professional journals, simulation exercises, interviews with practicing professionals, and the creation of an educational platform. Furthermore, all class work is taken as a cohort group to allow interns to receive peer support (Barnett, 1990). In a telephone interview, Dr. Neil Theobald stated that students assume a major role in their learning experiences. All interns must develop a topic or area of interest in which they feel a need to increase their competency. Each student then develops an action plan which is reviewed by faculty supervisors. The problem must be considered of value to the school in which the intern is working.

University-School Collaboration

In some preparation programs, collaboration, inherent in exemplary internship models, takes additional forms. Some preparation models include "grounding course work in schools and districts" (Murphy, 1993).

University of Utah

All EdD courses include a theory-research seminar paired with a field-based application course. The field site or clinic is the student's school of employment; here the focus is on problem solving and projects stimulated by the course work. Practicing field administrators holding the doctoral degree serve as part-time clinical faculty who help students identify problems or projects suitable for field application of course work. Also, the traditional dissertation is replaced by completion of a clinical research study (Ogawa & Pounder, 1993). Dr. David Sperry, in a phone interview, noted that student assessment includes creation and discussion of personal journals, mentor evaluations, observations by the university program director, and evaluations encountered in course work.

Hofstra University

Students as members of a "learning community" take their first five courses together. All of these courses are team taught by four faculty members and one teacher known as the "district partner," who is responsible for the problem-based experience. This team approach seeks to generate field opportunities in which the course work "unfolds" (Shakeshaft, 1993).

University of Connecticut

Much academic content is delivered in school settings in part because most students in the administrator preparation program live far from this rural university. By meeting at school sites, local school leaders can easily participate in classes. In addition, the program uses field trips to visit special programs, community service agencies, and legislative hearings (Milstein, 1993).

Arkansas State University

In the EdD leadership program, professors utilize three one-credit-hour integrative seminars consisting of field-based experiences to integrate the course work comprising the 33 credit hours of doctoral courses (Holifield, Cline, & Holman, 1995). For example, one doctoral cohort served a local elementary school by assessing the extent to which the school had accomplished programmatic goals outlined in the mission statement. Another cohort investigated the programmatic concerns of a staff at the local alternative school serving students identified as dropouts or potential dropouts with a wide range of academic and social problems. These cohort projects require university-school collaboration, numerous site visits for collecting data, and a published product presented to doctoral faculty and representative faculty from the cooperating sites.

SUMMARY

Even a cursory review of the literature on school administrator preparation reveals widespread application of collaborative, school-university, field-based, clinical experiences to integrate theory and practice. The forms that the integration takes might vary; internships, on-site clinical projects addressed in a particular course or block of courses during the period of the student's enrollment, and clinical research as an alternative to a traditional dissertation are some examples encountered in this review. Regardless of the form, students assume responsibility and accountability for successfully addressing problem-based activities actually encountered by school administrators on the job. Perhaps the high value now being placed on hands-on experience rather than shadowing programs, for example, is an appropriate response to criticisms that preparation programs have tended to ignore reality-based learning experiences.

REFERENCES

Barnett, B. (1990). School-university collaboration: A fad or the future of administrator preparation. *Planning and Changing, 21*(1), 146–153.

Barnett, B. (1991, October). *Incorporating alternative assessment measures in an educational leadership preparation program: Portfolios and educational platforms.* Paper presented at the annual meeting of the University Council for Educational Administration, Baltimore, MD.

Bridges, E. (1993). The prospective principal's program at Stanford University. In J. Murphy (Ed.), *Preparing tomorrow's school leaders: Alternative designs* (pp. 39–55). University Park, PA: University Council for Educational Administration.

Bridges, E., & Halliger, P. (1995). *Implementing problem based learning in leadership development.* Eugene, OR: ERIC Clearinghouse on Educational Management.

Gresso, D., Burkett, C., & Smith, P. (1993). Time is not of the essence when planning for a quality preparation program: East Tennessee State University. In J. Murphy (Ed.), *Preparing tomorrow's school leaders: Alternative designs* (pp. 109–127). University Park, PA: University Council for Educational Administration.

Holifield, M., Cline, D., & Holman, D. (1995). Is it real or is it memorex? Authentic simulations and curricular integration. In P. V. Bredeson & J. P. Scribner (Eds.), *Third yearbook of the National Council of Professors of Educational Administration. The professoriate: Challenges and promises* (pp. 154–161). Lancaster, PA: Technomic Publishing Co., Inc.

Mann, C. (1975). What peculiarities in educational administration make it difficult to profess? An essay. *Journal of Educational Administration, 13*(1), 139–147.

Milstein, M. (1993). *Changing the way we prepare educational leaders: The Danforth experience.* Newbury Park, CA: Corwin Press.

Milstein, M., & Krueger, J. (1993). Innovative approaches to clinical internships: The University of New Mexico experience. In J. Murphy (Ed.), *Preparing tomorrow's school leaders: Alternative designs* (pp. 19–37). University Park, PA: University Council for Educational Administration.

Mulkeen, T., & Tetenbaum, T. (1990). Teaching and learning in knowledge organizations: Implications for the preparation of school administrators. *Journal of Educational Administration, 13*(1), 139–147.

Murphy, J. (1993). *Preparing tomorrow's school leaders: Alternative designs.* University Park, PA: University Council for Educational Administration.

Muse, I. D., & Randall, E. V. (1994). The NASSP-Brigham Young leader preparation program: Partners in education. *NASSP Bulletin, 78*(559), 4–7.

Muth, R. (1989, October). Reconceptualizing training for educational administrators and leaders: Focus on inquiry. *Notes on Reform, 2,* 1–20. Charlottesville, VA: National Policy Board for Educational Administration.

Ogawa, R., & Pounder, D. (1993). Structured improvisation: The University of Utah's Ed.D. program in educational administration. In J. Murphy (Ed.), *Preparing tomorrow's school leaders: Alternative designs* (pp. 85–108). University Park, PA: University Council for Educational Administration.

Peper, J. B. (1988). Clinical education for school superintendents and principals: The missing link. In D. E. Griffiths, R. T. Stout, & P. R. Forsyth (Eds.), *Leaders for America's schools* (pp. 360–366). Berkeley, CA: McCutchan.

Shakeshaft, C. (1993). Preparing tomorrow's school leaders: The Hofstra University experience. In J. Murphy (Ed.), *Preparing tomorrow's school leaders: Alternative designs* (pp. 205–223). University Park, PA: University Council for Educational Administration.

Smith, S. (1993, November). *The ATLAS communities design: A comprehensive approach to school reform.* Presentation at the meeting of the Coalition of Essential Schools, Louisville, KY.

Thompson, S. (Ed.). (1993). *Principals for our changing schools.* Fairfax, VA: National Policy Board for Educational Administration.

Ubben, G. (1991). Strategies for organizing principal preparation: A survey of the Danforth principal preparation programs. In F. Wendel (Ed.), *Enhancing the knowledge base in educational administration* (pp. 7–26). University Park, PA: University Council for Educational Administration. (ERIC Document Reproduction Service No. ED 366 091)

Wiggins, G. (1993). Assessment: Authenticity, context, and validity. *Phi Delta Kappan, 75*(3), 200–214.

AUTHOR INDEX

Achilles, Charles M., 29
Achilles, Susan H., 29
Aguilera, Raymond V., 69

Barnett, Bruce G., 179
Basom, Margaret R., 179
Bell, Edwin D., 190
Blendinger, Jack, 231
Bradley, Fred, 258
Bradshaw, Lynn, 247
Bredeson, Paul V., 119
Browder, Lesley H., Jr., 16

Creighton, Theodore B., 131

Dagley, David, 87
Danzig, Arnold, 196
Dayton, John, 93
Dickinson, Gerald, 299

Edirisooriya, Gunapala, 268

Feuerstein, Abe, 113
Ford, Sharon M., 238

Fulton, Carol, 139

Geltner, Beverley B., 169
Guzmán, Nadyne, 214

Hendricks, Joen M., 69
Holifield, Mitch, 299
Hoyle, John R., 148

Johansson, Olof, 119
Johnson, Bob L., 49
Jones, Linda T., 231

Kaurala, Earl B., 208
King, Richard A., 76
Kowalski, Theodore J., 36

Levine, Linda, 157
Licklider, Barbara L., 139

Martin, W. Michael, 238
McCarthy, Martha M., 3
McDowelle, James O., 190
Murphy, Michael J., 238

Muth, Rodney, 214, 238, 289

Norris, Cynthia J., 179

Oates, Arnold, 148
Oldaker, Lawrence Lee, 87

Perreault, George, 247
Pignatelli, Frank, 157
Place, A. William, 36
Porter, Charles, 196
Price, William J., 169

Rehm, Robert, 289

Tracy, Jaclynn C., 169

VanTassel-Baska, Joyce, 279

Walter, James E., 103
Weller, David, 59
Wilkinson, Gayle A., 258

Yerkes, Diane M., 179